*

*

Also by Allan R. May

Mob Stories

Gangland Gotham

Welcome to the Jungle Inn

Crimetown U.S.A.

The Sly-Fanner Murders

*

PETRO
Cleveland's Handsomest Public Enemy

The Story of Julius Petro
and
His Collinwood Burglary Crew

Allan R. May

ConAllan Press, Cleveland, OH

Published by ConAllan Press, LLC
Cleveland, Ohio, USA

Library of Congress Cataloging-in-Publication Data

May, Allan R.
PETRO Cleveland's Handsomest Public Enemy
The Story of Julius Petro and His Collinwood Burglary Crew / by Allan R. May,
- 1st ed. p. cm.
Includes bibliographical reference and index.
ISBN - 13:978-0-9837037-6-1
LCCN 2022903928

1. Burglars - Cleveland - Northeast Ohio - Biography
2. Cleveland - Ohio - Biography
3. Police - Cleveland - Northeast Ohio - History
4. Mafia - Cleveland - Northeast Ohio - History
5. Organized Crime - Cleveland - Northeast Ohio - History
6. Mafia - Los Angeles - California - History

Cover Art by Mike Alexander
Design work by Connie May and Lynn Bycko

First published 2022

This book is dedicated to the memory of

My Big Brother

Gary Edward May
1955 – 2022

*

Table of Contents

Acknowledgments ix

Preface xi

Opening 1

Chapter One: Cleveland Birth 4

Chapter Two: Burglary & Murder: The "Bobby" Knaus Case 8

Chapter Three: Green Acres Casino Robbery 30

Chapter Four: Post-Bullet Hole Days 40

Chapter Five: "Very Strange!" Another Bullet Hole 52

Chapter Six: The Big Take-Down 62

Chapter Seven   The Strange Case of Dr. Spaeth 100

Chapter Eight: The Last Years of Julius Petro 117

Chapter Nine: The Petro Murder Investigation 137

Chapter Ten: The Friends of Julius Petro 236

Chapter Eleven: Alfred Calabrese, Paul Perotti & The "Red" Carpenter Story 301

Chapter Twelve: A Few Selected Biographies 357

End Notes 468

Bibliography 522

Index 524

*

Acknowledgments

I can't stress enough the help I received from Dennis M. Walsh, an attorney and author of *Nobody Walks*. I basically had no clue as to Julius Petro's activities near the end of his life in Los Angeles until Charlie Molino told me about Walsh's book. Over the past few years Dennis and I have become good friends and he has provided me with an incredible amount of information, not only about Petro, but also his cohorts on the West Coast, which included at one time Dennis's father. This book would be so lacking on the last part of Petro's life if it weren't for Dennis, his kindness, help and guidance.

I want to thank H. Carter Alden, who I call the hero of this book. After finding out he was still living in North Carolina, I called one Saturday morning in early 2019. I figured he had to be in his 80s and my concern was if he would still have his faculties and could even remember the events of that day back in August 1952. When I called, his wife answered the telephone. She told me he wasn't home; he was out playing tennis! That answered that concern. He and his wife were both delightful people and he contributed articles, pictures, and stories to the Petro saga.

James "Jimmy" Barber, a good friend, researcher and historian, was his usual terrific source of information. In addition to providing me with the information to reach Carter Alden, he also nailed down another address for me. There was someone I was looking for in California to see if they were still alive. Not only did he find them, but it also turned out they were living right here in the Cleveland area. I think if I asked Jimmy to find Hoffa for me, I wouldn't have to wait very long.

Charles R. "Charlie Moose" Molino remains my closest partner-in-crime after all these years. We're both slowing down. In addition to the friendship, "Moose" is my first contact anytime I'm looking for information. It's a good idea to bounce ideas off him on anyone I'm writing about, he seems to always provide something more about them to the story. I look forward to our continuing association in the years to come.

While working on the book in the early days, I met Louie Uhl, an Assistant U.S. Attorney with the Department of Justice in Scottsdale, Arizona. Louie provided me with a lot of technical help regarding the law and the trials Julius Petro was involved in. People who helped provide me with the photographs for the book were Brian Meggitt, Cleveland Public Library, who did an incredible job finding so many of the photographs used in the book. Lisa Sanchez, Cleveland Public Library, who came through in a pinch when I needed that one last photo. Elizabeth A. Piwkowski, Cleveland State University; Brenda J. Linert and Mike Semple, Warren *Tribune Chronicle*. Others who helped with articles and/or photographs were Marisa Minich and Jan Vaughn, Warren-Trumbull County Public Library, Linda Compau, and Dennis M. Walsh.

A special thank you to the folks who helped from Alliance, Ohio. D.J. Digianantonio, Rodman Public Library, who provided the many articles I needed on the Eldon Shoup murder and trials; and Barb Rogel and David Skolosh of St. Joseph Catholic Cemetery.

Another special thank you to a few others who provided assistance and / or counsel along the way: Christine Koren, Mary C. Krohmer, Gary E. May, Kathy Pastor, Rick Porrello, and Ellen Poulson.

Mike Alexander is almost like family. He stepped forward from Las Vegas, Nevada, and offered to help with the book cover and design and has become a good friend along the way. I look forward to future projects with him.

Lynn Duchez Bycko has served as an advisor and counselor, and has been one of my best friends for nearly two decades. In addition to helping to provide photographs for the book, she has provided my wife and I technical support in helping to get this book to the printer.

Last but not least, Connie May, my dear wife, has taken over the design work of my books, putting everything together before it heads out to the printer. We just celebrated 21 years together and I look forward to 21 more. I don't know what I'd do without her.

And of course, I want to thank the following family members, friends, supporters and those special people who keep me alive and get me through my day: Robin Carr, John Chechitelli, Rose Forster, Abby Goldberg, Mario Gomes, Jeffrey Kelman, Jerry Kovar, Tom Leahy, Lawrence L. Lynch, John Murray, Kim Novak, David Pastor, Steve & Susie Pultorak, Charly Ralph, Robin Stekkinger, James Trueman, Jan Vaughn, Charlotte Versagi and Fred Wolking. I'm at the age now where I need a medical staff to keep me ticking, so a special shout out to them: Dr. Crystal Lantz, MD, Dr. Christopher J. "Chip" Tighe, DPM, and Dr. Douglas P. Webb, MD. Dr. Webb has kept my eyes in check for the past 36 years and counting. And a special thanks to family members: "Ma" Scurec, Tammy Cabot, and the Vaciks – Nelda, Bob, Melanie and Robbie.

Thank you all – Allan R. May

PREFACE

I can't think of a better opening for this book than to have the hero of my story tell what actually happened that day. Hours after one of Warren, Ohio's largest robberies, H. Carter Alden and his mother Abbie came forward and identified the notorious Julius Petro and an accomplice as two of the men they saw fleeing a crime they weren't even aware had been committed.

It's doubtful that the Aldens had ever heard of Cleveland's number one public nemesis. If they had, then they might have been aware of the threats made to other witnesses who dared to identify Petro as having taken part in the crimes he was arrested for. Who would have blamed them if they decided to keep what they saw to themselves? At the time, Carter Alden had his whole life ahead of him, why should he stick his neck out?

But Carter Alden did, and when he finished testifying Julius Petro's world crumbled around him. His courtroom reaction on the day Carter Alden and his mother Abbie took the stand against him showed just that. After his indictment and arrest for the crime in October 1952, Petro would not see the light of freedom until the mid-1960s. By then, his reign of terror was over. And the policing agencies and citizens of Northeastern Ohio were grateful for that.

H. Carter Alden's Story

In August, 1952, I was a 19-year-old college student, home on summer break in Warren, Ohio. On the morning of August 14, I was driving my mother from our home to the branch bank of Union Savings & Trust Company on Woodland Avenue. As we drove up Oak Knoll Avenue, we were startled by a car racing around the corner of Montclair Street and speeding directly toward us. In the car were three men, each exhibiting excited, wide-eyed expressions. I looked at the driver's face, drawn to it by the excitement of the moment and his aggressive driving. My mother looked at both the driver and the front seat passenger. It was obvious to us that they were fleeing something.

We continued to the bank, discussing what those three men could have been involved with. My mother transacted her business and we departed. There was no indication to us that anyone there knew anything about a robbery of funds designated for their bank having occurred nearby just minutes earlier.

After leaving the bank, I drove my mother home and then went to play golf with some friends. When I returned home late in the afternoon, my mother told me what had happened. Our local newspaper (delivered in the afternoon) described it. The branch manager of that Union Savings & Trust was forcibly stopped and robbed of funds that were destined for that branch. The getaway car had not been found and there was no knowledge of the identity of the robbers. After discussing our part in witnessing the getaway (and the risks that we could be taking) we telephoned the Warren City Police. A couple of hours later, two FBI agents arrived at our home.

We described to them everything that we saw that morning on our way to the bank. They brought with them a packet of "mug shots" of several men. We were asked if we could identify any of the men in the photos as being occupants of the getaway car. My mother identified men in two of the photos as being the driver and the passenger in the front seat. I identified the same man that my mother had as being the driver. The agents asked if we would travel with them to Cleveland to view police line-ups.

The next morning, one of the agents drove us to Cleveland. During the drive up, the agent described how it would work. He carefully assured us that there was no reason to be frightened or intimidated, because those in the line-ups would not be able to see us. Once there, my mother again identified the driver and the front seat passenger in the line-ups. I identified the driver only. While returning to Warren that afternoon, the agent put names to the suspects that we had identified. Julius Petro was the driver and Joseph Sanzo was the front seat passenger. He also briefly described their criminal histories. He discussed with us any concerns that we might have about appearing in court as witnesses against criminals such as Petro and Sanzo. He tried to reassure us by explaining that these men were being watched almost full time by the Cleveland FBI. He recommended, however, that we keep alert about our surroundings. If anything, at any time, seemed suspicious to either of us, we should call him right away.

In early September I returned to college. I did think about the upcoming trial and was somewhat concerned about it in anticipation. However, I was very busy with my mechanical engineering and naval classes, studying, and the social life, too.

I returned home in early December because my mother and I had been subpoenaed to appear at the trial. Each of us testified and identified Petro and Sanzo as before. I returned to college after our appearance in court. A week or two after my return, I was telephoned and then visited by a local FBI agent. He thanked me for my part in all the above described proceedings. He advised me that it was possible that Petro and/or Sanzo might try to retaliate against me. He assured me that he would monitor the situation. I was told to contact him immediately if I noticed anything suspicious or threatening. Fortunately, I found no need to.

During this time, my friends were very curious about our being witnesses and testifying at the trial, so I was involved in a lot of discussions about it. As time went by, I thought about it and discussed it less and less. I graduated from college, spent three years in the Navy, got a job, got married and had three children. I have been busy and enjoying family life, working, participating in sports, other activities, and now I am retired. Every now and then I have wondered about what ever became of Julius Petro and Joe Sanzo, but I was never so curious that I investigated to find out. Then, in the fall of 2018, I was contacted by Allan May.

My mother and I were always pleased that we were able to help the FBI and local law enforcement serve justice in this case.

Carter Alden

Abbie Alden

H. Carter Alden

Julius Anthony Petro was perceived by many to be on the fringes of the Cleveland Mafia. It was perhaps his wildness and notoriety that kept him from ever being considered for membership. He was more suited to operating on his own as a burglar and a robber, and with men of like spirit. Still, because of his Italian heritage and Collinwood upbringing, he would always be associated with the organized crime element in the city by the police and newspapers.

In January 1978, when hitman Raymond W. Ferritto confessed to killing Julius Petro, he was asked if he had to get permission from anybody to murder him, after all it was considered a "contract" murder. Ferritto answered his inquisitors, "Well, that all depends what kind of contract you're talking about. I mean if you're talking about one that comes from people in organized crime, then I would say you have to get permission. He [Petro] wasn't connected with any people other than that he knew them. It was one of his dreams to become one. But I know it to be a fact that he wasn't. So therefore, I didn't have to ask or tell anyone about it." Despite Ferritto's revelation, in the final years of Petro's life, and following his death, the newspapers seemed to always refer to him as a "mob enforcer."

In my two books about the Mahoning Valley, *Welcome to the Jungle Inn* and *CrimeTown USA*, Petro is mentioned briefly. In the Jungle Inn book, I'm embarrassed to say that I claimed Petro was a suspect in the robbery of the Mounds Club in Lake County in 1947. If he was, that would have been a neat trick, as he was sitting in a cell on death row at the time.

Over the years, Petro's name continued to pop up in my research on Cleveland crime. In 2011, an actor played him in a bit role in the movie, *Kill the Irishman*, a story about Cleveland underworld figure Danny Greene, based on the book by Rick Porrello. I decided to look at Petro and his activities a little more closely. Some of the things I discovered included:

- Petro was called Cleveland's "handsomest public enemy,"

- He murdered a young man in 1946 and sat on death row for 17 months.

- Petro pulled one of the biggest bank heists ever in the city of Warren.

- He was shot twice while involved in robberies

- Avoided having to go to prison for his crimes because he intimidated witnesses and they refused to testify against him.

I thought that was pretty good material for a book. But, another thing I discovered was Cleveland cops, as well as most cops throughout northeastern, Ohio, loathed Petro. You've heard the saying, "The cop would arrest a guy for spitting on the sidewalk?" Well, the deciding factor for me to write this book was when I read that a Euclid police officer once pulled Petro over, cuffed, arrested and jailed him, simply because he didn't believe he "would add much to the dignity of the suburb." How's that for great police work!

Instead of simply focusing on Petro, I decided to look into the key members of his Collinwood gang of safe crackers and thieves and, in addition, compiled some in-depth research on some of the other people – cops, robbers, a cop who became a robber – that somewhere along the line had rubbed shoulders with Petro.

That part of the book is followed by another chapter about an associate of Petro, who was involved in the murder of a local golf legend in Alliance, Ohio, during a burglary gone bad. When ratted out by one of the burglary crew, two members, who had nothing to do with the actual killing, were put on trial for their lives, while the other two received what amounted to a slap on the wrist.

Finally, in the last section, "A Few Selected Biographies," I've included stories of people who popped up in Petro's orbit, who had interesting lives and careers of their own. There were two fascinating characters I came across in my research. The first was Joseph Tholl, a self-taught handwriting and "questionable documents" expert, who was involved in a number of the Cleveland areas most celebrated murders and criminal cases. The second was Detective Lieutenant Thomas P. White, a no-nonsense Cleveland cop, who Petro tried to get even with by sticking pins in a voodoo-like image he created of the officer and kept under his pillow at Leavenworth Penitentiary.

Elements of Petro's most successful crime remain a mystery to this day. On August 14, 1952, a bank manager is Warren, Ohio, was transporting $71,000 to his branch when another automobile, containing three men, cut him off. Joseph Sanzo and another man, jumped out of the car and took the bag of money, while Petro remained behind the wheel. Two days before the robbery, an informant gave Lieutenant White the names of the three men, who were going to rob the manager. The third man, while known, was never arrested or named in the newspapers, and more than $69,500 of the money taken, was never recovered.

*

OPENING:

CLEVELAND HOOD SLAIN IN L.A.

It was January 1969 and the long, turbulent decade of the 1960s was beginning its last year. The country had witnessed being on the brink of war with the Cuban Missile Crisis, the assassinations of President John F. Kennedy, his brother Senator Robert F. Kennedy, and civil rights leader Martin Luther King, Jr. Each night people watched the six o'clock news as America was becoming split in two as the war in Viet Nam escalated.

In Cleveland, the city was dealing with its share of highs and lows during the first half of January. On the first, the Ohio State Buckeyes defeated the University of Southern California, who were led by Heisman Trophy winner O.J. Simpson, in the Rose Bowl by a score of 27 – 16. The New Years' Day victory propelled Ohio State to being named college football's National Champions for the 1968 season.

A "long-rumored shakeup" within the Cleveland Police Department became reality when Police Chief Patrick L. Gerity vowed to "clean up the town" with a major departmental restructuring program featuring "a plan unique in the nation and totally tailored to the needs of our city." Facing a room full of reporters and cameras, Gerity declared, "We are giving ourselves an opportunity to wage escalated war on vice and all its concomitant evils. We are going to arrest hard-core criminals. We are going to harass the professional criminal until he is behind bars or out of town. This is no shakeup," he stated. "It is simply a plan to build a more efficient department." Taking a shot at what he perceived as the problems of the past, he declared, "No police department should have units built around and for personalities."

On the same day Chief Gerity was expounding on his vision of a new police setup, a new Cuyahoga County Sheriff was taking office. Ralph E. Kreiger became the first Republican in 42 years to be elected county sheriff. Some 20 hours into his first day on the job, the new sheriff was still reorganizing the department, the jail and his office. All this was taking place against the backdrop of rumors that there would be a mass strike by deputies and jailers, mass firings, and a riot or jail break.

Despite the promises of new changes in local law enforcement, the next day a senseless and brutal murder was reported on the front pages of the newspapers. William Hairston, a well-known businessman, thoroughbred racehorse owner, and NAACP member, had just entered his place of business, the King's Men's Shop clothing store on Lee Road on the East Side. He was followed into the store by two men, who walked into the backroom after him. While one man began beating Hairston with a blackjack, the other pulled a revolver, placed it close to the businessman's temple and fired a bullet through his head. The vicious murder took place in the presence of three employees. The two men turned around and calmly walked out of the store. Police called the killing a "cold-blooded, pre-meditated murder." There was no attempt to even rob the store. Police eventually determined the killing was tied to the clearing house numbers racket in the city.

Sadly, this vicious murder would be topped a day later by one of the most infamous killings in the greater Cleveland area, that of Marlene Steele. The 37-year-old wife of Euclid Municipal Judge Robert L. Steele was shot to death in the couple's downstairs bedroom in their Miami Road home as her husband checked on their two sleeping sons upstairs. The murder dominated the front pages for days, but the case remained unsolved until the judge and two co-conspirators were betrayed by the hired gunman and convicted seven years later.

In Washington D.C., the National Aeronautics & Space Administration (NASA) named Ohioan Neil A. Armstrong commander of Apollo 11, the first manned mission to the moon. Along with Armstrong, NASA named Edwin A. "Buzz" Aldrin and Michael Collins to the crew. The mission would make history with a moon landing and walk seven months later.

The forecast for Thursday, January 16, 1969, was not typical of Cleveland, Ohio's mid-winter weather. Normal highs at this time of year for the city on the southern shore of Lake Erie were in the frigid single digits; not the 40-degree mark predicted for this day. As residents awoke to begin their day, the headline in the morning newspaper announced in bold letters:

CLEVELAND HOOD SLAIN IN L.A.

More than 16 years had passed since Julius Anthony Petro last made headlines in the city of his birth. Now, at age 46, his lifeless body was found slumped over in the front seat of his girlfriend's 1966 Cadillac convertible; the victim of a single gunshot wound to the back of the head. *Plain Dealer* reporter W. James Van Vliet wrote:

> Julius Anthony Petro, once called Handsomest Public Enemy No. 1, is dead at 46, struck down by a bullet in a car at Los Angeles International Airport. His crime career included everything from siphoning gasoline from parked cars to robbery and murder. His specialty was violence and daring intimidation of witnesses who threatened his precious freedom. Petro had three qualities necessary to a successful criminal. He was without fear. He was audacious. He lacked conscience.

It was reported that Petro had recently been working as a "muscleman and enforcer" for finance collection agencies in the Los Angeles area. In recent weeks, he was living with a 21-year-old prostitute from Chicago in a Van Nuys apartment. Los Angeles homicide detective Lieutenant Robert Helder told reporters, "Any one of 50 different individuals in the San Fernando Valley had good reason and the ability to kill him."

During the critical early days of the investigation very little information was discovered. On Saturday night, January 11, a man spotted Petro slumped over in the front seat of the car after parking in the space next to him. He assumed Petro was asleep and left him alone. When he returned from a flight the next night, he found Petro still slumped over in the same position and notified a parking lot attendant. When the attendant noticed blood, he called police. A member of the homicide unit stated they believe Petro drove alone to the airport and had met foul play there. There was no identification on the body, which had to be identified through fingerprints.

The killer of Julius Petro, and the details behind his slaying, would not come to light until almost nine years-to-the-day later, when a stunning revelation was made during an investigation into one of the Cleveland Mafia's most notorious murders.

Chapter One:

Cleveland Birth

Welcome to Collinwood

Collinwood consists of two large neighborhoods located in the far northeast corner of the city of Cleveland. The two neighborhoods are split down the middle by the railroads that run east and west and are known as North and South Collinwood. North Collinwood runs along the shore of Lake Erie and was historically a residential neighborhood. South Collinwood was traditionally an industry-heavy section of the city, dominated by the railroads. On January 21, 1910, North and South Collinwood were annexed by Cleveland.

South Collinwood for the first half of the 20th century was home to Irish, Italian and Slovenian families. Many found work at the massive Collinwood Railroad Yards. A wave of the Italian population relocated from what was once known as Big Italy in the Woodland / Orange Avenue section of downtown Cleveland. The central business district of South Collinwood is "Five Points." The area received its name from where East 152nd Street, Ivanhoe Road and St. Clair Avenue intersect.

Collinwood made national news on Ash Wednesday, March 4, 1908, when a fire erupted at Lakeview Elementary school. Known as the "Collinwood School Fire," 172 students, 2 teachers and 1 rescue worker died in the blaze; making it one of the deadliest school fires in the history of the United States. While it was widely reported that the back door, one of only two exits and where most of the victims were trapped, opened inward, an investigation revealed that to be false. Those who perished in the inferno, whose bodies could not be identified, were buried in a mass grave in historic Lake View Cemetery.

Another event, which garnered national attention, also involved a school. Located at the south-east corner of the "Five Points" intersection sits Collinwood High School, which for years provided an education to the many ethnic teenagers of the Collinwood neighborhood. By the mid-1960s, Blacks from the Glenville area to the west were moving into Collinwood and attending school there. While there were racial incidents at the school as early as 1965, the problem reached a peak five years later.

On April 6, 1970, an angry mob estimated at 350 to 400 people, mostly white high school students, gathered outside the school and began throwing rocks at the building. Staff and teachers herded the Black students to the third floor for protection. At 10:30 people from the mob began entering the school, but only ascended as far as the second floor before vacating the building. The next day, Cleveland Mayor Carl B. Stokes, the first Black mayor of a major city in the United States, ordered the school kept open. Cleveland police officers, supported by Ohio National Guard units, kept the peace.

During the first two decades of the 21st century, the population of Collinwood has remained predominantly Black, with the unemployment rate above the national average. It is estimated about one-third of Collinwood residents live below the poverty level.

In 2002, the Russo brothers, Anthony and Joseph – Cleveland's celebrated film directors, producers, screenwriters, and actors – wrote and directed "Welcome to Collinwood." Described as a "caper comedy," the film is about a group of small-time thieves, who attempt a safe-cracking at a jeweler's apartment. The film starred George Clooney, William H. Macy and Sam Rockwell. The plot of the movie in no way mirrored the efforts of Julius Petro and his Collinwood safe-cracking crew.

Described as the only "rotten apple" in the barrel, Julius Anthony Petro was born on June 13, 1922, the second child of John and Lydia Petro[1], who came to the Buckeye State from Italy. Julius and his two siblings, a younger brother Michael and an older sister Monda, grew up in the Collinwood area of Cleveland. While growing up, Julius developed a strong dislike of authority at an early age. His classroom education lasted until the ninth grade, when he quit school for good. From then on, his life was a steady diet of criminal activities, resulting in his becoming one of the city's most notable public enemies.

In 1933, when he was only eleven years old, Petro and four other youths attempted a rather Herculean feat by trying to steal a ton of aluminum scrap from an East Side electrical concern. The effort landed him in Juvenile Court, where his parents pleaded with the judge for clemency; he was given probation. It was around this time Petro obtained perhaps the only legitimate job he ever had, becoming a caddy at Highland Park Golf Course in Warrensville Township. Petro, who always had a pudgy physique, was called "Beef" by the older caddies at the course. It was a nickname he hated. When he got older, like Benjamin Siegel, who despised the nickname "Bugsy," Petro would administer a beating to anyone who dared to call him "Beef."

Automobile theft was the next item in Petro's criminal portfolio. In February 1939, he failed in this endeavor in Batavia, New York, located between Buffalo and Rochester just south of Interstate 90. What possessed him to travel out of state to test this new market is lost to history. The charge, however, was eventually dropped and the 17-year-old was handed over to Cleveland police. His next brush with the law also took place in New York State during 1939, when he stole $70 worth of merchandise from a hardware store in Buffalo. The police again returned Petro to Cleveland, this time he was sent to the Boys Industrial School in Lancaster, Ohio. Of his time there, one reporter wrote, "It was there that his lessons in serious crime began, and Julius was a good student." But this, too, was followed by another burglary gone-bad. A year after this release, he stole $300 worth of tires and automotive accessories from a store. Caught again,

Petro this time pleaded guilty in court and on January 17, 1941, was sentenced to one to 15 years in the Mansfield Reformatory.[2] During his time there, he befriended another Cleveland youth named Theodore "Bobby" Knaus, who was serving time since March 1941 for a burglary conviction in 1940. Petro was released on parole sometime before the fall of 1942.

Bertha's Café has stood for decades on the north-west corner of St. Clair Avenue and Marquette Street, a block west of the busy East 55th Street thoroughfare. A popular eatery and bar, the café, owned and operated by Bertha Cernigoz, was the target of several armed robberies over the years. While not yet a marquee name among Cleveland thieves, young Petro became the most famous of the holdup men to be connected with the café.

Petro's holdup, however, did not take place inside the two-story brick structure. On October 23, 1942, Bertha's daughter, Alice, was sent to a nearby bank, a normal Friday morning routine, to get money to cash the paychecks of local workers who frequented the place. After withdrawing $10,000, Alice was confronted by Petro and two associates, Andrew Haller and Joseph Horvatin, who proceeded to relieve her of the cash. On December 3, the Cuyahoga County grand jury indicted the three men for the robbery.

Petro and Haller were placed on the fifth floor of the Cuyahoga County jail, where they shared a cell with Ruben Mangine and Joseph Drago, the latter youth, 18 years-old, was just beginning a long criminal career in northeast Ohio. On Monday morning, December 7, the four prisoners refused to leave the cell to have breakfast. When the guards ordered them out, Mangine, the oldest at 27, acting as ringleader, began cursing the guards. This was followed by him and the rest of his cellmates setting fire to a mattress, then tearing the blankets to shreds and using the torn strips to tie the cell door shut.

Working together, six guards finally forced the cell door open and went inside only to be attacked by the four prisoners, who were using broom handles as weapons. The guards used their billy clubs to make short work of the breakfast insurrection, perhaps becoming a bit zealous in their efforts. When word of the jail "beatings" got back to Common Pleas Judge Frank S. Day, he requested that the court psychiatrist examine the prisoners. The four men claimed the guards viciously beat them with billy clubs and blackjacks, inflicting numerous injuries to them. Upon receiving the doctor's report, Judge Day ordered Sheriff Joseph Sweeney to conduct his own investigation. Sweeney was informed that the guards were armed only with regulation billy clubs, which they "used in self-defense."

Meanwhile, Michael A. Picciano,[3] attorney for Petro and Haller, claimed Petro was knocked unconscious by the guards and not provided with immediate care after the incident. Picciano used the event to request that the $10,000 bail on Petro and Haller be reduced so they could be released to see their family physicians. Judge Day refused to grant the reduction. When the investigation was completed, the judge exonerated the guards and commended them for the forceful action they took during the brief uprising.

Strangely, there was no mention in the local newspapers of what happened to Petro and his two companions for the $10,000 robbery of Alice Cernigoz. Petro, however, was deemed a parole violator and sent back to prison a few months later in March 1943. Five months later, he was transferred to "the Big House," the Ohio Penitentiary in Columbus and remained there until his release on November 22, 1944.

Chapter Two:

Burglary & Murder:

The "Bobby" Knaus Case

Early Morning Break-in

Around 2:00 on the morning of Tuesday, February 26, 1946, two burglars entered the Green Café, at 2460 Superior Avenue, using a rear door. The screws that held the hasp locking the door had already been removed from the inside. Two watch dogs, on hand to protect the place, remained oddly quiet, never once barking. After gaining entrance, the burglars encountered John Bush, a 61-year-old porter, who lived close by and did cleanup work at the place. The two thieves grabbed Bush from behind and forced him into a bathroom, where they bound his hands with adhesive tape, tied him to a drainpipe with a sash cord, stuffed a towel in his mouth, and placed another one over his head. The men then removed $3,700 that was hidden in an unused steam table in the kitchen, a secret hiding place that one of them obviously knew about, and an additional $417 from a small change box. From the cash register, a St. Francis medal[4] and a valve cap and parts were removed. The valve cap was the type used on automobile tires to cover the valve used for putting air into the tires. They also stole two handguns; a .38 Special revolver and a .32 semiautomatic; the latter item would become very significant.

The owner of the Green Café, Mrs. Marie Estrate, told police she was sure that she knew who robbed her. She had a son with a troubled past, whom she had just thrown out of her house, possibly leading him to seek revenge by robbing her café. On December 29, 1945, less than two months earlier, the 21-year-old was released from the Mansfield Reformatory; his name was Theodore "Bobby" Knaus.[5] Police were aware the delinquent knew Julius Petro and that they had become close companions since his release.

Mrs. Estrate also told detectives that on Wednesday, the day after the robbery, an automobile pulled up in front of her home at 5914 Vandalia Avenue, on the city's south side, about 11:40 p.m.[6] From the window, she said she recognized Bobby in the passenger's seat and Petro behind the wheel; neither man got out. She knew Petro because he was hanging out at the Green Café in recent weeks with her son and had dated her daughter, Dolores Knaus. This was the information police needed to confirm Petro was the accomplice, and they began an immediate search for the two suspects. It wouldn't be long before Petro was in custody.

Detectives arrested Petro at his home at 787 East 156th Street in North Collinwood, around 5:30 Thursday morning. They searched the house and his automobile. Inside the car, they found two spent .32 cartridges on the floor just under the backseat.[7] In the basement of the home, police found his leather jacket, containing $22, which they believed was part of the $4,117 stolen from the Green Café. Police also removed a St. Francis medal, a valve cap and a ring. Petro was taken to jail and questioned, but refused to admit to having any participation in the robbery. Police held him for investigation. Meanwhile, the search was still on for his suspected accomplice.

On March 1, Petro's attorney, Michael Picciano filed a writ of habeas corpus to get his client out of jail. Police responded by charging Petro with the burglary at the Green Café. By that time, Bobby Knaus had not been seen in four days. His uncle, whom he recently began to live with, told detectives he had not seen his nephew since the evening before the robbery. Knaus told his mother that same evening he was going to visit his girlfriend, who lived on Kinsman Road. When police questioned the young lady, she told them Bobby did not come over that night. With Petro now in jail and refusing to talk, by February 28 the case was at a standstill while police hunted Knaus.

In the eastern section of Cuyahoga County there exists a hilly, forest-covered ravine that occupies parts of four different cities: Cleveland, Cleveland Heights, East Cleveland and South Euclid. The area is bordered by Noble Road on the western side, where the headquarters of General Electric Lighting is in East Cleveland. The sprawling headquarters, not far from the northern entrance of the ravine, is renowned for its annual display of Christmas lights. The artistry, which began in the mid-1920s, draws thousands of visitors every year to the facility. Cleveland's famous Euclid Avenue makes up the northern border; Monticello Boulevard is the southern border; while the eastern border of the ravine is defined by South Green Road. Snaking its way through this wooded area is Belvoir Boulevard. In addition to the steep hill, which begins at Euclid Avenue and rises to the south, is a deep gorge through which Ninemile Creek winds the entire length. From the 1890s and into the 1970s the creek was a popular place for Boy Scout, Girl Scout and Campfire Girl outings and hikes. Deer, raccoons, skunks, possums, whistle pigs and other wildlife still inhabit the area, occasionally wandering into the surrounding neighborhoods in search of vegetation to consume. It remains a popular place for hiking and exploring.

Such was the case when two youths spent a late Saturday afternoon on March 2 exploring these woods. The two were following the creek down to a point a mile south of Euclid Avenue, and about 60 yards west of Belvoir Boulevard when they discovered a man's body lying partly in the water. The two boys quickly notified East Cleveland Police, who, just as quickly, notified Cleveland Police, "as the slain man was just over the line in the extreme edge of Cleveland." The newspaper surmised, incorrectly, that this was another mob-related murder reporting, "In typical gangland fashion four shots had been fired into" the body.

The dead man was soon identified as the missing and much sought-after Bobby Knaus. He was struck by one bullet in his upper left arm; another in the back of his left shoulder; a third struck him in the small of his back; while the fourth, the fatal slug, entered the base of his skull. Police found Knaus's overcoat and jacket on the Belvoir Boulevard pavement.

Detective Lieutenant Martin P. Cooney, head of the Cleveland Police Department's Homicide Unit, realized an irony regarding the discovery of Knaus. Cooney pointed out that, "This might be one of those rare cases where the murderer was actually in jail before the body of the victim was even found." This "irony" would one day come back to haunt Cooney. Confirming their belief they had the right man was the finding of a single spent cartridge from a .32 semiautomatic at the murder scene, the same caliber as the two recovered from Petro's car. Detectives believed the .32 automatic was the one stolen from the Green Café during the early morning robbery.

Early theories advanced by the police stated that since Petro was found with so little money on him, and that Knaus knew the secret location where the bulk of the money was hidden, that he had not shared the $3,700 with his accomplice. Petro may have found out about his shortfall in the division of the spoils from newspaper reports of the robbery. Once he found out he was cheated, he gave Knaus the "one-way ride." Also, police still thinking this was a gang-related murder, theorized that the gang may have murdered Knaus to keep his mouth shut, sensing that he might feel remorse for robbing his mother and could break down under police pressure.

On Sunday, Detective Inspector Charles O. Nevel let reporters know where the department stood in its investigation. Nevel announced they recovered a sack of coins from Petro's home containing many foreign ones that were identified as coming from the Green Café. The Bertillon Bureau had concluded that all three .32 spent cartridges, the two found in Petro's car and the third one found at the murder scene, were all fired from the same weapon. Detectives also recovered a .32 slug that had passed through Knaus's body and was embedded in the passenger side door. The last item Nevel revealed was that detectives were preparing to analyze mud found in Petro's car to see if it matched mud taken from where the murder was committed.

Nevel, Cooney and Deputy Inspector Kurt B. Gloeckner theorized that Knaus was killed late Wednesday night, sometime after 11:40 when he was last seen outside his mother's Vandalia Avenue home, or very early Thursday morning. The officers believed Petro drove Knaus to the Belvoir Boulevard location and shot him three times while he was inside the car, or while trying to escape from it. The final shot, the coup de grace, was fired into his head as he lay on the ground, which left behind the third spent cartridge found along the roadside (the fourth one was never recovered). They theorized Petro then dragged the body over to the edge of the ravine and rolled it in. He headed back to his North

Collinwood home, but instead of removing evidence from the car, he went inside and went to bed, only to have a rude awaking several hours later.

By Sunday, police had already charged Petro with the robbery of the Green Café. In addition to declining to make a statement, he was placed in a police line-up, where he defiantly refused to hold his head up. Police announced that the money had yet to be recovered.

Petro on Trial

When the murder trial of Julius A. Petro began on the first week of June 1946, it was a contemptuous one, pitting Assistant County Prosecutor Victor DeMarco against prominent defense attorneys Edward C. Stanton, the former long-time Cuyahoga County prosecutor, who served in that position from 1920 through 1928, and Michael A. Picciano, a former police prosecutor for the city of Cleveland. Common Pleas Judge Alva R. Corlett had the job of refereeing the verbal confrontations between the two legal teams.

If DeMarco was to prevail, he was going to have to do it with a totally circumstantial case. There was no smoking gun; in fact, there was no gun at all, none was ever recovered. There were also no eyewitnesses to place Petro at the scene of the murder. Defense attorneys would argue that the time of death established by the coroner was incorrect and that at the time of the murder, Petro was already in custody. DeMarco would have to build his entire case with circumstantial evidence, backed with a mass of scientific evidence delivered by expert witnesses on the subjects of micro-analytic chemistry and police ballistics, while having to prove every part of the indictment against Petro by inference. His most difficult job would be getting the jury to buy into it all.

Early in the trial, DeMarco accused the two defense attorneys of improperly obtaining police reports having to do with the case. Attached to the packet of documents in question was a note stating: "April 11, 1946. Given to Attorney Stanton by order of Inspector Costello c/o Kraws, Knecht 1063." The police officers, whose names were on the note, denied allowing the attorneys to view any of the reports. With access to the information, DeMarco claimed Picciano and Stanton had insight into the prosecution's case, and that by their cross-examination during the trial, it was obvious they had studied the data in the reports.

Inspector Timothy J. Costello, the old warhorse of the department, denied giving orders to anyone to hand over the reports to the attorneys. He told DeMarco, "They came in and asked me about them, and I said: 'See the chief.' I didn't tell anyone to give out the records." When "the chief" was questioned, George J. Matowitz declared that he had issued no order to allow the attorneys to view such records. He claimed he had not discussed the case or the record with either attorney.

Costello investigated who was on desk duty at Central Police Station on April 11 and confirmed with Officer Edward M. Craws that he had not given out any orders to reveal the records to anyone. Meanwhile, Patrolman Harold Knecht, whose name and badge number appeared on the note, was assigned to the record room at Central Police Station, where the records were stored. He, however, was on vacation at that time.

County Prosecutor Frank T. Cullitan, when questioned by reporters about the documents, stated. "There is no definite law forbidding the defense from seeing these records, and some contend they are public records. But this is a matter of ethics. Would the defense open up for us all the information they had prepared and collected from their witnesses before the trial?"

Key points and witness testimony that took place during the trial, which ran from the first week of June through June 19 included:

- It looked like an inside job to police after finding the screws to the door had been removed from inside the bar.

- Two watch dogs on-site to protect the property never made a sound, indicating they were familiar with who came in.

- A bartender testified the St. Francis medal and valve parts found in Petro's home belonged to him, he had left them in the cash register.

- A .32 automatic stolen during the burglary, but never found, was believed to be the murder weapon used by Petro.

- The .32 casings found in Petro's car and at the murder scene, along with a bullet removed from Knaus and compared to one found in Petro's car door, were found to be a ballistics match by police ballistician David L. Cowles.

- Mud from Petro's car was identical in chemical compound to mud found at the murder scene.

- Coroner Samuel R. Gerber, put the time of death between 66 and 72 hours before the body was found, which was a few hours before Petro was arrested.

The key part of defense counsel's case was to make the jury believe that Gerber's time frame was off thus showing that Petro was arrested and locked up before the murder took place. However, they failed to shake the coroner's testimony.

During the appearance of Petro's alibi witness, Donald Lemmo, he admitted in his testimony that on the night of the murder he was out on the "tavern circuit" until after 4:00 a.m. This was a clear violation of his probation and Judge Corlett immediately had Lemmo jailed for breaking his probation rules.

When Petro took the stand, he laid out an alibi for his activities on the night of the murder. The *Plain Dealer* reported:

> From midnight to 12:30 a.m. the night of Feb. 27-28 was at the Royal Castle hamburger stand at Five Points and from there drove to the Carnegie Auto Hospital, 7503 Carnegie Avenue S.E., where he threw the keys under the door and left his car.
>
> There, the alibi continued, Donald Lemmo, a former probation violator and burglar, picked him up and drove him to the Club Verdone, drinking spot at Mount Carmel Road S.E. and E. 110th Street, where they remained until 2:30 a.m. Then they went back to the Five Points hamburger place and left there to go to Petro's home, 787 E. 156th Street, where Lemmo and Petro talked a while – until 4:30 a.m.

Because of a shortage of ballistics instruments, the defense was allowed access to David Cowles tools, so Petro's "scientific counsel" could run tests on the shells and bullets. After spending a whole afternoon using the instruments, the "scientific counsel" was never put on the stand to testify.

On June 18, with closing statements completed, Judge Alva Corlett delivered a handwritten charge to the jury due to all the circumstantial evidence and inference delivered during the trial. The jury entered the deliberations room at 3:45 p.m., armed with exhibits from testimony that their verdict hinged on. Those items included spent cartridges, microphotographs of bullets and spent cartridges, dry mud samples, spectrograms of the mud samples, the St. Francis medal and valve parts.

After a trial lasting 16 days, it took the jury of four men and eight women just two hours and 15 minutes to reach a verdict. From the very first vote in the jury room, not a single juror had considered Petro anything but guilty of murder. But it took a total of seven ballots before they could resolve the issue of whether he was guilty of first-degree murder, which would send him to the electric chair, or second-degree, which would spare his life. The *Plain Dealer* reported:

> They split six to six over the death chair or a mercy recommendation at first. Then the mercy group was won over one by one until the final ballot was unanimous for a flat finding of guilty of murder in the first degree.

At the announcement of the jury's decision at 6:00 p.m., Petro "took the verdict without showing the merest shadow of emotion." Judge Corlett held up the sentencing until Petro's defense counsel could file a motion for a new trial and argue it before him. The following week the judge denied defense counsel's motion for a new trial and on June 27 sentenced Julius Petro to die in the electric chair on October 15, 1946. The prisoner was returned to the Ohio Penitentiary, but not to the general prison population, where he was once housed; instead, he was placed on death row to await his date with "Old Sparky," the death house nickname for the electric chair.

Another Murder Accusation

Back on October 8, 1945, just before 3:00 a.m., a trio of robbers tried to steal $50,000 from the City Terminal System's (CTS) – Woodhill carbarns, located at 3014 Woodhill Road. The robbery was foiled after one of the men shot James H. Peak, a 44-year-old dispatcher, in the back. During the ensuing commotion, another CTS employee set off an ADT alarm, recently installed at the insistence of the police, sending the trio of robbers into a panic and out the nearest door. Despite James Peak being listed in "fair" condition the night of the shooting, he died the next day from his wound. By Thursday, a $6,000 reward was being offered for information leading to the arrest and conviction of his killer. The Cleveland Transit Board put up $5,000 of this bounty, which the newspapers believed was the first time any branch of the city government had ever offered a reward. Despite an intense police search for the killers, no suspects were arrested, and the murder went unsolved.

More than a year passed. Then, on November 9, 1946, James LaManna, a resident of the Woodland Avenue / East 110th Street neighborhood, an area once known as Porrello Territory during the Lonardo-Porrello Corn-Sugar War back in the Prohibition days, walked into Central Police Station at 3:30 a.m. and confessed to being a part of the team that tried to rob the Woodhill carbarns back in October 1945. LaManna told a desk sergeant, "I want to see a detective. I have something to say about the Peak murder." When questioned by detectives, LaManna said that his conscious was bothering him and the killing of James Peak was preying on his mind, "because I believed in God and got religion." He claimed he was not the killer, and although he had a loaded revolver, he did not use it. "If the employees there would have started shooting, or the police had opened up, I would have surrendered," he stated.

According to LaManna's story, five other men were involved in the robbery. He and four others went into the barns, while the sixth remained in the get-away car. Once inside, LaManna said, "I went behind the [cashier's] cage. The next thing I knew I heard shots, and someone said: 'Let's get out of here.'" He confessed to detectives he participated in the robbery, "so I could get money to buy a beer license to open a restaurant."

LaManna named four of the five men who participated in the robbery as Julius Petro, Sylvester Papalardo, James V. Bocci, and Louis P. Bucci. The last member of the gang he knew only as "Skully." He alleged Bocci and Bucci were former members of the Detroit Purple Gang, but this was never proven, while the others were local men. On November 13, LaManna met with Detective Lieutenant Martin P. Cooney, head of the Homicide Squad. After asking for his parish priest, he repeated his confession in Cooney's office; but refused to sign it. LaManna was charged with first-degree murder.

The next day Bocci and Bucci were arrested in the company of Sam Papalardo, the brother of Sylvester, who had spent time in prison with one of the men. The men, one with 42 arrests, the other 24, were held 20 hours for questioning and then released after being told "to leave Cleveland by the fastest possible means." Being released around the same time were 22 men who were nabbed during a bookie raid at 1209 Superior Avenue. They were taken in and questioned about the whereabouts of Sylvester Papalardo, who was suddenly missing.

On November 16, Anthony DiMatteo, a.k.a. "Skully," was arrested in a Euclid restaurant and held as a parole violator. DiMatteo was paroled from the Mansfield Reformatory in March 1942 after serving about three years for an armed robbery. Six days later, DiMatteo was charged with first-degree murder. Both he and LaManna would be formally indicted for James Peak's murder on December 5.

Before he could be tried for first-degree murder, prosecutors had to be sure LaManna could be legally tried for the killing. On January 14, 1947, a sanity hearing was held before Common Pleas Judge Stanley L. Orr. The question was not LaManna's mental state at the time of the crime, but rather his current mental condition. During the hearing, psychiatrist's reports were presented as evidence as to the question of whether LaManna:

- Knows his present situation

- Appreciates the charge against him

- Understands the proceedings so as to be able to help build his defense

- Is able to counsel with his attorney

While the sanity hearing and its disposition were being decided, police in Newport, Kentucky, had a murder mystery on their hands. A 21-year-old man was found alive in a ditch after being shot five times. Taken to a hospital in Dayton, Kentucky, the man identified himself as "Mike Jacobs, a Cleveland gambler." He told police that four men forced him into an automobile and stole his wallet. He was then pushed into a ditch and shot. He claimed he was laying there for about 2 minutes before police arrived. The young man knew he was not going to survive and pleaded with police "that information that 'Jacobs' had been shot be given to 'Tony P.' at a Cleveland telephone number." Just before he died, Campbell County police were able to identify him as Louis P. Bucci, wanted in the murder of James Peak.

Police in Cleveland questioned Mr. and Mrs. Angelo Bucci, parents of the dead man. A family member told police the parents had not heard from their son in more than two years. Also questioned by police was Thomas Coreno, of Coreno's Funeral Home on Kinsman Avenue. He claimed he received a telephone call from a funeral parlor in Dayton, Kentucky, advising him that Bucci's body was being sent to him. He stated it was the first he had heard of the death.

Meanwhile, three days after LaManna's hearing, four psychiatrists concluded that he was unable to help with his defense or assist his counsel. Judge Orr declared LaManna insane and ordered him sent to the Lima State Hospital to remain there until he was "returned to sanity."

With no witness to testify against him, the charges against DiMatteo were soon dropped. Warrants against the others were obtained, but not a single person came to trial for the murder of James H. Peak, despite three people confessing to it. In addition to LaManna, in September 1948, George R. Andrews[8] of Pittsburgh claimed he murdered Peak. He also stated he murdered a Detroit girl earlier in the year. He was cleared after a psychiatric evaluation. In October 1952, a 37-year-old East Side man confessed to the murder. Detective Captain David E. Kerr investigated and found out the man was serving in the U.S. Army at the time of the slaying and later had received treatment at Crile Veterans Hospital for a mental disability. James J. LaManna passed away in January 1991.

The Fight to Save Julius Petro

On October 11, just four days before Petro was to be executed, Judge Alva Corlett granted an indefinite stay of execution for the condemned prisoner after defense counsel submitted "newly discovered evidence" in the case. The new evidence was an affidavit from former homicide detective Thomas Whalen.[9] In the affidavit, Whalen claimed, "Coroner Samuel R. Gerber told us that Knaus' body was in such condition that Knaus had died 60 hours before."

During Petro's trial, Picciano and Stanton had tried to shake the coroner on the time of death, which Gerber had established at 66 to 72 hours prior to his examination of the body at the county morgue. If it had been 60, this would have proved Petro hadn't committed the murder because he would have already been in custody. To warrant the granting of a motion for a new trial in a criminal case, based on the grounds of newly discovered evidence, it must be shown that the new evidence 1) discloses a strong probability that it will change the result if a new trial is granted; 2) has been discovered since the trial; 3) is such as could not in the exercise of due diligence have been discovered before the trial; 4) is material to the issues; 5) is not merely cumulative to former evidence; and 6) does not merely impeach or contradict the former evidence.

On November 15, 1946, a hearing was held in the courtroom of Judge Corlett on the new evidence gathered, based on former detective Thomas Whalen's affidavit. Whalen was in for a long day. There were several mistakes in the reporting. Beginning with the first sentence of a *Plain Dealer* article the next day which claimed Whalen, who had resigned from the detective bureau two months earlier, was "no longer on the police force." The article also reported that Whalen told the judge he was "fed up and quit [detective work] because he has three children to support." He allegedly told reporters afterwards he was going to practice law and had "a couple of other jobs."

The facts, however, dispute most of this. Despite a few bumps in his career, Whalen was a fine police officer and detective, who served the city at least until the mid-1950s, including working on cases in 1948 and 1949 where he was listed as a detective for the robbery squad. He earned a law degree from the Western Reserve School of Law in 1936, and while he may have handled some minor legal matters for clients, his name never appeared in the newspapers for handling any newsworthy cases.

This may leave the reader to perhaps wonder why Thomas Whalen agreed to making out the affidavit, which could have helped a convicted murderer and public enemy get out of prison. While admitting he had not testified at the June trial of Petro, he claimed, "I suppose it's going to be unpopular for me...to testify for the defense, but these are the facts. I'm not going back on my report. I made the report about four hours after the body went to the morgue. The facts are the facts."

During the hearing, Judge Corlett grilled Whalen about his comment in the affidavit that Coroner Gerber "told us that Knaus was dead for "approximately 60 hours." Corlett demanded to know, "What do you mean, 'the coroner told us?' Do you mean you and the others were told this, or were you using the 'editorial we and us?'"

Whalen replied. "That meant he told me. We always make out our reports that way."

Corlett inquired, "You have been a police officer nine years, and a lawyer since 1936." Do you mean to say that such reports can be used by attorneys if they want to exact evidence?"

Whatever Whalen replied, the newspaper didn't report. Corlett did not seem impressed with his testimony; he was disturbed by the fact that Whalen was present in the courtroom throughout the trial and could have been called by defense counsel at any time. Then they could have cross-examined Gerber as to the testimony of the detective. The judge was concerned about Whalen coming forward with his statement at the last minute.

Corlett suggested to Assistant County Prosecutor Victor DeMarco that he call other police officers who were at the county morgue that day to see if any of them heard Gerber set the time of death at 60 hours. The judge then continued the hearing until November 27.

When court reconvened, Judge Corlett overruled the motion for a new trial for Petro. Addressing defense counsel, the judge stated, "This was not new evidence. In the record of the trial are pages and pages of your cross-examination of Dr. Gerber, much of it on this very point. Whalen was around during the trial and could have been subpoenaed, and so could the records of the homicide squad. You also questioned other detectives who had worked on the case with Whalen. So, this is neither a new witness nor a new matter." Corlett did not set a new date for the execution, but Petro continued to remain on death row waiting for the next round of legal action before the court of appeals.

The next battle in the effort to save Petro took place on March 10, 1947, when Picciano and Stanton argued the case before the Court of Appeals. In addition to taking issue with the Gerber estimate of the time of death, they also claimed Judge Corlett "prejudiced the jury" with a remark about a Petro defense witness. During the June 1946 trial, the defense scheduled Donald Lemmo, a friend of Petro who was incarcerated at the Mansfield Reformatory, to testify on the defendant's behalf. The prisoner was brought to Cleveland and held in the County Jail until it was time to appear in court. When it came time for him to testify, they had to wait for him to be brought into the courtroom. When a question was asked about what the delay was, Judge Corlett responded, "The sheriff is bringing him down from the jail." At some point in the trial, the judge also referred to him as a "probation violator." On April 11, the Appeals Court upheld the conviction and refused to grant a new trial for Petro. A new execution date of June 23 was set. On May 9, his attorneys appealed the verdict to the Ohio Supreme Court.

After two failed attempts to obtain a new trial, time was running out on Petro. On June 26, 1947, a little over a year since his conviction, a *Plain Dealer* article announced: "Last Chance for Petro." The day before, the Ohio Supreme Court had decided to review the conviction. The court announced it would hear arguments after the summer recess.

The "summer recess" lasted a little longer than Petro anticipated. By the time the legal teams argued their case before the Ohio Supreme Court it was already November and Petro had been on death row for a year and five months, during which time he had watched five other inmates take the walk to eternity before him.

Before the state Supreme Court justices, the defense brought out their latest argument claiming the prosecutor had refused to provide them with a bill of particulars and that Corlett had upheld the refusal. When DeMarco got the chance to argue the state's case, he stated that the bill of particulars would have given "the defense a blueprint of the state's case" and with it an unfair advantage. The *Plain Dealer* reported, "Such bills are not ordinarily asked. The law says that the indictment need only to say what was the form and nature of the crime. But it also says the particulars may be requested by the defense." DeMarco then pointed out that the Supreme Court held just the opposite [view] and so had other appellate courts.

To DeMarco's surprise, on November 26, the Ohio Supreme Court granted a new trial to Julius Petro on what the *Plain Dealer* called, "a foggy point of law." The following month a reporter from the *Cleveland News* interviewed Petro at the Ohio Penitentiary. Petro told the reporter, "I spent 18 months in the same cell and only left three times, and those times to go to Mass. I was not afraid at anytime. I had faith in Almighty God, and knew that some day the truth would come out." While on death row Petro said he lost 25 pounds. Five prisoners were executed during that time. "The last ones I saw go were [Robert] Britton and [James] Griffin," Petro stated. He claimed he helped Griffin learn his Catholic catechism before he went to the chair.[10]

A Second Murder Trial

The second trial of the State of Ohio vs. Julius A. Petro for the murder of Theodore Robert Knaus was scheduled to begin on May 24, 1948. As the date approached, Petro was taken from the death row section of the Ohio Penitentiary and brought back to Cleveland and placed in the County Jail. Problems began ten days before the start date when a hunting jacket, called a key piece of evidence by the defense, turned up missing. Defense attorneys claimed the jacket belonged to Petro's brother Michael; despite being found in the convicted man's home. When detectives searched the pockets they discovered the St. Francis medal, the valve parts and $22.

Prosecutors said the medal and other items found in the jacket were stolen from the Green Café; defense counsel claimed the items belonged to Michael Petro. Attorney Picciano said, "Absence of the jacket would be prejudicial to the defense." He was not sure what steps would be taken if the jacket was not found. An immediate search was started by the property clerk in the prosecutor's office.

Assistant County Prosecutor Victor DeMarco would be trying the case again along with Thomas V. Moore. The error which earned Petro a second trial was "meticulously" taken care of by the two. DeMarco personally got involved in the search for the missing jacket. During the hunt, he realized some "vital" detective reports were also missing. These were the same reports that drew attention prior to the first trial when they ended up in defense counsel's hands for review. DeMarco demanded that Picciano and Stanton return them.

On May 18, during a hearing before Common Pleas Judge Frank J. Merrick,[11] attorneys Picciano and DeMarco took turns on the witness stand cross-examining each other on the question of, "Who saw that jacket last?" The contest ended in a draw, with neither attorney being able to recall what happened to the jacket. The hearing ended with Judge Merrick denying defense counsel's motion for a continuance.

The problems weren't over for the prosecution. Shortly after "jacket-gate," the prosecutors were informed that "loads of dirt" had been dumped into the ravine along Ninemile Creek near Belvoir Boulevard, changing the topography of the murder scene. Immediately "No Dumping" signs were placed at the site and local police were asked to give extra attention "to the death scene."

On Monday, May 24, the trial began before Common Pleas Judge Edmond Savord from Erie County. Savord was given the assignment to handle the second trial by Chief Justice Carl V. Weygandt of the Ohio Supreme Court because the "heavy murder docket" here could not be handled by the "few" common pleas judges free for such trials. The *Cleveland Press* reported, "Because of an old custom which dictates that common pleas judges up for election may not sit in Criminal Court in the election year, only two judges and Judge Savord, who has been sitting at Lakeside Courthouse for the past three weeks were eligible to hear the Petro case."

Jury selection got underway with a venire of 75 men and women. On the second day, DeMarco used his first preemptory challenge to excuse one of nine women tentatively seated. Soon, three more potential jurors were excused after admitting they were not believers in capital punishment. By the end of Tuesday, 11 jurors were selected, but only two members of the venire remained. A second venire of 75 would be brought in the next morning. Attorney Picciano questioned each potential juror "exhaustively," averaging 35 minutes per person. He asked each one if they would vote "not guilty" if it were proven that the murder was committed outside of Cuyahoga County? All answered, "Yes." When reporters asked him about this line of questioning, his brief reply was simply, "It's always a possibility." On Wednesday, a jury of three men and nine women were seated and sworn in.

On Thursday, after Savord denied a motion by Picciano to delay the trial until a piece of evidence – the hunting jacket – could be located, the jury was given a bus tour of the key sites that would come up in testimony during the trial. The locations included the murder scene along the Belvoir Boulevard ravine, the Green Café, and Petro's home in North Collinwood. The defendant went along for the ride, handcuffed to a deputy, but decided not to leave the bus at the Nine Mile Creek stop. If the dirt dumping at the murder scene created any problems, it was not mentioned in the newspaper reports. The next morning, both sides delivered their opening statements.

When testimony got underway, Coroner Samuel Gerber was one of the first witnesses to testify. From the beginning, the coroner's office had set the time of death for Bobby Knaus at between 8:00 p.m., February 27 and 2:00 a.m., February 28, 1946. The defense had to show that the time of death was three or more hours later, because by 5:00 a.m. on February 28, Petro was in police custody.

During Gerber's direct examination by DeMarco, he presented U.S. Weather Bureau official temperature charts that showed a high of 58-degrees and a low of 26-degrees during the period Knaus's body lay in the ravine. "Temperatures that cool," Gerber testified, "Would retard rigor mortis in its onset and disappearance and would prevent putrefaction." This, he stated, explained the fresh appearance of the body, not the later time of death that defense counsel was claiming.

Gerber set up a screen on the high desk of Judge Savord to show X-ray photographs of Knaus's body. He then pointed out where the bullets had entered and exited, and where fragments were left behind. At one point Stanton interrupted.

"I object. The photograph doesn't show the two particles he just referred to," he declared.

DeMarco responded, "And I object to your testifying!"

After Savord warned both sides that "this will be an orderly trial," Gerber pointed out the "particles" again and the trial continued.

Gerber also explained away a mystery on the coroner's report form, stating that the forms had been in use for 25 years and "failed to give exact terms." He said, "Where it says, 'time of death,' that means the time the official death report was made out – not the actual or estimated time the person died."

Dr. A.J. Kazlaukas, the deputy coroner, was worked over by attorney Stanton during his time on the stand. The wily defense counsel questioned him about rigor mortis to Knaus's stiffened ankles, only to show Kazlaukas that during his testimony in the first trial he was referring to his knees that had been rigid. As Stanton challenged the deputy coroner over the body temperature of the deceased, he asked whether or not there was a thermometer at the County Morgue, to which Kazlaukas answered that there was.

"But you didn't take the body's temperature?" Stanton asked.

"No," Kazlaukas replied.

"But that would be the only correct way to get the body's temperature, wouldn't it?" insisted Stanton.

"Yes, the exact temperature," Kazlaukas said.

Judge Savord, who "policed the trial sharply," ended the back-and-forth banter. Throughout the trial he kept a close eye on both tables, keeping "by play" and heckling between the two sides to a minimum.

Despite hammering away at the coroner's office testimony for two days, defense counsel was unable to break down the time of death for Bobby Knaus.

On Wednesday, June 2, after two contemptuous days of back and forth on the coroner's findings, the prosecution began questioning witnesses about the robbery at the Green Café. Marie Estrate, Knaus's mother, took the stand and testified, "I saw my son, Bobby, in the kitchen of the café that night with his girlfriend. The last time I saw him alive was when he borrowed my car and drove his friend home. I next saw him in the morgue." She broke down sobbing several times during her testimony. During cross-examination by Picciano, she was able to say exactly what the prosecutor had been contending, that her Spitz dog did not bark during the robbery because her son was one of the robbers and the dog knew him. "He was not friendly to strangers," she stated.

Mrs. Estrate was followed on the stand by her daughter Dolores Knaus. The pretty blonde-haired 20-year-old younger sister of the victim had once dated Petro. After his arrest and the discovery of the St. Francis medal in the hunting jacket, Petro told the police that Dolores had given it to him. When police brought her to the jail for questioning on March 1, the day before her brother's body was discovered, she told them she had never given Petro the medal. She now testified, "I asked Julius why he told them I gave him the medal?" She said Petro replied, "Don't believe them, they're lying." She also testified that in late December 1945, Petro, who by then was a regular at the Green Café, asked her how much money the bar took in on New Years' Eve. She said she told him, "It was none of his business."

Detective Edward Frindt, Jr. was called to tell the jury how he and his partner, Milo Sebek, found the spent .32 cartridges on the floor in the backseat of Petro's car. DeMarco used the location of the cartridges to prove his point about the firing of the .32 semiautomatic he claimed Petro used. By firing from the driver's seat with his arm extended towards a passenger to his right, the cartridges would have ejected out and to the right after being fired, which deposited them into the backseat area.

John Bush, the 61-year-old porter, who was bound and gagged before being tied to a drainpipe in the men's room, had passed away since the first trial. His previous testimony was allowed to be read into the current trial. DeMarco took the witness seat to read Bush's direct testimony before Stanton did the same while reading his cross-examination.

On Thursday, attorneys battled over bullets, spent cartridges and mud. In their questioning of state's witnesses, the *Plain Dealer* reported that Picciano and Stanton, "baldly hinted...that police had 'planted' bits of evidence along Julius A. Petro's trail to involve him" in the murder of Bobby Knaus.

Stanton attacked the testimony of Detective Milo Sebek, who testified to finding the empty cartridges and a lump of mud in Petro's automobile. "You knew a 32-caliber pistol was stolen in the Green Café robbery. So you knew what caliber of cartridge to 'find' in the car, didn't you?" Stanton declared. Stanton then demanded to know if it was Sebek or another officer who climbed into the car to investigate. Stanton wanted to show that the mud could have come from Sebek's shoe. His plan didn't work, as Sebek had already testified under direct examination of DeMarco that he wasn't at the murder scene along Belvoir Boulevard, so how could he have transported any mud from the ravine into the car while he searched it.

The fiery attorney then peppered Sebek with questions about Michael Carlin, whose St. Francis medal was stolen during the robbery and found in Petro's home. Stanton demanded to know if Sebek was in Carlin's room and if the

Green Café employee kept a lot of religious medals there? Sebek had already told the jury that he had never been in Carlin's room and simply replied, "I wouldn't know."

The state's next witness was auto mechanic Emil Jeney, who worked at the Carnegie Auto Hospital, 7503 Carnegie Avenue. Jeney was there when Sebek and other detectives found a bullet hole in the right door trim of Petro's car. Jeney removed the trim panel and found a .32 slug inside the door, as detectives looked on.

On Friday, June 4, as the murder trial reached the two-week point, Jeney was back on the stand. Picciano was about to question him about the valve cap found in the jacket in Petro's home. Police claimed the valve cap belonged to Michael Carlin and was stolen from the Green Café along with his St. Francis medal. During the first trial in June 1946, Petro testified that it came from a gasoline station run by his brother Michael. Now, Picciano had just built Jeney up as an expert on automobile parts and wanted him to tell the jury that the valve cap could have come from anywhere. He asked him if there were not "millions of such valve caps" all over the country.

Handing the cap to Jeney, the auto mechanic examined the cap and replied, "I've never seen a type like that in my life." Picciano's effort to nullify the valve cap as evidence was a failure and he quickly switched to another line of questioning.

The police believed from day one the robbery of the Green Café was an inside job, pulled off by Knaus and Petro. To prove this point, the prosecution called Joseph A. Kerns, a police expert who told the jury that the screws which held the café's door hasp, were unscrewed from the inside. "The door was not forced," he said, "because the screws were found clean of wood shreds and the threads still showed clean inside the screw holes after the robbery."

When the trial resumed Monday morning, Sergeant James K. Dodge, the police department's firearms expert, testified that the "fine grooving" on bullets retrieved from Knaus's body, matched the grooves on the bullet found in the door of Petro's car, indicating they were fired from the same .32 semiautomatic. He determined that the .32 semiautomatic they were fired from was either a Colt or Belgian-made model. Both of those models, he told the jury, "Out of some 200 brands of pistols" manufactured, have left angle rifling in the barrel.

Attorney Picciano attempted to raise doubt about Dodge's testimony in the minds of the jurors by asking the firearm's expert "is the science of ballistics infallible, sergeant?"

Dodge responded, "There is no science that is infallible."

The defense counsel tried to create doubt about the ballistics photographs entered into evidence in the trial. He read passages from a ballistics textbook and argued over the fact that the bullets were copper coated. "Doesn't the copper flake and make it harder to determine which gun it was fired from?" he inquired.

"Not in this case," Dodge replied, showcasing his expertise. "That kind of coating, such as Lubaloy,[12] is only about five-one-thousandths of an inch thick, but this is a full coating of 25 to 30 one-thousandths."

On Tuesday, the state put expert witness Dr. Irene Levis[13] on the stand. A consultant in spectroscopy[14] and microanalysis, Dr. Levis was under police protection. On Sunday, two days before her testimony, she received a telephone call from a man "who threatened vengeance if she dared to testify" against Petro. Police were investigating the threat, but so far, no leads had been developed in determining who the caller could be. The newspapers reported that several spectators at the trial were men with police records.

During the first trial, Dr. Levis testified to her analysis work on the mud samples collected from the murder scene of Bobby Knaus to those taken from the automobile belonging to Petro. Using micro analytic techniques, she was able to determine that based on their chemical ingredients, the soil samples were identical. Dr. Levis used the spectroscope to determine what chemical elements are present in a substance. In the second trial, after being given a police escort to and from the Criminal Courts Building, Dr. Levis discovered that the analysis she prepared for the first trial, like the hunting jacket, had disappeared and could not be located. During cross-examination, Picciano read aloud sections of her testimony from the first trial. At one point Levis screamed out, "I never said that! That's nonsense." She claimed a court reporter must have erred.

After Levis's testimony came that of Superintendent David Cowles, of the police department's Scientific Identification Bureau. Cowles fired a Colt .32 semiautomatic in the courtroom to show how the spent cartridge cases ejected from the gun. The demonstration proved that the shooter was sitting in the driver's seat firing the weapon towards his right, thus leaving the shells in the backseat, where police officers found them.

The state rested its case on Tuesday afternoon. Assistant County Prosecutor DeMarco had placed 50 trial exhibits into evidence, including mud samples, bullets, empty cartridges, spectrograms and photographs. Defense counsel objected to five exhibits, three of which were photos of the body of Bobby Knaus, which the attorneys deemed were "too gruesome." The other items were evidence envelopes that were labeled "property of Julius Petro." The attorneys claimed the items belonged to Julius's brother Michael and asked that their client's name be covered up. Judge Savord denied the requests.

On Wednesday defense counsel began their case by calling Donald Lemmo to the stand. He again testified how he followed Petro to drop off his car at the Carnegie Auto Hospital and then gave him a ride home around 3:00 a.m. on February 28. During cross-examination, DeMarco was loaded for bear, but Judge Savord quickly reined him in. In question was the fact that this same testimony, during the June 1946 trial, put Lemmo back in the Mansfield Reformatory for 14 months because it showed he had violated the guidelines of his probation. DeMarco wanted to make this point to the jury, but Savord would not allow him.

"Well, did you live in Mansfield in 1946?" DeMarco asked.

Judge Savord agreed to allow the question and Lemmo replied, "Yes."

The tricky prosecutor then inquired, "With whom were you living with there?"

"Object!" shouted defense attorney Stanton.

This time Savord sustained the objection and several others during a series of questions to show Lemmo was back in prison during this period. Finally, an exasperated DeMarco shouted, "Were you arrested and convicted of a crime?" Lemmo answered that he was arrested and convicted for a burglary in 1945.

Also taking the stand this day was Michael Petro. He told the court that he had seen his brother at the Royal Castle Restaurant at East 152nd Street and St. Clair around 11:40 that night. When questioned about the now infamous missing hunting jacket, he claimed it belonged to him.

The next day, Petro took the stand. The defendant repeated his alibi story from the 1946 trial, but this time with more detail. Petro now seemed more certain about the times and his movements back on February 27 and 28, 1946; going from restaurant to night club and from night club to repair shop. On cross-examination, DeMarco asked, "Have you refreshed your recollection since the last trial, Julius?"

"Yes," he replied.

"When did you do that?" DeMarco asked.

"I did that for 19 months," Petro replied, referring to his time in the Ohio Penitentiary.

The *Cleveland Press* noted that Petro "sprinkled his testimony with "yes, sirs" when he was on the stand. He wasn't the cocky youth of two years ago when he was sentenced to death in his first trial."

Michael Petro also took the stand again this day. He claimed he owned the St. Francis medal and the valve cap that were found in the now missing hunting jacket he left at his brother's North Collinwood home.

On Friday, the defense put their own expert witness on the stand to refute the testimony of Dr. Levis. During his direct testimony Dr. Clifford R. Keizer,[15] a Western Reserve University assistant chemistry professor, claimed there were differences between the mud samples placed in evidence by the state, compared to the analysis made during the first trial. Unfortunately, DeMarco "torpedoed" the testimony on cross-examination when he was able to get Keizer to admit:

- That mud samples used from Petro's automobile and from the murder scene in his analysis were not sufficiently exact for court purposes

- That he had failed to use a chemically clean spoon in extracting the earth samples

- That he used an unglazed mortar and pestle, which might have added extra chemicals to the earth samples

- That he failed to include a study of all the chemical elements in the samples

- And that he had not used any micro analytic measures of the quantities of the chemical ingredients

It was brought out, however, on cross-examination, that after two years of sitting in storage in vaults and drying, the chemical makeup of the samples could have changed.

Testimony from Petro's girlfriend, Olga Colucci, from the first trial was read by attorney Stanton, since she was unavailable to testify at the second trial. She had told of being with Petro from 4:00 p.m. on February 27, when he picked her up at her job, until he took her home at 11:00 p.m. From that time other alibi witnesses had filled in the time gap – in a restaurant, several bars and a Carnegie Avenue garage. The defense then called pathologist Dr. Harry Sneiderman, as another expert witness. He was called to refute the time of death given by the coroner's office.

When the defense rested its case, the only rebuttal witness called was Detective Edward Frindt, Jr. In checking Petro's alibi, Frindt retraced the time it took to drive from the Carnegie Auto Hospital to Club Verdone, clocking it six to eight minutes, not the 30 minutes as Petro and Lemmo had testified to.

The Thursday morning rebuttal was followed by closing statements by both sides. Stanton claimed Petro was already in jail when Bobby Knaus was murdered in 1946. He told the jury that the prosecution wanted to send Petro to the chair based on general rather than exact evidence.

DeMarco attacked Petro's alibi from every angle, declaring that he "coldly, deliberately" killed Knaus to get all of the loot they had stolen in the café robbery. In presenting the state's ballistic exhibits, he laid all the evidence out on a table before the jury. Ballistics experts David Cowles and James K. Dodge had shown that the empty cartridges in Petro's automobile, and at the death scene, showed the same breech markings, and that the "lands and grooves" on the fatal slugs matched a slug found in his passenger-side door. DeMarco repeatedly pointed out how the bullets and the spent cartridges cases found in Petro's car matched a cartridge at the death scene and the slugs removed from Bobby Knaus's body.

DeMarco then surprised the courtroom by ending his closing statement with, "The state would not tamper with the jury's right to extend mercy. The state will not complain if this jury decides to recommend mercy."

Petro's mother, Lydia wept as DeMarco described her son as a "cold-hearted killer." Julius Petro remained calm through the closing statements, occasionally swallowing hard. He whispered a prayer and crossed himself as DeMarco's closing statement came to an end. The *Plain Dealer* wrote:

His 19 months in a death cell worked drastic changes in the murder defendant. From a scornful, 180-pound rough-neck, whom his former comrades dubbed "Beef," Petro became a quiet, pious, slim (156-pound) figure of obvious humility. His prayer book became his main occupation.

Petro professed, "I went astray, but my religion came back to me down in that row."

Now it was the judge's turn. Throughout the three weeks and two days, Judge Savord cautiously tried to avoid even the slightest error that might derail the trial and make it necessary for it to be tried a third time. He watched both the principals and spectators like a hawk. He calmed any flare-ups between the defense and prosecution tables, he warned spectators for "snickering, grinning and talking." He drew a line between safe and unsafe questions that might have prejudiced the trial's outcome.

Judge Savord now charged the jury on both first-degree and second-degree murder, handing the case over to them at 3:45 on Tuesday afternoon. Hotel rooms were booked for the night in case the jury could not reach a verdict by midnight. Petro's second trial had taken 23 days, a week longer than his first murder trial back in 1946. It was now the longest murder trial in the history of Cuyahoga County.

The jury had the case for nearly for nearly 24 hours; deliberating it for 13 of those. Around noon on Wednesday, the jury presented a question to Judge Savord, "Does doubt about one link in the chain of the state's evidence justify a not guilty verdict? Or does certainty about the one strong link justify a guilty verdict?" The judge's answer provided little help. He advised them to "labor conscientiously to recall the law of the state as given in his final instructions" before they began their deliberations. With that, they trudged back to the deliberating room.

At 3:00 p.m., the jurors filed back into the courtroom and delivered a stunning "not guilty" verdict. Jury foreman, W.O. Hoffman later told reporters, "The verdict came on the 10th ballot. Trying to ascertain the time of death caused doubt, and so did discrepancies due to the frailties of police, such as the loss of some of the evidence." Hoffman did admit that the strongest part of the state's case was the ballistics portion. When the first vote was taken, Hoffman revealed, it was five for acquittal, three for guilty and four undecideds. At the point they asked the question of the judge, the split was seven for acquittal and five for guilty. In addition to their doubts about the time of death, they also were concerned about a lost analysis paper on which Dr. Irene Levis had written down the chemicals found in the mud samples in Petro's car and at the murder scene.

The *Plain Dealer* reported that when the verdict was announced, "Weary and tearful, some of the nine women jurors were deeply moved by the weeping of Mrs. Lydia Petro, the mother of the defendant, who was near collapse. She and the father, John, and son, Michael, who sold his interest in a filling station to pay for Petro's defense, never left the courtroom while the jury wrangled." Petro smiled and shook hands with his defense counsel.

After the verdict, Petro announced that he was "pledging" himself to a law-abiding life and going to work at his father's furniture business. "My father used to send me out on the truck when he was in the furniture business," he said. "I used to drive away and go swimming. I just wasn't responsible. But now I know that that kind of life doesn't pay. Nineteen months in death row and watching five men walk that last mile – men I ate their last meal with – taught me that it's no use. All I can do now is thank God, I'm here. I had faith because I know I was innocent. There are no atheists in death row."

DeMarco called the verdict "shocking" and said the jury was incapable of presenting any tangible reasons to support its decision. The irate prosecutor pointed out that the same defense counsel's arguments were the same in both trials. He declared Petro was acquitted on "exactly the same evidence that another jury weighed to convict him two years ago." DeMarco went even further declaring, "This was a bad jury. It didn't measure up. Scientific evidence went over juror's heads. They didn't understand what was going on."

After the verdict was announced, DeMarco called jury foreman Hoffman to his office and asked for an explanation of the jury's vote. "Hoffman just shrugged," DeMarco claimed. "He couldn't give me an aye, yes or no. He talked vaguely about inconclusive evidence, about conflicting testimony." Hoffman claimed jurors had doubts about the time of the murder and that Coroner Gerber's testimony was clouded by that of Detective Thomas Whelan's report, even though Gerber vehemently denied he made any such statement to Whelan. DeMarco was told by Hoffman that the finding of loot by police, even after it was identified by the café bartender who owned it, was not conclusive. As for the chemical analysis of the mud, Hoffman claimed that each side's expert testimony was "conflicting and confusing."

Hoffman said the state's strongest evidence was the finding of both the bullet and spent cartridges in Petro's car and matching these to the bullets in Knaus's body and the spent cartridge found near the death scene. DeMarco said he asked Hoffman: "If that's the case, then how could you acquit Petro? How did the bullet and shells get in his car?" DeMarco claimed, "Hoffman just shrugged his shoulders and walked away.

The prosecutor finished his rant by telling reporters, "Well, there is no doubt in my mind that this jury freed a guilty man. I never doubted at any time that Petro was the murderer."

Not all the news for Petro was good. He was a free man for only a matter of minutes before detectives grabbed him and took him to the jail to face charges for the actual robbery. Prosecutors announced they would attempt to show that some items owned by a Green Café employee, were the ones found inside the jacket found in Petro's home. In this case, he would again be represented by Picciano and Stanton; even though the two received only $500 apiece for their work in the second trial. Their compensation came from state funds from which the fees for the expert witnesses had to be paid, each of whom served two days and were paid $50 per day. The next day, Common Pleas Judge Frank J. Merrick set bond at $5,000 on these charges. When the attorneys posted it at noon, Petro found himself a free man for the first time since February 28, 1946.

Speaking briefly with a reporter from the *Cleveland Press*, when Petro was asked about the verdict he responded with this ironic remark: "Thank God. That DeMarco even had me believing at times that I was guilty. He's the greatest lawyer I've ever seen."

DeMarco had his own response. "Petro is a lucky guy!"

After reading DeMarco's comments in the *Cleveland Press* on Friday, Hoffman lashed out at the prosecutor. He told the newspaper, "I have been called by several of the jurors and we felt highly insulted by DeMarco's statements. He insulted 12 good citizens and we jurors think we did our jobs better than he did his. We couldn't tie the evidence presented by the state fixing the time of death in accordance with the bill of particulars. The majority of us believed Petro guilty but the state had not proved it. On the evidence, we had to free him."

Chapter Three:

Green Acres Casino Robbery

The First Shooting of Julius Petro
Around midnight, on Friday, September 17, 1948, a 25-year-old man was brought into Emergency Clinic Hospital[16] in Cleveland by his younger brother. Hospital personnel notified Cleveland police and soon Inspector Frank W. Story arrived and immediately identified the wounded man as Julius Anthony Petro. Doctors were treating him for wounds in the right chest and right arm; one of his ribs was shattered by a bullet. When Story questioned him, Petro claimed he was shot "accidentally while out drinking with the boys."

Police received conflicting stories from Petro's family. When they questioned Michael Petro, he claimed Julius had staggered onto the porch of his parent's home on Schenely Avenue in North Collinwood around 11:00 p.m., rang the doorbell and collapsed. When police questioned John Petro, the boy's father, they received an entirely different story. John Petro claimed neither son was at his home that night. He told police, "Mike phoned me at 10:30 and said Julius had been hurt in a fall. He asked for the car to take Julius to the hospital. Mike came, took the car about 11 p.m. and left without saying a thing." When police confronted Mike with his father's story, he just hung his head and refused to say anything. He was immediately held for questioning but released after a short stay.

Homicide detectives George Gackowski and Vincent Morrow received little help from the victim. He told them that he was drunk from a "two-day bender" and had no idea what happened to him. One thing Julius Petro did tell the detectives was he was treated earlier by another doctor, whom he refused to identify, claiming the physician had removed the bullet that had entered his chest. Doctors at the Emergency Clinic Hospital soon discovered otherwise – the bullet was still in Petro.

In an interesting piece of detective work, Gackowski and Morrow said they determined that Petro's wounds were caused by bullets fired from a .38 Special handgun. They claimed the wounds were at least six-hours old, based on discoloration around the edges. Their initial theory was that Petro, after his impassioned declaration to follow the straight and narrow path just 90 days earlier, was shot in revenge for the Bobby Knaus murder, or in a dispute over the sharing of the loot from one of several robberies the police believed the born-again robber was involved in since his June 17 acquittal. With Petro unwilling or unable to provide them with any further information, his $5,000 bond for the robbery at the Green Cafe was quickly increased to $25,000 by Common Pleas Judge Charles McNamee at the request of Assistant County Prosecutor Thomas Moore. Police then requested that Petro be transferred to the Prison Ward at

City Hospital (today Metro Health Medical Center).[17] The mystery of the shooting, however, would be short-lived.

Earlier that same Friday, the Green Acres casino was bustling with activity. Located in Struthers, Ohio, a city southeast of Youngstown in Mahoning County, the new gambling joint, which was reportedly in operation for less than thirty days, had opened to compete with its rival to the north, the Jungle Inn, located in Trumbull County. In attendance with the other patrons that night was a transplanted Mafia figure from Buffalo, New York, Joseph "Joe the Wolf" DiCarlo. The club was rumored to be run by local gambling figure Frank Budak, who had a well-known past.

Around 4:00 a.m. that Friday morning, five armed bandits wearing masks entered the casino where one of them shouted, "This is a stickup." There were approximately 250 patrons present, who were ordered to line up against the walls along with club employees. While three of the bandits kept everyone covered, the other two grabbed money off the gaming tables, including all the money left behind at the chuck-o-luck, roulette, and dice tables, and then they methodically searched the pockets of the patrons taking money, wallets, rings and anything else of value. The total haul was estimated at $25,000 to $30,000 (this figure was later reduced to between $8,000 and $10,000). One witness stated Joe DiCarlo was relieved of an expensive diamond ring by one the bandits. The robbery was eerily reminiscent of the infamous Mounds Club robbery, which took place in Lake County during September 1947, where an alleged $500,000 was taken by armed bandits.

When the robbers completed their work, they headed for a door leading to the outside where three vehicles waited. Before all could escape, someone in the casino opened fire with a revolver, emptying it at the fleeing intruders. As soon as the gunfire began, the patrons dove to the floor to escape any stray or ricocheting bullets. An eyewitness account said one of the robbers fell to the floor and crawled to the door where his accomplices helped him to one of the cars.

After the robbers fled, the patrons crowded towards the exits and poured out onto Broad and Bridge Streets, many looking for taxis to get them out of the area. In all the excitement, no one took time to call the Struthers police to report the incident. Instead, the bolting patrons told cab drivers what happened and by sunrise the story of the robbery was the talk of the town, seemingly being discussed everywhere with the exception of Struthers police headquarters.

On Saturday, Struthers police questioned John Sanko, whose position at the casino was not clear. One report said he identified himself to police as the owner, another claimed he was merely a bartender. Sanko was no stranger to law enforcement in the Mahoning Valley. His rap sheet started when he was just eleven years old after breaking the door seals on several Baltimore & Ohio railroad cars. On November 17, 1933, Sanko was stopped on the street while carrying money stolen from a filling station. He slugged his captor and broke free while the officer was requesting help at a police call-box. The officer fired a warning shot and when Sanko didn't stop, he was shot twice in the back. Sanko did two and half years in the Ohio Penitentiary and returned for a year and half more after violating his parole. In 1938, he was sentenced to 10 to 25 years for an armed robbery in Warren. His sentence was commuted by Governor John W. Bricker in January 1945, and Sanko was released a year later. Sanko became a close associate of Frank Budak and managed his activities when Budak was sent to Federal prison for tax evasion. Sanko was currently working for Budak at the Poland Country Club, where a Federal slot machine license was listed in his name.

By Saturday morning, word of the daring robbery reached Cleveland police, who contacted Struthers officials about the mysterious shooting of Petro. Struthers Police Chief Neil Gordon, Captain Woodrow Sicafuse and a patrolman escorted Sanko to Cleveland to see if he could identify Petro as one of the bandits. In the prison ward of City Hospital, where Petro was moved, Sanko said he could not identify the wounded man. Wearing a patch over his right eye, Sanko explained to police that one of the robbers hit him with the butt of his revolver, knocking him unconscious. He disclosed that he was "out cold" at that point and could provide no further details of the robbery. He also declared that none of the casino guards were armed, so it must have been a "gun-toting patron" who opened fire on the escaping bandits.

The Struthers police investigation revealed the building that housed the Green Acres was owned in part by Helen Tablack, wife of State Representative George D. Tablack, who was known as the "Little Caesar" of Struthers First Ward. In addition to the Green Acres, the building housed the Town Tavern and three apartments on the second floor. When asked who the Green Acres portion was leased to, George Tablack replied, "I don't recall the name."

It was not until late Saturday afternoon that Sanko made an official report to police about the robbery. In it, he claimed the robbers were "very fortunate if they got $4,000." Now, some 36 hours after the holdup, police finally had something, other than just rumors to go on, that a robbery at the club involving 250 patrons had taken place. As Struthers police began hearing from patrons who were present during the robbery, they discovered their stories didn't match with what they were told by Sanko. Eyewitnesses said it was a casino guard, positioned in a wire cage over the entrance door, who fired at the fleeing robbers. They claimed the guard held his fire to make sure his sight was clear of any patrons before he started shooting. Due to the glaring differences in the accounts from patrons to those of Sanko, the next day Struthers police arrested him on charges of being the keeper of a gambling casino.

By Sunday, none of the patrons had filed police reports regarding their losses. Struthers Police Chief Gordon pointed out that the victims of the Mounds

Club robbery also declined to file reports until they realized they could not collect on insurance claims without a formal police report having been made.

On September 20, City Hospital physicians planned to perform surgery on Petro to remove the bullet from his chest. It was hoped that the gun that fired the slug would be recovered, as this was the only chance police had to tie Petro to the robbery. No other slugs were recovered at the club. Petro, who was sitting up and reading in his hospital bed, became agitated when the attendants entered his room. Petro foiled their surgery plans when he was able to convince them that his condition had improved, less than 36 hours after being shot, to the point that the removal of the bullet was not necessary.

Dr. Walter S. Sellars, the assistant superintendent of City Hospital, told an anxious Detective Lieutenant David E. Kerr that, "We don't think any surgery is indicated, at least not at present. We have found out, especially in the war years with shrapnel wounds, that it isn't always necessary to remove the metal fragments." The doctor pointed out that it was normally the patient's decision to give permission for an operation. Struthers Police Chief Gordon was contemplating legal recourse to recover the slug. When Dr. Sellars was asked if police could "force" Petro to be operated on to obtain evidence, he responded that it was a "novel question," but one he didn't have an answer for. Sellars did say that a "forced" operation would require that someone assume legal responsibility for the outcome if something were to go wrong.

On Wednesday, September 22, Kerr decided that if Petro was well enough that he didn't need surgery, he was well enough to leave City Hospital. He was transferred from his hospital bed to less comfortable quarters in County Jail. There he sat while his family looked to find a way to satisfy his $25,000 bond. According to Kerr, Petro was placed in the hands of Cuyahoga County Sheriff Joseph M. Sweeney because Struthers Police Chief Gordon had failed to file any charges against the prisoner. In the meantime, Petro's trial for the Green Café robbery back in 1946 was scheduled to begin in two days.

On September 28, attorney Michael Picciano and bondsman Michael Kosser arrived at the court clerk's office and posted the $25,000 bond to obtain Petro's release. During the late afternoon, Petro was loaded onto a stretcher and placed in an ambulance before leaving the County Jail. Lieutenant Kerr believed Petro would attempt to find a doctor somewhere, possibly out of state, to remove the bullet from his chest. It was reported at the jail that workers there observed Petro in pain and "badly bent over" from the wound. Kerr's men trailed the ambulance from the County Jail and out along Memorial Shoreway before turning back.

Kerr was sure that the principals of the Green Acres casino would never sign a warrant to have Petro arrested. When Struthers authorities failed to send a warrant to keep Petro in the County Jail, Cleveland police interest in the case began to wane. But not all the efforts to seek justice against the robbers were finished. Hours after Petro began to rest comfortably in his own bed, the underworld gambling fraternity of the Mahoning Valley was on its way to Cleveland to extract revenge.

Sam Jerry Monachino

The same day Petro was released from jail, Sam Jerry Monachino, an alleged member of the robbery team that fleeced the Mounds Club and its patrons, and was a suspected accomplice of Petro in the Green Acres robbery, tried to sell a three-and-a-quarter-carat diamond ring for $1,000. Police theorized that word quickly got back to Joe DiCarlo his stolen ring had turned up. The wheels of mob justice were put in motion. Police believe Monachino was contacted by a man who expressed an interest in purchasing the ring. He requested a meeting to pay him that night near his home.

That Tuesday night, Monachino and his wife Margaret went to an East Side tavern, owned by Sam's brother, to watch the Cleveland Indians extend their first-place American League lead over the Boston Red Sox to two full games, with just four games remaining in the season. Indians ace Gene Bearden was on his way to an 11-0 drubbing of the Chicago White Sox with a 4-hit pitching gem. Margaret, who was eight months pregnant with the couple's first child, was reported at different times to be a former night club singer, or night club photographer. In recent months, she was said to be a waitress at a restaurant in the Cedar-Lee neighborhood of Cleveland Heights. Now, late in her pregnancy, she was not working.

The couple arrived home at 2555 East 127th Street around midnight. While having a cup of coffee, they were joined by Joseph Zingale, a friend. Shortly after 1:00 a.m., Sam told the two he was going out to purchase a newspaper. Margaret followed him out to the front porch, where he kissed her good-bye. He then walked off in a direction away from Larchmere Boulevard and any of the local stores, without a penny in his pocket.

Within minutes of his leaving the house, Margaret heard her husband cry out, "Honey! Honey! Help!" Despite being eight months pregnant, Margaret raced barefoot out of the house to aid her husband. She immediately encountered a scene where a gunman, dressed in a tan topcoat, was chasing and shooting at her husband, as Sam ran back toward the home. Several slugs soon felled Monachino, and as Margaret drew nearer, the shooter fired the last of his bullets into him as he was now lying prone in the gutter. The killer then pulled the lapel of his topcoat over his face and dry-fired the revolver at Margaret three times before running to a dark-colored sedan that was waiting for him.

By the time the police arrived Sam Jerry Monachino was dead; his lifeless body lying in the street. Two bullets had gone through his right arm, one creased his scalp, a fourth cut through his upper lip and nose, a fifth entered and exited his chest, while a sixth and fatal bullet hit him in the head, penetrating his brain.

Police questioned Margaret Monachino, but she could offer no description of the gunman other than his tan topcoat, because he had pulled the lapel over his face when he confronted her. Kerr, however, said he was not satisfied with the story provided by the Monachino's friend, Joseph Zingale; whom they held for questioning.

During the autopsy conducted by Dr. Sam Gerber, the slug was recovered from Monachino's brain, while another was found at the murder scene. The bases were intact and showed the rifling marks, but the noses of both bullets were distorted. Since Monachino was a known associate of Petro, the police were determined to tie Monachino to the Green Acres robbery and the wounding of Petro. One interesting thing turned up during the autopsy, Monachino did not have tuberculosis. Apparently, on several occasions when brought in for questioning, the reason he gave for being unemployed was he suffered from the debilitating disease.

The morning after the shooting, a woman walking her dog on nearby Fairhill Road found a Smith & Wesson .38 Special revolver on the tree-lawn in front of her home. The woman was the wife of Newton D. Baker III, the son of one-time Cleveland mayor and Secretary of War under President Woodrow Wilson, Newton D. Baker, Jr.[18] Lieutenant Kerr reported that the revolver contained six spent rounds. Police traced the gun and found that it was sold by the factory to a sporting goods store in Springfield, Illinois, before being purchased by a man who gave a fictitious Youngstown address.

After the autopsy and the discovery of the revolver from the Baker tree-lawn, police fired test shots to compare to the one recovered from Monachino, and the one found on the street at the murder scene. The rifling on the bullets matched, after which Kerr announced he was "Ninety per cent sure," the Monachino murder resulted from the holdup of the Green Acres casino.

Police were now hot on the theory that both Petro and Monachino participated in the Green Acres robbery. First, helping to tie the two men together was the fact that Sam A. Bevacqua, a cousin of Monachino, who was charged, tried and acquitted with him in two burglaries, attended the second murder trial of Petro and "tearfully rejoiced" when he was found not guilty of the Knaus murder. Next, without victims of the Green Acres' robbery willing to step forward, Cleveland detectives traveled to Ashtabula, Mahoning, and Trumbull Counties, as well as areas of Western Pennsylvania, where a series of gambling den robberies, and holdups of taverns and business places, including the Youngstown Hotel, had taken place. Victims of these robberies were shown a photo array of mugshots, which included Monachino and Petro. Kerr revealed that both men were identified as "very likely" suspects in those robberies.

After finding a pawn ticket for jewelry from a Youngstown pawnshop during a search of Monachino's home, police put together a theory of the motive behind his murder; that he had pawned Joe DiCarlo's stolen ring and was set up to be killed. In addition, it was reported that Kerr stated the revolver found at the Baker home, "was now known to be the firearm used by some person in the shooting that ended the Green Acres holdup." Kerr, still bitter about not being able to get the bullet from Petro's chest, lamented, "If we got that pellet we might have proved that the same gun was used at the robbery and in this murder." Kerr immediately sent two detectives to Youngstown Wednesday night to see what they could find out about the pawn ticket and the recovered revolver. The *Plain Dealer* reported that the officers were "blocked from running down their clews. The Bertillon and pawn shop records were locked up for the night and Youngstown Police Chief Edward Allen, Jr., was said to be out of town on a leave of absence."

The comments about the Youngstown Police Department touched a nerve in that city's legendary police chief. Eddie Allen declared that "all" of the city's police facilities were completely at the service of "any qualified investigators." Youngstown's Detective Chief William Reed said he received a telephone call from Lieutenant Kerr, who informed him that two Cleveland detectives would be there about 5:00 p.m. to consult with him. He waited until 7:00 for the officers to arrive. Reed denounced the *Plain Dealer* story. In detailing the work the Youngstown police had done, Allen stated:

> We determined that the supposed buyer of the gun was unknown and that the street address and the name were both fictitious. And we checked some pawn shop data and phoned it up this morning to the detective bureau as they asked.
>
> I was in a meeting at the time. But it was not necessary to get any special permission. Our record room staff is on 24-hour call.
>
> In the Green Acres case we offered our services to the Struthers marshal, but we couldn't do anything about that case. It was outside of our jurisdiction. Much to our chagrin we found that some of the patrons of that place were from our city, but we could not help on the case ourselves.

The day after the *Plain Dealer* article appeared, the Youngstown *Vindicator* reported that Cleveland homicide detective Arthur Willard "absolved the Youngstown detective bureau of charges that it refused to cooperate in the investigation. He said Cleveland police were fully satisfied with the efforts of the Youngstown police to aid in the hunt for the gun buyer."

One of the requests of Cleveland detectives to William Reed was to check the local pawn shops for any items taken there by Monachino. Reed came up with a watch and cigarette case Monachino pawned for $50 back on January 3, 1948, which he redeemed on July 12.

On Thursday night, police arrested three men, "all known cronies of Monachino," and all with criminal records, and held them in City Jail for questioning. Police were finding few leads as the investigation moved along. On October 6, a second .38 Special revolver was turned in by a resident after it was found at the corner of North Park and East Boulevards. It was a brand-new weapon with three shots fired. Kerr thought it possible that Monachino may have gone to his final appointment with the weapon, but the duration between the time he left home and returned, according to his wife, would not have allowed him to cover the distance to the corner where the revolver was discovered, at least not by foot. Police also found a Green Acres' robbery witness who identified Petro, Monachino and a third Cleveland man as "likely suspects" at the September 17 casino robbery.

Also on October 6, police picked up Joe DiCarlo outside the Hollenden Hotel[19] and brought him in for questioning. DiCarlo, who said he was in town to purchase tickets to a World Series game,[20] was rumored to have been a partner in the Green Acres casino. DiCarlo told Kerr that he had no ownership interest in the Struthers gambling den, but admitted he was there the night of the robbery playing barbut, a Greek dice game, but he could not offer any description of the men who robbed the place. When questioned about the ring, DiCarlo denied that one was stolen from him during the robbery. Asked why he wasn't wearing one now, the mob leader claimed he was having the ring's big diamond reset in another mounting for his wife.

Back in Youngstown, proving the age-old mob adage that "murder is bad for business," the operators of the Green Acres moved roulette, chuck-a-luck and other gambling equipment out of the casino and over to the Poland Country Club. Eddie Allen and the Youngstown police weren't sitting idle either. They, along with Mahoning County Sheriff Ralph E. Elser and Ohio State Liquor agents, raided the Poland Country Club. They found seven slot machines, which John Sanko had admitted to owning, and smashed everyone to pieces. Frank Budak, who was rumored to be the actual owner of Green Acres and the Poland Country Club, was a Federal parolee, having been convicted of tax evasion. Federal authorities would soon be looking into his activities.

Two days after the discovery of the second revolver, a convoluted tale appeared in the *Plain Dealer* after this weapon, too, was traced to Youngstown ownership. Kerr, who spearheaded the ownership search of the gun, hauled in three suspects – a gunsmith, croupier and gambling den owner – and held them for questioning. Kerr's investigation revealed that the revolver was traced from the Smith & Wesson Company factory in Springfield, Massachusetts, to Sandusky and then to Youngstown, where it was purchased by Robert Hildebrand, a former gun shop employee from Lowellville who purchased it in August 1947 from a local gun dealer. Hildebrand then sold the weapon to Raymond S. "Legs" Mashorda, a Youngstown resident who was a croupier at the Jungle Inn. In late 1947, Hildebrand went with Mashorda to the Jungle Inn where he watched him hand the gun over to "a part owner" of the gambling den who was never named, but always identified by the *Plain Dealer* as "the Cleveland Heights man." When questioned by Kerr about the exchange, Mashorda, while admitting that he worked for "the Cleveland Heights man," denied ever handing the gun over to him. When questioned by Kerr, "the Cleveland Heights man" denied ever having the revolver. Kerr did report that "the Cleveland Heights man" matched the description they were able to piece together of the man in the tan topcoat, who killed Monachino. Hildebrand and Mashorda were released after being questioned by Kerr.

On October 15, Youngstown police arrested Hildebrand and Mashorda. Hildebrand admitted to Allen that he had purchased 10 to 12 weapons and sold them to Mashorda, each for a $5 profit. Mashorda said he in turn sold them to his employers without realizing any profit. Mashorda claimed he had no idea why they wanted the weapons. When Chief Allen questioned Mashorda about the revolver discovered in Cleveland, he stated that he gave the revolver away, but he refused to say to whom, claiming if he did he "would be signing his own death warrant." The next day the two men were taken before Youngstown Municipal Judge John J. Buckley. Hildebrand pled guilty to unlawful sale of firearms and Mashorda to unlawful purchase of a firearm. Each was fined $200, with $150 suspended. No jail time was given. A few days later, Howard Trigg, owner of the Gun, Lock & Key Shop on East Boardman Street, which had once employed Hildebrand, was arrested for unlawful sale of a weapon. The charge was for selling a .38 Special revolver to Hildebrand without a police permit, just three days after he was fined in court. Trigg told Allen that he once sawed down shotguns and sold them to Mashorda.

In the meantime, mug shots of the three men questioned by Kerr were sent to Margaret Monachino, who had gone to stay with relatives in Nashville, Tennessee, for the last few weeks of her pregnancy. Kerr was notified the next day in a long-distance telephone call from a family member that Margaret viewed the photographs in her hospital bed, but did not recognize any of the men. The arrests would be the last ones made in the Monachino murder investigation.[21]

As for Petro, much to the chagrin of local police, he recovered from his wound and soon returned to his old profession. Months after his recovery, the *Plain Dealer* reported that, "Petro's bullet was of no use to police because it was split into ragged pieces and lodged in his ribs. It was said that removal would require a painful operation." Petro would later make the claim the reason he was shot was that he "was mistaken for Sam Jerry Monachino." As time went on, different stories emerged regarding the bullet in Petro's body; most of the stories initiated by the hoodlum himself. In February 1949, Petro gave this account to a *Plain Dealer* reporter:

He denied that he had refused to have the bullet removed from his chest. He said that he had been transferred from Emergency Clinic to the prison ward of City Hospital and that he had told police he did not want doctors there to perform the operation. "I told them I would agree if I could have the operation at Cleveland Clinic. After I was released I went to Huron Road Hospital, where a surgeon advised against having the bullet out. He told me the risk of surgery was greater than the risk of leaving it in." Petro always refused to explain how he had been shot, except to say that the shooting was "because of mistaken identity."

Chapter Four:

Post-Bullet Hole Days

On the Police Radar

With two major incidents now in his past, Julius Petro was well on his way to being one of the most sought after "persons of interest" on the radar of local police throughout northeastern Ohio. He was picked up repeatedly by Cleveland and East Side suburban police; most of these arrests resulting in a night in jail, then released without being charged with a crime. The breadth of the crimes in the incidents he was picked up for was an indication that Petro was spreading his wings in the criminal underworld. Of course, Petro didn't help his cause by tooling around in a flashy maroon 1948 Cadillac, even though he had no visible means of support.

Petro's first post "chest wound" arrest came on November 15 when he was the initial suspect brought in for the robbery of the Ohio Loan & Discount Company, at 247 Euclid Avenue. Petro was placed in a police lineup, but none of the robbery victims could identify him as one of the two holdup men. He was quickly released.

Just two days away from his first Christmas as a free man in the past three years, Petro was arrested on December 23, 1948. Perhaps it was just too much Christmas cheer as he and three friends were celebrating at George Hatton's Grill at the corner of East 55th Street and Lexington Avenue during the wee hours of the morning. Two Cleveland detectives showed up and began to question the men. When the four got "lippy" with the detectives, they were all placed under arrest. Taken in with Petro were Michael Delzoppo, Joseph Barbara and John Cirelli. Deputy Police Inspector Patrick Lynch must have been in the Christmas spirit as he allowed the men a "Yule Liberty" after determining the detectives "had nothing" on the four men. All were released after being "mugged" by the Bertillon Department.

Around 4:00 a.m. on January 11, 1949, two Cleveland Patrolmen, Edward Grieger and Pete Catavolos, spotted three men outside a tailor shop on Detroit Avenue near West 69th Street. When the trio saw the approaching officers, one man broke away and fled down West 69th. The officers questioned the two remaining men and then went off in search of the third man. They soon found him crouched down and hiding in a car parked on West 69th. He was not alone; he was keeping company with a set of burglary tools – a pinch bar, flashlights and several screwdrivers. At first, the man gave Grieger a fictitious name and then tried to bribe him. In addition to the burglary tools, the officers also found an unexplained list of auto license numbers in the glove compartment. Taken to City Jail, the "crouching man" was quickly identified as Julius Petro, after which he declared, "I ain't talking!" Police held him while they investigated the robbery of another clothing store, West Park Tailor Shop on Lorain Avenue, the previous day. Meanwhile, the owner of the car Petro was hiding in, Raymond Gentile[22] was brought in for questioning.

At the jail, Petro was questioned by Detective Charles O. Nevel. The old cop challenged him, "You spent 18 months in 'death row' and you are now alive and free. Why are you hanging around with men with records and out at all hours?" Petro shrugged and replied, "I know it looks bad, but I haven't been doing anything wrong since I was acquitted." Petro was released without being charged after "no criminal intent" could be proved.

Petro fed sob tales to reporters claiming he was unable to obtain steady work at his father's upholstery business due to customers refusing to trust him. He was unable to find other employment because "as soon as they learn my name they refuse to hire me." He claimed he once had to use an alias just to be fitted with eyeglasses because the optometrist refused to do the work once he found out who he was dealing with.

Five days later, two patrolmen arrested Petro at East 123rd Street and Euclid Avenue. Petro crashed a red light going 50 miles per hour and was driving with only a temporary permit. When pulled over, Petro demanded to know, "Are you guys trying to persecute me?" With him at the time were two 21-year-old women who claimed he had offered them a ride downtown. The women said that once he identified himself, they asked him to stop the car and let them out. They said Petro responded by stepping on the gas and saying he was going to show them a good time on the West Side. At Central Police Station, Petro claimed he was a salesman and lived at 17908 Schenely Avenue in Collinwood. After three hours at the station, Petro was allowed to leave after posting a $200 bond. The next day, Petro appeared in Municipal Court before Judge Edward F. Feighan. On the advice of his attorney, Edward Stanton, he pleaded guilty to speeding, running a red light and driving with only a temporary permit. Despite having five previous traffic violations on his record, Feighan declared, "This is a traffic court, not a robbery court." The judge fined him $20 and court costs. The next day the *Cleveland Press* blasted both Petro and the judge:

One of these days, Julius A. Petro is going to run out of his luck. He has used it up too fast even though he is only 26 years old. He could have been fined $200 and sentenced to jail for six months on each of the first two charges and given 10 days and been fined $25 on the third. We don't argue that Feighan should have thrown the book at Petro, even though that would have taken care of this bad boy for a while and kept him out of the hair of police. But fines totaling $20 obviously were inadequate. Why the coddling? We are sure that any decent, respectable and law-abiding citizen in there on the same charges and with five previous black marks, would have suffered much more than Julius Petro. But take care Julius, your luck is running out. You won't always come up before a Judge Feighan.

Less than a month later, Petro and a companion, James Zimmerman, were arrested on "general principles" after being observed driving around together during the early morning hours. During the mid-to-late 1950s, Zimmerman was a member of the Penn-Ohio Burglary Ring,[23] which included Mahoning Valley mob heavyweights Joseph Jasper "Fats" Aiello, Ronald D. Carabbia, Donald "Bull" Jones and Willie Napoli.

On February 22, Petro encountered Police Captain William Senkbeil of Brecksville, a suburb of Cuyahoga County, located south of Cleveland along the northern border of Summit County. Senkbeil stopped a 1948 Cadillac driving north on Route 21 (Brecksville Road) with three men inside. The car, driven by Petro, was pulled over by Senkbeil because "they didn't look good." The captain had no idea who the men were until after they were taken to the Brecksville Police Station and asked for their identifications. In addition to Petro, Senkbeil had hauled in Joseph Drago, who was involved in the "breakfast insurrection" with Petro in the County Jail 1942, and Salvatore A. Frederico, who had served a stretch in Joliet for an armed robbery in Illinois and was currently wanted for a bank robbery in Madison, Ohio, in 1933.

Upon learning the identities of his detainees, Senkbeil immediately telephoned Detective Sergeant Robert V. Slusser of the Cleveland Police Robbery Squad. The three men were soon on their way to Cleveland for questioning at Central Police Station. During the interrogation, the men admitted that they were returning from a trip downstate when they were stopped. They refused, however, to say which cities they had visited. Robbery detectives concluded that by the very fact "they were returning from a trip," was grounds for a thorough investigation of their activities. All three men were arrested and held for investigation of recent burglaries.

Petro told reporters he occasionally made trips to other cities in Ohio, "because that's the only way I can have any fun." The hood claimed Cleveland police were persecuting him by stopping him "at least twice a day" to search him and question him about his activities.

A Possible New Career

During the early morning hours of March 7, 1949, John Cesnik, owner of the Town House night club on Erie Street in Willoughby, a small city to the east of Cleveland, located in Lake County, was reading the morning newspaper when he heard a crash about 3:00 a.m. "I thought it was someone trying to break in," he told police. "I ran to the window, but I didn't see anyone or any car." Someone had tossed a stench bomb into the Town House. Cesnik said he had no idea who would want to bomb his place. He declared he had no slot machines or pinball machines, and that there had been no threats or signs of trouble with any patrons connected to the night club. He did state there was an offer to purchase the tavern, but no one pressured him to sell.

Cesnik telephoned the Willoughby Police Department. On his way to the Town House, Lieutenant James C. Coleman passed a 1948 Cadillac with two men inside. It was the second time he and the patrolman, who accompanied him, saw the car that morning. Coleman had noted the license plate number after the first spotting. Once he arrived back at the station, the lieutenant notified Cleveland police about the car, which belonged to Petro. Calls to Petro's home resulted in him agreeing to meet the officers near his home and then being taken to the Willoughby police station, where he was held for questioning.

While being interrogated, Petro denied being in the Cadillac and claimed he had sold the car to a friend. Shortly thereafter, police from the city of East Cleveland spotted the Cadillac on East 133rd Street. They impounded the car and held a suspect, turning them both over to Cleveland police. The suspect was a 26-year-old East Sider, who was often picked up for investigation. He had a misdemeanor record and had once deserted from the Army. Although not named in the newspaper articles, this fit the description and age of Anthony Paul D'Alessio.[24] Lieutenant Coleman said the suspect "looked very much like one of the occupants of the car" he had spotted. But the suspect and Petro both clammed up. Although police were running tests to see if an empty quart jar, they found at the Town House had fingerprints on it, no stench bomb ingredients were recovered from the automobile. There were also no eyewitnesses to link Petro, the suspect, or the Cadillac to the tossing of the stench bomb at the Town House night club. After two days in the Willoughby jail, Petro and the Army deserter were released due to lack of evidence.

On March 13, Bernard Chester, owner of the Hough Inn, located at 9215 Hough Avenue, went to Deputy Inspector James McArthur with an interesting story. On February 27, about nine days before the stench bombing at the Town House night club, Chester received two anonymous telephone calls warning him that stench bombs were going to be tossed into his place of business. On March 1, Julius Petro and a 34-year-old companion walked into Chester's cafe and claimed they knew the men who made the threats. Petro said he could "buy them off" for $400. Chester refused the offer and called police, even though Petro had warned him not to. When police questioned Petro and his cohort about the allegations, they denied having attempted to shake down the café owner. The companion claimed they were contacted and asked to manufacture several stench bombs by two men he refused to name. The next day, the *Cleveland News* announced that Petro was a key figure in an investigation into a new stench bomb shake down racket in the city. Police, however, did not have enough evidence to hold either Petro or his partner.

Sometimes, Petro was hauled in by police just because he showed his face on the street. Such was the case on April 13, 1949, after Cleveland police spotted Petro's "flashy and expensive" Cadillac as it "sped" out of a Royal Castle restaurant parking lot at 15109 St. Clair Avenue. After stopping the car, patrolmen questioned Petro and his two companions, Alfred A. "Allie" Calabrese and Anthony Paul D'Alessio. When one gave a false name, all three were arrested and held for questioning. While Petro was cooling his heels in jail, the police came across an old traffic violation from February 1946, where Petro had run a stop sign and pleaded guilty. Due to his arrest for the murder of "Bobby" Knaus, Petro was unable to appear in traffic court for sentencing the following month. Now, three years later, Petro went to court where he was fined $5 by Municipal Judge Edward F. Feighan for the traffic violation and then returned to jail until he could produce a driver's test receipt or valid driver's license.

On April 26, more than three years after the robbery of the Green Café, Assistant County Prosecutor Victor DeMarco asked that charges against Petro be dropped because "evidence of the robbery was weakened by the death of the victim, John Bush," the 61-year-old porter. DeMarco claimed Petro would have won an acquittal by default if the trial were further delayed. "This way," he claimed, "A new indictment can always be obtained if more evidence is found." In the article announcing the decision, Petro was referred to as "the death row graduate whom police lock up and release about once a week."

"You'll never make anything of it, copper," snarled Julius Petro as he found himself facing another arrest on May 23. This time he was picked up in an automobile while sitting next to a sack full of burglary tools. With him at the time was his close pal, Anthony D'Alessio. Petro let police know he'd be released in a short while. No one doubted him.

The next time Petro was picked up it involved a more sinister matter than speeding out of a Royal Castle parking lot. During June 1949, the National Industrial Laundries Company of Newark, New Jersey, a linen supply house, became involved in a price cutting competition with a Cleveland concern. By reducing costs by 20%, the Cleveland company had taken some 20 customers away from their East Coast competitor. The New Jersey firm tried to "reach an understanding" with their Cleveland rival, but was rebuffed.

The New Jersey linen supplier, which had previously operated here with only a small sales staff, decided to fight back by opening a local branch of the National Industrial Laundries Company. The company sent two executives, Herbert Tainow and Jerry Friedman, to establish the new office. Both men were living at the Sovereign Hotel[25] at 1575 East Boulevard, near the University Circle area.

During the early morning hours of June 29, a "high-explosive" blast destroyed Tainow's 1949 Chevrolet club sedan, parked outside the Sovereign Hotel, and broke 50 of the hotel's windows. While no one was injured, the blast sheared the limbs off nearby trees, scattered pieces of the automobile over the nine-story residential hotel, spreading debris over 500 yards, and woke hundreds of people in the surrounding neighborhood. When questioned by police,

Tainow said he could offer no explanation for the car bombing. He and his associates denied they had been warned or threatened since arriving in Cleveland. Deputy Police Inspector, James E. McArthur, however, said he was informed the men were warned by "local laundry interests" shortly after coming here that there would be trouble.

Just four hours after the bombing, Petro and a friend were arrested in a restaurant at East 105th Street and Superior Avenue, not far from the hotel, while they were eating breakfast. Both men claimed they were unemployed. Petro, however, had $70 on him, but refused to reveal where it came from. The other man had $250 stuffed in his wallet. The two were held for questioning the entire day before being released late that night. Police were left to wonder if the oft-arrested hoodlum was moving into a new line of business.

In the midst of a highly publicized scandal at Sonny's Show Bar (See next Sub-Chapter), came Petro's next arrest. On October 20, 1949, according to a *Cleveland Press* article, Petro was arrested and jailed for "merely driving out of a parking lot." Euclid Patrolman Dave Culmer recognized Petro as the man behind the wheel and stopped him and slapped the handcuffs on him because, according to the newspaper, the officer didn't believe this hoodlum "would add much to the dignity of the suburb."

As it turned out, it may not have been a run of the mill arrest. Petro and his 23-year-old companion, Martin E. Eschman, were both charged with being suspicious persons after Culmer found 20 boxes of "cheap cigars" in the car. East Cleveland Police reported a tobacco truck was broken into and robbed a few days earlier and 20 boxes of cigars were stolen. The men were turned over to the East Cleveland authorities. When that suburb couldn't pin the burglary on the two, they were returned to the city of Euclid to face the suspicious person's charges. On October 29, the men pleaded not guilty were released on $250 bonds. A trial set for November 12, but the charges were eventually dropped.

Sonny's Show Bar
On August 11, 1946, readers of the *Plain Dealer* couldn't help but be confused upon reading Glenn C. Pullen's entertainment notes in the newspaper's Sunday edition. Pullen, the popular entertainment gossip columnist for the newspaper, wrote an item about a new hot spot in Cleveland:

FORMER SERGT. ANGELO Lonardo, who won five major battle citations, blossomed out Friday night as the impresario of Sonny's Show Bar which opened at 12376 Superior Avenue N.E. It is a large but intimately decorated room, with music served by "Tops" Cardone's "Men of Note" and Bob Gaylord on vocals.

Readers must have wondered, how could this be true? Could Angelo Lonardo have gone off to war and come back a hero? Clevelanders knew Angelo "Big

Ange" Lonardo as the young man who avenged his father's 1927 murder by killing the man he held responsible. Convicted at trial, Lonardo, like Julius Petro a generation later, was granted a new trial at which he was acquitted. The last time Angelo Lonardo was heard from was when he was convicted of "extorting tribute" from the city's Black numbers operators and sent to prison in 1942. The mystery would be solved on December 29, 1949, when "Big Ange" Lonardo was on trial for trying to extort Black numbers kingpin Joseph Allen, which included the bombing of his automobile. He admitted during the trial that the Angelo Lonardo who obtained the liquor license for Sonny's Show Bar, was a cousin with the same name.

Sonny's Show Bar quickly became noted for its fine food and top entertainment. The latter provided by "Tops" Cardone, one of the most popular band leaders in town, and young crooner Bob Gaylord. The singer was in the process of dropping the Gaylord persona and going back to his real name, Joey Fatica, which he was known by when he was becoming a noted singer back at Patrick Henry Junior High School.

Despite the assorted underworld clientele that frequented Sonny's Show Bar, the place didn't draw a lot of negative attention from the newspapers. The only incident reported during its first two years of operation occurred on August 12, 1948. Three armed men entered the bar, guns drawn, with plans to pull a hold-up. Charles Sherman, a 78-year-old "special policeman," foiled the attempt by shooting and wounding one gunman and capturing another. During the shootout, Sherman was wounded in the hand and the third gunman got away.

One year after this attempted hold-up, Sonny's Show Bar was back in the news again; this time because it was being frequented by Julius Petro. By this time Angelo Lonardo and his cousin of the same name had sold the place. Lonardo would later claim he took the $45,000 he made on the sale and went to Florida for a four-month round of "horse-playing." It was now reported by state liquor agents that "police characters had taken over management of the night spot." The investigation was seemingly begun by *Plain Dealer* reporters during the summer of 1949. During their forays into the bar, they observed Petro "as a frequent and apparently non-paying patron of the bar." An article on August 29 revealed:

> It was observed that Petro's arrival at the bar at a late hour invariably was the signal for kowtowing by bartenders, who would set up drinks and proffer cigarettes. He was never seen to pay for his drinks.

A bartender, who fit the description of Anthony D'Alessio, told reporters that he was the "boss" of the bar. When reporters checked his police record, they found he had twice deserted from the Army and had spent a year in

Leavenworth Federal Penitentiary, before being dishonorably discharged. He record also showed he was a suspect at one time in connection with an armed robbery. Further investigation revealed that the current owner of the bar was Anna Uminski, who denied having surrendered control of the bar to "police characters." She claimed the operating of Sonny's Show Bar was in the hands of trusted managers, but she refused to say who they were.

In late August, State Liquor Enforcement Chief, Anthony A. Rutkowski, who two weeks earlier had led the well-publicized raid that closed the notorious Jungle Inn in Trumbull County, cited the liquor permit holder of Sonny's, charging the bar was operating under false ownership. The case was slated to be heard by the Ohio Board of Liquor Control in September. Sonny's was facing having its liquor license revoked.

On August 25, Sonny's was placed in receivership by Common Pleas Judge Joseph H. Silbert, who appointed William B. Webber receiver. Ironically, Webber's wife, Yetta was an officer of a newly formed corporation that was seeking to purchase the night club permit. Anna Uminski filed an application with the liquor department to transfer the permit to this new corporation called Sonny's Show Bar, Inc. The officers were listed as Jean G. Webber, as president, treasurer and sole stock owner, and Yetta L. Webber, secretary. Jean was the wife of Abraham B. Webber, the brother and law partner of William B. Webber. The two rented law offices in the Engineers Building, conveniently adjacent to the Cleveland area liquor office. An application filed for the transfer of the license was pending with the liquor department, but was nullified by the receivership action. The chief of the Ohio State Liquor Permit Department said the transfer would not have been allowed because the bar's D-5 liquor permit was due to expire on August 30.

When Jean Webber was informed of the citation issued by Rutkowski, she suddenly announced the deal was "all off, as far as we're concerned. I'm out of it altogether. If I had known there would be any commotion I would not have applied."

William Webber confirmed that the bar's previous owner, Ann Bochkoros, had taken judgment against Uminski after she defaulted on a mortgage payment, thus initiating the receivership action. As the receiver, Webber declared he would proceed to sell the bar to the highest bidder. Bochkoros was represented in the action by another Engineers Building lawyer, Aaron J. Frank, who also happened to be one of the incorporators of Sonny's Show Bar, Inc.

Four months later, in December 1949, not much had changed. The bar was still closed due to the cancelled permit. Webber had not sold the bar, but as receiver he was able to obtain a temporary restraining order against the state liquor department and asked that his appeal be heard immediately. In his request for the restraining order, Webber claimed that accusations by the state that Petro was in anyway an owner or manager of the bar were "fantastic." That charge, he declared, was based solely on a comment by Petro to police who stopped and questioned him. "That is certainly not evidence," Webber contended. "Usually, you have hoodlums using legitimate people as fronts and keeping it quiet that they have a part in a permit. Here you have a hoodlum saying openly that he has some part in a place run by legitimate people – and yet I don't know him. If he got some drinks in there or hung around, it was only because the owners were innocent people who had no way to check his record. He said he was a 'greeter' there, Why, I could tell anyone that I was manager of the Hollenden. That wouldn't be evidence."

Speaking for the police was Lieutenant John Mernagh, who took the stand to support the liquor department's contention that managing of the café was in the "hands of hoodlums." He told the Liquor Board that during the daytime Petro was in charge of Sonny's. On one of his routine stops by the police, Petro told officers he was on his way to a warehouse to purchase liquor for the bar. Mernagh also stated that Michael Petro, Julius's younger brother, worked as a bartender there, as well as several other "hoodlums" who described themselves as part of the management team.

At the end of the hearing, Franklin County Common Pleas Judge John R. King reversed the Board of Liquor Control in its refusal to renew Sonny's permit and granted a temporary court order to allow the bar to reopen. If the state appealed, it would be heard in the same court in Columbus where all state liquor board appeals were heard.

On Friday, March 10, 1950, more than six months after Rutkowski's citation of Sonny's Show Bar, a carload of police, including Deputy Inspector Michael J. "Iron Mike" Blackwell, headed for Columbus for a hearing to determine if the liquor permit was to be renewed. During the hearing, Blackwell testified that Petro told police that he was "in charge of the place" during daylight hours, and that another "police character was identified with the management at other times." Blackwell insinuated that a "muscling-in" had occurred at the bar.

The police did not receive the support of the Liquor Board, which refused to accept jurisdiction over the case on the grounds that the night club permit had expired last August 31, and a renewed application was not filed until August 29. The permit division then rejected the application that required renewal paperwork to be filed 15 days prior to the expiration date. Judge King, who had granted the temporary court order back in December, also heard testimony in this hearing. He ruled that the 15-day regulation could not be applied against the permit holder "in view of the circumstances of the case." The ruling effectively ended the battle by renewing Sonny's night club permit by court order. When the order was presented to Cole, he immediately issued the permit ending the six-month ordeal, much to the chagrin of Blackwell and the police.

Time Out for Marriage

Although it would not be reported in the newspapers until December 1952, Julius Petro got married for the first and only time during the summer or early fall of 1949. The object of Petro's affections was a 22-year-old former singer named June. Born in Cleveland, she grew up on the East Side maturing into an attractive red-head and a talented singer. June's good looks and her mezzo soprano voice helped to land her a job with the Stan Kenton[26] orchestra when she was just 18 years old.[27]

The *Cleveland Press* article reported that the "attractive former vocalist" performed with "big name" orchestras, indicating that Stan Kenton may not have been the only band she sang with. While touring the country singing, she met a musician, whom she soon married and had a son with named Darias. The birth of the child brought an end to her singing career and the marriage ended soon afterward. June returned to Cleveland and moved in with her parents in their home at 1635 East 86th Street. During the spring of 1949, June's cousin introduced her to Julius Petro "at a gathering." She later recalled that it was love at first sight. "He loved me, too," she stated, "and we were married a few months later. A justice of the peace married us and we have been living with my parents since [then]."

June claimed she knew nothing of Julius's past until after they were married. Then, "He told me all. He told of his mistakes, his time in jail. He wanted to leave Cleveland and start new in another city. He always wanted to work in a factory doing anything respectable. But I said no. I insisted we stay here and face up to his past. It was a tragic mistake on my part."

It wasn't long until trouble started, and old habits kicked in. "Julius would work two days here and there," she said, "but when they found out who he was he would be fired. I got a job as a waitress and have worked ever since. Julius liked to gamble a lot and occasionally he would win some money. Then we lived well. Dice, horses, barboot – he played them all. When he was out of town, he told me it was on business and I never asked him any more about it. He never brought any friends to the house, and we never went any place but to movies and occasionally downtown to dinner."

Around the spring of 1951, June had a second child; a daughter they named Juliet. Sometime after the marriage, Julius adopted Darias. June concluded her interview with *Press* reporter Bus Bergen by claiming that despite Julius's past, "I love him. No one else had any faith in him and for that I love him more."

"Luckiest Hoodlum in Town"

It was pretty much a standard practice for Petro, and the men close to him, to leave town in search of places to rob or burglarize. There had already been gambling den robberies attributed to Petro and his gang in Youngstown, Trumbull County, and places in Northeastern Pennsylvania. When he was younger, Petro was arrested for auto-theft in Batavia, New York. On March 24, 1950, Petro and two accomplices, Joseph Russo and Ralph "Bull" De Biase were arrested in Johnstown, Pennsylvania, after a failed safecracking attempt and a strong-armed robbery in which they got away with $43.

The evening began at the Sunshine Biscuit Company in Johnstown. The men attempted to crack the safe, which reportedly contained $1,000, but were unsuccessful. Not wanting to leave the city empty handed, the men parked their car and went looking for another score. They came across Elias Hanna, a store clerk, and assaulted him in his driveway. The men stole Hanna's wallet, which contained just $43, and left him with a broken nose. When police arrived, they noticed foot prints in the snow and followed them to where a car had been parked. Police recalled seeing a car with Ohio license plates on it parked there earlier. They began looking for the vehicle and soon found it and the men a dozen blocks from the crime scene. Hanna identified the men as his attackers and police found his empty wallet under the front-seat of the car. Police were also able to link mud and sand found on the men's shoes to mud and sand found outside the Sunshine Biscuit Company. All three were charged with robbery and attempted burglary. Petro was released on a $5,000 bond. The next day the *Cleveland Press* ran the following editorial:

Petro Just Can't Go Straight

It looks as if Johnstown (Pa.) police have Julius Petro behind the eight ball again. This young man, who spent 18 months in a death row cell at Ohio Penitentiary, apparently has not learned his lesson. He has been lucky and by twist and dodge has avoided spending more than a few hours in jail since a retrial cleared him on the murder rap. Cleveland police undoubtedly will breathe easier if Johnstown makes its robbery charges stick. He's obviously a tough guy who endangers society and should be put away.

Despite newspaper claims that the men were looking at five to ten years on the robbery and ten to twenty years on the attempted burglary, the results would be much different. According to the entry of the incident on Petro's rap sheet:

SAFECRACKING & ROBBERY – Johnstown, Pa. Arrested March 24, 1950. Disposition: Convicted Jan 10, 1951, placed on probation and told to stay out of Johnstown five years.

The only people "breathing easier" were Petro and his two companions. In addition to all the arrests of Petro, none of which resulted in any convictions, so far, police also believed he was "preying on" down-state dice games and was "shaking down" some businessmen in Cleveland. Nothing was ever proved, however, and nobody ever testified to anything.

There were certain signs in late May 1950 that this was not going to be a good summer for Julius Petro. He walked into a "large East Side hospital" coughing up blood. Doctors narrowed it down to two possible causes. One, Petro had contacted tuberculosis; or two, he was suffering from an irritation being caused by the slug that was still sitting in his chest from what authorities believed was a wound he suffered while robbing the Green Acres casino back in September 1948. The doctors told him they would need at least 30 days for bacterial cultures they took from him to develop. Despite information to the contrary, Cleveland Police Homicide Captain David Kerr was hoping that if Petro required surgery, they might recover the old slug inside him and all the secrets it might reveal. Nothing became of the incident.

Then, a few days later, it was déjà vu, all over again!

Chapter Five:

"Very Strange!" Another Bullet Hole

The Second Shooting of Julius Petro

This latest saga began on June 4, 1950, on a Sunday night. Joseph Carretta was a grocer and beer distributor in Alliance, Ohio, a city of about 22,000 residents located on the eastern border of Stark County, with a small portion of the city located in Mahoning County just to the east. Carretta lived in a nice home with his wife Florence and at least one son. Around 10:30 that night there was a knock at the Carretta's front door. When Joseph answered the door, a man he later identified as Julius Petro was standing there. Petro asked him if his son Frank was home. When Carretta said he wasn't, Petro left.

A short time later four men, including Petro, "smashed in." One man grabbed an iron, which was sitting out, and hit Joseph Carretta in the head, leaving a gash in his scalp. After demanding money from the couple, the gang moved to a wine cellar door, made up to look like a vault door. It would not come to light until four days after the attempted robbery that Carretta had $15,000 inside the wine vault. How the gang knew it was there, or why Carretta was targeted in the first place was never revealed. But, as the gang began to take a crowbar to the vault door, someone else "smashed in."

Fortunately for the Carrettas, an alert neighbor across the street had witnessed the home invasion and called police. Rushing through the Carretta's front door were four Alliance police officers. Confronted by the officers, one of the gang members declared, "Aw, this is just family trouble." A second later, the four gang members broke for the nearest doors and windows. Officer Edward Moretti fired at the fleeing Petro. One bullet went through his lower back and exited just above his right hip. This time no souvenir would be left in the hoodlum. Petro went crashing out through a Venetian blind-covered window with Moretti in hot pursuit. Petro's luck was working for him again. When Moretti hit the ground his service revolver went flying and he couldn't find it in the darkness. How the whole gang got away was never made clear, but one thing was for sure, Petro was the only one wounded in the escape.

Around 3:00 a.m. Monday morning, about four hours after the shooting, Petro and two members of the gang showed up at the home of Dr. Anthony LaPolla in Niles, Ohio, located north-east of Alliance in Trumbull County, just over the northern border of Mahoning County. LaPolla looked at the gunshot wound, as well as Petro's hand, which he had cut while jumping through the window. Some reports state the doctor placed bandages on both wounds, other reports state otherwise. The wounded man's main concern was about contracting lockjaw. When Petro and his companions inquired if the doctor had to notify police, LaPolla told them, yes. He also advised them to get Petro to a hospital as soon as possible. Before leaving, the good doctor provided them with two tubes of penicillin, a vial of lockjaw antitoxin and a hypodermic needle. These were later recovered from Petro's automobile, a cream and tan colored Pontiac coupe.

The gang left Niles and headed back to Cleveland, arriving at Petro's home at 17908 Schenely Avenue sometime between 8:00 and 9:00 a.m. Here the story gets a little confusing. The *Plain Dealer* reported that Petro's "mother summoned a brother, Michael," who arrived at his Julius's home with Sylvester "Studo" Papalardo, a "known crony of Julius and a man with a record. There is reason to believe that both men were with Petro earlier that night participating in the Carretta home invasion, and were the men who took Petro to the LaPolla home.

It was then reported that Petro asked his brother to get him "that doctor on Magnolia Drive." Michael made the telephone call and was told to bring Julius there. At the office of Dr. S. Maurice Simon, the physician immediately realized he was looking at a bullet wound and called police. The Petro brothers immediately cleared out, but not before the doctor's alert nurse got the license plate number of the car as they left. When police arrived, they were given the number, which was listed to Michael Petro at the Schenely Avenue address. They were also told by the doctor that "the man needs immediate medical care if he is going to live." When Dr. Simon later spoke with reporters, he told them, "I pleaded with him to go to the hospital or give himself up to police. He was lucky they caught him and got him to City Hospital. He would have died otherwise."

Back at the station, police immediately issued a nationwide "radiogram," requesting police everywhere to turn in news of any shooting, safe job, stickup or hoodlum war within a radius of 150 miles of Cleveland. Ironically, no word came from Alliance. Instead, the newspapers reported, "It was an anonymous radio listener who called Cleveland detectives to say a Niles doctor treated a gunshot wound, according to a downstate news broadcast." When Cleveland police checked with Niles authorities, they found out about Dr. LaPolla's late-night visitor. They were also told about "some sort of job over in Alliance." When they contacted Alliance police, they were finally informed about the Carretta hold up.

Cleveland police detectives soon arrived at the Petro home on Schenely Avenue. There they found Michael Petro and Sylvester Papalardo, who denied having made any visit to a hospital that morning. When asked where Julius was, Michael said he was in bed with tuberculosis. The detectives went into the bedroom and found Petro in bed. They pulled back the covers and saw the bandage on his abdomen and immediately called for an ambulance. Both Michael Petro and Papalardo claimed they knew nothing about the gunshot wound. Papalardo stated, "I heard Julius was sick and I came over to see him." With these responses there was no doubt why both men were hauled in and tossed in a cell.

When the police ambulance arrived, Petro refused to be carried out on a stretcher; preferring to walk out to the vehicle on his own like it was some badge of courage. The ambulance took him to Central Station instead of the hospital. Once there, he had to be helped inside by his brother and detectives as his knees buckled and his head drooped. Petro was placed under arrest. In the Detective Bureau, James McArthur, the chief, pulled aside Petro's clothing to look at the wound. The following exchange took place:

McArthur: Who shot you Julius?

Petro: I don't remember.

McArthur: When were you shot?

Petro: I don't know.

McArthur thought Petro was shot again while holding up another gambling joint somewhere outside of Cuyahoga County. Since the bullet had entered his back, the detective chief surmised he was shot while making his escape.

Petro was transported to the prison ward of City Hospital, where doctors performed exploratory surgery to see if any of his vital organs had been hit, none were. They did remove his appendix, which the newspapers claimed was "routine in abdominal operations now."

At the hospital Petro was questioned by David L. Cowles, the police department's ballistics superintendent. Petro told him he was shot around 4:00 or 5:00 a.m., in an attempt to distance himself from the 10:30 p.m. shooting in Alliance. When asked why, he now claimed it was because, "Somebody doesn't like me." Cowles finished by asking him what he was doing when the shooting started. "Minding my own business," Petro snapped.

Police were still looking for the clothes Petro was wearing when he was shot. They received a description of them from Dr. LaPolla, who by now had come forth after seeing a picture of Petro in the newspaper. The doctor told police that Petro was wearing a blue sports shirt and slacks. Police were not able to find the clothes during a search of his home, discovering instead only bloody towels and a handkerchief.

Joseph Carretta and his wife, the Alliance Police officers and Dr. LaPolla all said they would be able to identify the wounded man if they saw him again. With Petro in custody at City Hospital, that process began on Tuesday morning, June 6, when Carretta, his wife, and the Alliance policemen arrived at Central Police Station. They started by viewing Bertillon photographs of Petro and then looking at suspects in lineups. One of the robbers was identified as Michael Petro by both the police and Carretta. Two other men who were picked out of the lineup were identified as Sylvester Papalardo and Ralph "Bull" De Biase. The Alliance Police brought with them three "John Doe" warrants, charging assault to rob, in order to hold the three suspected companions of Petro. The suspects would later be taken back to Alliance to be viewed by an additional ten witnesses.

It was never explained by the newspapers how many people from Alliance actually came to look at the Bertillon photographs or view suspects in the line-ups. The only people named in the newspapers were Joseph and Florence Carretta and Patrolman Edward Moretti. In describing Michael Petro's presence in the police line-up, one newspaper claimed he was "identified by Alliance citizens," and that he would be taken back to Alliance to be "exhibited" in more line-ups before "10 new witnesses there."

Dr. LaPolla, who had already identified Julius Petro through a newspaper photograph, told police during an interview that Petro refused to be bandaged. The doctor said Petro then asked how long it would be before the un-bandaged wound would make him sick. LaPolla told him 24 hours. The gang paid the doctor $3 and got up to leave. As they were heading out, Petro told him, "I'm not afraid of dying."

As the information from Central Police Station began to reach reporters, one of the men from the *Cleveland Press* was allowed to interview Petro at City Hospital. He wrote:

Petro was stretched out on a bed in the City Hospital prison ward, occupied by three other hospitalized prisoners. A wide bandage engulfed his abdomen. A tube was inserted into his nose. He was not the cocksure, smiling talkative Petro who had been arrested so often in the past.

The reporter relayed the following exchange:

Petro: I was in the operating room for two hours. They took out my appendix, too.

Reporter: That's pretty good, getting an appendix operation on the city.

Petro: I've got hospitalization.

The reporter noted that the surgeon made no attempt to recover the slug from Petro's chest that police believed he received during the Green Acres robbery. The reporter then brought up the identification being made at Central Police Station:

Petro: They'd identify anybody. If you get in this bed, they'd identify you. They're crazy. I was nowhere near Alliance. I don't do anything like that. I don't steal. I'm working.

Reporter: Doing what?

Petro: Well – I'm working. I was getting along fine, then this had to happen.

Reporter: How did you get wounded?

Petro: I can't tell you. I don't know who shot me. That's why I didn't want to go to the hospital.

When asked about the other suspects who were also identified at the Alliance robbery, including his brother and two associates who were arrested, he responded:

Petro: They're crazy. My brother doesn't do things like that.

Reporter: Can I call anyone for you? Can I call your mother?

Petro: No, she knows how I'm getting along. And don't take my picture. I don't want any notoriety!

Police brought Joseph Carretta to the hospital where he again "positively" identified Petro as he was lying in his bed. Petro, "yelling denials and threats," told the grocer, "I've never been to Alliance in my life! You'd better be sure about it! You'd just better be sure!" Petro again declared, "They're crazy."

After Joseph Carretta's identification, Florence Carretta and Edward Moretti both viewed Petro and declared positively, "This is the man." Warrants charging Petro with assault to rob and breaking into an inhabited home to commit a felony were sworn out. The newspapers claimed the charges could carry penalties of from three years to life in prison.

By the end of the day, it was reported that the Cleveland Police were still shaking their heads over Petro's "cat-like" durability in three near-death incidents. "He still has six lives to go," one cop stated.

On Wednesday, June 7, Alliance detectives asked the Cleveland Police department to pick up a 28-year-old East Cleveland man, who was said to be a pal of Petro. Cleveland Police obliged, holding the suspect. The next day, Alliance Police released Michael Petro, Sylvester Papalardo and Ralph De Biase, after the remaining witnesses were unable to identify any of the three as having been involved in the robbery. Julius Petro remained the only "positively" identified participant in the Carretta home invasion. The Alliance Police, however, were still waiting to get the suspect the Cleveland Police were holding before witnesses, but he too would be released.

On Friday morning, Julius Petro was loaded into an ambulance and taken to the Stark County Jail's hospital ward. For some never explained reason, at his side were Alliance City Judge Harry S. Wykoff and Alliance Police Chief A.O. Lower. The ambulance took off escorted by a "cavalcade" of Cleveland police cars.

At the jail, bond was set at $25,000, but Petro refused to enter a plea to the charges and the arraignment was continued. When photographers attempted to take his picture, he pulled a sheet up over his face. On June 17, Judge Wykoff set an arraignment date of June 22 for Petro after finding out the prisoner hired Canton attorney D.G. Gennett to represent him.

On Thursday, June 22, Petro appeared in Alliance Municipal Court to be arraigned on two charges connected to the attempted robbery of local grocer Joseph Carretta. When the hearing opened, Carretta was asked if he "could identify anyone in the courtroom as one of the four men who invaded his home, slugged him and ransacked his house before police put the gang to flight?" Carretta looked directly at Petro before calmly answering, "No."

Petro's attorney immediately moved for a dismissal of the breaking and entering charge. Judge Wykoff, just as quickly, granted the motion. This was followed by Carretta withdrawing his assault to rob charge against the hoodlum. Petro stood up, embraced his mother and walked out of the courtroom a free man. Dr. LaPolla, who attended the hearing, was not called as a witness. Patrolman Moretti, who positively identified Petro as the man he shot as he escaped the Carretta residence, was not even mentioned during the reporting, as was the case with Carretta's wife, Florence, who had also identified Petro.

Later that day, a reporter reached Carretta at his store. The grocer told the reporter, Petro "was not the man who came to the door that night before the robbery. This man is tall. That fellow was short. This man is not as dark." The reporter then asked if Carretta was threatened or if anyone approached him to change his statement? Carretta answered, "No, no, no. It's my conscious. I couldn't see anyone sent away who didn't do it."

Cleveland Police were enraged with the ease in which the notorious hoodlum "beat the rap." Chief of Detectives James E. McArthur was especially outspoken in his disgust of what took place. He pointed out that Carretta had identified Petro from 20 different police photographs, and after seeing him face-to-face in City Hospital's prison ward. "What do you have to do to put this man away?" the Chief of Detectives declared. "This looks like the old story of witnesses being threatened directly or getting scared in their own minds about Petro and his gang. Maybe the only way you can take care of Petro is to catch him on the job and take proper police action!" Nobody seemed confused about what the obviously irate McArthur meant by "proper police action." He concluded with, "I don't believe in persecuting anyone, but the entire force will be watching this man. He'll be picked up wherever or whenever he's seen on the street. I'm satisfied this man will never go straight. Someday he'll kill a citizen or a policeman if he's not stopped soon."

Another outraged police official was the Chief of the Homicide Squad, Captain David Kerr. He also didn't pull any punches about his thoughts. "There was a fix on," he declared. It was "an open and shut case. Someone got to the witnesses." And from Harry Wykoff, the Alliance Municipal Judge in whose court the hearing was held and who allowed Petro to walk free after hearing just one witness, came the profound statement, "Very strange."

The Game Continues

East Cleveland would be the scene of Petro's next arrest when he was stopped on Hayden Avenue at 3:45 on the morning of July 9, 1950. He was driving a new canary-yellow Pontiac convertible and had an attractive "blond companion" at his side. East Cleveland Patrolmen Robert Allen and John McDonald, the arresting officers, claimed, "We recognized the car and stopped Petro." Not a difficult task, given the description of the vehicle. Petro told the patrolmen that his driver's license has been with his "personal effects" at Central Police Station since his last arrest. He confessed, "I'm afraid to go down to Central Station to get the license. They'll toss me in again." Neither Petro nor the blond had the $25 to pay the cash bond release. Brother Michael was called, and the couple left the station before 4:30 that morning. When Petro appeared in court on July 29, East Cleveland Municipal Judge Stanton Adams fined him one dollar.

As the date of Petro's trial in Johnstown, Pennsylvania, crept closer, the hoodlum began seeking help from the medical establishment to get out of paying his debt to society. In September 1950, Petro paid a visit to a specialist in Buffalo, New York, to see if he had a serious lung problem. The response was negative. It was not the answer he was seeking, so Petro went for x-rays at the Cleveland Clinic. The x-rays showed a minimal lesion on one lung, which doctors claimed was not unusual among "city dwellers" in Cleveland. A bacterial culture, taken in late May when Petro showed up at an East Side hospital coughing up blood, did develop traces of the tuberculosis bacillus, resulting in Petro routinely reporting to the city health department as a case to be sent to a county clinic for further examination. It was reported that he was in line for the Sunny Acres[28] waiting list if the germ continued to appear. Cleveland police, however, had no doubt that this was all a "dodge" by Petro to avoid his upcoming trial and pending prison sentence.

When the case finally came to trial in Johnstown in early January 1951, Cleveland Police were looking forward to Petro going away for a while. But it was not to be. Petro, De Biase and Russo were allowed to plead guilty to robbery after the burglary charge was dropped. In what a now shell-shocked Deputy Inspector James McArthur called, "The worst miscarriage of justice I've ever heard of," the sentence handed down to the three men by the judge was being placed on probation for five years and being told to stay out of Cambria County, Pennsylvania where Johnstown is located, for the same period of time.

Detroit Incident

Nothing seemed to stop Julius Petro – not bullets, trials or sickness. On March 7, 1951, the *Cleveland Press* announced that state and city police agencies were after Petro for a series of robberies committed in Cambridge, Ohio, a small city of 10,000 and the county seat of Guernsey County, located east of Zanesville in the southeastern – central portion of the state, at the crossroads of Interstates 70 and 77. Whatever brought Petro and his companions – Joseph W. Drago and Michael Grande – to this desolate area of the state was never explained. The newspaper reported that between September 1950 and February 1951, the gang pulled five burglaries that earned them $3,000. Police were helped after witnesses in Cambridge provided them with license plate numbers. Police believed the men were using one of three cars owned by Petro; a 1948 Cadillac, a 1949 Ford or a 1950 Pontiac. The burglaries took place at five small retail establishments located right on Cambridge's main street.

On March 22, five men were indicted by a Guernsey County Grand Jury. Three of the men, all from Cleveland, were identified as Vincent Innocenzi, Angelo Carmello and Edward Robert Stamphel, alias Angelo Marcellino. The other two men were Cambridge residents. Police were still looking for Petro, Drago and Grande, who had disappeared from their normal haunts.

The search for Petro ended on May 1, when the *Detroit Free Press* reported, "Holdup squad detectives arrested four hoodlums, including two fugitives from Ohio." In addition to Petro and Joseph Russo, Detroit police nabbed Albert S. Wright[29] and John Dulapa.[30] Police recovered three handguns from a specially built compartment hidden behind a clock in the dashboard of a car used by the men. Another handgun was recovered from a hollowed-out telephone book found in Wright's apartment where they were staying, located at 2690 West Boston Boulevard in a neighborhood north-west of the downtown Detroit area. It was never made clear if Petro, Russo and Wright were arrested in the car or at the apartment. The following day it was announced that two of the four handguns found were reported stolen during burglaries in Detroit in recent days, including the burglary of a night club in which $2,000 was taken from a safe. Detroit Police Lieutenant John Kellner told reporters the four had been under surveillance for a week after a detective spotted Russo and followed him to the apartment.

It's interesting to note that in its reporting on Petro, the Detroit newspaper got a few of its facts wrong. First, they claimed the Cleveland hood had been shot four times "in tangles with police." Then they stated that Petro was scheduled to die in the electric chair, "but the chief witness against him was proved insane." They obviously got the story of James LaManna mixed up with

Petro's retrial. On May 4, Recorders Court Judge Frank G. Schemansee ordered Petro, Russo and Wright each held under a $25,000 bond for carrying concealed weapons, an offense which carried a maximum penitentiary sentence in Michigan of five years.

Cleveland police traveled to Detroit, where it was reported that considerations were given to bring Petro and Russo back to Ohio to stand trial on indictments issued in Cambridge and Cleveland. It was then decided to find out what the Detroit courts could do with him first. On June 28, a jury of ten men and two women were sworn in to hear the case against Petro and the others. Detroit detectives testified that they watched the three men for several days before arresting them. They told the court that they were "shadowing" them because they were acting suspiciously and because they knew the men had police records.

There was not much coverage of the trial testimony in the local newspapers. The verdict received just slightly more attention. Late on the afternoon of July 3, after three hours and 15 minutes of deliberations, the jury returned finding both Petro and Wright guilty of possession and concealment of guns in a borrowed automobile, after which their attorneys promised they would appeal. Russo was found not guilty, but was quickly returned to Cleveland to answer for a burglary charge from which he jumped a $25,000 bond. Recorder's Court Judge Paul E. Krause set a sentencing date of July 17 for the pair.

Petro was still facing trial in Cambridge on an indictment as a member of the burglary ring there. Before sentencing time, it had yet to be determined if he would be returned there for that trial before serving his anticipated Michigan prison term.

On July 17, a stern-faced Judge Krause handed down a sentence to Petro and Wright of four-and-a-half to five years in prison. Krause announced, "I recommend these men serve the maximum time of this sentence with no chance of parole. From the record, and from all reports, they have never done anything useful to society since they were born." The *Plain Dealer* wrote, "Petro has been able to worm out of shooting scrapes with his life, out of prison sentences when convicted and out of criminal charges in clear-cut felonies." But no more!

To make matters worse for the pair, there was no appeal bond and no delay to the start of their prison time. Petro asked for a 20-day stay of sentence and the right to post bond while appealing his sentence. Both requests were denied, and it was off to the Michigan State Penitentiary they went. Authorities in Ohio couldn't help but be impressed with the lightning quickness in which Petro was sentenced and finally sent away; this time to do a solid four-and-a-half years behind bars. Or would it be?

Almost 11 months to the day after his conviction, the Michigan Supreme Court on June 5, 1952, granted Petro and Wright a leave to appeal for a new trial on their concealed weapons convictions. The *Cleveland Press* reported that

Petro's bond was set at $5,000, but he made no attempt to post it yet because it would mean being transferred to Cambridge, Ohio, to face trial on the burglary indictment issued there. Somehow, due to Petro's incredible streak of luck, the appeal for a new trial was never held and the charges against him in Cambridge were dropped. The Cleveland Police were simply left with nothing but to shake their heads at the turn of events, which always seemed to favor Julius Petro. Three years later, on April 15, 1955, without Petro or Wright present, the Michigan Supreme Court reversed the conviction of the two "for possession of guns in a borrowed car" ruling there was no proof that either man knew the guns were in the vehicle.

Less than two months after posting the $5,000 bond in Michigan, Petro was one of four men in two cars that pulled into Dave Creedon's Hi-Speed filling station on Route 20 on the afternoon of July 24, 1952, in Painesville, Ohio, a city of nearly 20,000 and the county seat of Lake County located on the eastern border of Cuyahoga County. As Mary Creedon, the owner's wife, pumped gasoline into one of the cars, a couple of the men entered the station to use the bathroom. After the men took off, Mary noticed that a cash box containing $817, which was hidden under the front counter, was empty. Having noted the license plate number while putting gas into one of the cars, she called police. Lake County sheriffs, with help of local police, soon stopped the two vehicles and arrested all four men. In addition to Petro, Anthony D'Alessio, Anthony DiVito and Philip Aliberti were arrested. The men were held under $5,000 bonds in the Lake County Jail. On September 12, all four men were indicted for grand larceny by a Lake County Grand Jury. Due to pending events, however, Petro would never be tried for the crime.

Chapter Six:

The Big Take-Down

Warren Heist

On the morning of August 12, 1952, Cleveland Police Detective Lieutenant Thomas P. White was making his rounds when he was approached by one of the many informants that helped police out on occasion. The man gave him the names of three Cleveland hoods who, according to his information, were "going to pull an awfully big job" two days later at a place outside of Cuyahoga County. White knew the "who, what and when," but he was missing the "where and how."

White immediately contacted the Cleveland FBI office and notified them of the impending robbery. The FBI notified him there was nothing they could do because they didn't know whether Federal jurisdiction would be involved. White couldn't do anything more himself other than to comb the city in hopes of finding another informant that could provide additional information.

Two days later White received a telephone call from the FBI. "This is it," he was told, a $71,000 robbery just went down in Warren.

Thursday, August 14, 1952, began as a normal day for Charles J. Foley, branch manager of the Union Savings & Trust Company in Warren, Ohio. The son of the Warren *Tribune-Chronicle's Church and Lodge* editor stopped at the bank teller's window and picked up a bag of money containing $71,000. The money, in denominations of $1 to $20 bills, was to be used for cashing patron's paychecks. It was Foley's weekly routine to vary the routes he drove to his branch in order to foil any robbery attempts. Foley's branch was located on Woodland Avenue. Shortly before 10:00 a.m., Foley was driving East on Market Street when he turned north on Kenilworth Avenue. Foley was about to become part of Warren's history.

Following Foley as he turned onto Kenilworth Avenue was a gray Oldsmobile sedan containing three men. Nothing appeared out of the ordinary...other than each man was wearing a burlap bag over his head. Once on Kenilworth, the Oldsmobile sped up to Foley's vehicle, cut in front of it and forced it to the curb. Two of the hooded occupants jumped out, one armed with a sawed-off shotgun, the other a .38 Special revolver. While the man with the revolver cursed at Foley and waived the gun at him; the other used the butt of his sawed-off shotgun to smash the passenger's side window of the car. The gunman then reached in and grabbed the bag of money.

Observing the episode was Mrs. Ida Campbell, of 171 Kenilworth Avenue, who was out hanging laundry. She came on the run when she heard the screech of Foley's tires braking to a stop as he was cut off. Once on the scene, she did more than just serve as a witness to the event; she memorized the license plate number of the Oldsmobile and was able to give a State Highway Patrol sergeant a full description of the vehicle, right down to it being either a 1949 or 1950 model.

The Youngstown *Vindicator* reported:

> Foley said that after the men had scooped up the single [cloth money bag] containing the money, they began to return to their Oldsmobile and then went back and insisted that he deliver to them [a second money bag].

It should be noted that when the case went to trial it came out in testimony that two bags of money were delivered the day before by Brinks, Inc. from the Federal Reserve Bank in Cleveland. That alone should indicate that the bandits received inside information for the robbery, a fact that was not discussed at trial. Workers at the bank, however, confirmed that Foley was only given one bag that morning.

Meanwhile, Foley assured the bandits that he had no second bag. Once the Oldsmobile and the hooded robbers took off, Foley ran to Ida Campbell's home and called the FBI, local police and bank officials. He then waited for the authorities to arrive.

The robbery of $71,000 was reportedly the largest theft in Warren since April 24, 1935, when Depression Era bank robber and kidnapper Alvin "Creepy" Karpis and two cohorts stole the $72,000 payroll of the Youngstown Sheet & Tube Company from a mail delivery truck.

Police quickly checked the best clue they had – the license plate number provided by Ida Campbell. They soon discovered the plates were stolen the night before in Toronto, Ohio, a small city of 5,000 on the eastern edge of the state along the Ohio River, just north of Steubenville, Ohio and Weirton, West Virginia.

State police and local authorities reacted quickly. They set up roadblocks in Columbiana County, located just south of Mahoning County, after a gray Oldsmobile was spotted near East Liverpool. County law enforcement reported that at a local roadblock there a vehicle fitting the description fled from authorities.

Despite the daringness and success of the robbery, the thieves made one major mistake, perhaps without even knowing it. As a state-wide alert was made for the bandits, Joseph D. Purvis, Assistant Special Agent-in-Charge of the Cleveland FBI office announced the FBI was joining in the hunt. A portion of the money stolen from the Union Savings & Trust Company was insured by the Federal Deposit Insurance Company, which meant this robbery was a Federal crime. Petro also wasn't aware that the serial numbers from $16,000 of the new bills taken were recorded. The *Plain Dealer* later wrote, "That any of the $71,000 could be identified was the FBI's ace in the hole. It was a tightly kept secret." Declaring, "We need all the help we can get," Paul J. Shine, Special-Agent-in-Charge of the Cleveland office, urged anyone with information in the case to contact local authorities. The FBI immediately printed circulars for local banks that identi-fied the serial numbers for the new $5, $10 and $20 bills. These were to be posted inside the tellers' windows so they could identify the money if it came through.

In Cleveland, Detective Chief James McArthur already had "insider infor-mation" from Detective Lieutenant Thomas White as to who the culprits in the Warren robbery might be. He immediately sent Detectives Allen W. Schultz, James W. Burke and Wilbert A. Wiseman to 1635 East 86th Street, where Petro was now living with his in-laws, and to the home of Joseph J. Sanzo. The detec-tives were there to greet both men upon their return home and took them into custody. Detectives grilled both of them as to their whereabouts during the past 48 hours.

On Friday, the day after the robbery, the FBI reported that the getaway car was discovered. Warren Fire Department Captain Clarence Hipple had gone to Trumbull Memorial Hospital to visit an ailing friend. There, just three blocks from the scene of the robbery, he spotted the gray 1950 Oldsmobile, that all of law enforcement in northeastern Ohio was looking for, in the hospital's parking lot. The car was stolen in Mansfield, Ohio, on Tuesday night. A search of the vehicle revealed no fingerprints were left behind.

That same morning both Petro and Sanzo appeared in police lineups at the Central Station. But by the end of the day both were released. Detective Chief McArthur refused to discuss anything that was revealed during the lineups or the interrogations. It was reported that another Cleveland man was being sought for questioning. Meanwhile, a preliminary hearing scheduled in Paines-ville for Petro and three others this day for the larceny at the filling station there, was granted a postponement. All would be indicted, however, the follow-ing month on September 12.

Investigation & Indictment

While the Warren robbery quickly disappeared from the newspapers, the FBI and the police were busy at work trying to solve it. On September 19, one week after Petro's indictment for the Painesville service station larceny, $500 of the stolen bank money was deposited by a real estate broker at an East Side bank branch. When questioned by police, the broker, Charles W. Schaefer, claimed he received it on the night of September 18 at the home of John Petro at 15725 Halliday Avenue NE, located a few blocks away from the Five Points intersec-tion in Collinwood. According to Schaefer, the money was to be used as a down payment for the Recreation Café at 12316 St. Clair Avenue,[31] a tavern John Petro and his son-in-law, Nicholas J. Tirabassi were negotiating to purchase. Tirabassi was married to Julius' sister, Monda, and lived with John Petro and his wife.

The next morning, Schaefer deposited the down payment in the North American Bank at 15619 Waterloo Road in Collinwood, where an alert teller noticed that the serial numbers on 25 of the $20 bills matched the numbers on the list of stolen bills provided by the FBI. Bank officials quickly notified the police. In addition to the 25 $20 bills, that were new and had the serial numbers the FBI was looking for, Schaefer also had deposited 25 additional $20 bills.[32]

Five days later, on September 24, 31 of the stolen $5 bills were discovered at the Bank of Ohio branch at 14707 St. Clair Avenue.[33] The $155 was deposited by a neighborhood delicatessen owner. Detectives were able to track the money back to the Grotto Inn at nearby 16136 St. Clair.[34] There, the owner, Louis Gattozzi revealed the bills had come from Joseph Sanzo, who had used them as a partial repayment on a loan.

On Saturday afternoon, October 4, police began rounding up the suspects. Julius Petro was the first one in custody, arrested at his in-law's East 86th Street home. Next to be nabbed were John and Lydia Petro, who police grilled for four hours before booking them for investigation. Sanzo was arrested early Sunday morning while in his new 1952 Oldsmobile, a vehicle police said cost $5,200. When booked, Sanzo claimed he was a truck driver.

Police quickly obtained a "secret" search warrant for John Petro's home, issued by Municipal Court Judge Louis Petrash. In a 2nd floor porch glider, detectives found $3,000 wrapped in newspapers and stuffed between the cushions. They also discovered $760 in Lydia Petro's dresser drawer.

When police questioned John Petro, he offered no satisfactory explanation of how he came to possess the 25 $20 bills stolen from the Warren bank manager. He was adamant that the $3,000 found in the porch-glider was his own legitimate savings that he earned as an upholsterer and income from two rental properties. "Julius never gave me anything but bills," John Petro told Detective Lieutenant Thomas P. White. He proved his point by producing two receipts. One in which he paid a $1,500 bond and another for which he forked out $500 for attorney fees. Both were for his son's connection to the Painesville larceny charge. John Petro acknowledged that Julius was aware of the secret cache he kept and was in the habit of borrowing from it and repaying it without his knowledge. What John Petro didn't let on was that the money provided to Charles Schaefer, the broker, had come directly from his wife's hidden stash, not his. Perhaps this was why White noticed a smirk appear on the face of Julius Petro as he sat listening to the interrogation.

During the grilling of Tirabassi, the die-setter claimed that Julius became enraged when he found out that the down-payment to Schaefer was made in cash and not by check. At that point he said John Petro tried to get the bills back by writing a check for $1,000 to the bank, even though he had less than $400 in his account. After the interrogations Detective Lieutenant White told reporters, "We know Tirabassi and John Petro. We know they are not the holdup men in the family." The most important part of the interview was about to come.

Police brought Lydia Petro into the interrogation room to confront her son. The weeping 57-year-old mother looked at her son and pleaded for him to, "Tell the truth." At this juncture, Petro turned to Detective Lieutenant White and stated, "I put it," admitting, as far as police were concerned, that Petro had put the $500 in stolen bills into his mother's "secret stash." He refused to say how he had come to possess the money. The admission was enough, however, to release his mother and father, as well as his brother-in-law.

Petro and Sanzo were held through the weekend and taken before Municipal Judge Andrew Kovachy on Monday morning. Petro was charged with concealing stolen property, the $500 in $20 bills; Sanzo was booked on a similar charge. The judge set bail at $10,000 and both men were off to the County Jail when they couldn't immediately make bond. Three hours into their jail stay the men posted bond and were released pending formal arraignment before Judge Kovachy scheduled for the following morning. Throughout the day and into Monday night the FBI worked with Cleveland police to "seal up" local charges while passing up Federal charges against the pair.

At the Police Court arraignment Tuesday morning, Judge Kovachy granted the pair, represented by Louis Fernberg, a continuance until October 29. If convicted on the state charges, the men were facing prison terms of one to seven years each. Both remained free on $10,000 bonds. Petro was suddenly facing three different charges in three separate cases, the others being in Detroit and in Painesville. "This is the best case we have ever had against Petro," claimed Detective Chief McArthur, who commented that $1,200 of the money was recovered here. Detectives felt this was finally going to put an end to Petro's "charmed career," that he would be facing a long prison term. But they also knew they had been wrong before...numerous times.

On Tuesday, October 14, the Cuyahoga Grand Jury began hearing evidence on Petro and Sanzo from a dozen witnesses, including FBI agents. The two men remained free on bail pending their October 29 hearing in Cleveland Municipal Court. Two days later, Petro and Sanzo were officially indicted by the grand jury for possession of stolen property – the cash from the robbery. Petro's indictment accused him of possessing $500 of the stolen money. Sanzo was indicted for spending $200 of the loot.

The two men pleaded not guilty on October 20 before Common Pleas Judge Harry A. Hanna. Petro's bond was increased to $20,000, Sanzo's to $15,000. Represented again by Louis Fernberg, the lawyer protested that the bond was too high and that Petro had never jumped bail despite his lengthy record of arrests. As what might have been expected, Hanna's reply was, "There's always a first time." That same day it was announced that the two men had been positively identified by three witnesses as having been in Warren on the day of the robbery.

The county grand jury indictment seemed more or less like a smoke screen as a Federal Grand Jury was also at work. In the week prior to Petro pleading not guilty to the county indictment, both of his parents, as well as Nicholas Tirabassi, appeared before the Federal Grand Jury. In all, Assistant U.S. Attorney Frank E. Steel called about a dozen witnesses to give testimony. Petro, whose county indictment was more akin to receiving stolen property, was now convinced that the robbery in Warren was being linked to him. On October 29, the day he was to appear in Municipal Court, the *Cleveland Press* announced that a "secret" indictment was returned by the Federal Grand Jury and that the newspaper believed it was against Julius Petro.

The next morning it was reported that Petro was being hunted by U.S. Marshals armed with an arrest warrant, which was issued late on the day before. There was a fear by local authorities that the hoodlum would flee instead of facing a 25-year prison sentence if convicted of the Federal charges.

During the early reporting of the "secret" indictment, Joseph Sanzo was not mentioned in connection with the Federal charges. It came as a surprise then that Sanzo was the first to be arrested. U.S Deputy Marshals Joseph Hovancek and Stanton N. Weegar arrested Sanzo as he entered his South Euclid home.[35] The two marshals followed this up with a visit to Petro's in-laws, where the hood was currently living. Petro was in bed, but exhibited no surprise. "We knew it was coming," he told the marshals, "We read it in yesterday's paper."

When Federal Court opened that morning, Petro and Sanzo were taken before U.S. District Court Judge Charles J. McNamee, where they entered pleas of not guilty "in scarcely audible voices." Familiar faces now represented the men – Edward Stanton and Michael Picciano. When McNamee set bond at $40,000 each, both attorneys objected until being told "curtly," the bonds would remain at $40,000. Petro and Sanzo were then on their way back to the County Jail.

The men's chances of raising the $40,000 bonds were slim. Stanton, representing Petro, said no effort was in the works to raise the bond. Currently, Petro was on $35,000 in bonds, which consisted of his Detroit and Painesville cases, as well as for the local charges in the Warren robbery. Picciano, counsel of record for Sanzo, simply stated, "We can't raise the bond for Sanzo."

On November 6, Picciano filed a motion asking for a bail reduction to $25,000, claiming his client's only criminal offense was a disorderly conduct charge in 1949. He insisted his wife and two children needed him for support. Judge McNamee agreed to the reduction and the following afternoon Sanzo appeared at the clerk's office in Federal Court with a professional bondsman. The *Plain Dealer* reported, "Sanzo was excited to the point he barely was able to write his name. He also needed coaching on the spelling of South Euclid putting down his address."

Three weeks later, Picciano tried another tactic. The attorney filed a motion for a separate trial for Sanzo, maintaining he could not receive a fair or impartial trial if he were tried with Petro. Picciano claimed in the petition that the criminal events in Petro's career were highly publicized and argued that jurors who had read the newspaper articles would be prejudiced against both Sanzo and Petro. The *Plain Dealer* reported:

> The lawyer also revealed that Petro, a hoodlum with a reputation for saying little to law enforcement officials, might have made "admissions" to the FBI. Picciano said there was "a strong possibility" that Petro might have made statements or admissions which, if accepted as evidence, might influence the jury against Sanzo.

The newspaper, however, claimed Petro and Sanzo were close friends and that the pleas in Picciano's motions were simply legal angles he was trying to exploit. Nothing was reported to indicate a falling out occurred between the two men. On November 26, five days before trial was scheduled to begin, Judge McNamee denied the motion.

Sanzo would remain out on bail for the entire length of the trial. During the early days of the trial, a *Cleveland Press* reporter sat down and interviewed Joseph Sanzo and his wife Jean after testimony had concluded for the day. The defendant talked about his life and about his "idol," Julius Petro.

Joe and Jean grew up together as next door neighbors on the East Side of Cleveland. Joe was a student at Collinwood High School, but quit when he was 16 years old and got a job. The following year he and Jean eloped to Kentucky. They were both 23 now and had two children.

"I first met Julius in a neighborhood beer joint, drinking coffee, around the first of July [1952]. We were introduced by mutual friends.

"I had heard about him for years. I had seen him driving around in his car. I'm telling you right now, even though we're in trouble together, what I know of Julius I like," Sanzo said.

Sanzo said their friendship developed during July. "We'd meet for coffee. We never went out together socially, though."

"In August this year, as they do every year, my hands and feet puffed up. Some kind of allergy, I guess. I couldn't even close my left hand. A doctor will prove that in court.

"I had to turn my dump truck business over to my kid brother and I did what I could that month to line up hauling business.

"The morning they say I was down in Warren with Julius, I was home eating breakfast at 9 o'clock," Sanzo claimed.

His wife, Jean then spoke up declaring, "I know he's not guilty, because he was home that day."

The Trial

On Monday, December 1, 1952, the bank robbery trial of Julius Petro and Joseph Sanzo got underway in Federal Court in Cleveland. Representing the government were U.S. Attorney John J. Kane, Jr. and Assistant U.S. Attorney Frank E.

Steel.[36] Defense counsel was Picciano and Stanton. Overseeing the trial was U.S. District Court Judge Charles J. McNamee.

The trial opened with 90 minutes of "sparring and intense quizzing" by Picciano and Stanton as they fought to seat the type of jurors they felt would best suit their case – one consisting mostly of women. For jury selection, a special venire of 70 men and women were called. After an initial selection of six men and six women, defense counsel proceeded to use its peremptory challenges to replace all the men with women. The government must not have been concerned with this aspect of the trial because the jury ended up consisting of 11 women and just one man; even the two alternates jurors were women. When jury selection was completed, the *Cleveland Press* commented that the 30-year-old Petro, "slick-haired and natty in a dark blue suit," looked pleased. Ironically, just one day into the trial it appeared that the case could end up being heard by an all-woman jury. Frank Alward, the only male on the panel, received news that his son had been diagnosed with polio. If it were decided that Alward be sent home, he would be replaced by one of the two female alternates.

In the government's opening statement, Frank Steel said that both defendants would "definitely" be identified as the men seen fleeing the scene of the robbery. Up until the start of the trial, the government had kept it from the newspapers that they had two witnesses who could identify the defendants as the men who sped away from the scene. Steel also stated that part of the case was the tracing of the new bills to Petro and Sanzo.

During defense counsels' opening remarks, it was quickly established that the defense for the two men would be based on alibis. Stanton declared, "Petro was nowhere near Warren on the day of the robbery. He was at home, and we are going to prove it. He is not guilty." Picciano told the panel, "On the morning of the robbery Sanzo got up at 8:30 a.m., ate a leisurely breakfast and then went to the Five Points area." He stated that Sanzo was a truck driver who suffered an "infirmity of the hands" in August and was unable to drive.

The government opened its case with a series of witnesses to establish the path the money took from the time it left the Federal Reserve Bank in Cleveland, on August 13, until it ended up in Charles J. Foley's hands the next day. L.A. Mines, vice president of Union Savings & Trust Company in Warren, testified he saw a crew of six guards from Brink's, Inc. deliver two bags on Wednesday and watched Foley leave with one bag on Thursday. Mines told the court that of the $71,000 in the bag, $16,000 of it was in new currency that was traceable due to its serial number sequence. He stated bank records showed that these traceable bills consisted of $5,000 in new $5 bills, $5,000 in new $10 bills and $6,000 in new $20 bills. Steel introduced the 25 new $20 bills and the 31 new $5 bills the government had recovered, and showed how they were identified as part of the cash stolen from Charles Foley.

Dan Campbell, a teller whose testimony may have cost the government some credibility points, testified that he received the two bags at his window and signed for them. He later corrected this testimony to suggest he may have been at lunch at the time and that another teller must have signed for them. Campbell did state that he placed both bags in a downstairs vault and the next morning personally handed the one containing the $71,000 to Foley to take to his Woodland Avenue branch.

George D. Hackley was an imposing figure as a Brink's, Inc. guard, who was in charge of the six-man crew that brought the money from the Federal Reserve Bank to Warren. He told the jury that the two bags, one with $71,000, the other with $32,000, were delivered to Union Savings & Trust Company at 11:10 a.m. Wednesday and the transfer took five minutes.

Throughout the afternoon testimony, defense attorneys "badgered" the witnesses as they traced the delivery of the bags of money to the Warren bank. The *Plain Dealer* reported, "They were demanding proof, outside of written records, that there was any money at all in the bag." L.A. Mines was asked if he opened the bag at any point and saw the money. He answered that he did not. Neither did bank teller Dan Campbell. The Brink's guard claimed he knew what was inside the bag by the tag that was attached to it. "You didn't actually see any money?" Hackley was asked. The guard agreed he hadn't because he wasn't supposed to look inside the sealed bag.

Steel's last witness in this matter was George W. Robey, a Federal Reserve Bank teller. Robey spent considerable time explaining how the cloth money bags were sealed with a cord and lead clasp and were to remain sealed until they reached their final destination. Steel made his point that there was absolutely no reason for the other witnesses to open the bags to see what was inside them.

Before trial ended this first day, Steel questioned the first witness in regard to the actual robbery. Mrs. Harold Auker, a housewife at home tending to her three children, discussed what she saw taking place a block-and-a-half from her home the day of the robbery. Like Ida Campbell, her attention was drawn to the incident by the screeching of tires. She then watched a man running with an object that looked like a stick to her, arriving at the passenger's side of Foley's automobile. The whole courtroom, it was reported, seemed like it was on the edge of its seat in anticipation of what she would testify to next. But all she proceeded with was, "Then I went back inside the house." Unfortunately, that's all she was witness to. Having picked up her mail, she went back inside to take care of her children. She did state that she and her brother-in-law later looked out and saw the back end of the gray Oldsmobile as it fled up Kenilworth Avenue. They were able to jot down the license plate number on a calendar.

At the end of the first day of trial, Sanzo, who was free on bail, went to retrieve his gray overcoat, which he had hung up near the jury box. The coat, however, was no longer there. Letting everyone within earshot know, Sanzo bellowed out, "Why, there's a thief in this place!"

During the second day of trial, Tuesday, a *Cleveland Press* reporter spoke to

FBI agents who stated that to-date less than $1,500 of the stolen money had been recovered from the robbery. They also admitted that they had made no headway in locating the remaining $69,500, of which $14,500 was traceable cash. The remaining $54,500 was older money, which could easily be passed because of its small denominations.

The government's plan for the second day of trial was to link Petro to the robbery itself. The jury, as well as the defendant and everyone else in the courtroom, were in for a big surprise.

Prosecutors Kane and Steel put on four witnesses over two hours, building up to what would be the appearance of their "secret star-witness." Beginning with Charles Foley, the assistant bank manager told the jury about the events leading up to the point where he turned onto Kenilworth Avenue and was forced to the curb and robbed at gunpoint. Next was Ida Campbell, the Kenilworth Avenue resident who was hanging out laundry and came running at the sound of the screeching tires that forced Foley to stop. She was followed by Samuel Brogden, Jr., a U.S. Postal carrier, who was delivering mail on the street. He saw the robbery by the hooded men take place from a distance. He drew laughter in the courtroom as he described hitting the deck and remaining prone on a resident's porch as the gray Oldsmobile sped up Kenilworth in his direction on its getaway. He watched as the car turned right onto Montclair Street.

The fourth witness was George Fisher, a local landscaper. His testimony, as well as Brogden's, was to show the bandits' getaway path after the robbery. Fisher testified that he was working on a lawn on Montclair Street when he heard the screeching tires of the Oldsmobile turning from Kenilworth on to Montclair. The car sped east on Montclair crossing Roselawn Avenue and then turned right on Oak Knoll Avenue, heading south back to East Market Street.

In all likelihood, once the robbers got back to East Market Street, they turned right and drove west five blocks to Trumbull Memorial Hospital, where the Oldsmobile was abandoned and discovered by Warren Fire Department Captain Clarence Hipple the next day. This meant that all the law enforcement roadblocks and reports of seeing the gray Oldsmobile in the area were all for naught. Petro and his cohorts were in a different car, if not two cars, within minutes after the robbery was over.

It was now time for the government's secret star witness to take the stand, a sophomore student at the University of Missouri by the name of Carter Alden. Home on summer break, the 19-year-old was driving his mother, Mrs. Henry Alden, ironically, to the Union Savings & Trust Company on Woodland Avenue. The two were headed north on Oak Knoll Avenue when the speeding Oldsmobile crashed the stop sign on Monclair Street, turned right and came barreling toward them from the other direction, nearly forcing them off the road. Alden testified that as the cars passed each other he saw the driver's face. "It was not hooded or concealed in any way," the young man testified. At the time, neither

Alden nor his mother thought much about the encounter. After going to the bank, he dropped his mother off at home and went out and played a round of golf. That evening, after reading about the robbery of Foley, his mother contacted the Warren Police Department.

Warren police quickly notified the FBI and the next morning Abbie Alden, and her son Carter were on their way to Cleveland in the company of FBI agent Stanley E. Peterson. The Cleveland police had picked up Petro the day before and were ready to have the Aldens view a special 5-man line-up.

In the courtroom, U.S. Attorney Kane asked Carter Alden what happened at the Cleveland Central Police Station that morning. "I picked out the driver of the car," Alden calmly replied. "It was Julius Petro."

An excited buzz erupted in the courtroom. The FBI and the Cleveland police had kept secret the fact that the college student had identified Petro as the getaway driver of the gray Oldsmobile, on the morning after the robbery took place. *Plain Dealer* reporter Ted Princiotto, who covered the trial, wrote:

> Mention of his name electrified Petro, who sprang like a wounded animal out of his chair muttering a low-toned denial of Alden's words. He rose only half-way from the chair and stood there momentarily. His manner came as a surprise to courtroom spectators who have watched his expressionless face for two whole days. Now it lit up with anger as he acted the hurt man.

John Kane allowed the excitement to die down before continuing his questioning, "Do you see the driver in the courtroom?"

"Yes," Alden answered.

"Which man was it?" Kane asked.

"The man in the blue suit," Alden replied, nodding toward Petro at the defense table, where the defendant sat in a blue suit with his jacket unbuttoned.

Petro was asked to stand up so Alden could verify his identification. The defendant arose in a "bear-like" movement. Nodding again, Alden confirmed that Petro was the man he saw behind the wheel.

In January 2019, the author contacted Carter Alden, now in his mid-80s and asked him to share his thoughts about the day of the August robbery and the subsequent trial in December, now some 66 years in the past:

- The part of the getaway that my mother and I witnessed took only several seconds, but I am very clear about the look I got at Julius Petro's face. He had a very excited and wild-eyed look as he sped by us, going in the opposite direction. I feel that the same was true in the case of my mother, in recognizing both Petro and Sanzo [Although both acknowledged that a third man was in the back seat, neither of them got a good look at him]. It was obvious to us that they were fleeing something.

- After reading about the robbery in the Warren *Tribune Chronicle* that evening, my mother and I discussed it. There was no hesitation in deciding that we needed to contact the police. We did have some concerns over getting involved in a case involving criminals, but we felt that we needed to do it. We called the Warren City Police and reported what we had seen.

- Later that evening two FBI agents visited us. We described to them what we saw and answered their questions. They showed us several photos of individual faces. I picked out one of these as the driver of the getaway car. My mother picked out the driver and also the person sitting next to him in the front seat. I was surprised that my mother could recognize both of them. At that time we did not know the names of Petro and Sanzo. (Author's note: Because of the information the informant had provided to Cleveland Police Detective Lieutenant Thomas P. White days earlier, the police and the FBI knew who the robbers were. They just needed a witness to put the faces to the men fleeing the scene.)

- Of my recollection of dealings with FBI agent Stanley Peterson; I remember him as being straight-forward, polite but business-like. I do not remember him being inappropriate in any way. I believe it was he who briefed me before my being cross-examined in the trial. He advised me to listen carefully to questions directed to me, and to answer them honestly, clearly and decisively. He also advised me not to offer information beyond what I was asked. I took this all as good advice, and tried to follow it.

- I was required to miss a few days of classes at University of Missouri in order to fly back to Cleveland and testify at the trial. I made the mistake of not notifying my professors of my reason for missing the classes. This hurt my grades in a couple of them. I regret having not informed them.

- One or two weeks after I had returned to college after the trial, I was contacted and visited by an FBI agent who was located in Columbia, Missouri. He had been informed of the trial involving Petro and Sanzo. He thanked me for my part in testifying. He advised me that, if I noticed anything suspicious or if I felt threatened in any way by anyone, that I should contact him immediately and they would take action to protect me.

The courtroom excitement "was still in the air," when defense attorney Stanton rose to cross-examine Carter Alden. It was late in the day and defense counsel would only get a few questions asked. The wily lawyer asked Alden about the speed of the Oldsmobile when they passed each other. Stanton was going to focus on how the witness could be so sure of his identification with the car flying past him at such a high rate of speed. Stanton asked him to describe the man behind the wheel.

"I described him as dark-complexioned, round-faced and well-built. I remembered his face," Alden replied.

"You don't know right now, sir, do you, if he had a hat on?" Stanton queried.

Alden answered that he did not know.

When court adjourned that afternoon, the jury was led out and then two deputy U.S. marshals escorted Petro away. As he was being led from the courtroom, two reporters he recognized were standing nearby. Petro inquired of them, "I was turned loose? Why didn't they charge me if he picked me out of the lineup?"

Petro would get his answer, but it would not come from the reporters. It came from John Kane, Jr., who spoke to a few of the newspaper people after court ended that day. He told them the story of what happened after the Alden's identification of both Petro and Sanzo in the lineup that day. On the night of the robbery, after Abbie Alden called the Warren Police Department, the FBI was notified, and agents visited the Alden's home where both Abbie and her son identified a picture of the driver from an array of eight to ten mugshots. Abbie also identified a photo of the man seated next to the driver. Neither picture included the name of the person who appeared on it. On Friday morning, FBI Agent Stanley E. Peterson drove the two to Cleveland to make positive identification during several lineups arranged by the Cleveland police at Central Police Station.

Afterwards, the FBI approached John Kane and requested an immediate arraignment of the two men, and that the robbery case be presented to a Federal Grand Jury. "Not so fast," was the reply from the cautious and experienced U.S. Attorney. "We still haven't got the $71,000," Kane stated. "We still haven't got the identity of the third robber. We will order Cleveland police to release Petro and Sanzo for 'lack of evidence.'"

Agent-in-Charge, Paul Shine, immediately devised and supervised a "cat and mouse" game using 12 FBI agents, assigned full-time to the case, to shadow Petro's and Sanzo's every move. In addition, over the next month, 29 other agents participated in helping to cover the pair. Throughout the balance of August and well into September, the agents tailed the men. Every time they were seen going into a store or shop to spend money, agents followed and collected the bills that were exchanged.

Agents collected the 31 $5 bills that Sanzo spent at stores in the Five Points area. Kane pointed out that Petro was a little more careful as he admitted having borrowed money from his mother's hiding place at home and then replacing it with the $500 in new bills. Here the story changes a little bit as the *Cleveland Press* reported, "Petro's mother's deposit of that money as a down payment on a bowling alley ended the FBI's game. They were forced to move in. Petro had to admit he put the money in his mother's home, or she would have been incarcerated." At the end of the day, however, Kane still had to acknowledge that more than $69,000 of the money was still unaccounted for.

On Wednesday morning, Carter Alden was back on the stand being cross-examined by Stanton. During questioning, Alden inadvertently remarked that the previous evening he had spoken to Warren police officers. During re-direct, Kane quickly got an explanation for this into the record:

Kane: Where did you talk to the police?

Alden: Why, they were at my home.

Kane: What were they doing there?

Alden: Why, Warren police sent two men to the home for protection all night.

The majority of Wednesday was spent by defense counsel trying their best to shake the testimony of Carter Alden, first, and then his mother, whose testimony came next. Mrs. Abbie Alden followed her son to the witness stand. She basically repeated Carter's story during direct examination. Abbie Alden was an excellent witness; her testimony was called "observant and specific." She described the man in the front passenger seat as follows: "His features were rather small. He had dark hair and his eyes were starey[37] and I noted particularly than his chin was rather small. He wasn't a full-faced man." In both the line-up in Cleveland, and in court, she identified Sanzo as the man in the passenger seat and Petro as the driver of the car.

On cross-examination, Stanton had Mrs. Alden retell when she first saw the Oldsmobile on Oak Knoll Avenue and had her place a mark on a chart he provided to indicate that spot. He then had her mark the position of the Alden's vehicle. Stanton then wanted her to show the point where the two cars passed one another. Mrs. Alden had estimated her son's speed at 20 to 25 mile per hour. It was estimated that the bandit's speed might have been as much as 60 or more. Mrs. Alden sensed what the attorney was attempting to do and stated, "If you want me to take more time, I'll figure it out. Maybe it's not quite accurate."

"You're right it's not quite accurate," Stanton shot back. "It shows on this map that you were going twice as fast as the other car."

Stanton next tried to rattle the witness regarding the identification of Petro. It came out during her son's testimony that neither of the Alden's knew the names of the men whose photographs they had identified on the evening of the robbery. Stanton tried to imply that Abbie Alden might have seen Petro's name in the newspaper account before being driven to Cleveland the next morning. "Did you see the article?" Stanton demanded, showing her a clipping from the Warren *Tribune Chronicle* dated August 15. The judge interrupted, bringing out the fact that Mrs. Alden was taken to Cleveland on the morning of the 15th and the newspaper was an afternoon publication. This coincided with Frank Steel's objection that counsel was "trying to infer" that Mrs. Alden was aware of the name before she arrived at the police lineup in Cleveland.

The *Plain Dealer* wrote:

> Similar exchanges marked the efforts of Stanton and Michael A. Picciano, the defense law-yers, to tear down or discredit the identification. When Stanton finished, the other defense attorney took over. Picciano concentrated on bringing out in minute detail all the happenings, using short quick sentences.

At the end of the day, however, the government called FBI Agent Stanley Peterson, whose testimony bolstered both of the Alden's statements. He told the jury that neither Mrs. Alden, nor her son "knew or was given" the names of the two men they had identified before arriving in Cleveland for the lineups.

Kane had called Peterson to explain how the Aldens were brought to the lineup at the Central Police Station and what instructions were given to them. Peterson related how the men in the lineup were assigned numbers from one to five. The Aldens were advised to tell him if they recognized any of the men in the lineup and to provide him with the number. "At no time," Peterson de-clared, "Were names mentioned."

The Aldens viewed the lineup separately. Peterson testified that Abbie Alden selected numbers that belonged to Petro and Sanzo. Carter Alden was shown the same men, but with different numbers, and he identified Petro as the driver of the Oldsmobile.

During cross-examination, Picciano asked the agent, "Did you give either of these boys an opportunity to confront the witnesses who picked them out?"

Peterson seemed confused as to whom the attorney was referring to as boys. "When you say boys, do you mean the defendants?"

Annoyed at the response, Picciano rephrased and asked, "You didn't have these boys brought out and have Mrs. Alden say, 'These were the boys I saw in the car?'"

Peterson replied that he had not.

At the end of Wednesday's session, Kane and Steel announced that they would begin to develop the second phase of their circumstantial case against Petro and Sanzo. On Thursday morning, the government called a number of witnesses to establish how John and Lydia Petro had come into possession of the stolen $20 bills. One of the witnesses, John Petro, was called to the stand as a reluctant witness. Under questioning from John Kane, Jr., he was forced to admit that he wrote a check for $1,000 in a vain attempt to recover the currency he had given to the broker Charles Schaefer.[38] Unfortunately for John Petro, his bank account only contained $337. John denied that his son had made him write the check.

In testimony provided that morning by Nicholas Tirabassi, the prosecutor tried to show that it was Julius Petro who suggested that a check be written in hopes of recovering the $500 in stolen bills deposited at the bank.

"Who suggested a check be written?" Kane asked.

"All of us did," Tirabassi replied.

During further questioning, however, Tirabassi confessed he had gotten "jumpy" and at one point told FBI Agent Robert H. Johnston that Julius was the one who suggested they write the check. Tirabassi admitted that he was too late in approaching Schaefer to prevent him from depositing the money the morning after he received it.

Also, in earlier testimony that morning, Charles Schaefer revealed that the Petros had contacted him about purchasing the Recreation Cafe[39] for $46,000. Schaefer said he went to the Petro home on the night of September 18. There, according to the *Cleveland Press*, he "received $1,000 in cash, which Mrs. Petro produced from somewhere inside the house.[40] Later, when Kane was questioning John Petro as to where his wife got the money, he answered, "I don't know where my wife got the money from. She hides it in so many places." The reply brought an outburst of laughter from those in the courtroom. While on the stand that morning, Schaefer also identified Sanzo as accompanying Julius Petro to his parent's home when he went there to discuss the tavern deal. This story had not come up prior to the trial and it was not made clear if this had occurred on the night the money was exchanged or at some earlier date.

During the John Petro examination, Kane questioned him repeatedly regarding events that occurred on September 19, the day after the money was given to Schaefer.

John Petro said, "When I came home from work the next day, Julius was at the house. Julius said, 'Daddy, how did you do with Schaefer?'

"I told him, 'we're buying the café, son, I gave him $1,000 in cash last night.'

"Julius said, 'How come you always pay in checks other times but this time it had to be in cash? Don't you know it's better to do business with checks?'"

Kane asked, "What else did he say?"

John Petro answered, "That's all he said."

It's of interest to note that, if this testimony was the truth, then it was obvious the reason John Petro didn't write a check to begin with for the $1,000 down-payment for the Recreation Café was he simply didn't have the funds in the bank to cover it. There was no explanation offered as to why he didn't tell his son that.

It was John Petro's testimony that no one forced him to write the check to retrieve the cash that Schaefer had deposited into the North American Bank; a task which would seem nearly impossible to pull off. The check, however, was written on September 19 by John Petro, the same day he had the conversation with his son, even though there was only $337 in the account. On this point, Kane hammered him, "So when you wrote the check it was worthless?" To which John Petro eventually acknowledged, "I guess so." When he gave the check to Schaefer, two days later, he still had only $337 in the account. On September 25, he deposited $906 into the account to cover the check.

Schaefer had just testified that when he took the check to the bank he received ten $100 bills, instead of any of the $20 bills John Petro was hoping to get back. By this time those bills were already in the hands of the FBI. The reason for this came from the testimony of North American Bank teller John Grdina earlier that morning. He told the court that he had spotted the new bills when Schaefer deposited them on September 19. He compared them to the FBI list and immediately notified the bank manager.

The government's next witness was Lydia Petro. The gray-haired 57-year-old mother of Julius Petro sat "weeping and wringing her hands," and, like her husband before her, appeared as a reluctant witness against her son. Mrs. Petro testified in broken-English and in a barely audible voice. She told the court she kept a cache of money hidden in her home, which she accumulated from savings from her husband's income. She claimed she never used the money herself, she just kept it hidden.

Lydia Petro's answers to most of the government's questions were a vain attempt at trying to defend both her son and husband. She claimed Julius did not know where her money was hidden, even though he had already told the police that he frequently borrowed from it, and paid it back, and that he had placed what turned out to be the stolen $500 there. She also stated that she was the one who rebuked her husband for using the money for the down-payment for the Recreation Café instead of writing a check. Lydia testified that it was also her idea to recover the $500 from the bank by using a check. Because of prior statements and earlier testimony her efforts proved to be a pitiful attempt to protect her family. There was no record in the newspapers of any defense counsel cross-examination.

Detective Lieutenant Thomas P. White was the government's key witness on Thursday afternoon. Answering questions from John Kane, Jr., White retold the events of October 4 when Petro was questioned at Central Police Station and confronted with his "weeping" mother. As she was led into the interrogation room, she told Julius, "Tell the truth!" To which Julius replied, "I put it." The *Plain Dealer* wrote:

> Coming from Petro, a hoodlum noted for giving little help to detective's inquiry session, the three-word utterance was made the most of by United States Attorney John J. Kane, Jr.

At this moment, an afternoon recess was called for by Judge McNamee, leaving some doubt as to what exactly the three words meant that Petro had done. When the recess was over, White was recalled and explained. "It was my understanding," he said, "That Petro had put the $500 in Lydia's hiding place."

Testimony of Detective Lieutenant Thomas P. White

U. S. Attorney John J. Kane continued his questioning of Detective Lieutenant Thomas P. White regarding his interrogation of Petro back on October 4.

White: I told Julio that his father, John Petro, had paid Mr. Schaefer $1,000 in cash as a down payment on a café and that $500 of that $1,000 had been identified as having been stolen in a Warren bank robbery on August 14. Julio asked me: "How do I know the money you traced to Schaefer is the same money my father gave him?" Then I explained to him how we traced the money back to Petro.

Kane: How did you trace it?

White: Mr. Schaefer told us he had gotten it from Mr. Tirabassi.

Kane: It had been in the bank?

White: Yes. Mr. Schaefer, after he left the Petros, had gone immediately to his home about 10 o'clock that night, and early in the morning he went to the bank and deposited $1,000 in the bank and there the $500 had been identified as having been taken in the robbery.

Kane: Did you tell him the police knew some of the serial numbers of the stolen money?

White: I did because I had a circular that had been put out by the Federal Bureau of Investigation listing the serial numbers, and I showed Julio Petro the listing of these serial numbers and I told him 25 20-dollar bills were included in the list of serial numbers traced to his father's home. I told him I knew his father had not stolen the money and that his mother had not stolen the money. I asked him how could the money get into that house?

He, at first, denied any knowledge of how the money got into his parent's hands. He said he didn't know where his parents kept their money. He didn't know if they had any money. Then he changed his story, saying that sometime in June he had been in his mother's home and in looking around the bedroom he had found a quantity of money concealed between sheets in a dresser drawer and he had gotten into the habit of using it in gambling.

I asked him how much money he had found in this hiding place, and he said he didn't know how much was there. He said he didn't know how much was there, but that when he went there he would take all of it and use it gambling and he would come back and replace it. I said, "Didn't you know how much was there?" and he said no. I said, "How did you know how much to replace?" and he just shrugged it off.

I asked him if he ever lost any money gambling, and he said he had not.

I said, "How if this money was traced to the robbery, how did it get in your mother's hiding place?" He said, "I probably put it there. I probably won it gambling."

I asked when was the last time you had taken any money and replaced it? He said a couple of months ago. I said you couldn't have replaced the money in view of the fact that the money had been stolen only August 14. He said, "Well, it was a couple of weeks ago." He had taken the money and gone out gambling with it. He said, "Somebody is trying to catch me in a switch." He said, "I know who it is, and if I have to go to court I will tell."

He said on one occasion, after he had been gambling and was settling up his account, he had taken money and gave it to the man running the game, and he said he gave him three stacks of money. I asked what denominations, and he couldn't remember. I asked whether new bills or old. He said he didn't know. I asked him how much money, and he said he didn't know. He said on another occasion he had borrowed $500 from a businessman downtown and that this may have been the money. I asked him who the businessman was, and he refused to name anyone.

I finally said to him, "Who put that stolen money in your mother's hiding place?" and he said, "I put it."

In retelling the events of that day's arrests and interrogations, White kept referring to Petro as "Julio." Finally, Kane interrupted him to get an explanation for this from the witness. White simply replied, "I thought that was his correct name."

White testified that Petro, "at first denied any knowledge of how the money got into his parent's hands. Then he changed his story, saying sometime in June he had been in his mother's home and had gotten into the habit of using [her savings] in gambling."

The detective lieutenant stated, "I finally said to him, 'Who put the stolen money in your mother's hiding place?' and he said, 'I put it.'" He insisted he won the money while gambling or implied that someone "put it in his possession" during a gambling game.

During cross-examination, Stanton asked White if Petro had not said he would "take the blame," rather than see his mother and father prosecuted for having the stolen bank money in their possession. Stanton barked, "Didn't he say, 'Tell me what you want me to say, and I'll say it?' That's when he said, 'I did it,' wasn't it."

White responded to the lawyer's tirade that he had only asked Petro to "tell me the truth." He did admit to conveying to him that his parents would be prosecuted, "unless he could explain how the money got there."

During the cross-examination, both Stanton and Picciano hammered away at White that police had searched the homes of Petro and Sanzo within a few hours of the robbery and had found nothing.

On Friday, December 5, the day after Detective Lieutenant White's testimony was completed, he finally revealed the events of August 12, when he had been notified of the pending robbery and who was going to be involved in it. The *Cleveland Press* reported, "Two of the three names the informant furnished were Julius Petro and Joe Sanzo. The third man, also a Clevelander, is not under arrest. He was the man in the back seat of the get-away car."

Defense Testimony

With Thursday morning's testimony focusing on Petro's family and their efforts to retrieve the "marked money," attorney Picciano requested several times that Judge McNamee remind the jury that the evidence and testimony involving Petro be disregarded when considering Sanzo's guilt or innocence.

The government's case against Sanzo began with the prosecution presenting evidence against him late on Thursday afternoon, December 4. Genevieve Spaulding, a teller at the Bank of Ohio on St. Clair Avenue identified the 31 $5 bills which she had received in a deposit back on September 24. Armed with the FBI flyer about the robbery, she matched up the serial numbers and notified her manager. She told the court that Henry Prijital,[41] a local delicatessen owner, deposited the money.

On Friday morning, Prijital took the stand and told the court that he had taken the money out of a cashbox owned by his brother-in-law, Gene Gattozzi, manager of the Grotto Inn at St. Clair Avenue and London Road. When Gattozzi testified, he said he knew both Petro and Sanzo "all my life," but claimed he only saw them together once at the Grotto Inn. Around August 1, he loaned $400 to Sanzo and was repaid within three weeks. Two weeks later he said Sanzo borrowed $500 more. Gattozzi said that Sanzo told him, "He was gambling and losing heavily." Three days later, Gattozzi said Sanzo paid him back and he put the money in a cashbox at the Grotto Inn. At this time, he told the court, he owed his brother-in-law, Henry Prijital money from a loan. He told Prijital to take the money from the cashbox. When Prijital deposited the money, the connection to the robbery was discovered.

With that testimony, the government rested its week-long case at noon Friday. The prosecution had called a total of 29 witnesses. As for the popularity of the trial, the *Cleveland Press* reported that not since Senator Estes Kefauver brought his traveling Senate Crime Committee hearings to Cleveland, during mid-January 1951, has the Federal Court House been so jammed. At least 100 people were turned away daily at the courtroom door of Judge McNamee. Those lucky enough to get in and find a seat (the judge allowed no "standees") would stay put during recesses in fear of losing their seat if they ventured off to a restroom.

On Friday afternoon at 2:00, following the mid-day recess for lunch, attorney Edward Stanton called the defense's first witness – Julius Petro. *Plain Dealer* reporter Ted Princiotto describes the appearance of Petro before the jury:

> Sitting in the slightly elevated witness chair, Petro made a striking, polished witness, except for his infrequent lapse into inept English. He spoke in a low tone, once or twice clearing his throat politely. For the occupation he gave – gambler – he was stylishly dressed in a tan, loosely fitting suit, white shirt and red-orange tie. His black hair, as always, was well groomed. Spectators and jurors alike listened closely as he denied being in Warren the day of the robbery or knowing anything about the $500 in stolen Warren cash found in his mother's savings' hiding place here.

Answering defense counsel's questions, Petro told the jury that on the morning of August 14 he awoke around 9 o'clock and left the house without waking his wife or two children. He got into his car to go see his brother, Michael, in the Five Points neighborhood. Michael was in the process of selling his shoe repair and hat shop and Julius met the buyer, Robert Igo, there. He had a loose heel on one of his shoes, which Igo fixed for him, charging him a dime. Petro testified he gave the man a quarter.

From his brother's shop he drove to his parent's home, in the same Collinwood neighborhood and spent the next three hours fixing a broken chair for them. When he was about to leave, his wife, June suddenly arrived with Juliet, their daughter. She was in an excited state as she informed him that Cleveland police detectives came to the house and searched their home and were now looking for him in connection with the robbery in Warren.

Petro testified that he drove to Euclid Beach amusement park[42] with June and Juliet, "to stay out of the way of police." Around 6:00 that evening, they arrived home in a taxicab, where police were waiting to arrest him.

Under questioning from Stanton, Petro denied urging his father to write a check for $1,000 in order to retrieve the $500 in marked bills paid to broker Charles Schaefer.

On cross-examination by John Kane, Jr. came the admission by Petro that he was in Warren four or five times during the six months prior to the August 14 robbery; Sanzo accompanied him on at least two of those occasions. Petro said the trips might have been as recently as August or within two weeks of the robbery. Kane seemed to focus his attention on Petro's being at Miller's Drug Store, which was located next door to the Union Savings & Trust Company bank.

"How many times were you in that drug store?" asked Kane.

"I don't know – I ate around there somewhere," Petro answered.

He claimed he was not even sure if he had ever been in Miller's Drug Store. Petro's story was that he had gone to Warren to borrow $2,000 from a man named Jay. Petro said he had lost a lot of money gambling and Jay had agreed to loan him the money. He claimed Jay "lived on the other end of Warren" and that the two of them never connected. He said he had not tried to find Jay since August 14, because he was "afraid to go back to Warren on account of the holdup." Petro stated he might have stopped to eat or buy cigarettes at Miller's along the way in Warren.

"Did you ever sit in your parked car in front of the drug store for several hours at a time?" Kane demanded.

"No, absolutely not," Petro replied.

At 3:45 p.m., Petro stepped down from the witness stand.

Both the *Cleveland Press* and the *Plain Dealer* commented about this line of questioning suggesting that "the FBI might have evidence putting Petro" at Miller's Drug Store, or at least in the parking lot, and that this was an "indicator that the Government did not close its case against Julius Petro with the ending of its direct examination."

Petro's mother-in-law, Mrs. Lillian Guentzler, was the final witness of the day. Mrs. Guentzler, a store clerk at the Higbee Company in Public Square, testified that Petro was home on the night of August 13. He had gone into the couple's bedroom to read and listen to the radio during the evening. The following morning, when she left for work around 9:00 a.m., she told the court, "I didn't see him, but I heard him cough."

Guentzler also testified that she purchased a 1951 Cadillac from Petro on September 1, for $2,800. She paid him $2,000, of which $1,000 had come from an insurance policy when her mother passed away. She still owed $800. She stated she made $35 a week at her job at Higbee's, while her husband was unemployed since October 15.

Under cross-examination, Kane asked her, "What does your son-in-law do for a living?"

"He hasn't done anything for a living since he came home in May," Guentzler lamented, apparently getting the month wrong. Petro was released from prison in Michigan on bail back in June.

The newspapers and many trial-followers believed Monday would bring an end to the trial. The *Cleveland Press* reported, "Almost an hour before the court session opened, all seats were occupied, mainly with sharp-dressed characters from the Five Points area. Closely they watched every move, every facial expression of Petro, a 'big name' at Five Points."

"What's been happening?" and "How's Julius doing?" were the common questions from corridor loiterers whenever spectators left the courtroom. FBI agents mingled among the hangers-on in the hall, or eyed them from the marshal's office from across the court."

On Monday morning, the defense was prepared with witnesses called to support the testimony of the two men that they were in Cleveland at the time of the robbery in Warren. Stanton finished his defense of Petro by calling Robert Igo, the man who had purchased Michael Petro's shoe repair and hat shop. The 31-year-old testified in support of Petro's alibi that the defendant was getting the heel of his shoe repaired at the time of the Warren robbery. During cross-examination, the prosecution was able to draw from Igo that Petro was in the shop at least ten times in the two weeks before the August 14 robbery.

At the conclusion of Stanton's defense of Petro, around mid-morning, it was reported that, "Petro's face lighted with the first smile he has flashed since the trial began."

It was at this point that the trial suddenly turned into a "battle of the surprise witnesses as it moved down the home stretch." Defense attorney Michael Picciano began the "battle" by calling as his first witness Dr. Alexander V. Spaeth, a skin-care specialist and graduate of Western Reserve University with offices at 10616 Euclid Avenue.[43]

Dr. Spaeth, who caught the government off guard, claimed that on the morning of August 14, at approximately 10:10 a.m., he was treating Joseph Sanzo's inflamed hands in his medical office. To refresh his memory, Spaeth brought with him the patient's Medical Record Card,[44] on which he had recorded the treatment he provided Sanzo.

The government attorneys were caught unaware of the crafty defense lawyer's move because he had already indicated that Sanzo was at a Five Points gasoline station getting gas a half-hour before the time of the robbery. In fact, defense witness Harry K. Peterson had testified to that. But they would not be deterred. Under-cross examination, Steel, incensed at the turn of events, snatched the card from the witness's hand and claimed it as evidence. Dr. Spaeth stated that he first saw Sanzo on August 12 and said his hands were in bad shape. On his Medical Record Card was a notation that Sanzo was to return in six days to see him on August 18. The *Plain Dealer* reported:

Steel looked at the card closely and then asked Dr. Spaeth why the date of Aug. 14, 1952, as printed by a rubber date stamp, looked as if it had been altered. The figure "4" was clearly written in by hand in ink over the obscured stamped digit.

Dr. Spaeth said that often happened and he himself had corrected the date by writing in the digit "4." He said mistakes occurred in adjusting the digits of the stamping device, a common kind used in many offices.

Steel wanted to compare the Medical Record Card to the doctor's appointment book. Dr. Spaeth said the book, a loose-leaf ledger, was back at his office. Judge McNamee recessed court for an hour and the doctor hailed a taxicab outside and returned to his office to retrieve it. When Spaeth returned with the appointment book, it showed that Sanzo had 10:00 a.m. appointments on both August 14 and August 18. The newspapers reported that Steel let the matter rest there and surmised that he would dispute the Medical Record Card when he presented his closing argument to the jury. They couldn't have been more wrong.

Critical Rebuttal

Now it was time for the government to strike back. This they did in rebuttal by presenting a witness who unleashed damaging testimony that apparently was held back purposely during the trial. Judge McNamee remarked that the witness's testimony properly belonged in the government's case "in chief." The judge, however, allowed the rebuttal testimony of a Miller's Drug Store cashier, based on the fact that Petro had denied during his testimony that he had ever been in the parking lot in front of the drug store.

Grace Wilson, described as a 27-year-old, auburn-haired divorcee and mother of four children, testified she saw Petro, Sanzo and a third man parked in front of the drug store "about 15 times" in the weeks before the robbery.[45] Steel had the witness step down from the witness chair and walk over to the defense table where she pointed to Petro and Sanzo and stated, "These two boys" were the ones she saw parked in a black Oldsmobile outside the drug store. She claimed she saw them over a three-week period just before the robbery. Grace Wilson had good reason to remember the men. She testified she believed they were following her. She told the court, "My boyfriend had been engaged. He was trying to break away from her and I suspected that perhaps someone was watching me for her."

During cross-examination Stanton tried to trap her with his questioning, but didn't have much luck. The defense attorney asked Wilson if she recalled seeing the trio in the black Oldsmobile on August 10.

"What was the 10th? She asked.

"Sunday," said a defeated Stanton, knowing his trick had failed.

"Then I wasn't there," she replied. She had previously testified she didn't work Sundays.

The government then called East Cleveland Police Detective Fred Schwenderman as another rebuttal witness. He testified that he saw Petro in a late model Packard on Hayden Avenue in East Cleveland around 7:00 p.m. on August 13, when both Petro and his mother-in-law, Lillian Guentzler, claimed he was home with his wife and children.

Also called in rebuttal was George H. Gehringer, a deputy clerk of the Probate Court. He was there also to refute the testimony of the mother-in-law, who had testified she inherited $1,000 from her mother when she died and used the money as half of the payment to Petro for the 1951 Cadillac she purchased from him. Court records showed that when Guentzler's mother died, the estate consisted of just an insurance policy worth $225.

Defense attorneys called their own rebuttal witness, Professor Max Morris of Case Institute of Technology, a mathematician. His contribution to the case was his testimony that witness Carter Alden would only have had 53/100th of a second in which to identify Petro as the getaway driver on Oak Knoll Avenue the day of the robbery.

By Monday night, the Medical Record Card that Dr. Spaeth had brought in for his testimony that morning was on a flight to Washington D.C. to visit the FBI's renowned scientific laboratories. There Special Agent George F. Mesnig examined the card. The following morning, Mesnig boarded a flight for Cleveland and was in court to share his findings. The FBI expert informed the jury that he had "photographed the card under infrared light to bring out invisible patterns of ink originally stamped on the card." Mesnig stated that in his opinion, a date stamp was originally applied to the card marking it "Aug. 18, 1952," not "Aug. 14, 1952" as Dr. Spaeth testified to the day before.

The special agent placed an enlarged photograph of the card on an easel in the courtroom for everyone to see. He then proceeded to show how Dr. Spaeth had used a pen to write the number "4" over the stamped date, which appeared as "thickly drawn" and "crudely made" on the enlargement. The doctor testified he had written in the "4," claiming he did so because the stamp didn't leave a clean imprint. He insisted, however, that he had written over the existing "4" left by the stamp, claiming the stamp had left a feint image. The *Plain Dealer* wrote:

> What was there originally, under the inked "4," was the crux of the alibi challenge by Mesnig. Mesnig said infrared light picked up traces of the original stamped figure. In his opinion, he said, the original figure had been either a "6" or an "8," making the date either Aug 16 or Aug 18. He added he believed it had been an "8," because it did not have the straight-backed stem of a "6" as printed by the same stamp.

At the end of Agent Mesnig's testimony, Judge McNamee called a recess to give Picciano time to determine how to counter the government's rebuttal witness. The defense counsel's surprise witness's testimony from the day before had just blown up in his face. Picciano had not counted on the government presenting their own surprise witness; an expert witness at that. At least that was what the *Plain Dealer* reported. "It was the kind of abrupt turn no lawyer likes to see his case take," the *Plain Dealer* declared. "Sanzo's lawyer, Michael A. Picciano was left dangling, without an expert of his own to counter the FBI." According to the *Cleveland Press*, however, Picciano actually had his own expert waiting in the corridor in anticipation of something the government might do. Joseph Tholl, "a Cleveland expert on questioned documents," viewed Dr. Spaeth's Medical Record Card of Sanzo under a large magnifying glass. But after viewing the FBI photograph of the Medical Record Card during the recess, the expert must have realized he didn't have a leg to stand on. At the end of the recess, the attorney told McNamee he would be calling no rebuttal witnesses.

Closing Statements

Judge McNamee immediately ordered the government to begin its closing statements. Steel began at 2:50 p.m., declaring, "You have these men identified, coupled with the fact that some of the stolen money has been traced to them. You're practical people, and you know that offenses like this kind are carefully planned."

Steel then walked the jury through all the key points of the planning. The testimony of Grace Wilson, seeing the men casing the bank and the movements of Charles Foley. The stealing of the gray Oldsmobile getaway car in Canton the night before the robbery and the "lifting" of the license plates in Toronto, Ohio. "What else shows the careful planning?" Steel asked. "The method of perpetrating the robbery – these men hid their faces. They pulled burlap masks over their faces."

This all led up to the morning of the robbery and the testimony of Charles Foley, Mrs. Harold Auker, Ida Campbell, Samuel Brogden, Jr., and George Fisher. Their testimony tracked the escape route of the bandit vehicle until it hit Oak Knoll Avenue. Steel then recapped the testimony of Carter Alden and his mother Abbie in passing the getaway car on Oak Knoll Avenue and positively identifying Petro as the driver and Sanzo in the passenger's seat. Then, with his voice rising, Steel told the jury, "If they're going to attack the credibility of the Aldens, I want you to consider what reason the Aldens would have for testifying as they have." Steel then rapped his knuckles on the table in emphasizing, "I think they're telling the truth."

Steel then attacked defense counsel's claim the getaway car was traveling at such a high speed that identification was impossible. "Your eyes," the prosecutor stated, "are such that photographs are inscribed in your mind. The Aldens told you the reason they remembered it is the car didn't stop and it swung over to their side of the pavement; they feared a collision." The prosecutor declared, "If the identifications are not correct, why was the money, $500 in stolen $20 notes taken in Warren, found in the Petro's house? Why was the money traced to Sanzo? Why do they bring doctored records to show Sanzo was not there? Why?"

After reviewing, one by one, the stack of paper documents introduced as exhibits by the government, Steel went for his closing. Claiming that Petro's big mistake was to hide the $500 in his mother's house with her savings, he stated, "Petro knew that his mother wouldn't use that money and for that reason the money would not show up in circulation. That's the working of his mind. He's one step ahead of everyone else." Petro couldn't have realized, however, that his mother and father would have used the money in their quest to purchase the Recreation Café.

Steel moved on to the testimony of Dr. Spaeth, recapping for the jury how the doctor's appointment book showed no appointment for Sanzo on August 14, but did show one for August 18, and that the defendant had paid for it. Then, on the other hand, the Medical Record Card showed an August 14 appointment, but not one for August 18. Yet on the Medical Record Card the FBI expert showed that the date was altered by the doctor, who wrote a "4" over the stamped date. "That makes it an absolute forgery," Steel declared. As the prosecutor spelled this out to the jury, Judge McNamee overruled vigorous defense counsel objections to Steel's statements. "Why did the doctor falsify his records?" Steel asked. "That wasn't his idea. What did he have to gain? Either he did it from a monetary gain standpoint or for some other reason I don't care to discuss at this time."

At the end of Frank Steel's 50-minute closing, defense attorney Stanton began his closing statement for Julius Petro, addressing the jurors as "fellow citizens." The *Plain Dealer* described Stanton as, "A peppery, bespectacled man with flapping necktie, he left little doubt as to his intent. At every turn he heaped doubt and more doubt, if he could, on the circumstantial FBI case."

Stanton's key points were to implicate Charles Foley in the plot, due to the belief that he had picked up two bags of money that day, a fact which did not bear out during testimony, even though there must have been some insider information for the gang to know there were two bags brought down from the Federal Reserve Bank in Cleveland.

The other point he attacked was the identification by the Aldens. Stanton spent much of his time accusing FBI agent Stanley Peterson of "suggesting" to the Aldens that Petro and Sanzo were the two men they had seen on Oak Knoll Avenue. He referred to it as "mental suggestion." Stanton again claimed that the Aldens "could not possibly" have identified Petro and Sanzo in the 53/100th of a second that the expert mathematician had fixed, based on the speed of the cars as they passed one another. Stanton cried out, "Lo and behold, when the FBI man came out to see the Aldens, what did he have in his pockets? What did he have but pictures of Julius Petro and Joe Sanzo and five or six more, who we don't know." Stanton claimed that Mrs. Alden had indicated that Peterson asked her to select men from the group of pictures "that would resemble the men we had passed." After this remark, both Steel and John Kane, Jr. objected. Judge McNamee ruled that the jury could decide for itself what Abbie Alden had said during her testimony.

The aging defense attorney ended his closing statement, and Tuesday's court session, with the following questions, "Where is the Warren police department in this case? Where is the other money bag? Who is the third man, if there was one?"

At 9:30 Wednesday morning, Picciano began his closing statement. He was faced with the damning testimony of the previous day from the FBI expert, George Mesnig. He pointed out Dr. Spaeth's reputation and integrity and offered, "We made no attempt to conceal that there was an alteration [to the record]. If you will observe, the day before was August 13. It is probable the stamp had not been changed the next morning. Sanzo's was the first appointment. Later the doctor discovered his mistake and changed it."

Picciano also attacked the identification by Abbie Alden and her son Carter, again based on the "split-second" glimpse of the robbers in the getaway car. Like Stanton before him, Picciano declared the prosecutor's whole case "rests on conjecture and supposition."

In Kane's closing rebuttal, the prosecutor had a few questions of his own for the jury to consider. "Mike Petro was supposed to have seen his brother, Julius that morning [August 14]. Where was Mike Petro? Why wasn't he here?" Kane then went after Sanzo's doctor's appointment alibi, pointing out that it wasn't the first alibi the defendant offered. "Sanzo said he was at a gas station that morning. The doctor says he was at his office at 10 a.m. How can he be in two places at once?" he asked.

At the completion of Kane's closing rebuttal, the jury received the judge's charge. Judge McNamee spent an hour in recital of the "evidence high points." The *Plain Dealer* pointed out, "Unlike state criminal courts, where the judge does not review the evidence, Judge McNamee devoted most of his hour-long charge to a marshaling of the evidence, putting the countless bits into a narrative."

Deliberations & Verdict

When McNamee completed his charge, the jurors left to have lunch at the Hotel Cleveland. When they returned, "they were taken down the marble-floored hall of the courthouse and upstairs to a loft-like chamber." There, the judge's bailiff, Alex P. Hughes, stood guard. Hughes didn't have long to stand. The jurors began reviewing evidence and exhibits at 2:05 p.m. and filed back into the courtroom at 3:40; a mere 95 minutes.

The *Plain Dealer* described the courtroom as a "grim, tense scene once the jury settled itself in the jury box." Judge McNamee received the verdict from jury foreman Frank A. Alward, the only male on the jury. At 3:42 he announced their decision – guilty! The *Plain Dealer* wrote:

Petro sat at the defense table, chin in hand, while Sanzo hunched over in his chair. When he heard Judge McNamee read the jury's verdict for him Petro sagged, and his mouth dropped open. Sanzo's head fell noticeably when his verdict was read next.

A clerk from the court's office polled the jurors, asking each one if the verdict was their own. One female juror was seen to wipe away a tear from under her glasses. Alward was the last to respond, nodding his head in agreement.

Judge McNamee then addressed the jurors. "The court says to you that in my opinion your verdict is supported by evidence and the law of this case. You are to be commended for your intelligent and courageous action. There seemed to be some impression that such a jury as this one, predominantly of women, might not act in accordance with the evidence and the law, that you might lack courage to do what ought to be done under the circumstances. By your verdict you have destroyed any basis for any such ill-founded presumption. I think you have learned a lot listening to the evidence in this case. You have seen how difficult it is in this complicated, modern civilization of ours for the law enforcement officers to obtain evidence against skilled, professional criminals who use all the mechanical contrivances and apparatus furnished to a modern civilization."

McNamee then called out, "Will the defendants come forward." Petro and Sanzo stood before the judge with Picciano and Stanton at their sides and guarded by three Federal marshals. The judge then asked if they had anything to say before sentencing was announced. The following exchange then took place:

Petro: Yes, your honor. I'm innocent. I had no knowledge of this robbery held in Warren, Ohio. I feel I have not been given a fair trial. As God is my judge, I stand before you an innocent man. I think they have convicted me on my past record. I asked for a lie-detector test, and I was denied this.

McNamee: Do you have anything further?

Petro: What can I say? Will you permit the lie-detector test? Will you give me the test? I will take the truth serum – I will take anything to prove my innocence. There must have been some doubt in your mind.

McNamee: There is no doubt in my mind whatsoever. You had a fair trial.

Petro: I don't want a sermon, McNamee. I want a lie detector test.

McNamee: Don't argue with the court. You're not here to argue with the court.

Petro: I thank you.

McNamee: I think too many words have been wasted on you, and I don't propose to waste any more. Your record has been such as to make it necessary to impose the maximum sentence under the law. Sentenced to 25 years.

At the moment the judge announced the 25-year sentence, June Petro cried out, "Oh, my God!" The *Plain Dealer* wrote, "Until that moment the wife, who had not taken the stand for her errant husband, was outwardly calm, almost to a fault. Her expression remained virtually unchanged, even when the finding of guilty was read. Only the judge's reference to a 25-year prison term reached the mark. It was then she cried out and buried her face in the shoulder of her mother-in-law, Mrs. Lydia Petro."

The judge then announced he was delaying sentencing for Sanzo and called for a presentencing report, since he did not have an extensive police record. Picciano, standing beside Sanzo, added, "Only disorderly conduct."

McNamee" implied strongly," however, that Sanzo may have tampered with defense witness Dr. Spaeth. The judge stated that Sanzo's "conduct in this case indicates his criminality did not stop with the commission of the robbery." Transcripts of the doctor's testimony, along with his office records, were to be reviewed by U.S. prosecutors Kane and Steel to determine if there would be any additional charges leveled against Sanzo and Dr. Spaeth.

The families of Petro and Sanzo "wailed and sobbed" in the courtroom as the verdicts and sentences were read. A throng of friends "carried on" inside and outside the courtroom. The wives, June Petro and Jean Sanzo, cried and "grabbed for embraces" from the two as U.S. Marshals led them away. Each day during the trial, Petro would always be taken back to the County Jail alone or shackled to another prisoner at the end of court for the day, while Sanzo, out on bail, was free to go home. On this last day, Petro, with a lit cigarette in his mouth, was handcuffed to Sanzo for the trip back to the jail.

Petro complained bitterly to reporters that the jury "convicted me on my past record." His police record showed that the oft-jailed hoodlum led a charmed career – many arrests, few convictions. The only portion of his record that could be made known to the jurors was the few convictions he had received. If his entire record of arrests had been presented to the jury, they might have requested another trip to the electric chair for him if given the opportunity. While that wasn't about to happen, one thing was for sure, Petro's charm for getting off hit a brick wall when he decided to tangle with the FBI.

The U.S. Marshals allowed June Petro, Jean Sanzo, the convicted men's mothers and a couple of male relatives to meet with the prisoners for a few minutes behind a screen in the Marshal's waiting room before taking the men to the County Jail.

Newspaper reporters also crowded around others for interviews afterwards. Defense attorneys Picciano and Stanton both promised to file motions immediately for a new trial. Stanton declared, "Of course I'll appeal, there is error in that testimony." If turned down, they would appeal to the higher courts.

Jury foreman Frank Alward told reporters the fate of both men was decided on a single ballot. He related, "We had one lady who held back before voting. She wanted to be absolutely sure. After we gave her all the evidence and answered her questions, she voted with the rest of us." Alward, whose son was diagnosed with polio on the first day of the trial also stated, "We never believed the doctor's testimony that Sanzo was in his office on the morning of August 14. After all the evidence presented to us, there was only one way to vote. We forgot Julius Petro's record. We convicted them on the evidence alone."

Judge McNamee ordered FBI Agent Robert Johnson to place the jurors in protective custody until the courtroom could be completely cleared. It was reported that this was the first time in local Federal Court history that such a precaution was ordered. Johnson took them into the empty courtroom of Federal Judge Paul Jones. The *Press* reported that, "Some of Petro's and Sanzo's pals remained in the hallway, banging the walls with their fists, cursing the judge, the jury, and the witnesses for the government." After 15 minutes the FBI finally ordered the "lingerers" out of the courthouse, and the jurors were released.

The women of the jury remained behind and had a brief discussion with Judge McNamee. At least three or four of them expressed concerns about retaliation. The judge advised them that if any of them were bothered in anyway, that they should notify the court, or the district attorney or the FBI, without delay.

On the day after the verdict was announced, the *Cleveland Press* printed this editorial:

This community, the state and the whole nation owe a great debt to a quiet Warren mother and her 19-year-old college student son.

It was they who clinched the case against those two enemies of society, hoodlum Julius A. Petro and his pal, Joseph J. Sanzo.

It would have been simple not to.

They were merely driving down a Warren side street when they saw a car crash a boulevard stop sign and then hurry past them.

That night in the Warren newspaper, they read of the $71,000 bank holdup and of the men who fled.

Sounded like the car they saw. Maybe nothing to it. Maybe just a lot of bother. Maybe it would involve them in real danger.

But they called the police.

And in that single act of helpful citizenship, these two made the one vital step that tied together all the months of difficult and careful police work.

Their identification closed the gaps and completed the case.

It was a bother, plenty of it. Interviews by teams of FBI men and detectives, trips to Cleveland for lineups of suspects, frequent questioning. The youngster even had to come back from the University of Missouri to testify.

There was danger, too. Bound to be when you deal with desperate criminals. It took courage to stand firm.

Mrs. Henry Alden and her son, Carter, stood firm.

Their decency and their unselfishness paid off yesterday when the Federal Court jury here found both men guilty.

It had taken the good people a long time finally to catch up with Petro, whose disgusting record goes back nearly 15 years.

But right prevailed last night.

Thanks, Mrs. Alden and thanks, Carter Alden. Thanks also to the thorough job of the FBI, and the skillful work of Cleveland detectives.

And thanks to the prosecutors, the jury and the judge.

A fine chapter in the book of justice.

Appeals, Motions & Imprisonment

The day after the verdict, the *Cleveland Press* announced incorrectly that Petro was to be imprisoned in the Federal prison on Alcatraz. The article stated, "FBI agents were tight-lipped about it, but they indicated 'The Rock,' in San Francisco Bay, was the likely destination of Cleveland's No. 1 hoodlum, whose 'beat-the-rap" luck finally left him flat late yesterday.

The *Plain Dealer* reported differently, stating Petro would be taken to the U.S. Penitentiary in Leavenworth, Kansas. They claimed once there, his background would be studied to see if he would qualify to be transferred to Alcatraz. The moves, however, would most likely have to wait until all routine post-trial motions were handled.

Meanwhile, less than 48 hours had passed since the verdict was read and defense attorneys were busy with their motions for a new trial. Picciano announced he was submitting his new trial motion based on "16 or 18 grounds," claiming the main one to be the judge's refusal to give Petro and Sanzo separate trials, "We still believe, "Picciano stated, "Petro's record and unfavorable publicity did prejudice to Sanzo."

On the weekend after the trial, local news affiliate WEWS televised a 40-minute program called *Report on Cleveland Crime*, at 1:45 on Sunday afternoon. Former Common Pleas Judge Roy W. Scott served as the program's moderator, which featured numerous Cleveland figures in law enforcement and the local judiciary community discussing the crime situation in the city. The highlight of the show was the awarding of three "Good Citizen" plaques, by the Cleveland Crime Commission,[46] of which two were presented to Abbie Alden and her son, Carter, for their role in helping to convict Petro and Sanzo. Abbie accepted both awards because Carter had already returned to school at the University of Missouri. The third recipient was Tinkham Veale II, the foremen of the Cuyahoga County Grand Jury, in recognition of the service performed by the 25-member panel. Appearing on the show that day were Cleveland Police Chief Frank W. Story, Cuyahoga County Sheriff Joseph M. Sweeney, FBI Special Agent in Charge Paul J. Shine, US Attorney John J. Kane, Jr., Cuyahoga County Prosecutor Frank T. Cullitan, Common Pleas Judge Harry A. Hanna, and Juvenile Court Judge William J. McDermott.

On Monday, December 15, Picciano and Stanton filed motions in Federal Court for a new trial for Petro and Sanzo. Stanton alleged 15 instances of error in the trial. Picciano's motion cited 16 trial and court errors, 12 of which were errors by the judge. One of the errors was a ruling denying a defense motion requiring Abbie Alden and her son "to submit to eye examinations to check the efficiency of their vision."

Picciano also stated that he had not been given sufficient time to examine the FBI's rebuttal evidence to refute Dr. Spaeth's medical records on Sanzo. This seemed ironic because Dr. Spaeth's testimony had come as a complete surprise to the government. The prosecutors, however, were quick to produce a rebuttal witness to claim forgery on the part of the doctor the next day. Picciano was seen conferring with Joseph Tholl during the recess granted to him by Judge McNamee, but when court resumed, defense counsel simply stated he had no rebuttal witnesses to call.

On Friday, December 19, everyone was back in Judge McNamee's Federal Courtroom for two hearings; one to hear Joseph Sanzo's sentencing, the other to hear the judge's ruling on a new trial. In sentencing Sanzo, Judge McNamee said he took into account the fact that Sanzo had only one other blemish on his record – the disorderly conduct case. The judge pointed out that under Ohio criminal law, armed robbery called for a minimum term of at least ten years, but he declared that the Warren robbery was a serious crime, which might have led to either bloodshed or murder. With that, he sentenced Sanzo to 15 years. The sentence provided Sanzo with a "first-time break," which meant, under Federal prison rules that he was eligible to apply for parole after serving five years, or one-third of his term.

In the other hearing, Judge McNamee denied Picciano and Stanton's motions for new trials, after which both announced they would file notices of appeal, within the 10-day timeframe, to the United States Court of Appeals. It could take months for the Appeals Court to review the case, and both Petro and Sanzo could choose to remain in Cleveland at the Cuyahoga County Jail. Picciano acknowledged, however, "The time they spend in County Jail will not count against their prison sentences," so they would not be making any such request.

By Monday, December 22, Picciano was back in Federal Court asking for an outside expert to examine the Medical Record Card of Sanzo. Despite already having Joseph Tholl on hand during the trial and not calling him, Picciano wanted him as the "expert" to analyze the medical record. The defense attorney held the opinion that the figure stamped on the card was not a "6" or an "8," but rather a "3" that had not been changed from the day before it was used on August 14.

In his motion, Picciano said Tholl told him, after a "cursory examination" during the trial recess, that the FBI's enlargement of the Medical Record Card "was out of focus." Tholl, however, did not take the stand to testify. Now, Picciano claimed that if Tholl's opinion supported his own theory that the number was a "3," then "it would be considered newly discovered evidence and would be cited as the basis for a new trial."

When talking to reporters after filing the new motion, Picciano was asked what would happen if an examination by Tholl supported the FBI's expert?

"Well, it might become a matter of professional relationship between a lawyer and his client," Picciano responded. "It would depend upon what conclusion the expert came to." He indicated the expert's findings would not necessarily become a matter of public knowledge. The attorney continued to insist he wasn't given ample opportunity to have an expert examine the Medical Record Card at trial. He charged that the FBI had no right to take the Medical Record Card out of the court's jurisdiction for an infrared examination at the Bureau's lab in Washington D.C. during a trial night recess. "It was highly irregular and highly improper," Picciano declared. "What would have happened if the airplane carrying the agent who had the card crashed? What if my client's life had depended on the card?"

The post-trial examination requested by Picciano was allowed by Judge McNamee. On December 29, Joseph Tholl began his experiments on the Medical Record Card of Joseph Sanzo. Referred to as an "authority on the authenticity of challenged documents," he used infrared light and special photographic equipment to examine the document. The examination took place at the Board of Elections, where his equipment was recently used in the investigation of voting irregularities. Deputy US Marshal Stanton Weegar, who coincidentally was one of the marshals who made the initial arrest of Sanzo, oversaw the work of Tholl, which was specified by Judge McNamee. In talking to reporters, Tholl emphasized that he was working "impartially" in this case and that his conclusions could result in the same conclusions the FBI expert arrived at.

The next day, Picciano told reporters the new tests on the Medical Record Card of Sanzo proved that the date on the card had not been changed. This contradicted the attorney's own declaration that the "4" had been inked in over a "3" from the date stamp that he insisted had not been advanced from the previous day. He claimed that the tests run by Tholl contradicted testimony from the FBI which helped convict Sanzo. "Our tests prove there was no stamped numeral at all under the inked '4.' That substantiates our contention during the trial, which we had no chance to prove."

Picciano, however, did not stop there. He then made a bizarre announcement stating, "I do not intend to ask for a new trial on the basis of the re-examination of Sanzo's medical record. There is plenty of time for that." He then stated, "Anyhow, we are working on something new in the case and that is taking all our time." Other than to say this revelation would set aside the bank robbery conviction of his client, he declined to elaborate on what the "something new" could be.

The day after New Year's 1953, Picciano and Stanton announced that they would travel to Cincinnati during the following week and request that the U.S. Circuit Court free their clients on bond while they waited for the court to hear their appeal. They would ask for the same bonds set by the Federal Court. Sanzo was free on a $25,000 bond until his conviction, while Petro had a $40,000 bond he couldn't meet. Indications now were that he could come up with the bond.

If the attorneys were successful, both men would be free for perhaps as long as seven months or more until the higher court made a decision. It also meant that Petro changed his mind about starting his prison sentence. It was reported that Petro had "expressed himself as anxious" to head off to prison to begin his term because County Jail time did not count against his sentence. He and Sanzo had recently declined to sign the paperwork that would allow them to be sent to prison while their case was being appealed. The choice they reportedly made could keep them in Cleveland, either free or in the County Jail. After announcing their bond request plans, Picciano stated he was going back to Federal Court to seek a new trial "on the basis of findings by Joseph Tholl." The attorney had yet to reveal his "something new" in the case.

Despite reports by the *Cleveland Press* that Petro would be sticking around, during the early hours of January 5 he was removed from his County Jail cell by U.S. deputy marshals and with Alex Clarco and James Zimmerman, was transported to the Federal Reformatory at Terre Haute, Indiana. There Petro was processed before being shipped off to Leavenworth Federal Prison to begin his 25-year sentence. The *Press* reported his removal from the County Jail "was carried out with such secrecy that even Sheriff Joseph Sweeney was surprised when he came to work and found Petro's cell empty."

On Wednesday, January 7, Joseph Tholl's findings were announced to the public and were the basis of a motion filed for a new trial for Sanzo by Picciano. According to Tholl's analysis, except for believing the underlying figure was either a "5" or an "8," he declared, "My findings are basically no different from those of the FBI. The only difference was in technical procedure." The *Plain Dealer* reported:

> Tholl subjected the office record to infrared photography and blue sensitive film. His conclusion was that somebody had made two ink-written alterations over the original stamp and reduced it to "a very faint impression which does not resolve itself into a legible figure."

Despite a conclusion that favored the government, Picciano used the analysis as the basis for a new motion to present to the court. He also filed a second affidavit where he repeated his previously overruled contention that the FBI's removal of the Medical Record Card overnight was "illegal, irregular and improper."

On Friday, January 23, Judge McNamee heard testimony from Joseph Tholl and George F. Mesnig. Attorneys Picciano and Stanton were present for their clients; the government was represented again by John J. Kane, Jr. and his assistant Frank E. Steel. Tholl testified that his examination showed the figure "8" handwritten underneath the figure "4" which Dr. Spaeth said he had written. Tholl said he could not determine what figure had originally been stamped on the card with the date stamp. He said the stamp left the printed marking, "Aug. 1_." Tholl also testified that the ink used to handwrite the "8" was consistent with the ink used in all the other writing on the Medical Record Card, while the "4" was made with a different ink.

After Tholl's testimony, FBI agent Mesnig took the stand. He also explained that he had found the same "8" inked in under the "4" during his examination, and although this was not testified to during the trial, it was included in his report dated December 10, which was introduced in evidence at the time he took the stand. He stood by his previous testimony that the stamped figure was either a "6" or an "8," but probably an "8."

When Tholl and Mesnig's testimony was concluded, McNamee dismissed the motions for a new trial for both men. He denied Petro's motion, based on Sanzo's alibi, which Stanton had filed claiming the FBI's "attack" on Sanzo's alibi had hurt his client. The judge observed "sharply" that Tholl's conclusions were more damaging to Sanzo's case than those of the FBI, claiming Tholl's finding "tends to impeach the witness," indicating Dr. Spaeth.

Trying to save face, Picciano made only one comment regarding Tholl's testimony. Tholl's confirmation that he could not decipher the original date-stamp impression was something the jury should have had the benefit of knowing. When Picciano tried to argue about the removal of the Medical Record Card, McNamee overruled his protests claiming that the card was a government exhibit.

Meanwhile, after his processing at the Federal Reformatory in Terre Haute, Petro was sent to Leavenworth to begin his 25-year stretch. Sanzo remained locked up in the County Jail while Picciano's motion was moving forward for a new trial. After Judge McNamee ruled against that motion on January 23, Sanzo found himself on his way to Terre Haute himself five days later to begin his 15-year sentence.

Picciano still had his appeal in to the U.S. Court of Appeals in Cincinnati with a request to grant Sanzo bail while the appeal was pending. In that appeal the attorney contended that the case presented "substantial questions of law" which entitled Sanzo to bail freedom. It was just the kind of legal language the court expected to see in order to grant the request. The newspaper noted, "Federal courts release convicted persons during appeals only when substantial legal questions appear to be involved."

Assistant U.S. Attorney Steel, perhaps thinking that bail would not be considered in Sanzo's case, did not oppose Picciano's motion for release on bail. Instead, he had advised the Appeals Court's office that if any argument was sought, he would appear and oppose the motion at a hearing.

On April 10, the U.S. Court of Appeals issued a one-page ruling pointing out that the government had not replied to Picciano's motion and concluded from his plea that "there are substantial questions to be presented in this appeal." To Steel's chagrin, the court did not ask for a hearing, it simply issued a ruling. The *Plain Dealer* reported:

One of Picciano's chief appeal points is a claim that Sanzo's identification as one of the robbers in Warren, O., on Aug. 14, 1952, was flimsy. He insisted Mrs. Addie (sic) Alden, a main FBI witness, had simply picked Sanzo out as resembling one of the fleeing gunmen.

The unexpected ruling actually caught both Steel and Picciano by surprise. The defense attorney had to go to work immediately to raise the $25,000 bail from a surety company for his client's release. He told reporters, "We're pretty sure we can raise the bail from the same people who furnished it before. But it looks like it will be sometime next week before we get him out."

Meanwhile, Steel was busy at work drafting a five-page motion asking the U.S. Court of Appeals to revoke its order granting bail. In the motion he addressed the Abbie Alden comments by Picciano claiming it was for the jury to decide the value of her testimony.

During the week that followed, the Appeals Court refused to revoke the bail decision. Steel said he would ask that the court expedite the case in view of the release of Sanzo. In most cases appeals took months to decide. The surety company supplied the $25,000 bond for Sanzo's release, costing him about $2,500. Picciano announced to reporters that Sanzo had signed the bond papers on Friday, April 17 and he expected his client to be released on Monday. Lost in the release frenzy was any word on Petro. When asked about him, Picciano stated only that "it would not be too late to file such a motion for Petro's release pending appeal."

As predicted, it would take months, nearly a year before the Appeals Court would make its ruling. On November 5, 1953, it was reported that Julius Petro was placed in solitary confinement in Leavenworth after seriously wounding a fellow prisoner with a knife fashioned from a filed-down saw blade. The *Cleveland Press* article stated that Petro would "go to Alcatraz as an incorrigible." The newspaper claimed he was originally slated for Alcatraz, but the transfer was being delayed by the "appeal action." The article, in providing a little bit of the story as to why Petro was in prison, finished with, "More than $69,000 still is missing. So is the third robber."

Despite being allowed out on bond, Joseph Sanzo couldn't refrain from staying out of trouble. During the early hours of Saturday, February 6, 1954, he was one of twelve people hauled in by police for investigation after a raid on a beer and wine tavern at 1909 Coltman Road. Two men were charged with selling liquor after hours.

On Monday, February 15, the U.S. Court of Appeals in Cincinnati affirmed the jury's guilty decision in the December 1952 trial of Petro and Sanzo. The court held that the convictions were "amply supported by the evidence" developed by FBI agents. On the key exhibit in the trial, the Medical Record Card brought in by Dr. Spaeth, the court ruled:

It was improper to send this exhibit out of the jurisdiction of the court without application to and approval by the court. However, the exhibit was sent directly to an agency of the federal government, was properly examined by a qualified expert and immediately returned to the custody of the court. The error, if any, was not prejudicial.

There was no mention, at least in the newspapers, about anything in regard to Abbie Alden's identification of Sanzo during her testimony.

When approached for comment, Picciano and Stanton remarked that they had "no conclusion" about their next step. Picciano explained their options as requesting a rehearing of the case from the U.S. Court of Appeals or to seek an appeal with the U.S. Supreme Court.

The attorneys did file an appeal to the U.S. Supreme Court, but they didn't have to wait long for a decision. On June 4, the U.S. Attorney's office was notified that the court refused to review the case. Julius Petro would become a bad memory for Cleveland and would not be heard from again during the 1950s. Joseph Sanzo immediately began counting his last days as a free man. He would soon be heading to Leavenworth to join his "idol."

Chapter Seven:

The Strange Case of Dr. Spaeth

The Trials of Dr. Spaeth – Part 1

The day after the verdict in the Petro-Sanzo trial was announced, back on December 10, 1952, the FBI was asked to conduct a complete investigation of Dr. Alexander V. Spaeth's alibi testimony by U.S. Attorney John J. Kane, Jr.

Spaeth was born and raised in Cleveland. He attended Western Reserve University, earning a Bachelor of Science degree, and completing his medical studies in 1931. After interning in Chicago, he studied abroad in Berlin, Germany, before returning to the Cleveland area where he was on the staff of Huron Road Hospital for a year. Over the last 20 years he specialized in dermatology. During this time, he married and became the father of three daughters, which he and his wife, Aranka raised in their beautiful Tudor home on Shaker Boulevard in Shaker Heights.

In their investigation, the FBI discovered the doctor had once before provided an altered document at a trial. Dr. Spaeth presented a $15,000 promissory note in a divorce case involving a friend, Dr. Joseph S. Somberg, an oculist (an outdated term for ophthalmologist or optometrist). It turned out Dr. Somberg was attempting to lower his alimony payments and divorce settlement demand to his soon-to-be ex-wife, Rose, by showing that he owed Dr. Spaeth a debt of $15,000, which was secured by his promissory note.

Rose Somberg's lawyer subpoenaed Spaeth to bring in the note. Spaeth obliged and the note was introduced as evidence. The lawyer turned it over for examination by a court expert on questioned documents. The expert was Joseph Tholl, whose infrared examination showed that the date, words and amount had all been altered. Tholl's report claimed the note had clearly been made out for $800, but was changed to appear as $15,000.

Fortunately for Dr. Somberg, the divorce case was settled before Tholl's findings could be introduced in court. During the Petro-Sanzo trial, Assistant U.S. Attorney Steel brought up the divorce case while cross-examining Spaeth, but Judge McNamee stopped the questioning before the phony promissory note could be introduced. When reporters tried to interview Spaeth by telephone about the story, he told them he had stopped making "newspaper comments" regarding the matter. He claimed, "misrepresentation and distortions" resulting from his recent trial appearance caused him "irreparable harm" and he would be making no further comments.

At the completion of the FBI's investigation, a Federal grand jury was requested by John Kane, Jr. During the grand jury inquiry, the following recitation of Spaeth's testimony from the Petro-Sanzo trial was used:

Q – Now I want to call your attention to this record. (Government's Exhibit No. 31, a card showing visits by Sanzo and treatment for his skin rash by Dr. Spaeth.) You have some changes there. Is that correct?

A – Yes.

Q – You have got Aug. 12. You have got Aug. Aug 14.

A – That's right.

Q – I want you to look at the record and indicate to the court and jury – in addition to the stamped date somebody has written over the stamped date on that particular day?

A – They have.

Q – Do you know what date was stamped before that was written there?

A – It was the 14th.

Q – How do you know that?

A – It was put in by myself at the time of the visit. That happens often, the stamp is incomplete, or fades and I write over it.

Q – When did you do that?

A – At the time of the visit.

The grand jury members charged in the final paragraph of their indictment: "That said testimony was not true and the defendant then and there knew said testimony was false and untrue."

On February 13, 1953, the 50-year-old doctor was indicted on the charge of giving a false alibi to Joseph J. Sanzo. During the brief plea hearing, he pleaded not guilty. After it was reported that the doctor's wife and daughters were traveling abroad in recent months, Judge McNamee ordered Spaeth's passport be placed in the custody of his attorney Parker Fulton.[47]

On March 2, attorney Fulton asked for dismissal of the indictment against his client claiming that Dr. Spaeth had not offered a "positive testimony" that would have warranted any perjury charges. Simply stated, the indictment did not state an offense, failing to allege that the doctor's testimony was material in the trial. From this request, prosecutors realized the indictment was improperly written. On June 22, Spaeth was charged again after the indictment was re-drafted. Three days later Spaeth pled innocent to the new indictment. At the same time Judge McNamee, because he had tried the Petro-Sanzo case, asked to be recused and requested the case be heard by Federal Judge Paul Jones. Spaeth remained free under a $5,000 bond.

Five months passed and in late November the trial was finally scheduled to get underway. On the surface it looked as if the trial would be a battle of experts in the field of document examination using infrared lights and special camera techniques. The key document in the case was the Medical Record Card established for the treatment of Joseph Sanzo's skin rash, which showed that he visited the office of Dr. Spaeth at 10606 Euclid Avenue on August 14, 1952, the date of the robbery in Warren, Ohio, in which he was convicted of participating.

Hearing the case was Judge Paul Jones, while the government was again represented by U.S. Attorney John J. Kane, Jr. and Assistant U.S. Attorney Frank E. Steel. Kane revealed that the government would call FBI expert George F. Mesnig and local Cleveland document expert Joseph Tholl to testify. On defense, attorney Parker Fulton was initially set to represent Spaeth, but in early September he was selected by Governor Frank J. Lausche to replace Common Pleas Judge Adrian G. Newcomb, who passed away in April. In his place was one of the city's most famous defense attorneys, William J. Corrigan[48] and associate counsel Timothy F. McMahon. Corrigan stated, "We intend to show the FBI made a mistake," and announced they would employ their own expert, A. Paul Tincher, a Cleveland lawyer and document examiner. The newspapers predicted the trial would last a week. Spaeth was looking at a maximum sentence of five years if convicted.

On Monday, November 23, after a jury of two men and ten women were seated, the trial got underway in the late afternoon. In opening statements, the government claimed it would show that the doctor's Medical Record Card, aka Government Exhibit No. 31, was altered not just once, but two times. McMahon, in delivering his opening remarks, told the jury they would prove the government's experts made mistakes in their analysis of the Medical Record Card.

Joseph Tholl was the government's first witness. The *Plain Dealer* reported, "Coming from Tholl, the testimony was ironic and went deeper into the case than the original FBI investigation of the doctor's medical card. Tholl originally entered the investigation to find loopholes in the FBI's case."

Tholl testified that in his examination he took 25 photographs, using infrared lighting, panchromatic film sensitive to all colors and another film sensitive to the color blue. This allowed him to reach the conclusion that he believed someone had written a figure "8" in ink on the Medical Record Card first and that this was the same ink which was used to complete the rest of the writing on the card. An attempt was then made to erase the figure "8" and a "blotched penned" figure of "4" was written over it, the original figure "8" was no longer visible to the naked eye, but discernable in several "extreme close-ups" of the document. His testimony left no doubt that "Government Exhibit No. 31" recorded a visit by Sanzo on August 18, 1952, not four days earlier.

While Spaeth listened intently and wrote down notes, defense counsel objected throughout most of Tholl's testimony. Corrigan insisted that the jurors must see for themselves what Tholl's photographs showed. Judge Jones agreed, stating that the jurors would draw their own conclusions after reviewing the exhibits.

On cross-examination, Corrigan attacked Tholl's qualifications as an expert, seeking to show that he was no more than just a photographer. Tholl held his own, replying that photography was only a portion of his body of work. Corrigan then tried to fire technical questions at Tholl, starting with asking for a scientific definition of light; trying anything to shake the expert's testimony.

On Tuesday morning, Joseph Tholl settled in for another three hours of cross-examination. *Plain Dealer* reporter, Ted Princiotto, covering the trial for the newspaper, wrote:

An old courtroom drama of expert witness verses the primed attorney furnished the day's script at the perjury trial of Dr. Alexander V. Spaeth in Federal Court. Firing questions with the persistence of a lawyer who has primed himself on another man's professional specialty, William Corrigan did not release his quarry until 2:30 p.m.

Ironically, there apparently was nothing noteworthy revealed in this alleged blistering as Tholl's name only appeared once more in the article. Tholl was followed on the stand by George Mesnig, who became the target of Timothy McMahon's equally intense cross-examination. When McMahon handed Mesnig a photograph that he had taken showing a four-and-a-half-time enlargement of the date portion of "Government Exhibit No. 31," the following exchange took place:

McMahon: You see a circle there, do you?

Mesnig: Yes.

McMahon: And in the upper right-hand corner, you see a small, curved line?

Mesnig: Yes.

McMahon: Can the jury see it?

Mesnig: I can't answer for the jury. I can see it.

McMahon then asked Mesnig to draw what he saw in the faint impressions of the photograph. Mesnig drew the bottom portion of the figure "8" and a curve to indicate an incomplete upper loop of the number. The drawing was important because it would be up to the jury members to see if they saw the same thing Mesnig did. The judge had already stated that this would be "the ultimate question" for the jury. The jury viewed copies of the exhibit as Mesnig testified.

Mesnig's testimony matched Tholl's regarding the first handwritten "8" on the Medical Record Card, prompting McMahon to ask why he didn't testify about it during the trial.

"I wasn't asked about it," replied Mesnig. Its existence was recorded in his report to the government attorneys.

When the testimony of Agent Mesnig was completed, the government rested its case.

Attorney Corrigan began the defense's case with the calling of three character witnesses for Dr. Spaeth. Two medical doctors and a chiropodist (podiatrist) testified to the defendant's "good" reputation as court ended this day before the Thanksgiving Holiday weekend.

On Monday, November 30, attorney A. Paul Tincher, a local handwriting expert, whose testimony was used at trials over the last 25 years, took the witness stand. He told the jury that he was convinced Dr. Spaeth had told the truth about writing the figure "4" over a date stamp figure "4" during his testimony at the robbery trial. From his tests, using photography, it was his opinion that the ink impressions relied on by the prosecutors and government witnesses were nothing more than a "gob of ink."

The next day Dr. Spaeth took the stand. For two hours Corrigan guided him through testimony. He told the jury that he treated skin rashes on Sanzo's feet and hands from August 12 to September 24, 1952, and emphasized that his records showed Sanzo was in his office on the morning of the robbery. Spaeth told the jury that when he testified at the robbery trial in December a year ago, that he did so from his records, not from "independent recollections."

Prosecutor Steel's cross-examination of the doctor would prove to be the highlight of the trial. Spaeth testified during direct examination that it wasn't until a relative informed him, that he knew he would be subpoenaed to testify at Sanzo's trial, about which, he claimed, "He knew nothing." Steel bored in trying to show that Spaeth knew he was going to be asked during the robbery trial if Sanzo had an appointment at 10:00 a.m. on August 14, 1952.

"How did you know they [Sanzo's defense] were interested in the time of 10:00 o'clock on August 14, unless somebody asked you?" Steel inquired.

Requesting a "yes or no" answer, Steel asked whether the doctor told the robbery jury he had consulted his appointment book "to fix the hour of the visit as 10:00 o'clock before coming to the courtroom."

When Corrigan objected, Judge Paul Jones stated that earlier in the doctor's testimony that morning, he had already testified that he had told the truth during the robbery trial. Jones asked the witness, "If you don't remember what you said, how were you able to answer your attorney that you testified to the truth?"

Spaeth disclosed for the first time that a "Mr. Contorono," a complete stranger to him, was the first to ask him for information about Sanzo's case. He said the stranger visited him twice on December 2, the day after the robbery trial began. On the second visit, the man brought an authorization from Sanzo to release a statement about his medical condition. According to Spaeth, it read:

> To whom it may concern:
> This will certify bearer (meaning Sanzo) was under my care and seen in my office during the period of Aug. 12 to Sept. 24, 1952, during which time I dis-advised against going to work because of painful hand rash. He visited my office once or twice weekly.

It was during this cross-examination that the bombshell dropped. Steel suddenly stopped his line of questioning and asked the doctor if he had a business card. When he answered, "yes", Steel asked if he could see it. Spaeth had a puzzled look on his face, but stood up and began searching the pockets of his suit for a card. He found one and handed it to the prosecutor. Steel had the business card marked as a government exhibit. He then read from the card out loud, "Office hours on Monday and Thursday 2:00 p.m. to 7:00 p.m." There was dead silence. It was not lost on anyone in the courtroom that Spaeth had testified that Sanzo had his appointment at 10:00 on a Thursday morning.

Spaeth's testimony ended the defense's case and the next day closing statements were given. Corrigan's strategy was to plant the seeds of doubt in the minds of the jury members. He did this by asking the following questions:

"Who is Sanzo?"

"What's Sanzo to him that he should lie for him?"

"What could Sanzo do for him?"

"Doesn't it strike you as preposterous that he should come boldly into court and tell a lie?"

"Where's the motive?"

During the defense closing, the aging attorney painted Spaeth as a "medical specialist," who operated a lucrative practice in dermatology and would have no reason to lie for a suspected bank robber. He claimed, "If he was going to fake an alibi, he wouldn't have brought in a card with an inked in "4." He could have made out a new card. It would have been the simplest thing in the world. Corrigan's final thought to the jury was, "Four dollars, that was his reward for this disgrace which has settled on his family and home."

Steel's closing focused on the facts in the case; the altered Medical Record Card, the business card showing Spaeth didn't even keep morning hours the day he claimed Sanzo was there, and now the mysterious "Mr. Contorono." Both the prosecutor and defense counsel attacked each other's document experts.

Late on Thursday morning, December 3, after five days of testimony, the jury received Judge Jones's charge. Corrigan asked that four sets of instructions be given to the jury. These instructions dealt specifically with the circumstantial evidence and the perjury requirements of direct proof. The *Plain Dealer* reported, "There is a specific statute requiring direct proof either by two witnesses or by one witness with corroborating evidence." Judge Jones deemed this standard of proof was met and rejected defense counsel's request that the rule be cited to the jury. The judge held that the evidence against Spaeth was "direct and positive." The jury went to lunch before beginning deliberations. Shortly before 3:00 p.m., after just 55 minutes of deliberations, the jury returned with a verdict of guilty of providing a false alibi.

Branded a liar under oath, in addition to a possible prison sentence of up to five years, Spaeth was also looking at discipline from the medical profession, which could possibly result in the loss of his medical license. When confronted for a comment, Dr. John H. Budd, President of the Academy of Medicine in Cleveland, advised that, "Any member of the academy who is found guilty of misconduct, either as a physician or as a citizen, is liable to discipline, of which there are various degrees." Spaeth remained free on bail and was allowed to return to his medical practice pending the passing of sentence by Judge Jones.

On December 9, defense counsel, seeking either a new trial or a ruling by Jones reversing the jury conviction, filed their motions. These included legal objections that were previously overruled by the judge. There were two key points. One, they charged that Spaeth was convicted on the basis of opinion or circumstantial evidence rather than positive or direct evidence as required to prove perjury. The second was that Judge Jones had erred in allowing the experts to tell the jury "what they saw beneath the visible material" on the Medical Record Card. They stated the jurors should have had the opportunity themselves to determine the disputed date with their own eyes.

The hearing of the motions and the sentencing was set for December 14, 1953. During a brief afternoon session, Judge Jones denied defense counsel's motion for a new trial. In a five-page ruling, he rejected defense arguments, reiterating his trial ruling that "the testimony of two experts of questioned documents was direct evidence" as to the altering of the Medical Record Card Dr. Spaeth kept on his treatment of Joseph Sanzo.

Jones then sentenced Spaeth to an 18-month term, declaring it was a "fair and just sentence." The sentence would make him eligible for parole in just six months. He refused to allow bail for the doctor while the case was being appealed, denying it on the ground that the appeal did not involve any "substantial question of law." Attorney Corrigan briefly stated that Spaeth had a heart condition, before turning to the doctor to furnish the details.

"I've been under the care of the Cleveland Clinic for a long time. I have a heart ailment and other disturbances and I am very ill," he claimed. He advised the judge that he was due for a checkup at the Clinic the very next day.

Jones, who planned to have Spaeth taken to the County Jail immediately to await his transfer to a Federal prison, agreed to delay the start of his sentence until 10:30 the next morning. He ordered Spaeth to bring in paperwork from the Cleveland Clinic doctors expressing their opinions "on what effect prison life would have on the doctor."

The next day, the response from the Clinic doctors was not reported in the newspapers, making it difficult to determine what affect they had on Judge Jones. The judge continued to deny bail, but postponed the start of Spaeth's sentence to allow his defense team time to seek bail from the U.S. Court of Appeals in Cincinnati. The Appellate Court agreed to allow Spaeth's release under a $5,000 bail that same day. The doctor would be a free man and continue to run his medical practice for as long as it took for the Appeals Court to review the case and make a decision, which could take up to a year...or longer.

Near mid-January 1954, there was a change in the 40-county Northern Ohio Judicial District. One year after taking office as President, Dwight D. Eisenhower's nomination for U.S. Attorney here was formally presented for confirmation to the United States Senate. Sumner Canary, a 49-year-old Cleveland trial lawyer, whose specialty was the defense of insurance companies in casualty cases as a member of the firm of Arter, Hadden, Wykoff & Van Duzer, would be sworn in two months later. Canary would be the first Republican to hold the office since 1933. John J. Kane, Jr. and Frank E. Steel busied themselves with their last cases.

The U.S. Court of Appeals didn't get around to reviewing the Spaeth case until December 1954. Representing the government at that time was James J. Carroll,[49] an Assistant U.S. Attorney appointed by Canary. The decision came down the following month. On January 25, 1955, the Appeals Court ruled in favor of the doctor and reversed the Federal Court's decision, agreeing with William Corrigan that the jurors should have been told more fully of the "high degree of proof" required in a perjury case. The higher court's ruling was a triumph for the aging attorney, who set the stage by telling the judge his client could only be convicted by "direct and positive evidence," claiming that FBI agent Mesnig's testimony was circumstantial.

The Trials of Dr. Spaeth – Part 2
On Monday, May 23, 1955, the second trial of Dr. Alexander V. Spaeth began. In an article that day, the *Plain Dealer* stated, "Trial testimony will cover the same scientific data but there will be a few more characters in the cast." On the government's side John J. Kane, Jr. and Frank E. Steel were replaced by two assistant U.S. attorneys, James J. Carroll and Russell E. Ake.

On the other side, Timothy F. McMahon would be handling the defense on his own. William Corrigan would no longer be involved in the defense of Spaeth. It wasn't because the wily old defense counsel, now in his late 60s, was too old, nor was he retired or ill. Corrigan was instead involved in what would be the most famous case of his legendary career; and again, it was another doctor he was defending. This time it was Dr. Sam Sheppard and it involved Cleveland's most infamous murder case, that of Sheppard's 31-year-old wife, Marilyn.

On the bench this time overseeing the trial was Federal Judge James C. Connell. The judge had made a name for himself 30 years earlier as the Chief Assistant Cuyahoga County Prosecutor. His boss during that time, ironically, was Edward Stanton. There was yet to be, however, one more new character in the cast.

During the first three days of trial the focus was on the chief piece of evidence: Government's Exhibit No. 31, the Medical Record Card of Joseph Sanzo, and was dominated by testimony from FBI agent Mesnig and Joseph Tholl. McMahon continued with the same objections and cross-examination questions as his predecessor.

On Thursday, the government called a total of just eight witnesses. Included this time was Charles J. Foley, the assistant bank manager who was robbed. His presence as a witness and what he testified to was not covered in the newspapers. Then the government sprung its surprise witness, convicted bank robber Joseph Sanzo. The witness was brought back to Cleveland secretly from Terre Haute Federal Prison in Indiana. Sanzo had not testified at his own trial, but here he sat ready to answer questions, "turning on the doctor who had aided him at his robbery trial." James J. Carroll asked Sanzo only a few questions:

Carroll: I am going to ask you whether you know the defendant in this case?

Sanzo: Yes, sir.

Carroll: If the defendant is in this courtroom, can you point him out?

Sanzo: Yes. Over there.

Carroll: Do you recall any of the events of August 14, 1952?

Sanzo: Pretty clearly, yes, sir.

Carroll: Tell the court and jury how you can recall that particular date.

Sanzo: That was the day I got picked up on my case.

Carroll: Tell the court and jury whether you were in the medical office of the defendant on Thursday, August 14, 1952.

Sanzo: No sir, I was not.

Carroll: I can't hear you.

Sanzo: No sir, I was not.

Carroll: You were not in the office that day?

Sanzo: No, sir.

Prosecutor Carroll turned to McMahon and told him, "You may inquire." With that the direct examination of the surprise witness was over. The cross-examination would not be so short and sweet. In fact, it barely got off the ground.

McMahon: Mr. Sanzo, you were tried in this Federal Court for a crime?

Carroll: Objection.

O'Connell: Sustained.

The judge ordered McMahon to "stop that line of questioning." Later, Mc-Mahon was able to get Sanzo to reveal he was in a Federal "institution." He inquired as to how he got there.

McMahon: What was your case?

Carroll: Objection.

O'Connell: Sustained

McMahon: When your case was heard, did you appear as a witness in your behalf?

Carroll: Objection...and obstruct the jury to ignore.

O'Connell: Objection sustained, ignore the question.

Judge O'Connell then addressed McMahon, "I must say to counsel, that on cross-examination, under the rules as he knows and we all know in Federal

Court, he must limit himself on cross-examination only to matters brought out on direct examination."

Despite the comment from the judge, McMahon still tried, unsuccessfully, to ask Sanzo if he was in Cleveland on the day of the robbery or whether he knew Harry K. Peterson, the gas station man at Five Points, who had testified at the robbery trial that he had sold gas to Sanzo about a half-hour before the 10 a.m. robbery in Warren. After Sanzo's testimony, the government rested its case.

On the morning after Sanzo's testimony, the *Plain Dealer* led off its article not with the shocking revelation that Sanzo admitted on the stand that he was not in Dr. Spaeth's office on the day of the robbery, thus destroying the testimony of his alibi witness, but rather with the fact that the doctor now had fodder for his appeal from his second perjury trial.

Because his cross-examination was curtailed by Judge O'Connell, attorney McMahon made sure he carefully noted for the record that the testimony he was attempting to develop had not been allowed. McMahon's careful noting took place during "hush tones" to the court stenographer during sidebars next to the judge. The *Plain Dealer* declared, "It doubtlessly will be cited if there is occasion for an appeal, court observers predicted."

Sanzo's testimony turned out to be the only new evidence presented at the second trial. But McMahon knew it was devastating to have the man his client was testifying for deny in court that he was in the doctor's office that day. The defense called its assortment of character witnesses and its own handwriting expert, A. Paul Tincher. The closing statements were delivered before and after the Memorial Day weekend. On Tuesday, May 31, the jury got the case after Judge Connell gave a 90-minute charge. The judge told the jury that in addition to the testimony of the experts on both sides, they could use their own judgement about what figure was on the Medical Report Card, as they were given the opportunity to examine the card under special lighting and lenses themselves. This time it took the second jury 30 minutes longer than the first jury to find Spaeth guilty again. At 4:40, the foreman of the seven-man, five-woman jury read the verdict as Spaeth sat showing no emotion. A short distance away, one of Spaeth's daughters cried on her mother's shoulder.

On Friday, June 3, after telling Spaeth that it was "very regrettable" that a member of the medical profession should seek to obstruct justice by false testimony," Judge Connell sentenced him to four years in Federal prison and fined him $1,000. Attorney McMahon provided medical records showing the doctor suffered from a "disabling heart condition." After reviewing the paperwork, the judge allowed Spaeth to remain free while McMahon appealed the case for a second time. Connell, however, doubled the doctor's bond to $10,000.

Nearly 11 months passed before the Appellate Court in Cincinnati rendered its decision. The verdict was reversed, it was again procedural errors that won Spaeth a third chance, the case sent back to Cleveland for a new trial. Attorney McMahon had been successful with his appeal. In reviewing the decision, the Appeals Court declared Judge Connell had committed "reversible error" in curbing the cross-examination of Sanzo. The higher court's ruling was:

The defense should have been permitted to subject Sanzo to rigid cross-examination. Sanzo had turned against his witness whose testimony – if believed – would have caused him to be acquitted of the charge of bank-robbery; for, had he been in the doctor's office on the morning of August 14, 1952, he could not have committed the crime of bank-robbery at Warren, Ohio, on that date. In all the circumstances, it would have been proper to permit careful scrutiny of Sanzo's motive for testifying against Dr. Spaeth. His testimony could well have been guided by his hope of an early parole as a reward for becoming a Government witness against appellant. It is not intended remotely to convey the impression that the United States Attorney might have promised Sanzo a recommendation for parole as a consideration for his testimony. Mere hope upon the part of Sanzo that he would be so rewarded would supply sufficient motive for his testimony against Dr. Spaeth.

Dr. Spaeth was contacted by a *Plain Dealer* reporter by telephone and made the following comments:

There was a terrible mistake made when I first testified from my office records in the Sanzo-Petro case that I have never been able to comprehend. I spoke only according to my office records. I spoke the truth to the best of my knowledge. The next thing I knew my whole world caved in on me.

I was never offered anything. I was subpoenaed by an attorney (for Sanzo) I did not know, to testify about a physical condition and treatment of one of a thousand patients I was treating at the time.

Since that time my family and reputation have suffered so terribly I can only say this decision of the appellate court has fortified my faith and belief in the American judicial system that the highest court will give justice. I have complete faith justice will be done and that I will be exonerated completely in the eyes of all my fellow citizens.

The doctor then made a startling revelation. He broke his silence and informed the reporter that before the second trial he turned down an offer to plead guilty in return for a lighter sentence. "I have maintained my innocence from the beginning," said Spaeth. "When I was offered virtually no penalty if I pleaded guilty prior to my second trial, I refused this offer because I was innocent."

The Trials of Dr. Spaeth – Part 3

Another eleven months passed before the next trial, the third in four years, of Dr. Alexander V. Spaeth vs United States of America began in April 1957. There would be a new judge, new defense attorneys and, most importantly for Spaeth, a new venue for the case to be heard. Spaeth, still claiming to be ill and under a doctor's care, filed a motion with the new judge, Paul C. Weick, to have the trial moved because he blamed both previous verdicts on prejudice generated by newspaper reporting. He insisted he could not receive a fair trial this third time unless it were held in the Northern District's western division in Toledo. In perhaps believing he would get his wish, the doctor hired a new defense team, which included two prominent defense attorneys from Toledo, George R. Hewes and Roger Smith. But Spaeth ended up only getting half of his wish. The trial was moved, but instead of going west to Toledo, it went east to Youngstown where Judge Weick was currently holding court to dispose of a "special docket" of cases. Federal cases in Youngstown were held in a courtroom located in the Main Post Office Building.

Heading Spaeth's defense team for this next round was Cleveland attorney Edwin F. Woodle. Opposing him for the government was Assistant U.S. Attorneys James J. Carroll, back for a return engagement against the doctor, and James C. Sennett, Jr. The returning Carroll told reporters, "We have as witnesses just about everybody we had before. It will be the same pattern of evidence, plus some new features." He declined to comment, however, if Sanzo would again appear as a government witness, stating only that he was "readily available."

After a jury of six men and six women were seated, testimony began on Wednesday, April 24. Joseph Tholl was the only witness to heard. This was not the handwriting expert's first court case in Youngstown, he had worked on several voter fraud cases in the city. During Tholl's technical explanation of the tests he used in his examination of Spaeth's Medical Record Card for Sanzo, the jury and attorneys relocated to a dark room in the Post Office, where an ultraviolet light was set up. There the jury was able to see the marks made by the different types of ink.

On Thursday, defense attorneys completed their cross-examination of Tholl. The government called six more witnesses this day including a former secretary of the doctor. Estelle Bulkley, described as a divorcee and grandmother, worked as Spaeth's secretary and receptionist from April to December 1953, months after the robbery trial. While she did not testify in the first or second trial, it was stated that, "persistent investigation work" by the FBI agents resulted in her unexpected appearance in the Youngstown courtroom. When she was called to the stand, Dr. Spaeth was taken "entirely by surprise." During her brief testimony, she stated that Spaeth had instructed her at one point during her employment to "take possession" of a book containing patient receipts from August 1952. She said she was told to take it home because "he did not want the FBI or even his own lawyer to learn of the existence of the book." The government rested its case at 3:15 that afternoon.

Before calling their first witness, the defense asked for a motion of acquittal, which Judge Weick quickly shot down. The first defense witness was A. Paul

Tincher. On Friday morning the jury was escorted back to the darkroom to view Tincher's exhibit under magnification. The defense attempted to show that the inked in "4" was not an attempt to write over an "8," but simply the doctor's effort to complete the stamped "4."

Character witnesses took up the afternoon session. Mrs. Madelyn Swim, Dr. Spaeth's 22-year-old daughter, testified that she worked in his office back in 1952. She described a "helter-skelter" record-keeping system that took place there because her father was so busy.

The defense rested its case on Monday afternoon. As in his second trial, Spaeth did not take the witness stand to refute any testimony of government experts or that of his ex-secretary. Closing statements began, and were completed by 10:45 the next morning. Judge Weick gave his charge to the jury and after having lunch, deliberations began at 1:55. The jury was allowed to go home at 5:15, but was back at 10:00 Wednesday morning. The first two juries arrived at a verdict after 55 minutes and 85 minutes respectively. At 4:55 on Wednesday, May 1, the third jury reached its verdict after ten hours of deliberations – guilty.

Convicted for the third time of committing perjury, the doctor's wife and two of his daughters broke down, weeping openly in the courtroom. Aranka Spaeth was at her husband's side for every day of the trial. Judge Weick delayed sentencing pending the filing of a motion for yet another trial. Spaeth remained free on a $10,000 bond. This latest conviction was sure to signal another round of appeals.

After the conclusion of the trail, the Youngstown *Vindicator* reported that Joseph Sanzo had refused to testify at the third trial because he "feared for his life at the hands of fellow prisoners." He claimed that after his testimony back in May 1955, he was "punched, threatened and tripped on a stairway" by inmates after he returned to the Terre Haute Federal Prison where he was serving his sentence. There was no comment from him as to why he testified in the first place.

On Monday, May 6, while appearing before Judge Weick for sentencing, attorney Edwin Woodle filed a new appeal for the doctor. In it, secretary Estelle Bulkley became the central figure due to her testimony about being told to remove the receipt book. In the appeal it stated Bulkley gave "testimony which was false," and that the doctor had evidence to "impeach and discredit" her story. Woodle stated that what she claimed on the stand was "in itself of sufficient importance to require a new trial." Judge Weick upon reading the request, put off the sentencing again until he could rule on Woodle's motion and on a pleading in opposition that was prepared by government attorney James J. Carroll.

Two weeks later, Woodle filed a brief demanding a fourth trial for the doctor citing trial errors. Attached to the brief was an affidavit in which Spaeth attacked his former secretary, claiming she had been "dismissed from her employment," after he accused her of "pocketing office receipts." The doctor claimed that she threatened "vindictive action" after being let go. Included in the filing were other affidavits, one from a patient of Dr. Spaeth, who claimed that money she had given to Bulkley was "not received" by the doctor. Another was from a former doctor from Bath, New York, who Bulkley had listed as a reference as a former employer when she applied for the position. The doctor denied she had ever worked for him. This was all part of "newly discovered evidence" which Spaeth was hoping would win him a new trial.

In the brief from Woodle, the attorney contended that "lack of motive was a fatal flaw in the government's case, that instructions to the jury were erroneous, and that the verdict could not be supported by the evidence because the evidence was circumstantial."

On January 14, 1958, Judge Weick refused the defense motion to grant a new trial and sentenced Spaeth to just one year in prison, which was less time handed down in the previous two convictions. He did not fine the doctor. The judge claimed he did not invoke a longer sentence, "because of the ordeal already experienced by the defendant." The doctor remained free on bond while appealing his latest conviction. A key point in Woodle's appeal was that his client was prejudiced because the trial was transferred to Youngstown and not Toledo.

The U.S. Court of Appeals in Cincinnati rendered its decision on August 22, 1958:

> On this appeal, we find no merit in the contention of appellant that it was reversible error for the district court to deny appellant's motions for transfer under rule 19 and for change of venue under Rule 21(a) of the Federal Rules of Criminal Procedure. We find no merit in any of the other assignments of error made by appellant. Appellant has been three times convicted by jury verdicts for perjury in the Sanzo case. The judgments of conviction and sentence in the first two trials were reversed upon grounds which in no manner gainsaid his guilt. There being no reversible error found in the record in the instant case, the judgment of conviction and sentence is affirmed.

Commenting on the Appellate Court decision, Woodle stated, "I was astounded!" He announced he would carry the matter up to the next rung and appeal to the United States Supreme Court, claiming the law permitted him three weeks to do so. Spaeth would remain free on bond.

Six months later, the Supreme Court responded. On October 20, James C. Sennett, who tried the third trial with Carroll, received a letter from the criminal division of the Attorney General's office in Washington D.C. announcing that one week earlier the Supreme Court had denied Spaeth's petition for a writ of certiorari, which allows appellants permission to present an appeal before the court. After being informed, Woodle claimed he would continue the legal fight "by taking any steps available to see that justice is done." His first step was to file a petition for rehearing with the Supreme Court. When questioned by reporters, Sennett said he was firmly convinced of Spaeth's guilt "because we always have held overwhelming evidence against him." Hence the three convictions!

At the same time the Supreme Court decision was announced, the Appellate Court sent a mandate to Weick ordering the one-year sentence the judge imposed be put into effect. If the judge were going to lessen the sentence, he had under Federal Court rules 90 days to do so. On October 27, Woodle met with Weick and James Sennett with a petition to either shorten his client's sentence or give him probation. In the petition it stated that Spaeth had suffered several heart attacks since his third conviction on May 1, 1957. Afterwards, Woodle told reporters that this meeting had nothing to do with his seeking a rehearing before the Supreme Court. He declined to say where that matter stood.

On December 4, Judge Weick denied Woodle's petition for the shortening of sentence or probation. The doctor was told he must report to the U.S. Marshall's office on Monday, December 15 to begin his one-year jail sentence. A dejected Woodle had little to say about the ruling, but stated he was "ready to do anything that can be done to keep my client out of prison."

On Friday, December 12, three days before Spaeth was to turn himself in, Woodle had a conference with Weick and Sennett in the judge's chamber. Weick denied a request from the attorney that his client be allowed more time before reporting to the U.S. Marshals in order to clear up matters in his practice; he claimed he was involved in several cases with patients that needed to be resolved. When that was denied, Woodle sprung another gem on them. The attorney claimed that the doctor had visited his office earlier in the week and was "in a state of near collapse." Woodle said he called a physician who ordered that Spaeth be hospitalized. Woodle now admitted that his client was currently in Doctors' Hospital[50] with a serious heart ailment and was too ill to report for prison on Monday.

The attorney was directed to bring into court a statement from the chief of staff at Doctors' Hospital with an explanation of Spaeth's condition at 10:00 a.m. Monday. He was told by Sennett that after it was received, Spaeth would be examined by a physician representing the court.

According to later reporting, Spaeth didn't enter Doctors' Hospital until December 15, the day he was actually supposed to report for prison. Two days later the *Plain Dealer* reported that Mrs. Spaeth had sold the Shaker Boulevard home in Shaker Heights for $11,000. In reporting on the doctor, the article stated, "His trip to federal prison awaits word from doctors that he is physically able to travel."

On January 22, 1959, Dr. Spaeth began his prison term when he was taken to the Federal Prison in Milan, Michigan, to serve a one-year sentence, despite his lawyer's pleas that it would kill him.

By 1960, after surviving his prison term, Spaeth returned home. His legal woes were not over, however. In 1962, Spaeth and his wife, Aranka ended up in tax court for payment deficiencies for the years 1953 through 1956. The short falls were the result of Spaeth deducting his attorney fees, which for those four years amounted to $22,477. The opinion of the court was, "It is well-established that legal expenses incurred in the unsuccessful defense of criminal prosecution are not deductible. We are aware of no sound reason for departing from this oft-announced rule now, and, accordingly the [governments] determination is sustained." In the case notes was the notation: "As a consequence of the perjury conviction, Spaeth lost his license to practice medicine."

The last time Spaeth was mentioned in the Cleveland newspapers came in April 1965 in a wedding announcement for their daughter Helene Rita. The announcement referred to Alexander and Aranka as "former Clevelanders" now of Sacramento, California. Alexander Spaeth died in Sacramento in August 1976.

Despite all the strange events that became the fabric of Julius Petro's life, perhaps none were stranger than the web woven by Dr. Alexander Spaeth. Despite another witness testifying that Joseph Sanzo was at a Five Points' gas station that morning; despite Sanzo recanting and testifying that he was not in the doctor's office that morning; despite the doctor's own business card that showed he didn't keep Thursday morning hours, despite two expert witnesses that testified another date had initially appeared on the doctor's Medical Record Card; despite testimony from an employee being told by Dr. Spaeth to take the patient receipts book home so the FBI wouldn't find it; despite an offer to plead guilty for "virtually no penalty;" and despite no comprehensible motive not to tell the truth, Dr. Spaeth, all the while suffering from a serious heart ailment, continued the charade and allowed his finances to be ruined, his career to be destroyed, and his family to be disgraced.

Chapter Eight:

The Last Years of Julius Petro

Prison Time in the 1960s

By the early 1960s the name Julius Anthony Petro was just a bad memory to most people in Cleveland and Northeast Ohio. He was behind bars, in one state or another, since October 1952, and in Federal prison, first in Leavenworth, then Alcatraz and later Atlanta. On April 17, 1961, Bus Bergen of the *Cleveland Press* reported Petro was in a new Federal facility. The article began, "Julius Petro, Cleveland's most violent criminal of the past two decades, is desperately ill in the Federal Medical Center at Springfield, Missouri. The doctors there say he is bleeding internally, but will give no further word." Petro obviously survived and it would be another two years before he was heard from again.

It is interesting to note that in Bergen's 1961 article he remembered Petro's sentencing in December 1952 differently from others who covered the trial, even though he was one of those who covered it. Bergen wrote that when the judge asked Petro if he had anything to say, he replied, "Yeah. Let's not have any of your lip. Gimme the 25 years and shut up."

In July 1963, while at the Federal prison in Atlanta, Petro apparently began a new career. Acting as his own attorney, he prepared a petition for Federal Court requesting his immediate release. In the petition he stated, "Relying upon the theory of law herein set forth, petitioner submits that he has satisfied a valid sentence of 20 years and now is entitled to his immediate release from custody."

Petro's contention was his sentence should have only been 20 years "because he had not put anyone's life in jeopardy." He had used a gun only to frighten bank employees. Now, with time off for good behavior, he claimed he had fulfilled his 20 years.

If those were the exact words of Petro, a couple of questions come to mind. Who were the bank "employees" that he frightened? Charles J. Foley, the assistant bank manager, was the only "employee" who encountered the robbers. Petro was identified as the driver of the gray Oldsmobile; his two passengers were said to have exited the vehicle with weapons and robbed Foley. If indeed there were three robbers, Petro would have had no reason to exit the vehicle, so at what point had he "used a gun to frighten" anyone?

Facts regarding Julius Petro's release from Federal prison are sketchy at best. A *Plain Dealer* article from February 10, 1967, stated that "Petro, 44, was paroled about a year ago from Leavenworth." That would have put his release date around February 1966. Perhaps more reliable was a Los Angeles, California, Police Department "Intelligence Report," from November 1968. In the report it states: "Subject has been on parole in California since 5-24-66, his parole ends

6/12/77." Assuming this to be correct, that meant Petro's time in Federal prison amounted to approximately 13 years and 5 months.

Whatever the case, Petro's time behind bars had done little to rehabilitate Cleveland's former Public Enemy Number 1. Once released, Petro moved to California, where his mother Lydia, father John and brother Michael had relocated. Julius initially moved into his parent's apartment at 5632 Kester Avenue in Van Nuys. There is no record of him ever returning to the city of his birth.

Petro's Post-Federal Prison Life

During the spring of 1968, Petro began a friendship / relationship with Christine Koren, a former Clevelander in her early 20s. Petro met her in a restaurant where she was working in Los Angeles. In conversation it came up that she grew up in Collinwood. By November, they had been at least companions for several months; it apparently wasn't a monogamous relationship for either one of them. On November 15, after having been drinking, Petro discovered Koren's diary, which had entries regarding "sexual intimacies" with a Dominic Rotundo. According to a police report, Petro "became enraged and began to beat her across the face and body with his hands. He called her foul names and spit on her. He refused to return the diary, and even threatened to mail it to her parents."

Koren claimed she found out about Petro's criminal past from newspaper articles her mother, who still lived in Cleveland, had mailed to her. Three days after the beating she filed a battery report against Petro at the West Hollywood police station. A battery warrant was issued the next day. During the ensuing investigation, police discovered that Petro could be returned to Federal prison to complete the 13-year-balance of his term if he was convicted of any criminal activity.

At the same time Petro was in a relationship with Koren, he was "cohabitating" at an apartment at 4657 Coldwater Canyon in Studio City with Roberta J. "Bobbi" Miller, a prostitute who used the name Dianne Winston at her "trick pad" at the Diplomate Apartments at 12360 Riverside Drive in Los Angeles. Petro apparently was a regular at the "pad," as he was "observed" there up until a month earlier when Miller was evicted for non-payment of rent. Miller packed up a few things and left in her Cadillac convertible.

The police investigation found that Michael Petro was running a dry-cleaning business called A-1 Martinizing at 8911 Sepulveda Boulevard in Los Angeles, not far from Los Angeles International Airport. Michael was reportedly involved in a loan-sharking operation and that big-brother Julius was called upon to provide muscle on occasion when borrowers didn't pay on time.

On November 20, police, while staking out his mother's home in Van Nuys, arrested Julius Petro when he arrived there with "Bobbi" Miller. He was taken to Central Jail and booked on the battery charges filed by Koren; bail was set at \$625. Petro was bailed out. No disposition on the case was reported, but it is possible Christine Koren[51] either dropped the charges, or that Petro was simply no longer alive to answer to them.

Petro in the Files of the FBI

Nearly all the information the FBI had obtained on Julius Petro came from agent interviews with informants. This information appeared in reports involving Los Angeles Mafia boss Nick Licata, burglar Frank J. Velotta, or the Cleveland, Los Angeles and San Francisco La Cosa Nostra (LCN) Families. In reviewing the FBI Freedom of Information Act Files, it seems apparent that most, but not all, of the information provided was received from one informant, who must have been pretty high up in the Los Angeles Family in order to be as close as he was to the family members his reported information came from. While the FBI hardly ever acknowledges who these informants are, this author wonders if it was Frank Bompensiero, who made a deal with the FBI sometime in 1967, right around the time Petro's name began appearing in the reports. The earliest mention of Petro came in a report filed May 4, 1967. The entry, under the Cleveland LCN Family, stated:

> As pointed out in San Diego letter to Los Angeles dated 4/26/67, entitled "ALADENA T. FRATIANNO, [names are always capitalized in the FBI reports] information has been received recently from the Los Angeles Office that LCN member JIMMY FRATIANNO, who was originally from Cleveland, has been observed meeting in the Los Angeles area with former Cleveland hoodlums, JULIUS ANTHONY PETRO, FRANK JOHN VELOTTA, NICHOLAS VALENTI, NICHOLAS J. TIRABASSI,[52] MICHAEL ANTHONY PETRO. [The informant would later make clear that these were friends of Fratianno "from the days he resided in the Cleveland area" and were not friends of the informant.]
>
> He [Informant] confirmed that JULIUS PETRO was recently paroled from Federal Prison after serving a long term on a bank robbery charge and that he was paroled to his brother, MIKE PETRO. He further admitted that FRANK VELOTTA is an expert safe burglar.

Frank John "Skinny" Velotta, by his own admission was a first cousin of Julius Petro. Like Petro, Velotta grew up in Collinwood. Velotta's name appeared in nearly all the reports where Petro's name was mentioned. In the Cleveland newspapers, there are almost no articles discussing arrests or burglary activities of Velotta. This could be because he was so successful in pulling them off. It could also be that since he was younger than Petro, that burglary targets were few and far between in Cleveland because of Petro and his Collinwood gang of safe-crackers.

Velotta was smart enough to know that when he moved around the country looking for lucrative jobs to pull that he needed to contact the local crime bosses, "known LCN members of authority," to let them know what his plans were, so as not to step on anyone's toes, and to give them a cut of the spoils.

Velotta, however, was not smart enough to keep his mouth shut and, like many mobsters and criminals, he would end up talking to a confidential informant. In discussions with these informants, he revealed such tidbits as that he sometimes dressed as a woman while casing an establishment he wanted to burglarize. Other times he dressed like an old man or wore some other disguise. His gang used walkie-talkies to relay information between the men inside the place being burglarized and the lookouts on the outside. He revealed that if they received information from an insider and it turned out to be "a good job," the insider would get a ten percent cut.

In a report filed on June 28, 1967, the case agent was interested in finding out if either Petro or Velotta had any involvement in the car-bombing murder of Gerald J. Covelli, a former member of the Chicago Outfit, who, according to which newspaper account you read, was either "blown in half" (Los Angeles Times) or "decapitated" (Chicago Tribune). In 1962, Covelli was a government witness against Chicago Outfit member James "Monk" Allegretti and four others. During testimony, Covelli exposed Outfit secrets with "an inside story of crime syndicate rackets" on the Northside. This taking place prior to the government's Witness Protection Program, Covelli was offered an opportunity to relocate to the West Coast. Things were fine until May 2, 1967, when Covelli's wife, Louise died under mysterious circumstances in the couple's Encino home. The publicity generated by her death alerted mob bosses in Chicago as to where he was hiding. The Chicago Tribune wrote, "Reports had been current in gangland circles that a key target of the Chicago mob was marked for death on the West Coast. But the identity of the target had not been determined." Covelli was returning to his Encino home at 10644 Royal Mount Drive in his 1965 Thunderbird when a ticking time bomb went off under the driver's seat. Both Covelli and his 25-year-old passenger Stephen Keno heard the bomb ticking. Covelli told his companion it was some kind of bugging device. Keno stepped out of the car just seconds before the blast, which possibly spared him his life.

Due to Petro's arrest after the June 1949 bombing of Herbert Tainow's automobile outside the Sovereign Hotel, he was being looked at as a possible suspect. Plus, both Petro and Velotta were hoping to score points with local Mafia leaders in order to gain acceptance into the "Honored Society." This was a point the informant would bring up several times during his conversations with the case agent.

Velotta had been arrested during an attempted burglary in Florida. Lawyer fees and flying back and forth for court hearings was starting to stretch his bank account. His concerns were apparent during a discussion with the FBI informant in a report filed on June 28, 1967:

Informant claimed he had no information to indicate FRANK VELOTTA or JULIUS PETRO or any of their associates in Los Angeles had anything to do with the COVELLI murder. Stated VELOTTA recently visited him and has been in telephonic contact with him and that he is under the impression VELOTTA is broke. Advised that FRANK VELOTTA is coming to San Diego on 6/26/67 to discuss with him his efforts to keep from being extradited to Florida, hoping that the informant would have contacts through SANTO TRAFFICANTE in Florida to help him.

In an update with the informant, filed in a report dated July 10, 1967, Velotta introduced a new burglar on his crew:

Informant stated VELOTTA last visited him 6/27/67, accompanied by RAYMOND FERRITTO. Identified FERRITTO as a burglar from Erie, Pennsylvania and an associate of VELOTTA. Stated that VELOTTA and FERRITTO drove from Los Angeles area to San Diego in FERRITTO'S 1966, gray Mercury station wagon, because VELOTTA'S 1965, black Cadillac recently caught fire and burned. VELOTTA collected $1,500 insurance money rather than have car repaired. Informant was of the impression VELOTTA in need of money at this time and specializes in burglaries only. Stated VELOTTA owns a ten-unit apartment house in the greater Los Angeles area. From comments made by VELOTTA, informant believes he purchased the apartment house and possibly some private homes as an investment with other associates. Informant believed two of these associates were RAY FERRITTO and JULIUS PETRO.

One could only wonder if the capital Julius Petro invested in the two dry cleaners and the apartment complex was part of the missing $69,500 from the Warren robbery in 1952.

Informant stated VELOTTA is an expert burglar operating with different hoodlums out of the Cleveland area. Informant believed RAY FERRITTO and ALBERT "Tubby" FIGER[53] were two of the persons with whom he operates. Informant was very doubtful that VELOTTA would ever become involved in a crime of violence such as kidnapping or the bomb murder of GERALD JOSEPH COVELLI at Encino, California on 6/18/67.

The informant updated the agent on Velotta's Florida woes. He stated Velotta was still looking for a connection to Santo Trafficante, "to pay off some public officials in order to kill the extradition process." During their June 27 conversation, Velotta told the informant that he recently heard through contacts in Cleveland that Al Polizzi, the former leader of the Mayfield Road Mob in Cleveland, who was now living as a retired millionaire in Coral Gables, Florida, could help him. Velotta told him Polizzi sent back word that if he was willing to voluntarily come back to Florida and plead guilty to the outstanding burglary charge against him he would only have to serve a six-month sentence.

Informant wanted to confirm with the case agent that his association with Velotta was fairly new and that they were not close. Apparently, the agent was trying to push the informant to find out information about burglaries being pulled by Velotta and his gang; something that Velotta would provide later.

Nearly eight months would pass before another report was filed on March 9, 1968. Informant received a telephone call from Velotta on February 21 stating he was in Los Angeles with gang member Alan Walch. [The reader needs to be aware that sometimes the FBI got gang members Alan Walch and Robert "Bobby" Walsh mixed up; something Jimmy Fratianno would do in his book *The Last Mafioso* written by Ovid Demaris.] The informant was advised at this time that Albert Figer had returned to Cleveland for a courtroom appearance "on some local case."

On March 6, the informant admitted to the agent that he and Jimmy Fratianno were receiving money from Velotta's gang from their burglaries. Here again, the author feels that Frank Bompensiero might be the informant. He and Fratianno were very close friends, and informant states that many of the conversations he reported were from places in San Diego where Bompensiero lived. Informant stated that he received about $1,500, but believed Fratianno got more. The informant gave some details about the robbery, but would provide a clearer picture of events at a later date. The case agent goes on to report:

VELOTTA is very anxious to gain LCN membership as it would greatly aid him in burglary jobs around the country. They have convinced VELOTTA that in the near future informant and FRATIANNO will have positions of power in West Coast LCN activities, which would help VELOTTA in his bid for LCN membership. The informant again denied personally participating in their burglaries and denied having any inside information prior to their committing a burglary.

Informant next met these burglars at San Francisco... They were staying at the Hilton Hotel in San Francisco from 1/15/68 through 1/29/68 and cased several jobs, including some supermarkets, but as far as the informant knows did not pull them off. During that time, informant received the impression they had a burglary score setup in the Los Angeles area with WALCH and FIGER and would be staying with JULIUS PETRO.

Informant advised that one of the members of this burglary gang is a former police officer, but could not recall which one. (This would have been Robert "Bobby" Walsh.)

Informant admitted that FRATIANNO was much closer to members of this burglary gang and admitted that FRATIANNO might be furnishing them inside information and contacts because of his need for money at this time.

It was also revealed in this report that Velotta was contacted by a New Orleans bank president. The case agent wrote in the report that Velotta "was in contact with TONY CORELLO" attempting to clear the job with him. No one by that name appears in any upper rungs of the New Orleans Crime Family at that time. It's more likely that he meant Anthony Carolla. Whatever the case, the job apparently was on hold at the moment.

The next report filed by the FBI was dated April 23, 1968. Under the New York Division the report pointed out that a bank burglary had taken place at Manufacturers Hanover Trust Company at 63-65 108th Street in Queens sometime during the weekend of March 22 to 24:

On 3/29/1968, New York furnished details of bank burglary involving use of highly complicated electronic gear MO to circumvent alarm system and considered FRANK VELOTTA as possible
suspect. Following instructions, informant called Los Angeles on 4/8/68 and requested VELOTTA
meet him in San Diego on 4/9/68. Velotta stayed overnight at informant's apartment (It should be
noted that Frank Bompensiero lived in an apartment in San Diego) and drove back to Los Angeles
with informant on 4/10/68. Informant does not believe VELOTTA participated in burglary at New
York on 3/22 – 24/68 for following reasons...

The informant laid out Velotta's travels for the past 10 to 14 days and they
hadn't included any trips to New York City. Velotta, however, did share these
tidbits:

VELOTTA has admitted to the informant in the past of having pulled big burglaries in New
York – New Jersey areas but claims he no longer operates back there as his MO is too well known and
he would be under too much observation by police authorities.

During his conversations with VELOTTA, informant learned from VELOTTA he has participated in a series of bank burglaries in Ohio and VELOTTA told the informant they specialized in
breaking into safety deposit boxes using torches, that VELOTTA specialized in getting around burglary alarm systems.

Informant recognized the name CIFFO (phonetic). Believes VELOTTA has mentioned in the
past having committed burglaries with him including one in the Miami area after which they were
arrested. It is on this burglary VELOTTA is now required for trial in Florida in November, 1968.

In fact, one of the trips was to New Orleans to investigate the bank burglary offer:

VELOTTA told informant he had traveled back to New Orleans with RAY FERRITTO and ALAN
WALCH [again this is more than likely Robert Walsh] to look over a possible bank burglary. Someone
had apparently set up the job for VELOTTA and VELOTTA indicated to informant it was an inside job
with knowledge of the bank president who was "in trouble with his bank." VELOTTA told informant
that he looked over the job and decided against it.

VELOTTA mentioned that while he had been in New Orleans area, he did not have the opportunity to contact LCN Member TONY CORELLO (sic) on this trip.

The report also contained the following comedic tale:

In this conversation VELOTTA told informant he had borrowed the car belonging to JULIUS
PETRO and that en route to Los Angeles they hit a deer and smashed up the car. JULIUS PETRO was
using VELOTTA'S car in the Los Angeles area and he also became involved in an accident, so VELOT-
TA had no car to use after arrival on the West Coast.

It was also in this report that the informant discussed in detail the burglary in which he and Fratianno received money from Velotta:

Informant stated that to his knowledge the last big burglary committed by VELOTTA was approximately a month before Christmas, 1967, which was a jewelry store "across the street from" a cleaning establishment operated by MIKE PETRO in the Los Angeles area. In his meeting with VELOTTA on 4/9/68, he learned VELOTTA planned that burglary with RAY FERRITTO and JULIUS PETRO. At the burglary scene on the night of the burglary, FERRITTO and PETRO "did not like the looks of things and wanted to back off" against VELOTTA's decision to go in. They called it off. VELOTTA became angry and sent back to Cleveland for two other burglary partners and they successfully burglarized the jewelry store obtaining jewelry with a retail value of about $400,000. After fencing it, VELOTTA received $22,000 in cash, according to VELOTTA – informant admits VELOTTA holds out on him as he hits him up for money. VELOTTA immediately left for Cleveland and Florida using his money to pay attorneys in Florida and one in Cleveland as well as giving money to his wife and two children in Cleveland, pay a $5,000 bond in Florida and getting his case postponed until November, 1968. By the time he returned to the Los Angeles area he had just enough money to live on and is now staying in an apartment operated by JULIUS PETRO who is his cousin.

A report dated May 10, 1968, updating the goings on with Frank Velotta began to show that the gang members were beginning to get under each other's skin:

Informant continues to maintain contact with VELOTTA and members of his burglary gang in Los Angeles. Advised that VELOTTA and RAY FERRITTO came to San Diego 4/25/68. He also admitted on the day before that JULIUS PETRO...drove down to see him accompanied by his girlfriend.

The informant claims that at this time JULIUS PETRO and FRANK VELOTTA are arguing with each other. They own the same rental property together on which property tax is now delinquent. JULIUS wanted the informant to use his influence on VELOTTA and convince him that he should not take the rental monies from this property and spend them but rather should use it to pay the property tax. From their remarks informant guessed their rental income is about $450 - $500 a month and that the property is owned by FERRITTO, VELOTTA and JULIUS PETRO but he did not know in what proportion.

He stated that he would arrange to see VELOTTA in Los Angeles on 5/6/68. He stated that this burglary gang is continuing to spend nights casing places but claimed that as far as he knows they have not as yet pulled off any recent burglaries and are in need of money.

Informant advised...that to his knowledge MIKE PETRO is a legitimate dry cleaning operator. He did not believe MIKE PETRO is involved in burglaries at this time and stated that if he gave this impression in the past, it was an error. Advised that in addition to the dry cleaning place he has in Los Angeles, about six or eight months ago he purchased and is now operating another dry cleaning place in Las Vegas.

The informant advised that in the Fall of 1967, MIKE PETRO and ALLEN WALCH [ROBERT WALSH]...went into a partnership – football bookmaking operation in the Los Angeles area. WALCH put $20,000 in cash which was part of his cut in a burglary payoff. Before the season was over they had lost their bank roll. The informant advised that according to JIMMY FRATIANNO, MIKE PETRO bought his dry cleaning place in Las Vegas with the money he stole from WALCH in this operation.

The informant sarcastically advised that MIKE PETRO is "a real business man." That he recently loaned WALCH [WALSH] $500 and charged interest. That at the present time MIKE PETRO has nothing to do with FRANK VELOTTA and is angry at him for pulling a jewelry store burglary in the immediate area of MIKE's dry cleaning store. The informant had the impression that at one time MIKE PETRO was a part of the gang but that he is of no use to them now and gets panicky.

At this time informant had no information concerning MIKE PETRO taking over the residence and furnishings of Los Angeles bookmaker BILL HOLT who reportedly lost his home to PETRO as a result of a shylock loan.

Informant advised at the present time VELOTTA is residing Los Angeles area with RAY FER-RITTO. He is driving a late model Lincoln Continental. VELOTTA and JULIUS PETRO are still feuding over the property they own together and RAY FERRITTO is in need of an ulcer operation.

The next report, dated June 4, 1968, had a brief listing about the gang under the heading of San Francisco Division:

Informant advised that while he was with VELOTTA on 5/9 – 11/68 he learned VELOTTA has been in contact with ABE CHAPMAN who is trying to interest VELOTTA in a supermarket burglary or robbery in the San Francisco area claiming he might be able to obtain as much as $150,000.00. VELOTTA has been to San Francisco to look it over and has discussed it with RAY FERRITTO, JULIUS PETRO, ALAN WALCH, and some other burglary member who is an ex-cop.

In a report filed on July 19, 1968, it seems obvious that this information was coming from a second informant. Information that wasn't being repeated was being reported wrong:

He stated that MIKE PETRO has been in Los Angeles since about 1946, but JULIUS PETRO has only recently arrived in the Los Angeles area while on parole. That MIKE PETRO has two dry cleaning places, one in Las Vegas and one in Los Angeles. That JULIUS PETRO is his partner, but does not draw any money until the places are paid off.

He advised that JULIUS PETRO, RAY FERRITTO and FRANK VELOTTA are partners in a jointly owned apartment house in the Los Angeles area. He had no information concerning RAY FERRITTO taking over bookmaker BILL HOLT's home as a result of a shylock loan to MIKE PETRO. He did not have any information at this time concerning RAY FERRITTO moving back to the Erie, Pennsylvania area.

We know that the first statement about Petro's brother Mike being in Los Angeles since 1946 is not accurate. His name appeared in articles about the murder of "Bobby" Knaus in 1946; he took Julius to the hospital after he was shot during the Green Acres robbery in September 1948; he was working at Sonny's

Show Bar in late 1949; he again took Julius to the doctors in July 1950 after he was shot by Alliance police during a home invasion robbery; and he was running a shoe repair business in Collinwood near Five Points in September 1952. The fact that Mike Petro was a suspect in the Alliance robbery of Joseph Carretta's home indicates that he was not always an innocent bystander to all of his older brother's activities.

In another brief item reported on the gang on August 23, the informant told about a recent trip by Jimmy Fratianno and Robert "Fat Bob" Tegay to Los Angeles. He states Tegay stayed overnight at the home of Frank Velotta, while Fratianno stayed with Julius Petro.

If there was a point during Julius Petro's time in California that things were looking up for him it came on October 7, 1968. Over a year earlier, on August 4, 1967, Nick Licata became boss of the Los Angeles Mafia Family after the death of the previous leader, Frank DeSimone. On Tuesday, September 24, the body of William S. "Billy" Amato, described as an "oft-convicted bookmaker," was found at 8:00 a.m. in a parked car at Huston Street and Bellingham Avenue, about three blocks from his Riverside Drive apartment. Amato had been shot once in the back of the head. His wife told police he left the apartment around 7:30 Monday night "to make a phone call because we don't have a phone."

Over the weeks that followed, no information came forth about the killer or the reason for the murder. Nick Licata was upset and wanted answers. According to an FBI informant update report on October 16, here is what Licata was planning to do:

> Informant told LICATA that his friend JULIUS PETRO might be a good man to make discreet inquiries among Los Angeles bookmakers in an effort to determine the identity of those ordering the killing. LICATA told informant to go ahead and make these arrangements with JULIUS PETRO, and that LICATA, would like to meet PETRO in the near future. Informant told LICATA that PETRO came here from the Cleveland area where he was considered a gunman with "guts." Informant advised that when JULIUS PETRO was a young man operating in the Cleveland area he robbed gambling joints, some of which were controlled by LCN contacts and that at one time a murder contract had been issued on him. Informant claims that JULIUS PETRO is not an LCN member, but that he would qualify because at one time he was in death row and "kept his mouth shut." Informant believed also that JULIUS PETRO, while in Federal prison, became acquainted with VITO GENOVESE and TONY GIARDANO (sic).[54]

It seems ironic that Petro "would qualify" for Mafia membership simply because he kept his mouth shut about a murder he committed solely on his own.

Before they broke up informant arranged with LICATA to meet in a few days so that he could introduce him to hoodlum JULIUS PETRO. They agreed to meet in a shopping center at Imperial and Crenshaw Boulevard.

Informant advised that on 10/7/1968 at 12:00 noon he met JULIUS PETRO at the Five Torches Restaurant in the shopping center at Imperial and Crenshaw Boulevard. He told PETRO that he was going to introduce him to the "top man" in the Southern California area. He told JULIUS that they were anxious to determine who was ordering murders of bookmakers and specifically who ordered the recent death of bookmaker BILLY AMATO. He told JULIUS to contact bookmakers in the Los Angeles area and put out the word that he is interested in starting a small book and wanted to know if it was safe to do so. He told PETRO to act "humble and cautious" in view of the recent AMATO killing and in this way he might be able to determine what element is controlling bookmaking to the extent of ordering killings. He told PETRO to criticize the LCN a little so that they would not suspect he was connected with them in this regard.

During this meeting with PETRO the informant told him not to hang around with "The Burglars" any more than he had to as he would get heated up with the police. PETRO told the informant that at this time VELOTTA was "up north in the Bay area" and that VELOTTA was accompanied by "The Irishman" and "The ex-cop from Cleveland," two of his gang members.

The following portrays a perfect example of how gang leaders communicated with people who were not connected with "Our Thing." They're very cautious to make sure they are not relaying instructions to an individual who could hurt them down the road. This was a practice that became more difficult for Mafia higher-ups as the FBI and sophisticated policing agencies began the use of undercover agents and high-tech recording devices.

At 1:00 p.m. on 10/7/68 they were joined at the Five Torches Restaurant by NICK LICATA at which time the informant introduced PETRO to LICATA. LICATA told PETRO to follow the informant's instructions, but did not discuss any details with him. The informant stated they had lunch together during which time LICATA discussed old times including his bootlegging days operating between Windsor, Ontario, Canada and Detroit. After lunch they broke up and each went their separate ways.

The remainder of FBI references to Petro in reports while he was still alive is scant. From a report filed on November 6, 1968:

Informant advised on 10/22/68 as follows:

Hoodlum JULIUS PETRO called him on the night of 10/17/68, advising that he had been successful in contacting Los Angeles bookmaker FRED SICA.[55] He requested a meeting with the informant on 10/18/68 in San Diego.

On 10/18/68, JULIUS PETRO and burglary gang leader FRANK VELOTTA came to San Diego in PETRO car, a used Cadillac.

From a report dated January 15, 1969, a week after Petro's murder, these notes appeared:

Informant advised that, on 12/21/68, he had a meeting with JULIUS PETRO... He gave to JULIUS, SLOAN'S home address and told him to send a "couple of mugs" to SLOAN's door to scare him but that no rough stuff was to be used.

Informant advised that, on 12/21/68, JULIUS PETRO reported that he had sent two men to SLOAN's apartment early in the morning. SLOAN opened the door but kept the night chain on. He was told to "get in line" and other verbal threats were made indicating that he was not to offer any further competition to the Desert Sands Casino. [They are referring to a local gambling spot, not the one in Las Vegas]

Informant claimed that JULIUS PETRO told him no rough stuff was used and no guns or weapons were employed, and that his men had not been in physical contact with SLOAN.

The informant did not know the identity of the men used by PETRO. Informant claimed that PETRO gave them $50.00.

In a report filed on January 15, 1969, the case agent reported:

The informant advised he was not aware of JULIUS PETRO's murder and did not know who had committed the murder

He furnished the following information on JULIUS PETRO in an effort to provide leads to solve this murder.

The informant claimed that he had recently learned from FRATIANNO that JULIUS PETRO and his brother MIKE PETRO, had approximately $150,000 outstanding in loan shark loans in the Los Angeles area, and that he had been using some "muscle" collecting these loans.

He also advised that JULIUS PETRO had been shaking down the owner of Sneaky Pete's, a restaurant or night club on the Sunset Strip in Los Angeles (owned by PETE ROONEY – a bookmaker from Pennsylvania). The informant advised that several months ago, an unexploded bomb had been found in Sneaky Pete's. Since that time, JULIUS PETRO'S brother MIKE, has become a hidden owner in Sneaky Pete's and, at the present time, has a hidden 20% ownership. The informant also advised that, according to FRATIANNO, JULIUS PETRO "muscled" a $3.500 loan from the owner of Sneaky Pete's

The informant advised that another hoodlum, who was angry at JULIUS, was the ex-cop BOB WALCH, (again this is incorrect, the ex-cop was Robert "Bobby" Walsh – the author has changed the name WALCH to [WALSH] throughout the rest of this paragraph so as not to confuse the reader) a member of the FRANK VELOTTA burglary gang, [in] Los Angeles. The informant advised that, in the fall of 1967, [WALSH] gave $25,000 to JULIUS and MIKE PETRO to use in a sports bookmaking operation they had set up and lost it all. [WALSH] believed that the PETRO brothers had set up phony losing wagers and defrauded him out of the money. He stated that [WALSH] has five children and is still living in Los Angeles and, in the past, has expressed anger toward the PETRO brothers. He advised that [WALSH] has been in contact recently with a sports bookmaker named SPARKY MON-ICA, a former partner of MIKE PETRO, and had learned that JULIUS PETRO was also shaking down SPARKY for $200 a week.

The informant also advised that, in the past, JULIUS PETRO has been used by the VELOTTA gang to help them in several burglaries, but they did not use him regularly as he was not depend-able. He stated that, in the past couple of years, JULIUS PETRO has been in partnership with FRANK VELOTTA and RAY FERRITTO, two members of the burglary gang, in the purchase and operation of two apartment houses in the Los Angeles area. As a result of this, there has been continued ar-guments between them over the expenditure of money for the upkeep of these apartment houses, and they lost one of the apartment houses for financial deficiencies. He believes this has caused considerable animosity among them.

The informant advised that, in his opinion, RAY FERRITTO had no use for PETRO and that FERRITTO is quite capable of murdering him.

He stated that, sometime during the past week of 1/6 – 10/69, FERRITTO took a plane back to New Orleans and is believed to be back in Louisiana at this time. He is back there to look over a burglary site and, if they decide to pull the burglary, VELOTTA will join him. The burglary is esti-mated to be worth about $100,000 and the tip has come from someone in the New Orleans area. (The informant claims he got this information on 1/13/69 from FRATIANNO and he did not have any more details regarding the place to be burglarized or the intended victim.)

In addition, the informant advised that JULIUS PETRO borrowed $2,000, interest free, from "Happy" MELTZER[56] about two years ago and has only repaid him about $500. He stated that MELT-ZER is another one quite capable of arranging PETRO's murder.

The informant stated that only recently LICATA quoted MELTZER as saying that JULIUS and MIKE PETRO were doing very well in their shylocking and gambling operations.

VELOTTA contacted the informant on 1/10/69 in San Diego and told him that he had not seen JULIUS PETRO in three or four days.

The informant advised the last time he had contacted PETRO was on about 1/3/69 when he talked to him on the phone and PETRO was in the Los Angeles area.

In summary, the informant claimed to have no positive knowledge of the murder but that PETRO had many enemies. He often got drunk and was a woman chaser and could have easily said something out of turn. He believes, however, that PETRO was too experienced to get trapped easily and that, in his opinion, whoever killed him was known to PETRO.

Meet Ray Ferritto

Raymond William Ferritto was never great at remembering names and dates, or even events for that matter, so one has to be careful reading his conversations and testimony. The book: *Ferritto: An Assassin Scorned* was written by Susan De-Santis Ferritto, Ray's third wife. Much of the story of Ferritto's life in the book had to have come directly from him. So that would account for many of the mistakes and missing pieces.

An Erie, Pennsylvania native, Ferritto, during the filming of the classic *Crime, Inc.* video series, discussed becoming a "made man" with journalist Martin Short. "Since I was a kid, that's what I dreamed of, it's what I always wanted... to be one of them," he stated. During the mid-to-late 1950s, he was arrested with four others after being caught burglarizing a gas station. Convicted and sentenced to prison, he was happy because he would be meeting "influential wiseguys from Philadelphia and the Warren-Youngstown" area of Ohio. DeSantis writes, "Ray knew there would be a lot to gain through their friendships."

Ferritto spent the better part of the next three years in Rockview Penitentiary[57] before being released sometime in 1960. After his release, DeSantis states he "arranged to meet up with his old inmates in Cleveland's Little Italy." There, she says, he rubbed elbows with James "Jack White" Licavoli and Cleveland Mafia Family boss John Scalish. She also claims he hooked up with, "The infamous Cleveland crew," consisting of Anthony "Tony Dope" Delsanter, Ronnie Carabbia, Frank Velotta, Julius Petros [sic], and Alfred "Allie" Calabrese and Robert "Bobby" Walsh;[58] the latter whom she describes as an ex-cop-turned-gangster.

The truth is, Petro could not have been part of this reunion of the "infamous crew" because he was in jail or Federal prison since October 1952, and did not see the light of day until the mid-1960s. While that seems like it may be a small mistake, it gets compounded in a story she relates where she writes that Ferritto dressed up as a priest and with Petro in tow drives to the home of a man who allegedly owed Licavoli $75,000. Just where and when this incident takes place is never mentioned. The debtor is described as a man nick-named "Bones," his real name was never revealed in her story. Using the priest outfit to fool the man's wife and gain entry to the home, Petro "held the wife at bay," while Ferritto finds "Bones" and tells him, "There is one of two people that are going to pay this debt...you, or your fucking widow." When the man became enraged at the invasion and the threat, he "bolted" and Ferritto, thinking he was going for a gun, shot him twice killing him. After assuring the wife that they meant her no harm, she gave them the combination to the safe, after which Petro tied her to a chair to give them time to escape.

Ferritto did become friends with Robert E. "Bobby" Walsh (See Chapter Twelve: Robert E. "Bobby" Walsh) after the ex-Cleveland police detective was released from the Federal Prison in Milan, Michigan, following a stint for counterfeiting in the mid-1960s. In Cleveland, Ferritto became involved in a burglary crew headed by Frank Velotta, which included Walsh, "Allie" S. Calabrese and "Butchie" Cisternino; the latter two Collinwood thugs. The men used the garage at Walsh's home in Highland Heights to practice opening safes.

In July 1966, after Velotta pulled up stakes and headed for southern California, Ferritto soon followed with his own family. He became good friends with "Bobby" Walsh, who had also moved out of Cleveland and headed to California in mid-1966. The two families became very close. Ray, his wife Bernadette, called "Bernie," and sons Victor and "Rayme" were frequent guests at the Walsh home, after they moved to the Porter Ranch section of Northridge, and enjoyed the swimming pool there. Walsh's sons became friends with the boys, as well as with Ferritto's nephew Frank Thomas, who would become a minor league catcher in the Pittsburgh Pirates' organization. In September 1967, the couples attended a performance by Connie Francis at the Ambassador Hotel[59] in downtown Los Angeles. Afterwards they were invited backstage to meet the singer.

Another person "Bobby" Walsh became friends with after arriving in California, was Julius Petro. In 2003, Christopher Walsh, "Bobby's" youngest son was brutally murdered. His oldest brother, Dennis, a defense attorney in Los Angeles, played a critical role in bringing his killers to justice. He wrote *Nobody Walks*, a book detailing the case, which was published in 2013. In the book Dennis talks about Petro, "Julius looked like a Warner Bros. gangster right out of central casting. He wore his jet-black hair slicked back. Dark and swarthy would be an understatement. Ten minutes after he shaved, it looked as if he hadn't shaved in a couple of days." Walsh compared Petro's looks to Hollywood personality Steve Cochran.[60] An actor whose first film role was in the movie series "Boston Blackie," a fictional character based on a short story series of the same name. In the short stories "Boston Blackie" was, ironically, a safecracker and jewel thief. In real life, Cochran had his share of run-ins with the police.

When the Walsh family first arrived out west, they rented a home on McKeever Street in Granada Hills from September 1966 until sometime in 1967. Petro was a frequent visitor at their home. Dennis Walsh told the author, "Ray Ferritto and Frank Velotta were comfortable coming to our house and being around my family. I never had that type of interaction with Julius. He would show up quite often at the McKeever Street house, however, they were always taking things from the trunk of an old green Pontiac they used and putting them in the garage; including duffle bags filled with burglary tools. Petro was mostly all business. I don't recall a lot of conversation when he would drive me to and from Notre Dame High School in Sherman Oaks when I was in the 9th grade. I was always happy when I got out of the car" Dennis compared being around a lot of his father's burglary partners to like those criminal figures portrayed in the hit television show "The Soprano's." They all had interesting personalities and were fun to be around, they were not just one-dimensional characters like many are portrayed in television shows and in the movies. Julius Petro, however, may have been the exception to the rule. He was neither the friendliest, nor most out-going of the lot.

After the Walsh family moved to Northridge, Petro stopped coming around. Dennis believed it was because he and his father got into an argument which ended with "Bobby" backhanding Petro across a table in a restaurant. The ex-cop had always been proficient with his fists. In addition, Dennis relates that Petro had once pulled a knife on Ferritto. Dennis told this author, "There was undoubtedly some bad blood all the way around there, but someone had to have squared the beef for the three of them to be together."

Ferritto, however, felt at ease while making himself comfortable in the Walsh home. Dennis Walsh related, "Although he always seemed very cool, he had an ulcer. While watching TV, he would loosen his belt and place four fingers inside his waistband and massage his stomach until he dozed off. He would often tell me, 'Denny, get me some Brioche, will ya please?'" Another story about Ferritto that Dennis revealed was, "One time my young cousin Neil, probably 3 or 4 years old, was missing. My aunt Mary Ann (my mother's younger sister) was quite upset. Ray finally found him over on the next cul-de-sac sitting on a fire hydrant and brought him home."

Years later, Ferritto told the District Attorney's staff that he flew out to Los Angeles supposedly to bail old friend Frank Velotta out of jail after he was arrested for a burglary. He claims Velotta was already out on bond when he arrived, and states he decided to stay in the area and "make this my residence." Ferritto stated that he met Julius Petro at the Los Angeles airport, and they soon got involved in "a few business deals," including the purchase of an apartment building and a cigarette vending business; the latter which never got off the ground. The former Erie burglar later recalled, "Through these few meetings that I had with him, I found him to be a little mentally disturbed."

Ferritto describes an incident that took place about six or seven months after he arrived:

It had to do over someone who had pawned a ring to his brother [Michael]. And when the fellow went back to claim the ring, his brother wouldn't give it up. I felt this was wrong. He [Julius] got all bent out of shape because he felt that I was taking the side of the fellow [whose] nationality was Irish over an Italian. And we had words and we had physical contact. And at that time he pulled a knife and I wrestled it away from him. And I knew then that I was gonna have a problem with him. It was either him or I.

At one time, according to Ferritto, Michael Petro got him and his brother together and made them shake hands and, using an old mob term, "forget-about-it." Ferritto says he agreed, "But...in my mind I didn't forget about it." Despite the uneasy truce, Ferritto had already decided that he was going to do away with Julius Petro.

It took a while before the Cleveland FBI office figured out where Walsh had relocated. Once they did, they notified the Los Angeles Police Department's Organized Crime Division of his presence there. In January 1967, Walsh, Velotta and Petro were indicted for conspiracy to commit burglary at an Alpha Beta Market located in Granada Hills. Along with them, the Los Angeles County Grand Jury indicted former Clevelanders Theodore Ricci and Richie Viccarone. The same gang was also believed to be responsible for five other Alpha Beta Market burglaries and two local post offices. A LAPD Intelligence report stated: *Robt. Walsh cases the prospective jobs and generally carries the tools. Frank Velotta is the wire man to bypass the alarms. J. Petro assists in the planning only – The type of businesses which suspects prefer are supermarkets, discount stores, and banks. Money or jewelry has been the object.*

Dennis Walsh remembers reading the newspaper articles about his father's arrest and cautiously spoke to him about it. He told him, "I remember you being at home that night on the couch. We were watching The Wild Wild West." In his book *Nobody Walks*, Walsh relates what happened next:

> The next thing I knew, I was in the office of renowned criminal defense attorney Barry Tarlow, telling my story. I testified at his trial at the Van Nuys Courthouse, where I would later practice as an attorney. I told the jury that my father was at home snoring on the couch the evening of the burglary while we watched TV. Although I testified truthfully, my father was convicted and wound up serving eighteen months in Chino state prison.

By the end of 1968, Petro was facing battery charges for his attack on ex-girlfriend Christine Koren. It was right around this time that there was an attempt made by Ferritto and Walsh to kill Petro by placing a bomb in his car. Jimmy Fratianno, in the book *The Last Mafioso*, again referring to Walsh as Walch, related a story that took place while he was staying at the apartment of Frank Velotta while on trial for one crime or another. Fratianno biographer Ovid Demaris states, "In the middle of the night, Walch and Ferritto come in the apartment and Ray's leg's all fucked up. He tried to put a bomb in Juli's car and it backfired. I think the cap went off." While the details of the attempt are sketchy, Dennis Walsh confirms it did happen in *Nobody Walks*. Walsh writes, "Ray was at our house in Northridge after that incident. His leg or his foot was wrapped up. He told my brother and I that he was painting and fell off a ladder. I never thought about that until later when the Demaris book came out. I do remember my mother tending to him. He would give me a few bucks to run to the store for him."

Robert Walsh was more than happy to help Ferritto out with planting the bomb in Petro's automobile. After the incident in the restaurant, Petro and Walsh had basically parted company. In the weeks after the failed bombing attempt, Petro started to muscle in on local bookmaker John G. "Sparky" Monica. Petro was trying to shake him down for money and Monica was scared to death. The bookmaker reached out to Robert Walsh, who informed Ferritto that the bookmaker "was offering money for whoever would take care of his problem." Ferritto and Walsh both suddenly saw an end to their own problem and a way to make money at the same time.

The Third Shooting of Julius Petro

The events leading to the demise of Julius Petro began on January 9, 1969. Petro drove to the home of "Sparky" Monica and knocked on the door. The houseboy, butler or whoever answered the door, advised him that Monica was not home and closed the door. Petro thought he was being lied to and responded by kicking the door open and running through the house looking for the bookmaker. Before leaving, Petro vowed he would be back.

Terrified, Monica called Robert Walsh and told him what happened, and that he wanted something done immediately. Ray Ferritto later recalled from his conversation with Walsh that Monica, "couldn't run his book because this guy was calling him up and threatening him and scaring the people that worked in his home and, I guess his wife – I don't know if that was his wife, but I understand it to be. And he was willing to pay."

Ferritto went to Walsh's house that night to discuss the situation. Walsh related in his initial conversation, that Monica said he would pay $3,000 to have Petro killed. Walsh told Ferritto about the amount before leaving the Walsh home that night and Ferritto agreed to go along with him "to do it." In addition, Monica offered Walsh 12% of his bookmaking business. Ferritto later stated that Monica had not come directly to him about Petro because he felt the two men "still had ties." Ferritto claimed, "He was afraid to come to me for fear that I might tell Juli what he had in mind."

Before leaving his home in Northridge to drive himself and Ferritto to the Sherman Oaks home of "Sparky" Monica around 8:00 or 9:00 o'clock that evening, Walsh grabbed a .32 revolver out of a bag containing some burglary tools. When Ferritto and Walsh arrived at the Monica home they were informed by the bookmaker that he wanted them to spend the night there. He was in mortal fear of Petro keeping his promise to return.

That night the men sat and discussed a plan to get Petro to meet them at the Los Angeles International Airport. The thinking was that it would be easier to kill him there in one of the parking lots because they were so big, there would be less people around and the noise of the airplanes taking off would help muzzle the sound of a gunshot. All they had to do was to come up with a plan to get Petro out there. As Ferritto and Walsh talked about the plan, Monica listened, but didn't participate. Ferritto recalled, "He didn't suggest anything. He just kinda like wanted it done. He didn't care in what way or what manner it was done."

According to Ferritto, by early the next morning, Friday, January 10, he had devised a plan to get their target to the airport. He told Walsh that Petro's "biggest fault is that he loves money. He'll do anything for money." The plan was to contact Petro and have him meet them at the airport because there was a diamond salesman arriving and Ferritto and Walsh were going to rob him. After the robbery, they would give Petro "the diamonds and let him go on his way and that we would meet him later." By "later" it would be conveyed to Petro to mean after he had fenced the diamonds.

After leaving Monica's house, Petro was called from a pay phone between

7:30 and 8:00 o'clock that morning. As Ferritto anticipated, Petro readily agreed to meet them at the airport in the United Airlines' parking area at the back of the lot. Around 9:00, Petro drove to the Los Angeles International Airport in "Bobbi" Miller's 1966 Cadillac convertible. He pulled into the United Airline's lot, tossed the ticket on the dash board and made his way to the backend area where he parked next to a palm tree.

Ferritto and Walsh were in a car a short distance away and watched as Petro parked the Cadillac. The two men drove to the airport in Walsh's blue Buick. Along the way the discussion turned to who was going to pull the trigger. Ferritto thought it would be better for him to get in the backseat, "so that [Petro's] suspicions wouldn't be aroused, because [Petro and Walsh] also did not get along." In the car, Ferritto emptied the cartridges from the revolver and wiped them down before placing them back in the cylinder. He also wiped the whole gun clean of prints. Both men had brought along a pair of brown cotton gloves.

Ferritto and Walsh walked over to the Cadillac and, as planned, Ferritto got into the back seat, while Walsh slid in beside Petro on the front passenger seat. Petro didn't seem concerned with both men were wearing gloves, perhaps he felt they needed them in the performance of the robbery they were about to pull off, or maybe his thoughts were simply focused on the money he was about to come into. The three men made small talk, while Ferritto waited for the next airplane to take off. As they spoke, Ferritto removed one of the gloves and began to wrap it around the revolver. An airplane soon took off and Ferritto was ready. He held the gun about six inches behind Petro's head and fired a single shot.

Apparently, as the old saying goes, "Third time's a charm." Julius Anthony Petro, "Cleveland's Handsomest Public Enemy," was dead.

Aftermath

According to Ferritto, the fatal shot did not result in much blood loss. Walsh got out and pulled the top half of the body down, so it was resting on the passenger side. Both men checked to confirm he was dead. For some reason there was a white pillow in the backseat of the car. One of the men placed it on the side of his face, covering his head. Before leaving the Cadillac, they removed the parking ticket and destroyed it. This way the authorities would have no idea when Petro had arrived in the parking area.

The two men got back in Walsh's Buick and left the parking lot. On the way to the closest pier, Ferritto took a screwdriver and removed every screw possible on the revolver. At the pier, he threw the gun parts in the water and the gloves into the trash. After the murder, Ferritto claims, "Sparky" Monica received a telephone call. Although he doesn't recall if he or Walsh made the call, the bookmaker was informed, "Don't worry about that – it was taken care of."

After dumping the murder weapon, Walsh drove Ferritto back to Glendale, where he had been sharing an apartment with Frank Velotta. Ferritto did not mention the killing of Petro to Velotta. He had always believed there was some kind of relationship between the two men. He said Velotta was some kind of "shirt-tail" relative.[61] Ferritto quickly packed a suitcase and Walsh drove him back to the airport, with Velotta in tow. Using the alias of Rini, Ferritto took a flight to New Orleans, where he stayed for a few days. While there, he received a telephone call from Velotta with the news Petro's body was found at the airport.

According to Ferritto, regarding the payment for his role in the Petro murder, he said Walsh was paid $3,000 of which he received $1,500. During Christmas time 1969, he said he received an envelope from Monica containing $2,000. In 1971, Ferritto was convicted of burglary, with "explosion," and sentenced to 15 years in prison and sent to the California Institute for Men in Chino, California. Also in Chino at that time was Jimmy Fratianno. During their time together Ferritto told him about murdering Julius Petro. It turned out to be a mistake for Ferritto, as he would one day have to confess to it a second time...to law enforcement. He was released from Chino in 1974. At that time, he said he saw Monica, who gave him another $1,500. Ferritto claimed that after splitting the initial $3,000 with him, Walsh was receiving 12% of Monica's bookmaking business. Ferritto states that since he decided to return to Erie, he let Walsh become the partner of Monica and collect the 12% all by himself.

In January 2022, Dennis Walsh was discussing the writing of this book with his younger brother Tim. During the discussion, Tim related for the first time, an interesting story that took place in the weeks after Ray Ferritto agreed to become a government witness. Sometime in the late 1960s, Ferritto built a dog house for the Walsh family's dog Rowdy, next to their home on Claire Avenue in Northridge. Shortly after Petro's murder, in January 1969, Robert Walsh told Tim to bury some guns under the dog house. In January 1978, when both Ferritto and Jimmy Fratianno agreed to become government witnesses, Tim visited his father, who was serving a term in Chino, and informed him. Although Robert Walsh never mentioned to Tim if the guns were connected to the Petro murder, he gave him a direct order, "Get rid of that thing." Tim understood.

There was no cause for concern, however, as Ferritto had lied to LAPD investigators and to Deputy District Attorney Ronald Carroll about what happened to the murder weapon, claiming he tossed it into the Pacific Ocean shortly after the killing. If he had told the truth, investigators surely would have paid a visit to the Walsh residence and turned Rowdy's home into a crime dig. After removing the guns, Tim, who at the time was a concrete contractor, buried them under a sport court, a combination tennis and racquetball court, at a home located south of Ventura Blvd., between Reseda Blvd and Topanga Canyon Blvd, in the San Fernando Valley, where they remain to this day.

Chapter Nine:

The Petro Murder Investigation

A 13-Year Investigation

By March 8, the murder of Julius Petro was at a complete standstill, virtually a cold-case. On this day Frank "Skinny" Velotta traveled to San Diego to meet with someone he did not realize was an FBI informant. Velotta let the man know that he had put together a new crew of burglars and that they had recently pulled a $100,000 burglary in the Los Angeles area a month and a half earlier. Velotta advised that they sold $100,000 worth of jewelry to a local fence there for $20,000 and split the money four ways. Velotta complained he had to use his cut to make payments to his lawyers and bondsmen. He also mentioned that he needed to remain in the Los Angeles area because he was subpoenaed to appear before a Federal Grand Jury investigating the murder of Julius Petro.

Velotta claimed he still did not know who murdered Petro and that he was still receiving regular telephone calls from Jimmy Fratianno in Phoenix asking if he had picked up any information about who killed him. The informant felt that Velotta knew something about the murder, but didn't want to discuss it. Once when talking about the murder he referred to it as "good riddance." He had mentioned that even though Petro was his first cousin, that what happened to him, "he had it coming." He also stated that prior to the murder Petro got into it with Ray Ferritto and had beaten him up. When Ferritto decided to talk to Velotta about that encounter, "Skinny" told him that "Julius was his first cousin, and he did not want to discuss it and that Ferritto should take whatever action he wanted to take against Julius and to leave him out of it."

The case agent added to his note that "The informant advised that because of the remarks [made by Velotta], it is his opinion that the chief suspect in the Julius Petro murder should be Ray Ferritto."

The informant had one last comment, he advised that Velotta stated Michael Petro "was afraid" and he had gone to Europe on February 25, and was spending most of his time in Las Vegas instead of Los Angeles these days.

One of the interesting stories that came out of the Petro murder investigation involved a highly publicized murder that took place in Cleveland in June 1968, that of Pierino "Pete" DiGravio.

In an FBI report dated January 15, 1969, the agent reports:

The informant also points out the possibility that the killing [of Petro] could be connected with the murder of PETE DI GRAVIO of Cleveland. (For the information of Los Angeles, on 10/23/68, the Cleveland Office advised that DI GRAVIO was killed by rifle fire on 6/21/68 while playing golf in the Cleveland area. Four shots were fired into him by an unknown assassin from the woods adjacent to the golf course. Since the early 1960's, DI GRAVIO had operated a shylocking business in Cleveland under the names, MDM Investment Company and DMM Investment Company, both located on Mayfield Road Hill in the heart of the Italian community.

The Cleveland informant advised in 11/66 that JULIUS PETRO, the former Cleveland bank robber, moved to Los Angeles after release from prison, and had come back to Cleveland for a conference with DI GRAVIO regarding the heading up of a loan shark business in Los Angeles with his brother MIKE.

DI GRAVIO had visited the Los Angeles area on several occasions, and his son resided in Los Angeles. DI GRAVIO'S son, WILLIAM, was arrested on 1/6/67 in San Diego for possession of marijuana and in Los Angeles on 2/8/68 for robbery. In May, 1968, PETE DI GRAVIO spent several weeks in California and eventually brought his son, WILLIAM, back to Cleveland with him.

One Cleveland source advised that, in his opinion, DI GRAVIO was killed as a result of something that happened in California during his last visit, but could not be more specific.

It should be noted that, when REDACTED visited St. Louis during December, 1968, he contacted Cleveland hoodlum, PETE LICAVOLI, in St. Louis and asked him about the DI GRAVIO murder to which LICAVOLI replied that he did not know who killed DI GRAVIO, but he believed he had been involved with some former Cleveland hoodlums in past posting or loan shark activities in Southern California and believed his murder had some connection with these activities.

At the end of this narrative was the following note:

The above information was furnished to the Los Angeles Division on 1/14/69 for evaluation and to assist in the solving of the JULIUS PETRO murder without compromising the identity of the informant.

On January 16, 1969, Lee Dye, a *Los Angeles Times* staff writer wrote:

A 22-year-old death sentence finally caught up with a man who was found slain in a plush convertible at Los Angeles International Airport. The strange story of Julius Anthony Petro, 46, reached a verdict climax last weekend. Police are still trying to unravel the story filled with mystery.

The "22-year-old death sentence" obviously referred to Petro's 1946 murder conviction for the "Bobby" Knaus killing, for which he was later acquitted. The article went on to question if the slaying was related to that long-ago murder. That, along with the fact that police believed Petro had driven someone to the airport, showed how little they knew about the murder.

Six months passed since the murder and then on July 9, a Los Angeles County Grand Jury began "investigating possible interstate racketeering ramifications in the gangland-style slaying" of Julius Petro. Called to answer questions before the grand jury was the 72-year-old Mafia boss of the Los Angeles Crime Family, Nick Licata, one of three ranking members of the mob family to be called. The other two were Jimmy Fratianno and Frank Bompensiero. The aging gangster was subpoenaed two weeks earlier and two days later respond-ed by entering Saint John's Health Center in Santa Monica for "an intestinal problem." U.S. Attorney Matt Byrne found out from Licata's physician that the medical tests run on the patient proved negative. He then obtained a court or-der for his appearance.

Licata showed up in court well-tanned, but appearing weak. After just 15 minutes in closed session with the grand jurors, he was taken before Federal Judge Jesse W. Curtis, Jr. by Byrne and two assistant U.S. attorneys. Judge Curtis was told that Licata was granted immunity from prosecution by the U.S. Attor-ney General. Licata's attorney asked for a postponement so Licata could return to the hospital, but Curtis denied the request. Instead, Licata was ordered back to the grand jury room to answer questions. Once back, he emerged five min-utes after re-entering, spoke briefly with counsel and then returned. Another five minutes passed and now it was the jurors who filed out, while Licata sat pleading, "I am an American citizen. I have the right to take the Fifth Amend-ment."

Back before the judge, one of the assistant U.S. attorneys read back the exchanges that occurred:

Question: Were you acquainted with Frank DeSimone prior to his death?

Answer: I would like to ask my attorney a question (This was when he stepped out for five minutes and then returned).

Question: What is your answer to the first question?

Answer: Well, he, my attorney, told me to decline and not incriminate myself in any way, shape or form.

The following are other questions Licata refused to answer:

Question: The jury has been advised that you were in fact acquainted with Frank DeSimone. Tell us what you know about the Apalachin meeting and Frank DeS-imone's attendance at the summit conference of Cosa Nostra leaders in New York in 1957?

Question: You heard about it, didn't you, Mr. Licata?

Question: You know, don't you, that Frank DeSimone was head of a criminal organization or group in Los Angeles?

Question: You know the nature and structure of that group, do you not?

Question: Do you deny that Frank DeSimone was head of a criminal group and you replaced Frank DeSimone as head of the Los Angeles family of the Cosa Nostra – or by whatever name it is known?

Licata simply indicated he would refuse to answer any questions. At the request of his attorney, a voluntary statement he made for the grand jury was read to Judge Curtis. The judge responded by ordering Licata back to the grand jury room to answer questions. Licata replied, "Your honor, I stand on the First, Fourth, Fifth and Sixth Amendments, which every citizen has a right to do."

Judge Curtis patiently explained that by answering the questions put to him by the prosecutors he could not incriminate himself because he had been granted immunity from prosecution by the court.

Licata insisted, "I don't feel like answering any questions whatsoever. The immunity proceeding is not in any law book in the United States. It's a way to force people to talk. I'm entitled to my rights, I'm a citizen of this country."

When Judge Curtis said he could be jailed for refusing to answer the questions, Licata replied, "I understand, your honor. That's your privilege. May I ask you one question? If I make a mistake and if I tell a lie, I still go behind bars, that's right?"

Judge Curtis answered, "Well, if you lie that would be perjury and it would be a separate penalty and offense."

Licata's final statement to the judge was, "I respectfully decline to answer any questions." Curtis responded by ordering Licata put in jail on a charge of contempt. He would have to remain there until the term of the grand jury expired in September 1970, or until he complied with the court order to answer questions.

On May 4, after the U.S. 9th Circuit Court of Appeals ordered Licata be admitted bail, the mob boss was released after Judge Curtis set bond at $2,500. Licata was ordered not to leave the Federal district and report to the U.S. marshal's office by telephone every Monday. After 72 days of freedom, however, the Appeals court revoked the bond and ordered Licata back to jail to finish his term. In September, Licata was indicted by a Federal Grand Jury for contempt of court for refusing to answer the questions of the grand jury. Conviction could result in fines and additional imprisonment. As for Petro's murder, it would be another seven-and-a-half years before it came up again. By that time Nick Licata was no longer around, having died on October 19, 1974.

Danny Greene Murder & Trials

On October 6, 1977, Cleveland witnessed its most sensational underworld murder, the car-bomb killing of Irishman Daniel J. "Danny" Greene in the parking lot of a suburban medical building in Lyndhurst. Law enforcement agencies throughout the county quickly worked together to solve the murder. Just 35 days after the bombing death, the Cuyahoga County Grand Jury indicted Raymond Ferritto for the murder. The next day, Ferritto surrendered to the FBI in Pittsburgh and began spilling his guts the same day. With the information supplied by Ferritto, on December 5, he and eight others were indicted for the murder of Danny Greene.

On January 13, 1978, Ferritto pleaded guilty to aggravated murder and aggravated arson in Cuyahoga County Common Pleas Court before Judge James J. Carroll during an afternoon session conducted in total secrecy. Assistant County Prosecutor Carmen Marino said the secret hearing was necessary because the U.S. marshals assigned to protect Ferritto feared for his life. Court officers did not confirm the hearing had taken place until 6:00 p.m., at which time the marshals had transported Ferritto out of the county to a safe location.

When reporters learned of the guilty plea, they questioned Ferritto's lawyer, Peter H. Hull. While acknowledging that the guilty plea could send his client to the electric chair, Hull confirmed that there was an understanding it could be withdrawn if Ferritto cooperated in the coming trial. Hull explained, "There is a plea agreement that after he testifies truthfully at the trial of the other conspirators, it is our understanding he will be allowed to withdraw this plea and plead to a lesser offense of manslaughter, for which he will serve five years."

Reporters sought out Prosecutor Marino, who confirmed the deal, then added, "And if he doesn't cooperate, he is in deep trouble." Ferritto was told if he doesn't tell the truth he could be executed.

On January 17, during a pre-trial hearing, the defense counsel of the indicted men received another blow when defendant Jimmy Fratianno was a no-show. Prosecutor Marino presented a waiver from him in which he relinquished his right to be present during arguments on pre-trial motions. Marino then explained that Fratianno was "under the protective custody of federal agents who are transporting him around the country for his safety." Fratianno's Cleveland attorney, Fred Jurek, seemingly unaware of what transpired, claimed he hadn't seen his client in a month.

Marino then confirmed the details of the Ferritto deal to the court. He said Ferritto's family would also be protected by Federal authorities. Defense attorney Leonard E. Yelsky, representing Angelo Lonardo, objected to the deal Ferritto cut, declaring he should be barred from the trial because "this man will be testifying with a magnum pistol at his head," referring to the fact he would face execution if he doesn't cooperate fully with prosecutors and tell the truth.

The next day, the *Plain Dealer* confirmed Jimmy Fratianno had indeed cut a deal with the Justice Department to testify against the men accused of the Danny Greene murder plot. He went one step further and agreed to cooperate with California authorities who were investigating the murder of Julius Petro.

On January 18, 1978, as part of a plea deal with the government, Ferritto confessed to the murder of Julius Petro nine years earlier. Ferritto was recommended as a hitman to kill Greene to the Cleveland Mafia by Jimmy Fratianno, who grew up in Cleveland's Little Italy neighborhood before heading west to Los Angeles. When Ferritto began implicating Cleveland Mafia members and associates who were involved in the plot to kill Greene, he also gave up Fratianno, who had been working as an FBI confidential informant. Ferritto was well aware that Fratianno knew about his role in the Petro murder. He had told him personally while the two served time in Chino together during the early 1970s. Ferritto had to come clean with this murder also or he could lose his deal with the government if Fratianno exposed it. He was told, in no uncertain terms, that if he did not fully cooperate with the government, or was caught in any lie, he could face going to the electric chair.

It should be noted here that when organized crime figures make deals with the government or local law enforcement, they are required to confess all their crimes and reveal all the murders they were involved in. One of the most publicized examples of this took place in 1991 with Salvatore "Sammy the Bull" Gravano, the underboss to Gambino Crime Family Boss John Gotti in New York. When Gravano made his deal with the government, he confessed to participating in 19 murders, even though he had only pulled the trigger in one. Less than five years after Ferritto made his deal, Angelo Lonardo, Acting Boss of the Cleveland Mafia Family due to all the convictions in the wake of the Danny Greene murder and ensuing trials, became the highest ranking member of the Mafia, up until that time, to become a government witness. When Lonardo gave up his murders, he revealed his participation in the murder of Dr. Giuseppe Romano, a Mafia boss of Cleveland in the mid-1930s. The murder, up until then, was a total mystery and was a cold case for 36 years. The reason the author brings these up is because Ferritto, in his deal with the government, only confessed to participating in two murders. In Susan DeSantis Ferritto's book about her husband, she describes the murder of a man nicknamed "Bones" by Ferritto in the early 1960s (See Chapter Eight; Sub-Chapter: Meet Ray Ferritto). While she also claims that Julius Petro was involved with this murder at a time he was actually in prison, it doesn't mean that Ferritto didn't do it with another accomplice. More disturbing is that in 2014 former Erie, Pennsylvania, police detective Dominick D. DiPaolo and Erie newspaper reporter Jeff Pinski wrote the book, *The Unholy Murder of Ash Wednesday*. Frank "Bolo" Dovishaw, a.k.a. "Ash Wednesday" due to a birthmark on his forehead, was a small-time bookmaker in Erie who worked for Ferritto after both left the witness protection program and returned home. Dovishaw played a small role in the murder of Danny Greene, testified for the government, and went into witness protection for a short while. The book is centered on the investigation of the brutal murder of Dovishaw inside his home on January 4, 1983. DiPaolo knew Ferritto since the future detective was just a teenager. The dedicated officer despised him his entire life. He wrote of Ferritto:

He was feared in many circles. He had killed – murdered – many times, casually, indifferently, and always gotten away with it. In January of 1983, Raymond Ferritto, 54, had been a long-established and confessed hit man for a regional mob that for many years spread its venom-saturated tentacles from Cleveland to Buffalo to Pittsburgh and Youngstown, with Erie, Pennsylvania, conveniently situated directly in the middle. Ferritto was even known as a journeyman killer in California. With literally no conscience and lacking even a single decency gene in his entire body, Raymond Ferritto is said to have killed at least 15 victims on contract hits.

When I spoke to the retired detective in the spring of 2021, he told me the hits were carried out in Pittsburgh, Detroit and Los Angeles; many of the latter carried out at the request of Jimmy Fratianno. Unfortunately, there were never any charges brought against Ferritto or the people who hired him.

Ferritto had already been caught in a lie about the murder of Greene. It was due to the carelessness of "Butchie" Cisternino in registering the cars used in the bombing that resulted in Ferritto getting caught. He was so angry about this he told authorities that it was Cisternino who was in the car with him when the bomb was set off that killed Greene, instead of Youngstown mobster Ronald Carabbia. On January 16, Ferritto was flown to Los Angeles, where he made a full confession at the District Attorney's office at which time he implicated Robert Walsh and John "Sparky" Monica in the Petro murder. State law enforcement officials in California and Ohio, as well as Federal authorities, agreed that although Fratianno had no direct role in the murder of either Petro or Greene, his testimony would be used to substantiate Ferritto's.

During the plot to kill Greene, the Cleveland Mafia made a connection with an FBI clerk and was bribing her to get the names of the bureau's confidential informants and other information. When Fratianno was told about this, by Cleveland Mafia boss James "Jack White" Licavoli, he realized he had a serious problem. Within a day or two of Ferritto's confession to the Petro murder, it was reported that Fratianno had made a deal with the Justice Department. In the reporting by the Cleveland *Plain Dealer* of the deal Jimmy Fratianno made, the newspaper claimed Petro was killed, "after a Southern California Mafia chieftain put out a death contract on Petro, California sources said." Obviously, the details of Ferritto's confession to the Los Angeles District Attorney had not been made public.

On February 21, 1978, less than four months after the murder of Danny Greene, jury selection began in the state trial held in Cuyahoga County Common Pleas Court before Judge James J. Carroll. The six defendants were Alfred S. Calabrese, Ronald D. Carabbia, Pasquale Cisternino, James T. Licavoli, Angelo A. Lonardo and Thomas J. Sinito. On March 30, during the opening statement of defense counsel Carmen A. Policy, who represented Carabbia, the attorney, in referring to the murder of Julius Petro, asked the jury, "Do you want to believe a cold, calculated killer who killed his friend in Los Angeles, or a respected family man such as Mr. Carabbia?" The prosecutors called Ferritto to the stand on Thursday, April 13 and his cross examination ended on Monday, April 17. On May 10, claiming that prosecutors had failed to provide enough evidence, Judge Carroll dismissed all charges against Alfred S. Calabrese.

On May 25, after 79 days, making it the longest continuous trial in the history of Cuyahoga County, surpassing even the Sam Sheppard murder trial in 1954, the jury delivered its verdict. Ronald Carabbia and "Butchie" Cisternino were found guilty of aggravated murder and aggravated arson, but not guilty of engaging in organized crime. The other three defendants were acquitted of all charges. On September 7, Judge Carroll sentenced Carabbia and Cisternino to life in prison.[62]

On May 19, before the first trial was over, Ferritto was taken back to Los Angeles to answer for the murder of Julius Petro. With four Federal marshals standing guard in the courtroom of Municipal Judge Gabriel A. Gutierrez, the 49-year-old Ferritto pleaded guilty to a charge of second-degree murder for the killing of Petro. Deputy District Attorney Richard Jenkins told Judge Gutierrez, Ferritto pled guilty to the second-degree murder charge in return for a promise that his sentence would be no more than five years and would run concurrently with a five-year sentence promised in Cleveland for the murder of Danny Greene, where Ferritto pled guilty to manslaughter. Deputy District Attorney Michael Brenner, when approached by reporters wanting to know more about Ferritto's confession, declined to comment stating, "That would reveal who hired him and that person is still a suspect." On June 2, two weeks after Ferritto's plea, a Complaint Felony, signed by Michael Brenner, was issued in the Municipal Court of the County of Los Angeles for the crime of murder committed by John Monica, "who did willfully, unlawfully, and with malice aforethought murder Julius Petro, a human being." The bail recommendation on the order was $100,000.

On the last day of May 1978, a second state trial began in Cuyahoga County Common Pleas Court. This time Judge Norman A. Fuerst was hearing the case. The defendants were John P. Calandra, Sr., who was to be a defendant in the first trial, but was dismissed due to health reasons, Kenneth Ciarcia and Thomas P. Lanci. Two other defendants, Anthony D. Libertore and Carmen S. Marconi, were Federal fugitives at the time. All the defendants were charged with aggravated murder, aggravated arson and engaging in organized crime.

Ferritto's testimony, on June 28 was short and sweet. He testified that during the year he stalked Greene, he met with Calandra about 20 times. He said during many of those meetings Calandra carried a little white poodle that had trouble breathing. As for the other two defendants, he didn't know either of them. In the end, Calandra was acquitted and Ciarcia and Lanci were found guilty of just aggravated murder. Fuerst sentenced both men to life in prison.

After testifying in the first two state trials, on January 15, 1979, Ferritto, as part of his plea deal, pled guilty to one Federal charge of traveling interstate to commit violence. In the U.S. District Court in Cleveland, with U.S. marshals guarding every door in the courtroom, Federal Judge Robert Krupansky sentenced him to five years in Federal prison, to be served at an undisclosed location and he was required to continue to testify at upcoming trials.

With the Los Angeles sentence handed down in May 1978 and the Federal sentence in January 1979, that was two down and one to go. On Friday, February 16, 1979, while under "heavy protection" by U.S. marshals, Ferritto appeared in Cuyahoga Common Pleas Court. After Ferritto withdrew his guilty pleas to charges of aggravated murder and aggravated arson, Judge James J. Carroll handed down a sentence of five years' probation for voluntary manslaughter for the death of Danny Greene.

Judge Carroll originally sentenced Ferritto to 5 to 25 years in prison, but after Assistant County Prosecutor Carmen Marino declared his life would be in danger in either Federal or state prison, the judge reduced the sentence. Ferritto's counsel, Peter Hull asked that his client be put in the Federal Witness Protection Program. The *Plain Dealer* reported, "Ferritto will be given a new identity and will serve the sentence under the federal protected witness program. If he survives the prison term he will be relocated at federal expense."

The Case Against "Sparky" Monica

John G. "Sparky" Monica was the Los Angeles bookmaker Julius Petro tried to muscle in on in January 1969, which resulted in his murder by Ray Ferritto and Robert Walsh. The case remained dormant until January 1978, when Ferritto confessed to it in the wake of the Danny Greene car-bombing murder in Cleveland. At that time, Ferritto gave up Monica as the man who paid $5,000 to have Petro killed, and Robert Walsh, who helped carry out the murder.

On June 2, 1978, a Complaint Felony was signed in Los Angeles Municipal Court charging Monica with Petro's murder. Nothing more was heard on the matter until the spring of 1979. On April 15, Robert S. Charney, who once worked for Monica, entered the Sherman Oaks home of Reta M. Wolkin, the former girlfriend of Monica, but as of March 1978 was officially his mother-in-law, and attacked her. Wolkin, described as in ill health and suffering from disabling arthritis, was "severely punched and kicked, then beaten with the heel of a shoe." All this took place in the presence of Lori Lynn Monica, John's estranged wife and Reta Wolkin's daughter. Lori was also struck several times by Charney, who warned her, "If she stays out of it she will not be hurt."

The *Los Angeles Times* determined "it" was the murder trial of "Sparky" Monica for the killing of Julius Petro. The newspaper stated, Reta was "slated to be the leadoff witness in the trial," and that Charney, "a former hot-tub salesman" was charged with four felony counts for the attack on her.

Charney was identified from a police artist's sketch prepared after descriptions of the assailant were provided by Reta and Lori. He was arrested after several days of investigation by the LAPD's Organized Crime Intelligence Division, which included helicopter surveillance of his home. Police charged Charney with assault with the intent to commit great bodily harm; attempting to dissuade a witness from testifying; burglary, and conspiracy to obstruct justice in the beating of Reta Wolkin. Charney was held in jail with bail set initially at $200,000 until Municipal Judge Gabriel Gutierrez reduced it in half, which Charney was still unable to raise.

The newspaper mentioned several times that Reta Wolkin was a witness to the murder of Petro. There was never anything written about what she witnessed or what she would testify about. This author believes she may have been in the home of Monica the night before Petro was killed and may have overheard the planning of the murder.

The Wolkin home was placed under 24-hour surveillance after the attack. On April 26, around midnight, three teenaged boys, 13, 14, and 15, decided to go for a joyride in the automobile of the mother of one of the boys. They apparently began by pushing the car down the street to get it away from the residence before starting it. The older boys were pushing the car, while the 13-year-old steered the vehicle. The boys were spotted by two police officers in a patrol car and ordered to stop. Instead, the two older boys fled. The 13-year-old was taken into custody at the scene, while the 14-year-old, whose mother owned the car, was found in a carport not far away.

The third youth, 15-year-old Carlos Washington, was not so lucky. He scaled a six-foot cinderblock wall behind the house heading into the backyard of the Wolkin home, which three police officers were there to guard. One officer shouted "Police! Freeze!" He didn't. Three shots rang out, one hitting the young man in the head. Washington was rushed to Sherman Oaks Community Hospital, where he was listed in critical condition. The initial reporting of the shooting to the newspaper people failed to identify the person's name, race or any details of what happened. Thirteen days later, Washington, who was still unconscious and being kept alive with a mechanical life support system, died. The police shooting drew immediate criticism as it came at a time when the police department was embattled in a controversy over its shooting policy and tactics. The incident not only gained state-wide attention, it was also reported in newspapers in nearly every major city across the country and in Canada.

On June 18, Reta Wolkin told newspaper reporters the police officers stationed at her home around the clock have become increasingly "brutal, mean and ugly," in the past three weeks. She offered nothing in the way of a reason that may have triggered this. She said when they first started working there, they were polite. But the situation rapidly deteriorated. "We have come to resent the officers," she claimed. "I have asked them to leave."

On October 18, the investigation into the death of Carlos Washington was made public. Deputy District Attorney Gilbert Garcetti,[63] who supervised the inquiry, announced, "Based on our analysis of all available evidence and applicable law, we have concluded that the very unfortunate and tragic killing of Carlos Washington was justifiable homicide under California law."[64] An attorney representing the Washington family said she intended to file a $5 million wrongful death suit against the city of Los Angeles and the officer involved.

The case against "Sparky" Monica had more problems in addition to the beating of a key witness and the tragic death of a teenaged youth. During a preliminary hearing on Wednesday, May 16, 1979, Municipal Court Judge George W. Trammell III refused a defense motion to close the hearing to the media, stating that the public had a right to know about the case and its possible Mafia connections. Little did Trammell know that his decision to fight the law would result in a two-year, nine-month delay in just getting Monica to be put on trial; not to mention the 13 years since the actual murder of Julius Petro.

Monica was represented by attorneys Barry Tarlow and Richard Fannin, who argued that "prejudicial publicity" would hurt their client's right to a fair trial. Fannin told the judge, "There is no way the public will not hear about the case. They will simply hear it at a later time." On Tarlow and Fannin's side was California Penal Code Section 868, which mandated that such hearings be held in secret out of the presence of the media at the request of criminal defendants, which allowed for a closed hearing. Trammell claimed the law was unconstitutional and violated First and Sixth Amendment rights. His position was the defendant's right to secrecy was outweighed by the public's rights in the Monica case because it allegedly revealed "Mafia entrenchment" in California.

Before the day was out, the 2nd District Court of Appeals ordered that Trammell be "prohibited from continuing any further preliminary hearing [in the case] except in conformity with Penal Code Section 868," or show cause. Trammell saw the higher court's edict as an "either-or" order. He claimed he could either proceed with the closed hearing and bar the media, or continue the case and show cause. He announced he would reschedule the hearing for the next morning at 8:30 and announce his decision at that time. The confident judge declared, "They haven't closed the door. If I take them up on the offer to show cause I will get a full-blown hearing."

On Thursday morning, Judge Trammell took up the challenge of the Appeals Court and said he would show cause why the preliminary hearing in a gangland slaying should not be closed to the public and the media. He then postponed the preliminary hearing until June 29, at which time he said U.S. Attorney General Griffin B. Bell was subpoenaed to appear as a witness for the defense. The judge defended his decision for a show-cause hearing before the Appellate Court stating, "this is a good case to test the issue on, and I want it litigated."

Deputy District Attorney Michael Brenner, who was prosecuting the case, stated he did not oppose the challenge to Penal Code Section 868, but told Trammell the district attorney's office desired to work out some "accommodation" with the news media representatives in order for the Monica trial to go forward. Brenner expressed his concerns because of Reta Wolkin, who he described as being in poor health and frightened for her life.

Tarlow declared the press would sensationalize the proceedings and turn it into a media circus. He said his defense would be based on showing that Jimmy Fratianno was responsible for ordering the murder of Petro.

On Friday, the 2nd District Court of Appeals refused to overturn the 107-year-old statute by declaring it "constitutionally should be decided by the California Supreme Court." The court backed away from making the decision because they decided that at the Appeals Court level it could risk the reversal of past criminal convictions, but it "urged the high court to review the issue." In the opinion of one of the justices, he said he believed the "state Constitution, which gives a defendant the right to a fair trial, should be interpreted to give the public a right to be present at the defendant's preliminary hearing." In essence, the decision ordered Trammell "to close the preliminary hearing under the provisions of Penal Code Section 868 and begin taking testimony."

After the court's decision, Trammell told reporters, "If in any way that order can be reasonably construed to give me the option to pursue on up to the Supreme Court, that is what I am going to do. I intend to do everything I possibly can legally to keep my courtroom open to the press." That's exactly the course Judge Trammell pursued.

On June 25, in a 22-page legal brief, Judge Trammell asked the California Supreme Court to strike down Penal Code Section 868. The key points of his brief were:

- The 107-year-old law violates both the California and U.S. constitutions

- Public trial guarantees are emasculated if a defendant can close a preliminary hearing without showing that having it open would harm his right to a fair trial

- That Penal Code Section 868 violates the separation of powers between the Legislature and the judiciary because it usurps the role of the judge in balancing the rights of the defendant with the rights of the public

A whole year passed without any action in the preliminary hearing. During the summer of 1981, the hearing was finally held and closed to the public. The hearing was to decide if Monica should be held to answer the murder charges in Los Angeles Supreme Court. During the hearing Ray Ferritto testified and implicated Monica, but Jimmy Fratianno did not appear. As for Reta Wolkin, it was reported that "a subsequent illness disrupted her courtroom appearances." A newspaper article commenting on Robert Walsh, reported that Ferritto's "alleged accomplice" had yet to be found by authorities and was believed to have fled the country.

The month-long hearing ended in late August. The public waited weeks and then months for Judge Trammell's decision. In early November, it was reported the decision would be handed down on November 6. When that date arrived, Trammell told attorneys for both sides he would make his ruling on December 18. Trammell later said the delay was due to having to deal with a series of defense motions.

Nearly two months passed and then on February 5, 1982, Judge Trammell ruled there was enough evidence to bring Monica to trial for the murder. The judge ordered him to appear on February 22 for his arraignment in Superior Court. Prosecutor Michael Brenner said it was "probably" the oldest active murder case in the history of Los Angeles. During the months leading up to the judge's decision, Robert S. Charney, who had attacked Reta Wolkin and her daughter, was tried and convicted on charges of assault, attempting to dissuade a witness from testifying, burglary and conspiracy to obstruct justice. His conviction was upheld; he served a prison sentence and was placed on probation. Meanwhile, from the time of his indictment in the spring of 1978, Monica had remained free on his own recognizance.

Around February 12, 1982, ten days before he was scheduled to go to court, Monica rented a car and drove to New Mexico, checking into a motel in Roswell. He stayed in the motel for three hours, made a long distance telephone call and left. Driving east, he passed through Carlsbad, New Mexico, where he was issued a traffic citation. Authorities believed he was headed for Odessa, Texas, where he may have had a girlfriend. On February 13, Monica was driving west on U.S. 70; he could have been headed back to Los Angeles.

While approaching Tularosa, New Mexico, a vehicle driven by 19-year-old David M. Gomez, made an illegal U-turn in front of Monica, who slammed into him, broadsiding the vehicle. Monica died instantly from massive head and chest injuries; Gomez and his passenger were treated for cuts and minor injuries. When authorities went through Monica's automobile, they found only a jacket and a pair of exercise shorts, no other clothing. Monica's death was reported in a one-paragraph article in the *Los Angeles Times*, some six days after the fatal accident. It wasn't until March 17, more than a month after his death, that an *El Paso Times* article appeared with more details of the accident and death of the late "Sparky" Monica.

The Non-Trial of "Bobby" Walsh

On February 13, 1982, Robert "Bobby" Walsh became the only person left to answer for the murder of Julius Petro some 13 years earlier. Nearly the whole time they were trying to get "Sparky" Monica into a courtroom from 1979 to 1982, Walsh was on the lam. By 1984, he was in custody and starting to do time for the crimes he had committed in 1980 and 1981. By 1993 he was about to be paroled, but he had one more issue hanging over his head – his role in Julius Petro's death.

Before he was released from prison, he contacted his son Dennis, who was now working as a defense attorney. The father asked his son to contact Ray Ferritto to see if he was going to testify against him in the Petro murder case. Dennis recalls the conversation:

> When I called Ray, sometime in 1992 or 1993, I did not know how he might react. His voice told me that he was pleased to hear from me. We chatted for a while before I got to the point of the call. I reminded him that the first time I ever drove on the freeway was with him on the way to Dodger Stadium after I had just gotten my driver's license.
>
> "I guess I shoulda had you driving when we offed that Irish prick," he said.
>
> Ray was referring to Danny Greene. After Ronnie Carabbia had detonated the bomb, Ray made the mistake of speeding away. A woman who heard the explosion had written down a partial plate number from Ray's car. That was the beginning of the end of the Cleveland Mafia.
>
> When I eventually got around to the Julius Petro murder, Ray told me that the L.A. District Attorney had tried to have him ordered to appear in California to testify, but a Pennsylvania judge refused to allow it.
>
> "Tell your dad not to worry, I ain't coming out there," he promised.

As an attorney representing his father, Dennis Walsh went to court and requested a speedy trial for his client, but the district attorney was unable to produce Ferritto to testify. Dennis Walsh relates that Ferritto never came to California and Robert Walsh never had to answer for his role in the killing. With that, it was case closed, and no one ever went to trial for the murder of Julius Petro.

Julius Anthony Petro – Cleveland's Handsomest Public Enemy

All photographs are from the Cleveland Public Library Photograph Collection, except where noted otherwise.

Julius Petro in the Cuyahoga County Jail in December 1947, after being granted a new trial by the Ohio Supreme Court for the February 1946 murder of Theodore "Bobby" Knaus. Petro spent 17 months on "death row."

Julius Petro at his re-trial during June 1948 for the "Bobby" Knaus murder. *CSU / Cleveland Press Collection*

Julius Petro signing paperwork on June 16, 1948, after being acquitted of the "Bobby" Knaus murder at his re-trial.

On Dec. 2, 1952, Petro heads back to the County Jail after the first day of trial for the $71,000 robbery of a Warren branch bank manager.

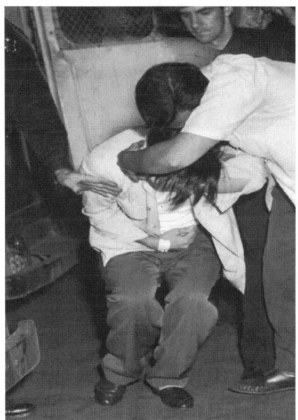

A few days after being shot by an Alliance, Ohio, police officer, on June 4, 1950, a wounded Julius Petro is assisted from a Cleveland Police paddy wagon by his brother Michael, while both try to duck the camera.

Julius Petro and Joseph Sanzo after their arrests on Oct. 6, 1952, for the daring holdup of a Warren branch bank manager and making off with $71,000.

Mrs. June Petro entering the Federal Courthouse for her husband's trial on December 2, 1952. She gave up a promising career as a mezzo soprano, singing for the Stan Kenton orchestra, for a three-and-a-half-year marriage to Julius Petro.

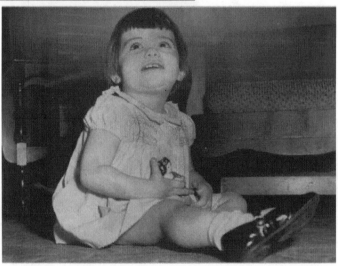

The marriage of June Guentzler and Julius Petro produced one off-spring, a daughter named Juliet.

From 1945 to 1965, Steve Cochran was a leading man of the stage, silver screen and television. Attorney and author Dennis M. Walsh, one of the few people interviewed who actually knew Julius Petro, claimed Cochran was the spitting image of the burglar. While one can easily see a difference between the picture of Cochran compared to shots of Petro from the late 1940s to the early 1950s, when he was in his mid 20s, Walsh didn't meet Petro until the mid-1960s, when he was in his early 40s. *IMDb*

The "Bobby" Knaus Murder

Located at 5393 St. Clair Avenue, just west of Marquette Street, sits what used to be known as Bertha's Café, from at least the early 1940s to the mid-1960s. Julius Petro was one of a trio of hoods who robbed the owner's daughter of some $10,000 on October 23, 1942. Arrested, convicted and sent the Mansfield Reformatory, there Petro would meet and befriend Theodore "Bobby" Knaus. *Google Earth*

Behind this undeveloped wooded area along Belvoir Blvd. runs Nine-mile Creek through a deep gorge, which snakes its way between Euclid Avenue to the north, and Monticello Blvd. to the south. Not far from here, on March 2, 1946, two young hikers discovered the body of Theodore "Bobby" Knaus, lying partly in the creek. *Google Earth*

5914 Vandalia Avenue, home where "Bobby" Knaus lived with his mother and the last place he was seen alive. *Google Earth*

787 East 156th Street, where Julius Petro was living at the time of the murder of "Bobby" Knaus. Evidence was removed from the home tying him to the Green Café burglary. *Google Earth*

Knaus Murder - Top Cops

Detective Lieutenant Martin P. Cooney, in charge of the Cleveland Police Department's Homicide Unit in 1946, realized an irony regarding the discovery of Knaus' body. He pointed out that, "This might be one of those rare cases where the murderer was actually in jail before the body of the victim was even found." This irony would one day come back to haunt Cooney. *CSU / Cleveland Press Collection*

Veteran Detective Inspector Charles O. Nevel kept reporters abreast of where the department stood in the Knaus murder investigation. Nevel announced they recovered a sack of coins from Petro's home containing many foreign ones that were identified as coming from the Green Café. He confirmed that the Bertillon Bureau concluded all three .32 spent cartridges, the two found in Petro's car and the third one found at the murder scene, were all fired from the same weapon.

Knaus Murder – Key Testimony

Dr. Samuel R. Gerber served as Cuyahoga County coroner from 1937 to 1986. His ruling of the time of death of Theordore "Bobby" Knaus would be a key point in both trials. *Cleveland State University*

Dr. Irene Levis, a consultant in spectroscopy and microanalysis, was under police protection after she received a telephone call threatening vengeance if she "dared to testify" against Julius Petro. *Cleveland State University*

Sergeant James K. Dodge, the police department's firearms expert. He testified the "fine grooving" on bullets taken from Knaus's body matched the grooves on the bullet found in the door of Petro's car. *CSU / Cleveland Press Collection*

Superintendent David Cowles, of the police department's Scientific Identification Bureau, fired a Colt .32 semi-automatic in the courtroom to show how the spent cartridge cases ejected from the gun, leaving them in the backseat of Petro's car where detectives found them.

Knaus Murder – Defense Attorneys

Defense attorney Michael A. Picciano, served as an Assistant Cuyahoga County Prosecutor under Edward Stanton from 1927 to 1929. In November 1933, he was appointed Chief Police Prosecutor. In June 1934, Law Director Ezra Shapiro removed three members of Picciano's staff, including his chief assistant, and two other assistants. When Harold Burton was elected mayor in November 1935, Picciano's prosecutorial career came to an end. He went on to have a long career as a defense attorney working many cases with Stanton. He died in April 1977. *CSU / Cleveland Press Collection*

Defense attorney Edward C. Stanton served four terms as Cuyahoga County Prosecutor from 1920 to 1928. During that time he handled some of Cleveland's most famous cases. Among them George "Jiggs" Losteiner, the murder of Dan Kaber, and the killing of Harold Kagy. In the Kagy case, the victim was in the company of William H. McGannon, Chief Justice of the Municipal Court, when shot. The day before Stanton took office, the murders of West Side businessmen Wilfred Sly and George Fanner took place. *CSU / Cleveland Press Collection*

Knaus Murder – Prosecutor

Assistant Cuyahoga County Prosecutor Victor DeMarco took a totally circumstantial case against two wily defense attorneys twice, winning the first battle and losing the second. The difference in the two cases, the jury. DeMarco claimed, "They freed a guilty man." Julius Petro said of DeMarco, "He's the greatest lawyer I've ever seen." *CSU / Cleveland Press Collection*

Knaus Murder – Judge

Cuyahoga County Common Pleas Judge Alva R. Corlett was more of a referee than a judge, as he handled the verbal confrontations between the two legal teams.

Green Acres Casino Robbery

Sam Jerry Monachino was referred to by the *Plain Dealer* as the "30-year-old jinx of the police," and "the cop-hating hoodlum." He was a suspect in the holdups at the Mounds Club in 1947 and the Green Acres casino in Struthers, in 1948. During the latter, it was alleged an expensive ring was taken from Mafia big-wig "Joe the Wolf" DiCarlo. The attempted pawning of the ring brought mob hitmen to the home of Monachino days later. *Cleveland Police Department Mug Shot*

Margaret Monachino heard her husband cry out, "Honey! Honey! Help!" Despite being eight months pregnant, Margaret raced barefoot out of the house to aid him. She watched as a gunman, dressed in a topcoat, chased and shot at her husband, as Sam ran toward the home. Several slugs brought Monachino down, and as Margaret drew nearer, the shooter fired the last of his bullets into him as he lay in the gutter. *CSU / Cleveland Press Collection*

2555 East 127th Street, the home where Margaret and Sam Jerry Monachino were living when Sam was murdered in the street. *Google Earth*

Green Acres Casino Robbery – Top Cops

Detective Lieutenant David E. Kerr, head of the homicide squad, was sure that the principals of the Green Acres casino would never sign a warrant to have Petro arrested. Kerr, bitter about not being able to get the bullet from Petro's chest, claimed they may have been able to prove the same gun was used in the shooting of Petro and the murder of Monachino.

When Inspector Frank W. Story was called to Emergency Clinic Hospital, around midnight, on September 17, 1948, he immediately identified a wounded man as Julius Petro. Doctors were treating him for wounds in the right chest and right arm; one of his ribs was shattered by a bullet. When Story questioned him, Petro claimed he was shot "accidentally while out drinking with the boys."

Cleveland Police homicide detective George Gackowski received little help from Petro. He told the detective he was drunk from a "two-day bender" and had no idea what happened. One thing Petro did tell Gackowski was he was treated earlier by another doctor, whom he refused to identify, that removed the bullet which entered his chest.

Green Acres Casino Robbery –
Youngstown Top Cops

Legendary Youngstown Police Chief Edward J. "Eddie" Allen. After reform candidate Charles P. Henderson was elected mayor of Youngstown in November 1947, FBI Director J. Edgar Hoover personally recommended Allen, the former Erie, Pennsylvania, police officer, to Henderson to clean up the crime-ridden city. *CSU / Cleveland Press Collection*

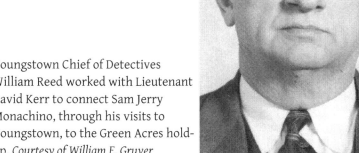

Youngstown Chief of Detectives William Reed worked with Lieutenant David Kerr to connect Sam Jerry Monachino, through his visits to Youngstown, to the Green Acres holdup. *Courtesy of William E. Gruver*

Green Acres Casino Robbery – Mafia Connection

Youngstown / Buffalo Mafia leader Joseph "Joe the Wolf" DiCarlo was born into Mafia royalty. His father was once the Mafia boss of Buffalo, New York. *CSU / Cleveland Press Collection*

The infamous Jungle Inn operated from the mid-1930s until it was raided and closed by state liquor agents in August 1949. *Bruce Birrell Collection*

Warren Robbery – 1952

Kenilworth Avenue in Warren, OH, scene of the robbery on August 14, 1952. Charles J. Foley, branch manager of the Union Savings & Trust Company, was robbed of $71,000 by Julius Petro and two others, near the home of Ida Campbell. *Google Earth*

Oak Knoll Avenue, part of the escape route. After making a right hand turn onto Oak Knoll Avenue from Montclair and heading south, Julius Petro almost hit a car containing H. Carter Alden and his mother, Abbie. *Google Earth*

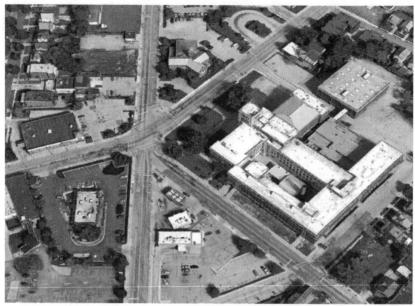

Aerial view of Cleveland's Five-Points neighborhood in Collinwood. St. Clair Avenue runs east and west; East 152nd Street runs north and south; while Ivanhoe Road intersects from the south east. Collinwood High School is the large structure on the right. *Google Earth*

The Grotto Inn, 16136 St. Clair Avenue, was in operation from 1935 until 2013, when it was gutted by a fire. Today it is a vacant lot. Joseph Sanzo exchanged recorded bills from the Warren robbery of bank branch manager Charles J. Foley there, helping to lead to his arrest in October 1952 for the crime. *Google Earth*

Warren Robbery – 1952
Villains & Victim

Julius Petro and Joseph Sanzo, two of the three participants in the
$71,000 robbery of Charles J. Foley, branch manager of the Union Savings & Trust Company in August 1952. The third man, known by police, was never named or arrested for the crime. *CSU / Cleveland Press Collection*
Joseph Sanzo. *Cleveland Police Dept. Mug Shot*

Charles J. Foley, branch bank manager of the Union Savings
& Trust Company, located on Woodland Avenue in Warren,
who was robbed of $71,000. Warren *Tribune Chronicle*

Warren Robbery – 1952
Top Cops & FBI

Detective Chief James McArthur dispatched detectives to the homes of Julius Petro and Joseph Sanzo to greet the pair upon their return from Warren on August 14, 1952.

Detective Lieutenant Thomas P. White was responsible for picking up, grilling and arresting Julius Petro and Joseph Sanzo for the Warren robbery in October 1952.

Paul J. Shine, Special-Agent-in-Charge of the Cleveland FBI office, immediately devised and supervised a "cat and mouse" game using 12 FBI agents, assigned full-time to the case, to shadow Petro's and Sanzo's every move. In addition, over the next month, 29 other agents participated in helping to cover the pair.

FBI Agent Stanley E. Peterson, assigned in the Mahoning Valley, met with the Aldens the night of the robbery. The following morning, he drove them to Cleveland where they picked Petro and Sanzo out of a police line-up. Peterson would have a tarnished record in the years to come. *CSU / Cleveland Press Collection*

Warren Robbery – 1952
Eyewitnesses

Abbie and H. Carter Alden are escorted by a U.S. Marshal on their way to the Federal Courthouse in Cleveland on December 2, 1952. Petro was stunned when Carter Alden took the stand. Petro had no idea he had actually been identified on the day of the robbery.

Warren Robbery – 1952
Prosecutors & Defense Counsel

U.S. Attorney John J. Kane, Jr. and Assistant U.S. Attorney Frank E. Steel would prosecute the case against Petro and Sanzo for the government. The two men were classmates, along with Don C. Miller at Notre Dame University. Miller was a member of the fearsome Four Horsemen of Notre Dame football backfield. When Miller was named U.S. Attorney in Cleveland, he brought in his two former classmates.

Louis Fernberg represented Petro and Sanzo through the arraignment. Petro may have already had Picciano and Stanton waiting on retainer for the trial.

Michael A. Picciano and Edward C. Stanton. *CSU / Cleveland Press Collection*

Warren Robbery – 1952
Federal Judge

U.S. District Court Judge Charles J. McNamee ran a commendable no-non-sense trial, despite various twists and turns put on by the veteran defense team. After a nine-day trial, it took the jury just 95 minutes to reach a verdict.

Warren Robbery – 1952 - Misguided Witness and His Nemesis

Dr. Alexander V. Spaeth was Sanzo's surprise alibi witness, claiming that the defendant was in his medical office the morning of the robbery. This, despite a previous alibi witness already testifying that Sanzo was at his Five Points gasoline station getting a fill-up at the same time. Spaeth produced an obviously altered Medical Record Card to support Sanzo's presence there. After the robbery trial, Spaeth was convicted of perjury in three separate trials, only to win retrials on appeal in the first two. God only knows why the doctor stood by his testimony, ruining himself financially and destroying his successful career.

Joseph Tholl, "a Cleveland expert on questioned documents," was contacted by attorney Picciano to be a rebuttal witness to the FBI document expert during the robbery trial. But after viewing the FBI photograph of the Medical Record Card during a recess, Tholl realized the doctor didn't have a leg to stand on. At the end of the recess, Picciano told McNamee he would be calling no rebuttal witnesses. Tholl would testify for the government in all three Spaeth perjury trials.

(L to R) Defense counsel William J. Corrigan, Dr. Alexander V. Spaeth and associate counsel Timothy F. McMahon. Even the legendary defense attorney William Corrigan could not help the misguided Dr. Spaeth. Corrigan retired from the case following the first trial after receiving a request to represent an even more infamous doctor.

Petro's Collinwood Gang - 1948 to 1952

Philip Aliberti, *Police Mug Book*

Anthony Paul D'Alessio, *Police Mug Book*

Ralph "Bull" De Biase, *Cleveland Police Dept. Mug Shot*

Joseph W. Drago, *Police Mug Book*

Vincent Innocenzi, *CSU / Cleveland Press Collection*

Dominic Mafrici

Thomas E. "Laughing Tommy" Rudelik, *Police Mug Book*

Joseph R. Russo

David F. Tiburzio, *Police Mug Book*

Associate Members of the Gang - 1952 – 1970s

Joseph J. Arrington,
Police Mug Book

Alfred A. "Allie"
Calabrese

Paul F. "Red"
Carpenter

John M. Delzoppo,
Police Mug Book

Michael Grande, *Police
Mug Book*

Joseph C. "Joe I."
Ilacqua. *Cleveland
Police Dept. Mug Shot*

Sylvestro "Studo"
Papalardo. *Cleveland
Police Dept. Mug Shot*

Charles C. Skubo-
vis, *Police Mug Book*

Anthony "Joe Blow"
Velletto, *Police Mug
Book*

Petro's Los Angeles Crime Connections – 1965 to 1969

Raymond W. Ferritto, became a good friend of Robert "Bobby" Walsh. In the mid-1960s, he took his family and relocated from Erie, PA, to the West Coast to be near him. There he also met Julius Petro, who he quickly grew to dislike. Ferritto ended up murdering Petro at the request of bookie John G. "Sparky" Monica. *Cleveland Police Dept Mug Shot*

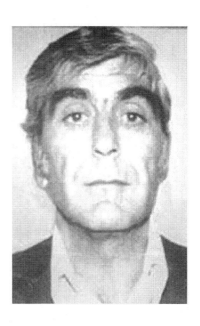

Frank J. "Skinny" Velotta, a Cleveland born burglary specialist and cousin of Julius Petro. He aspired to West Coast Mafia membership. Velotta died on February 12, 2005. *Cleveland Police Dept. Mug Shot*

Alan E. Walch found 1965 to be a busy year. In February, an eyewitness told police he saw him on East 101st Street as he gunned down Benjamin Feigenbaum, owner of the Seventy-Niner Café. Over that summer, Walch was called before a grand jury investigating violence in Local 17 of the Bridge, Structural & Ornamental Iron Workers Union. Acquitted of the Feigenbaum murder in October, the following year someone set off a bomb in Walch's wife's car. Walch needed a change of scenery and went to Los Angeles to visit his friend, Robert "Bobby" Walsh. *Cleveland Police Dept. Mug Shot*

Robert E. "Bobby" Walsh, was a one-time Cleveland Police detective, before retiring in 1956. When his and Frank Velotta's burglary activities attracted the attention of J. Edgar Hoover in the mid-1960s, he was forced to leave Cleveland and moved to Los Angeles. In January 1969, while Walsh sat next to Julius Petro in a Cadillac at Los Angeles International Airport, Ray Ferritto put a bullet in the back of Petro's head.

Robert E. "Bobby" Walsh
& Family

Robert E. "Bobby" Walsh in the mid-1950s when he was a detective in the Cleveland Police Department. *Courtesy of Dennis M. Walsh*

Robert E. "Bobby" Walsh and his partner, Detective Charles Tuite were inside the United Parking Service Co. at 1850 Prospect Avenue (present home of CSU's Wolstein Center) staking it out in January 1952. When a burglar returned, trying to pull off a repeat performance there, the detectives shot and killed him.

Dennis M. Walsh, attorney and author, helped put the people responsible for his youngest brother's death in prison. He captured the ordeal in his book *Nobody Walks: Bringing My Brother's Killers to Justice*. In asking Walsh if he knew Julius Petro, he told me, "Yes, he used to drive me to high school." Dennis has provided me with more details on Petro, Ray Ferritto, and his father, Robert "Bobby" Walsh than I could ever have gathered from books and newspapers. *Photo courtesy of Craig Endler*

Timothy Walsh paid a visit to his father after he had heard that old family friend Raymond Ferritto had made a deal with the government to spill his guts. At the time, Robert "Bobby" Walsh was serving a sentence in Chino. Tim was then sent to the dog house! *Courtesy of Dennis M. Walsh*

Los Angeles Mafia Connections
1965 – 1969

Aladena James "Jimmy the Weasel" Fratianno, was born in Naples, Italy, but grew up in Cleveland, Ohio. In 1937, he was convicted of a robbery and spent seven years in the Ohio Penitentiary. Once out, he headed to California, where he climbed the ladder in the Los Angeles Mafia Family, reaching the role of Acting Boss in the mid-1970s. He hooked up with several Cleveland burglars who had relocated there including Julius Petro, Frank "Skinny" Velotta, and Robert "Bobby" Walsh. *Los Angeles Police Dept. Mug Shot*

Nicholas Licata, was born in Sicily in 1897 and arrived in America in 1913. During the Prohibition years he was a bootlegger in Detroit. He left the Motor City for Los Angeles after offending Detroit Mafia boss Joseph Zerilli. In Los Angeles, he became close with boss Jack Dragna, and climbed the ranks. In 1951, he provided an alibi for Jimmy Fratianno after the murders of Anthony Brancato and Anthony Trombino. In 1967, Licata became boss of the Los Angeles Mafia family. *Mafia Wiki Website*

Pierino "Pete" DiGravio was a popular and well-liked money-lender who worked out of a Little Italy business office known as the MDM Investment Company. In May 1968, the government enacted laws to prevent loan sharks from lending money at exorbitant rates. On June 21, DiGravio was playing golf at Orchard Hills Golf & Country Club in Chesterland. On the 16th hole, a sniper hiding in the bushes opened fire and killed him. The FBI investigation into the death of Julius Petro alleged a connection to DiGravio, and a suggestion that the loan shark's death was related to events that occurred in southern California. *CSU / Cleveland Press Collection*

Murder of Danny Greene – 1977

Daniel J. "Danny" Greene, also known as the "Irishman," was a colorful character in the annals of Cleveland organized crime history. He was fearless, he was deadly, and he was hard to kill. Former Clevelander Jimmy Fratianno, who had befriended Ray Ferritto in Los Angeles and knew about him murdering Julius Petro, recommended him to Cleveland Mafia boss Jack Licavoli. The recommendation had two results. The end of Danny Greene, and the end of the Cleveland Mafia. *Cleveland Police Dept Mug Shot*

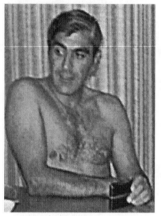

Raymond W. Ferritto was identified as a participant in the murder of Danny Greene shortly after the car bombing. Part of his demise was due to some shoddy car registration work by Pasquale "Butchie" Cisternino. Ferritto soon was spilling his guts. At the same time, Jimmy Fratianno was confirmed publicly as being an FBI informant. Because Ferritto had exposed his role in the Petro murder to Fratianno, Ferritto knew he would have to confess that killing to the government, and give up his friend Robert "Bobby" Walsh. *Photo courtesy of Dennis M. Walsh*

Ronald D. Carabbia could scarcely say he just went along for the ride. He was quickly exposed as the man sitting in the back seat, who actually pushed the button setting the bomb off that killed Danny Greene. He ended up having 24 years to think about that decision. Released from prison in 2002, he enjoyed nearly 20 years of freedom prior to passing away in December 2021, at the age of 92. *Youngstown Police Dept Mug Shot*

Pasquale "Butchie" Cisternino, along with Ronald Carabbia, were the only people convicted for the murder of Danny Greene. Cisternino was behind bars for 13 years before passing away in November 1990. *FBI Mug Shot*

Alfred S. "Allie" Calabrese was often mis-identified, even on this mug shot, as being Allie Calabrese, Jr. He and his father, however, had different middle names. Indicted for the murder of Danny Greene with eight others, he was the only defendant Common Pleas Judge John J. Carroll dismissed the charges against. *Cleveland Police Dept. Mug Shot*

James "Jack White" Licavoli was involved in underworld activities in St. Louis, Detroit, and Toledo before settling down in Cleveland. In 1975, upon the death of Cleveland Mafia leader John Scalish, Licavoli took over as boss. In the years following the bombing death of Danny Greene in 1977, the Cleveland Mafia family would be decimated in court cases. Licavoli was convicted of conspiracy to kill Green in July 1982 and died in prison on November 23, 1985. *Cleveland Police Dept. Mug Shot*

Wahoo Bar Burglary &
A Murder in Alliance
The Victim

Eldon E. "Pete" Shoup, while in high school, became a golfing legend in the Alliance area. At the age of 17, he was a qualifier for the National Junior Championship of the U.S. Golf Association. After school and time in the Coast Guard, "Pete" Shoup remained a local legend in Alliance and Stark County for his golf prowess. By February 1957, Shoup was 25-years-old, married, and he and his wife, Helen, had one daughter and another child on the way.

Eldon E. "Pete" Shoup's headstone at St. Joseph's Church Cemetery, in Alliance, Ohio. *Author's Collection*

Eldon E. "Pete" Shoup's Military Headstone, denoting his service in the United States Coast Guard, at St. Joseph's Church Cemetery, in Alliance, Ohio. *Author's Collection*

Eldon E. "Pete" Shoup murder scene, the home of Frank Wells, 2815 Ridgewood Avenue, in the Mount Union neighborhood of Alliance, Ohio. *Author's Collection*

Wahoo Bar Burglary &
A Murder in Alliance
The Villains

Alfred A. Calabrese and Paul Perotti, although neither man pulled the trigger that killed "Pete" Shoup, they were both involved in the burglary of the Wells' home. Both men put their families and friends through hell trying to concoct alibies in three different states to prove their innocence in the crime. In the end, they spent more time in prison for it than the two men responsible for the actual killing.

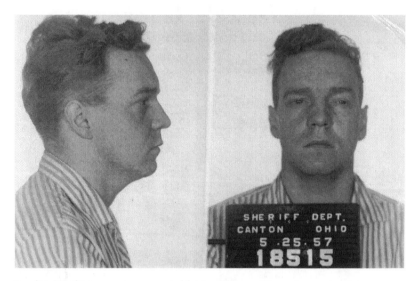

SHERIFF DEPT.
CANTON OHIO
5.25.57
18515

Paul F. "Red" Carpenter once told *Akron Beacon Journal* reporter Ray Warner, "I never was good at anything. I always felt like a weakling until I started running with the boys. Then I felt OK. I met the mob." Claiming his first marriage didn't work out, Carpenter stated, when it came to his second wife, he said, "I love her very much. I hoped if I could hold off talking about the Alliance thing – well. I just had in the back of my mind that if I held out maybe we would have a chance." It was because of Betty that he didn't confess to it after he was shot. But the murder "kept preying on my mind. I had to talk about it." Only because he had run out of people he could rat out.

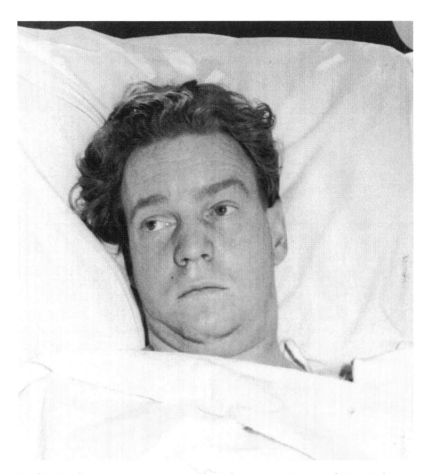

Paul F. "Red' Carpenter recovering in Lake County Memorial Hospital in Painesville. After calling "Allie" Calabrese for financial help, it came in the way of a gunman who fired three slugs into him and then buried him in a shallow grave. After crawling out, he informed Akron police about the Wahoo Bar burglary and named all the participants. But he had one more crime to rat out.

Wahoo Bar Burglary &
A Murder in Alliance
Top Cop & Prosecutor

Paul F. "Red" Carpenter, John S. Ballard, & Akron Police Captain Carroll Cutright in conference over the Alliance murder of "Pete" Shoup. When the Wahoo Bar burglary trial ended in a mistrial, "Red" decided it was time to rat out even more of his cohorts. He then confessed to the murder of "Pete" Shoup.

Summit County Prosecutor John S. Ballard, after graduation from high school, attended the University of Akron. He then enrolled at the University of Michigan Law School. During World War II, he served as an infantry lieutenant under General George S. Patton in Europe. After the war he became a Special Agent of the FBI, serving from 1949 until 1952. Back in Akron he studied law and became an Akron police prosecutor, before being elected Summit County Prosecutor from 1957 to 1964. He finished his public career by serving as mayor for the city of Akron from 1966 to 1979. Ballard passed away on April 21, 2012, at the age of 89. *Internet*

Ernest A. "Ernie" Foti headstone. Foti was once considered a top lieutenant in the notorious Akron gang headed by James LaFatch, which began operating back in the Prohibition days. He was one of the men convicted for the Wahoo Bar burglary. *Find A Grave*

Cleveland Police Department
Top Cops and Safety Directors

Michael "Iron Mike" Blackwell & Safety Director Eliot Ness

Then Lieutenant Martin P. Cooney, *CSU / Cleveland Press Collection*

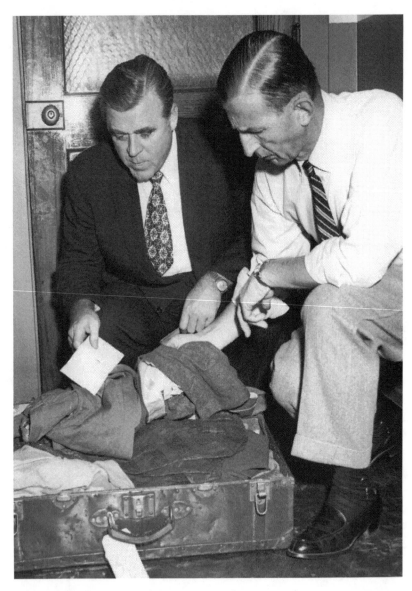

Cleveland Police Homicide Captain David E. Kerr and Inspector James E. McArthur

Cleveland Police Detective William F. Lonchar

Then Captain James E. McArthur in May 1948

Deputy Inspector James E. McArthur, Inspector Charles O. Nevel and Safety Director Alvin J. Sutton

Safety Directors John N. McCormick and Alvin J. Sutton

Safety Director William F. Smith

Then Cleveland Police Lieutenant Frank W. Story

Cleveland Police Detective Nathan Wachs

Detective Lieutenant Thomas P. White

Detective Lieutenant Thomas P. White

Thomas White's Squad Members

Detective William Kaiser

Detective Sergeant Harold C. Lockwood

Detective Samuel Mears

Detective Thomas E. Murphy

Thomas White's Mug Shot Book

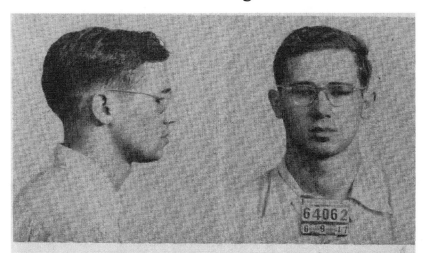

ALIBERTI, Philip   1951 E. 123 St.

27-5-9½-160--Lt. Comp. - Brn. Eyes - Brn. Hair - Med. Bld.

BURGLAR - Assoc. Ray Nero - Tony Dalessio

AUGUSTINO, Nate   5922 Tumey Rd.

38-5-6-145- Dk. Comp. - Brn. Eyes - Blk. Hair - Sl. Bld.

ROBBER - BURGLAR - Assoc. Joe Nunes, Etal.

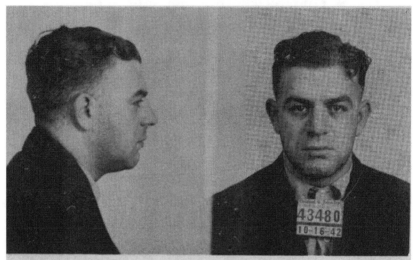

CILENTI, James   10919 Mt. Carmel

41-5-8-160- Lt. Comp. - Brn. Eyes & Hair - Med. Bld.

BURGLAR - BLACKMAILER - Bomber - Countefeit. Assoc. of

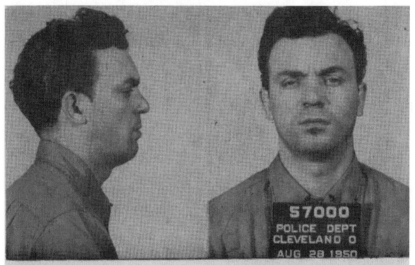

DALESSIO, Tony @ "DAGO"   12231 Wade Park

32-5-8-150- Dk. Comp. - Brn. Eyes - Blk. Hair - Med. Bld.

BURGLAR - SAFE MAN - Assoc. Jerry Pace

DELZOPPO, John Michael   20431 Nicholas, Euclid

23-5-9½-170- Dk. Comp. - Be. Eyes - Blk. Hair - Med. Bld.

BURGLAR - SAFE MAN - Assoc. Eugene Chiara

DI GRAVIO, Peter   2925 Fairmount Blvd.

28-5-9½-170- Lt. Comp. - Brn. Eyes & Hair

PIMP - GAMBLER - Assoc. Thieves

DRAGO, Joseph @ "BLAMPS"   1978 E. 123 St.

30-5-3-140- Med. Comp. - Brn. Eyes & Hair - Med. Bld.

BURGLAR - SAFE MAN - Assoc. any thief.

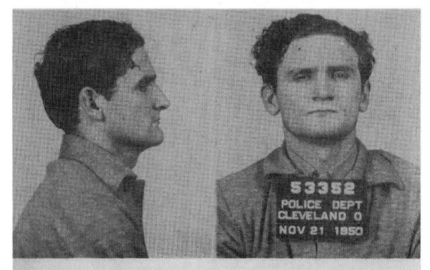

GRANDE, Mike @ "BANANAS"   1784 Crawford Rd.

31-5-5-125- Sallow Comp. - Brn. Eyes - Brn. Hair - Slim Bld.

BURGLAR - All around thief

INNOCENZI, Vincent   1646 E. 70 St.

34-5-9-180- Med. Comp. - Brn. Eyes - Blk. Hair - Med. Bld.

BURGLAR - SAFE MAN

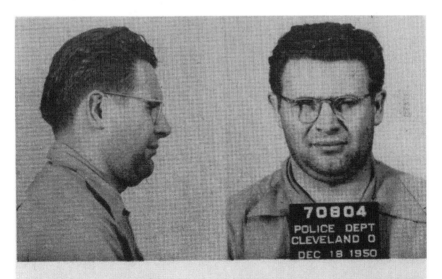

RUDELEK, Thomas   1094 E. 68 St.

30-5-11½-200- Med.Comp. - Brn. Eyes - Brn. Hair - Stocky Bld.

BURGLAR - SAFES -

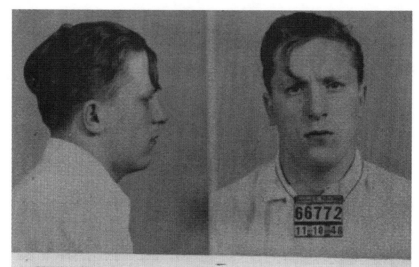

SKUBOVIS, Charles   Avon Lake, O.

29-5-9½-170- Lt. Comp. - Brn. Eyes - Brn. Hair - Med. Bld.

BURGLAR - ROBBER - Assoc. Jim Brooks, Etal.

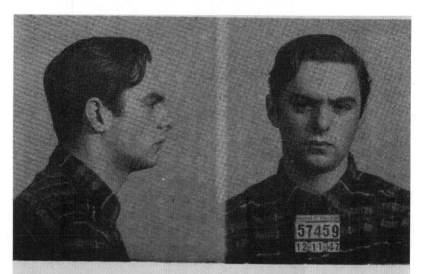

TARTAGLIA, Frank @ "RABBITS"   2063 Murray Hill Rd.

30-5-11½-160- Med. Comp. - Brn. Eyes & Hair - Med. Bld.

BURGLAR - ROBBER - Assoc. Dom Colosimo, Etal.

TIBURZIO, Dave   1381 E. 120 St.

31-5-8½-160- Dk. Comp. - Brn. Eyes - Blk. Hair - Med. Bld.

BURGLAR - STICK UP - Assoc. Joe Drago, Etal.

VELLETTO, Tony   1163 E. 148 St.

39-5-8-208- Stout,- Dk. Comp. - Blk. Hair - Brn. Eyes

BURGLAR - ROBBER

Prosecutors

Federal Prosecutor and later Common
Pleas Judge James J. Carroll

Then Assistant Cuyahoga County
Prosecutor Frank D. Celebreeze

Cuyahoga County Prosecutor
John T. Corrigan
Cleveland State University

Cuyahoga County Prosecutor
Frank T. Cullitan
Cleveland State University

Assistant Cuyahoga County
Prosecutor Carmen Marino

Assistant U.S. District Attorney
Robert J. Rotatori

Common Pleas Judge
John L. Angelotta

Federal Commissioner
Clifford E. Bruce

US District Court Judges Robert B. Krupansky and James C. Connell

Cleveland Municipal
Judge Mary B. Grossman
*Cleveland State
University*

Common Pleas Judge
Harry A. Hanna

Cleveland Municipal
Judge Andrew M.
Kovachy

US District Judge
Thomas D. Lambros

Common Pleas Judge
August Pryatel

. Common Pleas Judge
John M. Manos
CSU/Cleveland Press Collection

U.S. Magistrate Jack B. Streepy

Top Defense Attorneys

Attorney John P. Butler

Attorney Louis Fernberg

Attorney Parker Fulton

Attorney Albert R. Gamble

Attorney Fred Garmone

Attorney Gerald S. Gold
CSU / Cleveland Press Collection

Attorney Harry A. Hanna

Miscellaneous Criminal Associates

Nathan Augustino was a "gangland figure" wannabe. He was questioned in the bombing of the automobile driven by Joseph Drago on the night of May 6, 1955. *Police Mug Book*

Anthony D. Libertore was sentenced to life in prison after the murder of two Cleveland Police officers in 1937. In 1960, he was the only suspect arrested in connection with the murder of Vincent Innocenzi. *Warren Police Department Mug Shot*

James V. Cilenti was called "a jackal" by Common Pleas Judge Alva Corlett. He was a bootlegger, counterfeiter, suspected murderer, burglar, bomber, extortionist and all-around good buddy, business partner, and mentor to Sam Jerry Monachino. *Police Mug Book*

Peter "Petey Boy" Sanzo was the brother of Joseph Sanzo. Peter was involved in a burglary in Maryland in July 1964, with his brother and Alfred S. "Allie" Calabrese, the son of Alfred A., who was serving a life term for the "Pete" Shoup murder. *Cleveland Police Dept. Mug Shot*

Richard Callahan, became a member of Local 17 of the Bridge, Structural & Ornamental Iron-workers Union in the early 1960s. In January 1981, Callahan was convicted of murdering his wife, Fern, in May 1979.

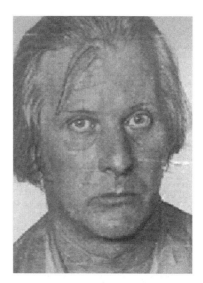

Charles M. Broeckel worked with two of northeast Ohio's most suc-cessful burglars – Amil Dinsio and Philip Christopher. He would one day rat them both out along with all of his other gang associates.
CSU / Cleveland Press Collection

Joseph C. "Joe I" Ilacqua - Biography

Joseph C. "Joe I." Ilacqua, despite coming from a respectable family, lived a life of crime. From a young age he was a Mafioso wannabe, but never made the grade. Still his resume was impressive – armed robbery, bombing, conspiracy, extortion, grand larceny, hijacking, parole violation, possession of burglary tools, possession of stolen goods, possession of stolen liquor, robbery, safe-cracking, sale of illegal liquor, and suspicion of murder. *Cleveland Police Dept. Mug Shot*

John B. Conte, Joe Ilacqua and a third man, aided by insider help, burglarized the Halle Bros. Shaker Square department store on April 23, 1963, getting $9,000 in cash. Ratted out by the insider, all three men did time. In September 1975, police in Austintown, Ohio, found Conte's badly beaten body behind a hotel there. Police discovered that when Conte left home, he told his wife he was going to meet Danny Greene to discuss the vending machine business. *Cleveland Police Mug Shot*

Irwin "Red" Mason, was a "floating poker game operator" since the early 1950s. His customers would start play on a Friday night and continue straight through to Sunday evening. By 1958, Mason's games had been chased by police "all over greater Cleveland." Mason apparently was also involved in moving stolen goods. After fencing some goods for attorney Lawrence Krasny in the early 1960s, Mason was ratted out by his own wife.

Joseph Bonarrigo was the step-son of Joseph Ilacqua. In 1977, Bonarrigo asked Henry A. "Boom-Boom" Grecco for a bomb to use on a rival in the vending industry. Grecco not only refused, he ratted Bonarrigo out to the intended target. On July 1, Grecco's body was found in Hudson Township. Bonarrigo was arrested and a year later was convicted, on June 28, 1978, and sentenced to life, but allowed free on bond until appeals could be heard. On February 24, 1980, Joseph Ilacqua called police to tell them his stepson was missing. Bonarrigo's body was found on March 6. *CSU / Cleveland Press Collection*

Home of Richard H. Moss. On April 27, 1975, Moss went into the attached garage where he noticed a "multi-colored" package on the front seat of his Lincoln. He picked up the package, walked around the car. Suddenly the package exploded in his hands. The 41-year-old Moss lay dead six feet from the rear of the car. Joe Ilacqua became a suspect in the bombing after it was discovered he was involved with Moss in a business venture called Slush King. *CSU / Cleveland Press Collection*

Albert H. Severino – Biography

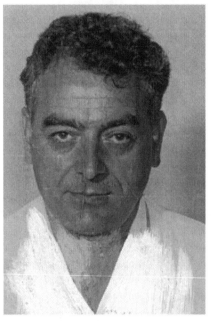

Albert H. Severino was described as one of Cleveland's "most accomplished burglars" during the 1950s. By July 1965, Severino was facing a slew of charges, including a Federal counterfeiting charge, and an extradition fight to avoid returning to New York State to begin a 5-to-10-year sentence for a burglary there. His legal problems ended on June 19, 1967, when a gunman fired four bullets from a .45 semi-automatic into him through his kitchen window. *CSU / Cleveland Press Collection*

Herman S. Pressman, was a Cleveland defense attorney who represented Lawrence Severino in a burglary case involving his brother, Albert, and Charles Skubovis. After Lawrence was acquitted, Pressman, perhaps, got a little to close to the case and was actually arrested for possession of stolen property that was involved in the burglary. Representing Pressman was William B. Mahoney, described as a "Buffalo criminal case attorney and powerful state Democratic leader." His brother, Walter J. Mahoney, was the New York State Senate Republican majority leader. Pressman got off. *CSU / Cleveland Press Collection*

Sonny's Show Bar Story

Joseph Allen was a numbers operator in Cleveland from the mid-1930s into the early 1950s. In 1949 he survived a muscling-in attempt by the Mayfield Road Mob which resulted in Allen's car being bombed. Around 1950 he built, what the *Call & Post* called, "The most fabulous ranch home ever built by a Negro in Cleveland." Located at East 146th Street and Bartlett Avenue, the cost, with furnishings, was estimated at $250,000. *CSU / Cleveland Press Collection*

Alex "Shondor" Birns, one of Cleveland's most notorious criminals, was entrenched in the numbers business for three decades, as well as many other criminal activities. After a failed assassination attempt by "Sonny" Coleman, "Shondor" wanted revenge. When Coleman made it known he was the shooter, Birns used the former Sonny's Show Bar, to launch his offensive. *Cleveland Police Dept. Mug Shot*

Anthony "Tops" Cardone was the featured act on opening night when, Sonny's Show Bar had its grand opening at 12376 Superior Avenue, on Friday night, August 9, 1946. Cardone's "Men of Note" performed at Sonny's into March of 1947. He reported at that time "his crew" was entering its 30th week there. Cardone had a long and successful career in the Cleveland area, and was a loved and respected member of the community. "Tops" Cardone ended his musical career in March 1984 at Masiello's Restaurant.

Clarence "Sonny" Coleman learned a valuable lesson as a wannabe assassin, if you shoot to kill and miss, don't shoot your mouth off. Days after missing Alex "Shonder" Birns with a rifle shot, Coleman was letting everyone know he was the man who pulled the trigger. The revelation took 20 days to get back to Birns, who had gone to Miami. It took even less time, 5 days, for him to retaliate. A one-time numbers runner for Birns, the 35-year-old was lucky to see 36.

The Angelo "Big Ange" Lonardo that Clevelanders knew was the young man who avenged his father and uncle's 1927 murders by killing the man he held responsible. Convicted at trial, Lonardo, like Julius Petro a generation later, was granted a new trial at which he was acquitted. In 1946, when Sonny's Show Bar opened, were people led to believe "Big Ange" had come back from overseas as a war hero, to run it? *Cleveland Police Dept. Mug Shot*

Glenn C. Pullen, the long-time *Plain Dealer* entertainment columnist, may have inadvertently led readers astray. His column stated: "FORMER SERGT. ANGELO Lonardo, who won five major battle citations, blossomed out Friday night as the impresario of Sonny's Show Bar which opened at 12376 Superior Avenue." "Big Ange" would actually clear up the mystery in court in December 1949, when he stated that the Angelo Lonardo that opened Sonny's was a cousin who had the same name.

Joseph Tholl
One of a Kind

Joseph Tholl, after graduating high school, attended the Cleveland Institute of Music, where he studied classical music and played the violin. While at the institute, he developed a second interest, handwriting. What he called his "hobby," other people might call his obsession. Tholl attended no college or trade school to learn this skill, but over the next 50 years he became an internationally known handwriting expert and document examiner.

Mariann Colby was responsible for committing one of the most despicable murders in the history of Cuyahoga County, that of 8-year-old John Cremer Young, Jr. in Shaker Heights on August 24, 1965. Joseph Tholl's role in the investigation was to help determine premeditated murder in the killing by confirming a forged name on a gun purchase was made recently by Colby. *CSU / Cleveland Press Collection*

Frank S. Day was elected Cuyahoga Country Recorder and was serving his third term when questionable payroll practices came to the attention of Cuyahoga County Auditor Ralph J. Perk. All county employees were required to sign their payroll record before being paid. The first issue Joseph Tholl encountered was 18 of the 65 signatures in the Recorders office were made by the same person. That was just the start, when the investigation was over it was discovered one employee was hired solely to perform work at Day's home, and another was a ghost employee.

On October 9, 1955, the body of a young unidentified woman was discovered in Brookside Park. Near the body was a note stating, "My mame [sic] Helen Carlin. Catch two boys. Because I would not drink." Good police work resulted in the woman being identified as 18-year-old Gloria Ann Ferry from Altoona, PA. Bizarre post cards arrived giving police misinformation to throw them off the trail. When the killer, Louis C. Statler was arrested, Joseph Tholl went to work, tying the "Helen Carlin" note, the post cards and a letter to an Altoona newspaper all back to Statler's handwriting.

Cuyahoga County Coroner Dr. Samuel R. Gerber stated during the early stages of the Cremer Young murder investigation that "the shooting could have been accidental or a deliberate act," and, on several occasions, suggested "the killing could have been the result of children playing with a loaded gun." On August 30, six days after the killing, Mrs. Mariann Colby asked if she could speak to Dr. Gerber alone. She then broke down and told the coroner her son Dane had shot and killed Cremer at her home that morning. But her story would soon change.
Cleveland State University

Cleveland Police Homicide Captain David E. Kerr, stares down at a suit case containing clothes, a newspaper edition from Altoona, Pennsylvania, and a name – Gloria Ann Ferry. Detectives were dispatched to Altoona where a local dentist confirmed through dental records the young lady found in Brookside Park was Ferry. Authorities there were able to give police all the details they needed of the likely suspect, Louis Statler, and the manhunt was on. Because it looked like a kidnapping, the FBI was brought in and on December 10, 1955, two months after the body was discovered, agents in Chicago arrested Statler.

John L. Kocevar, the unsung hero of the infamous raid on the notorious Jungle Inn back on August 12, 1949, found himself on the other side of the law in March 1967. The former chief executive officer of Cuyahoga County Sheriff James J. McGettrick, Kocevar was on trial charged with conflict-of-interest. Ohio state law prohibited county officials – elected or appointed – from having an interest in a contract for goods purchased by the county. Kocevar claimed he did not have an interest in the company, Tholl testified to signed documents that proved he did.

Norman Minor, a one-time Assistant Cuyahoga County Prosecutor, represented Frank S. Day at his trial, where he was charged with forgery and fraudulent payroll practices. On Monday, August 19, 1963, the trial began in Common Pleas court. After two days of testimony, Minor called for a sit down with prosecutor, John T. Corrigan. Day pleaded guilty to three counts, resigned his position immediately, and on sentencing day got 1 to 20 years. *CSU / Cleveland Press Collection*

George J. Moscarino was the lead prosecutor in the Cremer Young murder trial. The case was tried before a three-judge panel The motive? Mrs. Colby was angry because of Cremer's parents rejection of her son, and that Dane Colby didn't measure up to Cremer. In closing statements, Moscarino described her as "a scheming, devious, sexually starved woman," who lured the young boy to her home before murdering him and then attempting to conceal the crime, by blaming her own son. *CSU / Cleveland Press Collection*

In 1962, Ralph J. Perk was elected Cuyahoga County Auditor, before serving four two-year-terms as Cleveland mayor. The first Republican elected to a county office since the mid-1930s, what incensed Perk was that he had once lost to Day in the race for County Recorder. Perk knew a crook when he smelled one. Perk tried to work diplomatically with Day's office, but it was soon apparent that wouldn't work. Perk then ordered a complete and thorough investigation of the department. He then announced he was hiring Joseph Tholl to review the Recorder's payroll files. *CSU / Cleveland Press Collection*

Michael D. Roberts, a *Plain Dealer* reporter covering the trial of Mrs. Colby, explained the judges had found Mrs. Colby not guilty by reason of insanity on the basis of a 123-year-old English precedent known as the M'Naughten Rules. Roberts wrote, "Many legal authorities consider the law medieval in the light of progress made in psychiatry." In their written opinion, the three judges criticized the law they had before them, but none of them had the courage or foresight to challenge it and Cremer Young's killer went unpunished. *CSU / Cleveland Press Collection*

Shaker Hts. Police Detective Lieutenant Ralph J. Schaar along with Lawrence W. Doran, chief of the homicide unit of the Cuyahoga County Sheriff's Department, took charge of the Cremer Young murder investigation in the summer of 1965. Over the years Schaar had become a polygraph expert and was loaned out to other departments throughout northeast Ohio to conduct the tests. One of the more notable cases was the murder of Charles R. Clark, on Christmas Eve 1959, in Mentor, OH. Joseph Tholl was also involved in that case.

Eight-year-old John C. "Cremer" Young, Jr., left his home on the morning of August 24, 1965, at 3171 Warrington Road in Shaker Heights at 8:30. He was headed to a neighbor's house two doors away. The neighbor, Mariann Colby, called the Young residence minutes earlier and asked the boy's father if a jacket left behind at her place belonged to Cremer. Mrs. Colby's 9-year-old son, Dane, was classmates with Cremer Young at Onaway Elementary School, and they often played together. He was murdered shortly after entering the Colby home and his body left in Gates Mills. *CSU / Cleveland Press Collection*

Chapter Ten:

The Friends of Julius Petro

It is hard to read about the life of Julius Anthony Petro and not be drawn to comparisons with the 1970 crime classic *The Friends of Eddie Coyle*, by George V. Higgins. The novel, which takes place in Boston, Massachusetts, in the 1960s, is about a small-time gun-runner named Eddie Coyle who is being pressured by the local district attorney to give up one of his "clients" in order to catch a break on a three-year sentence he's facing. Called "one of the greatest crime novels ever written," it was followed by a movie of the same name in 1973 with Robert Mitchum playing the down and out Eddie Coyle. Both Coyle's and Petro's lives ended in similar fashion. Both were shot in the head while seated in a car with two other men whom they believed to be their friends. Neither saw it coming.

The men who went out on "jobs" with burglars and safecrackers like Julius Petro and Vincent Innocenzi numbered in the dozens. It seemed like the same crew never pulled two jobs together. How the men for these jobs were chosen, or even how the whole crew came together cannot be explained. There had to be a certain amount of trust between the men. More often than not, it was one member of the crew that was nabbed by the police, who in turn ratted out the others. Neither Petro, nor Innocenzi, escaped those accusations during their careers. Many times burglars opted out of being involved in a job simply because they didn't like or trust one or more of the other crew members who would be involved. Another element of the gang's burglaries, safecrackings and robberies was the "finger man." This was the person who would advise the gang of potential victims or businesses that could be "hit." These people would receive a percentage of the take if the job were successful, normally ten percent. Last, but not least, were the "fences," the men who purchased the stolen goods from the gang and then turned around and sold them.

Petro's Collinwood gang of yeggs had their heyday in the years following his release from death row. From 1948 until early 1953, according to Detective Chief James E. McArthur, the gang was responsible for "60% to 70%" of the safe-crackings and burglaries on the northeast side of the city, which earned them some $100,000. In addition to Cleveland and Cuyahoga County, the gang operated downstate Ohio, in western Pennsylvania and western New York. Lieutenant Thomas P. White claimed the gang was, "Systematic in its selection of places to victimize. It has waged concentrated campaigns – first against haberdasheries and then, in order, taverns, construction companies and dairies."

In 1952, Detective Chief McArthur organized a special unit of ten men to "prowl" the city during the early morning hours. Lieutenant White was second in command, while former homicide detective, Sergeant Harold C. Lockwood was placed in charge of the unit. For several months the unit staked out the suspected gang members, "cataloging their movements and noting their associates and meeting places." In March 1953, McArthur reported that of "some 40 members of the group, 15 have been tried, convicted and imprisoned on a variety of charges since last September." Included among the arrested was the top leadership of the gang, Julius Petro and Ralph De Biase.

White was worried about another element of the gang's activities. He was concerned about how the gang's successful burglaries were creating prestige for them among the juveniles in the Collinwood neighborhood. White added, "Their ability to recruit new members was bothering us more than anything else. But once they're put behind bars, they lose their luster as heroes." After the demise of the Collinwood gang's leadership, some former members organized new gangs, most notably Vincent Innocenzi, and continued their criminal activities into the 1960s.

Here are the key members that participated in Petro's Collinwood collection of yeggs.

Philip W. Aliberti

The only crime Philip Aliberti and Julius Petro were known to be involved in together was the stealing of the money from the cash box at Dave Creedon's Hi-Speed filling station on Route 20 in Painesville, Ohio, on July 24, 1952. At least that's the only crime that made the newspapers for the two.

The 1940 census showed 12-year-old Philip Aliberti living on Murray Hill Road in Little Italy with his widowed mother and five sisters. That year, Philip's 10-year-old sister, Lucy appeared in a *Plain Dealer* photograph with three other young girls dressed in the costumes they would be wearing as they followed the statue of the Blessed Virgin Mary along Mayfield Road during the annual Feast of the Assumption in Little Italy. Sometime since the 1930 Census, Philip's father Anthony and an older brother Vincent passed away. Without a father figure to guide him, Philip began a career in crime and became involved in Petro's gang of Collinwood yeggs.

While waiting for the Painesville filling station theft case to come to trial, Aliberti was part of a six-man crew that robbed the Clemmer Construction Company at 134 East Thornton Street in Akron on December 11, 1952. The men broke a lock on a gate and forced a backdoor open. Their inside information indicated they would find a $30,000 payroll in the safe. When they broke open the safe's door a tear gas bomb went off. The men simply opened the windows and waited outside for an hour while the gas dissipated. They returned to the office only to find $500 inside the safe.

Without revealing what led them to him, the Akron police soon arrested William E. "Red" Miller. The ex-con quickly started talking, confessing his role in the burglary, and ratting out his accomplices. Aliberti, Anthony DelGuyd,[65]

Joseph Sansavera and Frank Tartaglia were arrested and held under bond. Joseph Ilacqua, the last member of the crew, was being held in Cleveland as he was on his way to the Ohio Penitentiary, according to the *Akron Beacon Journal*, to begin a 1-to-15-year sentence on a burglary conviction. Akron Detective Captain John Struzenski claimed that all of the Cleveland men were "part of the Mayfield Road gang." Miller, he stated, "Served time in the Mansfield Reformatory and has admitted meeting one of the gang in that institution."

While Aliberti was out on bond for the construction company safecracking, his trial for the filling station robbery came up. On March 24, 1953, the 25-year-old, who was indicted for grand larceny in the theft of $817 from the station's cash box, was allowed to plead guilty to petit larceny. He received a 60-day sentence in the county jail and a $300 fine. In the *Plain Dealer* article announcing the sentence, he was referred to as "one of notorious Julius Petro's pals." The article went on to say, "Police believe Aliberti, an ex-convict, who two years ago beat a stabbing charge in Common Pleas Court here, has now become the boss of the gang led by Petro and later by Ralph (Bull) De Biase." Two days after Aliberti was sentenced, 25-year-old Anthony DiVito copped the same plea and received the same sentence.

On September 25, 1953, William "Red" Miller and Joseph Sansavera were found guilty of the safecracking at the Clemmer Construction Company. Although both men named several members of the Mayfield Road Mob in their confessions, both pleaded not guilty and went to trial. Neither would take the stand in their own defense, nor were any defense witnesses called. Both were convicted of grand larceny and breaking and entering. As the men were being led out of the courtroom, a spectator "hissed" at them saying, "Now you're not worth five cents." The *Akron Beacon Journal* reported that the implication of people in the Mayfield Road Mob they made, "was their mistake and the long prison terms they face are nothing compared to what will happen should the Mayfield mob decide to move in. Both knew it well."

Prosecutors were concerned the two men's refusal to testify on their own behalf would mean they won't testify at the trials of the other defendants in the case. In Miller's confession, he stated he met DelGuyd at the Mansfield Reformatory and he was his "contact" on the Clemmer job. He said DelGuyd assembled the burglary crew that did the actual work. On October 20, Aliberti, DelGuyd and Tartaglia were acquitted of the charges after Miller and Sansavera took the stand and refused to testify against them. The judge refused to have the confession read, ruling that, "The courts hold a confession is binding only against the men who make it."

In September 1954, Cleveland Police Detective Chief James E. McArthur was interviewed by Cleveland *Plain Dealer* reporter Sanford Watzman about the *Police Mug Book*. Going into its second edition, McArthur pointed out that of the 168 criminals in the first edition, "one-third are still more or less active, another one-third are in federal or state penitentiaries or have died (a few of natural deaths) and the rest have either 'retired' or left the city, having become too self-conscious under the 24-hour stare of the police department."

McArthur's chief aide, Detective Lieutenant Thomas P. White, stated he would like to keep the book to 100 mug shots, "so that the faces of all may be more easily memorized." Both men pointed out "the now defunct Collinwood safe gang," the largest single group in the old Mug Book were now missing. This was in reference to the recent imprisonments of Julius Petro and his associates Ralph De Biase, Sylvester "Studo" Papalardo and Joe Sanzo. White now wanted Anthony D'Alessio and Philip Aliberti, who he called "survivors of the Collinwood safe gang," as frontispieces[66] for the new volume.[67]

Lieutenant White wouldn't have long to wait for removing his frontispiece request. On Saturday morning, January 15, 1955, Aliberti and D'Alessio were arrested for the burglary of the Mills Jewelry Store in Carrolton, Ohio, located southeast of Canton in Carroll County. The two men, along with accomplices Michael Antonelli and Peter Guzzo, were spotted leaving the store by Carrollton Police Chief Hal Tasker, who "spread the alarm." The burglars made it to their getaway car, but soon got bogged down in a muddy field and had to continue their escape on foot through the snow. Chief Tasker was soon directing a 30-man posse he formed, which was now after the fleeing men, who were being tracked by the footprints they left in the snow. Three were soon captured by the State Highway Patrol and Carroll County officials. Antonelli, who apparently was moving at a much faster rate, was found 18 miles away. Law enforcement officials found a small safe containing $5,000 in diamonds in their abandoned car, along with other items packed into burlap sacks. The total take was estimated at $15,000. The men were arraigned before the Carrollton mayor and bound over to the Carroll County Grand Jury on a $10,000 bond.

The trial was described as "one of the weirdest" in the history of Carroll County. In the weeks leading up to it, Aliberti and D'Alessio were represented at various times by seven different attorneys. Common Pleas Judge Frank F. Cope, fed up with the continuous changes in representation, told the pair to settle on counsel or have none. On March 3, when the trial finally began, Aliberti and D'Alessio represented themselves. While both defendants cross-examined the state's witnesses, neither man took the stand in his own defense. After just 30 minutes of deliberations, the jury convicted both men for their role in the burglary. Antonelli and Guzzo had pleaded guilty earlier. All were sentenced to 1-to-15-year sentences in the Ohio Penitentiary.

In late November 1958, police were trying to clear out some of the repeat loiterers who were always hanging around after midnight at downtown night spots. On November 26, Philip Aliberti, described in the newspaper as a "burglar and leader of a gang of East Side thugs in the early 1950s," and Benedetto Contorno were arrested. Both were on parole and were held in the County Jail.

Detective Lieutenant White told reporters, "We're going to show people of this character that we won't stand for that kind of after-midnight activity. We're going to stop trouble before it gets a start."

It was the last time Philip Aliberti made the news.

Anthony Paul D'Alessio

D'Alessio's photograph has long adorned a wall in the detective roll call room and is entered annually in the police "mug book" of suspected criminals. – Plain Dealer article February19, 1957.

Known to be, "A henchman of the notorious Julius Petro," Anthony P. D'Alessio's first reported association with Cleveland's "handsomest public enemy" was in April 1949 when he was arrested with Petro and "Allie" A. Calabrese after they sped out of a Royal Castle restaurant on St. Clair Avenue. The next month, D'Alessio was picked up with Petro after police found a sack full of burglary tools in the car in which they were stopped. His last reported association with Petro came on July 24, 1952, when they were indicted in Lake County along with Philip Aliberti after stealing the cash box from Creedon's Hi-Speed filling station in Painesville.

D'Alessio's grandfather arrived in the United States during the great migration period of Italians during the latter part of the 19th Century. Sometime after he became naturalized, the grandfather returned to Italy to live. When his son, D'Alessio's father, was born in Italy, the boy had automatic status as an American citizen because of the grandfather's naturalization. D'Alessio's father lived in Campobasso, Italy, where he married, and Anthony was born June 10, 1922. The father came to the United States the next year, while Anthony and his mother arrived in 1929. Because the father did not reside in America prior to the birth of his son, the citizenship the father enjoyed could not be passed along to Anthony. With the path Anthony D'Alessio chose in life, this was going to present problems years later.

The criminal career D'Alessio embarked on tallied 18 arrests by the mid-1950s. During World War II, he was arrested several times for being AWOL, and once as an Army deserter. While most of the arrests resulted in minimal overnight jail stays, his most serious offense came in January 1955, when he was captured with Philip Aliberti after burglarizing the Mills Jewelry Store in Carrollton, Ohio. Both men were sentenced to 1-to-15-year terms. D'Alessio was released in March 1956.

During December 1956, D'Alessio was living in East Cleveland with his wife, Mary, and was the father of a 16-year-old son and a 9-year-old daughter. Working as a truck driver, he also owned a 1956 Cadillac. But his life was about to take a turn for the worst. During that month D'Alessio suffered three devastating setbacks. First, he lost his job as a truck driver. Second, he was in an accident in which he injured his back. The third event was the most tragic; his wife Mary died.

Unfortunately, things would get worse the following year. On February 18, 1957, D'Alessio was arrested and "ordered to give a good reason why he shouldn't be deported." John M. Lehmann, district director of the Immigration & Naturalization Service, said that due to his two convictions (his first one resulted in probation) showing "moral turpitude," he was being served with a deportation warrant. D'Alessio was notified by his attorney, Frank E. Steel, the former assistant U.S. attorney who helped send his friend Julius Petro to prison for 25 years, to appear in Lehmann's office. He was served with the warrant there and released on a $2,000 "conditional" bond. The terms of the bond stated it could be revoked if D'Alessio "is found associating with known criminals or if he leaves the state without permission." A deportation hearing was scheduled for March 20.

D'Alessio was incensed after his appearance. He shouted at reporters when he was released, "After 30 years here, all at once they tell me I'm not a citizen. Why? Because I went to the penitentiary? I always thought I was a citizen. And the only reason I did go to jail was because I didn't have a mouth piece at that Carroll County trial."

The initiation of the deportation hearings made Lieutenant Thomas White very happy. Now chief of "special services" in the Cleveland Detective Bureau, White called D'Alessio "an original target" of the long-term investigation that ended the Collinwood safe-cracking gang headed by Petro.

On March 29, Milton V. Milich, Special Inquiry of the Immigration & Naturalization Service, ruled that D'Alessio was an undesirable alien because of the two burglary convictions. D'Alessio remained free on the $2,000 bond pending the appeal of the Milich order. It would be a long appeals process.

While his attorney fought the deportation order D'Alessio went about his life. He found work managing several taverns over the next five years. In 1963, he was working as a manager and chef at Anthony's Restaurant & Bar at 1054 East 140th Street. In August, the owners made an application to the Ohio Liquor Control Commission to transfer a liquor permit. D'Alessio's employment there became the center of controversy, and the owners swore he would no longer be part of the operation. They promised authorities D'Alessio would be fired as manager and cook and a new one would be hired.

The Cleveland Police Department opposed the permit transfer, writing a letter to the liquor department with a warning, "because of his reputation in criminal circles, he has acted as a magnet by drawing many of his criminal associates as patrons to these various establishments" in the past. Despite the warning, the liquor permit transfer was allowed in September.

On December 6, 1963, D'Alessio discovered a theft took place at the bar after a cigar box holding $175 was taken. When police questioned D'Alessio, he described himself as the owner. Later that same month, he oversaw remodeling work done at the tavern. Five months later, on May 2, 1964, when police raided a dice game, he was behind the bar. On July 28, the liquor department contacted the Ohio Liquor Control Commission and advised they were misled. They charged "a false material statement' was made, referring to the fact D'Alessio was not to be allowed on the premises. This type of charge would normally mean the liquor permit would be revoked.

Like cases involving the Immigration & Naturalization Service, things moved at a snail's pace with the Ohio Liquor Control Commission. Some 16 months after the charges were filed, two members of the three-man commission met and dismissed the charge, ruling it was "not supported by evidence." The third member of the commission, who was also the chairman, was not present when the ruling was made. The *Plain Dealer* reported, "This is considered unusual, as in important cases no decision normally is made public until the absent member returns and has a chance to review the hearing record and casts his vote."

Nearly nine years after being ordered to leave the country, the deportation issue was still unresolved. *Plain Dealer* reporter Michael D. Roberts,[68] in an article which appeared on Christmas Day 1965, wrote that D'Alessio "has dodged deportation to his native Italy by running a maze of legal maneuvers:

> D'Alessio appealed to the U.S. Board of Immigration Appeals once before, tried the U.S. District Court here, and appealed that decision to the U.S. Sixth Circuit Court of Appeals. All pleas were denied. The U.S. Supreme Court also denied his appeal in 1961.

By now D'Alessio had a new "mouth piece," Harry C. Lavine. D'Alessio replaced Frank Steel with an attorney having more experience in handling deportation cases. Lavine's most notable victory came by successfully defending notorious Prohibition Era gangster Frank Brancato, who the government tried to deport in 1955. Lavine filed a motion in Federal Court on December 17, requesting additional time for his client to prepare his case for the U.S. Board of Immigration Appeals in Washington D.C. The motion was granted, and reporter Michael Roberts noted, "This apparently is his last chance to avoid deportation." In the meantime, D'Alessio was now on his third wife and had fathered another child.

On May 24, 1966, D'Alessio walked into a situation that could have turned fatal at the Park Lane Lounge at 16800 Brookpark Road.[69] By now, D'Alessio was running a vending machine operation headquartered on Chagrin Boulevard in Beachwood, known as Chagrin Cigarette Service Company. It's not clear if having his machines inside the lounge was his only connection to it. A newspaper hiring advertisement for barmaids at the Park Lane Lounge requested the applicants be interviewed at Anthony's Lounge at 1054 East 140th Street, where D'Alessio had managed and maybe still did. When he arrived that night, his brother-in-law, Anthony Bonarrigo was involved in an altercation over his "hurt feelings" with Robert P. Simmons, the manager.

As D'Alessio was about to enter, for some never explained reason, barmaid Patricia Joan Thompson tried to lock the door to keep him out. D'Alessio gave the door such a hard push that it knocked Thompson back against the cigarette machine, breaking her finger, dislodging a tooth and damaging the machine, which belonged to D'Alessio.

Inside the bar was Ronald Kaye, a former reporter for the *Plain Dealer*. He would later testify D'Alessio pulled a gun, aimed it at the ceiling and then lowered his arm and shot Simmons. Kaye followed this up with, "I don't know whether he aimed at Simmons, or whether his arm was just knocked and the gun just went off."

Bonarrigo told a different tale, one harder to believe. He claimed the gun belonged to Simmons and it went off while he was "grappling" with him. When being questioned about it, Bonarrigo refused to admit to pulling the trigger himself, claiming instead that it just "went off."

Simmons, who was shot in the arm, refused to identify the shooter and never went to court over the incident. He and Thompson later filed a personal damage suit against D'Alessio, but Simmons eventually left for the West Coast and the matter was dropped. In the end, the shooting would work against D'Alessio in his deportation case as it came up during several follow-up hearings and caused more delays to allow for "investigation" of the incident.

On March 20, 1969, the deportation case was now in its twelfth year, when yet another hearing was held. Daniel J. Shrull, a Special Inquiry immigration officer from Philadelphia, was hearing evidence about the Park Lane Lounge shooting. At the end of the two-hour session, D'Alessio's attorney, Harry Lavine, stated he would file for a suspension of the deportation order. Shrull responded to the lawyer, declaring, "This case has been dragging on for far too long. I will schedule another hearing for either April or May and perhaps at that time we can finally begin to make progress." The next month D'Alessio was looking for a new attorney after Harry Lavine passed away at the age of 74.

On the last day of June 1969, a van belonging to the Chagrin Cigarette Service Company was destroyed by a bomb as it sat in the company's loading dock over the weekend. The company, located at 896 East 152nd Street[70] in Collinwood, was across the street from the newly built Sixth District Police Station,[71] which was to have its official opening on July 1. When questioned by police, D'Alessio said he was not the owner of the vending machine company, just the manager. Technically he was correct; the company was in the name of his wife, Geraldine. When asked what he considered to be behind the bombing, he said he believed it was simply linked to others that had recently occurred in the Collinwood area.[72]

A year-and-a-half passed without anything new to report on the deportation proceedings. Then on August 13, 1970, D'Alessio's new council, former assistant U.S. attorney Robert J. Rotatori, went on the offensive and filed a writ of habeas corpus demanding the government "act speedily on its latest investigation or drop the whole matter." U.S. District Judge Frank J. Battisti set a hearing date of August 27 for the Immigration & Naturalization Service to show cause as to why the writ should not be issued.

Back in 1957, Milton V. Milich, then Special Inquiry Officer for the INS, ordered D'Alessio deported. In an ironic twist of fate, on October 2, 1970, Milich, back in the same position due to the retirement of Daniel J. Shrull, granted D'Alessio a hardship waiver to support his fourth wife, Geraldine, and their two children. The *Plain Dealer* reported that "Over the life of the proceedings, D'Alessio has gone through three lawyers, two wives, three immigration service district directors and three special inquiry officers. The D'Alessio case is one of the longest in the history of the service and serves to illustrate how immigration laws work, or can be made not to." On October 14, INS District Director Richard W. Ahearn announced the decision not to appeal Milich's ruling. After 13 years, D'Alessio was a "legal permanent resident alien."

"Terrific," said Rotatori, "Tony the citizen."

When reporters asked D'Alessio what he had to say after his long ordeal had ended, he replied, "With all due respect, I don't want to make no comments. I just want this whole thing to die."

Tony, however, was not the "citizen" Rotatori had stated. D'Alessio would need to stay "clean" for the next three years in order to apply for citizenship papers. D'Alessio had survived the 13-year deportation drama, but he would not live long enough to become a citizen.

Few details are known about D'Alessio's killing other than it was committed by Geraldine. Around 2:30 Sunday morning, on January 23, 1972, just 15 months after winning the 13-year legal battle to deport him, Geraldine shot Tony three times in the chest and stomach, after what was called a "family argument." The shooting occurred in the Roman Lounge, 29012 Euclid Avenue[73] in Wickliffe, a small city east of Cleveland in Lake County. Geraldine was arrested and a few days later bound over to the Lake County Grand Jury with bond set at $12,000. I could not find any more information.

Ralph "Bull" De Biase
"A pal of Julius Petro, Cleveland's ace of thugs, and himself a convicted burglar and a notorious night-prowling hoodlum." – *Plain Dealer* article January 3, 1953, describing Ralph "Bull" De Biase.

Ralph "Bull" De Biase[74] first came to the public's attention in March 1950 after being arrested in Johnstown, Pennsylvania, with Julius Petro and Joseph Russo. Their failed safecracking attempt there earned them $43, a conviction and a warning to stay out Cambria County, Pennsylvania for five years. A few months later, on June 4, De Biase was believed to be part of the home invasion team that robbed the residence of Alliance grocer Joseph Carretta. This botched attempt resulted in the second wounding of Petro, but the case was dismissed during the trial after Carretta claimed he could not identify Petro. Some articles would report that De Biase was Petro's successor as the leader of the Collinwood safe-cracking gang.

Less than a month after Julius Petro was convicted of the Warren robbery in December 1952, De Biase was arrested in his marquee safecracking adventure. For months the gang was busy pulling burglaries and hauling stolen safes back to a garage behind a home owned by De Biase's mother, in which she resided, at 15349 Yorick Avenue in Collinwood. The gang would bring the safe back during the early morning hours and crack it open inside the garage. The swag they collected from the burglaries was kept there along with an impressive array of burglary tools.

Sometime in November 1952, Cleveland police received a tip about the garage and began to stake it out. Key members of the stakeout team were Detective Sergeant Harold C. Lockwood and Detectives John Doyle, William F. Lonchar and Joseph Kolek. For weeks the detectives disguised themselves as workmen or soldiers to allow them free movement in the neighborhood without raising suspicion.

During the early morning hours of Friday, January 2, 1953, the gang stole a panel truck, that belonged to the Owens Flooring Company, from a filling station where it was parked awaiting some repair work. They then drove to the Western & Southern Life Insurance Agency at 18233 Euclid Avenue, where they broke in and stole a 1,200 pound safe. Arriving back at the Yorick Avenue garage around 2:15 a.m. were De Biase, James Buffa, and Benedetto "Benny" Contorno, Jr. As they began unloading the safe, detectives closed in. It wasn't exactly a Hollywood movie type of police bust. A squad car, with Detective Lonchar in the passenger seat, pulled into the driveway. Lonchar, with shotgun in hand, was ready to jump out and shout, "Police! Halt! The problem was the driveway was so narrow, he could not swing the door open wide enough to depart the vehicle. The driver had to back up and pull to the left in order for Lonchar to get out. By that time De Biase and Contorno had fled in one direction and Buffa in another.

De Biase and Contorno most likely ran to the latter's home, where the 23-year-old was still living with his parents and siblings, located just blocks away to the northeast, at 833 East 155th Street. It would have been better for them to just lay low there, but they didn't. They climbed into a dry cleaner's truck, which, according to Contorno, his brother had borrowed for his wife's dry cleaning deliveries. Minutes later a police car forced them to the curb on School Avenue, a couple of blocks north of Contorno's home. Buffa wasn't as fortunate. He tried to escape by running toward Yorick Avenue between two houses and was shot by John Doyle, one of the pursuing detectives; the bullet hitting him in the neck. The 31-year-old died from his wound on a resident's front lawn.

Buffa, ironically, was just released by Municipal Court, after having been charged as a suspicious person. His attorney, Louis Fernberg told Detective Chief James E. McArthur the day of his release, "We wouldn't kick if you held him on SOMETHING, but this is nothing." When Fernberg showed up in court the morning after the raid, he had yet to hear that Buffa was killed while trying to escape arrest. McArthur had the grim task of telling him. He began by stating, "We had your man Buffa on SOMETHING this morning."

On late Saturday afternoon, just four hours after warrants were issued to hold them for the grand jury, De Biase and Contorno, reportedly the "two ringleaders of an East Side safecracking gang," were released after both posted $10,000 surety bonds. Since the raid, police were scouring over the Yorick Avenue garage finding "loot" from burglaries that had been committed "every three or four days" during a recent crime spree.

On January 23, De Biase and Contorno were indicted by the county grand jury on three separate counts. The first was for burglary and larceny for stealing a safe, valued at $1,500 and containing $180 in cash, from the Western & Southern Life Insurance Agency. If convicted, the sentence would be 1-to-15-years in prison. A second count of receiving stolen property could result in a 1-to-7-year sentence. The most critical count was one for stealing the panel truck that they used to haul the safe to the Yorick Avenue garage. For this the men were looking at 1-to-20-years.

Representing De Biase and Contorno were Louis Fernberg and veteran defense attorney Fred W. Garmone. Both were still under $10,000 bonds and arraignment was scheduled for January 31. On Tuesday, January 27, Common Pleas Judge Frank J. Merrick met with Fernberg and agreed to keep the bonds at $10,000, provided the men agreed to trial at an early date. On the day of the arraignment, Fernberg told the judge that Garmone was out of town. After entering pleas of not guilty for both men, Fernberg said that he reserved the right of attacking the indictment.

Judge Merrick stated that because of the attack on the indictment, it would delay the trial while that matter was being resolved and thus it had broken the agreement he made regarding the bonds. A long discussion ensued and ended with Merrick increasing the bail for each man to $50,000, "to make sure they will be here for trial and we will have the trial at an early date." With that, De Biase and Contorno were marched off to the County Jail. By the time the trial began on Monday, March 9, both men were bonded out.

In addition to Fernberg and Garmone as defense counsel, Assistant County Prosecutor Thomas J. Parrino represented the state as trial began in the Common Pleas courtroom of Judge Merrick. De Biase sat through jury selection with an unexplained bandage on his thumb. Since nearly all the witnesses for the state would be police detectives, Garmone interjected into the potential juror's minds that there was currently a grand jury probe going on in the city involving police graft charges. He asked if they had been reading about "the conduct of policemen" in the newspapers.[75] The next day the jury was taken to the Yorick Avenue garage to view the scene, and afterwards opening statements were delivered.

Attorney Garmone's defense for De Biase was going to be a simple one. The *Plain Dealer* wrote on March 13, 1953:

He [De Biase] was at home in Wickliffe until about midnight Jan. 1 then he drove to Longo's restaurant at Five Points. There, he said, he met Contorno. They then went out to have the brakes fixed on a dry-cleaner truck which Contorno's brother, Ignatius, had borrowed for his wife's dry cleaning deliveries. Police picked them up as they drove the truck near the Yorick Road address, but they were going to a repair shop, not knowing of the police ambush which had just occurred.

Testimony began that afternoon with the state's key witness, Detective John Doyle. A pile of burglary tools – crow bars, bolt cutters, chisels, sledgehammers, and heavy-duty dollies – were brought in as evidence to show the jury. Doyle identified these items as having been found in the Yorick Avenue garage after the January 2 raid. He told the jury how detectives had done surveillance at the Yorick address, using walkie-talkies, binoculars and unmarked automobiles, keeping watch for several months.

The detective identified De Biase and Contorno as two of the men who fled through the backyard. Doyle told how he shot and killed James Buffa, after he refused an order to halt during his failed escape attempt. After he shot Buffa, Doyle removed an eight-inch long jump-wire from his jacket pocket, describing it as the kind used for stealing cars. Near the house, police recovered a two-tone blue sedan belonging to De Biase, which Doyle claimed was the same car the defendant drove to Yorick Avenue the day before when the jury viewed the crime scene.

On Wednesday, Detective William Lonchar took the witness stand and told his embarrassing story of being unable to get out of the police car due to the narrowness of the driveway. He said when they arrived in the driveway, he was able to identify the defendants and James Buffa in the glare of the car's headlights.

That same day, Assistant County Prosecutor Thomas J. Parrino presented evidence and called witnesses proving robberies of other local businesses. Found in the garage was an envelope of postage stamps stolen during a grocery store burglary. Also found were dozens of neckties taken from a tie shop.

When the defense began its case on Thursday, the plan was to convince the jury that De Biase was not the man seen running from the garage and that he had an injured right thumb at the time and couldn't possibly have helped move the heavy safe. Testifying for De Biase was Frankie Wallace, a former local featherweight boxer. Wallace, trying to add support to the tale De Biase injured his right thumb, stated he saw the defendant about 1:00 on the morning of January 2 with a cast on his right hand. Unfortunately, De Biase, who testified just before Wallace, stated he had a sore thumb the morning he saw Wallace, but the cast was not put on until January 4, two days later.

Next up was De Biase's brother Alfred. Telling the jury he had rented his mother's garage to a "Thomas Campbell," Alfred claimed he received three months' rent in advance. The defense was attempting to show that the stolen merchandise and the burglary tools belonged to someone else. During cross-examination by Prosecutor Parrino, the following exchange took place:

Parrino: When did this Campbell give you the rent money?

Alfred De Biase: In August.

Parrino: In what year?

Alfred De Biase: In 1952.

Parrino: Who was present at the time?

Alfred De Biase: Harry Truman.

The entire courtroom erupted in laughter after De Biase thought the assistant prosecutor had asked, "Who was president at the time?"

When Contorno took the stand, he told the jury he fell into the hands of the police while out "to get the brakes fixed" on a truck his brother had borrowed. During cross-examination, it was brought out that on March 2, exactly two months after the insurance agency burglary, Detective Doyle spotted Contorno's car on East 70th Street and pulled him over. With Contorno was Raymond Berkeley. That night the Ben Folkman Real Estate Company, at 2408 East 25th Street,[76] was broken into; the safe was cracked and the papers inside removed. When Detective Sergeant Harold Lockwood and Detective Doyle searched Contorno's vehicle, they found two metal wastebaskets and a half bushel-basket full of papers that were taken from the safe at the real estate concern. Asked by Parrino how they got in his car, Contorno replied, "I don't know. Someone must have put them there." Parrino was able to use the Folkman burglary as a "similar offense" in his case against Contorno.

On Monday, March 16, closing statements were given. During his comments regarding Contorno, Parrino told the jury, "If we caught him inside the safe, Contorno would tell you he was in there waiting for a streetcar." The jury didn't need much convincing, after a six-day trial, they reached a guilty verdict in just an hour-and-15-minutes, convicting the pair of burglary, grand larceny and operating a stolen truck. Jury foreman Norman Hammerle told reporters De Biase's sore thumb defense and Contorno's alibi didn't raise an iota of doubt. He said the jurors were unanimous in every vote. Afterwards, Judge Merrick told the jury, "You have seen a side of police work that you seldom hear about. It is very different from some of the bad things that you hear about policemen doing. You have seen evidence of some good police work, some heroic police work."

In a double whammy for Contorno, that same day a grand jury returned a brand-new indictment against him and Raymond Berkeley for breaking into the Ben Folkman Real Estate Company. Because a loaded pistol was found on the floor of Contorno's automobile, he was also charged with carrying a concealed weapon.

A week after the two men were convicted, Assistant County Prosecutor Saul S. Danaceau, recently elected officer of the Neighborhood Settlement Association, urged the social agency to begin immediate operations in Collinwood to curb the burgeoning teenage gang crime rate there. Danaceau told the executive board that, "Even with its hardest-boiled yeggs put in cold storage... the northeast neighborhood still has too many young thugs and too few youth agencies trying to steer the boys down the straight and narrow." He pointed out that a New York City youth board had a war chest of $2.5 million for which to hire trained youth counselors to break up gangs and work with families with youngsters who were on the fringes of the criminal element. A newspaper article listed the recent fall of "the heroes of the Five Points area." The names mentioned were Julius Petro, Joseph J. Sanzo, Peter Sanzo, Ralph De Biase, Benedetto Contorno, Philip Aliberti and the late James Buffa. Taking quick action, the executive director of the Neighborhood Settlement Association, Henry B. Ollendorff[77] announced to Danaceau, "You are now the head of a new project." The appointment did not include mention of a war chest.

One month after his conviction in the Western & Southern Life Insurance Agency burglary case, Contorno and Berkley were convicted for safe-tampering, burglary and larceny. In addition, Contorno was convicted of carry a concealed weapon. Both men bowed their heads as the verdicts were read. Judge Merrick again praised the work of the police. "You have viewed a demonstration of excellent police work by policemen who actually risked their lives to round up this gang," he began. "If the law provided for medals, I would be happy to confer them on the policemen. You have convicted two hardened and desperate criminals and you have arrived at the correct verdict."

On April 22, De Biase, Contorno and Berkeley appeared in court to learn their fate. Before the sentencing, defense lawyers and prosecutors met in Judge Merrick's chambers to hear De Biase's sordid last ditch effort to "dodge or whittle down" his pending prison sentence. There he told the judge that he had paid bribes to one of the officers to keep from being hauled in for investigation. He claimed the officer demanded $2,000 to get him off the hook for a robbery he committed in August 1952. De Biase said he told the officer he was "too poor" and that the officer got angry and decided to frame him. When Assistant County Prosecutor Parrino reminded him that a second detective had put him at the Yorick Avenue garage, De Biase suddenly remembered, "I paid him too."

Detective Chief McArthur told reporters De Biase's story was, "A pack of lies. If this guy was a meal ticket for some detectives, why would they try to put him in prison? And isn't it odd that the very ones he accuses are the ones who finally got him?" Assistant County Prosecutor John J. Mahon declared, "We will not investigate these charges. There isn't anything to investigate. This guy was on the stand in court. Why didn't he tell the jury all this and see if they'd believe him when it might have helped him?" Finally, County Prosecutor Frank T. Cullitan stated, "We certainly will not destroy the reputations of two police officers who won our praise for their work on this case. Not on the unsupported statement of a man with one of the worst criminal records in town."

It was obvious that the last minute rantings of a desperate man had little effect on Judge Merrick. De Biase was sentenced to a term of 3-to-42-years for burglary, larceny and operating a vehicle without the owner's consent. Contorno[78] received the same sentence, plus a 1-to-20-year term for the safe-tampering at the real estate company. His companion in that robbery, Berkeley received 3-to-42-years. The three men were denied new trials, but the judge allowed a stay of execution for all three while their attorneys prepared appeals. De Biase's bond was set at $50,000 and the other two were set at $25,000 apiece.

By mid-January 1954, all three men had lost their appeals and began serving their sentences. De Biase's appeals contention was that he was convicted on "inferences from inference." The Ohio Supreme Court refused to review the case. In an article announcing that he had lost his appeal, the *Plain Dealer* referred to De Biase as "the former buddy of Julius A. Petro, once king of the thugs here."

Joseph W. Drago

"Cleveland police have a standing order to pick up Drago should he be seen in parts of the city other than his usual haunts." – Plain Dealer, May 7, 1955

Joseph William Drago was born on February 3, 1924, in Pennsylvania. He lived for years in Little Italy at 1978 East 123rd Street, right behind Guarino's Restaurant. Like Julius Petro, Drago got into trouble at a young age. While spending time at the Boys Industrial School, a state reform facility in Lancaster, Ohio, located southeast of Columbus, Drago only 16, escaped with a 20-year-old from Columbus on October 10, 1940. On June 5, 1941, Drago again fled the institution, this time with five others. Two days later, Drago was one of two that were captured and returned. Whatever lessons he learned in the reform school didn't keep him from pursuing a life of crime as a career.

Two years later, now at the more mature age of 18, Drago faced Municipal Judge Louis Petrash after an incident involving future Petro cohort Angelo Carmello. The incident was the tossing of a stench bomb against the front wall of Nalepa's Café at 8316 Sowinski Avenue, between East 79th Street and Ansel Road. In court Carmello told the judge that he was riding in Drago's automobile on May 29 and threw the jar of stench liquid himself. He claimed Drago did not know that he had planned to do it. Judge Petrash acquitted Drago of the charges against him.

In February 1942, he was arrested for stealing an automobile. Later that year, in December, Drago was a cell mate of Petro in the County Jail after he was arrested for a burglary. It was here that Petro, Drago and two others staged the "breakfast insurrection" and received beatings for their efforts. Drago was soon back in reform school, this time it was the Mansfield Reformatory. By March 1944, he and Albert Severino, a future big wig in the yegg movement, were promoted to working at the honor camp at the local Soldier's Home. Apparently, they decided to slack off when they arrived there and soon were on their way back to the Mansfield institution for not "working satisfactorily."

In October 1945, Drago and Charles Presti were brought to Sandusky by sheriff's deputies on a warrant issued by the Juvenile Court. Both were arraigned on charges of contributing to the delinquency of two Homerville[79] youths, who were involved in a money theft.

Nearly six years passed before Drago was heard from again. In March 1951, Petro and Drago along with Michael Grande were wanted by police on arrest warrants charging them with breaking and entering in connection with a number of burglaries in Cambridge, Ohio, during 1950 and 1951. Somehow Drago was able to avoid indictment for the Cambridge burglaries and managed to fly under the police radar for the next four years.

Drago didn't surface again until the day of sentencing for Philip Aliberti and Anthony D'Alessio for the Carrollton jewelry store robbery. That evening, Drago and Anthony "Joe Blow" Velletto,[80] along with Joe Newman, an Akronite, were arrested in Knoxville, Tennessee. After Lieutenant Thomas White heard about the convictions and the arrests, both of which he provided information for to the out-of-town authorities to help achieve, he met with reporters at Central Police Station. The *Plain Dealer* reported the next day that, "The two Petro expeditionary forces were the last surviving remnants of the once-elusive gang that was driven from Cleveland by a stubborn program of police harassment," according to Lieutenant White.

The arrest of Drago and his companions was a classic tale. The three men checked into the Hotel Farragut on February 27. A couple of days later, the hotel clerk who registered them sat reading a "dime detective magazine" when he came across a mugshot of a man wanted for forgery, who he believed was one of the men he rented a room to. The man telephoned the local police and told them of his discovery. The police arrived and began questioning the men. The men told police they were on a leisurely trip to Florida to enjoy the last weeks of the winter season. Police were able to determine that the forger who appeared in the magazine was not one of the three men who had checked in. Police did discover, however, the men had registered under fictitious names while they were explaining their presence there. When detectives searched the men's car, they found acetylene torches and burglary tools. All three were held in the Knoxville City Jail on a $50,000 bail each, charged with possession of burglary tools and being fugitives from justice.

On March 5, Knoxville Acting City Judge H.O. Pollard dismissed all the charges against the men and released them after he was informed that none of them had any charges pending against them in Cleveland, and after police admitted under questioning that it was "impossible" to identify the tools as "burglary tools." Velletto told the judge he used the acetylene torches in his produce and flower business in Cleveland.

On May 6, two months after the Knoxville arrest, Drago was behind the wheel of his car, driving on the city's East Side with two companions, Richard A. Stewart and Arthur F. LaRiche. Around 8:30 that Friday night, the men were leaving the neighborhood of Euclid Avenue and East 116th Street (that stretch now known as Martin Luther King Boulevard) and heading toward the suburb of Euclid, further to the east. While driving on Lake Shore Boulevard, the men began to smell smoke coming from the engine. Drago pulled into a Euclid shopping center, where East 222nd Street merges with Babbitt Road. One of the men got out and lifted up the car's hood.

Suddenly a bomb, planted in the engine, exploded rocking the Euclid neighborhood. The *Plain Dealer* reported, "The explosion tore through the metal fire wall separating the auto's engine and front seat, buckled the dash board, smashed the windshield and blew off the hood." A piece of the car's engine casting was blown 25 feet away, tearing through the side of a parked automobile. Incredibly, none of the men were seriously injured. Drago and Stewart, cut and bruised, were taken to Euclid-Glenville Hospital and treated. They were then taken to the Euclid Police Station, where they were questioned and held for investigation. Within a couple of minutes after the explosion LaRiche hailed a passing cab, which delivered him to his Woodhill Road home. LaRiche may have scrammed due to still being on probation after serving four years for a payroll robbery in Buffalo back in 1950. Police caught up with him the next day and held him for investigation with the others.

Police immediately claimed the bombing was part of a "Cleveland gang feud." During the early hours of May 4, Nathan Augustino,[81] reported in the newspapers as a local "gangland figure," had his scalp creased by a bullet as he sat in his car at East 116th Street and Craven Avenue, miles south of the destination Drago claimed he and his companions started out from two days later.

The three men were fined $200 each for being suspicious persons and were released. The next month, on June 21, Drago and Stewart were two of four men arrested after "loitering suspiciously" in a car near the Williams' Service Garage at 4310 Chester Avenue.[82] Inside the car detectives found sledge hammers, bars and wrenches. The men were arraigned on charges of burglary tool possession with bonds set at $20,000 apiece.

Another five years would pass before Drago was arrested again. This time he was working with men with Youngstown connections. In September 1960, Drago was part of burglary crew that included Phillip "Fleegle" Mainer, Donald "Bull" Jones, George Florea, Joseph Weitzen and William Merrell. The men received information regarding Shontz & Myers, a clothing store in Sharon, Pennsylvania. On the night of the burglary, September 17, Drago and Mainer maintained a watch outside, while the other four entered the store. What the men didn't know was that the man providing them with the information was Sharon Police Patrolman Stanley Bombeck. The four inside the store were arrested immediately, while Drago and Mainer were able to flee.

By March 1961, the four arrested men had pled guilty, were sentenced by Pennsylvania authorities and sent to the Western Penitentiary outside of Pittsburgh. Drago and Mainer eventually surrendered in Youngstown, after being indicted for the burglary, and were fighting extradition from Ohio to Pennsylvania. Their attorney, Vincent P. Serman of Youngstown filed writs of habeas corpus for the two, claiming they each had alibis for the night of the robbery. The alibis were that Drago was in a Struthers gambling joint playing cards; while Mainer was in jail in Augusta, Georgia, on a traffic charge. Youngstown Common Pleas Judge Frank J. Battisti had denied the writs and, after Governor Michael V. DiSalle ordered their extradition, was ready to send the men to Pennsylvania to be tried pending an appeal. In late March, the 7th District Court of Appeals ruled in Battisti's favor. Attorney Serman then took the case to the Ohio Supreme Court, which refused to review the appeal. On June 8, Judge Battisti ordered the two men arrested immediately and sent to Pennsylvania.

On June 14, after a 14-month extradition battle, the two men appeared in a Mercer, Pennsylvania court and were arraigned for attempted burglary. Drago's bond was set at $40,000, which he posted and was freed; Mainer's bond was $60,000. On March 20, 1962, Mainer was found guilty of conspiracy and was sentenced to one to two years in the Allegheny County Workhouse.

On July 17, Drago took the witness stand during his trial in Mercer. He claimed that on the night of the burglary he was playing gin rummy in a poolroom in Struthers. His testimony was corroborated by Lenine "Lenny" Strollo, a tavern owner from Campbell, Ohio. The jury deliberated for three and a half hours before returning with a verdict of guilty. Attorneys announced they would ask for a new trial and the judge delayed sentencing, and Drago remained free on bond. On September 25, more than two and a half years after the burglary, Drago received a six to twelve month sentence in the Mercer County Jail.

After his release, Drago moved back to Cleveland. In the spring of 1964, he and Anthony Commorato were arrested for possession of burglary tools and breaking into an automobile. Both men were convicted at the end of May. On June 1, Common Pleas Judge Roy F. McMahon sentenced them both 1-to5-years in the Ohio Penitentiary. The judge then ordered that at the conclusion of that sentence, both men were to spend six months in the workhouse for breaking into the automobile. They were also fined $500 and court costs apiece.

Drago's next caper would prove to be the most lucrative of his career.

Friday, August 16, 1968, seemed like a normal day at the Lorain County Savings & Trust Company branch, located inside the Midway Mall Shopping Center north of Elyria. That is, until the Brink's Inc. guards showed up to make their daily routine pick-up – twice! At 11:10 that morning, two guards in Brink's uniforms and carrying side-arms appeared at the bank's inside walk-up window. Neither guard entered the bank. One guard stood aside, while the other spoke with a teller through a service window.

The teller asked the guard to sign a receipt book, which was normal procedure. The guard signed the name L.G. Waterhouse, who was a regular driver and pick-up man on the route. When the guard signed the wrong line in the book, the teller pointed it out to him. He then proceeded to sign on another wrong line. He was then asked to sign it a third time. The teller, as part of the routine procedure, then compared the signature to a list of Brink's employee-prepared signatures provided by the security company. Even though the signature appeared to be a match, the diligent teller checked with another teller for confirmation.

The second teller agreed with the match and the two of them proceeded to place two bags, stuffed with $5, $10, and $20 dollar bills, into a night deposit box; the money destined for the Federal Reserve Bank in downtown Cleveland. The guards removed the bags of cash from a sliding drawer outside the bank and soon disappeared among the shoppers in the mall.

Ten minutes later, another set of Brink's Inc. guards arrived. Once the tellers determined these were the real guards, they notified bank officials and the Elyria Police Department was called. The bank immediately closed and remained so until 3:00 that afternoon, during which time the FBI became involved. In a brief statement, a bank vice president announced that the guard impersonators made off with $93,000.

Nearly half a year passed before the robbery made its way back into the newspapers. On February 5, 1969, the Cleveland FBI office announced it made two arrests in the robbery of the Lorain County Savings & Trust Company. No details of how the men were tracked down appeared in any of the local newspapers. The FBI confirmed that 22-year-old Charles F. "Spider" Grisham was arrested at a Warren motel. Taken before U.S. Commissioner Clifford E. Bruce, Grisham's bond was set at $50,000. The second man Donald J. Coats of Brookpark, a suburb on the south-west border of Cleveland, was arrested at his Smith Road home. Referred to as the "inside man," Coats was one of the guards who arrived at the bank ten minutes after the robbery. Bond for Coats was set at $2,500, which he posted and was released.

Grisham was held in the Cuyahoga County Jail in Cleveland. The day after his arrest, attorney Gerald S. Gold went before Commissioner Bruce to get Grisham's bail reduced from the $50,000 that was set, claiming it was excessive. Gold told Bruce that $25,000 or $10,000 would be enough. "A person who has made a $25,000 bond is no more likely to try and escape then a person who has made a $50,000 bond," the attorney advised. Bruce disagreed and refused to reduce the bond, stating that bonds often were taken lightly by defendants and "this is a serious crime."

The FBI then announced a third man was identified, 27-year-old Joseph Diorio of Youngstown. Already a career criminal, Diorio was not hard to find, he was sitting in the Mahoning County Jail doing a 90-day stretch for receiving stolen property. U.S. Attorney Bernard J. Stuplinski stated that none of the money was recovered.

On February 12, a Federal Grand Jury in Cleveland returned indictments in the Lorain County Savings & Trust Company robbery. Indicted on charges of bank larceny were Coats, Grisham, Diorio and Joseph Drago. Assistant U.S. Attorney Harry E. Pickering stated that Diorio and Grisham posed as the Brink's guards; Drago was the get-away driver; and Coats "aided and abetted by supplying information about security arrangements." Drago was the only one not in custody. A fugitive warrant was issued for the 45-year-old, who was described as "a one-time associate of Cleveland underworld figure Julius Petro." Within 48 hours of being indicted, Drago was arrested by the FBI on Cleveland's East Side.

The day after the indictments were announced, against the wishes of U.S. Attorney Stuplinski, U.S. District Court Judge Girard E. Kalbfleisch reduced Grisham's bond from $50,000 to $25,000. Stuplinski's argument that Grisham was a "floater" who might disappear once released from custody, fell on deaf ears. Ironically, a few weeks later, on March 3, Clayton L. Grisham, the father of Charles, asked Kalbfleisch during a hearing, to revoke his son's bond. Grisham's father had pledged his property in order to secure his son's release. He told the judge, "My son was released on bond into my custody, but I never saw him during the two weeks of his release. He only came home in the daytime to shower and change his clothes when he knew I wouldn't be there." Clayton Grisham also testified that he had found two loaded hand-guns and ski masks in his son's closet a week earlier and notified Warren police about it.

Also appearing at the hearing was a representative of the United Bonding Insurance Company. He requested that the judge cancel the bond for Grisham on the grounds that he was a "poor risk." When Grisham's attorney protested the proposed cancellation of his client's bond, Kalbfleisch replied, "Anyone who would put his father through such an ordeal should have a bond set at $60,000," which he raised it to immediately.

When the case came to trial on September 23, it nearly came to a halt the same day before a jury could even be selected. After Grisham was brought into the courtroom in handcuffs, defense attorneys immediately requested that U.S. District Court Judge William K. Thomas dismiss a panel of 33 prospective jurors claiming it prejudiced his right to a fair trial. The judge met with defense attorneys and Assistant U.S. Attorney Harry Pickering. Thomas then denied the motion declaring that once a jury was selected, he would give instructions about a defendant's "presumption of innocence until the charge against him was proven beyond a reasonable doubt."

After a jury of eight men and four women was seated, opening statements by the government began on Wednesday, September 25. Harry Pickering told the jury that Donald Coats, the regular guard scheduled to make the pick-up on August 16 at the Lorain County Savings & Trust Company, delayed his arrival at the bank by stopping to shop. This gave his accomplices the time they needed to make the phony pick-up before he arrived ten minutes later. Diorio and Grisham made the pick-up, posing as the Brink's guards, with Diorio signing the receipt book for the money. Drago waited outside in the get-away vehicle. Pickering said that only $500 of the money was recovered, including a $5 bill which bore the stamp of a cashier from the bank, found at the Coats home on Smith Road.

When defense attorneys gave their opening statements the next day, counsel for Coats stated his client had never met any of the accused men prior to the robbery. He claimed the theft occurred due to the failure of bank personnel to observe security procedures.

On the first day of testimony, Pickering called a teller from the Lorain County Savings & Trust Company bank, who identified Diorio and Grisham as the Brink's guards who picked up the money bags from the deposit box. She recalled witnessing Diorio sign the receipt book in the wrong place twice. On cross-examination she said she identified the two men from FBI photographs, which she was shown again a few days earlier when she arrived at the Old Federal Building on Public Square in downtown Cleveland for the start of the trial.

For some reason the Cleveland *Plain Dealer* cut off its coverage of the trial, publishing its last article on September 27. During the defense portion of the trial none of the defendants took the stand. The closing statements came to an end on October 9 and deliberations began the next day. After taking the weekend off, the jury came back on Monday and delivered a stunning verdict, all four defendants were acquitted.

In a statement read by jury foreman Robert F. Bentley, the jury "censured the Lorain County Savings & Trust Company and Brink's Inc. for failing to enforce adequate security measures." The jury told Judge Thomas they were acting as "concerned citizens" in their criticism. Bentley declared that the fact the crime occurred at all was an indictment of both companies, telling Thomas neither had improved their security since the robbery occurred, causing the jury to arrive at the conclusion they were "acting irresponsibly in the public trust."

The jury concluded, "That this crime should ever happen the way it did borders on the absurd." When asked what led to the jury's decision to acquit all four of the defendants, in view of the eyewitness testimony that Diorio and Grisham walked away with the money, Bentley replied, "We just didn't feel the government had proved the charges against them." Beyond that, he would not elaborate.

In July 1970, a Lorain County judge ruled the men acquitted in October 1969 would have to stand trial again, this time under Ohio law for larceny by trick. All four men were indicted by the Lorain County Grand Jury in February 1970. Common Pleas Judge Leroy F. Kelly overruled Coats and Grisham's motion they could not be tried twice for the same crime. The judge set a trial date of August 24.

Arrest warrants were issued and served on all the men except Drago. After Drago refused to surrender himself, a Federal warrant, charging unlawful flight to avoid prosecution was issued on June 2. FBI agents finally arrested Drago in Farrell, Pennsylvania on November 13, 1970. There was no record of a second trial taking place.

It was the last time Drago was reported on in the newspapers. Drago died on January 11, 1997 at the age of 72. He is buried in Lake View Cemetery.

Vincent Innocenzi

"His ability to stay free while accomplices landed behind bars made him a king among thieves and brought him a host of enemies..." – Akron Beacon Journal, August 11, 1960

The Innocenzi family was no stranger to violent crimes. Two of the brothers were murder victims, a third died under what the family considered mysterious circumstances.

During the late 1930s, Edmond "Moe" Innocenzi was single and still lived at home with his mother and step-father; his own father, Adolf died in 1926. Innocenzi managed a White Front Provision Company;[83] one of a chain of butcher shops in Cleveland that at one time operated 13 outlets. At the time that Edmond managed the store, the chain was owned by Frank J. Hoge, a Cleveland bail bondsmen, who reached underworld fame in the late 1920s and through the 1930s as one of the top racketeers in the city. He and three others dominated the policy rackets here at one time and were known as the "Big Four." That ended when the Mayfield Road Mob decided to cut themselves in on the thriving business.

The shop Edmond Innocenzi managed was located at 7107 Central Avenue[84] at the corner of East 71st Street. The shop was mentioned in a July 8, 1940, *Plain Dealer* story in which famed Cleveland Safety Director Eliot Ness discussed a new police "Zone Boost Plan," in an attempt to stem the increase of burglaries, safecrackings and other crimes "not readily detected by touring police."

Ness's December 1938 plan of dividing the city into 32 "circular zones," patrolled by police cars equipped with two-way radios, resulted in a substantial decrease in robberies, assaults and purse snatchings because police were quicker to arrive at the scene. Criminals, driven to cover, now turned to burglaries. During the second half of 1940, the number of houses and stores broken into through windows and backdoors significantly increased. Police, on the move in their zone cars, seldom saw the rear entrances of these places and by the time they were alerted and arrived at the scene the burglars had fled. The point of the new plan, according to Ness, was that patrolmen would be required to "do more walking, watch more alleys and backdoors and get acquainted with all residents of each zone so as to spot strangers readily." In supporting the point about recent burglaries, the *Plain Dealer* listed the details of six recent break-ins; one of which was the White Front Provision butcher shop that Innocenzi managed. The article stated the burglars "entered by forcing a back door and $25.10 in cash, a check for $2.10 and a ham were stolen." In addition to this break-in, Innocenzi endured a number of hold-up attempts; one in mid-December 1940, when a man tried to rob him by threatening him with a razor.

On Friday, December 27, 1940, Lincoln McNealy, a Black man who lived around the corner, ten houses down at 2229 East 71st Street, purchased some meat from Innocenzi and refused to pay him. When Edmond demanded the money, McNealy threatened him with a knife. The following Tuesday afternoon, McNealy came back to the store around 5:30 while Innocenzi was out. When a woman walked in to purchase some meat, McNealy stepped behind the counter to help her. Innocenzi's 24-year-old assistant didn't try to stop him, later telling police he was "afraid of the man." The woman complained about the cut of meat she was given and as she argued with McNealy, Innocenzi suddenly arrived back at the store. Apprised of what was going on, Edmond took care of the customer and then ordered McNealy out of the shop. McNealy, refused to leave, however, and instead demanded 50 cents for waiting on the woman. At this point Innocenzi shoved him out the front door. McNealy's parting words were, "I'll get you later."

Just before 6:00 p.m., Innocenzi left the White Front Provision Company and walked out to the sidewalk. McNealy was waiting, hiding in a doorway next to the butcher shop. He suddenly stepped out and thrust a 10-inch-long knife blade into Innocenzi's side, saying. "I said I'd get you." Innocenzi crumbled to the sidewalk as McNealy fled around the corner and down East 71st Street. Police arrived and rushed Innocenzi to Mount Sinai Hospital where he died two hours later, but not before telling police the name of the man who stabbed him. On January 3, Edmond Innocenzi's funeral was held from the S.A. Conti & Son funeral home on Murray Hill Road in Little Italy. He was buried in nearby Lake View Cemetery.

Police quickly discovered the 29-year-old McNealy was paroled from the Ohio Penitentiary in 1938 after serving less than three years of a manslaughter sentence for which, ironically, he stabbed a man to death in 1936. Police arrested him at a relative's house on Hawthorn Avenue on January 2. McNealy signed a statement admitting to the killing, but claimed he was justified because Innocenzi had physically thrown him out of the store. The next month, McNealy went to trial where he was charged with first-degree murder. The jury must have believed his "self-defense" claim to some extent as they returned a verdict of guilty of second-degree murder. Common Pleas Judge Harrison W. Ewing sentenced him to life in prison. McNealy was eventually released and returned to Cleveland. He died in Akron at the age of 73 in February 1985, after a long illness. His obituary stated that he was "employed as a meat cutter."

Edmond Innocenzi's younger brother Vincent was nicknamed "the Horn," and "the Beak" due to his large nose. He was described as, "A man with a yen for fancy silk suits and a genius for staying out of jail." He first came to the public's attention in March 1951 for stealing a safe in Cambridge, Ohio. The theft took place during a rash of burglaries and safecrackings in that city, which occurred during the summer and fall of 1950. A *Plain Dealer* article stated, "At the time Cambridge police reported automobiles operated by [Julius] Petro and his gang were seen a number of times since the outbreak of the burglary wave there."

During a search for hoodlums at the request of the Cambridge Police Department, which included Petro, Joseph Drago and Michael Grande, police arrested only Innocenzi on March 7 and he was transported back to Cambridge. The next day, the Guernsey County Grand Jury heard testimony against Innocenzi for stealing a safe containing $65 from the Singer Sewing Company back on September 16, 1950. Innocenzi and an accomplice, Angelo Carmello, were held on $15,000 bonds. A third man, Edward Robert Stamphel, alias Angelo Marcellino, was also held. While the men were in the local jail, detectives from Zanesville, in Muskingum County, just to the west of Cambridge, questioned them regarding a number of safecrackings that took place in that city.

On December 19, 1951, Innocenzi pleaded guilty to the Cambridge burglary and safe tampering charges in Guernsey County Common Pleas Court. According to a *Cleveland Press* article, "Common Pleas Judge Delbert L. Tedrick gave him an indeterminate penitentiary sentence." After serving prison time, Innocenzi told his wife, Juanita, "Never, again" would he do anything that would put him back in prison. He was "scared" to go back. He was out by April 1953, because at that time police were looking for him for receiving stolen property. By that time Innocenzi had become the most wanted member of Petro's old Collinwood safe cracking crew, according to Detective Lieutenant Thomas White.

Innocenzi's most impressive burglary occurred in August 1953 when he was involved in the theft of a coin collection. Herbert Feinberg, according to police, was "recognized as one of the four principal coin dealers in the United States." At his home in San Bernardino, California, Feinberg stored nearly a ton of coins, mostly brand new uncirculated ones obtained after they were newly minted.

On Friday night, August 21, 1953, Feinberg took his wife and son out to a drive-in movie. While they were gone, several men entered the home by prying open a window to steal the coins. The following is a summary of the remarks from detectives at the scene as reported by the *San Bernardino County Sun*:

> The coins were stored in the Feinberg's den in a large wall case. The thieves took rolls of coins and money bags containing coins from this case. Sheets and pillow cases were stripped from the Feinbergs' beds. The sheets were placed on the floor of the den and the coins dumped onto them. The men then used the small red wagon of the Feinberg's 6-year-old son to haul the heavy sacks of coins out to a getaway car parked in an alley at the rear of the home. The burglars even took the 6-year-old's coin collection. Several men were believed to be involved in the burglary and that it was a professional job; the burglars knew what they were after, having taken some of the most valuable coins, while leaving others.

One detective surmised, "We think the burglars were surprised at their work." This was based on a money bag with $200 worth of new nickels being found in the middle of the living room floor by Mrs. Feinberg upon their return home that night.

The police chief said the burglary was "the biggest in San Bernardino" that he could remember. Feinberg initially placed the loss at $250,000, which represented the "collectors' value," while the face value of the coins themselves was around $55,000. Over the weekend, Feinberg adjusted the estimates to $70,000 and $35,000 respectively. He told police the coins were insured.

A side note to the robbery, the newspaper initially quoted a detective as stating that a 1913 Liberty Head nickel was "believed missing." Only five of these coins were minted, making it one of the rarest coins in American history. One can track the history of these five coins and their owners on the internet, but neither Herbert Feinberg's name, nor mention of the burglary, appear in the stories. The latest reported sales of these coins fetched one owner $3.7 million in 2010 and another $5.0 million in a private purchase in 2007.

While the theft was reported as the "largest single burglary ever perpetrated in San Bernardino," moving the coins proved to be a daunting task. The automobile transporting the burglars and the coins broke down on the way out of San Bernardino. Once they were away safe, disposing of the coins became the next problem. The shiny uncirculated coins looked so new the thieves resorted to "frying the coins in pans to make them look older."

After San Bernardino authorities wisely sought the assistance of the Los Angeles Police Department, the investigation began to move quickly. On September 14, a little over three weeks after the burglary, police arrested Harold F. Berthlaume, described as the ringleader of the burglary gang, and Martin E. Eschman, both of Los Angeles, and charged them with the theft. Within hours of these first arrests, police had five others, including the 17-year-old wife of one of the men, in custody. It was obvious after the arrest of Berthlaume and Eschman that someone must have been talking. The other arrests occurred quickly. There was not much mention in the newspapers about the investigation or the people arrested. Another topic that was never mentioned or explained was how the two Los Angeles burglars got involved with Vincent Innocenzi in the first place.

On September 16, William Krause was arrested in Cleveland. The next day, Innocenzi, who had made his way back to Ohio, may have been a little too curious as to what was going on out west. He called a bar in Los Angeles that he had frequented while he was out there planning the burglary. The bartender, who took the telephone call, contacted police who quickly traced it to a pay phone in a private club on Route 8, north of Cuyahoga Falls. Cleveland police were contacted, who enlisted the help of the Akron Police Department. Officers were sent to the café where Innocenzi was still seated in one of the booths. He and Krause, who had traveled to Los Angeles together the previous month, would soon be making a return trip.

Local prosecutors agreed to allow the case to be tried in Los Angeles, citing a provision in the penal code stating that either county, San Bernardino or Los Angeles, had jurisdiction in cases where items are stolen in one county and transported to another. A week later, Berthlaume, Eschman, Innocenzi and Krause were indicted by a Los Angeles County Grand Jury. Innocenzi and Krause were in the process of extradition hearings and would not arrive until mid-October.

On January 14, 1954, Berthlaume pleaded guilty to grand theft and received a sentence of one to ten years in the California State Prison. Innocenzi pleaded guilty on January 25. In addition to being sentenced to nine months in jail, he was placed on five years' probation.

Of the coins stolen in the burglary, Berthlaume told police he had "peddled" about $150 worth. At the time of his arrest, he still had $400 of the coins in his possession. None of the remaining coins were ever reported to be recovered.

As for the famous 1913 Liberty Head nickel, it was never again mentioned after the initial reports of the theft.

There were no reports on Innocenzi for the next two years. Then, in early January 1956, the Lorain County Sheriff's office wanted to question him regarding a $35,000 Christmas Eve safecracking job at the O'Neil-Sheffield Shopping Center in Sheffield, Ohio, located just west of Cuyahoga County along the shore of Lake Erie. Innocenzi, still on probation from the coin theft conviction, surrendered to Cleveland police after he found out he was a suspect in the robbery. The Lorain County Sheriff's Department released him after a polygraph test indicated otherwise.

On Friday, August 10, 1956, Innocenzi and three others were arrested in Mount Gilead, Ohio, a village 45 miles north of Columbus. A shopping center employee became suspicious of the men and wrote down the license plate number of the car they were driving and gave it to local authorities. Sheriff's deputies arrived and searched the automobile. They concluded the men "had enough lock opening devices to make a locksmith jealous." They found more than 1,000 blank keys, wax for making key impressions, key-making equipment, drills, and lock-jimmying devices. The men were arrested and held for investigation. With Innocenzi were Anthony "Joe Blow" Velletto, Thomas Rudelik, and Dave F. Tiburzio. The Marion Star newspaper, in reporting the incident, stated that, "The three Clevelanders [were] under $50,000 bond on burglary charges in Steubenville," involving a $10,000 burglary that took place there five weeks earlier.

On Tuesday, a Columbus Municipal Court judge set bonds of $20,000 apiece for the men. The newspapers linked the men to a series of burglaries in Northeast Ohio. In addition to their participation in the Sheffield safecracking, the newspapers also mentioned similar cases in Middleburg Heights, Youngstown and Barberton. Shortly after preliminary hearings for the men were continued, the *Akron Beacon Journal* reported, "Three fearful state's witnesses have asked officials and newspapers to withhold their names as they prepared to testify against the men, described as 'hardened, professional criminals.'"

On August 20, the Franklin County Grand Jury heard from a husband and wife, who watched the four men case a local store in Mount Gilead, and the testimony of the store employee who wrote down the license plate number of the men's car. After their testimony, grand jury members returned indictments against the four for possession of burglary tools.

Around 2:00 a.m. on October 14, residents near the Wintersville branch of the First National Bank & Trust Company in Jefferson County heard noises and called the Ohio State Patrol. When a patrolman arrived, he surprised two men who were trying to get into the bank through a rear door. The would-be burglars and the patrolman exchanged gunfire before the men fled and got away. Burglar tools were found near the back door and a half-block away a late model automobile without license plates was found. A check of the car showed it was registered to Thomas Rudelik. A search was soon on for him and Anthony Velletto, both of whom were arrested with Innocenzi at Mount Gilead. Innocenzi, meanwhile, was picked up Sunday night in Cleveland and held for questioning. Rudelik was captured and returned to the Jefferson County Jail, where Dominic Mafrici, another crew member, was still being held, to await trial for the Baron Café robbery (See Chapter Ten: Dominic Mafrici & David Tiburzio biography).

In May 1959, Innocenzi's name popped up in conjunction with that of Alfred "Allie" Calabrese and Paul Perrotti, who were serving lengthy sentences in the Ohio Penitentiary. Perrotti, according to the article, had allegedly been running a protection racket in Massillon, Ohio. A full scale war of words erupted in the local newspapers pitting Stark County Prosecutor Norman J. Putman against Perrotti and his attorney Earle E. Wise. During this period, Innocenzi and George Michael Florea were allegedly involved in the bombing of the Meinhart's Restaurant / Cigar store in Massillon. No charges were filed against either man, and no connection to crime in Massillon was ever traced to Calabrese or Perrotti.

On Monday, September 7, 1959, Innocenzi, George Florea and Joseph Jewell Arrington of Ohio, and West Virginian Paul Nathaniel Hankish were surprised by the local police around 3:15 a.m. while in the act of cracking a safe in the basement of the Community Supermarket in East Fairmont, West Virginia. Innocenzi, Florea and Hankish were arrested immediately and taken to jail. Police returned to the store Monday afternoon to find Arrington, a Black man with an impressive safecracking reputation, still hiding in the basement.

The next day, a night watchman from the Wheeling Country Club picked Hankish out of a police lineup. The watchman said he recognized Hankish because he had been handcuffed by him to a radiator after surprising a group of burglars at the country club back on August 24. Hankish had a record from running a numbers racket and operating a horse racing book in Moundsville, West Virginia. His underworld activities in the coming years left him with a notorious reputation in the state. Innocenzi, Arrington and Florea were soon back on the street after posting $15,000 bonds.

Innocenzi's next burglary took him back to a familiar place, Cambridge, Ohio. For this one, he was arrested and jailed in Cleveland in November 1959, after being identified as one of three men seen loitering near a supermarket in Cambridge. Shortly after being spotted, the store was broken into and $500 was taken following a safecracking. A man, who was taking a shortcut through the store parking lot, saw three men outside the store. He was able to identify Innocenzi from a photograph. After his arrest, the man picked him out of a Cleveland police lineup.

Before the month of November was over, Innocenzi was arrested after another safecracking, this time closer to home. On November 20, he was again identified by a witness who claimed he watched him leave a Fisher Food Company store at 8400 Euclid Avenue carrying a suitcase and in the company of two other men. After arriving to go to work, employees discovered Innocenzi's handiwork; management estimated he made off with $8,000. After being picked up by police and charged with safe tampering, Innocenzi was released under a $25,000 bond.

In February 1960, Innocenzi became the focal point of a court ruling involving "major procedural changes" in the handling of the Cleveland Traffic Court's docket. The battle involved the driving rights of Innocenzi after his legal counsel demanded that the court vacate a guilty plea he entered to a speeding charge more than a year earlier. His attorney, John P. Butler, a former assistant Cuyahoga County prosecutor, explained to Municipal Judge Theodore M. Williams that Innocenzi was misled into pleading guilty based on a blank, unsigned affidavit. The attorney argued that the blank affidavit constituted a nullity. Chief Police Prosecutor Richard F. Matia explained that the current practice of not signing affidavits was in effect for a long time due to manpower shortages in both the court clerk's office and the prosecutor's office. Matia advised that the issue of validity of other traffic affidavits could result in a number of citizens being entitled to a return of their fines. The next day, Judge Williams ruled in Innocenzi's favor stating that, "Merely because an individual pleads guilty to a non-existent affidavit, it does not validate his conviction." The judge said he believed if the same set of circumstances prevailed in other cases, fines could be refunded. Prosecutor Matia predicted that the ruling would necessitate "a major revision" of affidavit procedures.

Innocenzi received even better news on April 18, 1960, when the indictment for robbing the Fisher Foods store on Euclid Avenue was dropped by Common Pleas Judge J.J.P. Corrigan at the request of the county prosecutor's office. The decision came after the state's main witness claimed he now could not be sure of his identification. The *Plain Dealer* pointed out in its article that Innocenzi to-date had been arrested for 18 felony investigations and 14 misdemeanors.

Meanwhile, one of Innocenzi's burglary crew-mates was gaining publicity for the wrong reasons. In early May 1960, Special Agent in Charge of the Cleveland FBI office, Edward E. Hargett advised that Joseph Arrington was "becoming one of the most sought burglars in the country." It's interesting that Hargett's comment didn't explain if he meant Arrington was being "sought" by the authorities or "sought" by other burglars. Hargett became familiar with Arrington because the FBI arrested him three times on Federal fugitive warrants, each time for being a bail jumper. One of these arrests involved an armed robbery of the Alhambra Bowling Center at 10309 Euclid Avenue during 1958.

During the late spring of 1960, the trial for the supermarket break-in at Fairmont, West Virginia, the previous September, finally got underway. During the trial his lawyer claimed Innocenzi had met the other men in the store "because they wanted a place to hold a reunion." The jury didn't buy it and on June 8 Innocenzi was convicted along with George Florea and Paul Hankish. Arrington, who was arrested with them, had jumped bail; he was currently being held in Camden, New Jersey, after being arrested for a break-in there. Innocenzi was sentenced to a term of 2-to-10-years in the West Virginia State Penitentiary, but remained free on a $15,000 bond pending an appeal of his conviction.[85]

Innocenzi's increased criminal activity and time away from home on "jobs" put pressure on his family life. The fact that he had taken up with a young lady of "questionable character" didn't help matters. Audrey "Audie" Shaw, at 26 years of age, had a hard look to her. So hard, that she usually gave her age as 31 or 32 when she used the name Carla DeMarco, or another alias. While not referred to as a prostitute or a call girl by the newspapers, they reported that she was "known" in Akron, Youngstown and Warren, Ohio and Erie, Pennsylvania – the latter being listed as her hometown. On November 28, 1959, Shaw was arrested in Cleveland with Innocenzi and charged with "false hotel registration" after she checked into Fenway Hall at East 107th Street and Euclid Avenue using the name Mrs. Ann Paulette. Innocenzi was charged with occupying a room for the purpose of prostitution and lewdness. Both were released after posting $200 bonds. Word got back to Innocenzi's wife, Juanita, most likely due to an article about the arrests that appeared in the Sunday *Plain Dealer*. She filed for divorce charging cruelty and gross neglect the following month – but she failed to pursue further court action.

In January 1960, Innocenzi and Shaw were living together in a Liberty Township home on Roosevelt Drive, in Trumbull County. Innocenzi, described as a "dapper" dresser, was also particular about the furnishings in the places he lived. The home the couple shared had wall-to-wall carpeting and many modern features. The home was so nicely done that when Innocenzi was forced to leave, Philip "Fleegle" Mainer, another local Mahoning Valley burglar, moved in with his wife, a former nightclub dancer from Chicago. When Mainer was sent to prison, Mafia bigwig "Joe the Wolf" DiCarlo took up residence there.

The cozy living conditions between Innocenzi and Shaw didn't last long. Shortly after they moved in Shaw was taken to North Side Hospital, so severely beaten that she was in a coma for two days. Shaw told police she was injured in a fall from a moving vehicle. Despite the unmistakable signs of an assault, she refused to press charges against Innocenzi. Local deputies warned the safecracker "to stay out of Trumbull County." Officials believed the couple then rented an apartment above the Alibi Lounge at Boardman and South Phelps Streets in downtown Youngstown, although Innocenzi was still residing at times with his wife in a Cleveland area apartment. On February 1, Shaw, Innocenzi and two other men were arrested at a lakefront restaurant in Cleveland and taken in "for investigation."

On June 11, $20,000 was stolen during a burglary at Idora Park, Youngstown's popular amusement park. Six days later, Innocenzi was questioned by new Youngstown Police Chief Frank Watters. In early August, three associates of Innocenzi were captured in the middle of cracking open a safe in Napoleon, Ohio. The gang's lookout escaped causing some to believe it was because he had tipped off police to the crime; the lookout was alleged to be Innocenzi.

On Wednesday, August 3, Audrey Shaw checked out of a Cleveland hotel and went with Innocenzi to Akron where the two registered in a room together. The next day, Innocenzi, who was driving his wife's 1960 Chevrolet Impala, illegally parked the vehicle on State Street during rush hour and the Akron police had it towed. Innocenzi phoned professional bail bondsman John Sica of Akron, whom he knew from having supplied his bail in the past, and told him he had used his last dime to make the call. The bail bondsman went with Innocenzi to the police station, paid the $16.50 to cover the fine and towing cost, and loaned him $4 to get gas for the trip back to Cleveland. Sica would later tell police, "I didn't ask him what he was doing here. He was down and out – he only had a dime in his pocket. And he didn't seem nervous or under any strain."

That Saturday, August 6, Innocenzi was back with his wife and two young sons, at their home, a duplex at 9807 Easton Avenue, on Cleveland's south-east side. He and Juanita were watching television until 6:00 p.m. "He kept looking at the clock," she recalled. "At 7:30 he got up and said he had to meet a person. I never saw him again."

Four days later, on the afternoon of Wednesday, August 10, John M. Hall had just finished eating his lunch around 12:40. An employee of the Akron Metropolitan Parks for 24-years, Hall, who was part Delaware Indian and a World War I veteran, was on his way to mow a patch of tall grass with his tractor-mower along a lonely lane called Pump House Road in Virginia-Kendall Park, located in northern Summit County. Once there, Hall thought he saw a "bundle of rags" off to the side of the road. He soon realized he was looking at a corpse rotting away in the hot August sun; he quickly moved away so he would not disturb the area and notified sheriff's deputies.

The dead man's hands were in his pockets and clenched. His left hand held a Lincoln cent. Police also found five $20 bills in his pocket, despite the fact his wallet was missing. The body was taken to the Cleveland morgue after Summit County Assistant Coroner J.H. Dix's "routine death pronouncement," where positive identification was made through fingerprints. It was reported, "The dead man, whose body apparently had been there for three or four days, was widely known by all Northeast Ohio law enforcement agencies and had the reputation of being the area's number one safe expert, even acquiring a national reputation." The dead man was Vincent Innocenzi.

Where and when Innocenzi was killed was the subject of conjecture. While authorities agreed he was murdered – three .38 Special caliber slugs in the head – late Saturday night or early Sunday morning, there was a question of where the killing took place. George Vaughn, Summit County Chief Deputy, told the Youngstown *Vindicator* he believed the murder took place where the body was found. He claimed the amount of blood on the ground confirmed this. Meanwhile, the Cleveland *Plain Dealer* reported, "Summit County authorities said there was no doubt Innocenzi had been dumped there after being shot elsewhere." Sheriff Russell M. Bird thought the killing probably took place in Cuyahoga County. The continuing investigation would resolve that the murder took place where the body was discovered.

Juanita Innocenzi was brought to the Central Police Station in Cleveland for questioning. Mercifully, police did not take her to the morgue to identify the body, which was decomposing, and the head largely destroyed from the impact of the bullets. Not surprisingly, one of the first questions from investigators was why Juanita hadn't reported her husband missing. Hunched over and weeping, she replied it was not unusual for her husband to leave and not be heard from for several days. This comment, which appeared in the *Plain Dealer*, seemed at odds with a quote reported in the *Akron Beacon Journal*. That newspaper reported, "His wife, who had been working as a waitress, said, 'I loved him. Maybe he wasn't right, but he loved the kids. He never told me what he was doing, but he always called me when he was going to be away.'" Juanita also told detectives her husband, "didn't have a dime" when he left home Saturday night, this despite the $100 found in his pocket. Mrs. Innocenzi had some harsh words for her husband's murderer. "A snake is low," she stated. "But any man who would shoot another in the back is lower. He didn't have the nerve to look Vince in the face when he killed him." Juanita told police Innocenzi was a "good husband who loved his children." Also questioned was Armand Innocenzi, the victim's brother. He claimed he knew nothing about his brother's activities, calling him the "black sheep" of the family.

The Cleveland and Akron Police, as well as the newspapers representing those cities, had lots of questions for which answers could simply not be found. The *Akron Beacon Journal* asked:

Who were the men who drove Innocenzi to Barlow Road about a mile southwest of the intersection of Routes 8 and 303, marched him out of the car and down a woodland path?

Who were the men who ordered him to place his hands in his pockets and kneel down, then pumped three bullets in the back of his head?

Who were the men who left him there to rot – to be mistaken for a "bundle of rags" by John M. Hall?

"We shall probably never know," stated Cleveland Detective Lieutenant Thomas White, who was well familiar with Innocenzi and men of his ilk. Regarding the penny found in his hand, White related a tale that, "In the old gangland days, gangsters would use this as an indication that the victim either failed to split the loot from a job or had beaten them out of money." The detective chief went on to say that Innocenzi was known to be part of a "loose-knit" group of about 15 safecrackers and burglary men. The victim was killed "undoubtedly, over a quarrel about money. Probably some criminal arrangement fell through."

Chief Deputy Vaughn offered, "Possibly he knew too much...Perhaps he set up a job that didn't go right...Maybe he gave someone a bum steer...Could be that he served as a lookout for some guys and got away while they didn't...Who knows." One thing that was known, there was "speculation galore," just no real answers. Both Summit County law enforcement officials, Bird and Vaughn, were sure at least two men were involved; one who held the gun and the other who drove to the isolated part of the park.

The "bundle of rags" that Hall thought he saw turned out to be one of the custom-made English silk suits Innocenzi was known for wearing. He was also adorned in a custom-made shirt and wearing expensive loafers. A label inside one of the trouser pockets read: "This suit tailored expressly for Vincent Innocenzi."

Police hoped that by finding the Impala it might reveal some clues to the killing. A description of the automobile was given in the newspapers and announced on the evening news. When it was found on Thursday night, police technicians came up empty in the search for clues. Police theorized Innocenzi drove his wife's Impala to the parking lot of Chanel High School in Bedford, Ohio, and left it there, getting into another vehicle. The school was near a restaurant where Innocenzi told his wife he was going. Like his wallet, the keys were never found. A search revealed a pair of black leather gloves and a box of metal washers. Police claimed the washers were a "typical hoodlum trick" for cheating on long distance telephone calls. It should be noted that two other prominent mobsters with Cleveland / Mahoning Valley connections were also arrested for using washers and slugs. Leo Moceri, while a fugitive, was arrested in Hollywood, California, in 1952 for using washers in a Vine Avenue telephone booth. James Licavoli was once arrested while placing slugs in a vending machine in Florida.

In a bizarre piece of reporting the Youngstown *Vindicator* wrote, "Local law enforcement officials here learned today [August 11] that a special underworld meeting was called for last Friday in Cleveland. Innocenzi was reported to have attended the meeting with several local hoods." Neither the *Cleveland Press* nor the *Plain Dealer* reported this meeting. No other details of the alleged meeting were offered.

By Thursday morning, the investigation was in high gear...so were theories and speculation. One of the first "strong rumors" reported was that Innocenzi was attempting to muscle in on the bail bonding business in Akron. Two of the local bail bondsmen were questioned. John Sica, who had helped Innocenzi recover his automobile just days before his death, told investigators there was "never any indication that Innocenzi wanted to get into the bail bonding business in Akron." Liborio Percoco also claimed that he had never heard that Innocenzi was attempting to enter the business. "I don't see how Innocenzi could work that with his jail record," the bail bondsman stated.

On Friday, police took a "mine detector" out to the murder scene hoping to find the three .38 Special cartridges fired from the gun that killed Innocenzi. Their efforts failed. Meanwhile, the Napoleon, Ohio, robbery the previous month crept into the investigation. Police discovered a car there that they believed belonged to one of the burglary suspects that got away. After finding Innocenzi's body, deputies found a car that was stolen from Napoleon at the time of the burglary abandoned near the murder site. Investigators then focused on "every gangland connection that Innocenzi had in hopes of finding a possible clue to why someone might have felt Innocenzi had not come up with his 'share of the loot' from a job."

Sheriff's deputies had spoken to Audrey Shaw by telephone. She told them that she received a call from Innocenzi Saturday night before he left his house. He told her he had a meeting scheduled for 9:00 p.m. with two men, whom he didn't name, and that he would see her at the Akron hotel where she was staying and give her $100 before the meeting. She told him to go to his meeting first and then come to see her. That Friday, Shaw checked out of her hotel room and was never seen or heard from again; not even bothering to show up for Innocenzi's funeral, which took place the next day.

George Vaughn made plans to go to Warren to check out a lead. On the evening of Sunday, August 7, Warren police chased and stopped a speeding automobile containing Anthony Libertore and Cecil Angelberger. While the men were being held and questioned, detectives searched the area along the chase route and found a .32 caliber revolver and six sticks of dynamite in a waterproof bag that had been tossed in a ditch. The two men were questioned about the discovery 18 hours after they were arrested. After Angelberger passed a lie detector test he was released. Libertore also passed the test, but was immediately sentenced to a ten-day jail term for reckless driving.

Libertore had a notorious reputation in Cleveland, having been involved in the murder of two Cleveland police officers[86] while robbing a filling station in December 1937. Libertore received a life sentence, but was paroled in 1958. When Vaughn arrived in Warren to question Libertore, the cop-killer told the Summit County investigator, "I'm just the original hard luck kid. First, I'm stopped and arrested for nothing. Then they find dynamite in a ditch near where I was arrested. Now they think I'm connected with the murder of a guy I don't even know. The first time I ever left Cuyahoga County and broke parole, what happens?"

On Saturday, August 13, George Vaughn made plans to question Paul "Red" Carpenter, who was being held in the Stark County Jail for a murder in Alliance, Ohio. Vaughn was sure that Carpenter and Innocenzi had pulled a safecracking job at a Medina A&P supermarket back in early 1957, a fact the Medina sheriff confirmed, although charges were never pressed against either man. Vaughn felt confident he could get some answers, declaring, "Carpenter's life isn't worth a lead nickel, even if he gets out of jail. Maybe he'll do some talking." For whatever reason, however, Carpenter clammed up during a 35-minute session with the chief deputy sheriff. Other efforts to corral witnesses were also failing.

That same Saturday, the 39-year-old safecracker extraordinaire was laid to rest at Cleveland's famous Lake View Cemetery, in which such historic figures like President James A. Garfield, John D. Rockefeller and famed "Untouchable" lawman Eliot Ness have final resting places. Vincent Innocenzi rests on a small knoll not far from where older brother Edmond and his father Adolph are buried. In 1984, Vincent's brother, Harry joined him on the knoll.

On the day of the funeral the *Akron Beacon Journal* announced its theory of Innocenzi's movements on the night of the murder:

> He apparently met two or more men in Bedford, left his car in the parking lot and was taken to the murder site to "talk." Police believe that Innocenzi was then told to walk down Barlow Road with his back to his slayers. The first shot apparently spun him around and the other two were pumped into him after he fell to the ground. The penny may have been in his hand or he may have been made to keep it in his hand and keep his hands in his pockets by threat of the gun, they say.

Sadly, Vincent's death was not the only tragedy for the Innocenzi family that month. On August 19, less than a week after Vincent's funeral, Sylvio Innocenzi was found hanging in his Brooklyn Heights home. Police called his death "an apparent suicide." It was reported that the older brother was in poor health and distraught over Vincent's death and that he wrote a note and tied an electric cord to a rafter in his garage before stepping off the trunk of his automobile and hanging himself. Although ruled a suicide, family members felt there was foul play.

The investigation into the murder of Vincent Innocenzi soon fizzled out. No one was ever brought to trial for his killing. Despite the fact there was no information to connect him to the murder spree going on in the Youngstown / Warren area at that time, his death was still tied to the gambling activity there. His murder has been associated with the unrest that took place in the Mahoning Valley, which included the murders of eight other individuals, for the past 60 years.

In researching this book, I met with Vincent Innocenzi's son, Mario, a local businessman, during August 2019. He told me that his mother was pregnant with him at the time of his father's death. He grew up knowing little about his father's life, other than the stories he received from family members. Although the family spoke little about Innocenzi's murder over the years, Mario did offer a couple of interesting, if not tell-tale insights. At our first meeting he mentioned that years ago he had seen a report that claimed the Pittsburgh mob wanted his father dead because he and Sylvio had killed a Pittsburgh member. Although I had never heard that, I thought that it sounded plausible, as I always wondered why he was killed and what the connection was to the unrest going on in the Mahoning Valley at that time. It would also support his family's belief that Sylvio was also a murder victim.

During our second meeting, it got a little more interesting. He mentioned he had sent me a copy of a headline about the Pittsburgh mob member his father and uncle had killed. I hadn't received it. As Mario was looking for it on his cell phone, he starts to tell me they used a shotgun, and along with the Pittsburgh member, the guy's girlfriend was killed. Now this is sounding a little more familiar. He finds the article and says, "The guy's name is Sandy Naples." Mario had no idea who Naples was, or that the killing actually took place in Youngstown, so I knew he couldn't have been making this up, it was just a story that had been relayed to him when he was younger. Naples was killed in March 1960; Innocenzi was killed in August 1960. Although there is no proof to back this up, the time frame fits, and it certainly could explain a motive for Innocenzi and his brother's murders.

In addition, Mario also offered another tidbit. He said he was told that one of the guys from his father's gang set Innocenzi up to be murdered. The guy's name was Richard A. Stewart, who his dad always referred to as "Dickhead." His mother later told Mario, that on the night Vince left home for the last time, he got a telephone call and she heard him say, "I'll see you in a little while 'Dickhead.'" If she told this to the police during her interview with them, it never made the newspapers.

During the pre-dawn hours of Sunday, September 2, 1962, John Stoyka, an alert patrolman from Cleveland's Fourth District, foiled a bank burglary in progress at the Cleveland Trust branch at 5703 Broadway. Arrested were Innocenzi's West Virginia safecracking cohort Joe Arrington, along with Alfred Oponowicz and Charles J. Polizzi, son of Prohibition Era Mayfield Road mobster Charles A. "Chuck" Polizzi. Police recovered a .38 Special revolver from one of the men. It was soon identified as once having belonged to Innocenzi.[87]

Later that month Cleveland Detective Captain James Dodge went to Akron to check ballistics markings from bullets fired from the handgun with the slugs that were removed from Innocenzi. When he arrived at the Summit County

Sheriff's office, the bullets could not be found. A few days later, former Sheriff's Captain William Bickett, now a private investigator, found the bullets in his personal papers at his home. Bickett explained that every murder case he worked on during his time with the sheriff's office, he maintained a personal file for his own records because he was often called upon to testify in court.

On October 10, Dodge announced that Innocenzi was not killed with his own gun – the slugs were not a match. It would be the last hope in the murder investigation.

Dominic Mafrici & David Tiburzio

Sometime during the summer of 1956, Vincent Innocenzi put together a gang whose members had quite the criminal past. In fact, two were once tried for a vicious murder. The gang came to the public's attention in early July 1956. While Innocenzi escaped newspaper scrutiny, the remaining four armed members of the gang didn't. Arrested were Dominic Mafrici, Thomas Rudelik, David Tiburzio and Anthony Velletto.

Taking a look at Mafrici and Tiburzio ten years earlier, the *Tampa Tribune* reported on March 10, 1946:

> In a welter of knives and other weapons in which he dealt, Francisco Daniele, alias Frank Daniels, 52, semi-invalid antique dealer, was found murdered yesterday with a swastika decorated dagger plunged into the back of his neck in the cluttered bedroom of his little antique shop at 100 Magnolia Ave., near Grand Central.

Two young teen-aged boys sat waiting for Daniels to come out from his bedroom of his shop / home, called the Gay Nineties, some eight to twelve hours after he had been murdered. A *Tampa Tribune* advertising solicitor and a snack stand proprietor sensed something was wrong and entered his bedroom to check on him. Daniels, still in his pajamas, was found face down on the floor with a Nazi dagger driven to the hilt into his neck. The room was ransacked, and open boxes, clothing, coins and souvenirs were scattered about.

The newspaper stated Daniels had arrived in Tampa about two years earlier and opened the shop which "became a paradise for souvenir hunters." But recently, the disabled World War I veteran decided to move to Colorado for health reasons. It was rumored he had removed $800 to $2,000 from the bank and was preparing to leave. Missing from his shop was the money and 12 to 15 expensive women's watches.

A medical report showed the dead man was killed on the cot he slept on due to a blow from a heavy wrench which crushed his skull. After he was dead, the body was rolled onto the floor and the dagger, more likely a trench knife, was driven through his neck. The killer then used his foot to stomp on the dagger, driving it into the floor. The physician placed the time of death at 9:00 p.m. on Friday night; the body was discovered around 2:00 the next afternoon.

It was reported that three men visited Daniels on Friday. One was said to be the dead man's nephew, who introduced the other two as friends from his hometown – Cleveland. The death notice stated that Daniels was survived by two sisters and four brothers, all of Cleveland, Ohio. Before leaving Cleveland, Daniels had owned an antique shop on the city's east side.

The *Tampa Tribune* reported that the case was "moving slowly" and that "no headway was being made." But that was hardly the case. Police were doing an excellent job with the information they had gathered. Warrants for the arrests of the two men were issued in Tampa, where they were charged with first-degree murder. On Saturday, March 23, Cleveland Police Detective Lieutenant Martin P. Cooney, along with Detectives Emil Musil and Lawrence W. Doran, arrested 26-year-old Dominic Mafrici and 22-year-old David F. Tiburzio. It was not initially revealed in the newspapers that Frank DiAugustini was being held as a material witness, as authorities believed he may have been the one who actually planned the robbery.

On the night of the murder, Mafrici and Tiburzio were in the Gay Nineties shop when Daniels was showing James Dunn his collection of 1921-22 silver dollars. Daniels introduced Dunn, an acquaintance of his, to the two young men; whether he introduced him as Mr. Dunn or as Detective Dunn was not clear. Dunn had spent most of his career on the police force as a member of the pawn shop detail, which is how he met Daniels. Four months from retirement, Dunn was also a deputy court clerk. After the murder, Tampa detectives were able to trace Mafrici and Tiburzio back to the tourist court where they were staying with DiAugustini. One of them left behind a card in the shop with information about the tourist court, which included DiAugustini's name on the back. By the time Tampa detectives got to the tourist court, however, the men were headed back to Cleveland. Detectives found an automobile near the cottage the men stayed in, that belonged to a relative of Tiburzio, who had used it for the trip to Florida. When Cleveland detectives went to Mafrici's home, they found 65 of the 1921-22 silver dollars in a safe there. Tampa Detective Dunn came to Cleveland and picked Mafrici and Tiburzio out of a police line-up. Mafrici was soon identified as Frank Daniel's nephew.

By this time, Tiburzio's record showed he had served two-and-a-half years in Leavenworth Federal Penitentiary after deserting from the Army. Mafrici was currently on parole from the Ohio Reformatory in Mansfield, where he served two years of a 10-to-20-year sentence for the armed robbery of a filling station in 1939. He was released in 1941.

In late July 1946, Pat Whitaker, the attorney for Mafrici and Tiburzio, filed two motions to dismiss the indictment against his clients. The first was a technical one that involved a legislative act from 1933, which created the Hillsborough County Jury Commission, and involved how names were selected and drawn for the jury. The second motion to quash had to do with the indictment stating that each of the defendants "struck the deceased with a blunt instrument and stabbed him with a knife...but the cause of death is not alleged." The judge ruled against both motions, although he declared that both contentions could later be used for appeal if it went before the Florida State Supreme Court.

The trial began in Circuit Court on Monday, August 19, with jury selection. The state was represented by State Attorney J. Rex Farrior; defense counsel consisted of Whitaker, John R. Parkhill and Cleveland attorney Michael Picciano; hearing the case was Circuit Court Judge Curtis E. Chillingworth. During voir dire, attorney Whitaker asked every potential juror if they had any prejudices against people of Italian descent. None confessed to any. Testimony began the next day. The *Tampa Times* reported that the police officers described the defendants as "professional gamblers," and described their courtroom demeanor:

Older Mafrici sat hunched forward, intent and straining to hear the witnesses, as younger Tiburzio, slouched down in his chair, appeared uninterested in the testimony which might send them to their deaths.

In opening statements, Farrior told the jury they would be hearing lot of circumstantial evidence and that the State would be seeking the death penalty against the two men. In early testimony, it was obvious the defense was going to make the time of death a key issue. Throughout the trial Judge Chillingworth[88] had to referee the bickering that went on between Farrior and Whitaker.

On Friday, August 23, the jury got the case. At 11:30 that night, after just three hours of deliberations, the jury announced it was deadlocked at nine to three for conviction. The judge dismissed the jury and called for another trial.

The second trial began nine months later on April 7, 1947. Defense counsel and the prosecutor remained the same, but this time the case was heard by Circuit Judge L.L. Parks. The same theatrics continued between Farrior and Whitaker. After six hours of closing statements on April 11, the jury deliberated for just 30 minutes before returning a stunning verdict of acquittal for both men. Manfrici's courtroom celebration was brief. As he attempted to leave with family members, deputies surrounded him and took him back to the Hillsborough County Jail. Law enforcement in Cleveland had a warrant for his return for violating his probation from the 1939 filling station robbery. The judge ordered that the men's seized personal belongings be returned to them, this included the 65 silver dollars found in Mafrici's safe.

Nine years later, at 8:00 o'clock on the morning of July 8, 1956, the Baron Café in Steubenville, Ohio, located on the eastern border of the state along the Ohio River, 26 miles north of Wheeling, West Virginia, was burglarized for $10,000. Five armed gunmen, with their faces covered with handkerchiefs, forced their way inside the restaurant, and ordered three employees into a bathroom, where one gunman stood guard. "We could hear them working on the safe," one of the captives told police. "Then they locked us up in the basement and left." The two male employees quickly got out and telephoned police. Steubenville Police Captain Robert Cornelius stated that "five and possibly seven men" were involved in the burglary. "The employees of the restaurant said five were in the gang that entered the restaurant and indications are that two others were stationed outside," the captain told reporters.

A few hours later, four men were arrested at a roadblock at Ohio Routes 9 and 43 in Carroll County, after the State Highway Patrol sent out a notice about the café burglary in Steubenville, 33 miles southeast of Carrollton. A single patrolman, George Litt,[89] along with a "civilian auxiliary helper," arrested the four robbers without incident. All four men were taken to the Carroll County Jail. Innocenzi was not with the group. Since it was reported that five to seven men were involved, it's possible he fled Steubenville in another vehicle. At the police station, the men readily admitted to being ex-convicts, but denied having participated in the Steubenville burglary. When police searched the car, however, they discovered the $10,000 and several weapons.

The next day the four prisoners faced a judge. Anthony Velletto pleaded not guilty and was held on a $50,000 bond. Mafrici, Rudelik and Tiburzio refused to enter pleas until they obtained counsel. All were returned to the Jefferson County Jail. Three days later, they entered not guilty pleas and were held on $50,000 bonds. All of the men made bail and were soon back out on the street, with the exception of Mafrici, who was held as a parole violator.

One month later, on August 9, Rudelik, Tiburzio and Velletto were arrested in Mount Gilead, this time with Vincent Innocenzi (See Chapter Ten: Vincent Innocenzi biography). The four men were prime suspects in a number of recent burglaries around the state. Rudelik was sent back to the Jefferson County Jail where he shared a cell with Mafrici.

By October 1956, the trials for the four men arrested for the Baron Café robbery would soon begin. Mafrici was still being held without bail. On the night of October 26, with his trial only a week away, he was allowed out of his cellblock twice to make telephone calls to his mother in Cleveland, who was reportedly ill. He was returned to his cell the second time around 1:30 in the morning. An hour later a deputy noticed that the door to the cellblock was ajar. A quick check of the prisoners showed Mafrici had escaped. A state-wide alert was issued immediately. A faulty lock would be blamed for the escape. Alerted about the escape, Cleveland police kept an eye on Mafrici's home at 1945 East 123rd Street in Little Italy.

On October 30, the Baron Café robbery trials started. Anthony Velletto was first. The state's key witness in each trial was slated to be Carrollton Patrolman George Litt. Velletto was quickly found guilty. Thomas Rudelik was up next, he pleaded guilty (See Chapter 10: Thomas Rudelik biography). On November 26,

Jefferson County Common Pleas Judge John J. Griesinger sentenced both men. Velletto was given 10-to-25-years for armed robbery and 1-to-20-years for forcible entry of a safe. The judge ordered the sentences to run consecutively. Velletto quickly hired veteran Cleveland defense attorney John P. Butler to file a motion for a new trial. Rudelik was sentenced to 1-to-25-years.

When it was time for Tiburzio to go on trial, he was a no-show. This left the bail bondsman holding the bag for his $50,000 bond. In December, it was announced that Liberty Bonding Company of Youngstown was notified by the Jefferson County Court that it would have to make good on the bond.

From here, the scene switches to Buffalo, New York. Just before 5:30 on the morning of March 14, two men stood in the driveway of a quiet residential street. In the pre-dawn darkness, residents of the west-side neighborhood heard a man cry out, "Please, Tony, don't do it! Please, not that, Tony!" A volley of gunfire signaled the impassioned request was denied.

Police quickly arrived on the scene. A witness told officers he saw a tall thin man fire several times into the victim and then stood over the body for a moment to make sure the man was dead. Bullets entered the man's abdomen and head; a thumb was completely shot off. Police searched the body, but the man's wallet, as well as any jewelry or personal items were gone. Fingerprints were taken and delivered to the FBI. The bureau soon announced that Dominic Mafrici was no longer a fugitive from justice; the 37-year-old was now a murder victim.

Buffalo police believed more than one person was involved in the killing. They soon discovered a 1955 Chevrolet from Ohio parked near the murder scene. The license plates were reportedly issued to a Shirley Buffa of Cleveland. Buffalo detectives soon arrived in Cleveland. They were looking to speak to Anthony Buffa. Cleveland police had picked up Buffa the night before and interrogated him. Buffalo police already knew that Buffa was in their city just two weeks earlier and they knew he and Mafrici were friends. Despite the feeling that they had a good suspect, Buffalo police went home empty handed and Cleveland police released Buffa. The case turned cold quickly.

On April 16, a month after his long-time friend's murder, Tiburzio was arrested in Etna, Pennsylvania, a small borough in Allegheny County near Pittsburgh, by FBI and local police, for unlawful flight to avoid prosecution for armed robbery. A week later, Tiburzio waived extradition and was sent back to Steubenville. Like Rudelik before him, Tiburzio got the charge reduced from armed robbery to just robbery. On July 7, he pleaded guilty and was sentenced to 1-to-25-years in the Ohio Penitentiary.

It would be 17 years before Tiburzio was heard from again. In April 1974, after an investigation by the *Plain Dealer* into police corruption in the city, four police officers – Lieutenant Peter M. Mihalic, Sergeant Dennis N. Kehn, and Patrolmen Robert L. Buddie and James M. Doran[90] – were indicted by a Cuyahoga

Grand Jury and relieved of duty. The investigation alleged the men were involved with an East Side burglary and robbery ring, which had stolen $224,000 in money and goods during 1971 and 1972. In addition to the officers, ten accomplices were named. Among them were Tiburzio, Pete Sanzo, Phil Christopher and Charles Broeckel. The article indicated that at the time of the indictment, Tiburzio was serving time for another crime.

That was the last time David Tiburzio was heard from. He died on July 4, 1985, at the age of 61, while living in Euclid. He was buried in Calvary Cemetery.

Sam Jerry Monachino

At various times during the reporting of the Sam Jerry Monachino murder, the Plain Dealer *referred to him as the "30-year-old jinx of the police," and "the cop-hating hoodlum."*

From an early age, Sam Jerry Monachino seemed destined for a life a crime. It just wasn't clear how long that life would be. His first serious brush with the law came in 1938 when he was arrested for a burglary. Convicted, he was sentenced to the Ohio State Reformatory and served three years. Released in August 1941, he returned to Cleveland where he teamed with another career criminal, James V. Cilenti, who was nine years older. Cilenti had spent five years in Federal prison for possessing counterfeit money. The two men were involved in bootlegging and together ran a bar at 8215 Quincy Avenue called the Porto Rico Club. The two men would soon have a run-in with another Cleveland hood destined to have a short lifespan.

Peter LaDuca was not a good person. While in his early twenties, he and a friend, Santo Sgro, went on a double-date with two young ladies; aged 24 and 26. The women claimed LaDuca and Sgro tried to seduce them in the men's automobile. When the 24-year-old resisted, Sgro slapped her several times. LaDuca, a barber, pulled a straight razor from his pocket and threatened to cut her throat. When she got free from the car and ran, Sgro chased her, knocked her to the ground and kicked her in the face. The 26-year-old, terrified, "submitted" to LaDuca. Two months after being brought into court on felony charges of assault with intent to rape, LaDuca and Sgro walked free.

The next year, in April 1937, Peter and his brother Samuel were arrested for assaulting Joseph Messina. In court, Peter claimed Messina was engaged in unfair labor competition which involved stealing customers away from his barbershop by acting as a "house to house" barber.

By 1942, LaDuca was running a café at 12218 Madison Avenue in Lakewood, a suburb on the western edge of Cleveland, and still making enemies. The latest ones were Sam Jerry Monachino and James Cilenti. On October 12, it was reported that LaDuca and Monachino, while driving to the Porto Rico Club, got into an argument which turned physical. When they arrived at the club, LaDuca was dragged inside, given a beating and then dragged back out. Early the next morning his body was found with two bullet wounds in a field near 2256 East 75th Place, basically an alley that runs partly between East 74th and East 76th Streets, off Central Avenue, several blocks from the Porto Rico Club.

Five days after the killing, following an investigation by Detective Sergeant Martin P. Cooney, Cilenti and Monachino were arrested and charged with first-degree murder. Cooney claimed, "A personal grudge of long standing," was the motive for the killing. Police were holding as a material witness a man who drove LaDuca's automobile on the night he was killed. The investigation revealed Cilenti and Monachino threatened to kill LaDuca two weeks earlier in the Porto Rico Club. Coroner Samuel R. Gerber reported that LaDuca died of a gunshot to his abdomen.

Both men pleaded not guilty to first-degree murder at arraignment the day after their arrest. Lawyers for the two demanded a preliminary hearing, which was set for October 29. Seven months passed and on June 8, 1943, Common Pleas Judge Frank S. Day freed both men declaring the state failed to provide strong enough evidence to justify a trial. The case's dismissal left Cooney seething; he would not forget the two.

Before the month was over, both men were back in Municipal Court after liquor authorities found illegal whiskey and wine at the Porto Rico Club. In court, prosecutors were confounded when they discovered police had accidently destroyed the evidence against Cilenti. Judge Julius M. Kovachy discharged Cilenti, but police still had possession of the wine that Monachino was charged with possessing illegally. The judge fined him $100 and court costs and sentenced him to 30 days in the county workhouse.

When Cilenti and Monachino got together in 1941, in addition to bootlegging through their club, they were also involved in a number of local burglaries and bombings for extortion. One of the people working with them was Albert P. Lauerhaus. These activities continued through the war years. By 1945, Martin Cooney had risen in rank to Detective Lieutenant in the Cleveland Police Homicide Squad. Cooney, upset since not being able to produce a case against Cilenti and Monachino since the LaDuca murder, was biding his time, waiting for the next opportunity; the time was nigh.

The two hoodlums used a unique concept in the bombing / extortion racket. According to Cooney, "The gang went into action whenever it learned of private or business disagreements. Apparently without consulting either party to the dispute, they would bomb the home or place of business of one of them and then collect blackmail from the other party under threat of implicating him or her in the bombing." By 1945, there were at least 20 unsolved bombings attributed to the gang dating back to 1941.

The men were also responsible for pulling a number of burglaries in the Cleveland area. Two that helped bring the gang's activities to an end occurred at the homes of Charles W. Dougherty at 255 East 246th Street in Euclid, on October 26, 1945, and Emery Krizman, at 18004 Marcella Road NE, on December 2. Dougherty operated the Shore Club; Krizman ran a beer parlor at 916 Addison Road, a factory area just north of St. Clair Avenue. The burglars made off with an estimated $25,000 from the latter's home. On March 1, 1946, Cilenti, Lauerhaus, Monachino and Samuel A. Bevacqua were arraigned for the burglaries with bonds set high at $50,000 to $75,000.

Cooney selected Lauerhaus to lean on and he soon "yielded to police persuasion." A week later, he was the key witness in front of the Cuyahoga County Grand Jury spilling his guts about the gang's operations. One of the extortion plots he discussed involved two popular florists, Martin Orban and David Brunswick, who both operated florist shops on Carnegie Avenue in the shadow of the Cleveland Clinic. Lauerhaus testified they bombed Orban's shop on February 13, 1941, and that Brunswick paid extortion money to the gang to keep them from implicating him.

Despite what seemed to be an airtight case, Cooney would not quite get the results he was hoping for. In mid-June Cilenti, Monachino and Sam Bevacqua went on trial for the Krizman burglary. In a strange setup, a jury of eleven women and one man heard testimony against Cilenti and Monachino; while Bevacqua, who waived a jury trial but was tried jointly with them, would have his fate determined by Common Pleas Judge Frank J. Merrick. Prosecutors presented Lauerhaus as their key witness, as well as a resident of the Krizman home. On June 17, after hearing alibi witnesses for all three defendants, the jury found Cilenti and Monachino not guilty. After the jury's verdict, Bevacqua was freed by Judge Merrick. Monachino and Bevacqua were facing a second burglary trial for the Dougherty home break-in, while Cilenti would go it alone for the bombing / extortion case.

Days after the Krizman trial ended, Cilenti found himself on trial for extortion in the courtroom of Common Pleas Judge Alva Corlett. County Prosecutor James P. Hart and his assistant Victor DeMarco handled the case for the state, while Cilenti was represented by veteran defense attorney S.M. LoPresti and Gerard Pilliod. Hearing the testimony was a jury of five men and seven women; five of whom were school teachers.

Witnesses took the stand and described three separate extortion incidents. The first one involved a man who paid Cilenti $50 for getting his Warren, Ohio, teamsters' union card transferred to a Cleveland local. He said Cilenti then wanted another $30, which he paid. After Cilenti demanded another $50, he refused. He told the court Cilenti then threatened him by saying, "You have a beautiful child, and if you love that child you'd better do something about it."

The second threat involved a scared witness, who didn't want to testify. After he was assured of protection by Judge Corlett, the man told the court Cilenti offered to resolve a quarrel the witness had with two men, who had taken a shot at him. Afterward, he said Cilenti demanded that he sign a note for a down-payment on a new automobile for him. When he became reluctant, Cilenti had him sit in the new car, where a revolver was clearly visible in the open glove compartment. He said Cilenti talked to him about "people being scarred up or found dead under someone's porch." The witness stated that made him decide to sign the note.

In the last incident, Cilenti obtained $300 from a Mayfield Heights widow after bombing her neighbor's home and then threatening to implicate her for hiring him to do it.

During the defense portion of the case, Cilenti took the stand and testified that he was still "good friends" with four of the witnesses who testified against him and did not understand why they were accusing him of extorting money. On June 25, the jury came back with a guilty verdict. During sentencing Judge Corlett called Cilenti "a coward" and "a jackal," ordering him to serve two 3 to 17 blackmail terms, one at a time.

In the last trial, this one for the burglary at the home of James Dougherty, it was the same strange setup. Monachino was tried by a five man, seven woman jury, while Bevacqua waived a jury trial. The trial, again before Judge Kovachy, had the same result. Monachino was acquitted and the judge freed Bevacqua. Kovachy told Monachino, "The court wants to say to you that you are a mighty lucky man. You may go." To Bevacqua, he said, "This court cannot in good conscience, make a finding of fact contrary to the finding of 12 other minds. I am not clear in my own heart that they are right. But I cannot pit my finding of a jury of 12, to put my own judgement above theirs."

On early Sunday morning, August 22, 1948, two bombs exploded in East Side neighborhoods. One blast took place at the home of 17th Ward Councilman Charles V. Carr, the second at the home of Buster H. Mathews, a one-time numbers racket operator. Carr and his wife were out of town at the time; Mathews and two housekeepers "were hurled from their beds." A number of hoodlums were quickly brought in for questioning. On August 26, Monachino was brought in, questioned and photographed.

One month later, Monachino committed his last crime, an armed robbery of a casino in Struthers, Ohio, with Collinwood hoodlum Julius Petro (See Chapter Three; Sub Chapter: Sam Jerry Monachino, for the remainder of Monachino's story).

Thomas Eugene Rudelik

Thomas "Laughing Tommy" Rudelik was born on October 24, 1924, in Dilles Bottom, Ohio. Located in Belmont County, within Mead Township, it is described as an unincorporated community. It sits on what appears like a peninsula on the Ohio River that juts into West Virginia. On the other side of the river sits Moundsville, West Virginia. While still in his youth, Rudelik's family moved to the East Side of Cleveland; first to Addison Road and later to a house on East 68th Street. In June 1945, Rudelik enlisted in the Army and served until 1947.

Rudelik's activities involving the Baron Café burglary are covered in the Chapter Ten biographies of Vincent Innocenzi and Mafrici & Tiburzio. A month after that robbery, on August 10, 1956, Innocenzi, Rudelik, Tiburzio and Velletto were arrested in Mount Gilead for possession of burglary tools (See Chapter Ten: Vincent Innocenzi biography). A Franklin County Grand Jury indictment ten days later did little to slow the crew down. On October 14, "one of three or four" automobiles registered to Rudelik was found without license plates parked a block away from a Wintersville bank after a shootout in the early morning hours when a local patrolman exchanged gunfire with two men trying to enter the bank. Innocenzi was quickly arrested in Cleveland and Rudelik and Velletto were believed to be the two trying to get into the bank. Rudelik was currently free on a $50,000 bond for the Steubenville robbery, and another $20,000 bond for the Mount Gilead arrest and indictment.

On October 17, Rudelik forfeited his $50,000 bond when he failed to appear at the Jefferson County Jail in Steubenville to answer to the burglary at the Baron Café. At the hearing, one of his attorneys told the judge Rudelik called him and said "it was impossible" for him to appear today. Another lawyer asked for a week's continuance, but was denied. Rudelik didn't give an excuse as to why he couldn't make it, but the presence in the courtroom of an FBI agent, waiting to question him on the Wintersville botched burglary and shootout, may have had something to do with his decision to become a no-show. Anthony Velletto was also a no-show and forfeited his bond, too, no doubt trying to avoid the same questioning Rudelik was; Dave Tiburzio was free on bond. Rudelik appeared in court two days later with counsel, but was unable to post the new bond. Before being locked up in the same cellblock as Mafrici, the FBI questioned him about the Wintersville burglary attempt.

Mafrici was the only member of the burglary crew held in prison for trial since his arrest, due to a parole violation from a previous Cleveland conviction. But that was about to come to an end. On October 27, while Rudelik slept in the cell he shared with him, Mafrici calmly walked out while a deputy was in another part of the jail answering a telephone.

On November 27, the same day Anthony Velletto received his sentence, Rudelik pleaded guilty to the same charges. He received a 1-to-25-year sentence on the armed robbery charge and a 1-to-20-year term for forcible entry. The judge ordered the sentences for both men to be served consecutively. (See Chapter 10: Dominic Mafrici & David Tiburzio biography for their fate.)

Rudelik spent the next five years of his life in the Ohio Penitentiary. The next time he was heard from was in December 1963 when he was part of a burglary ring believed to have stolen $90,000 in cash and merchandise in the Canton area. The ring's success came to an end after a Canton woman noticed an unusual number of cars appearing at the house next to hers, which was abandoned. She began recording license plate numbers and turning them over to police. When Canton police provided the numbers to their Cleveland counterparts, the name Thomas Rudelik came up.

Rudelik was developing a reputation for participating in burglaries where gun fire was involved. The first incident occurred during the attempted bank break-in at Wintersville. The second took place on August 4, during the Canton robbery spree when the gang attempted a safecracking at a local bar. A bartender opened fire on the burglars, hitting Rudelik twice in the shoulder as he ran away. On December 12, with the Canton and Cleveland Police Departments working together, six men were arrested; three from Canton, and Rudelik and two Cleveland brothers, Milan and Daniel Kocevar.

Less than six months later, while out on a $5,000 bond from the Canton arrest, Rudelik was at it again. On Tuesday night, May 26, 1964, burglars broke into a farmhouse in North Royalton owned by Frederick C. Roth. The retired businessman kept his coin and stamp collections there. The collections were valued at more than $1.0 million. He did not live in the three-story barn-like structure because he feared it might be the target of burglars one day.

When burglars did show up at the farmhouse that Tuesday, they stole an estimated $12,000 in rare coins. While police were viewing the crime scene, they noticed a wicker basket and a satchel, both full of coins, which the burglars left behind. Thinking they might come back for them, suburban police from Broadview Heights, North Royalton and Parma staked out the farmhouse. On Wednesday night, police watched as an automobile drove towards the farmhouse twice before turning around each time. The third time the car approached, a man got out and walked toward the farmhouse. Suddenly he turned around and ran back to the vehicle. Police reacted immediately and rifle and shotgun fire permeated the night air. As the car took off towards Ridge Road, one of the tires was shot out. The vehicle came to a halt and the three men jumped out and began running into the woods. Police were able to catch one of the men – Thomas Rudelik. Police arrested him and questioned him at length, but Rudelik wasn't giving up his accomplices. It didn't matter; he was going to have his hands full for the remainder of the year with all the trials he had to face.

The trial for Rudelik's December 1963 arrest began in late August 1964. He and Milan Kocevar were charged with two counts each of breaking and entering, and two each of grand larceny; in addition, Rudelik was also charged with safecracking. On a more serious note, both men were facing a future trial for breaking and entering an inhabited dwelling, a conviction that could carry a life sentence.

On September 2, a Stark County Common Pleas Court jury in Canton found both men guilty on all charges. The judge allowed Rudelik to remain free on a $32,000 bond while awaiting sentencing. Less than two weeks later, his trial for breaking into an inhabited dwelling began. Facing the most serious charge of his criminal career, the jury received the case on the afternoon of September 15. Rudelik, who had lost the previous two cases and spent five years in prison, suddenly got cold feet. While the jury was deliberating, he slipped away from the courtroom. When the jury returned, the judge waited patiently for an hour for the defendant to return before having the jury render the verdict. Rudelik missed hearing his own acquittal. A later newspaper report said he had been hiding "somewhere" in the courthouse.

By mid-October, Rudelik found himself facing his third trial since late August. This one was for breaking and entering, grand larceny and auto theft. These charges again involved his Canton criminal activities, and he was back in a Stark County Common Pleas Courtroom. Again, he was found guilty on all of the charges. When it came time for sentencing on this latest conviction, Rudelik was again a no-show. This time the FBI was called in on a Federal warrant charging unlawful flight. On January 4, 1965, Earl E. Brown, Special-Agent-in-Charge of the Cleveland FBI office, announced Rudelik was apprehended at a friend's apartment in South Euclid.

The next day, in a Stark County courtroom, the 40-year-old Rudelik was given a sentence of from 5 to 77 years in prison. Ten days later, he received his final sentence for the earlier convictions involving the Canton burglary ring that stole some $90,000. Common Pleas Judge Paul G. Weber's sentencing brought Rudelik's total prison terms to 6 to 90 years.

That was the last to be heard of "Laughing Tommy." Rudelik passed away on February 2, 2008.

Joseph R. Russo

"I am the innocent victim of circumstances. Only I couldn't prove my innocence." - Joseph Russo after being found guilty of burglary of an inhabited dwelling and given a life sentence. – Plain Dealer – September 13, 1951.

By all accounts Joseph R. Russo was raised in a respectable Cleveland family. After getting married, the family he and his wife Antonio raised was just as respectful and law abiding as his own. But for Joseph his life was different. He had a long criminal career beginning when he was just 17 years-old. Russo had a string of arrests from 1922 to 1951, spending many years in jail and prison and in the end, he suffered a horrible death.

Russo was getting into trouble and serving time before his future burglary partner, Julius Petro turned two-years-old. The Boys Industrial School in Lancaster, Ohio, served as home to Russo before he reached the age of 15. Returning to Cleveland, Russo was more than fortunate that he lived to the age of 17.

During the early morning hours of Sunday, March 30, 1924, Russo, Michael Cragel and Carl Cardinala – all in their mid-teens – were burglarizing the home of Joseph David at 5808 Whittier Avenue.[91] Neighbors of David became aware of the break-in and telephoned him at his place of business, a confectionary at 4719 Payne Avenue,[92] located just a few blocks from his home. David rushed out of his store and raced toward East 55th Street, a block east of his shop. He ran into Cleveland Police Patrolman John J. Lynch, a beat cop. He quickly told the patrolman what was happening and gave him the key to his house.

In these days before radio communication and calling for back-up, Lynch ran down Whittier Avenue to the front door of David's house. He unlocked the front door only to find the intruders had fastened a chain-lock from the inside. Lynch, a big man, had no trouble breaking through the door. The patrolman suddenly found himself inside a pitch-black house with revolver in hand. Finding no activity going on in the downstairs, he headed for the staircase and started up to the second floor. Reaching the top of the stairs, Lynch was confronted by Russo and Cragel, both holding guns aimed at him. Russo suddenly dropped his revolver and raised his hands. Instead of opening fire on Cragel, the patrolman dove at him and, being much larger, easily knocked him to the floor and began wrestling him for the gun. While this was going on, Russo pulled a second handgun, which he had tucked in a back pocket, and attempted to shoot Lynch. The patrolman again refrained from using his own weapon and was able to grab Russo and rip the gun from his hand.

Lynch, now armed with four handguns and escorting two prisoners, proceeded to search the remainder of the upstairs. He soon found Cardinala in another room and disarmed him. The patrolman then marched his three captives down the stairs, out of the house, down the street and around the corner to the East 55th Street and Perkins Avenue police station.

At the station, Lynch and Officers Lloyd Trunk and Emil Koryta questioned the boys. During the interrogation they admitted to 15 local burglaries and three armed holdups. The three officers then went to a house on East 19th Street, where the boys claimed they were rooming. There the officers arrested two more youths, who were in bed, and found a cache of stolen goods. Discovered in the "pile of varied loot," officers found "eleven watches, four revolvers, a quantity of ammunition, cigarettes, razors, cuff links, flashlights, shoes, a ukulele, golf balls, roller skates, shirts, a Halloween mask, caps and blankets."

On Sunday morning, six victims of the youth burglary gang came to the East 55th Street and Perkins Avenue Police Station. There they identified property removed from the East 19th Street location as items that were stolen from them in recent burglaries; some which had taken place as recently as two days earlier.

While one might think being a suspect in a combined 18 burglaries and holdups, not to mention drawing a weapon on a police officer, would be enough to hold even a teenager in jail for some time; apparently that wasn't the case with Russo. On April 5, just six days after the armed wrestling match with Patrolman John Lynch on Whittier Avenue, Russo and a companion were shot at by police while trying to flee with a 10-gallon can of liquor near West 25th Street. After bullets came crashing through the windshield and others flattened tires, the two surrendered. Both were charged with transporting liquor.

On June 22, 1926, Russo was sentenced to two years in the Federal penitentiary in Atlanta and fined $400 by Federal Judge Paul Jones after a jury found him guilty of bribing Federal Prohibition Agent Albert Collins. On May 20, Russo had made a date to meet Collins at the U.S. Post Office where he handed him $200 to "fix a liquor case." At the post office, Collins introduced a "buddy" to Russo, while two Federal officers witnessed the exchanging of money. The "buddy" turned out to be Assistant U.S. Attorney John B. Osmun.

Russo spent just a few months in Atlanta before he was back in Cleveland and in trouble again. On Saturday morning, February 20, 1927, four masked men entered the Star Elevator Company at 2166 West 53rd Street to rob it. Present in the office at the time were seven officers and employees of the company. As the robbers entered one of them barked out, "Hands up!" One of the employees recognized his voice and immediately suspected who it was. Although never named, the man had "squint eyes and had worked at the plant occasionally." The seven men were herded into the company's vault, locked in, and left to suffocate. The robbers escaped with $650; a figure later reported to be $1,200.

The men locked inside the vault might have met a horrible fate if it weren't for the actions of a quick-thinking passerby. William F. Wehr was delayed at a nearby railroad crossing. While sitting in his car, he happened to glance into the Star Elevator office and saw the robbery in progress. He drove to the nearest police station and reported what he saw.

By the time the police arrived, the robbers had fled. Detective Lieutenant Frank Story was able to communicate somehow with the men inside the vault. Company president F.W. Blazy tapped the combination to him on the wall of the vault and the men were soon free. While the seven were being questioned, Lieutenant Story heard about the "squint eyed" employee. Story and Detective Lieutenant Harry Weis were soon on their way to the infamous "Bloody Corner," where the employee liked to hang out in a poolroom. The "Bloody Corner," at East 25th Street and Woodland Avenue received its name from the numerous bootleg murders that took place there during the mid-1920s.

As Story and Weis questioned the operators of the poolroom, in walked the "squint eyed" suspect. While being interrogated the man admitted his role in the robbery and quickly named his three companions. By early evening, less than ten hours after the robbery, all four suspects were in custody. The four men were Joseph Russo, Anthony Genaro, Joseph Luchenberg and Stanley Wojick. While the "squint eyed" robber was never specifically named, the one suspect who lived closest to the "Bloody Corner" was Wojick, whose address was 3436 Woodland Avenue.

On February 26, Genaro and Luchenberg pleaded guilty to the robbery charges before Common Pleas Judge Walter McMahon. Wojick decided to plead not guilty, while Russo had yet to be arraigned. After the robbery, a strong-box containing $2,500 in checks stolen from the Star Elevator Company, was found ditched on Schaaf Road, the men obviously dumping it there. That would not be Joseph Russo's last visit to Schaaf Road.

Russo received a long stretch for his role in the Star Elevator Company robbery. While incarcerated in the Ohio Penitentiary in April 1930, a fire started when oily rags on a roof in the prison's six-story West Block were ignited by a candle. The end result was one of the deadliest fires in United States history. A total of 322 inmates lost their lives and another 23 were hospitalized. Many guards refused to free prisoners when smoke entered the cell block. This resulted in the prisoners rioting and the prison reacting by bringing in soldiers from nearby Fort Hayes, as well as a troop of National Guardsmen. Machine-gun placements were set up, bayonets were fixed, and orders of shoot-to-kill were given. When the riot was quelled, many inmates were transferred to other prisons, among them Joseph Russo.

Back in Cleveland by January 1934, Russo and his brother Fred soon found themselves in trouble in a payroll padding scheme involving the Civil Works Administration.[93] Arrested and jailed, Russo was released after posting a $2,000 bond.

By the mid-1930s it was apparent that Russo was heading down a new path in his criminal career. On July 2, 1936, Federal Narcotics Agents staged a raid at the Hotel Edwin at 1302 Prospect Avenue.[94] During the raid Sidney Weiss ran out of the hotel, jumped in his automobile and attempted to escape. Agents gave chase and "had to wreck the car before capturing him." It wasn't made clear if they wrecked Weiss's car or the government automobile. The agents found $1,000 in cash in his pockets along with bank books indicating deposits of $7,800 during the past three months. In addition to Weiss, agents took Joseph Russo into custody. The next day, Federal Narcotics Agents announced they "have smashed one of the largest narcotics rings in northeastern Ohio." On September 10, Russo and Weiss were indicted for violating Federal narcotics' laws after charges were made by a Federal Grand Jury. Russo was convicted of selling narcotics and sentenced to the Federal penitentiary in Lewisburg, Pennsylvania, where he served two years.

Less than three years later, a *Plain Dealer* article describing an arrest on February 2, 1939, was an indication of just how far Russo had come in his new career. The article began:

Three men, one believed to be an agent for Joseph Russo, alleged leader of a Cleveland narcotic ring, were captured by police and federal agents last night in a downtown automobile chase after the fugitives had defied gunfire to dispose of 50 capsules."

The incident began at the corner of East Ninth Street and Woodland Avenue where two cars, one containing two Federal Bureau of Narcotics Agents, the other Detective Sergeant Martin Cooney, Detective Mason Nichols and "an anonymous investigator from the office of Safety Director Eliot Ness."

When Russo's "agent" stopped his car at the corner, two men came out of a drug store doorway and entered his automobile. The car with the detectives maneuvered into position to block an escape. Detective Nichols then shined his flashlight into the car and ordered the men to come out. Instead, the driver backed up the vehicle and began to drive south on East Ninth, despite Nichols firing three shots at the car. The Federal agents joined the chase and at Broadway and Central Avenue the car came to a stop and the men surrendered without incident.

On the front seat of the car agents found a single capsule containing a narcotic. The police and agents retraced the path of the chase and recovered a package containing 50 capsules lying in the street. The next day, newspapers reported that police had arrested Russo, who was held on a $10,000 bond after pleading not guilty to violating the state narcotics act. Newspaper articles claimed, "Detectives who arrested Russo and four alleged confederates declared they had smashed the largest narcotics ring in Cleveland."

On March 24, 1939, the *Plain Dealer* reported the previous day's conviction of Joseph Russo brought the successful prosecution of his drug ring to 16 out of 17 cases. Russo was found guilty of selling narcotics to Doris Schnaufer, a confessed addict. Schnaufer, under questioning from Assistant County Prosecutor Frank D. Celebreeze, claimed she purchased a narcotic from Russo for $1 on December 23, 1938; just one week after being released from Federal prison. The next day, she purchased $5 of narcotics from Frank Iacono, who was driven to meet her by Russo.

Russo was sentenced to 1-to-5-years in the Ohio Penitentiary by Common Pleas Judge Frank S. Day, but remained in the County Jail until a motion for a new trial could be heard. On May 13, Russo was bailed out for $3,000. On Monday, May 15, a motion for a new trial was denied by Judge Day. Russo's attorney said he would appeal the conviction. In Judge Day's chambers, the attorney was informed that he was given the wrong bond amount for Russo. His previous bond was $5,000, but Day was told it was $2,500, so he raised it to $3,000 for Russo while he waited for a ruling on his new trial. With Russo's counsel present in chambers, Day announced he was raising it to $6,000. He then picked up the telephone and called the clerk's office and ordered a capias, a writ for Russo's arrest, so the new bond could be imposed. In the clerk's office at the time of the call was Russo's bondsman, who overheard the conversation. Between Russo's lawyer and his bondsman, one of them informed him of the impending arrest.

At 6:00 p.m. Monday evening, Cuyahoga County Detective Harry S. Brown arrived at the Russo home to arrest him. Brown was flat out told, "He found out his bond was raised this afternoon, so he went to the fair." It wasn't the Cuyahoga County Fair that Russo allegedly went to; Brown was told he went to the New York World's Fair. The next evening, after numerous telephone calls were exchanged between Judge Day, Russo's attorney, the Deputy County Clerk and United States Fidelity & Guaranty Company, the bonding company, Russo walked into the County Clerk's office, put his signature on a $6,000 bond record and was on his way. There was no more talk about a visit to the World's Fair. But the circus was just beginning.

Despite the denial of a new trial, the appeals process was still dragging on in September 1939, when Russo's attorney filed a motion for a new trial based on newly discovered evidence. The motion for a new trial was heard by Judge Day on Saturday, September 9. During the hearing, Doris Schnaufer, testified that she gave false testimony about Russo because Detective Sergeant Martin P. Cooney had threatened her with a five-year prison sentence if she didn't. Assistant County Prosecutor Celebreeze requested time to investigate her claim before cross-examining the witness. Judge Day continued the hearing until September 23, but asked that Marian Patterson, a second witness, be brought in to be questioned. Patterson had also signed an affidavit claiming she had lied during her testimony at Russo's trial. She later repudiated it.

On Tuesday, September 12, Celebreeze approached Judge Day late in the afternoon. He asked the judge to place Schnaufer under bond to insure her appearance for cross-examination at the upcoming trial. Day told him to bring her in the next day. On Wednesday, Day and Celebreeze got into a heated argument after the judge found out that the prosecutor had held Schnaufer at the Central Police Station overnight. Judge Day ordered her immediate release and threatened to cite Celebreeze with contempt of court.

On November 25, 1939, despite Doris Schnaufer's testimony that she had lied during her testimony at the Russo trial, Judge Day denied his motion for a new trial based on newly discovered evidence. The second new trial hearing only served to delay Russo's appeal process. First was the Appeals Court, which ended up denying him. During his time as "drug ring leader," Russo seemed to pass the time by building his family to the tune of one a year from 1937 to 1940, with more to come. On June 20, 1940, almost 16 months after his conviction, the last of his appeals came to an end when the Ohio Supreme Court turned him down. It took Russo until July 15 to turn himself in at the County Jail.

Joseph Russo would not be heard from again for almost ten years. By the time he was arrested in Johnstown, Pennsylvania, on March 24. 1950, Russo had added a new chapter to his criminal career, that of yegg, and a new crew. The crew on that cold March night consisted of Julius Petro and Ralph "Bull" De Biase. At 43, Russo was the old man of the gang.

The trip to Johnstown was a failure from the beginning. A failed attempt to crack a safe at a biscuit company was followed by a strong-arm robbery attempt, which netted them all of $43. Local police tracked them down by following their footprints in the snow. The night ended with an arrest for robbery and attempted burglary.

As with nearly all burglaries, the names only make the newspapers when the perpetrators are caught. The names of the criminals seldom appear when the burglaries, robberies and safe-crackings were successful. If Joseph Russo participated in any successful burglaries after Johnstown, no one today is aware of them. On Christmas Eve 1950, a night Russo should have been home with his young and growing family, he chose to be out with an inexperienced yegg-wanna-be. The night, which began on a street oddly familiar to him – Schaaf Road – would be his Waterloo.

On a rather quiet Christmas Eve afternoon, Detective Inspector James E. McArthur received a telephone call from an anonymous caller informing him that the home of Abadallah Assad was to be the target of a burglary that night. Assad was the proprietor of the Outhwaite Delicatessen at 2539 East 55th Street. McArthur dispatched Detective Lieutenant Thomas P. White and Detectives Arthur Gerding, William Kaiser, Joseph Kolek and Samuel Mears, all veteran officers, to the Abadallah home at 1612 Schaaf Road disguised as deliverymen. They sent Abadallah and his family away as they "deployed themselves at points of advantage,"

That night, Peter Joseph Trovato, just 21 years old, arrived at the home with Joseph Russo and two other men. While the other two waited in the getaway vehicle, Russo and Trovato broke open a rear door and, once inside, went immediately to the basement. Their quick movements through the house and right to the safe in the basement were a clear indication someone provided them with a layout of the home. In seconds, they knocked the lock off the safe. Their speedy trek through the house left the detectives scrambling to catch up with them in the basement, but once ready Lieutenant White hit the light switch. "Well fancy meeting you boys here," said White. Although taken by surprise, the burglars had their guns at the ready and after a brief exchange of fire, the two surrendered with their lives intact. Their accomplices sped away the moment the first shots were fired.

The detectives shackled Russo and Trovato together. Lieutenant White asked the pair, "Why did you shoot at us?"

Russo replied, "The kid got excited,"

Trovato explained, "We didn't think you were police, we thought you were the people who lived here." As if opening fire on a man and his family in his own home was somehow more appropriate.

The two men were transported to the city jail, as detectives checked leads hoping to tie them to other crimes in the area. The getaway car, meanwhile, didn't get away completely unnoticed. A license number was obtained at the scene and the car was found in the garage of a man said to be a relative of one of the arrested men. He was soon in city jail, too.

After Christmas, Russo and Trovato were arraigned and charged with burglary of an inhabited dwelling, safe tampering, possession of burglary tools and shooting at policemen as they sought to arrest them. The most serious of the charges was the first one, the burglary of an inhabited dwelling. Both men could face life imprison on that charge alone. Russo was quickly on the street again after posting a $25,000 bond. He was soon in the wind.

Peter J. Trovato[95] pleaded guilty to all four charges in March 1951, asking for mercy on the charge of burglary of an inhabited dwelling. On March 30, before Common Pleas Judge Joseph A. Artl, Trovato was sentenced to 7-to-65-years in prison. Artl told reporters afterwards:

> I sent him to the penitentiary rather than the reformatory because it was evident that he had shot at the policemen intentionally and deliberately. There was a claim by the defense that Trovato became excited and fired at the arresting squad, but there was also evidence that he had used profanity between the shots, and that indicated that he knew what he was doing.

Russo, who had forfeited his $25,000 bond, had teamed up with Julius Petro again, this time in Detroit. The two were arrested there on May 1 after a string of burglaries (See Chapter Five; Sub-Chapter: Detroit Incident). At trial, Russo was found not guilty but quickly was on his way back to Cleveland for jumping bond in the Schaaf Road burglary.

On September 4, Russo made a shocking announcement. The *Plain Dealer* reported Joseph Russo, "43, said by police to be a charter member of Julius A. Petro's burglary gang, yesterday fired his lawyer and decided to plead his own case." Russo's attorney Alfred A. Frost told Common Pleas Judge Edward Blythin[96] that he had not received any payments from his client and that Russo did not want him to defend him at trial. Blythin excused Frost and questioned Russo. The judge wanted to know if the defendant was indigent and whether he needed court appointed counsel. Russo claimed he was not broke and that he owned his own home. He told the judge it was his desire to defend himself and Blythin obliged him.

Before the trial began, Russo filed a motion to have the trial transferred from Judge Blythin to another judge, claiming Blythin would be prejudiced because his son, Arthur was a detective on the Cleveland Police Homicide Unit. The judge overruled the motion.

Russo's trial strategy was to make the jury believe that by knowing in advance he was going to crack the safe in the Abadallah home, there was something corrupt in the Cleveland Police Department and he should be found not guilty because of this. During the trial, he would keep bringing out, in cross-examination of witnesses, the fact the Abadallah family knew their home was to be burglarized on December 24 because they had been told so by police ahead of time, thus creating entrapment. Defense experts claimed that for him to prove entrapment, he would have to show the police persuaded him to pull the job.

In his opening statement, Russo told jurors, "There is something behind this thing, and I mean to bring it out." It was obvious to Russo he was "ratted out," and he wanted to know by whom. During his cross-examination of Assad Abdallah, Russo tried to prove the witness "had links with the police," before the December 24 burglary. Abdallah testified he had not met detectives until just before the break-in. It was then he was told "someone was going to rob the house."

Despite taking careful notes and holding a gray loose-leaf notebook during questioning, Russo wasn't making much headway. Assistant County Prosecutor Harvey R. Monck, after multiple objections from the defendant / defense attorney, was able to get into evidence how Russo jumped bond and fled the state, forfeiting his bond, while the trial was pending. Judge Blythin ruled it was proper evidence, as flight was admissible as a fact for a jury to consider. While questioning Lieutenant White, Monck asked, "Did Arthur Blythin have anything to do with this case?" Russo shouted several objections, claiming the question was irrelevant. Monck responded, "You asked for this. We'll just put it in the record."

On Wednesday, September 12, Joseph Russo got his just deserts, as far as criminal justice was concerned. The jury of six men and six women deliberated 90 minutes before finding Russo guilty of all charges and refused mercy on the charge of burglary of an inhabited dwelling. Called before Judge Blythin and asked if he had anything to say before sentencing, Russo stuck to his beliefs claiming, "I am the innocent victim of circumstances. Only I couldn't prove my innocence."

Blythin told him, "You set out on a deliberate, dangerous, criminal career. This is just an example of what you are capable of and willing to do. I can't understand how people as intelligent as you would think you could outsmart the Cleveland Police Department."

Russo sneered at the remark and offered, "A corrupt police department."

"It is one of the finest police departments in the United States," declared Blythin.

Blythin then sentenced Russo to the maximum on each charge and then ordered the sentences to be served consecutively to give him the most time possible behind bars. Russo would have to serve a minimum of ten years...and then some. Russo was off to prison again, this time not to be heard from for nearly 17 years.

Little is known of what Russo did once he was released. What is known is that in August 1968, his life came to a horrible end. During the early morning hours of Sunday, August 25, Russo walked alone into the emergency room of Doctors' Hospital in Cleveland Heights. He was completely naked and carrying a bathrobe. He told medical attendants he was trying to prevent three men from setting fire to a house at 10100 Woodland Avenue,[97] owned by John DiGravio, the brother of Pierino "Pete" DiGravio, who was murdered two months earlier by a sniper waiting in ambush near the 16th hole at Orchard Hills Golf & Country

Club in Chesterland. Russo claimed the three men jumped him, poured gasoline on him, and then set him ablaze. By the time police arrived at the hospital they were unable to get any further information from him. There was no explanation as to what he was doing at the house at this early hour, or how he got there...or to the hospital for that matter. Police began an immediate search for his automobile. Russo was transferred from Doctors' Hospital to Lakeside Hospital of the University Hospital system. His condition there changed from critical to poor.

A few days later Maple Heights police, acting on tip, found Russo's automobile at the Southgate Shopping Center. Police towed the car to Second District Headquarters where they planned to search it for clues. Investigators found the 1968 Ford completely wiped of prints. Police were completely baffled. Some believed that Russo may have set himself on fire in an arson that went terribly wrong. The crime, if there was one, was never solved.

On August 28, Joseph Russo succumbed to the burns he suffered. The 60-year-old was buried in Calvary Cemetery on August 31.

Joseph J. Sanzo

Joseph J. Sanzo had his newspaper debut at the age of 20 when he was one of 12 gang members[98] who tried to force their way into the Emergency Clinic in Collinwood during non-visiting hours at the hospital. They were attempting to see patient Albert "Tubby" Figer, who was admitted there during the early morning hours of Sunday, May 23, 1949. The 21-year-old Figer had received injuries in "an unexplained street assault," in what police believed was an outbreak of gang warfare in Collinwood. During the remainder of that Sunday, 12 other young men, between the ages of 20 and 24, attempted to get into see Figer. Three of the men stopped by police were found to be carrying concealed weapons and were locked up. It was never made clear if the men were friends of Figer or members of a rival gang.

On Monday, Sanzo and the eleven others faced Municipal Judge Mary B. Grossman in Police Court. Later that month, on May 25, Sanzo and three others were fined $25 and costs by Municipal Judge Andrew M. Kovachy. Five of the men were released on bonds of $100 to $500 after pleading not guilty and having their cases continued until June 7. Meanwhile Judge Grossman set a hearing date of June 7 for the three charged with carrying concealed weapons.

Sanzo was not heard from again until after his arrest in early October 1952 for the Warren, Ohio, robbery he committed with Julius Petro (See Chapter Six). Both men were convicted and sent off to Federal prison. After serving nearly six years of his sentence, Joseph Sanzo was paroled in 1959. Did he go straight? When your self-admitted "idol" is Julius Petro, the answer is probably not. Sanzo and his younger brother Peter were working with Alfred S. "Allie" Calabrese, the son of a one-time friend and cell-mate of Julius Petro from the past. Two years earlier, young Calabrese was convicted of a burglary in Lake County and given a 1-to-15-year sentence. After serving one year, he was released on parole in January 1964. Peter Sanzo had a record of housebreaking and larceny.

In late July 1964, the three men burglarized a grocery store in Hagerstown, Maryland, making off with $3,400. On July 25, police arrested all three, but not before Peter Sanzo was shot and wounded. Police said Peter was being chased on foot when he decided to stop and shoot at his pursuers. Peter missed, the cops didn't. The three men were charged with burglary and larceny. Calabrese was held without bond for violating his parole in Ohio. The Sanzos were released on $15,000 bonds. Days later, a Federal parole officer announced that a violator's warrant was issued for Joseph Sanzo. There would be a hearing to determine if his parole should be revoked. He could be sent back to Federal prison to complete his 15-year sentence for the Warren conviction.

Both Joseph and Peter Sanzo received prison sentences for the Hagerstown burglary. They were still there in April 1966, when it was announced their partner-in-crime, "Allie" Calabrese was paroled back on February 23. Once back home, the Ohio Adult Parole Authority reinstated his 1964 parole from the Ohio State Reformatory. The superintendent of the Authority stated Maryland officials reported Calabrese "was sufficiently reoriented to justify his parole. We investigated his record and in view of the Maryland action decided his release was justified here also." So back came "Allie," where he became a pipefitter earning $5.16 an hour in Collinwood.

Nine years went by without any incidents being reported about Joe Sanzo...and then $47,000 worth of liquor disappeared.

On January 16, 1975, nearly 1,100 cases of gin, scotch, and vodka, valued at $47,000 were stolen from the TransAmerican Freight Lines, Inc. terminal at 530 Stumph Road in Parma. The interstate shipment of liquor had recently arrived from Louisville, Kentucky, on its way to three locations in New Jersey. One of the men involved in the theft was Robert L. Beavers of Medina, who recently purchased a farm there with a barn, where the stolen liquor was taken.

Beavers and his wife, Diane, helped distribute the stolen liquor, delivering it to the Golden Coin Lounge at 3936 Mayfield Road in Cleveland Heights, and the 20th Century Lanes & Tavern at 16525 Euclid Avenue in Cleveland. With the FBI on the trail, the *Plain Dealer* would later report, "Beavers avoided possible arrest Feb. 13 when he gave a statement to agents." The statement implicated Joseph C. Ilacqua (See Chapter Twelve: Joseph C. Ilacqua) and Ronald H. Sullenberger, who were indicted in April. Both men were still on probation from the hijacking of a truck loaded with 31,000 pounds of Pepto-Bismol in December 1970. Beavers promised to testify against the two in Federal Court on June 3. In the meantime, Beavers continued to work at Associated Transport Company, Inc. at 5400 West 137th Street in Brookpark, where he was employed as a dispatcher. Shortly after the indictments, Beavers and his wife began receiving threats.

Just after 7:30 on the morning of May 23, Andrew Sedlak, a co-worker of 12 years with Beavers, asked him for a ride home because the man who normally drove him had left early that day. At 7:40, the two men got into Beavers 1968 Cadillac. When Beavers started the car, a bomb wired to the ignition system exploded sending the hood of the car 100 feet into the air and knocking the hubcaps off cars parked nearby. The explosion cost Beavers his right leg and he also suffered an arm injury. Sedlak received several cuts and bruises, but was able to pull Beavers out of the damaged automobile. Both men were taken to Parma Community General Hospital, where Beavers was placed under the protection of U.S. Marshals.

When the FBI questioned Beavers in the hospital, he told them Sullenberger had visited him on May 7, and on two other occasions the week before the car bombing. He said Sullenberger was trying to talk him out of testifying. He also told them that he refused to drive Ilacqua and an attorney to his home recently to discuss the matter. FBI agents arrested Sullenberger at his Ridgewood Avenue home in Lakewood, on May 26, on charges of attempting to intimidate Federal witnesses, Beavers and his wife. Ilacqua, free on a $25,000 bond, was not arrested. Sometime, over the next two weeks, Sullenberger began talking to the FBI. On June 9, the intimidation charges against him were dismissed because of his agreement to cooperate with the government in the case.

On June 26, U.S. Attorney Frederick M. Coleman announced the indictments of Norman L. Bruening, Thomas L. Palumbo and Joseph Sanzo; charging them with conspiracy and possession of stolen goods, and indicating there could be additional indictments. At the same time, Ilacqua and Sullenberger were re-indicted with them. In exchange for his testimony against the defendants, Beavers was not re-indicted. The grand jury charged in the indictment that in February the five men met at Ilacqua's Grand Boulevard home in Euclid and split $20,000 among themselves. The case was scheduled for trial on September 15 in U.S. District Court in Akron. While Palumbo, Bruening and Sullenberger turned themselves in, Ilacqua and Sanzo failed to appear for their July 8 arraignment. Bench warrants were issued for both men.

At 7:44 on the morning of Monday, August 25, a call came into the Lakewood Police Department that a suspicious cardboard box was found on the porch of a resident living at 1428 Lakeland Avenue. Police realized as soon as they heard the name of the resident the call was not a hoax. The house belonged to Mr. and Mrs. Harry Sullenberger, the parents of Ronald Sullenberger.

On his way out of the house to work that morning, Harry Sullenberger spotted the cardboard box on his porch and immediately notified his wife to call police. When the Lakewood police arrived, they determined the bomb was made with ten sticks of dynamite, a detonator, and a timer. It had a 2.5 gallon can of gasoline resting on top. The timer was not ticking. Neighborhood residents told police they heard dogs barking about 3:00 a.m. Police determined that was probably the time the bomb was placed on the porch and a 45-minute timing device was set, but failed.

The police evacuated about 75 residents and cordoned off the street for 75 feet on each side of the house. The Cleveland Police Department's bomb squad was notified and Sergeant Victor Kovacic quickly arrived on the scene and analyzed the situation. Sergeant Kovacic, an experienced bomb disposal expert, decided to first remove the gasoline can from the bomb. He attached a cord to the can and, from some distance away, started to pull the can away from the bomb. When he did this, the bomb's timer began ticking again. Kovacic was able to stop the timer with less than two minutes remaining before the bomb detonated. He then extracted the detonator, disarming the device. A few days later, the sergeant received a well-deserved letter of thanks and appreciation from Mrs. Sullenberger.

Shortly after the Lakewood incident, an affidavit was presented to U.S. Magistrate Jack B. Streepy, which revealed that a "reliable source" told the FBI that Sanzo was "directly involved in placing the bomb which exploded in Beaver's car." On Saturday night, August 30, FBI agents arrested Joseph Sanzo while he was standing next to a wine rack in a drug store in Euclid. He was locked up in the County Jail to await a Monday morning arraignment in U.S. District Court. By this time, the U.S. Attorney's office in Cleveland had relocated Ronald Sullenberger.

Joseph Ilacqua was still on the loose. Now a suspect in three different bombings and two murders, on October 2, the FBI issued a warning about him to the public describing him as armed and dangerous. The notification stated agents believed he was still in northeast Ohio, probably Youngstown.

On Tuesday, October 28, the trial of the four men – Bruening, Palumbo, Sanzo and Sullenberger – was scheduled to begin in U.S. District Court in Cleveland. Hearing the case was Federal Judge Leroy J. Contie, Jr. The day began with Sullenberger being removed to a different courtroom where he pleaded guilty to two charges without the knowledge of the other three defendants. Next, Palumbo pleaded guilty to conspiracy to possess stolen liquor.

Then things got interesting. When Sanzo was arraigned after his late August arrest, Judge Contie set bond at $250,000, more than four times that of the other defendants, which the prisoner was unable to raise. After the pleas of the first two defendants this day, Sanzo's lawyer, Harry A. Hanna charged that since the FBI claimed his client was involved in the Beaver car bombing, the judge was prejudicial against him. In support of this, Hanna cited the judge's home was the target of a bomber 17 years ago. In 1958, when Contie was the solicitor for the city of Canton, his home was bombed after he led a crusade against gambling and prohibition and was credited with cleaning up the city. The bombing, however, went unsolved. Hanna declared the judge "might empathize with Beavers and the judge's sympathy might be reflected during the trial." The attorney claimed that the high bond the judge set for Sanzo was an indication of prejudice and argued that the court must not only be fair and impartial, but must avoid all appearance of prejudice. Judge Contie defended the high bond, stating Sanzo was a fugitive from justice after the indictment and cited his record for bank robbery, breaking and entering and parole violation. Contie said it was unreasonable to think a 17-year-old incident would affect his influence in the case and stated he presumed Sanzo innocent. Despite Judge Contie's strong feelings, he nevertheless recused himself from the case, which was immediately assigned to Federal Judge Robert B. Krupansky.

The next day, after having caused disruption in court the previous day by prompting the removal of Judge Contie, Sanzo delivered another surprise. Before the trial began, he pleaded guilty to one count of the two-count indictment, that of possession of $47,000 of stolen liquor. His co-defendant Norman Bruening pleaded guilty to conspiracy to possess stolen liquor. Sentencing was delayed on all four men pending background reports.

On December 11, 1975, Judge Krupansky sentenced Joseph Sanzo to six years in Federal prison. Norman Bruening received three years. Earlier, Judge Contie sentenced Ronald Sullenberger to six years and Thomas Palumbo to three. As of this writing, Joseph Sanzo is still believed to be living.

James Samuel Zimmerman

Zimmerman was a member of the Penn-Ohio burglary ring, a gang which was responsible for a number of safecrackings and an armed robbery in Warren during the mid-1950s. Known to his friends as "Jimmy Z," Zimmerman made news for the first time on April 15, 1940, when he was 18 years-old. He was with a group of friends, teenagers and one young adult, returning from a picnic at the North Chagrin Reservation in the Metropolitan Parks, south of Willoughby, in Lake County. Zimmerman, who was behind the wheel taking the four home, apparently was driving too fast and was unable to negotiate a curve on Strawberry Lane, a winding stretch of road inside the park. The car hit a tree. Zimmerman suffered a fractured jaw and facial lacerations; two other people in the car were admitted to Mount Sinai Hospital with serious injuries.

Later that same year, Zimmerman was involved in a burglary and larceny for which he was convicted and received a two-year suspended sentence. In 1945, he was arrested for an un-armed robbery and convicted. Sentenced to 1-to-25-years, he was paroled in 1946. Sometime in the 1940s Zimmerman became associated with the notorious James Petro.

On March 21, 1951, a drunken "Jimmy Zee" led police on a chase from East 9th Street all the way up to East 60th Street before being stopped. Police could only charge Zimmerman with intoxication, not speeding, because in recent years the courts in Cleveland held that traffic arrests could only be made by officers driving in marked vehicles. Later in the decade, on April 10, 1958, Zimmerman was fined $200 and sentenced to ten days in the County Workhouse for driving 100 mph on the East Shoreway.

In the early 1950s, Zimmerman was allegedly involved in the selling of heroin in Cleveland with Alex Clarco, who lived in and operated out of the Hotel Garfield at 3848 Prospect Avenue.[99] On May 13, 1952, Clarco collected $500 from Joe Romano, a reputed rackets figure who claimed he was "a big out-of-town" drug peddler, whose hangout was the Hotel Garfield. Later that day, Romano was told by Zimmerman where he could find the packet of heroin, which was hidden behind the Hotel Garfield. Unfortunately for Clarco and Zimmerman, Romano turned out to be an undercover agent.

Clarco and Zimmerman were arrested and went to trial on October 29, 1952; both were found guilty. The only evidence against Zimmerman was his thumb print on the envelope that contained heroin, as testified to by an FBI fingerprint expert.[100] Romano, whose real name was not made public during the trial, was the key witness. Zimmerman was represented by attorneys Anthony C. Carlin and Harry C. Lavine, who would represent him during his burglary trial some eight years later. Carlin argued there was no evidence that his client handled the heroin, and that he was simply doing a favor for Clarco by mentioning to Romano where the envelope could be found.

The Federal jury took just over an hour to find Zimmerman guilty on two counts of selling and possession of heroin; Clarco was found guilty of only selling the drug. Federal Judge Charles J. McNamee immediately sentenced Zimmerman to seven years in prison. After the verdict was read, Zimmerman turned around to face Romano, who was on the other side of the railing, and accused him of lying during his testimony. The lie involved Romano's testimony that he saw Zimmerman at the Hotel Regent, at East 105th Street and Euclid, Avenue (now a part of Cleveland Clinic). Zimmerman claimed he had not been at the hotel in the past two years. After an angry exchange of words, Romano walked away.

Based on this brief exchange, attorney Carlin filed a motion for a new trial. He took affidavits from three witnesses who overheard the conversation. On December 16, while Zimmerman was still being housed in the Cuyahoga County jail, a hearing on the motion for a new trial was heard. The affidavits stated that during their conversation, Romano admitted to Zimmerman that he might have been "mistaken" in his testimony. Claiming to have heard this was Zimmerman's sister, June; John Carlin, a law student and a younger brother of Zimmerman's lawyer; and a trial spectator. Judge McNamee asked Assistant U.S. Attorney Frank E. Steel for Romano's version of events. According to Steel, after Zimmerman told Romano that he hadn't been at the Hotel Regent in two years, the agent replied, "If it wasn't you, it must have been your twin brother." McNamee told the prosecutor to put the statement in an affidavit for the record, and then overruled the motion for a new trial. Zimmerman was sent to

Federal prison in Leavenworth, Kansas, and was paroled in December 1955. He would later tell reporters that he was "ashamed" to be linked with narcotics. He claimed he was just doing a favor for a friend and didn't know narcotics were inside the envelope he was carrying.

After his release Zimmerman became associated with the Penn-Ohio burglary ring. While it was never clear how many burglaries they were responsible for, in court and in the newspapers, they were only connected to four. The ring members were Joseph Jasper "Fats" Aiello, Ronald Carabbia, Donald "Bull" Jones, Willie Napoli and James Zimmerman. They were assisted by two rogue cops from the Warren Police Department – Harold Huff and Richard Stanley (See Chapter End Note #23).

Zimmerman, ironically, was the only member of the gang to be convicted of a burglary that the ring was accused of. By the summer of 1962, Trumbull County Prosecutor Lynn B, Griffith, Jr. had seen no reason to pursue additional charges against "Fats" Aiello and Ronnie Carabbia. Zimmerman's conviction was upheld by the 7th District Court of Appeals and was awaiting action by the Ohio Supreme Court. While many felt Zimmerman had a good chance of having his conviction over-turned, the 40-year-old Zimmerman just couldn't seem to avoid trouble.

On the night of August 16, 1962, Zimmerman boarded a flight to Chicago with future Cleveland Mafia enforcer Eugene "The Animal" Ciasullo. The men had checked their luggage at the airline counter in Cleveland. During a routine baggage search before being loaded on the plane, employees found handguns and ammunition in each of their suitcases. The Cleveland FBI was notified, who in turn contacted their counterparts in the Chicago office. After getting off the plane at O'Hare International Airport, Zimmerman and Ciasullo were approached by three FBI agents in the terminal while they waited for their luggage. One of the agents began questioning Zimmerman about some stolen bonds. He then inquired, "You have a reputation for carrying guns. Do you have any with you?" Zimmerman simply replied, "No, they're in our suitcases." Both men were arrested and charged with violating a Federal law which prohibits the interstate transport of firearms by a convicted felon. The two men told the agents they were in Chicago to collect a gambling debt. They were each held on a $15,000 bond.

In early October 1962, while Zimmerman was awaiting the Ohio Supreme Court to hear his appeal, he had another encounter with the FBI, this time at his home. On October 3, Zimmerman was arrested on a Federal indictment which charged him and ten others with conspiracy to transport stolen U.S. Treasury bonds, as well as other securities, in interstate commerce. Edward E. Hargett, Agent-in-Charge of the Cleveland office, announced the arrest after a bench warrant was issued in the U.S. District Court in Houston. The bonds were stolen during a safecracking. Nothing appears to have ever happened with this case.

By the end of October, the Ohio Supreme Court refused to hear Zimmerman's appeal on the 1959 State liquor store conviction, and he was off to prison. He returned briefly to face trial on the Federal charges of transporting a weapon across state lines as a convicted felon. His trial was heard before a Federal judge without a jury, and he was found guilty and sentenced to five years in prison to be served concurrently with his state sentence for burglary.

After serving his time for the State Liquor store burglary and the weapons charge, Zimmerman seemed to keep a low profile. His only arrests were for public intoxication in 1970, and driving while intoxicated and abusing a police officer in 1971. Despite his police record, Zimmerman found work as a part-time security guard at the Howard Johnson Motor Lodge at East 55th Street and the East Shoreway. But police believed he was into other activities, possibly loan-sharking. Security guards didn't own $90,000 homes, like Zimmerman did at 4595 Anderson Road in South Euclid; nor did they drive $10,000 automobiles.

In July 1974, Zimmerman made a brief appearance as a defense witness at the trial of Cleveland Police Lieutenant Peter M. Mihalic, who was on trial for burglary. The State's key witness was Charles M. Broeckel, a 20-year acquaintance Zimmerman knew from the Collinwood neighborhood in which he was raised. Mihalic was convicted for his role in a burglary ring which operated on the city's Northeast Side. In the week's following the trial Zimmerman had become "apprehensive and nervous" and began carrying a weapon.

On Monday night, September 30, 1974, Zimmerman left his Anderson Road home to meet a brother-in-law. It was the last time his wife, May, saw him alive. She telephoned police when he didn't come home, claiming that he always made a point of letting her know where he was if he wasn't going to make it home. She told police that she feared for his safety.

Around 3:00 Wednesday morning, police found Zimmerman's 1974 Lincoln Continental in the Howard Johnson's parking lot where he worked. The keys to the car were found on the ground a few feet from where his car was parked. The car appeared to have been ransacked and papers from the glove compartment were scattered about the inside of the vehicle. The newspapers described "Jimmy Zee" as "a personable, flamboyant ex-convict, best known for his safecracking forays. The police speculated his disappearance may have had something to do with his money-lending activities.

On Sunday afternoon, October 7, his body was found floating near the mouth of the Cuyahoga River. The body was pulled out of the water by officers from the Ports & Harbors Unit. The decomposing body was missing a finger. Zimmerman was known to have lost the little finger on his left hand. Although said to be wearing a gold ring, a diamond ring, and a watch, no jewelry was found on the body; instead, police found 75 cents in his pocket along with a pen inscribed "Merry Christmas or Happy Chanukah – Marty." The coroner ruled Zimmerman died from a single gunshot to the back of the head. Zimmerman was buried in Lake View Cemetery. Throughout the remainder of the 1970s, announcements appeared in the "In Memoriam" section of the *Plain Dealer* on the anniversary of his disappearance by family members.

Chapter Eleven:

Alfred Calabrese, Paul Perrotti & "The 'Red' Carpenter Story"

Author's note: This chapter of the story was the most difficult one to write. Information regarding the participants was hard to come by. Important factual details always seemed to be left out of articles that would have been helpful to tie the whole story together. The reporting from some of the newspapers was inaccurate and sometimes was inconsistent even when coming from the same publication. I have indicated in Italics my comments on events and when some of these missing pieces occur.

If Alfred Calabrese and Paul Perrotti were ever involved with Julius Petro in a burglary it must have been a successful one; their names never appeared with one another involving a burglary arrest. But they can be linked together if you consider their Collinwood connections and the age-old adage "guilt by association."

Alfred A. "Allie" Calabrese was introduced into the story of Julius Petro in April 1949, when the two were arrested, along with Anthony D'Alessio. Police stopped Petro's Cadillac after it raced out of a Royal Castle restaurant parking lot in Collinwood. When one of the men lied to police about his name, all three were on their way to jail. Two years later, "Allie" was arrested for burglary and larceny, but a grand jury refused to indict. One article claimed Calabrese was given probation for a burglary and larceny committed in 1955.

"Allie" and Paul Perrotti were friends. At one time, according to a *Plain Dealer* story on April 17, 1958, they were both employed by the St. Clair Builders Supply Company in Cleveland. Perrotti first came to the attention of Clevelanders on January 3, 1953, when it was announced he was one of nine men who were due to be charged that day with burglary and larceny after Cleveland police "went into the mop-up stage of a New Years' Night thug roundup." Included in the "roundup" were Ralph "Bull" De Biase and Anthony D'Alessio, former companions of Julius Petro. Perrotti's police record before that consisted of probation for safe tampering in 1952.

Meet the Wahoo Bar Burglars

Paul F. "Red" Carpenter, Ernest "Ernie" Foti, John J. Glassner, Arthur LaRiche and John Lexune were the men credited with pulling the burglary job at the popular watering hole. Even though Glassner and Lexune were in another part of town on the night of the burglary, they shared in the proceeds. Carpenter and John Glassner were introduced by John's brother William, the two men pulled at least ten burglaries together prior to the Wahoo Bar. Ernest Foti was once considered a top lieutenant in the notorious Akron gang headed by James La-Fatch, which began operating back in the Prohibition days. Arthur LaRiche had connections to several men in the inner circle of Julius Petro, including Joseph Drago, Dominic Mafrici and Richard Stewart. John Lexune was relatively unknown at the time of the burglary. Little is known about how all five men came together.

On September 8, 1955, Carpenter and the Glassner brothers burglarized the Automotive Supply & Equipment Company at 278 Water Street in Akron. The plan was to crack the safe, but William Glassner would later reveal, "The company had so many safes on the premises, we didn't know which one the money was in." The men didn't leave empty-handed; prominent among the things stolen were a number of items which could be labeled burglary tools. Over the next ten months, as Carpenter and John Glassner later testified, they were involved in nearly a dozen burglaries, utilizing the tools from the Automotive Supply haul.

In early June 1956, Carpenter was approached by Ernie Foti who told him that $12,000 was going to be locked inside a safe that weekend at the Wahoo Bar, located at 55 South Main Street[101] in Akron. Foti asked him if he would be interested in cracking the safe there. When Carpenter asked if he could bring in his friend, John Glassner, to help with the planning and serve as a lookout, Foti agreed. The plan was for the three men to "take" the bar on the night of June 10, using a key to the place that Foti had somehow obtained. Carpenter, Foti and Glassner were driven to the bar in a car owned by Mary Shaffer, said to be Glassner's girlfriend, even though he was married. Glassner had allegedly talked her into providing the ride. When the key didn't open the front door, the burglary was called off.

Carpenter met with Foti again the following week; this time Foti brought along Arthur LaRiche and John Lexune. During the early morning hours of Sunday, June 17, 1956, a meeting was held in the backyard of Carpenter's home at 67 West Street in Akron. Foti was present along with LaRiche, Lexune and Glassner. At the meeting, Foti told them the money was still in the Wahoo Bar's safe. They decided to pull the job that night. This time, instead of a key to the front door, they would have to climb on top of the building and cross over a few rooftops to a skylight on the roof of the bar. Foti claimed, "He had a sore back and couldn't climb, and that he didn't like heights." But he helped with the planning and volunteered to drive the car.

When Sunday night arrived, the five men met again at the Carpenter home. It was decided that Carpenter and LaRiche would be driven to the Wahoo Bar by Foti. Glassner and Lexune were not needed and instead were "dispatched to case" a South Akron market for a later burglary. This time, using a car owned by Carpenter's wife, Betty, Foti drove the two men down Malden Lane Alley about 10:45 p.m. Carpenter brought along an assortment of burglary tools and, as the men got out of the car, he told Foti to be back in 45 minutes. Carpenter and LaRiche ascended a nearby building, and then climbed over rooftops to the South

Main Street address, which housed the Wahoo Bar. From there they pried open a skylight and entered. Once inside, they cracked open the safe and removed the money. They completed their task in just 40 minutes, but Foti was 20 minutes late in getting back to the alley to pick them up.

The three men returned to Carpenter's West Street home, where Glassner and Lexune were waiting to split the money. Carpenter's wife, Betty, a waitress, made coffee for everyone, for which Foti gave her $70. Before splitting the money five ways, $900 was set aside for the "informant" who gave Foti the tip about the money being in the safe. This person was never identified.

On Monday morning, Fred Lieberman, manager of the Wahoo Bar, which was owned by his wife, Eleanor, discovered the burglary and all the damage caused in the break-in. At first it was reported that the take was $12,000. Another figure bandied about was $9,900 and that with the damages it brought the total to $12,000. On Wednesday, June 20, the *Akron Beacon Journal* reported two brothers were booked on open charges for the burglary. John and William Glassner were held without bond in Akron City Jail until formal charges could be filed against them. On Friday, the newspaper reported that the Glassner brothers and Paul Carpenter were charged with suspicion in Akron Municipal Court and the cases were continued with each man now under a $3,000 bond. On Monday, June 25, Ernest Foti was arrested, charged with suspicion, and also placed under a $3,000 bond. That same day, formal charges of burglary and larceny were filed against Carpenter and John Glassner; his brother William was still being held for suspicion. *In one of the ironies of the case, there was never anything reported in the newspapers as to what led to the arrests of any of the men.*

While they cooled their heels waiting until the next hearing to be held on July 17, Eleanor Lieberman, owner of the Wahoo Bar, was determined they were not going to use the money they stole from her to defend themselves on the charges. She stated the amount of money stolen was $12,841. The $1,846 police found on the men when arrested was attached by order of the Summit County Common Pleas Court; meaning the men would not have access to it.

By July 17, Carpenter and John Glassner, in addition to being charged with the Wahoo Bar burglary, were now charged with the burglary and larceny of the Automotive Supply & Equipment Company in September 1955. Tools stolen in that burglary were found abandoned in the Wahoo Bar. William Glassner, meanwhile, was still being held on suspicion charges. All three men had their cases continued. After Akron detectives told Municipal Judge Thomas M. Powers, they were convinced Foti was not involved in the Wahoo Bar burglary, his suspicion charge was dismissed, and he was released.

Both Glassners and Carpenter were formally indicted on July 26, for burglary and larceny of the Automotive Supply & Equipment Co. The owner said in court that the goods stolen from his company were valued at $784. All three men pleaded not guilty and went free under $3,000 bonds each. One week later,

John Glassner and Carpenter were back in front of Judge Powers for the third time in 18 days; this time they were indicted for the Wahoo Bar burglary.

Ernest Foti still had one issue to deal with. Back on April 15, 1956, while driving drunk, he hit a parked police car used by Akron Police Captain Carroll Cutright, an officer Foti disliked. The collision took place outside the Akron Police station, from where Foti was chased to Bowery and State Streets before being stopped and arrested. Police charged Foti with drunk driving, driving without a license and failure to stop after an accident; the last one creating a more serious hit-skip charge. Foti's wife, Mary, also filed a charge against him for non-support of herself and their four children.

When the case came before Municipal Judge Abner D. Zook on September 7, Foti's attorney claimed his client was so drunk he didn't even know he had been in an accident, and could not account for any of the events of that night. Judge Zook found Foti guilty of drunk driving and driving without a license; thus, freeing him of the hit-skip charge. Foti was fined a total of $125 and costs, but his jail sentence was reduced from 20 to 10 days, and he was given work privileges from 9 a.m. to 5 p.m. The judge allowed this so Foti could continue payments to his family, despite the fact that he didn't have a job. The newspaper pointed out that this was nothing new for Foti. His rap sheet showed a total of 16 arrests, but only three in which he was fined or did any jail time.

The only two suspects in the Wahoo Bar burglary were out on bond, and charges against a third were dropped. But Akron Police had not given up on the case; and the released men had not given up on their chosen professions.

A Murder in Alliance
The city of Alliance earns two mentions in this book. The first was when Julius Petro was shot there by Alliance police officer, Richard Moretti, during the commission of a robbery at the home of grocer and beer distributor Joseph Carretta, in June 1950. The second incident involved the senseless killing of a local sports hero, 25-year-old Eldon Earl "Pete" Shoup.

While in high school, "Pete" Shoup became a golfing legend in the Alliance area. At the age of 17, he was a qualifier for the National Junior Championship of the U.S. Golf Association. This honor allowed him to be one of the representatives of the district in the national tournament in Washington D.C. played July 27 to 30, 1949. Later that summer, Shoup placed high in the National Caddy Championship Tournament held in Columbus. After high school, he enlisted in the Coast Guard, serving from June 1951 to June 1954. While there he won two Coast Guard district golf tournaments held in Norfolk, Virginia. Once back home, "Pete" Shoup remained a local legend in Alliance and Stark County for his golf prowess. By February 1957, Shoup was married, and he and his wife, Helen, had one daughter and another child on the way. Shoup was working as an apprentice draftsman at Morgan Engineering Company.[102] Meanwhile, he continued to hone his golf skills as a member of Sleepy Hollow Country Club in Alliance, where he shared the course record with a score of 63.

Not much was known about Eldon's father, 49-year-old Earl Shoup. One article stated he was employed as a "craneman" at Transue & Williams Steel Forging Corporation. Another claimed he "helps Mr. Wells in his business dealings," while a third article claimed, "Shoup does part-time electrical work for Mr. Wells in a basement office" of the Wells' home. "Mr. Wells" was Frank E. "Red" Wells, who was well-known in the Alliance / Salem, Ohio area. He operated the 20th Century Cigar store and the Silver Bullet Café. The holder of a Federal Wagering Tax Stamp,[103] under the "principal" category, Wells, by his own admission, was "interested in gambling." *Wells interest in gambling was a continuing theme throughout the story of "A Murder in Alliance." Two things, however, were never brought out. One, what kind of gambling was he "interested" in, and just exactly what was it that Earl Shoup was assisting him with.*

Earl Shoup, also, had an apparent interest in gambling. He purchased a gambling tax stamp, under the "agent" category, at the same time Wells bought his. Both men, having purchased stamps in the spring of 1956, returned them to the mayor's office last July, along with ten other residents, after a public request was issued by the mayor for all stamp holders to voluntarily return them.

Around the last week of January 1957, Frank Wells left Alliance for a brief respite from the brutal Northeast Ohio winter. He drove to Coral Gables, Florida, with his wife and three daughters, where he kept a second home. While gone, he asked Earl Shoup to keep an eye on his "fashionable home" at 2815 Ridgewood Avenue, in the Mount Union neighborhood of Alliance, named after the local college of the same name.[104] Shoup would arrive between 8:00 and 8:30 p.m. each night, check the house, and then turn on a few inside lights so it looked like somebody was home.

On Thursday night, February 7, Earl Shoup stopped at the Wells home around 8:00, but left by 8:10. One report quoted him saying, "On a hunch – I decided to make a second check." Whatever the cause of that hunch, it would cost him dearly. Early reporting had Shoup driving to his son's home at 1048 ½ Arch Avenue, where he reportedly asked his son if he "wanted to take a ride." *The story of what happened between the time Earl Shoup left the Wells' home "by 8:10" and returned at 9:15, would take several twists and turns. It was never reported what the "hunch" was that caused him to return to the Wells' home, or why he went and picked up his son and brought him along. There was never any clear explanation as to why "Pete" Shoup was at the Wells' home that fateful night.*

During Shoup's absence from the Ridgewood Avenue home, police surmised two men arrived at the house between 8:10 and 9:00. It was believed they might have been dropped off on South Rockhill Avenue, which runs behind the Wells residence, by a third accomplice, who stayed in the car. Police found tire tracks where they believed the get-away car was parked. It must have been a muddy trek to the Wells home from South Rockhill Avenue, as investigators later reported "mud was found throughout the Wells home, as most of the house was ransacked." This indicates that the men had time, once inside, to look for valuables in other parts of the house. Police believed the men gained entrance by removing a screen from a basement window at the back of the house and forcing open the window. One man then climbed in and opened a door for his accomplice. Despite the ransacking of the home, the burglars spent most of the time in the basement, where a safe was located.

The *Alliance Review* wrote, "Police Chief A.O. Lower expressed wonderment on whether the elder Shoup had a 'feeling something was going to happen' at Wells' home." Shoup said when he arrived back, he drove to the rear of the home, got out and entered the back door. Once inside the hallway, he noticed the door leading to the basement was open. As he started down the stairs, he heard his son scream, "Dad! Someone is attacking me." At that instant, Shoup told police, a man raced from the basement and "brushed" past him. Shoup pursued the man, catching him just outside the back door. While Earl Shoup was wrestling with him, his son "Pete" was tussling with another. All of a sudden, the burglar on the ground, firmly in Earl Shoup's grasp, cried out in desperation, "Shoot the bastard!" The younger Shoup's assailant, who was armed with a revolver, fired three rounds at Earl Shoup, hitting him in the chest and hand. "Pete" tried to wrestle the weapon away from the man in an effort to keep his father from being killed. During the brief struggle, the burglar held the gun point blank to "Pete's" throat and pulled the trigger twice. The two burglars then ran off through the Wells' backyard. Police believed they headed west to South Rockhill Avenue, where a getaway car waited.

Earl Shoup picked up his son and carried him into the house. He called the police. Edward Moretti, the patrolman who put a slug in Julius Petro during the Carretta armed robbery back in June 1950, was one of the first officers to arrive, he found Earl semiconscious on a chair in the kitchen, and "Pete" slumped over on the floor in the dining room. Other officers quickly arrived, including Captain Laurence W. Lauer and Lieutenant Donald M. Cox. Both Shoups were rushed to Alliance General Hospital, where "Pete" died an hour later. Earl survived his wounds.

Police Chief Albert O. Lower told reporters that he believed the burglars knew the layout of the home and that the Wells family was on vacation. In one room in the basement, police found a medium sized safe[105] empty, lying on its side with the door removed, and a crowbar abandoned nearby. Also close by was sledge hammer, laying among some U.S. Savings Bonds, as well as other documents and a set of car keys. The burglars also ransacked an office next to the one where the safe was located.

The Ridgewood Avenue address was soon crawling with reporters. When one noticed some paper bags near the basement safe, he asked a police officer what was in them. His response was a terse, "Don't ask those questions." Reports and photographers, while permitted into the room where the safe was broken open, but they were refused entry into the room next to it, which was referred to as "the office." When one asked if they could open the door, just so they could get a quick photograph they were turned down, being told, "There are obscene pictures in there."

Frank Wells and his wife arrived home late Thursday night, or early Friday morning after taking a flight from Florida. He immediately told police that money stolen from the safe was of an undetermined amount. Mrs. Wells would check to see if there was anything else of value taken from the home. Frank Wells later placed the amount of money stolen from the safe at $1,000.

Technicians from the London Prison Farm[106] arrived at 4:00 a.m. Friday to assist in the investigation. They discovered insurance documents, bonds and personal papers littered across the basement floor near the safe. The investigators were able to retrieve three fingerprints from the "mud-spattered" safe. Neighbors, questioned in the vicinity, reported hearing five gunshots; three in rapid succession followed by two more. The technicians recovered one of the slugs at the rear of the garage door. Investigators would spend 72 hours on the scene – at the house and later interviewing Earl Shoup at the hospital. *The Salem News*, in a wrap-up of the investigation, wrote:

Investigators further said the work was done by amateurs. They base their opinion on the fact that the safe in the basement was clumsily opened in a matter (sic) not befitting a professional burglar; fingerprints were left behind on the safe; their tools were left and a size 11 overshoe was found in a field a short distance from where the assailants' auto was believed parked. The burglars dropped a total of $120 in currency and 60 cents in change as they made their getaway.

Stark County coroner, Dr. E.B. Mozes, completed his autopsy shortly before noon Friday. "Pete" Shoup died from a shot fired into the left side of his neck, which traveled downward shattering a rib and eventually ending up in a back muscle. The doctor recovered the .38 slug; now he needed the police to find the weapon to match it to. There were also marks on "Pete's" head, the result of being hit three times with the revolver.

On Saturday, Police Lieutenant Donald Cox questioned Earl Shoup at Alliance City Hospital. The *Alliance Review* printed this story about the questioning:

He [Shoup] told police he left there [2815 Ridgewood Avenue] about 8:10, made several stops and then went to his son Eldon's home to get the latter to help him carry 'some heavy equipment' into Wells' house. Shoup said he needed the help of his son because he had a rupture and could do no heavy lifting. The father and son arrived at the Wells home shortly after 9 p.m. and the shooting occurred [a] few minutes later.

Earl Shoup was also asked to provide a description of the burglar he wrestled with. He described him as 19 or 20 years-old; 5-feet, 7-inches tall, weighing between 145 and 150 pounds, with brown hair cut short.

On Sunday night "one of the largest crowds ever to view a body at the Myers Funeral Home" in Alliance came calling. The next day Eldon "Pete" Shoup was laid to rest after a funeral mass at St. Joseph's Church and burial in the church cemetery.

Over the next ten days, police brought in a few suspects, who were soon released. Police still thought that since the burglars knew the layout of the home, they were local figures, possibly gambling figures. They also believed that there were only two men in the house and made their getaway from South Rockhill Avenue, where the car was believed parked. On February 13, Frank Wells offered a $1,500 reward for information leading to the arrest and conviction of the slayer. At this point the newspapers were still reporting the burglary haul as $1,000. The case suddenly went cold, but would not remain so for long.

A Bizarre Shooting in Lake County

In the wake of the Wahoo Bar burglary, the Akron police conducted "an exhaustive search" of the establishment, and examined every piece of evidence for clues. One whole section of the bar was crated up and, along with the door to the safe, driven to Washington D.C. to be studied for prints at the FBI's famous laboratory. Despite this effort, the case remained stagnant until March 1957. Then Akron police devised a plan. They obtained secret indictments against the recently released Ernest Foti, along with Arthur LaRiche and John Lexune; the latter two recently deciding to make themselves scarce. Police arrested Foti and charged him with the attempted burglary of Emery's Market, at 2830 Copley Road, which took place weeks earlier on February 10. They claimed he was seen "fleeing the premises." The purpose of this ruse was to lull the remaining two members of the Wahoo Bar burglary crew into a false sense of "well-being," and to make them think they were no longer being investigated for the crime. The ploy apparently worked. On Monday night, March 18, police in Cleveland and Elyria arrested Lexune and LaRiche. The next day they were brought to Akron and held in the Summit County Jail.

Three nights after their arrest, Lake County sheriff's deputies received a telephone call from a man who said he had just been shot three times. Deputies raced out to Arcola Road and Route 20 (North Ridge Road), a rural area south of the community of North Madison near the Ashtabula County line. When they arrived at a filling station, they found a man in serious condition with bullet wounds of the neck, ribs, and thigh. He was quickly transported to Lake County Memorial Hospital in Painesville, where he was treated for three .38 Special caliber gunshot wounds.

He told law enforcement officers that around 10:00 p.m., while walking to an East Side restaurant, he was abducted by two men with guns, who forced him into a car at Euclid Avenue and East 105th Street. After arriving at a location on Arcola Road, he was shoved out of the car, shot three times, dragged 20 feet to a shallow grave on the grounds of an old foundry, and buried. He clawed his way out of the would-be grave, eventually got to his feet, and staggered a quarter-mile to the nearby filling station[107] where he called sheriffs' deputies. During the questioning, he told officers he was out on bond from a robbery in Akron – and that his name was Paul Carpenter.

During an investigation of the crime scene, near the Arcola Road foundry, deputies found a recently dug grave. They described it as "about two feet deep, 2 ½ feet wide and 4 ½ feet long." Deputies estimated that the hole, dug in rocky ground with lots of cinders, would have taken a half-hour to 45 minutes to dig. Based on the time-line Carpenter gave them, they believed it was dug in advance. With a little more searching they found a Smith & Wesson five-shot revolver with two live rounds in it, which had been thrown into Arcola Creek.

Authorities immediately speculated that since Carpenter was recently seen in the company of John Lexune, perhaps his partner-in-crime suspected him of ratting on him and LaRiche. But Carpenter told his inquisitors he could not give a description of the men who grabbed him, or even describe the car that drove him away. He maintained he did not know them and that they did not speak to him. He simply claimed his kidnappers' motive for the robbery and murder attempt was the $5 he had in his pocket. Despite this, he requested and received a police guard outside his hospital room.

Deputies wanted to question Betty Carpenter. She and Paul had recently been living at 10700 Helena Avenue[108] in Cleveland, a block away from St. Clair Avenue and East 107th Street. When deputies caught up with her on Friday afternoon, she told them she had not seen her husband since Thursday night when he left to go to a restaurant. The next she heard about him was Friday morning when she learned about the shooting from a radio news broadcast at 10:00 a.m.

On Friday morning, while Carpenter was recuperating in the hospital, an Akron common pleas judge set bond at $25,000 apiece for the recently arrested Foti, LaRiche and Lexune for the Wahoo Bar burglary. While it may seem rather odd that John Glassner and Lexune would be charged for a crime they played no part in, the state would hold that the two were actually looking for a place to rob or burglarize that night and the money they got would be pooled with what came from the Wahoo Bar. The first man to make bond was Lexune. Foti, unable to raise the money, instead filed a writ of habeas corpus with the 9th District Court of Appeals, claiming "his bail is too excessive and unlawful and that he is being imprisoned without legal authority." Prosecutor John S. Ballard promised he would resist all efforts by Foti to receive a lower bail.

Four days after the attempted murder, Carpenter was released from the Lake County hospital and immediately arrested by Lake County sheriffs' deputies. He was taken to the county jail and held for investigation. By now, he had dropped the robbery story and was claiming the shooters "just got the wrong man." Akron police, by now, had changed their theory of the shooting. Instead of believing the attempted murder was for turning on his cohorts in the Wahoo Bar burglary, they believed it had something to do with his Cleveland activities since being released.

On April 19, Carpenter and John Glassner pleaded guilty to two counts of breaking and entering and one count of possession of burglary tools for both the Automotive Supply & Equipment Company break-in and the Wahoo Bar burglary. William Glassner pleaded guilty to one count of breaking and entering, and one count of possession of burglary tools in the Automotive Supply & Equipment Company case. The charges carried sentences of 1 to 15 years and 1 to 5 years, respectively. Common Pleas Judge Clande V.D. Emmons delayed sentencing at the request of the men's attorney, George Hargreaves until the probation department could file their reports.

Wahoo Bar Burglary Trial – Part 1

On Thursday, April 25, 1957, the trial for the Wahoo Bar burglary in June 1956 got underway in the courtroom of Judge Emmons. Representing the state was Summit County Prosecutor John S. Ballard; the defense attorneys were Paul C. Laybourne of Akron (representing Foti); Casmere K. Batule (Lexune) and Nicholas Brinsky (LaRiche) both of Cleveland. That morning at the courthouse there was a change in procedures. In the week since pleading guilty, word leaked out that "Red" Carpenter and his wife, Betty were both going to testify. As courthouse personnel and spectators (limited to 20) entered the courtroom, they were frisked by sheriff's deputies. Men and women alike were patted down; women's purses were also inspected. All remained in the dark until Prosecutor Ballard delivered his opening statement. "A defendant in this case," he stated, "made a threat that if one of the witnesses for the state dares to testify in this case 'they'd get him or they'd get his wife.' You will hear more about this at the proper time."

Before this, while jury selection was still in progress, a telegram reached the courthouse from Toledo requesting that defendant John Lexune be arrested and held for a $32,000 payroll holdup of the Libbey-Owens-Ford Federal Credit Union in that city back on February 1. In addition, Lexune was also wanted for another armed robbery in Toledo at a W.T. Grant store where $5,000 was taken. When Akron Police Captain Carroll Cutright asked Judge Emmons to revoke Lexune's bond during a recess so he could be arrested on the Toledo charge, the judge replied that he could not do so while court was in session.

After jury selection, which consisted of five men and seven women, and opening statements, Carpenter was one of the first witnesses called by the state.

During his 45 minutes on the stand that afternoon, he identified all three defendants as having taken part in the Wahoo Bar burglary. Carpenter told the court his version of the burglary and the events leading up to it. He told about meeting Foti in early June, bringing in John Glassner, and the failed attempt to get into the Wahoo Bar with a key.

Carpenter related the story of a second meeting with "Ernie," at which time Foti showed up with Arthur LaRiche and John Lexune. As Carpenter told this to the courtroom, Lexune barked out, "He's nuts," from the defense table. As the witness continued his testimony, Lexune then shouted, "You're a liar!" At this point, Ballard objected loudly and Judge Emmons halted the trial long enough to warn Lexune there were to be no further outbursts.

From there, Carpenter told about the meeting at his home on July 17, and gave the details of the robbery that night. He told how he and LaRiche got on top of the building and crossed roof-tops to get to the Wahoo Bar before opening the skylight and making their way inside. Finishing their task in just 40 minutes, they were forced to wait outside in the alley for Foti to return for them. He stated how John Glassner and Lexune were not needed to go on the Wahoo caper and instead were sent to a South Akron area to case a market for a later burglary. Back at the house he described a jubilant scene as the five men, Glassner and Lexune had returned from their mission, split up the money, while his wife, Betty served coffee.

It was at this point in his testimony that Carpenter tried to clear up the dispute over how much money was actually taken. The first witness that afternoon was Fred Lieberman, the Wahoo Bar manager. He claimed to have known of $12,481 being in the safe. Police had reported the amount at around $9,900. During his testimony, Carpenter claimed the total the men split among themselves was $10,500.

On Friday morning, Carpenter was back on the stand. During questioning by Ballard, he claimed he decided to "talk" after he was shot and left for dead in March. By early April, he advised Ballard that he was ready to cooperate. He told the court that while taking a shower Wednesday morning, April 24, Foti came by and "told me I had better not get on the stand and testify, and my wife had better not, or I'd find myself in a lot of trouble."

During cross-examination by Paul Laybourne, the defense attorney elicited testimony from Carpenter that since leaving the Army in 1948, he held no steady job, and over the past two years had committed about ten burglaries. He stated that the tools he used in the burglaries he had stolen from the Automotive Supply Company in 1955. The tools, brought into the courtroom as an exhibit, were called by one newspaper, the "finest assortment of burglary tools ever displayed at a Common Pleas Court trial." He said he had lived with his current wife, Betty for a year before their marriage in September 1956. He testified she worked as a waitress at the Tangier Restaurant, but quit ten days before he burglarized it. He insisted she was not involved in the "job,"

Laybourne asked, "Then you were living off the proceeds of burglaries and the wages of a woman not married to you?" To which Carpenter answered, "Yes."

Throughout his morning testimony, Carpenter said repeatedly he made no deals with the prosecutor or the police to keep his wife from being indicted, nor had he obtained any leniency for himself. Carpenter remained on the stand for the majority of the day, maintaining a calm exterior despite what the *Akron Beacon Journal* called "withering cross-examination" from defense counsel. Betty Carpenter took the stand briefly before court ended for the week.

During his usual parting statement to the jury, reminding them not to read or think about the case, Judge Emmons added, "If you are disturbed or molested or anyone attempts to contact you, call me at once or contact the prosecutors' office or the Akron Police Department."

Over the weekend, witnesses from the Libbey-Owens-Ford Federal Credit Union holdup in Toledo were brought to Akron to view Lexune. Toledo police detective Edward Meeker reported that witnesses "positively identified" him as one of the participants. Meeker told reporters if Lexune was acquitted of the Wahoo Bar burglary he would be immediately taken to Toledo for trial.

On Monday morning, April 29, Betty Carpenter's cross-examination continued. Described as "a 30-year-old, petite, platinum-haired restaurant / night club waitress," she had been referred to as a night club singer in some articles. At one point Betty joked about the articles describing her as a singer. "I can't carry a tune in a bucket," she said. "I'm a waitress and I've never done any singing." Betty was given a blistering cross-examination by defense attorneys. Among the accusations she was hit with were:

- Being a bigamist, because she lived with a man for five years, having two children with him, which constituted a common-law marriage by Ohio law, before she married Carpenter

- That she bought an automobile with money her husband received from his burglaries. She claimed she used her own money and provided the car title to prove date of purchase.

- Being accused of "fingering" the Tangiers Restaurant burglary for her husband, quitting just before the break-in. She denied the allegations and claimed she quit after a dispute with the manager after she showed up late for work.

- That she married Carpenter so she wouldn't have to testify against him. She claimed she did not know anything about her husband's past until she read about it in the newspapers.

Betty Carpenter handled the defense attorney's attacks as coolly as her husband. At one point, it was a defense attorney that Judge Emmons had to admonish about raising his voice. Before completing their cross-examination, one attorney asked, "Isn't it true you have said you would do anything to help your husband?"

"Anything but perjure myself," she responded.

Despite denying any deals with the police and the prosecutors, multiple times while "Red" Carpenter was on the stand, a defense attorney asked Betty if she was aware of her husband making any application for probation for turning state's witness. Prosecutor Ballard stood up and declared Carpenter had made no such application.

Just before lunch, the defense asked Detective Lieutenant Woodrow Meadows, during cross-examination, why LaRiche was kept in solitary confinement for 30 days. The officer replied, "To keep him away from Foti." The response was not expanded upon.

On Monday afternoon, the state called its last witness. John Glassner, the 33-year-old partner of Carpenter, took the stand and admitted to participating in eight robberies with him. He stated he once served 27 months in the Ohio Penitentiary for pandering. Near the end of his testimony, attorney Laybourne asked him what he did with the money from the Wahoo Bar heist. The witness replied he spent part of it on bonds.

"Government bonds?" queried Laybourne.

"Oh, no – jail bonds – to get out of jail," said Glassner.

Like Carpenter before him, Glassner denied receiving anything for his testimony. The defense claimed Glassner was "lying for leniency."

On Tuesday morning the trial opened with Prosecutor Ballard resting the state's case. Defense counsel's first witnesses were four members of the LaRiche family. Ballard objected strenuously to their testimony, arguing that Foti was the only defendant who filed an alibi defense for the night of the burglary. After Laybourne claimed the purpose of the testimony was to impeach Carpenter, his wife and Glassner, Judge Emmons allowed the questioning to continue. LaRiche family members claimed Arthur spent the night celebrating the Feast of St. Anthony of Padua at Holy Rosary Church in Cleveland's Little Italy neighborhood. Marilyn LaRiche, the 13-year-old daughter of the defendant, recalled, "We had lots of sausage and pizza and stuff."

Ernest Foti took the stand in his own defense during the afternoon. Much had happened since the burglary at the Wahoo Bar. Foti and his wife, Mary had separated, but did not divorce. She was living in Galion, Ohio, located west of Mansfield. She filed suit in Medina County for non-support of herself and their four children. A grand jury indicted him on the non-support charges. Foti was also charged with breaking into an A&P supermarket in Medina, allegedly with Paul Carpenter, and was scheduled to appear in mayor's court on July 2. Any trial in Medina would have to come after the outcome of the Wahoo Bar burglary trial.

On the stand, the 44-year-old claimed the only reason he knew Carpenter and Glassner was because of his bookmaking operations at Ascot Park.[109] He claimed both men were bookies, and both owed him money. Foti refuted the testimony of both Carpenter and Glassner that he was involved in the Wahoo Bar burglary. In keeping with defense counsel's theory the prosecutor offered deals to Carpenter and Glassner to testify, Foti claimed Detective Captain Carroll Cutright had promised him leniency for a confession. When questioned about his alibi defense, Foti delivered the following story, as reported by the *Akron Beacon Journal:*

> The night of the burglary, he picked up his girlfriend about 9:00 when she quit work as a waitress in a downtown restaurant. They went to her Wills Avenue apartment. She changed clothes. They went to a veteran's club, a suburban night club, and then went to an all-night restaurant to eat. The rest of the night was spent in the girl's apartment. He often stayed there, or with his mother, who lived at 187 Wheeler Street.

During his direct testimony, Foti denied ever threatening the Carpenters. When defense counsel finished their questioning, Ballard took over. Suddenly, Foti's memory wasn't as sharp on cross-examination as it was on direct. He had trouble remembering any of the addresses he lived at over the past five to six years, He said he had many jobs, but his main occupation during that period was "as a sometime bookmaker, poker dealer and seller of numbers books." In discussing his criminal record, he had one felony conviction, for which he served prison time, along with a "long string" of misdemeanors dating back to 1931.

Ballard then asked him about his legal occupations. Foti said he had worked as a television repair and installation man. He claimed he worked at the job with his brother, Louis. Ballard continued to delve into this in an attempt to show that Foti had helped install a television set in the Wahoo Bar. This was vehemently denied by the witness.

During trial Tuesday afternoon, it came out that attorney George Hargreaves, who represented Carpenter and Glassner, had received threats on two different occasions regarding the case. The threats were delivered to Hargreaves on April 11 and April 15, both by telephone, one at his home, and the other at his office. The veteran defense attorney reported the threats, but otherwise ignored them. Hargreaves appeared with both clients in court on April 19, when they changed their pleas to guilty.

On Wednesday morning, the defense called their last witness, John Lexune. The 39-year-old was an admitted alcoholic and ex-convict, who served time in the Ohio Penitentiary from 1939 to 1944 for auto theft. He claimed to having met Carpenter and his wife a couple of times. One time he met with Carpenter and John Glassman in a Cleveland bar, where the two men asked him to provide them with an alibi for a "certain night." Lexune said he declined the request because of his criminal record.

Lexune testified he did not meet LaRiche until they were in the County Jail after their March 18 arrest. As for Foti, Lexune stated he "thinks he remembers seeing him" when he was in the Ohio Penitentiary. After Lexune's cross-examination, the defense rested their case.

On Wednesday afternoon, Ballard surprised the courtroom by calling Arthur LaRiche's wife back to the stand as a rebuttal witness. Pregnant with her fourth child, Mrs. LaRiche repeated her story about being with her husband and family at the Feast of St. Anthony in Little Italy on the night he allegedly took part in the robbery. She repeated the story of attending services at the church and then going to the parish hall in the church basement for pizza. She said there was no entertainment going on and recalled no orchestra or dancing.

The next rebuttal witness called was the Reverend Paul Rebol, assistant pastor of Holy Rosary Catholic Church. Father Rebol testified that in celebration of the Feast of St. Anthony that night there were no services, just the traditional fireworks, dance, and raffle. A teen-aged orchestra played music for parishioners to dance to in the parish hall. He said he did not recall seeing either Mrs. LaRiche or her daughter, Marilyn, at the church that night.

Father Rebol also testified to something else. He said several weeks before the trial, he received an anonymous telephone call from a woman who asked for the date that the Feast of St Anthony was celebrated on the previous June. The woman claimed a "relative" was in trouble and this information could help them.

After Reverend Rebol, John Glassner's wife, Ella Jean took the stand. She was called to refute Foti testimony that he had never been in the Glassner home, Mrs. Glassner testified he visited them three weeks prior to the June 17 burglary.

The last rebuttal witness was Detective Captain Carroll Cutright. He denied promising Foti leniency for a confession, as the defendant testified to on Tuesday. The last order of business was the recalling of Detective Lieutenant Woodrow Meadows to report on Mary Shaffer. The girlfriend of John Glassner, whose car was used during the ill-fated first attempt to burglarize the Wahoo Bar, had not appeared in court to testify. Meadows reported police were unable to locate her.

On Thursday morning, both sides gave their closing statements. After lunch, Judge Emmons gave a 37-minute jury charge, before handing the case to the jurors at 2:49 p.m. By dinner time there was no verdict, and the group went out to eat. By 10:00 p.m. there was still no verdict, and the judge allowed the jurors to go home for the night. The jury returned the next morning. By 4:40 that afternoon, they were still far from unanimous on any defendant and told the judge they were hopelessly deadlocked. Emmons had no choice but to discharge the jurors and order a new trial.

Jury foreperson, Mrs. Olive Johnson, later announced the voting as follows: Foti, 9-3 guilty; LaRiche and Lexune 8-4 guilty. She told reporters the main issue during deliberations was a "widespread disbelief of the state's witnesses." They, "being the type of people that they were," she stated, "we felt their word could not be taken in finding anybody guilty on their say so." According to Mrs. Johnson, the jury's take on the matter was Carpenter and Glassner only testified in order to "drag in" Foti, Lexune and LaRiche. The group felt the two men were trying to provide an alibi for Betty Carpenter, who they thought had a more prominent role in the burglary. What made them reach that conclusion was not revealed by Johnson. One week later, however, the *Akron Beacon Journal* reported, "Some persons connected with the prosecution of the Wahoo Bar burglary case explain the hung jury by saying that one juror had a past criminal record and another was a relative of one of the defendants. If that's true, the prosecutor should say so – out loud."

After the dismissal of the case, all three defendants were questioned about the results. Foti said, "Next time there'll be more witnesses," to prove he was nowhere near the Wahoo Bar on the night of the burglary. LaRiche declared, "I am innocent and I believe this bears out my innocence." Innocent or not, he was the only defendant not to take the stand in his own defense; instead, sending family members to deliver perjured testimony for him. Lexune's comment was, "I don't want any more women on my jury, that's for sure."

And so, a second trial was scheduled for mid-June, but much would transpire before that came along.

Who Killed "Pete" Shoup

Paul "Red" Carpenter was a free man up until the time he crawled out of a shallow grave near Arcola Road in Lake County back on March 22. Since then, he pleaded guilty to his role in the Automotive Supply & Equipment Company burglary and the Wahoo Bar burglary and agreed to testify against his accomplices. He was hoping that when the three men were found guilty, he could do his time and move on with his life. When the case ended in a mistrial, he suddenly felt his life starting to unwind. On Saturday night, the day after the jury announced it was deadlocked, Carpenter became unhinged. His new crime revelations would make the Wahoo Bar burglary pale in comparison.

Carpenter began unloading his conscience to Chief Deputy Gobel Waddell. His reasoning was clear. "My life isn't worth a plugged nickel. If I have to go to the chair for this, okay. At least my slate will be clean. They'd kill me anyway if I got out," he declared.

Out of Carpenter's mouth soon flowed the details of how he murdered Eldon "Pete" Shoup back on February 7, during a burglary at the home of Frank E. Wells in Alliance. The accomplices he named were Alfred A. "Allie" Calabrese, the getaway car driver; Paul Perrotti, one of the two men who ransacked the house and broke open the safe; and Raymond A. Paone, the "finger man" for the burglary. After naming three of his four accomplices, police in those jurisdictions were notified and all three were quickly apprehended. The last accomplice Carpenter named the police didn't have a hard time finding; he was sitting in the Summit County Jail. Arthur LaRiche was the second man in the house and the one who "brushed" past Earl Shoup to get out of the basement. He was also the one who called out, "Shoot the bastard!"

Carpenter readily confessed he killed "Pete" Shoup and wounded his father, Earl. He claimed he "got panicky," while using a gun for the first time during a burglary. After Carpenter spilled his guts, things moved quickly. Alliance and Cleveland authorities were notified Saturday night. Cleveland police arrested Perrotti in a local night club; and apprehended Calabrese, who was found hiding behind a wardrobe at his home. Alliance Police Lieutenant Donald M. Cox and Patrolman Joseph Short were dispatched to Akron. Upon returning to Alliance, they went to the Fireside Inn on East State Street, a place Ray Paone was known to frequent, and arrested him.

On Sunday morning, Chief Deputy Waddell contacted Prosecutor John Ballard, Captain Carroll Cutright and Sheriff's Captain Harry Lesher. He had Carpenter repeat to them his story of the night before:

On the night of February 6, Ray Paone, who lived in Alliance, took Carpenter, LaRiche and Perrotti to the home of Frank Wells, who was in Florida with his family. Paone told them there was a "lot of money" in the residence. Paone knew about the arrangement for Earl Shoup to be keeping an eye on the house, and that he arrived each night between 8:00 and 8:30 and turned on some lights. When the men were about to park, a neighbor turned on his porch light to let their dog out. That was enough to frighten the burglars away.

The next day, February 7, the Cleveland men drove back to Alliance in two automobiles. This time Alfred Calabrese was with them. The four men (Paone did not join them on the second night) met at the Fireside Inn, a bar on East State Street, before heading to the Naborhood Inn on West State Street. There Perrotti left his automobile. From there, Calabreeze drove them in Carpenter's car to the Wells' home, arriving, according to Carpenter, about 9:00. At some point LaRiche handed Carpenter a .38 Special revolver, that belonged to Calabrese, and was told he would be the lookout.

There seemed to be some confusion, at least in the newspapers, as to what role Alfred Calabrese played in the burglary. Early reporting of Carpenter's confession had Calabrese entering the house, as opposed to being stationed in the getaway car cruising the neighborhood.

Carpenter was very specific when he stated that LaRiche, the oldest member of the burglary team, "Gave the orders on the job." Carpenter stated, "Calabrese would be driving the car back and forth down the block while the job was pulled by LaRiche and Perrotti." By the time the men arrived, Earl Shoup had already been there and left. "All looked clear when we came to the house," Carpenter commented.

After LaRiche, the smallest of the men, got through the rear basement window, he opened a back door and let the other two inside. LaRiche and Perrotti headed down to the basement where the safe was. Carpenter left out the part about one or both of the men ransacking the house and leaving a mud trail behind in it. Carpenter said he was initially in the main floor hallway when he heard the Shoups arrive. He said he hollered into the basement for LaRiche and Perrotti to, "Lay low, cut out the noise, but apparently they didn't hear me, because they made quite a racket."

Carpenter's story of what happened next was quite different from the one Earl Shoup told police. From the *Akron Beacon Journal*, This was part of Carpenter's confession on Saturday night, May 4, after telling his accomplices to cut the noise:

> The elder Shoup heard the noise and investigated. Carpenter edged onto the back porch, surprised Eldon Shoup and held him at gunpoint. "Next thing I knew, LaRiche was running out of the basement with Shoup (Earl) right behind him," said Carpenter. He said LaRiche had a cardboard box stuffed with money. He said the elder Shoup caught LaRiche and wrestled him. They were on the ground and Shoup was winning. Carpenter said LaRiche cried out, "Shoot the b_____." Carpenter said, "I was panicky – it was the first time I ever used a gun on a burglary." He said he shot the elder Shoup "two or three times" in the chest and hands. Eldon Shoup leaped at Carpenter, who admitted firing out of panic and young Shoup fell dead.

From the *Alliance Review*, this was part of Carpenter's tale on Sunday afternoon, May 5:

> Carpenter said Eldon Shoup entered the Wells home first, followed by his father who went to the basement. Carpenter said he approached Eldon and warned him to be "calm and cool," and was taking Eldon to the basement when LaRiche ran past them, followed by Earl Shoup. LaRiche and the elder Shoup started to tussle in the back yard and LaRiche yelled, "shoot, shoot," Carpenter related. Carpenter said he fired a shot at the elder Shoup and when the younger Shoup lunged at him, he also shot Eldon.

Carpenter and LaRiche then fled through backyards toward the railroad tracks with the cardboard box of money from the safe. Carpenter claimed the box was too heavy to run with, so they took a roll of bills from it and hid the rest under a tree in a field near the New York Central Railroad tracks. Carpenter claimed he threw the gun into the field. *Since Frank Wells had already told police only $1,000 was taken, one has to wonder how heavy a box containing $1,000 could weigh, unless it was all in coins.*

At some point while this was going on, Perrotti ran out of the basement and found Calabrese. Carpenter related from a conversation with Perrotti, that the two of them claimed they remained in the area for some time, circling the Wells' home looking for him and LaRiche. They watched as police cars and an ambulance arrived at the home. *If this was true it wasn't very smart on their part. Police would have noticed the same car circling the block and would have stopped them to find out what they were doing there. If that occurred they certainly would have noticed the mud on Perrotti and questioned the men.*

Carpenter claimed he and LaRiche "ran and walked" until daylight, ending up on Route 30 and found a phone from where they called a friend in Canton, who came and picked them up. They got a hold of Perrotti after he had arrived back in Cleveland, who then drove to Canton and picked up the two.

After describing the Alliance murder and burglary, Carpenter said that Alfred Calabrese was responsible for the attempt on his life back in March. He said he telephoned Calabrese and told him he needed money. Calabrese gave him instructions to meet someone near Painesville about pulling a job. Carpenter said he met the man, but all he got was three bullets. After surviving the murder attempt, he said he walked into Ballard's office ready to talk about the Wahoo Bar burglary. After that, it was fear and bitterness that led to his latest confession.

On Sunday afternoon, Akron Police Captain Carroll Cutright and sheriff's deputies drove Carpenter to Alliance where he confessed everything to Alliance Police Chief Lower. Earl Shoup was brought to the police station where he identified Carpenter as one of the intruders at the Wells' home on the night of February 7. *There was no mention of Earl Shoup ever being given a mug shot to identify LaRiche, the man he wrestled to the ground. Shoup had already given police a description of the man and clearly stated he was 19 or 20 years old. In reality, LaRiche was the old man of the robbery crew at 39 years of age.*

While there, with local police officers, the group searched the area behind Frank Wells' home along the railroad tracks. The search party was unable to find the money or the murder weapon. Chief Lower announced he would borrow a mine detector and a huge magnet from the arsenal in Ravenna and continue the search for the revolver.

On Monday, Prosecutor Ballard held a news conference with the media to go over the details of the case. At one point, he brought Carpenter in to "make sure everything was straight." One detail, at least in the *Alliance Review*, was different. When the men went down the first night, February 6, there was "an unidentified fourth man" that accompanied them. Whoever this individual was, if he did exist, was never brought up again.

After the news conference, Carpenter gave a candid interview to *Akron Beacon Journal* reporter Ray Warner. He told the reporter, "I never was good at anything. I always felt like a weakling until I started running with the boys. Then I felt OK." Claiming his first marriage didn't work out, Carpenter stated,

"She was a good wife, but I was a lousy husband." When it came to his second wife, he said, "I love her very much. I hoped if I could hold off talking about the Alliance thing – well. I just had in the back of my mind that if I held out maybe we would have a chance." It was because of Betty that he didn't confess to it after he was shot. But the murder "kept preying on my mind. I had to talk about it."

Carpenter told the reporter, "I've never been what you'd call a steady responsible citizen – but I always had a job." Once he met John Glassner, Carpenter felt he had found his calling. He claimed he had finally discovered something he "was good at." Since that introduction, he and John Glassner were involved in nine burglaries together. But it also meant something else to Carpenter. It was through John Glassner, "I met the mob," he said.

On Monday afternoon, Ray Paone, co-owner of United Billiards on East Main Street in Alliance, was arraigned. He pleaded innocent to first-degree murder, and asked for a preliminary hearing. The *Alliance Review* wrote he "reportedly" served time for a burglary charge some 20 years earlier. Carpenter claimed the Alliance poolroom operator was the finger-man in the burglary and served as a finger-man for other jobs the gang carried out. Later Chief Lower described those jobs as three burglaries at local businesses, a burglary at one doctor's home, and the robbery and slugging of another doctor. After they were scared away from the first burglary attempt at the Wells' home, by the neighbor's dog on February 6, they left their burglary tools under Paone's porch and then picked them up the next night, according to Carpenter. Another item, brought up only in the *Alliance Review*, on Monday, the newspaper claimed, "Chief Lower reconstructed the entire story, both before and after the murder, on the basis of statements by Carpenter and Paone." This was the only mention of Paone cooperating with authorities before the trial. He had pled innocent at arraignment that morning.

That night, Alliance Police Lieutenant Cox and Patrolman Short picked up Calabrese and Perrotti without incident from Cleveland, and brought them to the Alliance City Jail. On Tuesday morning, both pleaded innocent to first-degree murder charges during arraignment in Alliance Municipal Court. They were held in the city jail until Carpenter could be brought in from Akron and questioned in front of the two.

Shortly after Carpenter arrived in the city under heavy guard Wednesday afternoon, he was brought face-to-face with Calabrese and Perrotti. In the meeting with Akron and Alliance police authorities, and Stark County Prosecutor Norman J. Putman and some of his staff, Carpenter retold his story of the burglary and murder. Calabrese and Perrotti denied even knowing Carpenter and remained silent. Authorities in the room were reluctant to comment on anything that was accomplished. Afterwards, Carpenter was taken into Municipal Court, where he pleaded guilty to first-degree murder and was bound over to the Stark County Grand Jury. Calabrese and Perrotti were then off to the Stark County jail. Carpenter went back to the Summit County jail, as Prosecutor Ballard announced that due to the upcoming retrial of the Wahoo Bar burglary case, both Carpenter and LaRiche would remain in solitary cells in the Summit County Jail. It was reported that Carpenter also made a statement in front of LaRiche, once back at the jail Wednesday, accusing him of participating in the burglary / murder.

Meanwhile, the search for the murder weapon continued. On Tuesday night, the search was focused behind the Wells' home for the gun used to kill "Pete" Shoup. Alliance auxiliary police, with the help of a large magnet from the Ravenna Arsenal, were combing through fields behind the house. For some reason Alliance Police Chief Lower believed the gun used to shoot Carpenter back on March 21, was the same gun used to kill "Pete" Shoup. That gun was retrieved from the Lake County authorities and taken to the Ohio Bureau of Criminal Identification in London. A bullet fired from the revolver was compared to a slug recovered from Shoup's body, but the rifling didn't match. Chief Lower was considering borrowing a mine detector from a state construction crew in Columbus to continue the search.

On May 13, the Stark County Grand Jury indicted Calabrese, Carpenter, LaRiche and Perrotti on two counts each. The first count was for the first-degree murder of Eldon "Pete" Shoup; the second for "burglary of an inhabited dwelling in the night season." Paone was indicted for the latter count only and released on a $10,000 bond two days later.

On May 20, Calabrese and Perrotti pleaded innocent to burglary and murder charges before Stark County Common Pleas Judge John Rossetti. Both men continued to be held in the county jail without bail. Paone pleaded innocent to the "nighttime" burglary charge. Carpenter and LaRiche were not released from the Summit County Jail to attend the arraignment.

Wahoo Bar Burglary Trial – Part 2
With the second Wahoo Bar burglary trial less than a month away, the defense was already looking for ways to discredit Paul Carpenter. Nicholas Brinsky, one of the two Cleveland lawyers on the defense team, made a request to the Common Pleas Court for a check on Carpenter's mental condition. Prosecutor John Ballard agreed to the evaluation. Judge Emmons also agreed, and a psychiatric evaluation was ordered on May 23. Brinsky then asked that a team of Cleveland psychiatrists conduct the examination. To this the judge said, no. He would have the conducting of the examination done by three Akron doctors. Whatever the results were, they didn't find their way into the newspapers, but nothing prevented Carpenter's participation in the upcoming trial.

By the time the new trial was scheduled to begin on June 17, the first anniversary of the burglary, all three defendants had been indicted for crimes elsewhere. Foti was indicted in Medina County for non-support, as well as for questioning in the A&P supermarket burglary. Lexune was indicted by the Lucas County Grand Jury on June 12 for the $32,000 holdup at the Libbey-Owens-Ford Federal Credit Union in Toledo. LaRiche faced the most serious charge after being indicted with Carpenter for the Eldon Shoup murder in Alliance last February.

Ballard told reporters he "will proceed substantially" as he did in the first trial. But noted there could be a few surprises. He advised he had done "lots of digging on this thing." Newspapers speculated that the surprise could be the results of Carpenter's psychiatric evaluation.

One thing was sure; the proceedings in the second trial would be nastier. The first day of trial was dominated by jury selection. Things got nasty right away. The defense started it by asking potential jurors if they'd believe a prostitute rather than a circumspect housewife, an obvious reference to Betty Carpenter. Prosecutor Ballard, seeing that the defense was already trying to paint his witnesses in a bad light, responded by telling prospective jurors he'd prefer to use only civic leaders and Sunday School teachers as witnesses. "But the problem is that unless the police surprise burglars in the act, it's impossible to have witnesses unless they are burglars themselves, or people who associate with burglars," he stated.

Defense lawyer Paul Laybourne jumped right back into the attack pointing out that the state's key witness, Paul Carpenter, "confessed to 10 burglaries here, and a murder in Alliance." He also stated that in addition to confessing to numerous burglaries and serving prison time for pandering, John Glassner had also robbed a church.

The jury selection ended with a panel of seven men and five women. After the jury was sworn in, opening statements were next. The state said it would present witness testimony substantially the same as provided in the earlier trial. Defense counsel responded by applying terms of "frame up" and "pathological liar" in describing the witnesses the state would present. The first witness called was Fred Lieberman, who described for the jury how the bar looked the morning he opened up after the burglary.

One difference in the second trial was the testimony of Mary Shaffer, the witness police could not find during the first trail. *There was never any mention in the newspapers as to where she was while police searched for her.* Described by the *Akron Beacon Journal* as "an attractive girl driving school instructor," the girlfriend of the married John Glassner told about the first attempt to break into the Wahoo Bar, which took place a week prior to the actual burglary. Shaffer related the story of driving Carpenter, Foti and Glassner to the Wahoo Bar on June 10, 1956. She said Glassner stood guard as Foti and Carpenter tried to unlock the front door. "I found myself in a situation with which I could not cope," she told the jury. She claimed she was relieved when the key failed, and everyone went home. A week after the first attempt, she said Glassner put some "tools" in the trunk of her car and again on the day after she heard about the burglary of the bar's safe. Shaffer identified a quilt, introduced into evidence, as having been wrapped around the burglary tools that were placed in her trunk.

Detective Lieutenant Woodrow Meadows was called to describe the investigation the police were conducting. During cross-examination, Laybourne asked him if Glassner was promised anything in return for his testimony.

"I told him the truth always pays, but I made no promises," he stated.

Laybourne then said, "I will ask you if Detective Sergeant Carroll Cutthroat made any promises."

Prosecutor Ballard immediately objected. He then admonished defense counsel, "You know you are the only person who calls him Cutthroat." Laybourne asked the question again using Cutright's correct name and his actual rank of captain.

John Glassner went through a more vigorous cross-examination during the second trial. Attorney Laybourne got Glassner to admit that after he was released on a $3,000 bond for the Wahoo Bar break-in, he was involved in three more burglaries; only this time he was armed with a 16-gauge shotgun. After he posted bond, Glassner received numerous threats from people police believed to be members of his own gang. Detective Lieutenant Meadows loaned him the shotgun for protection. At one point the following exchange took place between Laybourne and Glassner:

Laybourne: How many more burglaries have you committed since the police recommended your release on a $3,000 bond? Was it more than one?

Glassner: Yes.

Laybourne: Was it more than two?

Glassner: Yes.

As Laybourne attempted to discover which places were burglarized and what was taken, Glassner declared, "I refuse to answer!"

Ballard objected to the line of questioning, stating that the witness was being asked to testify against himself. Judge Emmons sustained the objection.

Glassner was then asked by defense counsel why he needed a shot-gun when all the men he was testifying against were in the county jail. He replied, "Amazing things happen in jails."

When Carpenter took the stand for the second trial, he had a different story to tell. During direct examination, he told the jury how upon returning from service in Germany during World War II, he attended the University of

Akron, taking both day and night classes to prepare for a career. He said that up until 1954 he had never committed a felony. He was then led through all the details of the Wahoo Bar burglary and the roles of the three defendants, as well as Glassner's.

During cross-examination by LaRiche's counsel, Nicholas Brinsky, he was asked why he didn't turn state's evidence in order to get probation. "I didn't have hope of that, but I was trying to get myself out of this mess and start my life over."

When questioned about the jobs he pulled with Glassner, after they were both bonded out, he declined to provide any information Glassner had accompanied him. Brinsky told him, "Glassner has already said you were with him." Carpenter thought it funny that here he was trying to protect his old friend and Glassner had already testified against him.

Then the most ironic testimony of the trial came out. Carpenter said that after being released on $3,000 bond in the Wahoo Bar break-in, his plan was to stage a few more burglaries so he could "get started in a different sort of life." One of those burglaries led him to Alliance and the murder of "Pete" Shoup in February, which led him to being taken for a one-way ride by Cleveland gangsters in March, which further led him to becoming a state's witness against his accomplices in the Wahoo Bar case. In short, Carpenter had murdered a young man, was almost a murder victim himself, was re-jailed, and then was charged with and confessed to first-degree murder, all in an attempt to rehabilitate his life.

Carpenter stressed he had steadfastly denied involvement in the Wahoo Bar burglary until after being shot and buried alive. Defense counsel asked whether he thought that any of the three defendants he was testifying against had anything to do with the plot to murder him. Carpenter answered, "I want to say only that I do not know the name of the man who shot me."

On Friday, Ernest Foti took the stand and delivered an alibi that had changed considerably. After picking up his girlfriend at work and driving to her home at 370 Wills Avenue to change clothes, he now claimed her home was at 104 Dawes Avenue. When pressed for an answer for the difference in the addresses by Ballard, Foti responded, "Well, one address is almost across the street from the other – it's just around the corner." The biggest change was that Foti claimed he was "so drunk" that he couldn't possibly have been involved in a burglary that night. He claimed he didn't know either LaRiche or Lexune, and was at two different night clubs when the burglary took place. Foti did admit during cross-examination that Father Duffy Post No. 4, one of the places where he was drinking, was "less than three blocks from the Wahoo Bar."

LaRiche again did not take the stand. While his wife and daughter Marilyn were both present in court, only Marilyn testified, again claiming that her father was with them at Holy Rosary Church that night.

Lexune was the last to take the stand. When questioned about his arrest for the armed robbery in Toledo back in February, he claimed he was not in that city at all during the month. He also testified he had only met Carpenter three times and hardly knew him. During cross-examination, however, Assistant Summit County Prosecutor Sam Bell got Lexune to admit he was contacted by Betty Carpenter for help after her husband was arrested. Bell also got him to say he and Carpenter attended a boxing match together.

As testimony came to an end that Friday afternoon, Judge Emmons again cautioned the jurors. During the weekend break at the first trial, his concern was about the jurors being "disturbed or molested" by anyone trying to contact them and for them to call the prosecutor's office, the Akron police or himself if they were. This time he had a different message, he simply told them, "Let nothing happen which might make it necessary to declare a mistrial after we've been here all week."

On Monday morning, Ballard had a surprise rebuttal witness. Albert Gottfried, treasurer of the Libbey-Owens-Ford Federal Credit Union of Toledo. The prosecutor called him to refute Lexune's testimony that he was not in Toledo in February. Gottfried positively identified Lexune as one of two men who robbed the credit union on February 1 of $32,000 during an armed robbery that took less than three minutes. When Gottfried pointed to the defendant in the courtroom, Lexune jumped up and shouted, "You're wrong!"

After both sides rested their case that morning, closing statements began and continued through the afternoon. One thing both the prosecution and the defense seemed to agree on in their closings was that the verdict pivoted on whether or not the jury believed the word of 13-year-old Marilyn LaRiche, over the testimony of two confessed burglars.

On Tuesday morning, after jury instructions from Judge Emmons, the jurors were given the case. Late that afternoon, after just five hours of deliberations, the jury returned with a verdict of guilty for all three defendants. The newspaper reported that after the verdict was read, Judge Emmons "scorched" the earlier jury, which had disagreed on the first case just 53 days earlier. Emmons told the jurors, "There was another trial at which the jury stood 9 to 3 and 8 to 4 for conviction. I'll never [understand] how they arrived at this position. Yours was the only verdict you could reach. I'll never understand the misfeasance and malfeasance of that first jury. I congratulate you and the prosecutor. You have done a splendid job." The judge deferred sentencing pending a decision to appeal by all three defendants.

In an article announcing the conviction, the *Akron Beacon Journal* made an interesting comment, which had not been reported previously in the newspapers. They reported:

In a stranger-than-fiction chain of circumstances, the state held Northern Ohio gangsters thought falsely that Carpenter had informed on Foti, LaRiche, and Lexune.

Carpenter was taken for a ride, shot, and left for dead in a shallow grave at Painesville. He dug his way out, was returned to Akron, and gave a full account of all his crimes.

It was then revealed that it was Glassner, not [Carpenter], who had given police the information that led to the arrest of Foti, Lexune and LaRiche.

On July 5, 1957, Foti, LaRiche and Lexune were each sentenced to a 1 to 15 year term for burglary and a 1 to 7 year term for grand larceny by Judge Emmons, who then ordered the terms served consecutively. As each man was sentenced, Emmons asked them if they had anything to say. Foti, who went first, had nothing to say. But the judge had something to say to him. When Emmons was on the Akron Municipal Court bench some 25 years earlier, Foti came before him. "I warned you then," he stated, "that if you didn't change your associations, you would end up in the electric chair." Emmons repeated the same warning; again, without any response from Foti.

Lexune was next, but whatever he "hissed" out at Emmons, neither the judge nor reporters understood. Last was LaRiche. The only defendant who refused to testify in court, and instead sent his wife and 13-year-old daughter to the stand to deliver perjured testimony for him, finally had something to say. "I am innocent," he claimed, rising to his feet, "and time will bear me out." Emmons, waved the runty burglar back to his seat and declared, "You were the worst of the lot!" On July 11, four deputies loaded Foti and Lexune into two cars and were off to the Ohio Penitentiary in Columbus to drop them off. LaRiche, who had another trial to contend with, was left behind with Carpenter in private accommodations at the county jail.

None of the newspapers were quite sure where Arthur LaRiche was between the time of his conviction for the Wahoo Bar burglary and his trial for the Shoup murder. Some newspapers claimed he was in the Summit County Jail, some said it was the Stark County Jail, others reported he was already serving his Wahoo Bar term in the Ohio Penitentiary.

On July 19, John J. Glassner faced judgement day. He pleaded guilty to eight Akron burglaries before Common Pleas Judge Emmons. Before announcing sentence, Emmons heard from the prosecutor and two of Akron's ranking officers.

Prosecutor Ballard spoke before "a rather terse courtroom audience," unveiling new and interesting details of the case. Ballard said that it was Glassner who provided the first tip in the Wahoo Bar break-in. Most people believed it was Paul Carpenter who spoke first and that his shooting was the result of his ratting out the members of his Wahoo Bar burglary crew. Ballard told the court that "late last year" during his appearance before the grand jury, Glassner "revealed the existence of a big time burglary ring here." Since this took place near the end of 1956 it does not explain who originally implicated Carpenter and the Glassner brothers in the Wahoo Bar break-in less than two days after it occurred. In addition to the break-ins at Wahoo Bar and the Automotive Supply & Equipment Company, Ballard claimed Glassner also implicated Lexune in the Libbey-Owens-Ford Federal Credit Union in Toledo. *This is an interesting point because it was never reported Lexune was arrested and in the Summit County Jail prior to March 1957. Where did Glassner obtain the information he revealed to authorities prior to the robbery in February 1957.*

The Akron officers who also addressed Judge Emmons were Captain Cutright and Lieutenant Meadows. They both related that Glassner was such an important witness to the case they felt the need to arm him while he was out on bond. They revealed threats were made against not only Glassner, but his wife, children and attorney.

After hearing the testimony of Ballard and the officers, Judge Emmons sentenced John Glassner to five years' probation. Emmons explained that he knew Glassner's life was in danger for cooperating with the police. He claimed, "Torture by the men Glassner helped send up, if not death, would await him in the Ohio Penitentiary." Certain conditions were also laid out by the judge. First, that Glassner continue to cooperate with the police, including testifying in the Lexune robbery trial. He must also keep himself employed, report monthly to his probation officer and keep from associating with anyone with a criminal past. Cutright commented after the conditions were laid out that, "No man ever had a better reason for staying out of trouble."

Also coming before the judge that day for sentencing was William J. Glassner. Judge Emmons postponed sentencing until he received a report from the probation office. William didn't return for sentencing until September 12, when he pleaded guilty to breaking and entering and possession of burglary tools for his role in the Automotive Supply & Equipment Company break-in. The judge also sentenced him to probation.

"Pete" Shoup Murder Trials

By summer's end, a November date was set for the "Pete" Shoup murder trial in Canton. As the day came near, pre-trial motions began making news. On Halloween, attorney Earle E. Wise, lead counsel for Calabrese and Perrotti, filed a motion seeking statements Carpenter made to authorities in the Shoup killing. Wise claimed the statements were not "confessions" because they weren't signed. He also said allegations were made in the statements regarding the whereabouts of his clients at times which could be disproven. Arguments were heard on November 8, at which time the judge denied the motion.

On November 13, attorney Wise filed a "notice of alibi" defense for the two defendants. The *Plain Dealer* reported, "The law requires a notice of alibi be filed at least three days before the scheduled date of trial to allow time for an investigation by the prosecution." The alibi notice claimed both men were at the Millersburg Military Institute in Millersburg, Kentucky, on February 7, visiting Alfred S. Calabrese, the only child of the Calabreses, a second-year student at the school.[110]

The filing of the alibi notice created the next problem in the case. On November 15, Common Pleas Judge George N. Graham granted a 3-day continuance for Stark County Prosecutor Norman A. Putman. With the trial scheduled to begin on Monday, November 18, the prosecutor requested the continuance for additional time to check the alibi defense counsel had provided. That same evening, a Friday night, attorney Wise and co-counsel Ray Marchbanks, Jr. went to the home of Judge Graham to voice their displeasure. Wise claimed the notice of alibi was filed six-days ahead of trial, instead of the required three, and that the prosecution was not entitled to additional time. In fact, it was only filed five days ahead of trial and what the defense attorney left out was that the journey to check out the alibi not only involved Millersburg, Kentucky, it also extended to Pensacola, Florida. Judge Graham granted a new hearing on the matter to take place the next morning.

During the Saturday morning session on the continuance, Wise made accusations that the prosecutor had threatened and intimidated an alibi witness in an effort to keep him from testifying. At a follow-up hearing on Monday, Putman brought the witness, who was allegedly   threatened, into court. The man denied he was ever threatened by Putman or his staff. The continuance stood, and the start of trial was moved to Thursday, November 21.

On Wednesday, with jury selection set to begin the following morning, The Massillon *Evening Independent* reported:

A first-degree murder trial marked by bitter pre-trial skirmishes between the opposing attorneys will get underway Thursday in Stark County Common Pleas Court. The pre-trial bitterness is expected to color the trial proceedings. [While] the opposing attorney's...personal differences are expected to arouse as much interest as the defendants themselves.

The highlight of Thursday morning's jury selection process came when Prosecutor Putman received a telephone call that his 5-year-old daughter's recent illness was diagnosed as chicken pox. The doctor making the call advised Putman to spend the night at his parent's house. Shortly into the afternoon session, Putman had an outbreak of red blotches on his skin. At the close of court that day he visited a doctor's office; but was back in the courtroom Friday morning.

Throughout the questioning process in trying to seat a jury, Putman asked each prospective juror, "Would fear for the safety of yourself or members of your family prevent you from following the evidence of the case and instructions of the court?" The answer always came back, no.

After a day-and-a-half of jury selection, Judge Graham swore in a panel of eight men and four women before noon on Friday. After the swearing in, the judge gave the normal instructions to them of not discussing the case with anyone, or listening to broadcast accounts of the trial, or to read any newspaper accounts. "You are to judge this case solely on the basis of evidence presented in this courtroom," Graham told the panel.

On Friday morning, there was additional security in the courtroom. Five armed auxiliary deputies were present, two of which took up positions at the back of the courtroom, while the other three were in "strategic places" elsewhere. No reason was offered for the additional security, other than it was requested by Putman.

By mid-afternoon Friday, the jurors were on their way by bus to Alliance to visit the Wells' home on Ridgewood Avenue. While there, jury members were forbidden to ask questions as they toured the grounds and basement of the home. Also on the tour were Calabrese and Perrotti, brought there in a sheriff's deputy car. Apparently, there were no restrictions on them. While Perrotti was in the basement, he was heard to say, "As God is my judge, I have never been in this house before." Calabrese was heard to make "a similar statement" in the basement, also. Having never been reported to be in the home, his utterance was likely more accurate.

On Monday morning, November 25, opening statements were delivered. Prosecutor Putman stated, "Evidence will show that Perrotti, Calabrese, Alfred LaRiche and Paul Carpenter entered into conspiracy to rob and did commit the burglary," and that the killing of young Shoup was a "natural consequence of the unlawful act." He claimed that testimony, "will show that this crime is the work of syndicated, professional criminals." He told jurors to be, "Prepared to vote the death penalty." He then gave a 25-minute outline of the state's case. Wise, meanwhile, reserved the right to withhold his opening remarks until the defense began its case.

Raymond Paone, by now had decided his best chance of avoiding a long prison term was to cooperate and testify for the state. As the first witness called, he testified to "fingering" the Wells' residence for the gang. The married father of two lived in Alliance for the past 15 years, where he operated United Billiards. Paone opened by telling the court that as late as Thursday, June 21, he was receiving death threats to keep quiet and not testify. In describing that call to his home he stated, "They told me to keep my mouth shut or I would get it." Questioned about Carpenter, he testified that he met Carpenter two years earlier at a New Year's Eve party in Canton. Carpenter and his wife later visited the Paone home in Alliance. Paone stated, sometime in 1956, "Carpenter came back by himself and asked me if I knew of any jobs concerning big time gamblers that he might pull." Paone told him about Frank Wells' operation and said he kept an office and a safe in his basement; he also told him that Earl Shoup helped take care of Wells' gambling business. On a return visit, Paone stated, Carpenter brought Arthur LaRiche along and the three of them discussed a burglary plan. Paone claimed a "deal" was made at the Fireside Inn and he was to get 10 percent. When Putman asked if he ever got any of the money, Paone responded, "No, I didn't want it. Eldon "Pete," was a good friend of mine." Paone admitted that after the murder he took a trip to California, claiming he did so only because, "I was a real good friend of Eldon's."

There was little doubt Paone knew both Wells and Earl Shoup. In newspaper articles listing the names of the Federal Wagering Tax Stamp purchasers in Alliance from 1953 to 1955, were the names Albert and Raymond Paone, sandwiched between Frank Wells and Earl Shoup. Since Paone knew the layout of the house and where the safe was located, it was obvious he had been inside. In addition, he also knew when Wells would be out of town and that Earl Shoup would be acting as caretaker, while the Wells family was gone. Paone seemed to know, right down to the hour, what time Shoup came to the home and what he did while he was there. On the afternoon of February 6, he met Carpenter, LaRiche and Perrotti at the Fireside Inn, where they planned the burglary. From the witness stand, Paone identified Perrotti as one of the men at the meeting. The men went over the layout of the house and who was to do what. Paone then drove the men to the Ridgewood Avenue home to drop them off. Once they pulled up, however, they were scared away by the neighbor's dog, and decided to call off the burglary until the following day. The next night, Calabrese took the place of Paone as the driver on the burglary team. There was no indication as to why Calabrese replaced Paone. Under a brief cross-examination, Paone was very clear about one thing regarding the burglary, "I set it up," he admitted.

Paul Carpenter took the stand next. With little interruption from Putman, Carpenter was free to tell his story. The story, as he told it, was a bit chopped up. He began with the details of what happened that fateful night. "Calabrese was driving my car. He dropped the three of us off at a railroad crossing near the Wells home. We first discussed the burglary in connection with a job at the Medina Super Market. Then I and LaRiche contacted Paone and Perrotti on February 6," he testified.

"We met Calabrese in a Cleveland social club. LaRiche, Perrotti, and I went to the Fireside Inn, and we called Paone at the billiard hall. Paone took us to Wells' residence and said, 'his partner takes care of the business.'" Carpenter said that while Paone drove them around, he showed them where Earl Shoup lived and told them what kind of car he drove. He then said when they arrived at the Wells home, they were scared off by a neighbor's dog. After their plans fell through, they headed back to Cleveland where they met Calabrese in the social club. He agreed to go back with them the next night.

The following night the four men drove to Alliance in two cars. The plan was for Calabrese to use Carpenter's car and drop the men off near the Wells home. He would disappear for 30 minutes, but then come back and circle the neighborhood every 15 minutes until the men completed their work. Carpenter said he remained on the first floor as a lookout after LaRiche and Perrotti went to the basement. *There was no comment as to where they were dropped off, or how one or all of them got so muddy, nor was there any comment about the ransacking of the rest of the house or how it got so muddy.*

"A car drove in the alley," Carpenter continued. "I hollered downstairs for them to be quiet. I saw a man come to the door. He had trouble unlocking it. The first man went to the basement. The second man stood outside, and I grabbed him." *This story was different from the earlier ones he told.*

After the shooting, he and LaRiche raced away, down the railroad tracks, with a cardboard box full of money. "We decided to get rid of the gun and money. We ditched the gun and money, but I thought of not having any cash, so I went back and picked some up," Carpenter stated.

So begins another mystery about the night. There was never an amount agreed upon as to how much was taken that night. Wells claimed it was $1,000. Other estimates put it at as much as $10,000. Wells would have been best served if the amount had only been $1,000, otherwise, he and Earl Shoup would have been answering questions from the IRS. Unless the $1,000 was in coins or loose $1 bills, how much of a problem would it have been to shove the cash in their pockets, after all it was February and they must have had on winter coats with pockets in them. If Carpenter and LaRiche didn't take the money with them when they fled, then one, or both, more than likely, came back later and got it. Also, there apparently was no consideration given to the fact that Perrotti could have run off with some himself.

Carpenter ended his morning testimony by saying he and LaRiche made it to Minerva, Ohio, on foot before they "started backtracking" to Cleveland. Minerva is almost 13 miles straight south of Alliance.

Carpenter's afternoon testimony that Monday, about the gang's attempt to silence him, was another one of the big mysteries about the case. The smaller town newspapers claimed Carpenter testified the attempt on his life was due to his cooperation with the police on the Wahoo Bar burglary. By nearly all accounts, however, Carpenter didn't confess to any authorities until after the murder attempt on his life. There was also an indication that some of the newspapers had concluded the Wahoo Bar burglars and the Alliance burglars were all part of one big gang. There was no proof Calabrese or Perrotti had connections to any of the Wahoo Bar gang other than LaRiche. Although LaRiche lived in Elyria, he was an "East Sider," born in Little Italy. He was living on Woodhill Road in May 1955, when a bomb went off under the hood of a car he was riding in with Joseph Drago and Richard Stewart (See Chapter Ten: Joseph Drago biography). Despite LaRiche's connection to both burglaries, it was the Alliance murder, not the Wahoo Bar burglary, for which Calabrese wanted Carpenter silenced.

Another thing that changed about the story to murder Carpenter, was after he confessed to murdering "Pete" Shoup, the attempt to kill Carpenter all of a sudden involved only one gunman that night, not two as he originally stated. There was never any report of him ever naming the gunman or even offering a physical description of him.

Carpenter testified he called Calabrese and told him that he needed money. Calabrese told him to go to a supermarket near Painesville on the night of March 21, and "size up the place for an attempted hold up." *Based on this, it would seem more than likely that he drove himself out there to meet the unidentified person who shot him. Another version would come out later that someone picked him up on the East Side and drove him out there to look at the supermarket before shooting him.*

On cross-examination from Wise, Carpenter said he believed Calabrese set-up the attempt on his life and that, "A man he had met previously, but did not recognize, shot him three times and dragged him to an open grave." Carpenter offered that he believed his name was "Jerry."

The story Carpenter told to the jury on Monday, about the burglary and murder at the Wells home, was pretty much the same one he gave to Chief Deputy Waddell at the Summit County Jail, but with more detail at times. He talked about being given the gun he used to kill "Pete" Shoup by LaRiche, and standing guard near the backdoor when the Shoups arrived. Then being told by LaRiche to shoot Earl Shoup, while the two men tussled. He described after the shooting how he and LaRiche fled along the railroad tracks, hiding the money under a tree, and tossing the gun into a field. To this, he added that when the two men reached Route 30, they found a telephone and called a "Lou Batista" in Canton, who came and picked them up.

Also testifying on Monday were Earl Shoup and Frank Wells. Both men answered questions about gambling. Wells, when asked about his occupation at the time of the burglary / murder, stated he was "interested in gambling." While he was in Coral Gables, Florida, he said Earl Shoup, who was employed at Transue & Williams, was helping to oversee the gambling activities in his absence. Wells, the owner of the 20th Century Cigar store and the Silver Bullet Café in Alliance, said Shoup also took care of his house, with help from Nordi Vitalune, one of his employees from the cigar store, making sure the lights and furnace were on. Wells stated that he had planned to be in Florida for a month and was gone for two weeks before the murder and burglary took place. Since his return, he and his wife were divorced. During this testimony, Wells claims that before he left for Coral Gables, there was $6,500 in the safe, and that Earl Shoup had some money of his own in a separate compartment.

During Earl Shoup's testimony, he claimed he was at the Wells home earlier that day, and then drove to Canton. Later, when he returned to the Wells home, between 9:00 and 9:15, with packages of "treasury tickets," he brought his son. Earl Shoup testified he parked the car in the Wells' garage and that Eldon stayed there while he went into the house. "When I got out of the car, he was sitting in the car...I didn't see him until after the shooting," Shoup stated. He said he was in the basement when he heard Eldon call to him, "Watch out Dad." *This is completely different from the stories Earl Shoup and Paul Carpenter gave* regarding "Pete" Shoup's activities at the house that night to authorities back in February and May. In Earl Shoup's previous stories he said in one that he made several stops after leaving about 8:10, in both stories he said he drove to his son's house to pick him up. If he did go to Canton, the round trip would have taken him an hour. As for "Pete" Shoup's presence there, the Alliance Review reported on that first day of testimony, "He merely accompanied his father to the Wells residence that night."

After the shooting, in which Earl Shoup testified he was wounded in the right chest and left thumb, he helped his son into the house. "My son started to dial a number and then passed out. Then I dialed the Police Department for an ambulance," he said. He then stated he went to the basement and checked the safe. He claimed there was about $10,000 in the safe, some of the money his, and that all of it was taken. He and Wells both swore "Pete" Shoup had no connection to the gambling operation. This tale is the second one in which Earl Shoup puts himself in the basement, yet neither time does he mention seeing Paul Perrotti there. There is never any mention, not even speculation, as to how or when Perrotti made it out of the basement.

The last witness on Monday was Dr. E.B. Mozes. The Stark County Coroner testified Eldon was shot in the left side of the neck, near the collar bone, and that the bullet was recovered from his chest. It was introduced into evidence.

A result of the first-day testimony from Paone, Wells and Earl Shoup was the sudden need for Prosecutor Putman to let the newspapers know he was conducting a murder trial, not a gambling probe. He claimed, "any investigation of gambling activities testified to...will have to wait until the trial is completed." Putman told reporters no effort has been made to investigate the gambling operations brought out during the trial. He declared, "Our first duty is to conduct these murder trials involving an alleged Cleveland syndicate of professional burglars. We cannot jeopardize or threaten the testimony of state witnesses by any investigation of petty criminals."

On Tuesday morning, Alliance Police Lieutenant Donald Cox took the stand and testified he was in charge of transporting Calabrese and Perrotti from Cleveland to Alliance the day after their arrests. He stated both men told him that at the time of the burglary and murder they were in Florida, and neither man mentioned being in Millersburg, Kentucky. He said he wasn't aware of the Kentucky alibi until he read about it in the newspaper at a much later date.

Several other officers followed Cox to the stand that morning. Included in this group was Patrolman Howard Best, called to talk about the size 11 overshoe found in the field outside the Wells home. Carpenter had mentioned in his testimony, the day before, that he had lost an overshoe. Attorney Wise objected stating it was Carpenter's shoe, and Carpenter was not on trial, so it had no connection to this case. Judge Graham sided with defense counsel and the overshoe was not introduced.

Captain Lauer testified Mrs. Earl Shoup "was the first civilian" to arrive at the Wells home. She was contacted by Patrolmen Edward Moretti and Carl Vestal. The rest of the officers gave descriptions of the crime scene, including seeing the basement window pushed in, papers scattered about the basement and the finding of a spent bullet at the west end of the garage. *There was no testimony about the mud that was splattered all over the house during the night the burglary and shooting took place, which was reported on by the* Alliance Review.

On Tuesday afternoon, Akron Police Captain Carroll Cutright delivered some of the most compelling testimony of the trial. Cutright stated that back on March 29, a week after the attempted murder of Carpenter, the victim was in the Summit County Jail, held by his own request for protective custody. Carpenter asked to make a telephone call, which the captain approved. Cutright then listened in on an extension.

Cutright testified Carpenter gave the operator a number listed for 16320 St. Clair Avenue in Cleveland. It was said to be the home address of Russell Calabrese, but Alfred A. Calabrese was living there. A man who answered the telephone identified himself as Al Calabrese. Carpenter addressed himself to Calabrese as, "the man from the grave." Calabrese replied to Carpenter, "We didn't have anything to do with it, it was the syndicate's idea. We are trying to get into the syndicate and they practically had a gun at our backs." He added, the "syndicate is very pleased with your work and I have a present for you." During the conversation, Calabrese asked Carpenter, "You didn't tell anything about the S and S case did you?" Cutright heard Carpenter answer, "No, but everything is in a will in a safe deposit box. If anything more happens to me everything will be known."

Cutright told the jury he did not know at the time what "S and S" meant, but since then he has interpreted it to mean "Shoup and son." While it was never brought out whether or not Carpenter knew Cutright was listening in on the call, this is a pretty clear indication that he did not. Carpenter later confirmed that "S and S" meant "Shoup and Shoup."

On Wednesday morning, the state rested its case. Attorney Wise immediately made a motion for a directed verdict of acquittal to Judge Graham, which was over-ruled. It was at this point defense counsel Wise delivered his opening statement. He told the jury the testimony they would hear would prove that at the time of the burglary and murder his clients were on their way back from Millersburg, Kentucky, where they had visited Calabrese's son. Wise reserved the right to recall some of the prosecution's witnesses for cross-examination, and would call ten defense witnesses to prove that neither man was in Alliance at the time of the burglary / killing. He claimed it would be shown that Paul Carpenter had "beautifully framed" the defendants, because he held them responsible for the attempt on his life.

The first defense witness was Paul Perrotti, who began his testimony by telling the jury that he was 33 years old, married, and the father of a 5-year-old daughter. He worked at St. Clair Builders in Cleveland, and had known Calabrese for five years. While he confessed to a prior criminal record – convicted in 1952 of breaking and entering, safe tampering and grand larceny for which he was placed on probation – he threw in that he was honorably discharged from the armed services.

He then told the jury about his movements in the days prior to the Shoup murder. He testified that he, his wife, Margaret, his daughter and another man drove from Cleveland to Pensacola, Florida, leaving on January 28, 1957, with plans to visit his wife's sister and her husband. The trip was scheduled because Perrotti and his wife were to serve as God Parents to his sister-in-law's new child during a January 31 baptism. On that date, they were joined by Calabrese and another man. Attorney Wise then introduced a baptism certificate to prove that the defendant and his wife were at the ceremony.

Perrotti then testified that Calabrese, who had arrived late on the night of January 31, needed to have the brakes on his car fixed. Perrotti claimed he helped pay for this. Perrotti discussed his stay there, and said that on February 6, the day the prosecutor claimed he was in Alliance, he, Calabrese and the other two men, visited Sister Pauline, a Catholic nun, who was his second cousin, at a parochial school in Pensacola, taking her a box of candy. He said she gave them a tour of the facility.

Perrotti said he decided to come home with Calabrese and the other two, while his wife returned to Ohio with relatives. Perrotti and the other three left Pensacola about 11:00 p.m. on February 6, with a planned stop in Millersburg, Kentucky, to see Calabrese's son, a student at the Millersburg Military Institute. After driving all night, they arrived in Paris, Kentucky, about 6:00 p.m. the next day. He said Calabrese called the school from the restaurant to make arrangements to see his son. Perrotti claimed they left the military school approximately 40 minutes after arriving. At 9:00 p.m., about the time of the Shoup killing, his party had yet to reach Cincinnati. They would not arrive in Cleveland until 3:00 or 4:00 on the morning of February 8.

Here again is another unexplained part of the story. Who were the two men that arrived in Pensacola with Calabrese on January 31? If these two men were with Calabrese and Perrotti in Florida and Kentucky when the Alliance activities were taking place, they would have made excellent witnesses for them. The men, however, were never named in the newspapers and did not appear at trial as witnesses for the defense.

Following his rather brief examination, after lunch Wednesday, Perrotti was cross-examined until 4:00 p.m. by Prosecutor Putman. The *Plain Dealer* called it a "cat and mouse" battle as Perrotti was hesitant with his responses and not sure about many details. Putman, trying to prove that the alibi of the two defendants was not true, grilled Perrotti about the exact location of the military school and what he saw when he arrived there. Many of the prosecutors questions were answered with, "I don't remember exactly." As to when they arrived, Perrotti replied, "We arrived at the academy after 6:00 on February 7. It was daylight and Calabrese was driving. Calabrese was in the academy building about five minutes before coming out with his son. Captain Pumphrey (an instructor and coach at the school) also came out and I was introduced to him. I only know Pumphrey and wasn't introduced to anyone else," he said. Perrotti told the prosecutor they left about 6:30 or 7:00 p.m. and arrived back in Cleveland around 3:00 or 4:00 a.m. Some of the newspaper reporting indicated Perrotti focused his responses more on where he wasn't, than where he was.

Another matter Putman questioned him about extensively was his involvement in the Collinwood Construction Workers Social Club in Cleveland, which he claimed he and Calabrese organized a year earlier. It opened during the summer of 1956, and construction workers went there to "play cards, rummy and poker." He stated he was an officer of the club and paid the rent. Perrotti, however, couldn't recall what office he held, the names of any of the other officers, or whether records were kept of expenses and membership rolls.

After having Thursday off for the Thanksgiving holiday, on Friday morning, the cross-examination of Perrotti continued. Both Calabrese and Perrotti were collecting unemployment compensation since December 1956 after being laid off from St. Clair Builders. Putman said records showed they each made the required weekly visit to the unemployment office on February 5; the day before the first effort to burglarize the Wells home took place. These visits required, under state law, each applicant to appear in person and to sign the application form.

Since this was a day Perrotti claimed he was in Florida, the prosecutor wanted to know how he could be in two different states at the same time. Perrotti said his brother went to the office and signed for him that day. As Putman delved deeper, the defendant immediately began his "I don't remember" routine again in response to questions, but was quick to point out, however, that Calabrese, who was with him in Florida, also had a brother sign for him that day. Putman declared he would have additional witnesses on the matter and call a Cleveland compensation official to the stand.

Perrotti was followed to the stand by Chief Petty Officer William B. Choma, his brother-in-law and the father of the baptized child. Choma testified of dining at the Chief Petty Officer's Club with the two defendants on February 5 and 6 in Pensacola. Choma also stated that he, Calabrese, Perrotti and the other two men attended a basketball game on February 6, before the men left for Kentucky between 9:00 and 10:00 that night. During cross-examination, Choma stated that a parish priest from Pleasant City, Ohio, had visited his home in Pensacola, but he did not recall just when, nor did he recall the priest's name.

After lunch, the defense called Sister Pauline, a Roman Catholic nun of the Benedictine Order. She was called to support the defendant's alibi that they were with her for a tour of a parochial school in Pensacola where she taught first grade. Prior to Putman's cross-examination of Sister Pauline, a five-minute recess was called. During that time, Perrotti broke down in tears and was led out of the courtroom by deputies. Calabrese walked over to the nun and kissed her hand. Once the trial resumed, Putman asked the witness how she could be so sure about the timing of the visit. She replied, "I'm positive the boys visited the school the week before I telephoned my mother on February 14." She pointed out that was her mother's birthday, and she calls her every year. Sister Pauline claimed, "I haven't talked to anyone before the trial about the telephone call."

Sister Pauline recalled that two days later, Margaret Perrotti paid her a visit. Margaret Perrotti then took the stand and confirmed the visit for Attorney Wise. This was done solely because Perrotti and Calabrese had returned to Cleveland two days earlier. The next witness was Frank Parker, a cook at the Chief Petty Officer's Club who testified that the defendants had dinner there on the night of February 6.

The day's testimony ended in controversy when attorney Wise told Judge Graham two of his witnesses, who were subpoenaed from the Ohio Penitentiary, did not show up because someone called the prison and said it was not necessary to bring the men to Canton. The judge recessed the trial until Monday and released the jury. Then the fireworks began.

Prosecutor Putman told the judge he wanted the record to show the telephone call not to bring up the prisoners did not come from his office. Wise disagreed. "That is what the warden said – that it was from your office!" the attorney shot back. Judge Graham wanted the matter resolved. Wise's statement in court was he had the witnesses subpoenaed, "but that the warden had just called him and said that the prosecuting attorney's office called and told them (the prison officials) they were not to bring them up."

Ohio Penitentiary Warden Ralph Alvis was then called, and he flat-out declared Wise's statement was a lie. He said "some attorney's office" in Stark County called Wednesday morning and wanted the two witnesses at the trial by 1:00 p.m. Friday. Alvis told the person calling prisoners could not be removed to Canton, or anywhere else for that matter, without subpoenas and he had not received any. When Alvis didn't have the subpoenas by Friday morning, he called the prosecutor's office. A clerk in Putman's office told him she knew nothing about the subpoenas. The following exchange then took place:

Putman: Did anybody from my office tell you just to forget about it?

Alvis: No, sir.

Putman: Did anybody from my office tell you it wouldn't be necessary to bring the men up?

Alvis: No, sir.

Putman agreed with Warden Alvis that Wise's accusation was a lie. He pointed out it was the second time Wise made "known malicious, false statements about the conduct of the prosecuting attorney" during the trial.

On Monday morning, a photograph was introduced showing Perrotti at the baptism rite of his nephew in Pensacola. It was never made clear who provided the picture. It may have come from the first defense witness called that day, Miss Thelma Choma. A bank clerk from Pleasantville, Ohio, located some 30 miles east of Zanesville, Thelma was Perrotti's wife's sister. She drove the Perrotti family, and the unnamed friend, down to Florida, leaving Ohio on January 28. She testified to seeing Calabrese, after he and his friend arrived on January 31, and having dinner at the Chief Petty Officer's Club one night. She drew a diagram of the Choma home for the court. Under cross-examination, she testified that on February 6, the Pleasant City priest was at the Choma home, along with two other priests and her brother, who "introduced them around." She testified the priests arrived in the afternoon and remained for supper that evening. When told that during the previous week, when Putman cross-examined her brother, William Choma, he provided "detailed explanations and descriptions of his guests and activities" the day of February 6, but failed to mention any of the three priests. Thelma Choma suddenly "became vague on certain details of the visit." At the end of her testimony, Putman reserved the right to recall her. William Choma was asked to come back to the stand to answer questions about the priests. He told Putman he didn't know the names of any of the priests, even though one had baptized his son a week earlier, and he was not sure when they visited; though he thought one visit had taken place over the summer. Neither Paul Perrotti nor Calabrese testified to seeing any priests at the Choma home on February 6.

A picture was beginning to form that Calabrese and Perrotti were indeed in Florida the last week of January 1957, and had gone to Kentucky – but had left several days earlier than they said they did. Thelma Choma testified she drove Perrotti family members and one unnamed man down on Monday, January 28. Calabrese and his unnamed friend met them at the Choma home late on Thursday, January 31, the day of the baptism. If they would have left Saturday night, February 2, that would have put them in Paris, Kentucky, the next evening, during which time they saw Calabrese's son and Captain Pumphrey. The ride home would have had them arriving at 3:00 or 4:00 a.m. on Monday morning and would put both men at the unemployment office the next day, February 5, as well as in Alliance on Wednesday and Thursday nights, February 6 and 7. At the time of the trial it was nearly ten months since the trip to Florida. The only solidly undisputed date was January 31, the day of the baptism, and there was a picture to support that.

Following Thelma Choma to the stand was Frank Stredrick. In late September, Stredrick, a Black man, was in the Summit County Jail, held to the grand jury for a break-in at the Star Inn Café on West Bartges Street.[111] Acting in the role of a jail house snitch, he testified he met Carpenter at the jail, where other prisoners referred to him as a "rat." Stredrick claimed Carpenter told him he believed Calabrese and Perrotti were responsible for the attempt on his life back on March 21. He said he was told by Carpenter the two men were not involved in the shooting, but "this is the only way I can take 'em with me."[112]

Attorney Wise then called Alfred Calabrese to begin his testimony. The defendant testified for nearly five hours, his time on the stand was spent mostly reaffirming the alibi claims made by Perrotti the week before. He denied being with Carpenter in Alliance in February, when "Pete" Shoup was killed, and denied shooting Carpenter in Painesville back in March. When Putman questioned his role in the shooting of Carpenter, Calabrese admitted he was a "contact man" between Carpenter and another person "setting up a mark," and confirmed it occurred near Painesville. The following exchange then took place:

Putman: Why didn't you help justice and inform police when you knew these men committed a crime?

Calabrese: At times you have to keep your nose clean.

Calabrese swore he never pulled any jobs with Carpenter, but admitted meeting him "four or five" times during January 1957. He said the two exchanged telephone numbers at the Collinwood Construction Social Club. Calabrese stated he was on probation for "driving a motor vehicle without the owner's consent" when he left for Florida, but claimed he had his probation offer's consent to travel there. He said he stopped in Millersburg to see his son on the way down to Florida.

The cross-examination turned grueling on Monday afternoon. Putman questioned the witness at length about his activities from the time he left Cleveland, on January 30, until he returned on February 8. Calabrese's ability to afford his son's attending the military school was a big part of the prosecutor's inquiry. As questioning turned to the claim he filed for unemployment benefits, Putman asked if he got a check for $36, to which Calabrese responded, "I think I did." The defendant then stated the cost to send his son to school was $1,500 annually. He also claimed he drove a 1956 Oldsmobile. Calabrese was asked if a Captain Leslie Blankenship at the military academy inquired into his ability to keep up payments for his son's tuition there. Putman then asked if the witness had $10,000 in his bank account. Calabrese answered, "I haven't the slightest idea."

When asked about Arthur LaRiche, Calabrese answered he met him about a year and a half earlier at the Italian Club in Cleveland. He also admitted that LaRiche played cards at the Collinwood Construction Social Club, where Calabrese and Perrotti were both members. During questioning about the March 21 shooting of Carpenter, Calabrese claimed he called Perrotti after hearing of the incident. Putman asked him why he didn't call the police instead of his friend, Perrotti. Calabrese replied, "It was none of my business."

On Tuesday, December 3, the two prisoners from the Ohio Penitentiary, Joseph Pittacora and David Suarez arrived and took the stand. Both men, from Chicago, were charged with burglarizing Belinski's Jewelry store in Canton.[113] They were being held in the Stark County Jail back in May, one charged with grand larceny and the other possession of burglary tools, when Calabrese and Perrotti arrived at the jail after their arrests in Cleveland. Also there, after having just been arrested in Alliance, was Ray Paone. Both Chicago men testified Paone failed to recognize Calabrese and Perrotti when they were brought to the jail, despite the fact Paone met Perrotti, Carpenter and LaRiche at an inn near Alliance to discuss the burglary, before the drive to the Wells home on the night of February 6. This begs the question, since Paone and Perrotti were from different cities in Ohio, but were accused of being involved in the same burglary, why would either man risk acknowledging the other, which would only solidify a connection between the two. Plus, Paone had already testified he never met Calabrese. Prosecutor Putman did not care to cross-examine either man.

The defense's final witnesses were Captain Benjamin H. Pumphrey and his wife. A math teacher and basketball coach at the military school, Pumphrey testified he knew Calabrese because he had met him on several occasions. During 1957, the captain recalled seeing him twice; the first time was on Wednesday, January 30. Asked by Wise how he was so sure about the day, the witness responded, "I remarked at the time that it was too early in the week for him to take his son for a weekend, but he told me he was on his way to Florida." The second time was "after supper" on the night of February 7, around 6:20. *For the first time in the reporting of the* Alliance Review, *the newspaper acknowledged the existence of the two mysterious men that came into the story. The newspaper reported, "Pumphrey testified further that Calabrese, in the company of Perrotti and two other men, returned Feb. 7 on Calabrese's trip back to Cleveland." Other newspapers had reported the presence of the two, always unnamed men, that appeared. It is not for certain exactly how and when they both got there. One newspaper report claimed they arrived with Calabrese on January 31. During Perrotti's testimony it was reported he left Ohio with one of the unnamed men. Some newspaper reports even had them with Calabrese and Perrotti when they visited Sister Pauline. It would not be until months later that one man was named, and the other was referred to only by his nickname.*

Pumphrey recalled that on the February 7 date, "I asked Mr. Calabrese if he knew a Tony Hughes, a boxer in Cleveland. Mr. Perrotti overheard the conversation and said he knew him and Mr. Perrotti and I talked." Pumphrey also stated the three men discussed getting some balls and bats at the school for the baseball team. Wise asked the captain to identify the two men in the courtroom, which he did.

During cross-examination, Putman focused on trying to show both Pumphrey and the jury that the captain was mixed up on his dates and that Calabrese and Perrotti were at the military school a week earlier than the witness recalled. *If Putman was correct, and all four men were there on Wednesday, January 30, then Perrotti's whole alibi about driving to Florida with his family was contrived. There was never any explanation as to why Calabrese, and the man he showed up with in Pensacola on January 31, were even invited to join the Perrotti family for the blessed event. What seems more likely to have happened was that the men left Florida earlier than they claimed to; either Friday, February 1 or Saturday, February 2. That would at least account for Captain Pumphrey's recollection of meeting Perrotti and having the conversation he claimed to have had with the men.*

Finally, Pumphrey told the court that he remembered the Wednesday date because as the men were driving off, his wife came home. She had been in Lexington, Kentucky, on a shopping trip. The captain said he and his wife had an argument about her spending.

Mrs. Pumphrey was the last defense witness. She, too, knew Calabrese and after the news broke of his arrest, she was sure her husband would be called as a witness. She testified that a good friend of theirs had a baby and she wanted to go to Lexington to purchase a present. She said when she got home that night, she saw her husband standing outside the school as a car was pulling away. She thought her husband was out there "just spying" on her, as she took her packages into the apartment. Pumphrey's wife, who did not see any of the men, said her husband later remarked to her, "Calabrese had just been there." The only difference between Pumphrey's testimony and Perrotti's was the captain claimed they arrived after dark, while the defendant claimed it was still light out.

Defense counsel rested their case at 2:00 p.m. Tuesday afternoon. This apparently took Putman by surprise as he told Judge Graham he would not be prepared to present rebuttal witnesses until 1:00 p.m. Wednesday. Attorney Wise jumped on this and told the judge the defense was ready to move forward with closing statements and submit the case to the jury. Graham refused the prolonged delay and told Putman to be ready by Wednesday morning at 9:00.

On Wednesday, five rebuttal witnesses took the stand for Prosecutor Putman. The first witness, Paul Carpenter, was recalled to refute the testimony of Frank Stredrick. Carpenter said he knew the jail house snitch, but denied telling him that Perrotti and Calabrese were innocent and that he wanted revenge for their alleged part in his shooting in Painesville.

Also recalled was Ray Paone, who, like Carpenter, was put on the stand to refute testimony of two jail house snitches, Joseph Pittacora and David Suarez. The two men testified when Calabrese and Perrotti were brought to the Stark County Jail, Paone told them he didn't know either one of them.

The third rebuttal witness, an important one, was Betty Malen, who worked at the Ohio Bureau of Unemployment Compensation office in Cleveland. She testified application forms for benefits were signed and filed in Calabrese's and Perrotti's behalf on February 5, at the Cleveland office. She claimed the application for Calabrese was signed and sworn to her by him in her presence, and she dated and signed it herself at that time. In response to a question under cross-examination from attorney Wise, she said, "I am speaking from the record. I could not identify either man and I could not possibly remember each individual person whom I see." However, she witnessed the signature as it was written and it matched Calabrese's previous applications.

Putman's next witness was Father Simeon Fetzko, of St. Michael's Byzantine Catholic Church in Pleasant City, Ohio, one of the three priests at the Choma home on February 6. Putman told the judge of Fetzko's importance, claiming he was a "witness that was hidden by the defense." The priest was scheduled to deliver Mass that morning in Pleasant City at 9:00 before he could begin his journey to Canton. When Judge Graham called a recess, Prosecutor Putman made an application that a court commission be sent to Dallas, Texas, to take a deposition from the Reverend John McGonagle, another of the three priests who paid a visit to the Choma home on February 6. McGonagle, of Birmingham, Alabama, was currently in Dallas on sick leave from the church. Putman claimed that it was "absolutely vital" to the case. Judge Graham was concerned that by granting the application it would stretch the trial out another week, because the prosecutors, defense counsel, the two defendants and the necessary guards would have to travel by train to Dallas. He said he would reserve his ruling until after hearing the testimony of Father Fetzko that afternoon.

During the recess Perrotti sought out William McCarty, city editor of the *Alliance Review*, who was in the courtroom that morning. He had a statement for the editor:

"I want you to know something. One favor I want to ask. Regardless of the outcome of the case. I want the wife, and mother and father of the fellow who got shot to know that I had nothing to do with the incident, I was never in that house. I've said a prayer every night for him."

At 1:00 p.m., Father Fetzko took the witness stand. He testified that he took a vacation on February 3 and arrived in Pensacola on February 6. He had been invited to the Choma home because of "hometown connections" to Pleasant City. Father McGonagle, a seminary classmate of Fetzko, who happened to be in Pensacola at the time, came to the Choma home to meet him. "We had quite a reunion," Father Fetzko announced, stating that the Navy chaplain, who baptized the Choma baby, also arrived. Fetzko was asked if he saw the defendants Calabrese and Perrotti while he was at the home, or if their names were mentioned at anytime while he was there. To the first question Fetzko replied, "No." and "I don't recall," to the second one. During cross-examination by Wise, Fetzko stated Father McGonagle could testify that he hadn't seen the two defendants at the Choma home. That answer basically shot down Putman's request for the trip to Dallas.

Colonel Leslie Blankenship, head of Millersburg Military Institute, was the last rebuttal witness called. He was questioned about the manner in which Captain Pumphrey had determined the date he last saw the two defendants. Blankenship felt Pumphrey was mistaken about the timing. Blankenship was president of the Millersburg Military Institute. He testified that, apparently, at the time Pumphrey was requested to be an alibi witness, that he approached the colonel seeking to determine the day he actually saw the two defendants. Blankenship said Pumphrey told him he "remembered the date of an academy basketball game against Herrodsburg on February 8, when they discussed an earlier visit by Calabrese." The colonel later realized he was in Washington D.C. on February 8 to attend a military school meeting. Blankenship told the court he informed Pumphrey of his "mistaken memory," and together they tried to determine the date of the actual visit, resolving that it was actually January 30, the night before students were given a long weekend pass from Thursday to Sunday. The colonel said Pumphrey later came back to him, claiming it was February 7, because he remembered a shopping trip his wife took.

The last item of business that Wednesday afternoon regarded the admission records provided by Betty Malen, from the Ohio Bureau of Unemployment Compensation. Defense counsel, while admitting that the signatures of Calabrese and Perrotti were valid, stipulated that they did not agree the documents were signed on a specific date or in the presence of Malen, as she had testified. They claimed the documents were signed by the defendants before leaving for Florida and were taken to the unemployment office by their brothers.

On Thursday, closing statements were delivered after both sides agreed to a maximum of two hours apiece. Attorney Wise in his closing pitted the testimony of Carpenter, who he continually referred to as, "The star of the show," against two key defense witnesses. He asked the jurors questions like, "Would you take the word of Carpenter against that of Sister Pauline?" or "Would you take the word of Carpenter against that of Captain Pumphrey?" Wise told the jury:

"The star of the show," he arrived with fanfare and without a bit of remorse, proudly says "I shot the man." "The star of the show," again without remorse, wants to take others to the electric chair because he thinks others set him up to be killed.

During the state's closing, Thursday afternoon, Putman focused on the fact the men were in Cleveland on February 5, filing for unemployment and could not have been in Florida. The defense argued the two had signed the application before leaving and left them with brothers to submit at the unemployment office. Putman pointed out neither of the brothers testified. "Where are these brothers?" he asked.

To his surprise, the answer came ringing out from the gallery, "They're in the hall outside!" Mrs. Mary LaRiccia, Perrotti's sister, announced.

Judge Graham immediately admonished her and ordered her out of the courtroom. As she got up to leave, she again stated, "The brothers are out in the hall." This time Graham ordered her held in contempt. She later apologized to the judge, who dismissed the charge.

After closing statements, Judge Graham delivered his instructions to the jurors. The *Plain Dealer* explained the guidelines for the guilty penalties. "Conviction of first-degree murder carries a death sentence unless mercy is recommended, in which case the convicted person is eligible for parole after 20 years. Second-degree murder and house burglary in the night season [sometimes referred to as burglary of an inhabited dwelling in the night season] carry life sentences, like first-degree murder, but the person is eligible for parole after 10 years," the newspaper reported.

The case went to the eight men and four women at 3:20 that afternoon. The jury deliberated until 5:00 p.m. then went to dinner. From 7:00 until 9:05 p.m. they continued the deliberations and then told the judge they were hopelessly deadlocked. Polled by Judge Graham, all but one juror said they would never come to an agreement. After two days of jury selection, seven days of testimony, four hours of deliberating and after six ballots the case ended in a mistrial at 9:23 that night.

One juror revealed the results of the balloting, stating it was seven to five for acquittal throughout, without any switching. The *Alliance Review* reported another "source" claimed there was considerable switching and the first ballot taken showed nine to three for acquittal, while the final ballot stood at eight to four. Judge Graham was asked why he pulled the trigger on discharging the jurors so quickly, as opposed to bringing them back Friday morning for more deliberations. The judge replied, "The jurors made definite statements that there was no possibility of reaching a verdict if they were kept together. It would be abusive discretion on the part of the court to make the jury do something it didn't want to do."

The defendants appeared "shocked and downcast" by the decision. Neither spoke with reporters. Perrotti talked to his wife briefly, and kissed her goodbye before being led back to the county jail with Calabrese by deputies.

Prosecutor Putman stated the case would definitely be retried as soon as the press of other cases in his office will allow.

On Saturday, December 7, attorney Wise wasted no time in attempting to get his clients out of jail. He filed bail motions for both men, which gave him three days to file briefs for Judge Graham. Prosecutor Putman's office immediately announced any granting of bail would be opposed. Putman, meanwhile, wasted no time himself announcing that a second trial would begin on February 10, 1958.

A hearing on the bail motion was held December 12, and was denied by Judge Graham. One week later, defense counsel for Calabrese and Perrotti announced they would appeal the dismissal of the jury in the first trial to the 5th Ohio District Court of Appeals. Wise and Marchbanks claimed that "in light of the evidence presented" the judge should have directed the jury to deliver a verdict of not guilty. Prosecutor Putman stated he will move ahead with the second trial preparations despite the appeal.

On January 14, 1958, Helen Shoup, the widow of Eldon "Pete" Shoup, filed suit in Stark County Common Pleas Court for $364,800 in damages. Alliance attorney Gus Tarian, who filed the suit, claimed that Shoup's death left Helen and her two children, two-year-old Regina Ann, and nine-month-old Eldon Peter, without support. Named in the suit were Paul Carpenter, Arthur LaRiche, Raymond Paone, and "others."

The 5th Ohio District Court of Appeals heard arguments on attorney Wise's motion regarding a directed verdict of acquittal on February 5. The court gave each side two days to file briefs, and said a decision would be rendered after Monday, February 10, the day the second trial was to begin. Stark County Common Pleas Judge Paul G. Weber, scheduled to hear the second trial, immediately ordered it postponed until a decision could be made by the appeals court. A venire of possible jurors was dismissed.

Prosecutor Putman stated, possibly as a ploy because he knew Calabrese and Perrotti were anxious to gain their freedom, the decision to delay the trial could result in a wait of "many months." He rightfully pointed out that if the appeals court ruled against the defense, the case could be taken to the Ohio Supreme Court and the back and forth could take months before a ruling came down. The ploy worked. Attorney Wise abandoned his appeal on February 6, making some of the same points Putman made. Wise stated he was, "reluctantly dismissing" the appeal because it would be "unfair to our clients, who are innocent of this charge, to insist on going ahead while they languish in the Stark County Jail." Wise said the decision by the appeals court could mean two trips to the Ohio Supreme Court, by whichever side lost the ruling, before a final decision could be rendered. He estimated this alone would result in another year in prison for Calabrese and Perrotti. Wise then called for an immediate trial.

The Massillon *Evening Independent* reported that Prosecutor Putman "took a dim view" of Wise's demand for an "immediate trial," during his announcement withdrawing his appeal. Putman stated, "Calabrese and Perrotti had already been given their chance for a speedy trial. Our office rescheduled the second Calabrese – Perrotti trial as soon as we could and we were ready to go forward. It is the defense attorney's doing that the trial was postponed." He went on to say Wise "interposed this appeal into the issue apparently with the purpose of taking our attention off the trial preparation and forcing us into the court of appeals." The prosecutor said many other defendants were awaiting their right to a speedy trial and Calabrese and Perrotti would just have to wait their turn. He pointed out that as a result of the postponed second trial, his office had no trial work scheduled for the following week, "in the face of one of the longest waiting lists of defendants in the court's recent history."

Despite the long waiting list of defendants, Putman re-scheduled the second Shoup murder trial to begin April 1. When the trial began that Tuesday, all the players were the same with the exception of the judge. Common Pleas Judge George N. Graham was replaced by Paul G. Weber. Defense counsel of Earle E. Wise and Ray Marchbanks, Jr. were still using an alibi defense. Prosecutor Putman and Assistant Stark County Prosecutor Jacob F. Hess, Jr. were hoping for a win this time.

The first 12 jurors were selected by noon on Friday. The panel consisted of seven men and five women. The afternoon session was spent selecting an alternate juror. During the afternoon, *Plain Dealer* reporter John Beaber got an opportunity to conduct interviews with the two defendants and their wives. What follows is some of the comments and observations from those interviews:

Paul Perrotti: "I think about my wife, daughter, mother and the people who have helped me at trial." The balding, sleepy-eyed former truck driver said he had nothing against Paul Carpenter. "He must think I know who shot him, but deep in his heart, he knows that I had nothing to do with that thing in Alliance."

Alfred Calabrese: The slender, dark complected former cement mixer operator, showed no malice toward Carpenter or Raymond Paone. Calabrese, an excellent dresser even to the extent that his glasses matched the color of his suit, shoes, socks and ties, said simply that he wants "justice done."

Margaret Perrotti: The defendant's wife, who sat in the courtroom each day, said, "I'm more numb than in the first trial, if the state couldn't prove its case in the first trial, why should they have to be tried a second time?" She said she doesn't work and would be a "pauper" if her two brothers, Albert and Peter Choma were not paying expenses for her and her daughter, 6-year-old Carolyn, who is attending kindergarten. "I wouldn't dare work because Carolyn has never been told Paul's in jail. She thinks he is away on a special job and won't be home till it is over."

Anna Calabrese: The reporter said Calabrese's wife had not been to the new trial. She is working at the TAPCO[114] plant in Cleveland.

Author's note: Much of the testimony in the second trial was a repeat of what was said during the first trial. I have focused on items that were new or different.

On Monday, April 7, the jurors were taken to the Ridgewood Avenue home of Frank Wells to view the crime scene. This time, there was no report of Calabrese and Perrotti being there to provide commentary. After lunch, Prosecutor Putman gave his opening statement. Attorney Wise again held back his opening until the state rested its case. In the afternoon, Stark County Coroner, E.B. Mozes was the first of the state's witnesses. He was followed by the state's key witness, Paul "Red" Carpenter, who repeated his story of shooting "Pete" Shoup, as well as the attempted murder of himself.

The next morning, Paul Carpenter was cross-examined by attorney Wise. When defense counsel asked him if he was offered a deal for his testimony, before he could answer, Judge Weber interrupted and asked, "Did anyone ever offer you your life for testifying in this case?" Carpenter replied, "No, sir. No one ever promised me my life." The only new twist to Carpenter's testimony involved his calling Lou Batista, his Canton friend from a restaurant near Minerva, after he and Arthur LaRiche fled from the Wells' home that night. Putman called Marjorie Totten, a waitress at the Breezeway Restaurant on Route 30, east of Minerva, to substantiate Carpenter and LaRiche's presence there, and his making the telephone call. Afterwards, Putman called Marie Garland, a telephone operator from Malvern, who recalled placing the call to the Batista residence between 3:00 a.m. and 4:00 a.m. on the morning of February 8.

After that, the testimony of Frank Wells and Ray Paone took up the rest of Tuesday morning. During the afternoon session, Paone, who now described himself as a "former" poolroom owner, again broke down on the stand while telling the jury that "Pete" Shoup was a friend of his. He said he had no idea that he would be with his father at the house that night. Paone stated he was supposed to receive 10% of the "take" for fingering the job for the burglars, but because his friend was killed, he did what he thought was the noble thing and didn't accept any of the money. Paone, like Carpenter earlier, was asked by Wise if he was "offered any deals" for testifying. Paone said, "No." *The newspaper coverage mentioned at both trials how Ray Paone reacted on the stand when talking about "Pete" Shoup, his "friend." This brings to mind that there was never any mention of emotion being expressed by "Pete's" father, Earl Shoup. Surely he bears some responsibility for his son being there that night; offering different reasons for his presence. During his testimony, I was struck by the fact that as "Pete" sat there mortally wounded, his father got up and walked down the basement to check the safe.*

On Wednesday afternoon, the state rested its case after calling 21 witnesses. The last person called was again Akron Police Captain Cutright.

Wise then delivered his opening statement, before calling Paul Perrotti as his first witness. Perrotti repeated the same story he told during the first trail, including the appearance of the two mystery men, who had spent eight straight days with Calabrese and Perrotti. This time Perrotti identified the man who drove to Florida with his family as Mike Credico. The man who arrived with Calabrese was only identified by his nickname "Nipper." The next day, Perrotti spent the entire morning on the stand under cross-examination from Putman, who attempted to breakdown his alibi or to discover discrepancies in it from the first trial.

Thursday afternoon was taken up with the testimony of Alfred Calabrese. The questioning continued through Friday morning; most of it on cross-examination. While most of the questions "fired at him" were the same as in the earlier trial, many of the responses were now different, consisting solely of the three-word answer, "I don't remember." The *Evening Independent* reported, "Both he and Paul Perrotti...were much more hazy (sic) on details of their alibi than they were at their first trial last November," if it were possible to be so. The only new thing in Calabrese's testimony this time was a claim he made that he received an anonymous telephone call threatening him and his son. Before he could provide any more details, like when he received the call or who may have made the threats, court ended for the day and it was not covered further in the newspapers. Also, sometime Friday afternoon, Father Fetzko took the stand and repeated his testimony about being at the Choma house on February 6, but not seeing either of the defendants.

On Monday morning, April 14, the brothers of Alfred Calabrese and Paul Perrotti, apparently left standing in the courthouse hallway during the first trail, took the stand. Ralph Perrotti testified that the brothers "often signed unemployment compensation blanks for each other when one was out of town." When Anthony Calabrese was on the stand, he testified that he signed the unemployment compensation report for Alfred back on February 5, 1957, while his brother was in Florida. During cross-examination, he told Putman he had lied to get the $33 in unemployment compensation for his brother. Putman asked if he would lie to get his brother $33, wouldn't he lie "to save his brother's life." Anthony answered, "No." When Ralph Perrotti was asked the question, he gave the same answer.

Anna Calabrese, Alfred's wife, was also called to the stand. Like her brother-in-law, she was not a witness at the first trial. Whatever she was questioned about, however, was not reported in the newspapers. On Tuesday, the defense called witnesses from the first trial, including Captain Benjamin Pumphrey and Sister Pauline. Afterwards, the defense rested. If any rebuttal witnesses were called the newspapers did not report it.

On Wednesday, closing statements were presented to the jury. In a strange directive to the jurors, defense counsel Wise told them the defendants must be given the death penalty or should be found innocent. Prosecutor Putman didn't ask for the death penalty, but said the evidence warranted such a verdict. After instructions from Judge Weber, the jury received the case at 5:23 p.m. They deliberated for two hours and 45 minutes that evening before heading over to the Hotel St. Francis for the night.

The jury returned Thursday morning and continued deliberations at 9:00. After 45 minutes, they arrived at a verdict. Calabrese and Perrotti were found guilty of first-degree murder. Instead of giving them the death penalty, as their own attorney demanded, the jury recommended mercy for the men. Unlike the first trial, where at least one or two jurors divulged how the balloting went, there was no indication as to the number of ballots taken in the second trial. The only rumor was that one juror, who voted for conviction, held out for conviction without a recommendation of mercy. Judge Weber delayed sentencing pending the filing of a motion for a new trial. *Plain Dealer* reporter John Beaber wrote, "Paul Perrotti and Alfred Calabrese this morning took their life-saving murder conviction in stunned silence except for one apparently sneering remark Perrotti made to Calabrese. But their relatives and friends went through waves of emotions." What the "sneering" remark could have been was never revealed.

The *Plain Dealer* also noted, "The verdict carries a life sentence unless the governor commutes the sentence after 20 years. In that case, the two convicted men will be eligible for parole five years after the governor's action."

On Saturday, April 19, attorney Wise filed a motion for a new trial for Calabrese and Perrotti with Judge Weber. The motion charged 14 errors in the conduct of the trial. Judge Weber was cited for several errors and for again overruling a defense motion for a directed verdict of not guilty, claiming the guilty verdict was "not sustained by the evidence and was contrary to the law." Also included were irregularities on the part of Prosecutor Putman and state's witnesses. Judge Weber denied the motion for a new trial and on April 30, imposed life sentences on both Calabrese and Perrotti. Wise immediately announced he would appeal to the 5th Ohio District Court of Appeals. The two convicted men, who were still sitting in the Stark County Jail since May 1957, were scheduled to be transferred to the Ohio Penitentiary in a week to ten days.

Shoup Post-Trial

The day after the verdict, the $364,800 wrongful death suit filed by Gus Tarian, the attorney for Helen Shoup, was back in the news with one change. The word "others" in the suit was now changed to Alfred Calabrese and Paul Perrotti.

On April 29, 1958, Arthur LaRiche, who was to go on trial for the murder of "Pete" Shoup next, appeared in Stark County Common Pleas Court to seek new court appointed council. The trial was scheduled for early September and would be followed by the cases against Raymond Paone and Paul Carpenter. Judge Weber appointed Harry W. Schmunk and Nicholas G. Caplea, both Canton attorneys, to represent him at county expense. LaRiche claimed he could not afford an attorney and that the ones who represented him previously were engaged by his family. Numerous attorneys had offered to represent him, but LaRiche stated in court, according to Putman, that "he had lost confidence in them because they didn't believe him, and wanted him to testify for the state in the Calabrese-Perrotti trial.

A new mystery in the "Pete" Shoup murder popped up the day after the sentencing. The effort to unearth the murder weapon through extensive search and the use of a powerful magnet failed. But that didn't stop two local youths, aged 13 and 15, from finding a .38 Special revolver. According to one report, "A gun, rusty and bearing signs of long exposure, was found by two boys," not far from the residence of Frank Wells. Alliance Police Chief Lower said the pistol was believed to be the one used to kill "Pete" Shoup. The mystery is due to the fact the boys found the gun on April 12, in the middle of the second trial, and it was turned over to Prosecutor Putman two days later. Chief Lower said he was told "make no comment" about the finding of the gun. When news broke about the discovery on May 1, Putman and Lower declined comment. The *Evening Independent* reported, "If the gun found in Alliance does prove to be the one used in the murder, it is expected to strengthen the state's case against the two remaining defendants." Unfortunately, the finding of the gun is not mentioned again, meaning there was no public confirmation as to whether or not it was the murder weapon.

On July 16, *Plain Dealer* reporter Fred Mollenkopf revealed to Cleveland readers a recent scam that was going on in the city. He wrote, "Another energetic crop of salesmen selling "benefit" tickets for police figures who are in trouble or in jail has turned up in Cleveland." This latest benefit drawing was for Paul Perrotti. Cleveland detectives found the tickets after stopping two relatives of Perrotti and Alfred Calabrese. The one-dollar tickets advertised the drawing of three television sets to be held at the Collinwood Construction Workers Club, at Evangeline Road and Mandalay Avenue. The drawing was scheduled for Sunday, August 3.

Detective Lieutenant Thomas P. White said the ticket was taken from the automobile of the stopped relatives. "Judging from the number on this one [2050]," he said, "There is a lot of them out [there]." White pointed out that in June, Detectives William Lonchar and Steve Vrabel "picked up a flock" of benefit tickets after stopping Joseph M. Petrangelo[115] at East 71st Street and Superior Avenue, who was selling them for a $10 steak dinner to raise money for himself as he was facing trial for another armed robbery.

On Friday, November 15, 1958, Arthur LaRiche went before Stark County Common Pleas Judge George N. Graham and pleaded guilty. La Riche was to go on trial Monday on charges of first-degree murder in the death of "Pete" Shoup and burglary of an inhabited dwelling during the night season for the break-in at the Wells home in Alliance. LaRiche decided to get the best deal possible, so he skipped the trial and made a plea. He first pled guilty to the burglary charge, which carried a life sentence, but a possibility of parole after 10 years. Then, in yet another mystery in the case, he was allowed to plead guilty, not to first-degree murder, but instead to first-degree manslaughter, for which he received a 1 to 20 year sentence. The terms were to be served consecutively, after completion of his sentence for the Wahoo Bar burglary.

Shortly after the conviction of Calabrese and Perrotti, defense counsel filed their appeal to the 5th Ohio District Court of Appeals. On April 22, 1959, the appeals court responded and upheld the conviction of the two.

With three of the five members of the Alliance burglary crew now serving long sentences in the Ohio Penitentiary, only two were left to be tried, Paul Carpenter and Ray Paone. On April 24, 1959, the *Akron Beacon Journal* ran a front-page article with the headline, "Carpenter Gets Top Jail Care To Keep Him Alive." The article claimed Carpenter was living a life of isolation in the Stark County Jail waiting for a trial which, "probably won't start for at least another year." The reporter on the story, Pat Ordovensky, claimed authorities in Stark County were keeping him in jail in order to prevent him from being killed. Prosecutor Putman said the delay in trying Carpenter was due to all the appeals involved in the Calabrese and Perrotti convictions. Putman was concerned that when Carpenter was shipped off to the Ohio Penitentiary he would become a target, not only of Calabrese and Perrotti, but of any prisoner who had a distaste of squealers. Should Carpenter be killed in prison or threatened so badly he would be afraid to ever talk to authorities again, it could create a problem if any of the appeals for a new trial were granted for Calabrese and Perrotti and he was need-ed to testify again. While the total appeals process played out, Putman declared, "We want Carpenter right where we can keep our eyes on him."

While Putman's comments were reasonable and understandable, what he said next bordered on the absurd. "These aren't ordinary criminals – this is the Mafia. This gang is a second cousin to Murder, Inc., which killed Anastasia." Putman apparently wasn't up to date on his "Mob history." Murder, Inc., for all intents and purposes went out of business when Abe "Kid Twist" Reles ratted out the gang in 1940. Albert Anastasia, who was the boss of what became the Gambino Crime Family, was murdered in a barbershop chair in a downtown Manhattan hotel 17 years later on October 25, 1957.

Reporter Ordovensky went on to write, "Deputies at the County Jail are do-ing everything they can to keep Carpenter healthy. He is kept away from other prisoners as much as possible and is allowed no visitors. When a reporter tried to interview Carpenter this week, he was told politely, but firmly, 'Nobody talks to this boy.'" This left the reader to wonder if the "no visitors" rule applied to Carpenter's wife Betty. For the record, after she was questioned following the shooting of her husband on March 22, 1957, she was never mentioned in the newspapers again.

On May 19, 1959, Meinhart's Restaurant / Cigar store at 65 Erie Street in Massillon, was bombed. The bombing was the sixth in recent months in the county, and was believed to be part of a wave of bombings in Stark County re-lated to gambling shakedowns there. The *Akron Beacon Journal* jumped on Pros-ecutor Putman's "second cousin to Murder, Inc." comment and used it in the article. Putman stated that he believed the bombings were being pulled by "the gang of which Paul Perrotti, Paul Carpenter and Vincent Innocenzi were members." The *Evening Independent* reported an investigation that centered on individuals who were suspects in the recent bombings were seen at Meinhart's in the past few days. Two people connected to the cigar store were current holders of gambling tax stamps.

On July 31, 1959, Calabrese and Perrotti's defense attorneys filed their appeal with the Ohio Supreme Court. The appeal included the charges of judicial error in the trial, in which Judge Weber made "certain incidental statements" that prejudiced the jury against the defendants. On October 21, the high court conducted a hearing on the case and agreed to review it. On February 10, 1960, the court heard the appeal. During the hearing, attorney Wise asked for the reversal of the first-degree conviction stating the men did not receive a fair trial. Prosecutor Putman, while addressing the justices, asserted, "justice has been done in the case," and he argued for the high court to uphold the decision. After hearing the appeal, the Ohio Supreme Court on March 2, 1960, affirmed the convictions in a 4 – 0 decision. Less than 24 hours later, attorney Wise announced that he would file a motion for reconsideration with the high court of Ohio. This was just a "preparatory" step to filing an appeal with the U.S. Supreme Court.

The motion for reconsideration was denied. At this point attorney Wise called on a seasoned veteran of defense counseling. To file his appeal to the U.S. Supreme Court, Wise brought in one of the men who had delivered Julius Petro to freedom after 18 months on death row back in 1948. Michael Picciano helped Wise draft the appeal which was filed with the highest court in the land on June 24. The process consisted of the U.S. Supreme Court first ruling on whether or not it will accept the case for hearing. Then, if accepted, the court will consider the merits of the case itself. On October 11, 1960, the two-and-a-half-year appeals battle waged by Calabrese and Perrotti came to an end when the U.S. Supreme Court refused to review the case.

The decision opened the door for trials for Carpenter and Paone, the last two men indicted in the Alliance burglary and murder case. Prosecutor Putman announced he would ask the court for a reduction of charges against the two men because they cooperated with law enforcement in convicting their three accomplices in the murder of "Pete" Shoup. By now, Carpenter had been in one jail or another since March 25, 1957; Paone was free on a $5,000 bond. Putman stated he would ask that the charge against Carpenter be reduced to second-degree murder and the charge against Paone, "be changed to some undetermined lesser offense."

On February 6, 1961, four years to the day when Paul Carpenter and Ray Paone sat in a car outside the home of Frank E. Wells ready to burglarize it, only to be scared off by a neighbor's dog, they were sentenced for the crimes that occurred the next night. Paone was sentenced to a term of 5 to 30 years after pleading guilty to a charge of burglary of an inhabited dwelling in the night season. It was not the reduced charge that Prosecutor Putman had discussed, however, Judge Paul Weber did not impose a life sentence, giving the defendant a lighter sentence instead. Paone would be eligible for a parole hearing in three years and four months. Paul Carpenter pleaded guilty to second-degree murder in the death of Eldon "Pete" Shoup, and the burglary charge. Judge Weber sentenced him to two life sentences in the Ohio Penitentiary; one for the murder, the second for the burglary of an inhabited dwelling in the night season. Weber ordered them to be served concurrently.

Later that day, Carpenter was driven to Akron to be sentenced on his guilty pleas there for the break-ins at the Automotive Supply & Equipment Company and the Wahoo Bar, and for the possession of burglary tools. As he entered the courtroom of Common Pleas Judge John M. Kelly, he was approached by reporters. While most prisoners seem to lose weight in jail, reporters stated, "The smiling, good looking Carpenter" had grown pudgy. "I'm going on the assumption that eventually I will be returned to society," he said. "I expect to train for some occupation so I can make my living when I get out."

Judge Kelly sentenced Carpenter to two terms of 1 – 15 years for the break-ins and a 1 – 5 year term for possession of the burglary tools. The judge ordered the terms to be served concurrently with the Stark County sentences.

Prosecutor Putman said the prisoners would be sent to the Ohio Penitentiary in the next four or five days. He said he had written a letter to Warden D.C. Sachs requesting Carpenter and Paone be kept separated from the other prisoners serving sentences there who were involved in the Wahoo Bar and the Shoup murder case. He suggested the men be housed at the Junction City or Roseville[116] facilities near Columbus.

Aftermath

During the Wahoo Bar trial, Cleveland attorney Casmere Batule argued his client John Lexune should have been charged with receiving stolen property instead of burglary; the latter crime carrying a stiffer sentence. On August 2, 1957, he filed a notice of appeal. Lexune still had bigger problems.

Back on February 1, 1957, four "heavily armed men" entered the Libbey-Owens-Ford Federal Credit Union in Toledo at 9:40 a.m. shortly after a Brinks, Inc. armored car dropped off money there to cash company paychecks. A fifth man reportedly waited in a getaway car nearby. The men had disguised themselves by wearing stockings, dark glasses, a scarf, and one donned a Hitler mustache. Albert Gottfried, the secretary-treasurer, said two of the men walked into his office and demanded, "We want the bundle that Brinks just delivered." Gottfried told the robbers the money had already been separated and put into drawers. This irritated the men, who began cursing and terrorizing the seven employees and several customers, ordering them to stand against the wall. The thieves emptied six cash drawers, leaving behind all the coins, including several hundred silver dollars. Before leaving, they pulled out all the telephone lines except one, which Gottfried used to call police. The men made off with an estimated $32,000,[117] in a stolen automobile, which they abandoned several blocks away. In April 1957, while Lexune was on trial for the Wahoo Bar burglary, Albert Gottfried and others picked Lexune out of a line-up at the Summit County Jail.

According to the police investigation, Lexune received the information about the Brinks drop-offs to the credit union from Charles G. Radd. Overhearing this was John Glassner, which he soon revealed to Akron police. *Assuming this to be true, then Glassner, Lexune and Radd all had to be locked up at the same time before the February 1 robbery, which could only mean Lexune had to have been jailed for the Wahoo Bar burglary and released well prior to February 1957. This was never reported in any of the newspapers.* When Radd was questioned about the conversation in court, he denied he had ever spoken to Lexune. Both Lexune and Radd were indicted by a Lucas County Grand Jury for armed robbery on June 12. Charles Radd went on trial for perjury on September 11. The state's key witness was John Glassner. Before taking the stand, Glassner told Lucas County Common Pleas Judge Thomas D. Stahl he was "warned" not to testify against Radd, and had received several threats by telephone against his life. Judge Stahl told Glassner that unless his answers meant self-incrimination, he could face contempt charges if he refused to answer questions. Glassner[118] proceeded to tell the court about overhearing Radd tell Lexune about information he had regarding dates when several large money deliveries would be made to the Libbey-Owens-Ford Federal Credit Union in Toledo. Charles G. Radd,[119] at this point, seems to disappear from the credit union robbery story.

On the last day of 1957, the 9th District Court of Appeals upheld the convictions of Ernie Foti and John Lexune. The court confirmed the convictions without opinion. Lexune continued to serve his term in the Ohio Penitentiary with the Toledo credit union robbery charges looming ahead of him once he was released.

According to a report in the Marysville, Ohio, *Journal-Tribune*, Lexune might have decided to join the rat-fest with Glassner and Carpenter. On February 13, 1958, the newspaper reported that George Stryanka[120] was arrested in Cleveland in connection with the Libbey-Owens-Ford Federal Credit Union Robbery. When police entered his Middleburg Heights home they found "two loaded guns, a portable key-making machine, a code book of auto keys and a strip of celluloid used by burglars to jam door locks." The article stated Toledo police accused Stryanka of the robbery after John Lexune implicated him in the holdup. Stryanka and Lexune were no strangers. On April 7, 1956, three armed men walked into the Urick Foundry Company in Erie, Pennsylvania, and herded several employees into a closet before walking out with a $12,000 payroll. Two of the men suspected of the robbery were Lexune and Stryanka; the third was Arthur LaRiche.

The trial for Stryanka in the Toledo robbery was held in May 1958. His attorney filed a notice of alibi defense and was able to convince the jury that Stryanka was indeed working at his Middleburg Heights home on the morning of the robbery. During cross-examination of witnesses, defense counsel was able to bring out discrepancies in the testimony of two eye-witnesses. After being acquitted, it was quickly pointed out that Stryanka was going to be held for Pennsylvania authorities for the Erie payroll robbery. Stryanka remained a guest at the Lucas County Jail until October 2, when Pennsylvania authorities decided to drop the case.

John Lexune served his time for the Wahoo Bar burglary conviction and was released from the Ohio Penitentiary. He moved into a home on Lake Shore Boulevard in Bratenahl, a suburb surrounded by Cleveland along the coast of Lake Erie. In July 1961, Toledo authorities asked Bratenahl police to arrest and hold Lexune for the credit union robbery. On August 11, the Lucas County Grand Jury refused to indict him for the crime that took place more than four years earlier and Lexune went free.

John Lexune's name did not appear in the newspapers for any crimes again. Perhaps he ended up going straight. At some point he relocated to the West Coast. He died while in his late 80s on December 22, 2005, in Los Angeles.

After his release from prison Ernest Foti returned to Galion, Ohio, where his wife, Mary and family resided. Indications are that the couple had reconciled; there were no reports in the newspaper of any divorce. Foti found legitimate employment working for the City of Galion at its disposal plant. There were no more reports of Foti getting into trouble. On January 13, 1969, Foti was involved in a two-car collision. It was determined that the accident resulted due to the negligence of Mrs. Elizabeth McLeod of Galion. Foti received serious injuries in the accident.

On August 29, 1969, after a week at University Hospital in Columbus, Ernest Foti died at the age of 55 from complications from an aortic aneurism. He left behind his wife and four children. The funeral was held on September 2 at St. Joseph Catholic Church in Galion. Foti was buried at Mt. Calvary Cemetery in Galion.

Four months after her husband's death, Mary M. Foti, the administrator of her husband's estate, filed a lawsuit on January 4, 1971, against Elizabeth McLeod, charging that her negligence caused the death of her husband. The suit was for $55,000 and costs and was claimed for herself and her four children. In April, the suit was settled out of court by McLeod. Before the end of 1971, Mary Foti filed another law suit, this one against the Bureau of Workman's' Compensation and the City of Galion as the employer of her husband. Her application for a workmen's compensation benefit in his death was denied. The bureau claimed she had provided no proof that his death resulted from an injury received during the course of his employment.

As for Paul Carpenter, while in prison he trained himself to be a "jailhouse" lawyer. After filing paperwork in the late 1960s to vacate his 1961 burglary sentence, the case ended up in Summit County Common Pleas Court in January 1970. After hearing arguments, Common Pleas Judge Daniel Quillin vacated the sentence because Carpenter did not have an attorney present. In the ensuing years, the sentencing was never appealed and by the late 1960s his right to do so had long expired. Quillin vacated the sentence, but immediately resentenced Carpenter to the same term. The legal gymnastics allowed Carpenter to now appeal the sentence. In the re-sentence, Quillin gave him credit for not only all the time he had served in prison, but also for the time he was held in jail before sentencing. During the hearing, Carpenter helped argue his case before Quillin, after which the judge said he "showed impressive abilities as his own attorney."

It was never made clear what Carpenter hoped to achieve with this appeal. He had confessed to two burglaries, plus he was serving a life sentence for the murder of "Pete" Shoup. Whatever his reasoning was, it was the last time Carpenter made news.

By the end of the 1960s all of the convicted men from the Wahoo Bar burglary had either died or settled into a legitimate career, except one. On April 18, 1975, Arthur LaRiche, now 57 years old, was one of 19 men arrested in two states for the theft of a $352,000 trailer-load of Levi Strauss blue jeans in Cincinnati back on December 19, 1974. A semi-trailer, loaded with the blue jeans, was stolen from a Southern Railway siding in Cincinnati and found empty and abandoned in Twinsburg, Ohio, several days later. Arrested with LaRiche was Pasquale "Butchie" Cisternino, who, on May 25, 1978, would be convicted for his role in in the murder of Cleveland gangster "Danny" Greene and sentenced to life in prison. On June 25, 1975, LaRiche was found guilty in Federal Court in Cleveland of the theft.

Arthur F. LaRiche died on October 18, 1985, at the age of 68. He is buried at Lake View Cemetery.

Whatever Alfred Calabrese and Paul Perrotti did after their releases from prison was not public knowledge. Neither man seemed to have been in trouble with the law again. On February 17, 1986, Calabrese died. He was buried in All Souls Cemetery in Geauga County, where he rests with his son Alfred S., a suspected murder victim in 1999, and his wife Anna, who passed away in 2011. Resting in the same cemetery is his former partner in crime Paul Perrotti, who died on March 24, 2012, at the age of 87.

Chapter Twelve:

A Few Selected Biographies

Abbie Carter Alden & H. Carter Alden

There was a group of citizens who were true heroes on August 14, 1952, for coming forward to report what they had seen of the brazen armed robbery of Charles J. Foley, branch manager and assistant treasurer of Union Savings and Trust Company, in Warren, Ohio. Of those citizens who reported what they witnessed to the police, Abbie Alden and her son Carter were the only ones who could make first-hand identification of Julius Petro and Joseph Sanzo. Their testimony was key to sealing the fate of this safe-cracking career criminal from Cleveland, who used threats to witnesses as part of his modus operandi for staying out of prison.

Abbie Carter was born in Norristown, Pennsylvania. She graduated from Ursinus College, a private liberal arts college located in Collegeville, Pennsylvania, where she met her future husband, Henry H. Alden. They were married shortly after they graduated; the couple would have two children, Virginia and Carter. The Aldens moved to Warren in 1930 to be closer to Henry's father and other family members who lived there. Henry's father was minister of the First Reformed Church in Warren at that time. Carter remembers his mother, Abbie as, "A very helpful, sweet and caring Mom, who volunteered regularly for our church and also for the hospital." Henry Alden passed away at the age of 54. Abbie outlived him by 33 years and died at the age of 87 on March 28, 1994.

H. Carter Alden was born in Warren, Ohio on May 30, 1933, at Trumbull Memorial Hospital (ironically, the site where Julius Petro switched getaway cars after the robbery). He proudly states that, "My dad was a 10th generation descendent of John and Priscilla Alden, who had come to the new world on the Mayflower; so I am 11th generation." He attended Warren public schools through ninth grade, before enrolling at The Choate School in Wallingford, Connecticut. The private Episcopal college-preparatory boarding school, in addition to its most famous alumni John F. Kennedy and his older brother Joseph, was also attended by Hollywood personalities Michael Douglas, Paul Giamatti and James Whitmore. After the school became co-educational and changed its name to Choate-Rosemary Hall in 1971, the following personalities could claim alumni status: Glenn Close, Jamie Lee Curtis and Ali McGraw.

Alden graduated from The Choate School in June 1951, and that fall enrolled at the University of Missouri – Columbia on a Navy ROTC scholarship. Early in the summer of 1952, he took his first "Midshipman" cruise, on the heavy cruiser USS Des Moines. The dates of the cruise were approximately mid-June through the end of July, during which the ship visited England and Northern Ireland. He recalls, "This was new and exciting to me. Then I returned from this just a week or two before the bank robbery, which was also exciting, but in a much different way."

After graduating from Missouri with a degree of B.S. in Mechanical Engineering, Alden received a commission as Ensign in the U.S. Navy. Committed to serve three years, he was assigned to the USS Eaton (DDE 510), known as a Fletcher-class destroyer, with a "home port" of Norfolk, Virginia. When he reported aboard the Eaton, at Norfolk Naval Shipyard in Portsmouth, Virginia, the forward third of the ship was being rebuilt, having recently been involved in a collision with the battleship USS Wisconsin.

Alden spent all three years of his naval service on the Eaton, serving in positions in the gunnery department. During his third year, he was promoted to Gunnery Officer. He recalled his time in the Navy as a great experience, allowing him to visit many interesting places in the world. In November, 1958, at a dress-up dance at the Little Creek (Marine amphibious base) Officers' Club, he met Frances Tharrington, a graduate of UNC-Chapel Hill, who was teaching school in Portsmouth, Virginia, whom he would later marry.

On June 6, 1959, he was released from active duty in the Navy. In August, Frances moved to Charlotte, North Carolina, to take a teaching job in the Charlotte-Mecklenburg school district. Alden soon followed and found work at Piedmont Natural Gas in Charlotte in October, 1959. In addition to four years working for Piedmont, he worked for a sheet metal fabricator, an engineering-construction firm, and then as a manufacturer's representative at an engineered products sales firm. Alden retired at the age of 65 in May, 1998.

In a note to the author, Alden wrote, "Frances and I are still very happily married. She is still irresistible to me. We have three children (but no grandchildren). Outside interests: I love sports, participating and watching. I gave up golf two years ago. I still play tennis two or three times per week. I love singing in choirs.... have been in various church and school choirs since I was eight years old. I have been in our church choir for 58 years. I enjoy reading, gardening, yardwork, and I tolerate "honey-do" projects. Frances and I have loved traveling, but now it is limited to visiting children and relatives." The couple celebrated their 60th wedding anniversary on February 12, 2020.

William Amato & Steve Calcavecchio

Amato was born Biagio (William Sam) "Billy" Amato on June 3, 1919, in Cleveland, Ohio. He grew up in Cleveland's Little Italy neighborhood and attended local schools through his first year of high school. In March 1926, William's father Calogero passed away at the age of 40. His mother, Angela, was pregnant at the time. On June 19, she gave birth to a son, Charles. Tragically he died a week later. In May 1943, William enlisted in the U.S. Naval Reserve, serving as a coxswain until his discharge in October 1945. By March 1947, he was working part-time as a bartender in Little Italy.

Steve Calcavecchio was born on November 14, 1919, in Cleveland. He also grew up in Little Italy and in his teenage years became a local boxing sensation. Fighting under the name Steve Cala, in two Golden Gloves tournamnets as a bantamweight, he won the 112-pound championship in 1935. The next year he was runner-up in the flyweight division. He moved to Oakland, California, for a while and participated in the Amateur Athletic Union tournament, where he was runner-up in the featherweight division.

In 1938, Calcavecchio was convicted of malicious mischief in Modesto, California. Instead of prison time, he was transferred to a state mental institution in Stockton. That November, the California State Athletic Commission suspended Calcavecchio indefinitely after he was "adjudged as physically unfit." When Calcavecchio was released, he returned to Cleveland where he got into trouble again. On September 16, 1939, he was arrested for an unarmed robbery of $41 at a service station on the corner of East 191st Street and Lake Shore Boulevard. He pleaded guilty and received a suspended sentence and was put on probation for three years. He turned his attention back to boxing, this time deciding to go professional. In March 1940, he was signed to a scheduled six-round bout at Public Hall against newcomer Joey Pirrone. The upcoming bout was the talk of the town. Joey, the younger brother of former middleweight contender "Beltin' Paul" Pirrone, was making his professional debut. On March 27, Pirrone decked Calla with an upper cut to the chin. If it wasn't for the bell, Pirrone would have had a 1st round knockout. But Calla was no quitter. The *Plain Dealer* wrote, "A Pier 6 lightweight number listed for six, wound up at 1:56 of the fourth, with Mayfield Road's Steve Calla a clean knockout winner over the Broadway sector's Joey Pirrone."

Called the "hottest prelim number of the season," matchmakers scrambled for a rematch. Fight promoter Steve Brickman got both sides to agree to a five-round follow-up fight for the night of May 16. In the second bout, Pirrone again put Calla down early, this time an eight-count with a left hook to the chin in the second round. Cala got up and finished the fight, but Pirrone hung on to win a five-round decision. It may have been Calcavecchio's last fight.

On July 14, 1941, Calcavecchio enlisted in the Army. An article in the Honolulu Star-Bulletin on September 13 stated Calcavecchio was a member of the

8th Field Artillery Division, assigned to Battery B, at the Schofield Barracks on the Island of Oahu. Less than three months later came the sneak attack on Pearl Harbor by the Japanese. Calcavecchio survived the strafing and bombing on his barracks. When he was discharged from the Army on May 21, 1942, the paperwork stated he had a "nervous disability." In March 1947, he was employed at Thompson Products, Inc., the forerunner of TRW, Inc.

On Saturday night, March 15, 1947, Amato and Calcavecchio were out shooting dice together at the Midway Café, at 12308 Mayfield Road[121] in Little Italy. Among the other players was Otto Ignatius Lombardo, the 21-year-old son of Joseph Lombardo, a popular local grocer. He came from a large family and his six siblings were well liked throughout the neighborhood. But Otto was known to be a bully. Despite his father describing him as "a good boy," Otto had a darker side, besides just being a bully. He was arrested in July 1945 for raping a 16-year-old girl in Cleveland Heights. The charge was later reduced to "contributing to the delinquency of a minor."

Calcavecchio was aware of Lombardo's reputation first hand, having been kicked in the balls by him a year earlier and threatened; Amato was about to get his own first-hand knowledge. During the dice game Lombardo lost $20 and became enraged. Nobody knows what instigated the confrontation, but Amato and Lombardo got into an argument. Lombardo ended up punching Amato in the eye and then picked up a knife and threatened him. The *Plain Dealer* reported that, "Friends broke up the fight," but just whose friends they were wasn't indicated.

After the fight Lombardo left about 9:15 and took his wife to the movies. After they arrived home, he borrowed $10 from her and went back out. Lombardo went to the Italian-American Brotherhood Club, at 12024 Mayfield Road. There are two different accounts of what he did there. One says he got involved in another dice game, the other was he played poker. Whatever he was doing, he got lucky because he ended up winning $85. At the same place were Amato and Calcavecchio. After the fight earlier that evening, Calcavecchio went home and picked up a Polish-made semi-automatic pistol, which he purchased in San Francisco from another soldier upon returning from his tour of duty in the Pacific. Now came the big mystery of the night – did the two men go to the Italian-American Brotherhood Club figuring that Lombardo would be there, or was it just coincidence that he showed up. The two of them were there into the early morning hours, taking off with another older man before Lombardo left. The three walked to the corner of Mayfield Road and Murray Hill. After a brief discussion, the older man went on his way. Amato and Calcavecchio stayed at the southwest corner of the intersection knowing that Lombardo would have to pass them on his way home.

About 15 minutes passed since Amato and Calcavecchio arrived at the corner before Lombardo left the club. It was 4:00 a.m. He walked south up the hill headed to 12208 Mayfield Road, the grocery store his father owned. Lombardo and his wife of eight months, lived in an apartment above the store at which he was employed as a clerk. When he got to the corner at Murray Hill, he came face-to-face with Amato and Calcavecchio. Angry words were exchanged before Calcavecchio pulled his gun and fired seven shots at Lombardo, hitting him six times. Amato raced to his family's home at 2023 Murray Hill Road, literally just feet from the corner of Mayfield Road. Within five minutes, Calcavecchio joined him there and spent the night.

People inside the Midway Café, a couple doors down from where Lombardo was killed, heard the shots and ran outside. One person saw the victim on the ground while the gunman fired into him, before racing up Murray Hill following another man. Two witnesses from the café got Lombardo into a car and raced over to nearby Lakeside Hospital of University Hospitals, but it was too late. The young man was dead on arrival. When the coroner, Dr. Samuel R. Gerber, autopsied the body he found two fatal wounds through the head. Lombardo was also hit twice in the left leg, once in the right leg and once in the left hip.

As a crowd started to gather in the street, someone went and told Frank Lombardo, Otto's older brother. He quickly arrived on the scene with a shotgun, ready to seek revenge. Friends of his took the shells from him and left them on the ground, which only served to confuse the police, who believed both assailants had been armed. Police later found the shotgun and when Frank Lombardo was questioned, he told them what happened and how the shells ended up there.

Police recovered the spent cartridges from the semi-automatic at the murder scene. Shortly after daylight, a seven-year-old boy found a Polish nine-millimeter Radon semi-automatic handgun near a garbage can at the rear of 2029 Murray Hill Road, almost next door to the apartment where the Amato family resided. On Tuesday, David C. Cowles, of the police scientific investigation bureau, confirmed that the cartridges found on the street matched with cartridges fired from the Radon semi-automatic.

By Monday, Cleveland Police basically knew who was involved in the shooting of Lombardo and long interrogations were in progress. Both Amato and Calcavecchio claimed they had left the Italian-American Brotherhood Club, with another man, while Lombardo was still there. All three were being held by police. What had police stumped was the role, if any, of the "52-year-old man" who had accompanied Amato and Calcavecchio out of the club and over to the corner of Mayfield and Murray Hill that morning. The *Plain Dealer* wrote:

A second man held for questioning is an ex-bootlegger, 52, believed to have operated the crap game where the fight occurred. Up to a late hour this man would not even tell police his name, although they know him well. He was once accused of murder, and once during the prohibition era he was shot in a bootleg feud. On that occasion he would not name his assailant. Police searched his home, found two revolvers, ammunition and a blackjack. Still he would not talk.

It turned out to be a tense few days in the Little Italy district. Detective Inspector Charles O. Nevel assigned the entire detective squad to the case. With the Lombardo family being well liked and respected in the neighborhood, police feared a "wholesale outbreak of violence" on the hill, with vendettas to follow. He then asked famed Detective Lieutenant Charles Cavolo, now with the auto bureau, for his assistance due to his deep ties to the community. Cavolo quickly realized that even though detectives correctly suspected that the identity of the killers was no secret in the neighborhood, the prevailing sentiment was "You stay out of it, we'll settle it ourselves."

Cavolo gave credit to Detectives Lawrence W. Doran and George Gackowski for achieving the first break in the case. On Tuesday night, after 11 straight hours of "sullen silence," Amato confessed his role and claimed that nobody else was involved other than the "triggerman," who he refused to name. He told them the "52-year-old man" had departed from the corner before Lombardo arrived. At the end of the interrogation, Amato told the two detectives, "Now you know all the facts. Go ask my mother who came home with me." When detectives questioned Amato's mother, Angela, she told them that Steve Calcavecchio, had spent the night there.

When he was told initially of Amato's confession, Calcavecchio shrugged his shoulders and continued to remain silent. On Thursday afternoon, Cavolo again questioned Calcavecchio, who this time confessed to him. He told the lieutenant about the fight that occurred a year earlier, and then about Lombardo punching Amato at the dice game. He said when they met at the corner of Mayfield and Murray Hill that morning, "angry words were exchanged." That's when Calcavecchio pulled the pistol and began firing. He told Cavolo, "He was too enraged to remember how many shots he fired." Late Thursday, first-degree murder warrants were obtained for the two men and Detective Lieutenant David E. Kerr, head of the homicide squad, and Charles Cavolo made the arrests. Kerr told reporters, "Conspiracy and pre-meditation were evident on the part of both Calcavecchio and Amato throughout the night," thus justifying the first-degree murder charges. The county grand jury indicted the men on March 31.

Otto Lombardo's body was taken to the S.A. Conti & Son funeral home at 2110 Murray Hill Road.[122] On Thursday, March 20, the funeral service was held at Holy Rosary Catholic Church, where 500 people attended. The funeral procession was led to nearby Lake View Cemetery by three truckloads of wreaths and flowers. Otto's mother Frances fainted at the gravesite.

Amato and Calcavecchio would be tried separately for the killing. The murder trial of Calcavecchio began on Monday, June 16, in Common Pleas Court before Judge Charles J. McNamee. Assistant Cuyahoga County Prosecutor John J. Mahon, handled the case for the state; the defendant was represented by Stephen M. Young and Gerard Pilliod. Jury selection was completed on Monday and the panel, six men and six women, was taken to the site of the murder in Little Italy that afternoon.

On Tuesday, opening statements were made by each side. During the police investigation it was brought out during the questioning of Frank Lombardo that his younger brother Otto had once threatened to kill Calcavecchio, and that he often used a gun to kill rats behind the store on the block, which included his father's grocery store. The defense attorneys used these statements to contend that their client "shot a notorious gun-toter in self-defense.

The key witness for the state was William Amato. He made for a reluctant, but not hostile witness. Prosecutor Mahon dragged out of him that he knew Calcavecchio had a gun on him as they stood together that morning at the corner of Mayfield and Murray Hill Roads, admitting he had seen it in his pocket after entering the Italian-American Brotherhood Club. At the corner, he testified that he saw Lombardo "come at Calcavecchio, swearing and reaching for his pocket." When he heard the first shot, he got scared and ran home. Calcavecchio followed, arriving in four or five minutes, and stayed all night. During cross-examination, Amato admitted to lying to police and holding out for two days before confessing his role in the murder of Lombardo.

When Calcavecchio took the stand on Wednesday, he told the court Lombardo was a bully and he was scared that Otto would kill him. He repeated that Lombardo had come at him at the corner that night reaching for his back pocket. Although no weapon was found, Calcavecchio was quick to point out Lombardo had grabbed a knife during the earlier encounter with Amato.

After a trial of three days, the jury took eight hours to reach a verdict. The newspaper wrote, "A middle-of-the-road minority in the jury held out for second-degree murder and won its argument." After the verdict was announced at 6:00 p.m., Judge McNamee called Calcavecchio before the bench and asked if he had anything to say before sentence was announced:

Calcavecchio: I was fighting for my life.

McNamee: Have you anything else to say?

Calcavecchio: I didn't know what I was doing.

McNamee sentenced him to life in prison, which meant, on a second-degree murder conviction, Calcavecchio could be paroled in ten years. Attorneys Young and Pilliod must have been grateful. They announced no motion for a new trial, or any appeals would be made.

The second trial, for William Amato, did not take place until October 3. This one was held before Common Pleas Judge Samuel H. Silbert. Defense counsel was the same, but this time the state was represented by Assistant County Prosecutor Thomas V. Moore. It was a short trial.

Steve Calcavecchio was brought in from the Ohio Penitentiary and testified as a defense witness, during which he accepted full blame for the murder. After just one-hour of deliberations, the jury returned with a not guilty verdict. Amato jumped out of his chair and headed for the jury box until defense attorneys subdued him and told him to await Judge Silbert's discharge decree. Because Calcavecchio had gone to Amato's home after the shooting, a charge of harboring a felon could be made against Amato, but the prosecutor chose not to.

On July 9, 1957, the now 37-year-old Calcavecchio was granted parole. He was released from prison on August 22. On December 27, 1988, Steve Calcavecchio passed away at the age of 69. In the death notice he was also listed as "Calla," the last name his son had taken. Ironically, Calcavecchio traveled the same path Otto Lombardo had in death. The funeral home was now the Conti-Vitantonio Funeral Home, the service was held at Holy Rosary Church, and interment was at Lake View Cemetery.

As for William Amato, after his acquittal, he felt the urge to get out of town; perhaps he needed to leave for "health" reasons. In the mid-1940s, Anthony "Tony" Milano had established a residence in Los Angeles. During the time West Coast mobster Mickey Cohen was in Cleveland, he and Milano had become friends. In Cleveland, Milano operated the Italian-American Brotherhood Club. It's quite possible that Amato knew Milano through the club or from the neighborhood and sought out some career advice from him. Whatever the case, Amato soon became a resident of Los Angeles, California.

It wouldn't take long for Amato's name to appear in another newspaper, this time the Los Angeles Daily News. On May 4, 1949, Amato was one of six men arrested for suspicion of robbery during a vice raid at a pool hall at West 3rd Street and Lucas Avenue in Los Angeles. One of the men arrested, Joseph Anton Kaleel, was a gambling associate of Mickey Cohen. According to the article, while sitting in the "jug," the men played "coy," covering their faces with their hands or handkerchiefs when any newspaper photographers ventured near. One used a newspaper to fashion a mask with two eye holes in it.

In addition to the suspicion of robbery pinch, police records dating back to 1948, showed Amato with arrests for burglary, assault with a deadly weapon, and at least ten arrests on gambling or bookmaking charges. The Los Angeles Times reported these arrests:

- 1949 bookmaking, sentenced to three months in the L.A. County Jail

- 1961 bookmaking, sentenced to one year in the L.A. County Jail

- 1963 assault with a deadly weapon, given one-year probation

- 1963, bookmaking, fined $350

- 1964, bookmaking in San Gabriel, sentenced to 10 days in jail and fined $50

- 1964, gambling in Los Angeles, sentenced to six months' probation

By 1965, it seemed like Amato's best days were behind him. One report described him as a "Big-time bookie in the early 1950s" but in the mid-1960s he was only a "minor operator." In September 1968, Amato was working for a brewery on an "on-call" basis, three days a week. He had no telephone at home and had to run out to find a pay phone when he needed to make a call. That was the case on the night of September 23 when he left his home at 12360 Riverside Drive to call someone. Within minutes of him leaving his apartment, a little before 7:00 p.m., he was dead. Amato's 1963 white Thunderbird was found on the street corner of Huston Street and Bellingham Avenue, just a few blocks from his apartment. Amato was found sprawled in the front passenger seat with a bullet wound in the back of his head. Nobody in the neighborhood heard a shot fired, so chances are the fatal bullet was fired elsewhere before his killers parked the car and left. The belief was Amato knew the people he let into his car. There was no identification on the body, he was identified from the car's registration and then confirmed by fingerprints.

William Amato was buried in Holy Sepulcher Cemetery a few days after his murder. In death, another mystery arose. On the Find-A-Grave website for Biagio (William Sam) Amato, is a note stating, "He married Dorothy Sue Webb on February 24, 1965 in Nevada. They had three children during their marriage." That would have meant the couple had three children between February 1965 and September 1968. The children's names were marked "private" on the site. The website also indicated that Webb lived from 1932 to 1971. On the Ancestry.com website, however, it states that on February 24, 1965, William S. Amato married Sybil Milissa Totman in Nevada, not Webb. In support this, the *Los Angeles Times* report on his murder states, "Detectives went to the Amato apartment and informed his wife, Sybil, of his death."

Jack Gotch, an investigator for the District Attorney's Office speculated that Amato was killed by someone he knew because he wasn't paying off on the bets. He also stated, "He operated alone, but there could have been a gangland connection." This seems apparent from the FBI informant that introduced Julius Petro to Nick Licata, on October 7, 1968, just two weeks after the murder. The Los Angeles Mafia boss wanted Petro to find out who murdered Amato. Ironically, three months later, Petro's life ended the same way Amato's did; being shot in the back of the head by someone sitting in the back seat of a car while he was in the front seat. The killer being someone he knew.

In February 1969, Los Angeles detectives arrested two men – Jack C. Fronte and Luigi Gelfuso – for the murder of Amato. Police believed an unpaid loan-sharking debt was behind it. The two men were described as "gangland enforcers." The police investigation revealed Amato owed $25,000 to either a New York or Los Angeles loan-shark. Both men were charged with the murder and held in jail without bond. On April 15, the case came to trial before California Supreme Court Judge Adolph Alexander. As the prosecutor was presenting the case to the jury, defense attorney Daniel Busby requested a dismissal of the charge due to insufficient evidence. The judge responded he could not do that under the California Penal Code, but then made the comment, "If the jury finds the defendants guilty, he would set the verdict aside." The District Attorney's Office then agreed to waive the jury and the case became a court trial. After evidence was presented, Judge Alexander ruled it was insufficient to convict and Fronte and Gelfuso were found innocent.

Joseph C. Ilacqua

During his long criminal career, he was known to the police and his associates as "Joe I." Joseph Charles Ilacqua earned his first rap sheet entry in 1949, when he was arrested for grand larceny. He gained his first notoriety in early 1953. In the wake of Julius Petro's 25-year prison sentence for the Warren robbery of assistant bank manager Charles J. Foley, the police were cracking down on the remaining members of Petro's nefarious gang of Collinwood yeggs. At the time, police believed there were 15 to 18 members or associates of the gang that were not in prison. In February 1953, Ilacqua was ratted out by William "Red" Miller as having participated in the six-man safe-cracking crew that broke into the Clemmer Construction Company in Akron (See Chapter Ten: Philip Aliberti biography). Before Ilacqua could be indicted in that case, he was arrested and held in Cleveland for possession of burglary tools. He was later convicted of both crimes and served three years in the Ohio State Reformatory.

"Joe I" next made news following a raid at a 1950s version of the Prohibition Era "speakeasy" on Superior Avenue. Five days after the raid, Ilacqua turned himself into police and admitted he was the third operator of the illegal bar. During the raid, on January 19, 1958, Ilacqua "ducked out a rear door," with three bottles of whiskey, as state liquor enforcement agents entered the illegal bar early on a Sunday morning. Ilacqua and Mrs. Sue Bonarrigo were charged with the sale of illegal liquor. Sue Bonarrigo was the former Susan Mary D'Alessio, the younger sister of Petro cohort Anthony Paul D'Alessio. She would one day become Mrs. Joseph C. Ilacqua.

On October 19, 1961, a "neatly dressed, good looking" man knocked on the door of Dr. Otto W. Blum at his fashionable West Side home at 11530 Edgewater Drive. Mrs. Blum opened the door to find a caller wearing a dark hat, sunglasses and carrying a briefcase. The man claimed he was delivering "special medicine" that was ordered by the doctor. Once inside, the 55-year-old doctor's wife was attacked by the man; hit in the head with a telephone, and kicked before being gagged with a towel. While this was going on, a second man entered and began searching for jewelry and money. The Blum's 65-year-old gardener and a housemaid were also given a beating by the robbers, as a third man stood watch outside the home. The take was estimated at $10,000.

The robbery had eerie similarities to one that occurred the previous month, at the home of Sam D. Magid. Sam and his wife Hilda were active in affairs related to the Jewish community in Cleveland Heights. Magid was at one time president of Yale Auto Parts, Co., he was now associated with Realty Operating Co., 1836 Euclid Avenue. Magid was also co-owner of Hotel Sorrento in Miami Beach, Florida, which he advertised heavily during the winter months for people to come and spend their vacations for just $11 daily per person. On September 14, a man telephoned the Magid at 3477 Severn Road. The caller spoke with Hilda and asked if he could drop off a lease for Sam at the house, explaining it would be easier than having to drive it downtown. Ten minutes later the doorbell rang. Hilda opened the door to a man in a suit, carrying a briefcase. He told Mrs. Magid he was the man who just phoned her. No sooner had she let him in that he drew a gun and told her, "If you cooperate you won't get hurt."

The men bound Hilda's hands behind her back with clothesline and forced her to lie on the living room floor with her face in the rug. The intruder then opened the door to let two accomplices enter. When asked where she kept her furs and jewelry, she wisely told them. While one man guarded her, the other two ransacked the bedrooms on the second floor, breaking open locked closets and a cedar chest.

Then the situation got frightening. When the men were unable to find a diamond bracelet that they obviously had prior knowledge about, which was purchased for her by Sam for $10,000, they threatened to kill Hilda before she disclosed where it was hidden. In addition, the robbers pulled two diamond rings from her fingers, took $200 from her purse, and took diamond cuff links and a wristwatch, which belonged to Sam. The furs and jewels taken from the Magid home had a value estimated at $50,000.

Just days after the robbery at Dr. Blum's, the wife of Irwin "Red" Mason paid a visit to the Akron Police Department. For reasons unknown, she revealed the names of the members of the Blum robbery crew, and claimed that while her husband was the mastermind of the crime he did not participate in the actual assault and theft. On October 27, police arrested attorney Lawrence A. Krasny. The father of two young children graduated from Miami University in Ohio before attending Western Reserve University Law School and Cleveland Marshall Law School, from which he received his law degree; he passed the Ohio bar exam in 1959. Krasny hung his shingle in the Leader Building at Superior Avenue and East 6th Street downtown and lived in a home in Cleveland Heights. That same night, 28-year-old Howard Green, employed as an appliance salesman at Green's TV & Furniture Store, owned by his father, at 880 Hough Avenue,[123] was arrested at his East Cleveland home. In 1960, Green was found guilty of assaulting a police officer. Both men were placed in a police line-up at Central Police Station and identified by Mrs. Blum, the gardener, and the housemaid, as well as a few neighbors of the Blums.

When police searched Krasny's automobile, they discovered a dark hat, a handgun, sunglasses, and a briefcase. In his Leader Building office, they found a notepad with the name "O.W. Blum" written on it. When questioned about the notepad, Krasny denied knowing the doctor. Police noticed that Krasny's hand still "bore tooth marks." Mrs. Blum said she had bitten him while he was gagging her with the towel.

The two men were also placed in line-ups viewed by several victims of other recent robberies. None of these victims could place the two at the scene of these other crimes. Police believed, however, that Krasny was involved in the $50,000 robbery of jewels and furs from the home of Sam Magid, back on September 14. Police were told Krasny had shown the stolen items to "Red" Mason and informed him they were from the Magid robbery. Mrs. Mason told police she was introduced to Krasny at a restaurant, where she and her husband were dining. By now, Cleveland police were looking for "Red" Mason, who was thought to have fled to Hartford, Connecticut, where his first wife resided.

On October 30, Municipal Judge Hugh A. Corrigan released Green and Krasny after reducing their bails from $20,000 to $10,000. This came after their lawyers convinced the judge their clients had ties to the community and were "unlikely" to leave town. On November 9, Krasny pleaded not-guilty to charges of armed robbery, assault with a dangerous weapon, aggravated assault, and receiving stolen property. The last charge involved the robbery at the home of Sam Magid. Krasny and Magid both lived in Cleveland Heights less than a mile from one another. Krasny was represented by attorney John P. Butler. Green also pleaded not-guilty to the first three charges, which involved only the robbery at the Otto Blum residence.

From there, things only got worse for Krasny. Before the month was out, Krasny was named in two additional indictments totaling 56 more charges. The first was for two counts each of forging and cashing 27 American Express money orders, stolen during the burglary of an IGA Supermarket in North Eaton, Ohio,[124] during February 1961. The second indictment was for two counts of grand larceny by trick.

Meanwhile, Irwin "Red" Mason had come under heavy police scrutiny. It wasn't the first time. Since the early 1950s, Mason was a "floating poker game operator." His customers would start play on a Friday night and continue straight through to Sunday evening. Lieutenant Martin Cooney recalled years later, Mason would always have three or four women at his games. In fact, it was a woman from Shaker Heights who got Mason in trouble for the first time back in 1954. She told police her son lost $25,000 at one of Mason's games at a Bratenahl estate he rented on Lake Shore Boulevard. When Mason's landlord, a retired priest, found out about the poker game he evicted him. Over the next three years Mason was arrested some 40 times for gambling. In October 1957, after raiding a second floor apartment at 13711 Kinsman Road, police arrested Mason after he climbed out a window and was found sliding down a tree. By 1958, Mason's games had been chased "all over greater Cleveland."

After the Krasny apprehension, police arrested Mason twice in mid-November, both times in response to statements made by his wife. Following the first arrest, he was released after posting a $1,000 bond. Mason was hauled in again a short time later and questioned about his wife's claim that Krasny had shown the two of them stolen furs and jewelry from the home of Sam Magid. Mason made a statement confirming what his wife said about being shown the stolen goods by Krasny. The statement could not have made Krasny's wife, Marcia happy. Mason claimed this viewing took place in the apartment of Krasny's girlfriend. Krasny, who was arrested on November 22 for questioning about the stolen money orders, was already in jail. Officials from the jail brought the two men together, and Mason identified Krasny and made the accusation about the apartment encounter in front of him. While all this finger-pointing was going on, a "third suspect" in the Blum home invasion turned himself over to police on November 25, saying he heard police were looking for him in connection with the robbery.

On February 16, 1962, standing with his new counsel, attorney Fred W. Garmone, Lawrence Krasny pled guilty to armed robbery, two aggravated assault charges and receiving stolen property. Charges against Krasny for forging and passing the stolen money orders were dropped in the plea agreement. Common Pleas Judge Thomas J. Parrino cancelled the $10,000 bond and remanded him to the County Jail until sentencing. On March 30, Howard Green pleaded guilty before Judge Parrino to armed robbery and aggravated assault. On the recommendation of the assistant county prosecutor, the charges of receiving stolen property in the Sam Magid case, and an apartment robbery in Shaker Heights, were dismissed due to insufficient evidence.

On April 10, Judge Parrino sentenced Krasny and Green to 11 to 30 years each in the Ohio Penitentiary. After Assistant County Prosecutor Daniel DeRocco recited a list of the offenses committed by the two men, Parrino declared, "This court has never heard a story of lawlessness and viciousness such as this." He told Krasny that he had degraded his profession, disgraced his family, and was destroying his own life. Krasny asked to be sent to the reformatory in Mansfield out of concerns of being viewed as an informer, "among the hardened lot at the penitentiary." Back in November 1961, after Mason confronted Krasny in the County Jail and ratted him out regarding the Magid robbery, Krasny got even by telling police about Mason's role in the North Eaton burglary involving the theft of the American Express money orders; thus, preserving the age old adage about "No honor among thieves." Judge Parrino had the final say, however, and had "no qualms" about his decision to send Krasny to the penitentiary, declaring, "That is what he deserved." On May 3, less than a month after Krasny was sent away to prison, his wife Marcia sued for divorce in Common Pleas Court after eight years of marriage. The charges were neglect and extreme cruelty. She asked for custody of both children.

Next up was "Red" Mason. Arrested and bonded out twice in November, by March he was on the run. Wanted for questioning for his involvement in the stolen money orders that Krasny had exposed, Mason fled the state and was captured by the FBI in Denver on April 9 with help from the local police there. His wife was arrested by Akron police for forging signatures on some of the stolen money orders. She had pled guilty on April 1 and was expected to testify against her husband. A question arose about her ability to do that since their marriage did not involve a formal ceremony. Prosecutors pondered that if a common law marriage existed, then "Red" Mason had remarried without being divorced from his first wife, meaning he could also face bigamy charges.

On April 11, Mason, still out in Denver, was indicted by the Cuyahoga County Grand Jury for forging signatures on nine stolen money orders, as well as receiving stolen property worth $15,000 from the home of Sam Magid. Incredibly, shortly after Mason's arrest in Denver, he was freed on bond there. On May 3, Mason surrendered to Detective Sergeant Norman Ferris and Detective William Mueller in front of the Criminal Courts building on East 21st Street. Ferris told reporters that Mason, who drove in from Denver, had not technically jumped bond because he was not actually due in court until May 4.

On October 29, 1962, Mason pleaded guilty before Common Pleas Judge Daniel H. Wasserman to forging names on the nine stolen money orders worth $750. Judge Wasserman cancelled his $5,000 bail and remanded him to County Jail to await sentencing. The assistant county prosecutor recommended the dismissal of nine counts against Mason for passing the money orders and another count for receiving stolen jewels and furs from the home of Sam Magid. No one was ever brought to trial for the armed robbery of Hilda Magid at her home. Only Krasny was given time for receiving stolen property. On November 9, Wasserman sentenced Mason to one to 20 years in the Ohio Penitentiary. Mason's counsel asked the judge for probation for his client so he could relocate to California. Wasserman denied the bizarre request declaring he was not sending Ohio's "troubles" to another state; perhaps because he was concerned about getting theirs back in return.[125]

With Krasny, Green and Mason off to prison, the focus returned to the "third suspect." On March 7, the "third suspect" was finally charged. Joseph Ilacqua was indicted for taking part in the robbery at the home of Dr. Otto Blum, and a second robbery at the apartment of Adolph Weisfeld at 16727 Van Aken Boulevard. A year after the other three were serving time, "Joe I" was still out on a $50,000 bond with no trial date in sight.

On April 23, 1963, the Halle Bros. Company Shaker Square store was burglarized for $9,000 in cash and $4,000 in checks. Detectives investigating the break-in were suspicious of how the burglar alarms at the rear entrance and safe were bypassed. The detectives suspected the security company's involvement and began questioning employees of the Morse Signal Service. On April 29, police arrested William Suveges,[126] who immediately "spilled his guts." He told them his motivation for the crime was to obtain money for his youngest child's medical expenses for treatment of a congenital heart ailment. Suveges said he was promised a $3,000 share of the take, but had received nothing.

Charged with burglary and larceny, he implicated three men: Joseph Ilacqua, who the newspapers identified as Suveges's "step-brother," John B. Conte and Jesse Lynn. Ilacqua was out on bond in the Dr. Blum robbery case; Conte was awaiting trial in Federal court for transporting stolen goods; Lynn had fled town, but was apprehended in the city of California, Missouri. By the next day, when all four men were indicted by a Cuyahoga County Grand Jury, only "Joe I" was not in custody. Ilacqua was later arrested, and by the end of the year the Halle Bros. burglary trial finally began. On December 19, all three men were convicted of three counts each of burglary and larceny. William Suveges pleaded guilty and was placed on probation. Common Pleas Judge Bernard Friedman sentenced each man to three terms of one-to-15-years to be served concurrently. While Conte and Lynn headed off to the penitentiary, Ilacqua went back to the County Jail to await trial for his role in the Dr. Blum robbery and the Adolph Weisfeld apartment robbery, both of which took place more than two years earlier. There he sat and waited...and waited.

Another 15 months passed. Then in April 1965, Ilacqua's attorney, Moses Krislov, subpoenaed Cuyahoga County Prosecutor John Corrigan to testify in Common Pleas Court as to why his client was still being held without being brought to trial. Krislov wanted the 1961 robbery indictments against his client dismissed on the grounds that Ilacqua was denied his constitutional rights to a speedy trial. Assistant County Prosecutor Robert H. Hanna told Common Pleas Judge August Pryatel that neither Krislov nor Ilacqua had ever requested a speedy trial. On April 21, Judge Pryatel denied the motion to dismiss. The judge declared the Ohio and U.S. Constitution guarantees the right to a speedy trial only if the accused demands one. The next day, Judge Hugh A. Corrigan, presiding judge of the Criminal Branch of Common Pleas Court, ruled that all delay requests, regardless of being made by the defense or the prosecutor, must be approved by the presiding judge, in court, and with the accused present. Prior to this, attorneys on either side could obtain a continuance by requesting delays from the office of the court's assignment commissioner.

Prosecutors here were currently facing another problem that could affect many of their prior cases, including the latest conviction of Ilacqua. In late April 1965, the U.S. Supreme Court ruled, in a 6 to 2 decision, that judges and prosecutors were barred from making comments to juries regarding a defendant's constitutional right not to testify. In the ruling, Justice William O. Douglas declared, "Comment on the refusal to testify...is a penalty imposed by courts for exercising a constitutional privilege." Prosecutors across the country were outraged by the decision and claimed the high court was bending over backwards to protect criminals. Ohio was one of six states that permitted a judge or prosecutor to comment to the jury about a defendant's failure to testify. In May, the Court of Appeals had already reversed one decision made in Cuyahoga County Common Pleas Court involving William Pollard, who was sentenced to 20 to 40 years for violating Ohio's narcotics law. The trial record showed that the assistant county prosecutor in that case brought up Pollard's refusal to testify during his summation. Pollard's co-defendant had testified and both men were found guilty. Pollard's court-appointed defense counsel, James R. Willis was aware of the high court's consideration of a defendant's right not to testify when he filed his appeal, and the Appellate Court had no choice but to reverse Pollard's conviction; his co-defendant's conviction was upheld.[127]

Another case the Ohio Supreme Court was considering an appeal on was that of Joseph Ilacqua for his December 1963 conviction for the Halle Bros. store robbery. The appeal was on the grounds that prosecutors reminded jurors that Ilacqua did not testify during the trial. Both co-defendants John Conte and Jesse Lynn had taken the stand. County Prosecutor John Corrigan was concerned about the Superior Court making its ruling retroactive, which could tie up the court with retrials for years. Corrigan declared that the high court had overreached its authority. He stated, "The Supreme Court in the last few years seems more intent on preserving the rights of criminals than the rights of the average, law abiding citizen. The thief, the burglar, the murderer, the rapist are the ones being protected by the court, but the court does not seem to realize that fact. Who is to protect the citizen?"

Nearly a year passed, in February 1966, "Joe I" was granted a new trial in the Halle Bros. burglary case. Judge Harry Jaffe set bond for Ilacqua at $100,000, which he was unable to produce. The newspapers reported that in 26 months of appeals, both the Common Pleas Court and the Appellate Court had refused to set bail due to the fact Ilacqua had jumped bail in 1962 after being indicted for the Blum and Weisfeld robberies. Ilacqua's time served in the County Jail, the newspapers pointed out, would not count toward his sentence if he were to be convicted again in a new trial for the Halle Bros. burglary.

On July 7, 1966, a *Plain Dealer* headline announced, "Record-Holder Joe I Is Undergoing Retrial." In going to trial again for the Halle Bros. burglary, the newspapers proclaimed Ilacqua was a two-way record-holder in Cuyahoga County. The first record was that no prisoner had a longer stay in Cuyahoga County Jail than Ilacqua, who had currently been there from December 1963 to July 1966, so far. "Joe I's" second record was that he was the first man in Cuyahoga County to be retried due to the recent U.S. Supreme Court ruling regarding the mention of a defendant's refusal to testify. During his lengthy stay in the County Jail, Ilacqua worked as a helper in the kitchen.

The Halle Bros. burglary retrial took place in the courtroom of Common Pleas Judge Francis J. Talty. Assistant County Prosecutor George J. Moscarino, who had also prosecuted the first case, represented the state and Robert W. Jones of the Public Defender's Office represented Ilacqua. During the first day of testimony, the states key witness was William Suveges. Under questioning from Prosecutor Moscarino, Suveges said the Halle Bros. burglary was planned in his apartment with the other three men present. Under cross-examination, however, Suveges admitted that after his arrest he was able to identify police mug shots of John Conte and Jesse Lynn, but not one of Ilacqua.

On July 8, Jesse Lynn was brought in from prison to testify against his former burglary partner. He told the court that because of "Joe I's" broad shoulders, he was used to "boost" Lynn up in order for him to climb through a nine-foot high window in order to break into the store. Lynn said that once inside, he removed cash and checks from the store's safe, which had been left unlocked by Suveges. Afterwards, $9,000 in cash was divided among Conte, Ilacqua and himself, at "Joe I's" home. John Conte did not testify against Ilacqua.

After a six-day trial, a jury of six men and six woman deliberated for three hours on July 13 before handing "Joe I" a third record. He was now the first man in Cuyahoga County to be reconvicted after being granted a retrial because of the U.S. Supreme Court's recent ruling. Judge Talty sentenced Ilacqua to a term of 2-to-22-years in prison. The newspapers made it clear that Ilacqua still had two armed robbery charges from 1961 to answer for. If he ever did, there was no record of it in the newspapers.

The three-plus years "Joe I" spent in prison did nothing to alter his career path. On December 3, 1970, Ilacqua was a member of an eight-man robbery crew that hijacked a piggy-back trailer loaded with what the men believed to be pharmaceuticals. The rig was bound for a Revco Drug Store distribution center from the Erie-Lackawanna Railway Company yard at 3030 East 55th Street at 7:30 in the morning. The men then drove the trailer, belonging to the Rock Island Lines, to the Lester Tavens & Company at 7711 Woodland Avenue, which was owned by one of the robbery crew.

By 8:15 a.m., "Joe I" was breaking the seal on the door of the trailer, which contained 31,000 pounds of Pepto-Bismol. The gang was going to need as much of the upset stomach and nausea medicine as they could consume because in addition to the stomach medicine, the trailer contained the ultimate belly ache – five FBI agents. During the ensuing arrest of seven of the gang members, one of the men, Ronald H. Sullenberger resisted and was shot by one of the agents. He was taken to St. Luke's Hospital, where he quickly recovered. In addition to Ilacqua, Sullenberger and Lester Tavens, agents arrested Charles A. Setzer, a tractor-trailer owner who drove the stolen rig; Phil Christopher, the future "Superthief;" James J. Celeste, listed as unemployed; and Michael J. Ryan, a wig salesman. Later that day, Hilmon R. Akers was arrested at his place of work, the Erie-Lackawanna Railway Terminal. Ilacqua and Setzer were released on $20,000 surety bonds; the rest on $5,000 personal bonds, set by U.S. Commissioner Clifford E. Bruce.

The men were facing interstate theft charges, which carried a maximum sentence of ten years and a $5,000 fine. U.S. Magistrate Jack B. Streepy said the FBI was alerted to the theft and the five "inside" agents were followed to Lester Tavens & Company by several car loads of agents, who assisted in the arrests. On December 15, a Federal Grand Jury indicted all eight men, each on a two-count indictment.

On June 10, 1971, U.S. District Judge Thomas D. Lambros handed down sentences to six of the men who had pleaded guilty. In what the newspapers referred to as split sentences, Ilacqua, Setzer and Sullenberger received six months in prison and five years' probation, due to their prior convictions. The judge said any violation of their probation would result in the men being returned to prison to serve the remaining nine and a half years of their sentence. Celeste, Christopher and Ryan all received three years' probation. Both Akers and Tavens pled not guilty and were awaiting trial.

By the time "Joe I" was heard from again it was early 1975, when the business of crime in Cleveland was booming. By July 4 of that year, 11 bombs had been set off in Cleveland, causing at least two deaths. The first fatality occurred on February 27 in Beachwood, a suburb located on Cuyahoga County's southeast side.

Richard H. Moss and his brother Stanley K. Moss were no strangers to crime. In 1966 both brothers were being sought by the FBI for the "theft, sale and transportation" of 585 shares of Reynolds Metal Company stock, valued at $60,000, taken from the law office of attorney James B. Ceris in Ambridge, Pennsylvania, on May 7. Stanley, eight years older than Richard, was arrested by FBI agents on November 19; Richard turned himself in days later. On November 23, both men pleaded innocent to the crime before U.S. District Court Judge Girard E. Kalbfleisch, who released the brothers on a $2,000 bond. Stanley was quickly taken before U.S. Commissioner Clifford E. Bruce and charged with forging the endorsement of another man on a $25 U.S. Savings Bond.

In January 1968, Assistant U.S. Attorney Robert J. Rotatori accused the men of trying to sell $31,000 of the stolen stock after forging the name of the real owner during a hearing in U.S. District Court, where the brothers and a third man pleaded guilty. On April 19, Federal Judge Thomas D. Lambros sentenced the brothers to five years of probation and ordered them to make full restitution.

In the years following the conviction, the Moss brothers seemingly got their act together. They ran M&G Enterprises at 3252 Lorain Avenue, an importing business. Richard Moss must have been successful because by the mid-1970s he owned an $80,000 home in fashionable Beachwood; his vehicles included a 1973 black Lincoln Continental and a 1974 Corvette. Along the way he married Roberta Strawn Golden, a beautiful and talented woman who graced the Cleveland Orchestra's violin section from 1962 to 1984.

Around 9:00 on the morning of April 27, 1975, Moss went into the attached garage where he noticed a "multi-colored" package on the front seat of the Lincoln. He picked up the package, walked around the car and called out to Roberta, who was in the kitchen, asking her what was in the package. Suddenly the package exploded in his hands. As Roberta ran screaming from the house, neighbors rushed to the scene to help. The 41-year-old Moss lay dead six feet from the rear of the car. The blast caused damage to the ceiling and door frame of the garage, and broke windows in the home next door.

During the ensuing investigation, police revealed that Moss and his brother were involved in several businesses in addition to their importing company. One newspaper reported they were involved in vending machines and had recently tried to venture into pinball machine activities. The result of that effort caused both brothers to receive numerous threatening telephone calls warning them to stay out. The Department of Justice began investigating the bombing as a possible link to the Northern Ohio Bank, which had gone defunct less than two weeks earlier. One of Moss's business partners was Harvey Rieger, an attorney who lived in Pepper Pike, another fashionable and wealthy suburb of Cleveland, located next to Beachwood. A former director of the Northern Ohio Bank told investigators that loans were made to Rieger and confirmed that Moss was a partner in a venture partly financed by the bank. One newspaper report stated that Federal investigators were looking into companies Moss was associated with when police found certificates of deposits and worthless stock was used for collateral to obtain loans from the bank. Attorney Rieger was of prime interest after it was reported that several cashier's checks, he had converted from his account, resulted in there being no money to cover them. The bank's failure was blamed on poor management of loans.

Law enforcement could find no link to the killing of Moss and his business interests, nor to the March 11, 1974, murder of Detroit businessman Harvey Leach, whose company was also connected to failed loans involving the Northern Ohio Bank. The 33-year-old Leach was believed to have been knocked out and then had his jugular vein cut with either an axe or a hatchet, before being thrown in the trunk of his Lincoln Continental Mark IV, which was left in the parking lot of a Southfield, Michigan, office building. The murder took place just one day before Leach was to get married. During the investigation into Leach's death, one of the names that surfaced was that of Detroit Mafia leader Pete Licavoli. Two other names that came up in the investigation of the Northern Ohio Bank loans were Michael W. Frato[128] and Dominick E. Bartone.

With the Northern Ohio Bank unable to provide any promising leads to the murder, and with the underworld connections, which had popped up in both Cleveland and Detroit, the investigators soon were looking at links to organized crime. In 1972, a new business was opening in the Cleveland area called Slush King. The new concern advertised it was looking for people who could make a minimum investment of $1,625 for a new business "with a proven success pattern." Sometime before January 1975, Moss was involved in a business that dealt with franchising the machines used in making the flavored crushed ice cones for Slush King. His business associate in the venture was Joseph Ilacqua. The newspaper, when discussing the association, pointed out that Slush King was being investigated. For what, was never mentioned in the article. A *Plain Dealer* article on October 5, 1975, proclaimed, "The business, called Slush King, is under investigation by grand juries in Pennsylvania and New York and a federal grand jury in Cleveland." Despite the alleged investigations, nothing ever tied "Joe I" to the bombing of Richard Moss, whose murder – with no suspects, not even a motive – quickly became a cold case and dropped out of the headlines.

While the incident with Richard Moss was going on, Joe Ilacqua made the news again following the announcement of his involvement in the theft of 1,097 cases of liquor back in January 1975 from the Trans America Freight Lines, Inc. terminal in Parma (See Chapter Ten: Joseph Sanzo biography). During the time police were looking for Ilacqua for the car bombing of Robert Beavers and the planting of a bomb on the porch of Ronald Sullenberger's parent's Lakewood home, another murder came to light.

On September 19, 1975, police in Austintown Township, one of the 14 townships of Mahoning County, found the body of a man who was bound and gagged before being beaten to death and left behind a motel. The body remained unidentified for two days until a Mentor woman reported her husband was missing since September 17. The husband was John B. Conte, one of Ilacqua's accomplices in the Halle Bros. burglary back in April 1963. Conte, who was convicted and incarcerated for other crimes since then, was released from prison in 1972 and was still on a parole that was to continue until 1978. When Conte left home, he told his wife he was going to meet Daniel J. "Danny" Greene to discuss the vending machine business. Police were looking for Greene to question him, but were told he was out of town. They also wanted to question Joseph Gallo, but he was in hiding since the bombing of Danny Greene's Collinwood home / office at 15805 Waterloo Road back in May. The police found themselves 0 for 3 when they wanted to talk to Conte's "close friend" Ilacqua, as he too was in the wind. Police later theorized that Conte was killed in a trailer used by Greene. No one was ever arrested for the murder.

By the fall of 1975, Joe Ilacqua was still on the loose. He was wanted for the January hijacking of the liquor shipment, for which he had already been indicted; the bombing of Robert Beaver's automobile, in which the victim lost his right leg; the planting of the bomb at the Sullenberger home; and for questioning in the murder of his friend and former burglary accomplice, John Conte. Plus, he was still on probation for the infamous Pepto-Bismol hijacking. On October 3, the FBI issued a warning that Ilacqua was armed and dangerous and that anybody seeing him was to notify the police or the FBI immediately. The warning said the 46-year-old Ilacqua was "6 feet 1 and weighs190 pounds. He has graying black hair and brown eyes." The FBI believed he was in northeast Ohio, most likely in the Youngstown area. That weekend in the Sunday *Plain Dealer* "Spotlight" section, reporter Mairy Jayn Woge wrote two long articles, one about Joseph C. Gallo, the other about Joseph C. Ilacqua. The article on "Joe I" listed all the events he was currently wanted for and why. The Gallo story outlined the search for him in regard to the bombing attempt to kill Danny Greene on May 12, 1975.

On March 22, 1976, after more than nine months as a fugitive on the run, Ilacqua was arrested at the Holiday Inn hotel on Rockside Road in Independence, where he had checked in four days earlier. It was reported that an informant tipped off the FBI to his whereabouts. Ilacqua faced Federal Judge Robert Krupansky the next day. Despite the urging of Assistant U.S. Attorney Theodore Gale for a $1.0 million bond, the judge set it at $300,000 and Ilacqua was off to the Lake County Jail.

Just 44 days after his arrest, "Joe I" was facing trial in U.S. District Court in Akron. It was nearly 16 months since the robbery of the liquor from the Stumph Road terminal. Since Ilacqua was only being tried for the theft, government prosecutors were not allowed to mention the car bombing, which cost Beavers his right leg, nor were they allowed to mention the bombing attempt at the parent's home of Ilacqua's accomplice, Ronald Sullenberger. By now Beavers, his wife Diane, and their three children were relocated in the Federal Witness Protection Program. Sullenberger, who was convicted the previous year, was serving time in an unknown location while his family had also been relocated.

Ilacqua was being represented by Paul Mancino, Jr., who argued that having Beavers before the jury would be prejudicial; despite the prosthetic leg, he still walked with a pronounced limp. U.S. District Judge Leroy J. Contie, Jr. handled this issue by bringing Beavers into the courtroom before the jury was seated that morning. During questioning by Assistant U.S. Attorney William J. Edwards, Beavers stated that Ilacqua and four other men brought the tractor trailer containing the stolen liquor to his farm around 12:30 on the night of January 16, 1975. He helped unload it and placed it in his barn. Beavers told Edwards he and his wife dropped off 11 cases of the booze at two East Side suburban night spots, and was paid $80 for his work. Without mentioning the May 23 car bombing, he said he agreed to cooperate with the government a month later after being questioned by the FBI. At the end of his four-hour testimony, Judge Contie said he needed to discuss a legal situation with attorneys from both sides. He used this ploy to excuse the jury so Beavers could leave the courtroom unseen by the jurors.

Ronald Sullenberger was brought in from the prison where he was secretly being held. He testified to helping steal the truck and taking it to the Beavers' Medina farmhouse.

After a four-day trial, Ilacqua was found guilty of conspiracy and possession of $44,000 worth of stolen liquor. Normally, he would be facing a maximum of 15 years in prison and a $15,000 fine. But this is when it got interesting. "Joe I" was about to set another one of those "firsts" he was becoming known for.

Prior to the trial, and unknown to Judge Contie, Prosecutor Edwards and Edwin J. Gale, a government attorney with the Strike Force Against Organized

Crime, filed a sealed petition requesting Contie to impose additional confinement for Ilacqua if convicted. This unusual procedure was required under the Federal Dangerous Special Offender Statute, which allows a judge, for just cause, to increase a sentence by up to 25 years.

The announcement caught Ilacqua and his counsel off guard. Mancino declared he would fight the petition and appeal the case if Contie tried to impose the additional years. "I feel it is unconstitutional in the way things are used," the attorney claimed. "It can be used arbitrarily if you don't like the guy." Judge Contie announced he would hold a separate hearing after he received the probation department's report. At that time, he would determine if an additional sentence should be imposed.

On June 25, 1976, Contie handed down a sentence of ten years to Ilacqua for possession of 1,097 cases of stolen liquor. He also sentenced him to five years for conspiracy, but ordered the sentences to run concurrently. He dismissed the government's motion for additional time, claiming they failed to explain why the prisoner should be considered dangerous. Despite the judge's ruling, Mancino said he would appeal the conviction.

By February 1980, less than five years into his ten-year sentence, Ilacqua was out of prison. On February 24, Ilacqua notified police that his stepson was missing. Three days earlier, Joseph F. Bonarrigo, an employee of Arthur Frank Construction Company, left his Stevenson Road home in Collinwood to visit his wife in the maternity ward at Euclid General Hospital. He never made it.

On Thursday, March 6, police were called to a vacant home at 971 East 79th Street,[129] around 5:15 in the afternoon. In front of the garage lay the body of a man stuffed inside a green plastic garbage bag, a detail that would not escape police attention once they found out who the man was. The body was discovered by a carpenter who was working to refurbish the house, located two blocks south of St. Clair Avenue. The dead man's hands and feet were bound, and he had been shot five times in the head. The decomposing body was identified by fingerprints the next day as Joseph Bonarrigo's.

In 1973, Bonarrigo first came to the public's attention when he was a 22-year-old employee of the Cleveland Division of Streets. On the night of July 23, he was involved in altercation with another driver at the corner of Cliffview and Olympia Roads, just down the block from Bonarrigo's Cliffview Road home. Both men accused each other of running the other off the road, jumping out of their cars with guns in hand, and engaging in a heated argument. The man in the other car, however, was off-duty Cleveland Patrolman Ronald L. Turner, a member of the controversial "Mod Squad," who had a colorful record as a police officer in the city. Weeks earlier, on June 28, Turner and his partner Jerome E. West were in a shootout in which Jose Miquel Rayes was fatally wounded in a house on East 39th Street near Payne Avenue. The shooting was ruled justifiable.

During the July incident, according to Turner, he and a friend were driving north on Cliffview Road about 11:00 p.m., when an automobile driven by Bonarrigo coming south, forced them off the road. Bonarrigo stopped, backed up and then jumped out of his car "waiving a revolver and shouting obscenities." Turner sent his friend running to call police and then got out on the passenger-side of the vehicle to confront Bonarrigo. He said he tried to disarm him, but was struck in the face with the revolver. At this point Turner drew his own revolver and fired several times, hitting Bonarrigo in both legs.

The sequence of events related by Bonarrigo were that both he and Turner jumped out and began an argument that lasted about ten minutes; after which the off-duty officer opened fire. Police found a .22 revolver on the ground about ten feet from where Bonarrigo fell. When asked about this gun, Bonarrigo claimed, "I didn't pull a gun. I don't know where the gun came from. It could belong to Turner's friend. But it was not mine." Bonarrigo was taken to Huron Road Hospital in fair condition. He was arrested and placed under police guard. On July 26, less than 72 hours after the shooting, Chief Police Prosecutor Everett A. Chandler, who a month earlier ruled the killing of Rayes justifiable, exonerated Ron Turner in the wounding of Bonarrigo. At the same time, he dropped a charge of assault and battery against Bonarrigo.

On the night of June 23, 1976, some of the patrons at Guerino's Bar at 15634 Kipling Avenue ambled outside, perhaps to catch a breeze coming down the street on this early summer night. The two-story brick structure was tucked away between residential houses in the South Collinwood neighborhood. According to reports, about eight or nine men began to get "rowdy and loud." Police were soon called. When Sergeant John Hageman, Jr. and Patrolman Richard L. Putney arrived, they figured the easiest course of action was just to tell the men to go back inside the bar. Instead of obeying orders, the men responded with obscenities and a fight ensued. Hageman called for reinforcements.

The troops quickly arrived and at least half of the men from the bar fled. Police arrested Kenneth Argie, Joseph Bonarrigo, Alfred S. "Allie" Calabrese, and Glen Pauley, charging them with aggravated rioting and disorderly conduct. It took a year before the case was heard. Early in the trial, Argie pleaded guilty. When the jury completed their deliberations, they found that Calabrese and Bonarrigo "had persisted in their disorderly conduct after being warned to stop," and found them guilty of "a fourth-degree misdemeanor." They decided Pauley had not persisted and found him guilty of a "minor misdemeanor."

In the year following the bar incident, Bonarrigo would cross paths with Henry A. Grecco, which would result in tragic consequences for both men. Known as "Boom-Boom," unlike Youngstown legendary boxing hero Ray Mancini, who earned his famous moniker from knocking out opponents in the ring, Henry Grecco earned his nickname by building bombs.

Grecco came to the attention of Cleveland authorities when he was 41 years-old. Living in Marsol Towers in Mayfield Heights, at one-time a predominantly Italian suburb on the eastern edge of Cuyahoga County, Grecco was arrested by the FBI and charged with impersonating an investigator for the Federal Deposit Insurance Corp on September 24, 1975. Grecco and an accomplice tried to swindle an elderly West Side man out of $10,000. The case was later dropped.

In 1977, the results of a two-year investigation came to light on March 11 when Federal prosecutors from the U.S. District Court in Cleveland indicted Grecco along with Dominick E. Bartone for conspiring to sell 1,000 submachine guns, 18 automatic pistols and other "implements of war," to two undercover agents in Florida during 1975 and 1976. Indicted the previous September was Morton H. Franklin of Lyndhurst. The case was scheduled to come to trial on June 7.

In the midst of the ongoing bombing war in Cleveland, another life was taken. Around 4:15 on the morning of April 5, 1977, Enis Crnic, whose address was listed as 827 East 141st Street the same as a suspected headquarters of the Hell's Angels motorcycle club, was wiring a bomb to the ignition of John M. Delzoppo's car. The dark-green Oldsmobile was parked in a lot near East 206th Street and Shawnee Avenue, not far from Delzoppo's home at 20608 Chickasaw Avenue in Euclid. Sylvester Yockey, the resident agent-in-charge of the Federal Alcohol, Tobacco & Firearms Bureau, described what he believed happened next: "We feel that Crnic had the bomb all hooked up and inadvertently touched a hot lead and it went off."

The blast killed Crnic instantly and left DelZoppo's Oldsmobile a mangled mess. Police believed the bombing attempt was similar to the one that was made against Alfred S. "Allie" Calabrese on September 14, 1976. In that mishap, Calabrese's neighbor, Frank Pirsio was killed when he went to move "Allie's" automobile. Calabrese and Delzoppo had done time in prison after both were convicted in Federal Court in October 1968 of robbing the Society National Bank branch at 18325 Euclid Avenue of $27,720. Police also believed that the maker of the bomb that killed Crnic, and who was sitting nearby in a getaway car waiting for the work to get done, was Henry Grecco.

On May 31, 1977, Summit County deputy sheriffs found a blood-soaked automobile belonging to a girlfriend of Grecco on Isabel Avenue in Twinsburg Township around 2:30 in the afternoon. Police believed that Grecco was an associate of Teamsters Union official John A. Nardi, the victim of a "bombing war" blast two weeks earlier on the afternoon of May 17. The girlfriend, Nancy Spehar filed a missing person's report the day before, Monday, May 30, claiming she had not heard from Grecco since 4:00 p.m. Sunday. She said Grecco had called at that time and said he was at the Italian American Citizens Club at 18114 St. Clair Avenue and would be coming to her Belvoir Boulevard home in South Euclid soon. It was her 1973 Toyota that was found in Twinsburg.

The next day, a *Plain Dealer* article stated that deputies said the keys was still in the ignition and "a large amount of blood was on the passenger's side of the front seat." The article went on to say that Cleveland intelligence unit detectives were looking for Grecco to question him about the Nardi murder. A source close to the investigation said Grecco had connections to both Nardi and the people who were trying to kill him.

Friday came and Grecco was still missing. Through the newspapers, police made public several items from their investigation. In her Sunday afternoon telephone conversation with Grecco, Nancy Spehar revealed that Grecco told her he would be dropping off a friend, who lived on nearby Cliffview Road, before coming home. Shortly after the phone call, residents along Wayside Road, near East 166th Street in South Collinwood, heard three gunshots. Two people told police they saw a man exit a white-over-blue 1970 Buick, walk to a blue Toyota, shove the driver into the passenger seat and take off. One witness recorded the license plate number of the Buick. Police traced it to a brown-over-green Buick that had been in a Youngstown used-car lot since January. Police could not locate the man who sold the car.

On July 1, a month after Grecco had disappeared, a man taking his dog for a late night walk found a body behind bushes near Feldt Road, a street which dead-ended off Ohio 91, three miles south of I-480 in Hudson Township. The body, stuffed in a green plastic garbage bag, was found about a mile and a half from where Spehar's blue Toyota was found on Isabel Avenue in Twinsburg Township. A.H. Kyriakides, the Summit County coroner, said the man died from a bullet wound to the head and a fractured skull. While the coroner stated he would try to make a positive identification later in the week, an announcement by Cleveland intelligence unit chief, Lieutenant Andrew S. Vanyo made the point moot. The Lieutenant revealed that Grecco's driver's license and social security card were found on the body.

While the newspapers were still hot on the theory that Grecco's disappearance had something to do with the murder of John Nardi, Lieutenant Vanyo must have known otherwise. He was quick to point out, "This is just another murder. Maybe a falling-out among thieves... It's been fairly quiet since Nardi died. I think an uneasy peace has been made." Seeming to confirm this statement was the arrest of a suspect in the days ahead.

On Saturday, July 9, Joseph Bonarrigo was arrested for the murder of Henry Grecco. On Monday, he was arraigned and charged with aggravated murder with bail set at $100,000. An affidavit filed that day stated Bonarrigo and several others had given a rival in a vending machine dispute a beating. Bonarrigo wanted to kill the rival and approached Grecco with a request to build a bomb. Not only did Grecco refuse to build it, he allegedly told the intended victim of Bonarrigo's plan to kill him.

On Thursday, June 22, 1978, the aggravated murder trial of Joseph F. Bonarrigo got underway in the courtroom of Common Pleas Judge James F. Kilcoyne. That morning, the jury of six men and six women was taken to 837 Wayside Avenue, where police believe Grecco was shot to death; then to Isabel Avenue in

Twinsburg Township where the blood-stained car of Nancy Spehar was found; and finally, to the Hudson Township location, off Route 91, where Grecco's decomposing body was found.

Nancy Spehar was the state's first witness. She told the jury about the events of the day Grecco disappeared and her conversations with him throughout. She was followed to the stand by the state's key witness, James Paolucci, who lived at 837 Wayside Avenue at the time of the murder. The two-story brick structure sat at the corner of Wayside Avenue and East 166th Street; a sprawling manufacturing company ran the length of East 166th. A driveway to the parking lot ran down the west side of the apartment. In the front of the building, a shared wooden porch stretched across the front of the building on the second floor. Paolucci's identity was kept a secret since the day of the murder. During his testimony, two U.S. Marshals were posted in the courtroom. Below are the keys points of his testimony:

- Around 5:00 p.m. on the afternoon of May 29, Paolucci heard "popping" sounds and stepped out onto his porch on the second floor to investigate.

- He saw a blue Toyota parked in the driveway to his right below. A man's head was leaning out the driver's side window with blood streaming down the door.

- A man, who was standing nearby, got into a Buick and left. At that point, Paolucci went back inside his apartment and called police.

- When he returned to the porch and looked out, he saw the man who left in the Buick had returned and got out of the car carrying a blanket.

- He watched as the man opened the driver's side door of the Toyota and pushed the body over to the passenger-side of the front seat. He then covered the body with a blanket.

- The man then got in behind the wheel of the Toyota and backed it out of the driveway. The Buick, driven by another person, followed the Toyota.

Assistant County Prosecutor Herman H. Marolt then asked Paolucci to point out the man he saw that day. The witness pointed to Bonarrigo.

On Wednesday, June 28, the jury deliberated for two hours and twenty minutes before finding Bonarrigo guilty of murdering Henry Grecco. Judge Kilcoyne immediately sentenced him to a 15-year-to-life term. The judge, however, set bond at $25,000, allowing Bonarrigo his freedom while his lawyer filed an appeal. Twenty months later, while the case was still being appealed, Bonarrigo, a father of four, was now himself a murder victim.

In June 1982, Franklin R. Fencl of Richmond Heights, described as "a window washer and member of the Hell's Angels," was indicted for Bonarrigo's murder. Nearly two years later, in April 1984, Fencl's case gained notoriety when it was discovered that former Cuyahoga County Sheriff and current Cuyahoga County Common Pleas Judge James J. McGettrick was arrested in chambers and accused of accepting a $5,000 bribe involving Fencl's case. The sting investigation, initiated by agents of the Alcohol, Tobacco & Firearms bureau, came five months before Fencl was to go on trial before McGettrick on September 11. Recovered in the judge's home was $5,000 in marked bills. On January 16, 1985, McGettrick pleaded no-contest. On February 8, the disgraced former judge was sentenced to four years in prison. Suffering from prostate cancer, McGettrick requested shock probation in May, but was denied. On June 30, he suffered a heart-attack at the Orient Correctional Institute, and was taken to the Ohio State University Hospital in Columbus. On July 17, while still there recovering, he suffered a fatal heart attack at the age of 68.

The sting against McGettrick went down without either Fencl or his attorney knowing anything about it. After the judge's arrest, Fencl's case was turned over to Common Pleas Judge Ralph A. McAllister. Back in 1973, Fencl was convicted of aggravated assault and concealing a stolen automobile. Three years later he was convicted of receiving stolen property. He made local headlines in April 1982, after trying to spit on Euclid Municipal Court Judge Robert Niccum, during a court appearance for shoplifting. The judge gave him a sentence of 65 days; five for shoplifting, the rest for his courtroom conduct.

On August 31, 1985, after a plea deal with prosecutors, Fencl was allowed to plead guilty to involuntary manslaughter in the death of Bonarrigo, under a provision of the law that permitted a guilty plea without admission of guilt. According to the newspaper report, "Authorities said they believed the killing capped a drug-related dispute." In 1984, Fencl was arrested for shoplifting a $29 pair of shoes. Because of his previous convictions, he was given a two-year sentence, but he remained out on bond until the murder case came to trial. Perhaps adding insult to injury for the Bonarrigo family, Judge McAllister not only sentenced Fencl to two years in prison for killing Bonarrigo, but he ordered the term to run concurrently with the two years he received for shoplifting the shoes. Fencl died in 1993.

By the fall of 1982, Joseph Ilacqua had managed to remain out of the crime headlines for over six years. That all changed on September 20, when "Joe I" was arrested along with John J. "Skip" Felice, Jr., a former officer of the International Brotherhood of Teamsters Locals 73 and 293. The two men were charged in an extortion scheme that involved forcing Thomas D. Ganley, a successful local automobile dealer, to provide them with $10,000 and a vehicle in exchange for his life. Felice was also charged with embezzling $5,200 from Locals 73 and 293.

According to the indictment, Ganley was approached in April 1981 by Felice who told him "high-ranking organized crime figures" wanted him dead. Felice offered to get the "contract" on Ganley's life cancelled, but he wanted paid. Felice received two payments of $5,000; one in May 1981, the other in February 1982. Included in this payoff, Ilacqua received a 1981 Oldsmobile 98 Regency, which was owned by Ganley's Leasing Division.

The indictment followed an 18-month investigation by a special Justice Department Strike Force Against Organized Crime grand jury. Special Agent-In-Charge of the Cleveland FBI office, Joseph E. Griffin, called Ganley a "very courageous individual" for going to the FBI and giving them information about the extortion plot. Griffin credited the recent conviction of Cleveland Mafia boss James T. Licavoli for prompting victims of organized crime to step forward. He claimed that while Ganley was receiving protection, he had not entered the Federal Witness Protection Program. On September 21, U.S. District Court Judge Alvin I. Krenzler set bonds of $50,000 for Felice and $200,000 for Ilacqua. Both were soon back on the street.

Eight months passed before the case came to trial. The key evidence was conversations secretly taped by Ganley. Defense attorneys Robert J. Rotatori and Paul Mancino, representing Ilacqua, filed a motion to keep the tapes from being introduced as evidence. Back on April 7, 1982, the FBI seized the Oldsmobile that was being driven by Ilacqua. Strike Force attorney David Bauer stated, "The lease was invalid because it was obtained under duress, there were no lease payments made and there was no signature on the lease to make it valid." The purpose of the seizure, however, was to force Ilacqua to call Ganley so their conversation could be taped. The defense lawyers maintained the FBI failed to seek a proper search warrant to take the car, which in turn forced the telephone calls to be made.

On Friday, May 20, 1983, four days of pre-trial motions came to an end with both men accepting plea deals. In the morning, Ilacqua pleaded guilty to conspiracy to extort. The government agreed to concessions in accepting the plea. They agreed to dismiss the same "habitual or dangerous special offender petition" they requested in Ilacqua's possession of stolen liquor conviction back in June 1976. They also agreed not to recommend a sentence to the court.

Early that same afternoon, Felice, after he and his defense counsel, Ralph D. Sperli spent several hours listening to the tapes, pleaded guilty to conspiracy to extort $10,000 from Thomas Ganley; and to illegally controlling and acting as an officer of Teamster Local 293 within five years of his 1978 conviction for embezzlement. The charges of extorting $10,000 from Ganley, and two counts of embezzling from Locals 73 and 293, were dropped.

On July 15, Judge Krenzler sentenced Ilacqua to four years in prison. He still faced an additional six years as a parole violator. Felice was sentenced to five years on the extortion conspiracy charge and fined $2,000. He was given another year, to run concurrently, on the charge of illegally controlling Teamsters Local 293. During the sentencing, defense attorney Sperli told the court that Felice was operated on recently for intestinal cancer and a subsequent report indicated the cancer had spread to his lymph glands. He claimed his client had a 40% chance of survival. Strike Force Chief Steven R. Olah told the judge that the illness should not prevent Felice from going to prison because Federal prisons had medical facilities. Olah also stated that Felice was leading a normal life of late and had recently organized a baseball league. Sperli also talked about Felice's good standing in the community and presented several letters attesting to his good character. Included with the letters were ones from Sam Miller of Forest City Enterprises, and former U.S. Congressman Ronald M. Mottl. Judge Krenzler stated he would make a recommendation to send Felice to the Federal prison in Louisville, Kentucky.

The conspiracy to extort conviction may have been "Joe I's" last criminal hoorah. Ilacqua passed away on November 20, 2005. He was 76-years-old.

Albert H. Severino & Charles Skubovis

Albert H. Severino[130] was described as one of Cleveland's "most accomplished burglars" by Lieutenant Thomas P. White. By the mid-1950s it was estimated that burglaries Severino and his crew pulled earned the gang $100,000. Members of the Severino burglary gang included Vincent Innocenzi, Charles Skubovis, Richard Stewart, Joe Arrington, and George Florea.

Albert Hubert Severino was born on June 22, 1921, in Batavia, New York. He grew up in a family of 13 children, the youngest of six brothers. From all accounts, he was the only black sheep in the family. His first run-in with the law came in 1938 when he was 17 years-old. He was arrested in Waycross, Georgia, where he was charged with "being a hobo." Given a sentence of four months and a fine of $15, the judge agreed to suspend both on the condition he leave town. During World War II, he registered for the draft in February 1942. Despite being described as a "good father" and provider, one newspaper article claimed he was a "wrathful man when angered, [and] once kicked his wife Ellen, who was in a hospital for five days with head and rib injuries."

From the mid-1940s until 1957, Severino had arrests for auto theft, robbery, and false application for an automobile title. While he was said to be in the "tree business," he somehow honed a skill in collecting and enhancing burglary tools and forming a gang of yeggs. One of the first people he began working with in the mid-1950s was Charles Clarence Skubovis.

Skubovis did not exactly have a successful burglary career to date. In May 1953, Skubovis, Paul Heim and Charles Whited were captured by Brooklyn, Ohio, Police Captain Thomas C. Murphy outside a local restaurant in the Cleveland suburb. Murphy found burglary tools in the automobile the men were in. Heim immediately tried to bribe a police officer with $200. Brooklyn Mayor John M. Coyne charged the men with possession of burglary tools and bound them over to the Cuyahoga County Grand Jury.

On April 15, Skubovis was released on a $5,000 bond from a housebreaking and larceny arrest. Less than a week later he was arrested on April 22 by police in Columbia, South Carolina. A rookie police officer there saw two men enter a flower shop around midnight after being dropped off by two women, who parked around the corner. The officer called for help and two patrol cars quickly arrived. Inside the flower shop, police arrested Skubovis and William Michael "Peter" Rooney, a well-known Cleveland criminal, as they attempted to burglarize it. Outside, police arrested two women; one was Rooney's wife, the other Skubovis' girlfriend. When the women saw the police arrive, one of them threw nine money orders out the window. While in custody, police overheard the two men talking about "a big Cleveland jewelry job," that had just been pulled. Cleveland police were immediately notified, and the next day Detectives Thomas E. Murphy and Edward Walsh were on a plane to South Carolina to question the men about a $160,000 burglary at Wolland's Gold & Silver Shop at 1272 Euclid Avenue[131] in Playhouse Square. At the time he was arrested, Rooney was wearing two diamond rings and a diamond stickpin. Murphy and Walsh photographed the jewelry and took it back to Cleveland with them, but a Wolland's company official, who viewed the photographs, determined the items were not stolen from them in the recent burglary. It was discovered that the nine money orders, tossed out the car window by one of the women, were tied to a burglary on March 28 in Cleveland at the Friedman & Hellman law office at 2609 Lorain Avenue.

On July 16, 1957, Skubovis was found guilty of a burglary that took place at Bobbie Brookes, Inc. at 1545 East 23rd Street. He remained free pending a hearing on a motion for a new trial. The judge in the case denied the motion, but through a series of legal maneuvers by attorney John P. Butler, Skubovis was able to remain free.

On April 29, 1958, Severino and Skubovis met their Waterloo. During the early morning hours of April 28, the two entered the owner's office at the T.J. Clarke Box & Label Company[132] at 45 Norwood Avenue in Jamestown, New York. After breaking into the safe, the burglars stole antique watches stored in special mounting boxes, California gold coins, and another assortment of rare coins. The take was estimated at $10,000 at the time. The burglars headed back to Cleveland.

The next night they had the misfortune of running into a squad of men under the command of Lieutenant Thomas P. White. Sergeant John Popovich along with Detectives Robert Clifton and James Sweeney had just arrested three hoods, shooting one of them Joseph M. Petrangelo, as they attempted to rob the Play-Mor Bowling Alleys at 686 East 140th Street in North Collinwood. While looking for a fourth accomplice, they began searching streets in the neighborhood. Two blocks away from the bowling alley, the detectives came across a black Lincoln they recognized as one of Severino's automobiles. It was parked on Eaglesmere Avenue, outside the home of Severino's brother Lawrence. When the detectives checked it out, they found Skubovis hiding on the floor of the backseat and arrested him. They then waited for Severino to appear, which he did after some time, and they arrested him and his brother.

The next morning, the car and the Eaglesmere Avenue home were searched by Detective Sergeant Harold Lockwood and Detective Edward Walsh. Inside the car were items taken in the T.J. Clarke Box & Label Company robbery in Jamestown. In the house they found a sophisticated collection of burglary tools in a converted coal bin. The *Plain Dealer* described the find:

> The equipment included telephone sets with hundreds of feet of wire, apparently used by lookouts on burglary jobs; heavy duty electric drills; welder's torches and tanks for both heavy and

light metal cutting; a large electric impact tool which acts as an air hammer on concrete; and various cutting tools and sledge hammers. Each tool was fitted with a special hook, used for dropping it into narrow openings (a hole cut in a roof, etc.). Most of the tools were carried in containers resembling women's overnight cases or specially made wood boxes covered with oil cloth.

Veteran detectives agreed the tools and equipment confiscated was the largest, most elaborate collection of burglary tools ever to be brought into the detective bureau. By the end of the week, the men were charged with possession of burglary tools, arraigned, and out on bonds of $50,000 apiece.

On May 9, the Cuyahoga County Grand Jury indicted the three men on the possession charge. At the same time, Albert Severino and Skubovis were charged with the Jamestown, New York, burglary. Skubovis celebrated his indictment by getting drunk with his girlfriend and hitting a police car driven by Patrolman Richard Borowiak on Cedar Road in Cleveland Heights. While the officer cuffed Skubovis and put him in the car, the girlfriend tried to claw Borowiak, for which she was charged with assault and intoxication.

More than three months passed before Severino and Skubovis had an extradition hearing, which they were fighting. On August 19, the pair met with their attorney Adrian B. Fink,[133] three Cleveland detectives, and a Jamestown district attorney. The two were charged in New York State with first-degree grand larceny and third-degree burglary for the T.J. Clarke Box & Label Company break-in. Paul Tague, Jr., executive secretary to Ohio Governor C. William O'Neill, overhearing the session, ordered a second hearing after determining that "the great amount of evidence submitted required considerable study."

Then things got bizarre. Cleveland attorney Herman S. Pressman, who represented Lawrence Severino, told police he had retained David L. Cowles, the retired head of the Cleveland police scientific identification unit, as an expert witness and wanted permission to examine the evidence the police had. "Not so fast," responded Cowles when questioned by the newspapers. He said he had talked to Pressman, but no agreement was reached. When Chief Assistant Cuyahoga County Prosecutor Saul Danaceau was informed of what occurred during the hearing, he explained that at such hearings the merits of the case are not to be discussed, and that there are only two issues to be decided:

1. Is the accused the person named in the charge?
2. Was he in the accusing state when the crime occurred?

On September 4, the extradition hearing continued. Despite Jamestown District Attorney Sidney Hewes' objections, the defense called two expert witnesses. Dr. Harry Nash, assistant professor of physics at John Carroll University and David Cowles. Both men testified that the materials found on the clothing of the defendants could have come from somewhere else besides the robbery scene.

A month after the hearing, six unexploded sticks of dynamite were found in a canvas bag by Thomas White outside the lieutenant's home in Euclid. Among the people rounded up for questioning by police were Severino and Skubovis. On October 9, the extradition hearing continued in the courtroom of Common Pleas Judge Donald F. Lybarger. Detective Henry E. Dombrowski, Cleveland police ballistics expert, compared slides taken of the trace materials from the defendants clothing and matched it to materials from the scene of the Jamestown robbery. On October 15, Judge Lybarger upheld the extradition of Severino and Skubovis to New York to face charges.

At this time, Skubovis, who was still out on bond after having been found guilty of burglarizing the Bobbie Brooks Company on East 23rd Street, lost his appeal and had his appeal bond revoked. He was sent to the Ohio Penitentiary to begin serving his sentence. On January 7, 1959, Skubovis and the Severino brothers went to trial on the possession of burglary tools charge in the courtroom of Common Pleas Judge John J. Mahon. County Prosecutor John T. Corrigan represented the state, and defense counsel was Norman S. Minor, John P. Butler, and Herman Pressman. After a three-week trial, the jury was handed the case on January 28. After six hours of deliberations, the jury of seven men and five women found Skubovis and Albert Severino guilty, and acquitted Lawrence Severino. Judge Mahon held off sentencing until a motion for a new trial could be heard. Skubovis was remanded immediately because he was serving a penitentiary sentence; Mahon also remanded Severino to the County Jail and set a hearing to determine if his bond should be revoked. On February 13, Judge Mahon sentenced both men to five years in the Ohio Penitentiary.

In another twist, after two months in the Ohio Penitentiary, Severino was transferred to the Marion Correctional Facility. Reporters were told all "candidates" for Marion have to be screened in Columbus by a "classification committee," before an inmate can be moved to a less secure prison. Police claimed they had never heard of a prisoner "on whom a detainer had been placed by another state" being allowed to be assigned to an honor-type branch of the prison system. It should be noted that back in March 1944, Severino was serving a sentence in the Mansfield Reformatory with Joseph Drago. The two were moved to the "honor-camp" at the Soldiers' Home in Erie County. Both young men were returned to the reformatory after officials at the camp determined their efforts there were not deemed satisfactory.

A new drama entered the case on August 27, 1959, when attorney Pressman and Richard Stewart, a member of the Severino burglary ring, made a trip to Jamestown. The two men stopped at the Chautauqua Transfer & Storage Company, where Stewart went in and left a suitcase at the facility. The clerk became suspicious after Stewart provided a fictitious Jamestown address and then drove off in an automobile with Ohio license plates. The clerk called police and a short time later police stopped the car in Ripley, New York, located on the shore of Lake Erie, near the Pennsylvania border. When police checked the suitcase, they found antique watches stolen from the T.J. Clarke Box & Label Company in Jamestown. Stewart and Pressman were charged with breaking a New York State law involving "buying, receiving, concealing or withholding stolen or wrongfully acquired property." The two were booked into the Chautauqua County Jail in Mayville, New York. Stewart at the time was under a Federal indictment for selling counterfeit money to an undercover government agent. Both men pleaded not guilty the next day. Pressman was released after posting a $5,000 bond; because of the counterfeiting charge, Stewart's bond was set at $25,000.

On the morning of Thursday, September 17, 1959, a preliminary hearing was held in Jamestown, New York, which, to a conspiracy theorist, had all the earmarks of a political cover-up. Reporters were barred from the session without any indication as to which side made the request. Witnesses heard included an FBI agent and Jamestown attorney, Michael Lombardo, who had represented Pressman at his arraignment. Representing Pressman at this hearing was William B. Mahoney, described as a "Buffalo criminal case attorney and powerful state Democratic leader." His brother, Walter J. Mahoney, was the New York State Senate Republican majority leader.

During the afternoon session, in which reporters were allowed to attend, the clerk from the Chautauqua Transfer & Storage Company testified about Stewart checking the suitcase. He said he did not see Pressman at that time and would not see him until after the men were arrested. City Judge Lester W. Berglund said he would not make a decision about sending the case to the grand jury until the preliminary record was transcribed.

During the week of September 14, Severino and Skubovis were scheduled to be moved to the Chautauqua County Jail. Skubovis, for some reason never made public, resisted the sheriff's deputies when they tried to remove him from the Ohio Penitentiary. When he was told he could make the trip "peacefully or in leg irons," he chose the former. On Monday, September 21, four days after the preliminary hearing and before any decision was announced by Judge Berglund, Severino and Skubovis pleaded guilty in Chautauqua County Court, where they were both represented by Michael D. Lombardo, who had served as a defense witness for Herman Pressman four days earlier. County Judge Rollin A. Fancher set September 28 as sentencing day.

The newspapers reported that court observers found it highly unusual the defendants pleaded guilty, risking additional prison time on top of what they were already serving. What was even more unusual was that Assistant District Attorney Sidney T. Hewes claimed that the guilty pleas came as a complete surprise to him, despite the fact that Cleveland police officers involved in the arrest had not even been subpoenaed to appear to testify at the trial. On September 28, Severino and Skubovis were each sentenced to 5-to-10-year terms in Attica

State Prison. Both were then returned to Ohio to serve out their burglary tool possession sentences.

On October 3, Judge Berglund of Jamestown released Pressman from court custody with a warning that "other interested parties still had recourse to legal action against him and might attempt to hold him for the grand jury." Stewart, meanwhile, was held for the Chautauqua County Grand Jury. When Stewart came up for trial on March 28, 1960, he was represented by attorney William Mahoney. County Judge Fancher allowed him to plead guilty to a misdemeanor because he "had nothing to do with the burglary and larceny." He remanded him to jail until sentencing.

On September 30, 1960, Cleveland police officials were dealing with the Ohio Pardon & Parole Commission on the upcoming parole of Charles Skubovis. He had served the minimum of his two felony sentences, one year and 11 months, when he was scheduled to be paroled on October 13. In addition to letters from Lieutenant White, Chief Frank Story and Inspector Richard Wagner protesting the parole, County Prosecutor John T. Corrigan wrote the following letter to the commission:

> It seems to me that if hardened, confirmed criminals, hoodlums of a most despicable type, of which this man is one, serve a minimum of time, then the efforts of the police department, prosecutors and courts are rather meaningless and certainly shallow, to say the least.
>
> I cannot conceive that this man should in any manner be treated as a first offender and in my opinion, since he has chosen this way of life and has not manifested a departure therefrom, he should be held in the penitentiary for a period as long as possible under the law. This, I believe, is the least that is owed to the public of this state.

On October 13, 1960, the parole was rescinded by the Ohio Pardon & Parole Commission. Skubovis would be kept in prison four more years before he was paroled on November 12, 1964. One week after his parole, a Chautauqua County Judge in Mayville turned down his motion to have the five-to-ten-year sentence in New York State set aside and ordered him to prison. When Skubovis got out of prison he may have gone straight; he certainly didn't do anything that brought him into the public eye again. He was living in Sheffield Lake when he died on November 1, 1981. He is buried in Lakewood Park Cemetery, in Rocky River, Ohio.

Albert Severino finished his Ohio sentence on February 13, 1964, five years to the day of his sentencing. He began an immediate legal fight to stop from being extradited to New York State to begin his sentence there. In Franklin County Common Pleas Court in Columbus, he refused to waive extradition and was released on a $5,000 bond. Representing Severino in New York was attorney Mahoney, who was asking that his client be put on probation or allowed to serve his New York sentence in Ohio. A letter from an Ohio Penitentiary employee was sent to Prosecutor Sidney Hewes in Jamestown. The employee wrote an extremely complementary letter about Severino, finishing it by saying, "He will do well if released." When Warden E. L. Maxwell was asked about the letter, and if it was normal for his employees to issue such a note, he replied, "It is usual for a prisoner to obtain a letter like this when he is leaving. I imagine Severino coached and sponsored the project." He then pointed out that the person who wrote the letter had only been employed there for three months. Maxwell then added that the letter "should not be misconstrued as any recommendation in regard to any action by any other law agency. I don't think that he has changed much in the five years he was locked up here. He still travels on the fringe of the law." On April 17, 1964, Franklin County Common Pleas Judge Dana F. Reynolds denied Severino's writ for habeas corpus and ordered him to return to New York to face sentencing. The court battle raged on into the summer.

In early August, Severino was arrested after a drive-in restaurant operator in Ashtabula got suspicious of a $20 bill handed to him and recorded the license plate of the man who gave it to him and notified police. When sheriff's deputies stopped him near Madison, Ohio, they found $2,000 in counterfeit $20 bills under his front seat. Severino appeared before U.S. Commissioner Clifford Bruce. He was charged with passing and possessing counterfeit money, and released on a $1,000 bond.

A month later, U.S. Secret Service agents busted the leaders of the counterfeit ring by arresting three men in two Cleveland hotels. The men were apprehended with $60,000 of the phony $20 bills. William K. Deckard, Agent-in-Charge of the Secret Service here, reported that about $200,000 in counterfeit bills were produced in a Cleveland printing shop. The Secret Service first learned of the bogus $20 bills after Severino's arrest in August.

By July 1965, Severino was still under a $5,000 bond fighting extradition to New York to begin his 5-to-10-year sentence for the Jamestown burglary, and was still out on a $1,000 Federal bond in the counterfeiting case. On July 24, a safe containing $2,500 in cash was stolen during a burglary at the Star Home Pride Bakery at 18320 Lanken Avenue.[134] A man, claiming to have heard talk of a safe being dumped in the Euclid Creek Reservation, notified police and the empty safe was found the next day. When police questioned residents of the area, some claimed to have seen a black Cadillac and a white panel truck in the park area. Knowing that Severino used vehicles matching those descriptions, they went and questioned him and quickly made an arrest. In the panel truck, police discovered papers that were kept in the safe, some partially burned, a bolt from the safe and some matching paint chips. None of the money was recovered.

The next day, Severino was charged with five felonies – breaking and entering, burglary, forcing entry of a safe, grand larceny and possession of burglary tools. When arraigned before Common Pleas Judge Frank Celebreeze he was placed on a $100,000 bond. On August 5, Severino was bound over to the Cuyahoga County Grand Jury, by Common Pleas Judge Hugh A. Corrigan, who refused a lower bond request by attorney John P. Butler. Severino remained in County Jail for four-and-a-half months until December 16, 1965, when Judge Charles W. White, over the objections of Judge Celebrezze, lowered the bond to $50,000 after then public defender Elmer A. Giuliani argued the bond was excessive.

A year and a half went by without any of the cases being finalized. On Monday, June 19, 1967, Severino appeared with his attorney, James R. Willis, in the Payne Avenue Courts Building, where Common Pleas Judge Francis J. Talty granted him a final trial continuance on the Star Home Pride Bakery burglary, setting a trial date of July 25. Once back home at 19005 St. Clair Avenue, his wife Ellen recalled, "Albert was very nervous. He always wanted to be alone when he was that way." Ellen took her 13-year-old daughter Denise, boarded a bus, and went to her sister's house on Fulton Road on the West Side. Early that evening, Severino called James Willis to discuss the case. Around 1:00 a.m. Tuesday morning, Ellen and her daughter were driven home by her nephew; her sister went along with them. When they reached the house on St. Clair, Ellen found both the front and back doors locked. When the nephew raised the kitchen window to remove the screen, Ellen recalled, "I saw some holes that hadn't been there. Denise went in. She saw Albert on the floor. My sister Mrs. Horvath, ran to him, raised his head. It was bloody. I thought someone had beaten him. But he was dead."

Police were called and quickly arrived. They found Severino's body between the kitchen and living room, face up and covered in blood. People in the neighborhood said they heard gunshots shortly before midnight. Police theorized that someone appeared at the kitchen window and called to him. When Severino leaned on the window sill, the killer fired five times through the screen with a .45 semi-automatic. Severino was hit four times; three bullets hit him in the chest and one in the hip. Five spent cartridges were found outside the window.

A couple of interesting items came out when police questioned family members. Ellen Severino revealed that, "For the first time in seven years our police dog was tied in another place where Albert thought it would be cooler for him." It wasn't exactly beastly hot that day. The forecast called for temperatures in the mid-70s and a cool night. This leaves one to wonder if the killer knew ahead of arriving that he would not have to be concerned with either family members or the police dog. The other item, reported by the *Plain Dealer*, stated a question was asked whether Severino was an informer for the Federal government. Without identifying the person, other than referring to them as "she," the newspaper wrote, "A member of the Severino family [replied] he was never brought to trial on a counterfeiting charge here in 1964." She followed that up with, "Draw your own conclusion."

Adding to this interesting exchange was a revelation made after the murder by U.S. Secret Service Agent-in-Charge, William Deckard. He said when he was interrogating Severino after his arrest for counterfeiting, any answers he gave us "he would write on a small tab and hold it up for us to look at, and then eat the slip the note was on. He thought the room might be bugged, so he ate the paper."

On Thursday, June 22, the day Severino would have turned 46-years-old and less than 72 hours after the murder, the *Plain Dealer* released an article titled, "Severino Probe at Dead End." Albert H. Severino was buried in All Souls Cemetery in Chardon, Ohio.

Sonny's Show Bar

Located at 12376 Superior Avenue, Sonny's Show Bar had its grand opening on Friday night, August 9, 1946. The bar and restaurant, according to an article, listed "Former Sergeant Angelo Lonardo...as the impresario" of the city's new entry in the entertainment business. This Angelo Lonardo was a nephew of the infamous "Big Angelo" Lonardo, who had avenged his father and uncle's October 1927 murders during the Lonardo/Porrello Corn Sugar War, and had risen to the position of Acting Boss of the Cleveland Mafia in the early 1980s. After being sentenced to 100 plus years on drug charges, Lonardo "flipped" in 1985 becoming the highest ranking member of the Mafia at that time to become a Federal witness.

Some three years before Julius Petro's apparent takeover of the place, Sonny's Show Bar was riding high. Opening night at Sonny's featured "Tops" Cardone's "Men of Note" and Bob Gaylord as vocalist. Gaylord, the stage name of Joey Fatica, honed his "pipes" while a student at Patrick Henry Junior High School. During his first few weeks at Sonny's it was reported, "His amiable crooning of laments figuratively toppled the moon-struck gals off their high stools...much to Joey's own surprise."

As for "Tops" Cardone, his career in the Cleveland music scene became legendary. Born Anthony S. Cardoni on May 23, 1921, it was reported that Cardone began his musical career "at the tender age of 10." That meant his career in the entertainment business lasted 53 years. Known as a "singing accordionist," Cardone got his first big shot in December 1945 when he appeared at Ben Ross's Penthouse, a cocktail lounge at 10011 Euclid Avenue,[135] with headliner Bessie Brown, "Cleveland's Queen of the Blues." Cardone's "Men of Note" performed at Sonny's into March of 1947. He reported at that time "his crew" was entering its 30th week there. A week later, it was reported that "Tops" Cardone was making his first downtown appearance. One reviewer wrote his "melodious little band, including Vic Warren's tenor and Leo Leta's guitar, is shaping up excellently at Joe LaRocca's Roxy Musical Bar," pointing out that Cardone was the new maestro there.

In October 1948, it was reported that Cardone "and his likeable dance crew are roosting in the Biscayne Club," located in Playhouse Square. Just three months later, came the report that he had disbanded his orchestra and joined Cleveland's polka king, Frankie Yankovic. After touring for nearly six years with Yankovic's band, Cardone formed an instrumental trio and was "baptizing the Alhambra's new Algiers Room," in April 1954.

Over the next 30 years Cardone appeared at numerous venues around Cleveland and Cuyahoga County. These engagements lasted weeks, months and sometimes years. Among these venues were Tassi's Skyway, at Brookpark Road and Rocky River Drive (1959); Continental Ballroom, 13929 Euclid Avenue, East Cleveland (1960); Alcazar Hotel, Cedar Avenue, Cleveland Heights (1962); Sahara Motor Hotel, Euclid Avenue and East 32nd Street (1964); Owen's Plantation, 15357 Euclid Avenue, East Cleveland (1965); Ottino's Restaurant, 6036 Mayfield Road, Mayfield Heights (1965 to 1974); Charter House, 24800 Euclid Avenue, Euclid (1975-76); Shaker House, 3700 Northfield Road, Highland Hills (1975); and Masiello's Restaurant, 5851 Mayfield Road, Mayfield Heights (1975 to 1984).

In addition to his musical skills, Cardone was an excellent golfer and in 1970 hosted, played in and several times won the "Tops Cardone Open Invitational." A few years later, he broadened this into a Florida golf tour during the winter months; golfing by day and performing at night.

In July 1974, Michael Ward, a writer and associate editor of the *Plain Dealer* Action Tab, stated that one of the keys to Cardone's success was "the ability to move with the times without forgetting the best of the past." Cardone told him during the interview that, "I play things that people can relax to, regardless of how old or how new they are." Ward also explained:

Nine years ago when the sciences of music and electronics were still largely divorced, he spotted the trend. Therefore, he hooked up his cordovox (in brief, an electronic accordion) to a speaker and a rhythm box and was ready for the age when the single entertainer blossomed.

At that time Cardone had been playing at Ottino's on Mayfield Rd. for two years. By most standards that was a long engagement, but it was one that was to go on for nine more years.

During the interview Cardone stated, "I traveled for eight years, during that time I made four records with Doris Day, including 'You Are My Sunshine.' For six years I had a contract with Columbia Records, and I also appeared on the Arthur Godfrey, Kate Smith, Faye Emerson and Cesar Romero television shows."

"Tops" Cardone ended his last gig at Masiello's Restaurant in March 1984. Perhaps it was to retire or just have more time for golf. He lived another 18 years before passing away on October 6, 2002 from abdominal cancer.

Back to Sonny's. In December 1949, Angelo Lonardo was on trial along with Charles Amata, Joseph Artwell and Nick Satulla for trying to extort Black numbers kingpin Joe Allen. In testimony on December 29, Lonardo explained that he and a cousin of the same name had sold Sonny's Show Bar for $45,000. He did not elaborate when or to whom it was sold.

On May 20, 1951, after Julius Petro and friends were driven away, the entertainment columnists announced that Sonny's "Showboat" was purchased by Nick Zlaket, who renamed it the Mirror Show Bar. Zlaket at one time was the building superintendent of the Central Police Station and operated several restaurants in the downtown area. Advertisements that month named the Chick Alberto Trio, the Tempo Tones and the Musical Jestors as scheduled performers there.

The Mirror Show Bar made the news in April 1952 after the arrest of Marvin Cornacchion. There was an altercation at the bar during which Cleveland

Patrolman Francis Sherman was roughed up by four men. After his arrest, Cornacchion alleged he was beaten in his cell by Sherman. When the prisoner filed charges, the FBI was called into investigate. Joseph D. Purvis, acting agent-in-charge, said agents investigating the matter would determine if civil rights laws were violated. A few days later, Sherman was cleared during a departmental hearing. In court, following a bench trial just days later, Municipal Judge Andrew Kovachy acquitted Cornacchion claiming police had not provided sufficient evidence to convict.

On November 7, 1955, U.S. revenue agents seized and closed the Mirror Show Bar for non-payment of delinquent cabaret and payroll taxes. Cleveland collections chief of the agency, Harry X. Robinson reported the bar and its assets would be put up for public sale to help satisfy $28,000 in cabaret taxes and $7,000 in past due income withholding taxes. Twenty days later, a legal notice advertised the sale of the Mirror Show Bar.

The Trennen Company purchased the bar and kept the Mirror Show Bar name. Advertisements for barmaids and waitresses were published in the papers during the spring and summer of 1956. The ads wanted "colored and white" and "attractive and neat" applicants. In December of that year, the Trennen Company was fined $50 after a man reported he ordered a 70-cent drink and was not charged taxes.

In the mid-1940s, Charles Lee Lester, a Black teenager, was on his way to becoming a Cleveland boxing legend. At 16 years of age, he was the top contender for the Golden Gloves Heavyweight title, weighing in at 230 pounds. Helping to bring Lester along was one of the best boxing teachers and trainers in the country, Johnny Papke. In February 1944, while fighting in the semi-finals for the Cleveland Golden Gloves Heavyweight title in the Novice Division, Lester knocked out an opponent with one punch 24 seconds into the bout. Three days later he won the championship with another knockout.

In May, he scored a second round knockout to win the heavyweight title in the Cleveland Amateur Boxing Trainers Association program, which Papke helped found and served as first president. In February 1945, fighting at 258, Lester again won the Cleveland Golden Gloves Heavyweight title, this time in the Open Division. From there it was off to the National Amateur Athletic Union bouts. Lester entered the bouts at 240 pounds. Reaching the championship bout on April 4, Lester was knocked down twice in the first round, each time taking a nine count. In the second round he did the same to his opponent. After an impressive showing in round 3 he won on a decision receiving his first AAU Heavyweight title.

In February 1946, he won his third straight Cleveland Golden Gloves Heavyweight title, and second in the Open Division. He now prepared to make it back-to-back National AAU titles. On April 10, he did just that. Afterwards, the newspapers claimed Lester would go pro in the fall of that year. But there was very little coverage of Lester's professional career. In March 1947, he faced Sid Peaks in Chicago. A newspaper article at the time claimed Lester had won 13 professional fights in a row before heading into that bout. Although Lester was the favorite in the eight-rounder, he was knocked down seven times before the bout was over in round 3. On April 28, he faced Peaks again, only to be knocked out in the sixth round this time.

On March 28, 1950, Lester ended a scheduled five-round fight with a vicious kidney punch to his opponent in the first round. The fight was on the under-card of the Middleweight Championship bout between Jake LaMotta and Chuck Hunter, won by LaMotta. Later that year, on a card sponsored by the *Cleveland News* Christmas Toyshop Fund, Kid Gavilan won a decision over Youngstown's Tony Janiro. Lester had a four-round bout scheduled against a Detroit heavy-weight, but it was cancelled due the length of the other bouts. On June 17, 1952, Lester may have had his last boxing match. In a fight in Newark, New Jersey, he was outpointed during an eight-round bout.

Charles Lee Lester disappeared from the media and the public view. The only time his name appeared in the newspapers was when they published a by-year listing of previous Cleveland Golden Gloves champions and AAU champi-ons. On April 17, 1959, in a *Plain Dealer* article mentioning Lester, the newspaper reported he had "served time for rape, assault and battery." If this was true, there didn't seem to be any previous articles that reported the crimes.

On March 19, 1959, the Cleveland police had a mystery on their hands, "Who Shot at Alex Birns?" Alex Birns, better known to Clevelanders as "Shondor" Birns, was a menace to society since the early 1930s. Deeply entrenched in the numbers business for nearly three decades, as well as many other criminal ac-tivities in the city, Birns had risen to the top of Cleveland's Public Enemy list. On the night of March 19, Birns arrived at his home at 16913 Judson Drive, in the Lee-Harvard area on the city's southeast side. As he got out of his car, someone fired a shot at him, narrowly missing him and leaving a bullet-hole in his garage door.

Police did not find out about the incident until April 8, when Birns was in Miami, Florida. Police arrested Clarence "Sonny" Coleman[136] a 35-year-old ex-convict, and released him after questioning. Police also brought in a friend of Coleman. During questioning, the man blurted out, "I didn't shoot that rifle!" This certainly aroused police suspicion, as the fact that a rifle was used in the shooting had yet to be made public. When Birns returned on April 9, police were anxious to question him. Birns presented a slightly different tale, stating he was shot at around 8:40 p.m. on March 20, as he was about to get into his rented Chevrolet. He would later claim the shooting occurred "several weeks" before that. Birns also made it clear to officers he would not file a police report, nor would he testify if anyone was charged.

Less than a week after Birns' return, Clarence Coleman would learn a valuable lesson: If you take a shot at "Shondor" Birns, don't follow it up with shooting off your mouth. Coleman's bragging about the deed, led to his initial questioning by police. By the time Birns returned from Miami, he was also aware of the identity of his assailant. Coleman, a Black man, had served Federal and state prison terms for the possession and sale of narcotics. One of the jobs he acquired after he was released was as a numbers runner for Birns, a position he obtained through his friendship with Fred Stitmon. A former muscleman for Birns, Stitmon was an enforcer for the "Big Five" clearinghouse operators in 1956 and 1957. He was once tried with Birns and three others for blackmail and the bombing of Donald King's[137] home. He also had a record for armed robbery, auto theft and burglary. Stitmon and Coleman became friends after the latter's release from Federal prison in early 1958, so close were the two that Stitmon allegedly named his second child after him. But local gossip had it Coleman was recently fired by Birns for some indiscretion.

On the night of April 13, Coleman went to the Mirror Show Bar where he said he planned to meet friends who lived around the corner from the bar at 1317 East 124th Street. Once inside the bar, Coleman spotted Birns drinking at the bar and "not caring for any trouble which might have arisen over his alleged attempt on Birns' life," made a quick telephone call and left. From the Mirror Show Bar, he walked toward his friends' home on East 124th. Along the way he noticed a two-tone Chevrolet parked on the west side of the street. A Black man got out of the car and approached Coleman. As he got near, Coleman reported, "He pulled the gun. I jumped high. If I hadn't, the first shot would have hit my chest. It hit my leg instead." When Coleman landed, his leg buckled, and he rolled toward the corner of a building as the gunman continued to fire. After the last shot, Coleman looked up and saw the Chevrolet was now on the east side of the street. "I could see Birns was driving," he said. "The light was good." When the gunman got in the car, the dome light on the car's ceiling provided even more light for Coleman to see who was driving, As the car slowly moved down East 124th. Coleman dove through a window at the home of his friends and from there called the cops.

Police arrived and transported Coleman to Lakeside Hospital. Back at the Mirror Show Bar, officers questioned the owner, William Lynch, a friend of Birns, and a waitress. Both stated that Birns was in the bar around midnight. Then they questioned the bar's bouncer, who told them he had seen Birns drive south on East 124th Street at the time Coleman was shot. The next day William Lynch fired the bouncer. The bouncer was the former boxer, Charles Lester.

Three men were arrested after showing up at the scene of the shooting, two of whom were the friends Coleman was going to see at the 1317 East 124th Street address where he jumped through the window. All were arrested the next day. Birns was arrested at his home. He admitted to Homicide Captain David E. Kerr he was at the Mirror Show Bar, but claimed to know nothing about the shooting. Police searched Birns' home and confiscated a .22 rifle with a telescopic sight and several boxes of ammunition. The next morning, after Birns made a statement to detectives, he was being led from the Homicide Bureau to an elevator when he was suddenly confronted by several photographers. The irritated Birns, holding a handkerchief to hide his face, hollered at them, "You've got 9,000 of these already. Why take one when a guy's been in jail all night?"

Police quickly arrived at a theory that the shooter was brought in from out of town. Their support for this was that Birns allowed himself to be seen at the Mirror Show Bar only because he was there to "finger" Coleman for the hitman. Cleveland Detective Chief Richard R. Wagner told reporters, "We've never been able to place Birns so close to a crime scene as in this one. The fact that he was in that bar – according to witnesses and his own admission – is unusual in Birns' history. Knowing Birns, it seems the only reason he would allow himself to be seen that close is that he had to identify Coleman for the gunman." Wagner reasoned that a Cleveland hood hired for the job, would have known Coleman. The next day, Birns was released on a $5,000 bond.

On April 17, the newspapers announced Charles Lester, "a 290-pound witness," placed Birns at the scene of the shooting. "Lester definitely strengthened our case," Detective Chief Wagner announced. The same day, it was also announced Birns' case received a continuance due to his attorney, Fred W. Garmone being tied up with another trial.

On May 1, the Cuyahoga County Grand Jury returned an indictment against "Shondor" Birns in the shooting of Coleman. Before Birns could even be arraigned, Coleman went to the police at 5:00 a.m. on May 3, and asked for protection. Police questioned him and held him in jail for several hours before he asked to be released. He told a reporter that he got "a little nervous," and that there would probably be no trouble. "I felt some pains in the old wounds, man. I was hurting, man, and I was feeling pretty nervous," he declared. The nervousness came while Coleman was at the Hotel Belden, at 1903 East 70th Street, visiting with Fred Stitmon. During their conversation in the lounge, he heard that two "strange men" were asking for him.

Three days after the indictment, Birns appeared for arraignment in Common Pleas Court, with his bondsman in tow. He pleaded not guilty to the shooting-to-wound indictment. Common Pleas Judge William K. Thomas doubled his bond to $10,000 and Birns was released. The next day, after Coleman claimed he heard "someone trying windows and doors" at his residence at 3277 East 123rd Street, police provided a full-time guard for him. A few days later, on May 7, Detectives William Lonchar and Harry Sargent stopped a taxicab shortly after it left Birns' home. Inside was Fred Stitmon. The significance of the visit would come to light later.

Coleman, at his own request, was being held as a material witness at Metropolitan General Hospital, in the prison ward. On June 4, he asked to be released because he was bored. The upcoming trial was scheduled to begin June 15. Birns' attorney, Garmone filed a motion with the court that his client would offer an alibi defense.

On Monday, June 15, trial began in Common Pleas Court before Judge Joseph H. Silbert. The state was represented by Cuyahoga County Prosecutor John T. Corrigan and Assistant Prosecutor Harvey R. Monck. A jury of eight men and four women was selected and plans were made to have them visit the scene of the shooting on East 124th Street and the Mirror Show Bar on Superior Avenue.

After the jury was sworn in, Corrigan made a surprise move asking Judge Silbert to triple Coleman's bond, which was set at $5,000 for him as a material witness. Coleman's attorney, Albert R. Gamble told Judge Silbert his client now could not identify Birns as the driver of the car that sped off with the gunman who shot him. Back in October 1957, when Fred Stitmon was tried with Birns and three others for the blackmail of Donald King and the bombing of his home, he was represented by Albert Gamble, a Black attorney. Police believed the meeting at Birns' home with Stitmon on May 7, was to get him to have Gamble make either threats or promises to Coleman in order to get him to change his story.

Silbert set the new bond at $15,000 after Coleman had no objection. When court attaches stated Coleman had little chance of raising the high bond, Corrigan declared that, "If he gets that $10,000 for this new bond I'm going to know where that money comes from." The prosecutor stated that when Coleman was questioned after Gamble's revelation, he said he had no intention of changing his story.

The next day, the state had a new problem to contend with. Charles Lester, the ex-boxer and bouncer at the Mirror Show Bar, was reported missing following his statement to Homicide Detective Frank Dimperio on April 16, about seeing Birns in the bar that night and driving away on East 124th Street. Police searched daily for Lester to subpoena him to testify. Police reported back to the prosecutor that not even his mother has heard from him.

It was odd that no mention was been made of Lester since he gave his statement to the police and was fired from his job. Missing now for two months, when reporters questioned Prosecutor Corrigan as to when Lester was going to appear, he replied, "I don't know if he will. We don't know where he is. But we certainly would like to have him."

During trial that Tuesday, Coleman was the state's first witness. On the stand he refused to identify Birns as the driver of the car and denied all previous statements he made to police. He even refused to admit he saw Birns in the Mirror Show Bar the night he was shot. Prosecutors Corrigan and Monck were able to have Coleman designated as a "hostile" witness, and obtained Judge Silbert's permission to "refresh his memory" from statements he made to police. Coleman admitted to making the statements, but claimed, "I did make those statements, but they're false. I'm under oath now. I created those answers for purposes of my own." He concluded his testimony by claiming he had not seen Birns anywhere the day of the shooting and did not know if Birns was even in the car in which his assailant escaped.

Monck demanded to know who Coleman talked to after assuring Corrigan and the assistant prosecutor that he had no intention of changing his story. Coleman admitted he spoke with his attorney, Albert Gamble that morning, in his hospital room at the jail. Monck then attempted to establish, through the questioning of Patrolman Jerry Kreiger, Coleman's words after being the first officer on the scene. When Birns' attorney objected on the grounds of hearsay, Corrigan immediately cited a ruling by the Ohio Supreme Court, which allowed an exception to the rule. The ruling was "the words of a victim of a startling occurrence, while he was still under the nervous shock and excitement of the occurrence and without time for reflection, could be repeated as testimony by witnesses who heard them." The trial recessed for the day before Monck could question the witness further. Outside the courtroom, after his testimony on Tuesday, Coleman claimed he refused to name Birns due to his "mother's welfare" and not having the courage to "stick to his original tale" that Birns was driving the car that night.

The next day, before testimony began, attorney Gamble appeared before the Court of Appeals with a writ of habeas corpus stating that his client was being held under "excessive bond," and had completed his testimony. Back in Common Pleas Court, Coleman was back on the stand and now identified Birns as the man he saw inside the car, and that he had also seen him in the Mirror Show Bar that night.

During cross-examination, Garmone tried to discredit Coleman, bringing up his past criminal record. At one point during his heated cross-examination, Garmone told the judge he was dizzy and asked for the court to be recessed for the day. In earlier testimony that day, both the barmaid and the owner of the Mirror Show Bar testified to Birns being in the bar that night between 11:30 and midnight. William Lynch was also questioned about Charles Lester. Lynch told the court that Lester hadn't worked at the bar since the night of the shooting. That was because Lynch had fired him the next day after he told police he saw Birns driving south on East 124th Street at the time of the shooting.

Also testifying was Detective Steve Hospodar, who arrived at Birns' home after the shooting that night. He said the engine of Birns' car was still warm despite the fact Birns claimed he was home watching television. At Lakeside Hospital, Coleman told Hospodar that Birns was the man driving the car.

On Thursday, Birns took the stand in his own defense and denied having been involved in the shooting of Coleman. He admitted to being at the Mirror Show Bar and seeing Coleman there, but did not speak to him. He claimed he left about 11:45 and drove home where he watched the movie, "Full Confession," a 1939 drama about a priest who convinces a man to come forward to save an innocent man from going to the electric chair.

The trial was recessed until Monday, because Garmone had a previously scheduled Probate Court appearance. That day, however, the Court of Appeals heard testimony about the habeas corpus writ filed by Coleman's attorney, Albert Gamble. During the day-long hearing, County Prosecutor Corrigan was called to the stand along with Lieutenant Martin Cooney and Sergeant Carl De-Lau to emphasize the importance of Coleman to the state's case. At the end of the hearing, the Court of Appeals rejected the habeas corpus request.

On Monday, June 22, Birns was back on the stand, where he underwent 40 minutes of cross-examination by Corrigan, who questioned his more than his 50 arrests. The defense rested and closing statements were delivered by both sides before Judge Silbert gave his instructions to the jury. After four hours of deliberations, the jury returned to the courtroom at 10 p.m. and delivered an acquittal. The jury foreman said the decision was based on two factors. They found the testimony of Coleman not believable, and they had trouble believing the state's time line between Birns' leaving the Mirror Show Bar and his arrest at home.

On July 24, a month after Coleman was released following the trial, he was stopped by Elyria police in Lorain County, for driving without headlights. Police searched his car and found a handgun under the front seat. Coleman told police he was carrying the gun because of "Shondor" Birns. He was in fear for his life. Coleman was charged with carrying a concealed weapon. In December, he pleaded guilty and was sentenced to one-to-three in the Ohio Penitentiary. In January 1965, Coleman was convicted of accepting a stolen television from a narcotics addict. The judge gave him a sentence of one-to-seven years. It was the last time Coleman made the news. He died in September 1982.

Alex "Shondor" Birns continued with his criminal career up until the mid-1970s. Birns met his doom in spectacular fashion on Easter Eve, March 29, 1975, when he was blown in half after entering his car outside Christie's Lounge near West 25th Street. It was widely believed that Irish gangster Danny Greene was responsible for Birns' farewell party – it was a blast.

As for Charlie Lester, many thought he would resurface after the trial's verdict. He didn't. He never made the news again, not even in blurbs over the years about "Shondor" Birns. Whether he was killed or moved out of the area forever is still a mystery to this day.

Sometime during the early 1960s the Mirror Show Bar became the Kit Kat Show Bar. The heyday of the club was over, and the place attracted minors and the dregs of the neighborhood. Throughout the 1960s, the only time the bar was mentioned in the newspapers was when state liquor agents raided it for serving minors; arresting both the purchaser and the bartenders or barmaids who served them.

There is nothing left of Sonny's Show Bar today. The area of Superior Avenue on which it stood, is a vacant lot.

Joseph Tholl

Joseph Thal was born on April 6, 1909, in Toledo. Ohio. He took up the playing of violin at an early age. By the time he was sixteen, he was president and con-certmaster of the Woodward High School symphony orchestra in Toledo. After graduating high school, he attended the Cleveland Institute of Music, where he studied classical music and continued to play the violin. While at the institute, he developed a second interest, handwriting. What he called his "hobby," other people might call his obsession. Although he attended no college or trade school to learn this skill, over the next 50 years he would become an internationally known handwriting expert and document examiner – but, not as Joseph Thal.

Sometime prior to enlisting in the Army in 1942, Joseph Thal changed his last name to "Tholl." I based this on the fact that according to the 1940 census, he was still using the name Thal. But there is no record of his military record at Ancestry.com and the first mention of him in the Cleveland newspapers in February 1947 identifies him as Joseph Tholl.

In 1955, he told reporter Sanford Watzman, "Some people tinker with ma-chinery, and others collect antiques. My hobby has always been handwriting, and I've made a vocation out of it, which I enjoy very much." As for his study of music and playing the violin, he claimed he still plays "to keep myself from go-ing crazy." The work and training of a handwriting expert and document exam-iner is far more complicated than most people can imagine. *Plain Dealer Sunday Magazine* contributor Dwight Boyer wrote in August 1962:

> Tholl's work is considerably more involved than the simple analysis of handwriting. Scientif-ic examination and evaluation of questioned documents and handwriting is a broad field requiring extensive knowledge of ultraviolet and infrared photography, variations of typewriters and type, latent markings, stains and an extensive knowledge of papers, inks, stamps and pens of all kinds... steel point, fountain and ball point. The study of handwriting, also involves knowledge of physiol-ogy, psychology and pathology because all sometimes have some bearing in the handwriting of an individual during varying conditions of stress or health.

Tholl began the study of handwriting in 1930, and by 1933 "was expert enough" to examine some documents. It would take 20 years before he could make a full-time career of his passion. To support himself he picked up an oc-casional gig playing his violin, and also earned a living as a photographer. He soon specialized in aerial and legal photography. Three months after the United States entered World War II, Tholl enlisted in the Army on March 9, 1942. He served as a handwriting expert for the Army Air Corps and worked in photo-graphic reconnaissance at Peterson Field in Colorado Springs, Colorado, with the base's legal and intelligence officers. He was soon sent overseas to work in such Pacific Theatre locations as Biak, New Guinea, the Philippines, Okinawa and Japan. Tholl was honorably discharged in December 1945.

On October 15, 1948, Tholl married Ina Marie Hoover; both lived in Cleveland Heights at the time. In addition to the money he was getting for his document examination and photography work, by now Tholl was supplementing his income by giving professional talks and lectures on his specialty as an expert in his field. He was a sought after speaker addressing various groups like Kiwanis Clubs and the Photographic Society of America. In an article advertising one of his programs, it stated his talk included a conversation about typical forgery situations, uses of ultraviolet and infrared photography, as well as a lighting and focusing discussion with notes on processing.

In April 1952, Tholl testified at the perjury trial of Anna J. Sprunk, a former clerk of Sheffield Lake Village, in Lorain County. The case, which garnered much media attention, was transferred to Ashland County Common Pleas Court. Sprunk was accused of forging a fictitious signature in a real estate deal, which helped her to earn $4,000 from the purchase of a city land sale. Tholl testified that Sprunk's handwriting matched the fictitious name on the purchase agreement. Sprunk denied to the grand jury that she signed the documents, thus creating the perjury indictment. Jurors found her guilty. The judge gave her a 1-to-10-year term in the Marysville Woman's reformatory, but suspended the sentence.

During the late summer and fall of 1952, Tholl became involved in a massive ballot forgery case resulting from the spring primary. The publicity he received from his work propelled his career to a new level. His work on voter fraud cases was one of the crimes that would occupy a great deal of Tholl's time over his career. In September 1952, he worked with Thomas B. Crisafi, a special vote fraud investigator for Ohio Secretary of State Ted W. Brown. A "definite pattern" of fraud was discovered in several wards in the county following the 1952 spring primary. Tholl came across a situation in Ward 1 – Precinct 1, where 76 out of 82 votes were written by the same hand. The practice used was called "short-penciled ballots." On many of the ballots, the voters had not voted in all the races. The May primary ballot featured races for county commissioners, U.S. senators and state representatives, but it was the precinct committeeman position that drew the most fraud. Many voters were simply not interested in the precinct committeeman contest and didn't vote on it. The poll worker, using a short pencil that could be hidden in their hand, would mark an X in the box for their candidate in the section left blank by the voter. Another trick was for the poll worker to put a piece of lead under their fingernail and use it to mark ballots. In some cases, the poll worker would mark an X in his candidate's box, even if the voter had selected the other candidate. This would invalidate the vote for that race on the ballot, thus reducing a vote for the candidate the voter chose.

The investigative work was tedious. According to the *Plain Dealer*, the search for "bad X marks" proceeded in an assembly-line fashion: (1) a corps of vote-counting veterans scan every ballot, precinct by precinct; (2) an official checks and screens suspected ballots; Joseph Tholl, handwriting expert, then examines the questioned ballots; (3) bad ones result in a subpoena call for all booth workers involved; (4) handwriting samples and testimony are taken; (5) Tholl compares those samples with the bad ballots; and (6) results are turned over to prosecutors overseeing the case. Later, at the prosecutor's office, files are started consisting of polygraph test results, results of further questioning, and police data added to appropriate files. Booth workers were sometimes found to have criminal records.

Tholl explained that the "scoffers," who thought they could get away with the short-penciling, were mistaken if they thought an X placed on a ballot could not be traced to its maker among a group of possible vote-snatchers. He explained his process:

> There are 40 characteristics by which an X can be classified. Often in Probate Court, where a will is contested, the question is about the X made by an illiterate testator. There you have only one X to go on. In some of these ballots we get a dozen examples. I have reduced the 40 different characteristics to the 10 most important ones for convenience of these checkers. And they are doing a good job of finding the differences.
>
> Pressure, the type of lead or ink, the size, extra little hooks, the different weights of the two bars making up the cross, wavering lines and curved ones, the slant of the crosses and so on have caught a great many vote thieves.

Another problem Democratic County Chairman Ray T. Miller had to address was that certain Democratic officials were registered outside the precincts they lived in. One man was forced to move to a room at the Hotel Statler after being told he could not claim a locker at the Cleveland Athletic Club as his legal residence.

By October, the investigation came up with the first "stolen election." The contest was for Republican committeeman in Ward 32 – Precinct X. The short-penciling took place at a polling place located at East 185th Street and Lake Shore Boulevard. Tholl told the Board of Elections that someone had "retraced hundreds of X marks all over the ballots." It was also noted that for the first time during the two-month fraud probe a witness refused to provide a handwriting sample of his name and his Xs for the election board. Chairman Ben C. Green and board member Dan W. Duffy asked poll worker Mike LoSchiavo why he had refused to mark Xs on a sample ballot for the board:

LoSchiavo: I refuse because it might contaminate me.

Green: Might what?

LoSchiavo: Well, how do you pronounce that?

<u>Duffy</u>: Incriminate.

<u>LoSchiavo</u>: Yeah, I refuse because it might incriminate me.

In the end more than a dozen people were convicted of voter fraud. The probe produced 91 bags of ballots from the May primary to be reviewed for a possible recount. The Board of Elections, however, decided there would be no recount until after the November 4 election, which was still a month away. The reason for this, the board claimed, was that, "Such an operation would take $100,000 and 8,000 workers." No recount occurred.

The perjury trial of Dr. Alexander V. Spaeth (See Chapter Seven), which began in November 1953, gave Tholl his big break, providing the documents examiner with the most publicity he had received to-date. The case, in which the first two trials ended in convictions only to be overturned on appeal, would finally be resolved after a third conviction in May 1957. After appeals were exhausted, Dr. Spaeth was sent to prison in January 1959.

Tholl worked from an office he created in his home at 58 Bellview Avenue in Chagrin Falls, where he and Ina lived. On August 2, 1955, Assistant Safety Director Robert H. Johnston announced Tholl was hired by the Cleveland Police Department as an examiner of questioned documents. He was recommended for the job by Detective Chief James McArthur to fill a void caused by the death of Clarence L. Hawkins back on February 2. Hawkins, originally a Municipal Court reporter, joined the detective bureau after being appointed a civilian member by special city legislation. During his 25 years with the detective bureau, he worked under five detective inspectors handling a number of responsibilities, one of which was serving as the department's "unofficial" handwriting authority.

In this new part-time position, Tholl would serve as analyst, consultant, witness in court, and training officer in the department to examine questioned documents. He was to be paid $1,800 per year. Tholl was placed under the direction of Deputy Inspector Thomas A. Murray, and scheduled to be in the police laboratory on Tuesdays, but to be "on call" for other situations.

Tholl's next big case was the murder of an 18-year-old girl. On October 9, 1955, a man picking mushrooms in Brookside Park, at Fulton Road and Dennison Avenue, found the body of a young lady covered in leaves in a deep deserted ravine. Police arrived and found the "faceless," partially clad body, with a note beside it. The body was estimated to have been there for six days. Police were unable to determine her identity or the cause of death, even after the autopsy. The note, for the most part, was destroyed from exposure and from the leaves, but what investigators were able to glean was, "My mame [sic] Helen Carlin. Catch two boys. Because I would not drink." A description of the girl, who was missing two front teeth, was sent to police agencies across the country and a day later was being reported in newspapers nationwide.

On October 14, Coroner Samuel R. Gerber, after days of extensive medical tests, concluded the girl died due to asphyxiation from manual strangulation, and ruled her death a homicide. That same day, an experiment using polarized light at the General Electric laboratories failed to reveal any more information from the note found beside the body.

Days passed with leads coming in about missing girls from several states. The investigation heated up after luggage discovered left behind at the Hotel Statler came to the attention of the police. The contents revealed the name Gloria Ann Ferry. Also found in the luggage was a newspaper from Altoona, Pennsylvania. Detectives were immediately dispatched to that city in the south-central part of the state. A dentist there soon made positive identification through dental records the body was that of Ferry. A confirmation from fingerprints followed.

The attractive teenage girl was a housekeeper for Louis C. Statler, a 69-year-old resident of the city, described as a "dappy" dressing, diminutive ex-convict, street cleaner and former carnival wrestler. Newspaper articles portrayed a sordid picture of Gloria by family members as the third of nine children, who felt unloved and was looking for a better life when she answered Statler's newspaper want-ad for a housekeeper and child care provider. The child, a 12-year-old called Tony, was described at various times as either Statler's son or grandson. Another rumor had it that a woman had just dropped the child off there one day and never returned for him. Sometime after taking this job, Gloria actually moved into Statler's home. More than 50 years older than her, Statler at times would refer to Gloria as either his wife or daughter. In mid-August, Gloria was found walking the streets with Tony at 1:00 a.m. She told the police she was "put out" of the home by Statler. Altoona police arrested Statler on August 20 and charged him with contributing to the delinquency of a minor. Tony was removed from the home by a juvenile court judge. Ferry was going to testify against him about Tony when the case was scheduled for a hearing the first week of October. For a while, Ferry was held in the Blair County Jail in Altoona as material witness. She was then released to her mother. Mary Ferry revealed that within a week of her daughter's release, Gloria was receiving threatening letters. It was reported Statler was enraged because Tony was taken away from him.

Investigators from the Altoona police found out Statler came back to the city shortly after killing Gloria Ferry to visit Tony. Statler was clearly on the run now and was believed to have been in Canada, Chicago, and as far west as California. The FBI was brought into the case as Statler had obviously crossed state lines in order to avoid prosecution. The Cleveland investigation revealed Statler and Ferry were in the city between September 26 and October 3, which was the day they believed he murdered her. They stayed in at least two downtown hotels together and were seen by more than a dozen witnesses on the street and in diners. Several arguments between the two were overheard.

Homicide Captain David E. Kerr received a postcard from the suspected killer who sent it in an apparent effort to throw police off the trail. The note read:

> The girl Helen Carlin is from Chicago ILL. She came with us by car with two sailors and is a dope fiend. We read in papers about her death. Her home is on North Clark St. We heard one sailor call her Helen.

On November 25, Statler was identified as being at a hotel in Gary, Indiana, where he stopped at the front desk to borrow stationery. He then used it to write a letter to the Altoona Mirror newspaper in another attempt to throw investigators off his trial. Shortly thereafter, FBI agents in Chicago tracked him down, surveilling him for several days before making an arrest on December 10, as he walked along West Van Buren Street, a few blocks west of the Loop.

Statler was brought back to Cleveland in January 1956, and indicted for the murder in February. In April, court-appointed attorneys for Statler – Dan W. Duffy and David Ralph Hertz – asked Common Pleas Judge Felix T. Matia for a jury to determine if their client was sane before his murder trial. On May 14, after hearing the testimony of three staff members from Lima State Hospital for the Criminal Insane, Judge Edward Blythin ruled Statler was "presently sane" and mentally competent to stand trial for first-degree murder. Trial was scheduled for June and assigned to Judge Joseph H. Silbert.

After several delays, the trial began on June 25. Statler's counsel asked for the case to be heard by a three-judge panel instead of a jury. Judges Matia and Silbert, along with Common Pleas Judge John J. Mahon heard the case. Assistant County Prosecutor Saul S. Danaceau represented the state. During the trial, the prosecutor brought in a parade of witnesses who saw Statler and Ferry in various parts of the city together. It was a circumstantial case, however, and the key piece of evidence was the note found near the body, because only the killer could have left it and to determine who that was the state called Joseph Tholl as the 35th and final witness.

On July 3, Tholl took the stand and sealed Statler's fate. He tied the handwriting from the "Helen Carlin" note left next to the body to postcards the defendant mailed to throw off the police and to the letter sent to the Altoona Mirror.

Defense counsel, in presenting their case, did nothing to refute the prosecution's witnesses. They were solely banking on rebuttal witnesses to say their client was insane or, at the very least, incapable of telling the truth. Their biggest problem was that their client wanted to take the stand in his own defense. His attorneys were against it and told the judges so. But Statler had already told reporters, "It's my life and not Hertz's." He railed that he was being framed by false circumstantial evidence, which only he could refute.

On Friday, July 6, after calling a doctor to refute the coroner's finding that Ferry died of strangulation, defense counsel announced, "The defense rests." The three common pleas judges all stared directly at Statler. After a brief awkward moment, Judge Silbert advised Statler he was declared sane and could decide whether he wanted to testify himself. Silbert then stated the decision not to testify must come from the defendant. He called a recess so Statler could confer with counsel. When the recess was over, Duffy told the court that Statler "has seen the wisdom of our arguments. He will not testify."

Silbert ordered Statler to approach the bench, where the following conversation took place:

Silbert: This court wants to make sure that what Duffy says is your desire.

Statler: [Incoherently] In the condition the last couple of days, my nervous condition...I've got to overcome that. But I'm inclined to agree with both attorneys...

Silbert: Being inclined is not sufficient. If it will help your nerves any, we will recess until Monday morning to give you an opportunity to compose yourself.

Statler: I appreciate that opportunity. I really do.

As deputies began to escort Statler out of the courtroom, Hertz suddenly demanded the trial be suspended until a second inquiry could be made about his client's sanity. The motion was greeted with a terse refusal by Silbert.

On Monday, Statler made a clear decoration that he would not be taking the stand. Attorneys for both sides then gave their closing statements. At 1:30 the judges began their deliberations, returning at 4:00. They found Statler guilty of first-degree murder, but granted him mercy, sentencing him to life in prison. The judges felt Statler's actions before and after the murder showed clear premeditation and that the killing was not the result of an impulsive reaction; thus, proving he was sane. Silbert said the defendant's advanced age was the main factor in their decision not to impose the death penalty. "We recognized that he's never going to live long enough to get out of the penitentiary."

On September 18, 1956, Tholl was elected president of the Ohio Association of Questioned Document Examiners. In later years, he became a member of the American Academy of Forensic Science. During his career he gave some 75 seminars regarding his techniques, and had more than 35 articles published in professional journals. At the peak of his career, he estimated he was involved in more than 3,000 forgery cases each year.

In January 1960, Tholl became involved in one of Ohio's most bizarre murder cases. On Christmas Eve 1959, Charles Clark, an engineering executive, scoutmaster, and Sunday school superintendent was shot down by a sniper while standing in his kitchen with his wife and 12-year-old daughter. When police questioned Lois Clark, his wife, she revealed she had been engaged in a series of sexual trysts with four different men. Floyd E. Hargrove, her latest lover, was arrested three hours after the shooting. Hargrove made two confessions and, under the influence of sodium amytal, which he asked to have administered, revealed the location of the murder weapon in the Chagrin River. Despite this, and Tholl's confirmation that a forged name on a receipt for a .22 bolt-action rifle was in his script, in June 1960 a Lake County Jury found Hargrove innocent of the murder.

Andre Alessando138 had a sordid past, which began in the late 1940s as the proprietor of the Lucky Star Café, opened in May 1946 at 3842 Scovill Avenue.[139] In July 1948, two narcotics detectives and a Federal narcotics agent sent an informant into the Lucky Star after reports of marijuana being sold there came to the attention of the authorities. The informant was able to purchase ten marijuana cigarettes. The café's night club permit was revoked, and the place was ordered closed in February 1949. After appeals were denied, the Lucky Star went out of business in late 1950. In June 1951, attorneys for Alessandro were able to bring action to set aside the revocation order after the drug informant, who by now was serving a narcotics conviction in the Ohio Penitentiary, had his testimony challenged. The bar remained open until February 1955, still racking up violations. The newspapers claimed the Lucky Star "holds the long-distance record for operating under court restraining orders." But once the Ohio Department of Liquor Control chief, Edward J. "Eddie" Allen, the former mob-fighting police chief of Youngstown, got involved, the luck of the Lucky Star Café ran out.

This didn't stop Alessandro. He simply began running the Cavalier Bar at 1800 East 17th Street,[140] which was owned by his uncle, August Luizzo, who, due to poor health, was trying to transfer the liquor permit to his nephew. Just like the Lucky Star, the Cavalier Bar was soon a target of police complaints. The latest charges included refilling bottles, false material statements in applications for a permit, and unsanitary conditions. Unlike selling marijuana to supplement his income, Alessandro came up with a new scheme. He became a "key member of a trio of forgers who specialized in faking church raffle prize checks."

During the fall of 1960, Assistant County Prosecutors John T. Patton and Bernard J. Stuplinski presented evidence against Alessandro in Common Pleas Court. He had participated three times in the forging of checks on churches. On two of them he forged the name of a clergyman. The forgeries were confirmed by Joseph Tholl, who also found six other checks forged by Alessandro, who had his underlings cash the checks. When the case came to trial in November 1960,

Alessandro was facing nine counts of forgery and nine counts of negotiating forged instruments. With Tholl's testimony, the jury came back in less than two hours with a guilty verdict. That's when Common Pleas Judge Roy F. McMahon threw the book at Alessandro. The penalty for each charge carried a penalty of 1-to-20-years. The judge sentenced him to a 9-to-180-year term, ordering the forgery sentences to be served consecutively.

Beginning in mid-December 1960, Tholl was embroiled in another election squabble in the Mahoning Valley. This time it involved the race for county commissioner in Trumbull County between Republican Dr. W.A. James, who was completing his first four-year term, and the Democrat challenger Joseph J. Baldine, who had served six two-year terms as mayor of Hubbard. Dr. James won the November 8 election by 26 votes, but was not declared the winner due to the contesting of the count by Baldine. While Baldine received a "good vote" in the machine tabulation, he lost by a wide margin after the counting of the absentee vote. Baldine paid $2,300 for a recount, which resulted in three additional votes for Dr. James, giving him a 29 vote margin, and being named winner on December 10.

Baldine then hired Joseph Tholl to examine the results, having no comment on just what he expected him to find. On December 31, Secretary of State Ted W. Brown voted with Republican members of the Trumbull County Board of Elections on procedural issues to conduct a fair investigation into the fraud charges raised by Baldine in the voting for county commissioner. Brown's vote favored the contacting of the State Bureau of Criminal Identification & Investigation[141] to conduct the fraud probe into the election, but meant he was against the hiring of Tholl to assist the state agency. Tholl had helped investigate voter fraud charges at the request of Ted Brown in the past.

The contest of election suit was being heard by Common Pleas Judge William Wayne Badger of Holmes County, located southwest of Canton, sitting in by special assignment. At question were 2,300 absentee votes in general, but in particular the ballots from the Trumbull County Home and the Trumbull County Tuberculosis Hospital. Jacqueline Booth, a registered nurse at the County Home testified she aided some of the residents with the marking of their ballots and, in addition, had marked some for them herself. She also stated she had either aided the voter or made marks herself on the identification envelopes in which the ballots were placed after the residents voted. In addition, assistance was also given filling out the cards mailed to the board of elections to obtain the absentee ballots.

For the investigation, Tholl was hired by Baldine, while Maurice A. Nernberg, a prominent Pittsburgh attorney and handwriting expert, represented Dr. James. In his work, Tholl examined all aspects of the absentee voting that took place at the County Home, including marks on the cards for the ballot requests, marks on the identification envelopes, and the marks on the ballots themselves.

In court, on January 21, he testified his conclusion was "a number of X marks on the ballots showed a similarity."

Due to Judge Badger's schedule, the trial didn't convene again until February 2, 1961, when Tholl testified to some "double voting" he found on both sides. Tholl said he came to Warren at the request of Baldine to examine absentee ballots. He claimed he "was not told what to look for and had no idea that certain voters had not marked their own ballots, as charged by Baldine." The next day, Dr. James' expert, attorney Nernberg, took the stand and declared, "It is impossible to compare an "X" on an absentee ballot to one on a specimen ballot and tell whether they were made by the same person and positively identify that person."

On February 14, Hugh L. Leggett, superintendent of the Ohio Bureau of Criminal Identification & Investigation, who was advising Ted Brown on the Trumbull County situation and had attended all the hearings, advised the Secretary of State the testimony did not provide any indication there was any fault on the part of the Trumbull County Board of Elections. "Certain irregularities occurred at the tuberculosis hospital and county home on the part of employees in the institutions, but the board of elections had nothing to do with the irregularities," Leggett stated.

The *Plain Dealer* wrote, "Leggett reported testimony offered by Joseph Tholl, Cleveland handwriting expert for Baldine, and M.A. Nernberg, Pittsburgh handwriting expert for James, was confusing to the court. Tholl said he could identify Xs marked on ballots by comparing them with Xs made on specimen ballots, but Nernberg said such an accurate identification could not be made."

Leggett seemed riveted on pointing out that there was nothing that could be blamed on the Trumbull Board of Elections, as he repeated, "No negligence on the part of the board of elections was brought out." He pointed out that the Board of Elections could not be charged with knowing there was some irregularity in connection with the notarizing of documents applying to ballots cast by sick and disabled persons. Regarding testimony some residents of the county were aided in marking Xs on ballots, Leggett said the superintendent of the home should have called the Board of Elections for help, which is required by Ohio law.

When the hearings were over, Judge Badger said he has taken the case under advisement and, after reviewing briefs requested from both sides, would render a decision. On April 7, Judge Badger, in his ruling, accepted Tholl's testimony over Nernberg's as to the "similarity of absentee ballots cast," that the ballot markings were made in the same handwriting. The judge then ruled "that aid or assistance could not be provided to anyone voting, except that prescribed by law, namely assistance from two dully authorized clerks from the Board of Elections." With that, Judge Badger threw out 51 votes from voters at the Trumbull County Home cast for Dr. James, and 10 votes cast for Baldine, all from the absentee ballots. He stated that six or seven votes cast for Baldine were notarized by a notary public, "who had an interest," therefore he invalidated those, too. The judge declared Joseph Baldine the winner of the election, by 12 votes, in the commissioner's race.

Was Joseph Tholl developing a following from his work? Perhaps the following will illustrate that he was. Carl Stern was a 24-year-old radio talk show host working at KYW Radio in Cleveland during 1961. Shortly after Tholl's testimony during the Trumbull County election suit, he was a guest on Stern's "Program P.M." talk show. Tholl was first of two guests on the night of March 9, appearing for 20 minutes at 10:10 p.m. If you're wondering who the second guest was, it was William O. Douglas, Associate Justice of the U.S. Supreme Court. As for Carl Stern, he went on to a journalism, law and broadcasting career, and earned just about every news broadcasting award known to man.[142]

A *Plain Dealer Sunday Magazine* article from August 19, 1962, showed how well-known Joseph Tholl had become. The article described him as an "internationally known handwriting expert." In addition to handling cases in the northeast Ohio area and the Mahoning Valley, Tholl helped solve cases in Canada, Germany, and India. Tholl told the writer he was currently handling about 500 cases each year, with the bulk of his work being done in the basement laboratory of his Chagrin Falls home.

Tholl was aware that many people were fascinated by his work and would like to get into the field, but claimed as they began to understand how extensive and tedious the learning was, their interest began to wane. In the article, Dwight Boyer wrote, "Detecting a forged signature is not always as easy as the layman imagines. Tholl points out that 'just a signature is often not enough evidence. But with a representative amount of the individual's handwriting specimens, the style can be as distinctive as a fingerprint. The number of letters in the alphabet makes the forging of a long document by hand almost an impossibility... if it comes before the scrutiny of experts."

Tholl's most famous case came in June 1963, when a recommendation was made by County Auditor Ralph J. Perk and his chief accountant Warren D. Riebe, that he be hired to assist in a payroll investigation in the office of County Recorder Frank S. Day. Perk, a future four time two-year-term mayor 1971-77, was the first Republican elected to a county office since the mid-1930s. Frank Day on the other hand was a Democrat, serving his third four-year-term in the Recorder's office.

During the Depression Era years of 1929 to 1936, Frank Day was seldom employed. In 1936, he entered politics and lost in a bid for the Ohio Senate. In 1941, he won a Senate seat without the backing of either political party. The *Plain Dealer* chalked up the win to him having the same name as Common Pleas Judge Frank S. Day, but also acknowledged, "The 'Day' name has been magic in Ohio for decades.[143]

In 1945, he resigned from the Ohio Senate's liquor control and political subdivision committees he was a member of, claiming he should have been appointed to a labor committee, where he "could do the most good." He blamed the Democrat minority for giving him a "raw deal." Ironically, that same year he ran a red light in Cleveland and was arrested for drunk driving. He pled guilty, was fined $150 and received a 30-day suspended workhouse sentence.

Leaving politics, he worked as a spot welder for the Auer Register Company, a heating and furnace contractor, from 1946 to 1952. In 1952, he decided to use his "magic" name once again and ran for Cuyahoga County Recorder. He told reporters, "Sure, I don't know anything about the job, but I want a chance to prove I can do it. I may not do well...but, after all, give me a chance." Attorney John F. McCrone ran his campaign and was rewarded with the job of chief deputy recorder when Day won. He later gave Day a much needed refresher course in basic accounting procedures. Day would win re-election without party support in 1956.

In 1954, Day threatened to resign after he charged Ray T. Miller and other Democratic leaders with interfering in his operations. He claimed Miller brought pressure on him to keep a long time female employee he had fired. Asked why he didn't resign, Day stated, "My wife talked me out of it." In 1955, some of his employees claimed they were pressured into making contributions to a "voluntary collection" to purchase Day a wrist watch for his birthday.

One of the things opponents questioned Day about was his citizenship. Day wasn't sure where or when he was born, claiming accurate records weren't kept "in those days." In 1958, Prosecutor Corrigan, after an investigation requested by the Citizen's League, discovered that Day was born in Cuba, where his father, an American soldier, was stationed.

McCrone and Day had a falling out in 1959 resulting in McCrone being fired when he charged his boss with malfeasance after he destroyed several chattel mortgage records. Two other employees were also terminated, including Day's sister-in-law. McCrone was replaced by Anthony J. Lysowski.

In the 1960 election, Day defeated Ward 13 Councilman Ralph Perk, which would set off future fireworks between the two. In 1961, Day laid off two employees claiming he didn't have the funds to pay them. He then promptly approved $13,000 in pay raises for 66 other employees.

The 1963 investigation began after discrepancies in signatures on payrolls in Day's office were found. Separate investigations were already underway by the State Auditor and Cuyahoga County Prosecutor John T. Corrigan. With the bi-monthly payroll, employees were required to sign a payroll sheet before receiving their checks. The signatures were to verify they earned the money they worked for. At each county office, the official in charge was responsible for certifying the accuracy of the payroll.

Tholl was called upon to check the signatures on the payroll records to see if they matched the signatures on file for the employee. It didn't take Tholl long to recognize a problem. He noticed on the June 15 payroll that 18 of the 65 names had similar signatures, meaning one person signed for all of them. When questioned, Day's personal secretary, Evelyn Prusak, admitted the handwriting belonged to her. She told a reporter, "When I prepared the payroll, I would go through the office and if employees were on coffee breaks, sick or on vacation, I would sign for them. I have nothing to be ashamed of. I will submit to any lie detector test. I will talk to the county prosecutor or state auditor."

There were three signatures by Mrs. Prusak which drew the most scrutiny. The first was for Frank C. Cushion, who had died on June 9. Tholl's examination revealed Cushion was also issued a check for the June 30 payroll. The second was John Edvon, who nobody seemed to know. When questioned, Prusak said he worked in her office, but refused to discuss him, or explain why she endorsed his check. A search of Edvon's name as an employee of Day or the Recorder's office failed to turn up in any local city directory. As soon as this came to light, Perk received a letter from Frank Day stating that Edvon had resigned. The last signature Prusak made was for Michael Kascak. Listed as a deputy recorder, he was reported to have spent most of his time at Day's Parma Heights home doing remodeling work.

On July 3, Perk sent Warren D. Riebe, his chief of general accounting whose signature appeared on all the paychecks, to see Day's chief, Anthony Lysowski, to obtain information regarding John Edvon. Lysowski, who had previously refused to answer any questions about Edvon from newspaper reporters, told Riebe that "he had no address, withholding statement or any other confirmation of Edvon's employment." That same day, Recorder Day refused to make any comments to the media and referred all questions to his new counsel, Norman S. Minor.

Corrigan, who was preparing to present information to the Cuyahoga County Grand Jury as soon as possible, also wanted to talk to Edvon, who he identified as a plumber living in North Royalton. Newspaper people, who were hot after the elusive plumber, were told by his wife he was on a fishing trip and to her knowledge had never worked for the county and did not know Frank Day.

Corrigan also wanted Michael Kascak, the deputy recorder who doubled as a handyman at the Day home, investigated by the grand jury. When questioned about Evelyn Prusak signing the names of 18 employees to the payroll sheet, Corrigan said he wasn't interested in pursuing that matter because, "she acted under the direction of Day and there is no evidence of complicity on her part or of any knowledge of illegality."

Records showed John Edvon appeared on the payroll as a deputy clerk making $541.66 a month, making him one of the five highest paid people in an office of 65 employees. He was on the payroll since April 16. Questioning of other employees in the Recorders office revealed that none of them had ever seen the man.

On Independence Day evening, County Auditor Perk ordered a complete and thorough investigation of the Recorder's office payroll records going back to January 1953, when Frank Day first took office. Perk announced the hiring of Joseph Tholl to review the payroll files for the ten-year period. He assigned Edward C. Kumerow, a former FBI agent, to work with Tholl as a deputy auditor and to guard Day's books. Tholl would be paid $10 an hour "for his professional services," which included his technical and photographic equipment, as well materials and supplies. Tholl's normal fee was $250 per day. Perk later hired Leonard C. Kamerer to the investigative team. A deputy auditor, Kamerer worked previously as a secretary for six different safety directors of Cleveland, including Eliot Ness, William Smith, Alvin Sutton and John McCormick.

It didn't take Tholl long to find discrepancies in some of the old records. Working with Kumerow, the two were finding discrepancies in names, brief tenure on the job and strange signatures. A new issue came up in the Edvon investigation. Prusak said she had endorsed all four of his checks, but Tholl was only able to match two of her signatures, "I don't know who signed the others," he said. The checks totaled $985.32.

As Perk was exerting effort to bring additional evidence to light, Prosecutor Corrigan suddenly announced his case was "wrapped up." He said his office could not conduct any further inquiry into the payroll records due to manpower, but would "pursue any new or additional evidence brought before him." Corrigan, a Democrat, then appeared to deliver a political shot at the Republican Perk by stating the auditor's predecessor John Carney, a fellow Democrat, had the "machinery" that would have caught the checks made out to Edvon. Corrigan took another swipe, stating witnesses had already contributed statements concerning the questionable signatures made and that paying Tholl $10 "was a waste of money and a duplication of effort."

Perk went on the offensive at that point and responded that it was Tholl, not Corrigan's office that discovered and substantiated "the fact that there were suspicious signatures on the payroll. These people, knowing Tholl's reputation for accuracy, came forward and admitted they were the ones who made the signatures. Without Tholl, there would not have been any revelations." Perk then defended himself against Corrigan's "machinery" comment by pointing out that the payroll clerk that handled those matters was the same one Carney had employed in the position. "In fact," Perk declared, "all personnel in that department are unchanged."

After several days, Corrigan was able to track down John Edvon, who was on a fishing trip at Pymatuning Reservoir on the Ohio-Pennsylvania border in Ashtabula County. Edvon told the prosecutor he had no knowledge his name was being used on the Recorder's payroll records. He did, however, state that back in the spring he performed some plumbing work for Day at his North Royalton home on Lawnsdale Drive. He also stated that on hand helping him, for the two days he was there, was Michael Kascak.

On July 9, Michael Kascak appeared before the grand jury and quickly turned on his employer, stating his desire to turn state's evidence against Day. Two days later, Frank Day was indicted on 27 counts of forging payroll checks, passing the forged checks, receiving money fraudulently from the county payroll, and certifying a fraudulent county payroll. He pleaded not guilty to the charges before Common Pleas Judge William K. Thomas and posted a $2,000 bond. He then went back to work, despite demands countywide, and numerous newspaper editorials calling for his resignation.

With the trial scheduled to begin on August 19, a fund was started in mid-July in Day's office to help with his legal expenses. While Corrigan acknowledged the fund was not illegal, he called it "most reprehensible."

On Monday, August 19, the trial began in Common Pleas court. The first order of business was attorney Norman Minor's motion for a change of venue, which was denied by Judge Thomas. Despite ordering a venire of 150, a jury of six men and six women was seated quickly. In his opening statement Minor stated, "Lax? Maybe. Careless? Perhaps. But stealing money by putting a fake employee, John A. Edvon, on his payroll? No, a thousand times no!" As if that wasn't enough, Minor added, "Edvon wanted a job. They gave him a job. He endorsed his first check and asked them to cash it for him. The checks came through and were cashed. The money piled up in the safe."

On Tuesday, John Edvon testified he had never applied for any job with the county. He said that in mid-April he went to the 11030 Lawnsdale Drive address of Day to look at a plumbing job. On May 1, he came and performed the work over a two-day period, receiving assistance from Michael Kascak. When the work was completed, he said Day gave him a pay voucher, made out with his name, and told him, "Here. Sign this and I'll get you some money." A week later Day gave him $80.

Evelyn Prusak's testimony filled most of the day Tuesday. She took the stand in "a blue maternity dress, tearful and upset." She had been demoted to routine office work since the payroll scandal burst into the news. Prusak gave testimony about Edvon and Michael Kascak. She stated Day approached her in April and said, "He had a friend he was putting on the payroll, that this friend had been unemployed and had a disability, that he felt sorry for him and wanted to do something for him, and that he had five children." Day then advised her "that Mr. Edvon was out at his home helping Mike [Kascak], and that when he was done there he'd be brought down to work in our storeroom." But Edvon never turned up in the flesh.

Day and a deputy recorder obtained a job application form and turned it over to her to file. She said the application told of "Edvon's politics, church and ethnic background but mentioned no family." During cross-examination, Minor asked her how she knew how many tax exemptions to use? She repeated, "I was told by Mr. Day he has five children."

On Wednesday morning, the third day of the trail, testimony came from a number of neighbors, who were witnesses to all the improvements going on at the Day home. One of the neighbors, a housewife in the mold of the Gladys Kravitz character from the "Bewitched" television series, was keeping an eye on Kascak because she thought "Day was being gypped because his yardman was idling away so much time." Once she found out Kascak was doing personal work for Day while on the county payroll, she began logging all of his activities. She must have been chomping at the bit to testify and was scheduled to take the stand Wednesday afternoon.

Before lunch on Wednesday, attorney Minor was cross-examining a witness and asked him if he could telephone his office for some information during the lunch period. Judge Thomas approved the request and offered, "Go ahead. You can use my office to make the call. Or rather, the county's office. It's the county's not mine," he stated, while stifling a grin.

After lunch, Day, Minor and Corrigan had a sit-down. The testimony that morning was devastating to the defendant and he and counsel saw no way out. The three men met with Judge Thomas and crafted an agreement on a guilty plea. At 2:35 court reconvened and, with the jury out, Day was called before the judge where the following exchange took place:

Judge Thomas: Do you plead guilty to counts 5, 13 and 24?

Day: Yes, I do.

Judge Thomas: Do you do this freely and voluntarily?

Day: Yes.

Judge Thomas: And with the full realization of the possible consequences?

Day: [Nodding] Yes.

The three counts were:

- On April 16, 1963, Day made and certified a payroll with Michael Kascak's name on it as deputy recorder, though Kascak was working weekdays at Day's home, not for the county.

- On May 1, 1963, Day made and certified a payroll bearing Edvon's name, knowing that Edvon was not working as a deputy recorder.

- On June 1, 1963, Day had John Edvon's name endorsed illegally on a paycheck made out to the plumber.

In addition to pleading guilty to 3 of the 27 counts, Day resigned, effective immediately, and forfeited $985.32 of his salary to cover the payments the county had made to John Edvon. Judge Thomas declared, "A public office is a public trust. He pleads guilty of violating his public trust. There remains only sentencing to prison. The public good demands it." Sentencing was set for September 24, following a presentencing report from the court probation department. Day was allowed to remain free on his $2,000 bond. Despite the guilty plea, when attorney Minor and his client faced reporters afterwards, they both refused to admit Day had done anything wrong.

On the day of sentencing, Minor asked for probation, claiming Day was a sick man and may not live out his term. In reviewing the presentencing report, one thing stood out in Judge Thomas's mind, Day had told the probation officer he allowed Kascak to work on county time as a handyman at his Parma Heights home because he felt "it was common practice to do so."

Judge Thomas told Day, "In that one sentence you show how utterly unfit you are to hold public office." He then sentenced Day to a term of 1-to-20-years in the Ohio Penitentiary. In December 1963, Day was transferred to the Roseville facility to serve out his sentence at what Warden E. L. Maxwell called "an old man's jail." The warden said Day had an "honorary prisoner status and has been assigned to no particular work detail." In August 1964, Day's bid for parole was denied. His next consideration was in August 1966, at which time he was granted parole. Frank S. Day died on September 19, 1974 at the age of 67. He was buried in Louisiana, where he grew up.

In August 1965, Joseph Tholl, hailed as "Chagrin Fall's internationally known examiner of questioned documents," was one of the key speakers at a joint meeting held in Ottawa, Canada, of the American Society of Questionable Document Examiners and the Royal Canadian Mounted Police Crime Detection Laboratories, a week-long affair. For Tholl's part he prepared a program showing his new techniques in handwriting identification, and held a discussion in experimentation with a new Eastman-Kodak product in the use of "critical analysis of inks."

If the Frank S. Day case was Tholl's most famous case, then the murder of John C. Young, Jr. was his most infamous. On the morning of August 24, 1965, the 8-year-old boy left his home at 3171 Warrington Road in Shaker Heights at 8:30 to stop at a neighbor's house two doors away. The neighbor, Mariann Colby, called the Young residence minutes earlier and asked John C. Young, Sr. if a jacket left behind at her place belonged to "Cremer," the boy's middle name, which he used to distinguish himself from his father. Cremer and Mrs. Colby's 9-year-old son, Dane, classmates at Onaway Elementary School, often played together.

By late morning, Cremer had not returned home. His mother Nancy, a member of the Junior League of Cleveland, called the Colby home but no one answered. Calls to the homes of a dozen other friends of Cremer in the neighborhood proved fruitless. At 12:10 p.m., about three-and-a-half hours after leaving home, and ten miles away, Cremer's body was found by David Griesinger, a Harvard College senior, who was out walking his two labrador retrievers in a wooded section between roadways of Gates Mills Boulevard, not far from Old Mill Road in the well-to-do village of Gates Mills. The dogs discovered the body 150 feet from the west side of Gates Mills Boulevard.

The body was removed to the Cuyahoga County Morgue. Two Shaker Police officers were dispatched to the Young's home to break the bad news to John Young and take him to the morgue to identify his son's body.

The young boy was shot in the back of the head at a range of two inches with a .32 caliber handgun. Cuyahoga County Coroner Dr. Samuel R. Gerber, after noting the absence of blood where the body was recovered, determined Cremer was killed elsewhere and his body left in the wooded area. Law enforcement believed the murder took place in Shaker Heights and Detective Lieutenant Ralph J. Schaar, along with Lawrence W. Doran, chief of the homicide unit of the Cuyahoga County Sheriff's Department, took charge of the investigation. Dr. Gerber said the shooting could have been accidental or a deliberate act.

The cold-blooded murder of the popular and well-liked little boy, whose parents were socially prominent in the city, was a front-page news sensation for days. The newspapers had a field day covering every aspect of the investigation. The Shaker Heights police did an excellent job of investigating the murder and looking for suspects. Shaker Heights Police Chief Carl R. Longstreet put together a questionnaire for patrolmen to canvass the neighborhood with. In this open appeal for help from the public, he asked for their theory of what could have happened. The chief later explained he had a strategy that the question might prompt the slayer or someone with knowledge of the slaying to reveal information that only the killer would know. Longstreet told reporters, "A thorough examination of rubbish collected from every home in a four-block area produced nothing of value." In hopes of prodding the killer to turn their self in, police advanced the theory of the shooting being an accident and the moving of the body a panicked reaction. Dr. Gerber, on several occasions, suggested the killing could have been the result of children playing with a loaded gun.

Television and newspaper reporters naturally rushed to the Young's home for stories. Cremer's grandfather, Richard Hawley Cutting, a prominent Cleveland architect, showed off a recent report from his grandson's time at summer camp at Hawken School. He had received a mark of excellence for integrity, honesty, compatibility and attitude. Cremer had won a "boy of the week" honor for popularity, voted on by his fellow camp attendees. He was also captain of the baseball team. His father said Cremer, "Was absolutely reliable, never wandered off without telling his mother where he was going. He would call her up if he was at neighbors."

Although both the police and newspapers refrained from speculating on a suspect, it was hard to ignore something that occurred on the day of the murder. When police questioned Mrs. Colby about the early morning phone call regarding the jacket, she told them, "Cremer had stayed overnight here last spring and I was sure it was his jacket. I walked out and asked him. We talked in the driveway. He said it wasn't his. Ordinarily Cremer would have come in and played with Dane. But he walked away. He looked as though he had someplace to go." Later that day, John Young and a detective went to the Colby home to view the jacket, a black and white windbreaker. He said it belonged to Cremer. He recalled his son was with him when the jacket was purchased and the boy really liked it. Nancy Young said, "He was so proud of it. It was the only one in the neighborhood. He didn't miss it because he didn't need it [during the summer months]." Despite the glaring differences about the jacket, police had no motive, and no weapon and continued the investigation.

On the morning of Thursday, August 26, a private service took place at Lake View Cemetery, where Cremer was laid to rest. At 1:30 that afternoon, a ten-minute memorial service was held at St. Paul's Episcopal Church at Fairmont Boulevard and Coventry Road in Cleveland Heights. The family was ushered in and out through a private entrance.

As the days passed and no suspects were found, the police began to press Mariann Colby a bit more; after all, she was the last person to see Cremer alive. On Monday, August 30, she voluntarily took a polygraph test at the coroner's office. Police theorized her responses were "inconclusive" due to her nervous condition and she agreed to take another one within 24 to 48 hours. On Wednesday, September 1, eight days after the murder, Mariann was at the detective bureau in the Shaker Heights police station. At the start of the session, Coroner Gerber advised her, "You are entitled to the advice of an attorney and your husband." She replied she wasn't interested in speaking to a lawyer or getting advice from her husband." She was then questioned for five-and-a-half hours by Lieutenant Schaar, Coroner Gerber, County Detective Doran and Shaker Heights Detective Thomas A. Geschke. At 3:45, Mrs. Colby asked if she could speak to Dr. Gerber alone. She broke down and told the coroner her son Dane had shot and killed Cremer at her home that morning.

Mariann told police a bizarre tale about the morning of the shooting. She said she retrieved a .32 revolver from a buffet in the dining room and, for some reason she could not explain, loaded it. She then took the five-shot revolver and placed it on a cabinet in the kitchen and covered it with clothing that needed to be washed. When Cremer arrived at the Colby home, after Mariann's call to John Young, he and Dane began playing at the side door landing. Gerber related what

Colby told her next. While she was in another room, "she heard an explosion or the firing of a gun. She went to the place and saw Cremer lying on the floor. She looked at him, and saw he was beyond help. She didn't say he was dead. She sent Dane upstairs and took a coat from the closet and wrapped Cremer's body in it."

Before removing the body from the house, she wrapped it in a plastic dry-cleaning bag. Mariann carried him out to the car, an old blue Buick Century station wagon, and placed his body on the floor of the backseat, hanging shirts on the window so no one could see inside. She then drove "aimlessly" out Shaker Boulevard and could not remember how she arrived in Gates Mills. She carried the 59-pound body of the boy 150 feet into a wooded area where it was later found by Griesinger's dogs.

When asked about the gun, Mariann said she purchased it three years earlier at a West Side gun store for "no definite reason." She claimed her husband didn't like guns, so she never told him about it. After the shooting, she concealed the revolver, along with a box of cartridges, in a package of ground meat and hid it in a deep freezer. She offered no explanation of how her son found the weapon on the kitchen cabinet, or any reason for how or why he had shot Cremer. She then dictated, read and signed a statement that her son had shot and killed Cremer Young.

Everyone bought the story of Dane, the "slow learner," killing his friend, Cremer, for no discernable reason. Case solved. Even with all the holes in Mariann's statement, police made no arrest and she and Dane were allowed to go home. They were picked up by her husband, Robert W. Colby, a space program engineer at TRW, Inc. He had heard about the latest news on the car radio while going to pick up Mariann. When he asked her why she never told him about Dane shooting Cremer, she told him, "I didn't want to upset you." When he asked her about the gun, he received the same answer.

What would become of their son? How would the law handle him? What about Mariann? Would there be charges against her for withholding information in an investigation, tampering with evidence, or a slew of other violations? Tomorrow would be another day.

Police recovered the .32 revolver that evening from the Colby home, right where Mariann said she hid it in the deep freezer along with the cartridges. Police immediately began tests on the weapon and attempted to track down where she had purchased it, from whom, and most importantly when.

Mariann had readily agreed to meet with Detectives Doran, Geschke and Schaar the next morning to retrace her steps to Gates Mills, and willingly returned to the detective bureau to "clear up the inconsistencies in her statements." They took her out to the Gates Mills site where Cremer's body was found. The detectives peppered her with questions as her story kept changing. Back at the station, her details about what happened the day of the shooting were changing, too. The gun she had loaded and hid among the clothing, she now claimed was in a coffee urn on a breakfront in the dining room.

The bad news for Mrs. Colby came when ballistics tests came back on the gun. The tests showed that it required 15 to 17 pounds of pressure to fire the .32 double-action revolver. This meant it was physically impossible for 9-year-old Dane to have fired the weapon that caused Cremer's death.

Mariann's next admission was the shooting didn't take place at the side door landing, but while she was picking up and moving clothes in the kitchen area. The gun went off accidentally as she was standing five to six feet away. By 11:30, the police had wrapped up the case.

Based on all the information police gathered, and with all the lies they heard from Mrs. Colby, at 3:15 Thursday afternoon they charged her with first-degree murder. Within an hour of being charged, she pleaded innocent before Judge John A. Corlett in Shaker Heights Municipal Court. After a request for her release on bond by her attorney, Gerald S. Gold, which is not allowed in first-degree murder cases, she was taken to the Cuyahoga County Jail.

One of the elements of pursuing a first-degree murder case against Mrs. Colby was to show there was premeditation on her part. The fact she lured Cremer to her home before shooting him was one of those elements. Police wanted to show she purchased the gun she used to kill him recently, as this would be another important element. This is where they were going to need Joseph Tholl.

Investigators tracked down Burdell Willsey, a Medina gun dealer, who sold the .32 revolver. He was currently on a five-year Federal probation for failure to register firearms information. The records he was able to pull on the sale of the weapon, based on the serial number, showed it was sold to a "Nancy C. Russell" on April 17, 1963, two years and five months before the murder. Willsey, whose record keeping was described as being "in a confused condition," seemed to want to help investigators and reporters. He told Donald L. Bean, the *Plain Dealer*'s chief police reporter, "I might have sold her [Mrs. Colby] the gun or I may have sold it to this Russell woman and somehow it may have wound up in Mrs. Colby's hands."

Willsey said he was questioned the previous night by agents of the U.S. Internal Revenue Service. The address for Nancy Russell was the 3900 block of Spokane Avenue SE, in a stretch that runs between Pearl Road and West 41st Street. Willsey told investigators he could not remember the woman. Two families named Russell lived on Spokane Avenue, but told the *Plain Dealer* there was no Nancy Russell related to them. When government agents showed him a picture of Mariann Colby, Willsey didn't recognize her. He told reporter Bean, "I studied and studied that woman's picture and it rang no bells." He did say the gun was purchased from the Strongsville store he owned at one time, which matched Mrs. Colby's claim of purchasing it from a West Side gun shop. While Willsey did not recall selling the box of Smith & Wesson cartridges, found in the deep freezer, to Colby, he did confirm that the handwriting on the box was his.

On September 10, Tholl examined the handwriting of Mariann Colby to see if it matched the "Nancy C. Russell" signature. "They are similar," he told news people, "but I have asked Shaker Heights police for more material." On September 16, Tholl announced the findings of his investigation. It represented good and bad news for the prosecution. The good news was he made a complete identification of Mariann Colby's handwriting and determined she was the person who signed the receipt for the purchase of the .32 revolver as "Nancy C. Russell." The bad news was the purchase was confirmed as being made in April 1963, destroying the theory she bought the gun recently as part of the plan to murder Cremer Young.

The first-degree murder trial of Mariann Colby began on Tuesday, March 15, 1966. On the advice of counsel, she requested a trial before a three-judge panel. Gold figured since all her neighbors wanted to hang her, his chances of getting 12 jurors to acquit her were nil. He figured he would have a better chance of convincing three men in black robes that she was insane rather than a lynch mob. The three common pleas judges selected were John L. Angelotta, Donald F. Lybarger and John M. Manos. The state was represented by Assistant County Prosecutors George Moscarino and Leo Spellacy, while Gold and Thomas J. Barnard comprised the defense counsel. The defense attorneys entered pleas of innocent and innocent by reason of insanity. To Moscarino, he was simply presenting a case of cold-blooded premeditated murder. The motive? Mrs. Colby was angry of the Youngs' rejection of her son, and that Dane didn't measure up to Cremer.

The judges visited the Colby home on Warrington Road. The house was now for sale, and Robert Colby and Dane had moved to Euclid. After going to the site where the body was found in the woods off Gates Mills Boulevard, they returned to Lakeside Avenue Courthouse, which would draw huge crowds on a daily basis during the trial. The first witness called was Gates Mills Chief of Police Fred Fenohr, who testified about the finding of Cremer's body in the wooded area by the college student and his dogs just after noon on August 24.

Coroner Gerber was the second witness called by the state. When he began to discuss Mrs. Colby's September 1 statement about Dane shooting Cremer, attorney Gold objected immediately. He moved to have the written statement suppressed. Gold had argued at preliminary hearings that his client was denied representation. The judges granted Gold the privilege of questioning Dr. Gerber about the statements before they were introduced. During that questioning, Gerber explained to Gold that Mrs. Colby was told numerous times she should have a lawyer, and this was recorded by the stenographer who was present during the questioning. Prosecutor Moscarino also told the court that on September 1, Mariann had not yet been arrested and it was her idea to come to the police station to be questioned.

On Wednesday morning, Gold's motion to have Colby's statement about her son suppressed was overruled by the judges. Dr. Gerber was allowed to continue his testimony regarding Mrs. Colby's September 1 admission. The state entered as evidence the .32 handgun as well as a picture of it wrapped in the ground beef. Gold again objected, stating Mrs. Colby was not advised of her right to object to a search of her home. The judges overruled this objection, too. On Wednesday afternoon, when state testimony turned to Mrs. Colby's admission of guilt, Gold again took to the stand in an effort to suppress her oral confession from September 2, in which she claimed to have accidently shot Cremer. He gave a timeline of his requests to see his client that day while she was being questioned. Charles P. Durra, a family attorney for the Colbys, took the stand and said he tried to telephone Mrs. Colby at 12:15, but was not successful. Gold then argued that anything Mrs. Colby said after 12:15 was obtained illegally. He testified he arrived at the Shaker Heights police station at 1:30, but was refused permission to see his client until 3:15 that afternoon.

On Thursday morning, Gold's efforts paid off as the judges ruled Mrs. Colby's September 2 oral confession was inadmissible because it was obtained after 12:15. Also on Thursday, Mr. and Mrs. Young took the stand. Nancy Young stated the friendship between her son and Dane caused friction between the two families. John Young testified that Mrs. Colby was "concerned" because Dane was not permitted to stay overnight at the Young's home. At one point, John Young spoke to Robert Colby and said they "mutually decided the boys would not play together as much as they had. Bob Colby was somewhat upset by my indication to Cremer that Dane had somewhat babyish tendencies."

On Friday, March 18, the state produced two surprise witnesses, who had been shielded from the media. Robert Enterline, a Warrington Road resident, testified he saw Mrs. Colby backing out of her driveway between 8:30 and 8:45 the morning of the killing. Lois Berry, a domestic servant working for a Gates Mills family, told the court that about 9:00 a.m. on August 24, she saw a blue station wagon parked near the place where Cremer's body was found. She recalled she saw shirts hanging in the right-side window of the vehicle.

Much of the proceedings were taken up by attorney Gold's desperate attempts to suppress Mariann's two statements to investigators. Attention to these motions played out through all four days of the trial during the week. Each time, Gold was allowed to take the stand or call witnesses in support of his suppression efforts. On Thursday morning, the judges ruled that anything Mrs. Colby had said to investigators after 12:15 on September 2 was inadmissible. On Friday afternoon, the issue was taken up again. During the Friday session, Robert Colby, who had been waiting outside the courtroom all week, was called as a witness, but only to support Gold's timetable of September 2.

Detective Thomas Geschke then took the stand and said he was having a cheeseburger and coffee lunch with Mrs. Colby at noon on September 2. He testified that Lieutenant Schaar advised him at 11:30 a.m. that Mrs. Colby "confessed." With this testimony, the judges reversed their decision to suppress Mrs. Colby's confession to shooting Cremer. This allowed for Schaar to be called to the stand and tell the 3-judge panel the story of Mrs. Colby, after being told the results of the trigger-pull test, admitting she accidently pulled the trigger killing Cremer.

The state rested its case on Friday, after which the defense requested the first-degree murder charge be dropped and the trial continue as a second-degree murder case. The motion was overruled by the judges.

When the defense began their case on Monday, March 21, there was no way they could refute the evidence presented by the prosecution. All they could hope to do was to convince the judges Mrs. Colby was insane at the time of the killing. They called just three witnesses, two psychiatrists and a psychologist, to try to make their point.

Dr. Lily Brunschwig, a clinical psychologist at Hanna Pavilion of University Hospitals, who examined Mariann twice at the Cuyahoga County Jail, claimed the defendant was psychotic, having "an abnormal feeling of superstition, distrust and persecution." She was followed to the stand by Dr. Arthur L. Rosenbaum, of University Hospitals, who, despite having five sessions with Mrs. Colby, was making his debut in a first-degree murder case. He traced her problems back to 1952 and characterized the defendant as "a chronic schizophrenic, a split-personality, who sometimes locked her mother in her room and at times was quite cruel in punishing her only child. The psychiatrist portrayed her as "an incurable sick woman with deteriorating mental processes."

When Dr. Rosenbaum returned to the stand the next day, he testified that Mrs. Colby purchased the weapon in order to "kill a man who had rebuffed her love." He said she was known to follow this man, who was never identified, when he was on a date. The doctor stated she was severely ill mentally and "pathologically interested in another person." Dr. Rosenbaum claimed Robert Colby was aware of her involvement with this other man, having received a phone call from him late one night, but made no attempt to intervene.

A third doctor, Charles DeLeon, a psychiatrist, also from Hanna Pavilion of University Hospitals, told the judges Mrs. Colby, "lives in a fantasy world of hate, fear, hostility, suspicion and delusion." At the end of his testimony, the defense rested their case. Neither Mrs. Colby, nor her husband, Robert, took the stand.

After the testimony of the three doctors, one was left to wonder how Mrs. Colby was able to get out of bed in the morning, let alone devise a murder plot and carry it out to the point of keeping the police at bay for over a week.

On Wednesday, March 23, the prosecutors called Dr. David Sprague, head of the psychiatric unit of Lakewood Hospital as a rebuttal witness. He had three sessions with her. During his testimony, he stated on cross-examination that Mrs. Colby may have had a "psychotic episode" on the day of the murder, and "that cannot rule out the possibility that disturbed thinking played a part in her act." He called Mrs. Colby a borderline personality, a person "who lived on the edge of normal and psychotic." Neither statement proved helpful to the state.

The question that needed to be answered was whether or not Mrs. Colby was sane at the time of the crime. The *Plain Dealer* explained, "Ohio law states that even a mentally disturbed person must be found guilty if he [or she] knows right from wrong at the time the crime is committed." Someone not knowing right from wrong would not have gone through the lengths that Mrs. Colby did to cover up the crime if she was insane at the time she committed it.

Dr. Wilfred M. Gill, head of the psychiatric clinic of Cuyahoga County Common Pleas Court, was the last scheduled rebuttal witness and testified Thursday morning. Dr. Gill was perhaps the most experienced of all the expert witnesses. He testified he had examined 750 people accused of committing first-degree murder during his career. He told the court Mrs. Colby was suffering from a minor mental disorder – "passive-aggressive personality, aggressive type," but he was emphatic that she was not psychotic and was able to reason at the time of the killing. Judge Lybarger asked, did Mrs. Colby understand the "social value implication" of the shooting? Dr. Gill, replied "Yes, but she just didn't care."

In closing statements, both the prosecutors and defense counsel seemed to tear Marianne Colby apart. Moscarino described her as "a scheming, devious, sexually starved woman," who lured the young boy to her home before murdering him and then attempted to conceal the crime, first by blaming her own son, and then claiming she shot him by accident. He closed by asking the judges, "Would you want Mrs. Colby living next door to you?"

Gold simply continued to push his agenda that she was insane despite the fact the only people to buy into that were the doctors he put on the stand. He asked the judge to send her to Lima State Hospital with the following send off, "Mrs. Colby is lost. She has lost her battle not only in the court but against psychic disintegration. No matter what the court does, Mrs. Colby will be in institutions for a long, long time."

After closing statements, the three judges began their deliberations at 5:00, Thursday afternoon. After three-and-a-half hours, they had not reached a decision. On Friday morning, they continued their deliberations before coming to a verdict an hour-and-a-half later. Before they could deliver it, they had another matter to deal with. The packed courtroom was in the process of being cleared of all spectators. An anonymous caller had threatened the life of Mariann Colby. Lieutenant Schaar told reporters, "It was a male voice threatening to shoot her if a verdict of not guilty by reason of insanity was returned." Everyone coming back into the courtroom was searched for weapons. When the panel returned, presiding Judge Donald Lybarger warned spectators, "There will be no demonstrations whatsoever in this courtroom. Guards have been placed among you to see that this order is carried out."

Mrs. Colby was then asked to come to the bench. As she approached the judges the heel on her right shoe broke off. Judge Lybarger read the decision of the court telling her she had been found not guilty by reason of insanity and she would be committed to the penal institution for the criminally insane. He finished his address by saying. "Mrs. Colby, we leave you to heaven." He then quickly waved her out of the courtroom.

"What the hell does that mean?" questioned John Young, from his seat in the back of the courtroom.

Lybarger said the verdict was unanimous, but made no further comment, other than to say copies of the verdict would be available later.

Plain Dealer reporter Michael D. Roberts explained the judges had found Mrs. Colby not guilty by reason of insanity on the basis of a 123-year-old English precedent known as the M'Naughten Rules. Roberts wrote, "Many legal authorities consider the law medieval in the light of progress made in psychiatry." In their written opinion, the three judges criticized the law they had before them:

> Unless and until some trial court under proper circumstances has the courage to point the way to a better method of submitting to the triers of the facts the issue of the insanity of the accused when insanity is tendered as a defense, then Ohio will continue to adhere to criteria which more and more are challenged as being false.

It was immediately apparent the triumvirate of judges who heard this case did not have the "courage to point the way to a better method." When the state rested its case, attorney Gold knew his attempts to get the case thrown out with his many motions citing illegally obtained evidence had failed. At that time he seemed willing to throw in the towel for a second-degree murder conviction for his client, which would have kept her out of the electric chair. The state prosecutors should have supported it. At least 8-year-old Cremer Young and his family would have received some justice. They obviously weren't going to receive it from the judges, who, by the way, overruled Gold's motion to reduce the first-degree murder charge.

As Mrs. Colby was shipped off to Lima State Hospital on March 28, it was left to be seen what was to happen to her now that her future was left to heaven. If Gold's prediction held true that this broken insane woman who, "lost her battle not only in the court but against psychic disintegration," and was going to be in "institutions for a long, long time," then maybe she deserved it, but only if Gold's definition of a "long, long time" meant just five years and seven months for the taking of a young boy's life.[144]

In March 1967, Tholl was a witness in the conflict-of-interest trial of John L. Kocevar, the former chief executive officer of Cuyahoga County Sheriff James J. McGettrick. Kocevar, when he was just 25 years-old, was an agent of the Ohio Liquor Enforcement Department and the unsung hero of the infamous raid on the notorious Jungle Inn, which took place on August 12, 1949.[145] Kocevar climbed the ranks in the department and eventually became the agent in charge of the Cleveland district.

On April 8, 1963, James J. McGettrick, in his eighth term in the Ohio House of Representatives, was selected by the Cuyahoga County Central Committee to replace Joseph M. Sweeney, as Cuyahoga County Sheriff. Sweeney passed away on January 25 at the age of 84. Four days later, McGettrick chose John Kocevar to be his chief executive assistant. An editorial in the *Plain Dealer* called the appointment of McGettrick a political one, but claimed that some of the reservations they had about McGettrick were removed by his selection of Kocevar.

Things would change. The newspaper never seemed happy with the way the new sheriff was running his office. Spending by McGettrick was a main concern. On November 21, 1965, the proverbial "shit hit the fan" in a front-page Sunday *Plain Dealer* headline article, by Donald L. Barlett in which the newspaper revealed an on-going and wide-ranging investigation into improprieties going on in the county sheriff's office. Key among the areas being investigated was that Kocevar had a business interest in Kitchen Reddy Foods, Inc., which advertised as providing "Frozen Prepeeled Precut Potatoes, with a Full Line of Frozen Foods." The company had been around since 1958, originally as Redi Taters, Inc., before adopting the current name in 1960. There is no record of how John and Rita Kocevar got involved in the company, let alone how they became board members and shareholders. The concern had a contract to provide meals for prisoners at the Cuyahoga County Jail. Ohio state law, however, prohibited county officials – elected or appointed – from having an interest in a contract for goods purchased by the county. Penalties included a prison sentence of 1-to-10 years. The newspaper uncovered a tax document from March 1964 showing that John Kocevar was Secretary of Kitchen Reddy Foods, Inc., and his wife, Rita was the vice president and a 50% stockholder in the company. The jail had been purchasing fish and french-fries from the company since January 1964, and had paid them nearly $4,000.

When the *Plain Dealer* reporter questioned Kocevar, he denied being an officer of the company or that he had a financial interest. Asked if he had ever been an officer, he replied, "I really wouldn't remember." He did acknowledge his wife's position and financial interest. The next day, County Prosecutor John Corrigan announced he would be initiating his own investigation of Kocevar's connection to Kitchen Reddy Foods to see if he was violating the state's conflict-of-interest law.

Among the other items reporter Barlett revealed, was that two sheriff's deputies were assigned to a stakeout at the frozen food plant at 1825 Scranton Road, to watch for a suspected burglar. The plant was located in an area of Cleveland that falls under Cleveland police jurisdiction. On January 9, 1965, the two deputies, along with two Cleveland detectives arrested an ex-employee after he came out of the building with $30 of frozen shrimp. Barlett also revealed he saw Kocevar driven to the Kitchen Reddy Foods facility in an unmarked sheriff's car. Barlett got to a telephone and called the sheriff's office and asked for Kocevar. He was told he was unavailable because he was in a meeting.

The reporter also contacted Kitchen Reddy Foods attorney William E. Mahon. The attorney was a close friend of Kocevar and represented him, too. Mahon told Barlett that Kocevar served as Secretary in 1963, but submitted his resignation in December that year. When asked why his name appeared on the March 1964 tax document, Mahon replied, "If his name is there, it's a mistake. I have his resignation right here in the corporation record books," which the attorney said he planned to turn over to the prosecutor's office.

The story played out all week in the newspapers until November 26. Kocevar met with Sheriff McGettrick that day seeking a leave of absence from the department. What happened next neither would tell the media, but McGettrick obviously turned Kocevar down and a heated argument ensued. This resulted in Kocevar resigning, turning in his badge, and cleaning out his desk. At the time, the newspapers reported that Kocevar was the highest paid law enforcement officer in the county, making $16,000 a year. McGettrick provided reporters with a statement announcing the resignation, but offered no details and answered no questions. Prosecutor Corrigan quickly addressed the resignation, stating it would not affect his investigation into the conflict-of-interest accusations. On March 4, 1966, Kocevar was indicted by the Cuyahoga County Grand Jury. He pleaded not guilty before Common Pleas Judge Harry Jaffe, who set bond at $500.

Kocevar's trial did not begin for another year. On March 13, 1967, a jury of six men and six women were seated in the Common Pleas Courtroom of Judge Perry B. Jackson. William Maher represented the defendant. Assistant County Prosecutors Patrick G. Lazzaro and Dennis J. McGuire represented the state. In his opening statement Lazzaro said Kocevar served as an officer of Kitchen Reddy Foods, Inc. during the same time he worked in the sheriff's office – April 1963 until November 1965. Attorney Mahon claimed that his client "severed his connection" with the frozen food concern in December 1963.

Among those testifying for the state on Tuesday was the county's purchasing agent, who said he received a letter from McGettrick on September 18, 1963, asking that Kitchen Reddy Foods be placed on the bid list. He stated that the frozen food company filled its first order on January 21, 1964. When McGettrick was questioned about the letter, he could not recall writing it and stated that neither he nor Kocevar had authority to order food for the jail, that it was handled through the county commissioner's office.

An agent from the Ohio Department of Taxation testified that Kitchen Reddy Foods sent a report to his department dated March 4, 1964. The report identified B. Joseph Linnen as president and treasurer, Rita Kocevar as vice president, and John Kocevar as secretary. Attorney Mahon objected to the admissibility of the documents, a ruling Judge Jackson said he would withhold until the state finished its case.

On Wednesday, an official from Society National Bank testified that since April 1965, Rita Kocevar deposited 24 checks over an eight-month period into the Kocevars' joint-checking account. Then over a five-month period, ending on November 8, 1965, John Kocevar made four withdrawals totaling $4,000. The money Kocevar withdrew, along with money from Joseph Linnen, was said to purchase stock control of Area-Wide Paging Systems, Inc., a paging service using portable beeper-type devices. With Kocevar as president and Linnen secretary-treasurer, they held 105 of 115 shares of stock in the corporation. Paid advertisements appeared in the *Plain Dealer* showing the company was located in Suite 229 of the Lincoln Building at the south-east corner of East 6th Street and St. Clair Avenue in downtown Cleveland,[146] long-time home of Pat Joyce's restaurant. The advertisements appeared frequently in 1965, right up until the time the *Plain Dealer* released their expose on the sheriff's department, derailing Kocevar's career there.

Later that day the prosecution called Joseph Tholl. At question was a document sent to the Cleveland Trust Company requesting a mechanical signature service for payroll checks. It was dated October 1965. The document had the Kitchen Reddy Foods, Inc. name on it and listed John Kocevar as Secretary and was signed by him. Tholl verified that the signature on the document was Kocevar's and that all the signatures on the checks withdrawing the $4,000 from the joint checking account were his, as well. While attorney Mahon acknowledged the signature on the Cleveland Trust Company document was Kocevar's, he claimed his client "signed many blank forms" at Kitchen Reddy Foods before he resigned.

During a half-day session on Thursday, Donald Barlett, the investigative reporter from the *Plain Dealer* took the stand. Barlett, now working for the Chicago Daily News, told the court he saw Kocevar enter the Kitchen Reddy Foods facility about 3:30 p.m. on October 21, 1965, some 23 months after Kocevar said he had resigned.

On Friday, when the state rested its case, Judge Jackson admitted all the documents into evidence with the exception of the tax report from March 1964, for which he was still withholding his ruling.

When John Kocevar took the stand on Monday, March 21, his plan must have been to plead ignorant to everything that was going on. Under direct examination by Mahon, he claimed he had nothing to do with the food supplied to the County Jail; he resigned as secretary of Kitchen Reddy Foods before taking the job in the sheriff's office; and "I think my wife was," when asked who was on the board of directors at Kitchen Reddy Foods.

During nearly five hours of cross-examination, he made the following statements:

- He knew very little about Kitchen Reddy Foods

- He wasn't sure what the firm did, "I just saw them [the jail] getting the potatoes. I didn't know where they went."

- While his wife Rita was a stockholder in Kitchen Reddy Foods, he didn't know what she paid for it or that she owned 50%

- He didn't know what his wife earned at Kitchen Reddy Foods

- Even though he introduced Joseph Linnen as a friend of his to Mc-Gettrick, he didn't know the sheriff wrote a letter to county commissioners asking that Kitchen Reddy Foods be out on the county bid list to supply food

- He didn't know who the directors of the company were, even though he was one of them

Prosecutor Lazzaro asked Kocevar, as Secretary you must have known something about the firm's operation. Kocevar replied, "Whenever they gave me papers to sign, I would sign them." He claimed that was the case with the mechanical signature service letter, which was signed in October 1965, more than 30 months after he resigned from the company.

Testimony was completed on Tuesday and closing statements were delivered. Mahon hammered the table as he continued to insist his client had no interest in Kitchen Reddy Foods after accepting the sheriff's department job. The prosecution claimed that in addition to Kocevar being directly involved as Secretary in Kitchen Reddy Foods, he indirectly benefited by using his wife's compensation from her vice president's position to gain central control of Area-Wide Paging Systems, Inc.

After Judge Jackson delivered his charge, the case was in the jury's hands for deliberation. After an eight-day trial, the jury deliberated two-and-a-half-hours between 10:30 a.m. and 3:12 p.m. on Thursday. After taking just one vote they returned to the courtroom with a verdict of guilty.

The jury simply didn't buy Kocevar's story that he had no interest in Kitchen Reddy Foods, not to mention only scant knowledge of the company's operations. After the verdict was read, jury foreman, Robert G. Brown, said the decision "all hinged" on one document, the one Joseph Tholl verified that Kocevar had signed dated October 1, 1965, for the mechanical signature service.

Judge Jackson deferred sentence until after ruling on a motion for a new trial from Mahon. After denying the attorney's request days later, Mahon said he would appeal the decision; he would lose. In the meantime, on June 1, 1967,

Judge Jackson, noting that Kocevar had lost a public position of trust, told him, "I believe you have suffered sufficiently." He then placed him on two years' probation.

On January 28, 1968, Tholl's wife, Ina, passed away at the age of 68. During her life she had been secretary to the dean at Spencerian College, where she also taught bookkeeping and shorthand. Later she was a secretary in the sports department of the *Plain Dealer*. She and Joseph were married for 20 years. He later married Josephine Rodenbaugh.

In the early 1970s, Tholl got a taste of Cleveland's organized crime world. Cleveland police contacted him following the killing of rubbish hauling company owner Michael W. Frato by Daniel J. "Danny" Greene on November 29, 1971. During the investigation after his death, Frato's wife, Susan, turned a letter over to police consisting of newspaper and magazine clippings pasted on a sheet of paper stating:

If there are any more waves created in this town by this senseless violence you will be annihilated. This advice has been mailed to all three of you punks. We did not build this town to have it destroyed by punks. Believe it or not.

The other "punks" were never identified. The address on the letter, mailed to the Frato home, was handwritten. After studying the handwriting Tholl determined that it did not belong to Danny Greene, but, believed instead, it was written by a woman. Danny Greene pleaded self-defense in the shooting and Common Pleas Judge Herbert R. Whiting agreed, telling the jury to find Greene not guilty.

In a 1972 article by *Plain Dealer* writer Allen Wiggins, he noted, "There are not too many Joseph Tholls around. Tholl himself says he is a member of a dying breed. In the whole country, he says there are only three or four examiners like himself who use all the forms of analysis in attacking the authenticity of documents and signatures."

Now in his 60s, Tholl would continue to be involved in several high-profile cases over the last ten years of his life.

April 1972 – In the spring of 1972, Tholl testified in a bribery trial involving Philip S. Gaeta, former Cleveland streets commissioner, and William A. "Sonny" Harris, former secretary to the service director. Both were on trial after being indicted on ten counts of soliciting and accepting bribes to allow privately owned trucks on the city payroll. Tholl testified on April 6 that Gaeta's payroll record signature matched the endorsement he made on a check covering a bribe he accepted. Both men were convicted.

May 1972 – Tholl participated in the investigation of a "larceny by trick" scheme involving Nunzio R. Calvo, a member of the Cuyahoga County Soldier's Relief Commission. Tholl discovered a dozen vouchers with falsified signatures.

Calvo was indicted in August, along with four Cleveland merchants. A second indictment in December charged him with 50 counts of fraud and conspiracy. In January 1973, Calvo pleaded guilty to 12 counts. In March he was sentenced to 2-to-17-years in the Ohio Penitentiary.

August 1972 – Tholl was called upon by Cleveland City Council Clerk Mercedes Cotner to study petitions submitted seeking to reduce the size of City Council. Cotner sought Tholl's help after noticing multiple signatures that seemed to be made by the same person. After reviewing 8,000 of 29,000 signatures, Tholl confirmed that he found a number of invalid signatures. Proponents of the referendum to reduce council from 33 members to 15 needed 23,012 signatures to get the amendment on the November ballot. It was Cotner's responsibility to verify the petitions. Tholl charged that many of the names forged appeared to be done so by the petition circulators. He determined that as many as 161 petitions, containing 3,000 to 4,000 names could be involved. The attempt to reduce city council failed, but nine years later, in 1981, Cleveland voters agreed to reduce council from 33 to 21 members.

August 1972 – Before the month was over, Tholl found himself in "an obscure basement office of the Statehouse" in Columbus, searching for forged signatures on petitions to repeal Ohio's graduated income tax. Tholl indicated some people signed the petition for themselves as well as for family members. It was reported that in some counties an individual filled petitions simply by copying names from a voter registration list.

March 1976 – A Federal Grand Jury in March 1976 used Tholl during an investigation of the Cuyahoga Metropolitan Housing Authority (CMHA). Tholl discovered five forged leases in which authorities believed CMHA employees cooperated with Cleveland numbers racketeers at the King-Kennedy Estates. The apartments were allegedly used for selling numbers and "other illegal activities," while the rents were subsidized with Federal funds.

May 1978 – During the recall of Mayor Dennis J. Kucinich, the mayor hired Tholl to examine questionable signatures on some of the recall petitions in May 1978. The question of who was going to pay Tholl for his work was brought up in the newspapers. When Tholl first began working for the police department his contract was for $1,800 a year. Now, 23 years later, he was making $8,400. On August 13, Kucinich survived the recall attempt by the slimmest of margins, a mere 236 votes out of more than 120,000 cast.

August 1980 – Tholl's last important action came in August 1980 when the Citizen's League of Cleveland and the League of Women Voters were the proponents of a charter proposal that would replace Cuyahoga County's three county commissioners with an executive and nine assemblymen, elected from districts. Petition inspection charges and counter charges seemed to dominate the process. All Joseph Tholl needed to look at were just ten petitions before declaring, "These are completely phony." Signatures on the ten petitions appeared to have been written by the same person in blue, black and green ink. "You've got a real good case of fraud here," he said. "There's no doubt about it. It's flagrant." In November, the proposed home-rule charter was soundly defeated. Some 29 years later, in November 2009, in the midst of a highly publicized county corruption scandal, the voters approved a new form of county government. The charter replaced the three county commissioners with an 11-member council.

As Tholl's career was winding down, he moved to Peninsula, Ohio, with his wife Josephine. In late 1981 or early 1982, he spent several days in the Cleveland Clinic for a respiratory ailment. On February 4, 1982, at the age of 72, Joseph Tholl died in his sleep.

There were no college or university degrees adorning the walls of Joseph Tholl's home office. There weren't any courses to be taken, so he didn't earn any degrees from the field of endeavor he loved and devoted his life to for nearly 50 years. But his love of that field and his professionalism was the product of his own work and drove his desire to learn everything that he possibly could to expand his knowledge. He succeeded and moved to the top by the sheer force of being able to "prove he could prove things."

Alan E. Walch

In 1949, when Alan Walch turned 18, he must have made a decision he was going to lead a life of crime. Over the next 16 years he was arrested nine times and was twice convicted for burglaries. It was not until February 1965, however, that Walch made his mark as a Cleveland criminal.

Benjamin "Ben" Feigenbaum was no stranger to violence. In August 1963, Ben and his brother Paul were the targets of a group of teenagers and were beaten near a drive-in restaurant at 8300 Euclid Avenue, near the old Cleveland Play House. Ben and his brother-in-law, William Maltz had purchased the Seventy-Niner's Café sometime in the early 1960s. Located on the northeast corner of East 79th Street and Hough Avenue, the bar earned a notorious reputation and would one day become a landmark in Cleveland crime history.

On May 12, 1962, two young men from Lorain County, who were driving around the Hough neighborhood enjoying a case of beer, stopped in the bar to relieve themselves. Both walked into the place around 2:00 a.m., each with a bottle of beer. When William Maltz went into the bathroom and saw both of them drinking there, he ordered them to leave. As the two left, 18-year-old Dennis A. Hemming picked up a beer bottle and struck Maltz in the face with it. The bottle broke the left lens of the glasses Maltz was wearing, cutting his face. Maltz grabbed a revolver and began beating Hemming about the head. He claimed that while defending himself the "gun discharged accidentally."

About an hour later, Hemming was pronounced dead at Mount Sinai Hospital from a gunshot to the head. Maltz was listed in satisfactory condition with sever lacerations around his left eye and was under police guard. As for Hemming's companion, he staggered out of the bar unaware that his friend was no longer accompanying him. He drove to the home of a relative, spent the night there, and returned to his home in Elyria later that day. After hearing of his friend's death, he made a visit to the Lorain County authorities. In the end, the police ruled the shooting justifiable and Maltz was not charged.

Around 6:30 on the evening of February 10, 1965, James A. Banning, a 16-year-old *Plain Dealer* newspaper delivery boy, was out collecting money from his customers in the East 101st Street neighborhood. As he walked down East 101st, across from two apartment buildings, he thought he heard two firecrackers explode. He later recalled:

> I looked to my left, across the street, and saw flashes and heard three more explosions come from inside a red and white Pontiac. Then a man, who had been leaning into the car on the passenger side backed out of the car. I was curious, so I crossed the street and approached the man. He had his right hand in his pocket. I got within two feet from him. He told me, "Turn around and go down the street." I did what he said.

Banning walked to Lamont Avenue and doubled back through an alley between the two buildings. By the time he got to East 101st, people were already gathering around the automobile. Banning soon spotted the object of their curiosity. Lying with his legs across the front seat with the rest of his body slumped down outside the car, his head resting on the cold sidewalk, was 53-year-old Ben Feigenbaum. The bar owner had been shot five times in the head, but was still alive and moaning when Benning arrived at the automobile.

Feigenbaum was quickly removed to nearby Mount Sinai Hospital where he pronounced dead. Police theorized that Feigenbaum knew the man he was talking to, as he made no attempt to pull a .38 Special revolver he had tucked in his pocket. Police questioned other witnesses present who reported seeing two men fleeing the scene in a dark colored car. The building's custodian told police that the car had been parked there before, usually during the morning hours. He said he had left notes on the vehicle asking that the driver not to block the apartment's driveway.

Customers back at the Seventy-Niner's Café told police that two men were in the bar and left around the same time Feigenbaum did, sometime between 6:00 and 6:30. A search was immediately begun for "a white man, about 35 years old, 5-foot-9 and wearing a light tan top coat."

Lieutenant Carl DeLau, head of the Homicide Unit, assigned four detectives to the case. From talking to associates of Feigenbaum, police learned that he was worried and depressed during the weeks leading up to his murder and was drinking heavily. Detectives also wanted to know why he was showing up at the apartment buildings on East 101st Street, almost every morning for the past few months.

On Friday, February 19, nine days after the brutal murder, Police Prosecutor Edward V. Cain issued a first-degree murder warrant against Alan E. Walch. Lieutenant DeLau refused to discuss what led to Walch's arrest other than to say they had "more than sufficient grounds on which to charge him." While police questioned and released several more men, they seemed to be focused on Walch. On February 26, he was indicted for first-degree murder by the Cuyahoga County Grand Jury.

During the summer of 1965, Walch also made news for something other than the upcoming murder trial. Cuyahoga County Prosecutor John T. Corrigan was heading a grand jury investigation into labor union violence in the Cleveland area. One of the unions the grand jury was investigating was Local 17 of the Bridge, Structural & Ornamental Iron Workers Union, whose members had endured beatings, bombings, and car burnings in recent months. Walch was referred to as one of Local 17's stewards during the investigation; the police labeled him one of the union's "enforcers." A report released by the grand jury stated:

Nine witnesses confronted the grand jury with a major obstacle by invoking the Fifth Amendment to the United States Constitution. They refused to answer questions on the ground that they might incriminate themselves. Even after Judge Hugh A. Corrigan ruled that they must answer specified questions, which he held were not incriminating, most of these witnesses were hostile or were not cooperative beyond complying with the judge's order.

The reluctant witnesses were led by Thomas E. McDonald, Local 17's business representative and president of the Cleveland Building Trades Council. The other witnesses, whom the *Plain Dealer* referred to as the "Nine Iron Men – With Rusty Voices,"[147] were Richard Callahan, Phil Christopher,[147] Paul Lyons, Dan Harding, William Gates, Richard A. Stewart, Alan E. Walch and Gordon Womack. All were members of Local 17, with the exception of Womack, who had just been released from the penitentiary.

The investigation revealed that Walch and Richard Stewart accompanied McDonald to a national iron workers convention in San Francisco in November 1964. Photographs in a convention publication showed the three men together. In Cleveland, some of the members of Local 17, who refused to allow the use of their names, claimed that Stewart was soliciting funds from them to aid in Walch's defense.

Walch appeared before Corrigan and the grand jury on July 15. Ten minutes later, after refusing to answer questions, he was being led out. As deputies escorted him, he shouted at Prosecutor Corrigan, "You give everyone else a lie detector test; why don't you give me one?" As Walch was being led back to the County Jail, he spoke to news reporters. "I didn't answer anything in there and I won't answer any questions until my wife and I get a lie detector test about this first-degree murder charge." Walch had been confined to the County Jail since his arrest for the Feigenbaum murder.

With his trial scheduled to begin on Monday, September 13, Walch's attorney, John P. Butler, finally filed a formal notice of his client's alibi defense on the Friday before. The attorney stated, "From 4 p.m. until 9 p.m. on February 10th, Walch was moving his family from 14012 Lake Shore Boulevard to 19121 Nottingham Road."

The trial began with jury selection; a venire of 125 were summoned for questioning. Since this was a capital murder trial, some potential jurors were excused because they objected to the death penalty. The process lasted a week. Hearing the case was Cuyahoga Common Pleas Judge Earl R. Hoover. The prosecution was handled by Assistant County Prosecutors George J. Moscarino and Robert H. Hanna.

On the weekend before testimony in the trial was to begin, Walch's wife, Maryanne gave birth to the couple's first child, a son at St. Ann's Hospital. On Monday, September 20, a jury of eight man and four women were seated and sworn in. The jury was then put on a chartered bus and driven to the murder scene on East 101st Street. While the attorneys for both sides followed in different vehicles. Attorney Butler insisted to Judge Earl Hoover that Walch be taken out to the scene. "The jury has never seen the place," Butler stated, "and neither has my client." Walch was loaded into a prowl car by the sheriff for the trip east. Hoover turned down a second request from Butler that the jury be allowed to visit the neighborhood after sunset. He claimed identification would have been harder to make after sundown.

On Tuesday morning, James Banning was the first witness to testify. He pointed out Walch as the man he saw backing away from the passenger side window of Feigenbaum's automobile on the night of February 10. The young man said he could not identify the second man at the scene, who was standing about 100 feet away. Banning said that although it was dusk and that he was only up close for four seconds, he had watched the man for 35 seconds while walking toward him. He said he had no problem picking him out of a line-up a few days after the shooting.

The next day, Mrs. Lulu Middleton, a 25-year-old barmaid at the Seventy-Niner's Café testified. She didn't offer a ringing endorsement of the place, stating the bar was frequented by "dope addicts, prostitutes and underworld characters." She said she often found hypodermic needles, eyedroppers and syringes that were left behind in the bar's restrooms by addicts. These same addicts often brought in items to sell Feigenbaum, such as sewing machines and radios, to get money to support their habit.

Middleton, who was separated from her husband, said she was having an affair with Ben Feigenbaum; he bought her gifts such as a fur piece and a wrist watch. She said Feigenbaum often had arguments with his brother-in-law, Bill Maltz. Three weeks before his murder, she said Feigenbaum was depressed and began drinking heavily. "The night he was killed, Benny was supposed to have dinner with me at my apartment. I went to a store near the bar to buy food. Benny was to wait for me. When I got back to the bar, he was gone," she stated. One of the key points of Middleton's testimony was that Walch "frequented" the bar.

On Thursday, Detective Adelbert O'Hara took the stand and testified that Walch was arrested on February 16, six days after the murder, at the Jones & Laughlin Steel Corporation, where he was employed by an erector firm. On February 10, "He said he had worked until 4 p.m., picked up his wife around 4:30 at East 9th Street and Euclid Avenue, drove home and stayed home that night." O'Hara said the following day Walch was questioned again. This time the story was, "He left work at 11 a.m., in order to move furniture into his new apartment." Walch claimed two friends were helping him at his new Nottingham Road apartment and, after his wife arrived home, they returned to the previous apartment at 14012 Lakeshore Boulevard to get clothes and other items. O'Hara stated that one of the men helping him was Albert "Tubby" Figer. Lulu Middleton had testified that Figer was in the Seventy-Niner's Café between 4 and 5 p.m. the day Feigenbaum was murdered.

O'Hara stated that on February 17, he and Walch and several detectives went to the Nottingham Road address and searched the apartment. They found a .32 revolver and a light-tan jacket with a blood stain on it. Banning had testified that Walch was wearing a beige jacket when he saw him at the murder scene. On Monday, September 27, the last day of the prosecutor's case, Mary Gowan, a senior medical technologist with the Cuyahoga County coroner's office, testified about the stain found inside a sleeve on Walch's jacket. Her examination, the day after it was discovered by Detective O'Hara, "revealed it to be blood." Questioned by Prosecutor Moscarino, Gowan stated, "I'm positive it was human blood and that the blood had been on the jacket for days, perhaps weeks, as contrasted to months." When asked by the prosecutor, Gowan stated that in her opinion, it was possible the stain could have come from blood spurting from a gunshot wound. On cross-examination, Butler got the technologist to admit that blood spurting from a wound would more than likely land on the outside of the jacket as opposed to inside the sleeve; and that it could have come from an accident on the job.

On Tuesday, the defense began their case by attacking the victim, Benjamin Feigenbaum. One of the first witnesses, Feigenbaum's nephew Abe, said that the owner of the bar kept two sets of books, "One for the business and the other to cheat on government taxes." The nephew testified that he and his brother had bought out William Maltz's share in the bar earlier in September. Abe Feigenbaum also testified that his uncle did not know Alan Walch or Richard Stewart. It was not explained how the nephew would have known this. The nephew also claimed Maltz and Ben Feigenbaum were "enemies" who often "argued violently" with each other. The witness said his uncle thought that Maltz was cheating him out of some of the weekly income. He also said that Maltz didn't like the fact that his uncle was dating the barmaids.

Butler also put on witnesses to try to prove that the murder scene was dark that night and Banning and other state's witnesses could not be positive as to what they saw.

After a day attacking the victim, Butler turned his attention to attacking the police, or more pointedly, the methods used by the police. Abe Feigenbaum claimed during his testimony that while being questioned by Lieutenant Carl DeLau, head of the Homicide Unit, the officer told him, "We have nothing on Walch or [Richard] Stewart, but they are rotten enough to have done it." Aris Roberts, a barmaid at the café, claimed she was held in jail for two days after not being able to identify pictures of suspects when questioned by police. She was shown photographs by Lieutenant DeLau. She testified, "After I told him I couldn't recognize the pictures, he locked me up without any charge." Fingerprinted and photographed, she was released two days later after signing a "suspicious person" waiver.

In an attempt to discredit the testimony of James Banning, Butler called Gustav Landsman, an ex-Cleveland police officer. Landsman testified that back on February 16, the day Banning was questioned at Central Police Station, he passed Banning twice in a third-floor hallway. Landsman claimed that Banning looked at him, but in court last week could not identify him. While this seems like a petty point, it turned even more ridiculous on cross-examination when Landsman admitted he had been fired from the police department in August after having been caught moonlighting. He was now working as an ironworker. It was also brought out that he grew up in the same Hough neighborhood as Walch and was friends with the defendant since childhood.

On Monday, October 4, Mary Ann Walch, the defendant's wife, took the stand. She was described as "pale and thin," having just given birth to the couple's first child two weeks earlier. She testified that her husband was at home watching television when she arrived after work at 5 p.m. They watched a movie, "Hell Canyon Outlaws," until 6:30, at which time he received a phone call and left to go to their new apartment on Nottingham Road.

Another witness called this day was Al Spagnola, a friend and neighbor of Walch. A fellow ironworker, Spagnola stated he saw Walch and two other men carry a stereo unit into the Nottingham Road apartment at 7:00 p.m. the night of the murder. Under cross-examination, Spagnola admitted he denied knowing Walch when questioned by police after the murder. He said he was arrested in connection to the killing and held two days for investigation. Spagnola also claimed he was once a jewelry salesman in Philadelphia before moving to Cleveland. When asked by Prosecutor Hanna to name any wholesale jewelry dealers in that city, he couldn't recall the name of a single one.

Thursday began with a surprise witness called by attorney Butler. Lyman Treat, a resident at the apartment building where Feigenbaum was murdered in front of, took the stand. He testified that he was walking home along East 101st Street at the time of the shooting. He claimed that he thought the men he saw leaving the scene of the crime were both Negroes. Under cross-examination, he stated that as he was standing by the death vehicle, "another car parked somewhere behind it roared away. The man in the right front seat resembled Walch."

Also on Thursday, Alan Walch took the stand. After a few early questions the following exchange took place:

Butler: Did you kill Ben Feigenbaum?

Walch: No.

Butler: Did you know Ben Feigenbaum?

Walch: No.

Butler: Do you know anyone who knew Ben Feigenbaum?

Walch: No.

Butler: Were you ever in the Seventy-Niner's Café?

Walch: Once, in 1959.

Walch testified that on the day of the murder, he was employed as an iron-worker and left a construction job at Jones & Laughlin Steel at 11:00 a.m. Richard Stewart, a friend and union steward working the site, drove him to the plant gate, and dropped him off at his car. He drove to his apartment at Nottingham Road, changed clothes, and drove to a tavern on Ivanhoe Road. Around 3:30, he borrowed a Jeep panel van to move a phonograph to his new apartment from Lake Shore Boulevard. "I was home at 5 p.m." he claimed. "I don't even know what Ben Feigenbaum looked like," he stated. One of the other things Walch claimed was that on the day he was picked out of a police line-up by Banning, the other four men he appeared with were either taller or shorter than him. On cross-examination, the two prosecutors hammered away at Walch about the two sets of statements he had given to detectives, the first one being that he picked up his wife after work that afternoon and they stayed home all night.

On Friday, the last day of testimony, the prosecution called two police officers as rebuttal witnesses. Detective James Mooty, who had worked as a beat patrolman in the neighborhood where the Seventy-Niner's Café was located, testified that he had seen Walch numerous times at the bar in November and December of 1964, and up to the first week of February 1965 when Feigenbaum was killed. "I didn't know his name," Mooty said, "but he often looked disheveled and in need of a shave."

At that, Walch jumped to his feet and shouted," That's a damned lie!"

On cross-examination by Butler, the attorney wanted to know why this information hadn't been volunteered earlier.

"I didn't know Walch was on trial," Mooty stated. "I found out when prosecutors called me in. I picked out a photograph of Walch from one of 15 I was shown."

The second witness was Homicide Detective Frank Dimperio. He testified that on March 19, he questioned Paul E. Lyons, an ironworker and one of the members of Local 17 who was questioned along with Walch over the summer during the grand jury investigation. He testified earlier for the defense he had telephoned Walch at the approximate time Feigenbaum was shot. During the March questioning, however, Lyons told the detectives he hadn't seen or talked to Walch that day.

On Monday, October 11, after 15 days of testimony, closing statements were delivered. During jury instruction, Judge Hoover advised the panel they could return with four possible verdicts: guilty of murder in the first degree, with or without mercy; guilty of second degree murder; or not guilty. Jury deliberation began at 7:45 that evening. At 10:40 p.m. a verdict of not guilty was reached. After the verdict, the jury foreman announced, "We believe we acted as good citizens. We agreed not to reveal our deliberations."

Walch was "elated," his attorney was thankful to the jury, and the prosecutors were disappointed and "extremely surprised," claiming the verdict "was not consistent with the evidence." No one was ever held to answer for the murder of Ben Feigenbaum. The most surprising fact about the whole case was that at no time during the trial, nor at any time leading up to it, was a motive for the killing offered. Tragically, the next time the Seventy-Niner's Café[148] made news, it would be a national story.

Eight days after the verdict, Paul Lyons was indicted for receiving $600 worth of jewelry from an armed robbery in August that took place at Mullins Jewelry Store at 11018 Lorain Avenue. Lyon's pleaded not guilty, ironically, before Judge Earl Hoover, who released him on a $2,500 bond. In the article announcing the plea, the newspaper referred to Lyons as a "major defense witness" for fellow ironworker Walch.

Lyons was indicted a second time a month later on November 19. This time it was for three counts of perjury involving his testimony during the Walch trial. While giving his alibi testimony for Walch, Lyons claimed he drove from Lakewood, a suburb on the western edge of Cleveland along Lake Erie, to Chesterland, in Geauga County to the east of Cuyahoga County. With today's upgraded freeways and roads, the travel time is listed as 41 minutes during normal driving times and conditions. In winter rush hour, Lyons claimed he drove it "in less than 50 minutes." On November 24, Lyons pleaded not guilty before Common Pleas Judge Charles W. White and was freed on a $25,000 bond. Things didn't get any better for Lyons in the new year. On March 3, 1966, he was picked up on "a secret indictment," and was now charged with armed robbery in the theft at the Mullins Jewelry Store. Later, Lyons would be acquitted of both the robbery of the jewelry store and of receiving stolen property.

During the Cuyahoga County Grand Jury investigation of violence among local ironworkers a year earlier, one of the criminal activities the panel was looking into was a number of car bombings involving vehicles belonging to union members. On August 24, 1966, this crime came home to roost for Alan Walch. That evening, Walch, his wife, and son were at home in their apartment at 1925 Cliffview Road[149] in Collinwood. Suddenly a bomb, placed on the passenger side of Mary Ann's 1962 car, exploded in the parking lot behind the apartment complex. In addition to destroying the Walch's vehicle, four other automobiles in the lot were damaged.

On March 1, 1967, Richard Callahan, a fellow member of Local 17 of the Bridge, Structural & Ornamental Ironworkers Union, was with two friends at

Peterlin's Lounge at 5501 St. Clair Avenue. The men ordered drinks, but were re-fused credit by James Fabrick, the owner. Callahan, a former city Golden Gloves boxing champ at 160 pounds, had once brawled with two Cleveland police offi-cers and a civilian, was infuriated and grabbed Fabrick. At the same time, Cal-lahan's friends, also ironworkers, pulled handguns and aimed them at Fabrick, his partner Joseph Peterlin, and a barmaid. During a brief scuffle, a shot was fired into the ceiling and police quickly arrived. When threats were issued by Callahan and his friends, the bar owners told police nothing had happened. The next day the bar received a number of threatening telephone calls. On April 24, Callahan and his two fellow ironworkers were indicted. Callahan was charged with intimidating a witness, while the other two were charged with carry con-cealed weapons and aggravated assault with a deadly weapon.

Two weeks later, on May 7, Callahan was found in front of 17813 Detroit Avenue by a Lakewood patrolman. Callahan's brother, William told the officer he had been hit by an automobile. The police officer didn't have to be a doctor to see that Richard Callahan was shot three times; the bullets hitting his right arm and left thigh. The wounded man, shot with a .22, refused to tell police what happened. Callahan recovered from his wounds. At his trial for the bar incident, he and the other men were found not guilty after Fabrick and Peterlin responded with "I don't remember," to every important question put to them by the prosecutor.

On January 28, 1981, Callahan was sentenced to 15 years-to-life in prison for the murder of his wife, Fern, back on May 27, 1979. The two had just re-turned home from a party and, according to Callahan, an intruder entered the home and killed his wife with her own pistol, and shot him in the foot.

The perjury trial against Paul Lyons began in late April 1967. Held before Com-mon Pleas Judge John J. Mahon, Assistant County Prosecutor Francis E. Swee-ney's key witness was Common Pleas Judge Earl Hoover. Lyons was represented by attorney John P. Butler. During his testimony, Hoover stated that he had per-sonally sworn in Lyons and that he was a "very important" witness for Walch. The defense's first witness was Alan Walch.

After a six-day trial, the jury deliberated for ten hours over a Friday and Monday before reaching a not-guilty verdict on May 8. Attorney Butler claimed the charges were a "vindictive retaliation" for Lyon's testimony in the Walch trial. Afterwards, Lyons told reporters, "You have no idea what an indictment like this can do to a man. I've become an alcoholic. My wife was going to commit suicide. I spent all my savings."

Lyons didn't have much time to celebrate the legal victory. Two weeks later, on May 21, he received a knock on the door of his Clifton Boulevard home at 3:00 in the morning. After determining the reason for the late night call, Ly-ons put away the .22 pistol he carried for protection. Lyons stated that the man said he wanted his help in getting a job. "I let him into the house and poured him a drink," he said. "We were seated at the table having a conversation about a matter. He pulled out a gun and my wife jumped between us." Nadine Lyons was shot three times. The 38-year-old mother of four was pronounced dead on arrival at Lakewood Hospital at 3:40 a.m.

Paul Lyons was shot three times, once in the stomach and twice in the left arm. At the hospital, he told his daughter, Paula what happened. He claimed he had never seen the short, stocky man before, but knows who he is. As he was being wheeled into surgery, he said, "I shouldn't have let him in." Lyons told police someone from out of town was hired to kill him, but he refused to help the police in any way.

During a search of the Lyons' Lakewood home, police found the .22 handgun and immediately checked it to see if it was the one used in the recent shooting of Richard Callahan. With Lyons still refusing to tell police who came into his home that night and shot him and his wife, police believed he may have killed his wife himself, and then hired someone to shoot him to cover up the murder; or that the hitman may have been hired to kill the wife and then wound Lyons.

Paul Lyons recovered from his wounds and was released from the hospital. No one was ever arrested for the murder of Nadine Lyons. She was buried in Lakewood Park Cemetery. In July 1967, Lyons was arrested for intoxication and creating a disturbance inside a downtown bar on Payne Avenue. He told police two men were following him around and, he predicted, he would "get hit." During the fall of 1967, Lyons and his three sons moved to Windsor, Ohio, located in the southwest corner of Ashtabula County. It was believed he found employment as a construction worker.

On February 13, 1968, police noticed an abandoned 1964 Buick parked at Phelps Avenue and 12th Street in the northwest section of Cuyahoga Falls in Summit County around 5:30 that morning. Police kept an eye on the car and after discovering it belonged to Paul Lyons, "a former ironworker and police figure," they took a closer look. Detectives discovered a spent .32 bullet, a blood stained jacket and two pairs of eyeglasses. They also found a "foreign matter" splattered about the car which they later determined to be brain tissue. Summit County Prosecutor James V. Barbuto announced investigators were now searching for a body.

The jacket, found in the car, had gunpowder burns, indicating to police that it may have been used to muffle the sound of gunshots. Police wondered if Lyons may have faked his own death, and were not convinced he was killed. Police studied blood samples to see if they could match them to Lyons' type, and checked the glasses to see if they matched his prescription. On February 27, a young girl on her way to the store for her mother, tripped and dropped her purse down a sewer. Her brother came to the rescue and removed the grating to recover it. The recovery effort revealed something else – a .32 revolver.

Cuyahoga Falls police quickly arrived to retrieve the gun and perform a complete search of the sewer, which was located a block north of Phelps and 12th Street, where Lyons abandoned car was found. Inside the sewer, police recovered a set of car keys which fit Lyons vehicle.

A week later, on March 5, Chris Nielsen, a rural mailman, was driving his mail truck on Brandywine Road in Sagamore Hills, located in the northwest sector of Summit County. It was a bright day and the sunshine reflected on a shiny object on the side of the road. He stopped to see what it was and discovered a cigarette lighter and several coins. Looking over the side of the road and down a ravine, Nielsen spotted the body of a man at the bottom of an eight-foot ditch with his feet pointed up the slope. The mailman quickly notified police from a nearby home.

Police arrived and removed the body to the office of Summit County Coroner Dr. A.H. Kyriakides, who confirmed through fingerprints the body was that of Paul Lyons. The coroner determined he died from four bullet wounds; three in the back and one at the base of the skull behind the left ear, all fired from close range. The coroner also discovered another bullet lodged in Lyons' diaphragm, which he determined was from the gunshot wound he received the night his wife was murdered. Police said the motive for the shooting was not robbery as they found an expensive diamond ring, as well as a wedding ring, a wristwatch and $30 on his body. While there was no wallet, police did find an alphabetized address book. Lyons was dressed for construction work, having on thermal underwear, a blue work shirt and pants and brown work boots, but no jacket.

The funeral service for Paul Lyons was held on March 8. His death notice stated he was a member of Structural Iron Workers' Local 17. He was buried next to his wife in Lakewood Park Cemetery.

Three months after Lyons' funeral, Alan Walch was back in the news. In San Mateo, California, the FBI was on the trail of two fugitives from Cleveland, Theodore R. Ricci and Richard P. Viccarone. On Saturday night, June 15, 1968, they raided a motel and found the two men. To their surprise, they also came across three more Clevelanders, John M. Delzoppo, Frank J. Velotta and Alan Walch. With help from both the San Mateo and Los Angeles Police Departments, all five men were arrested.

Ricci and Viccarone were held on $100,000 bond; both were wanted back in Cleveland. They, along with Velotta, were also wanted in Los Angeles on a burglary charge. Walch and Delzoppo were booked for possession of burglary tools. They were soon released "for lack of sufficient evidence."

Walch remained out of trouble and out of the news until May 1971. Walch had been arrested with Frank Velotta, Raymond Ferritto and Joseph J. Dorando in Los Angeles, for involvement in the theft of a coin collection, which took place back in October 1968. The coins belonged to Dr. William Harper of Sherman Oaks and Julian Lavin of Granada Hills. The next month, Dr. Harper saw his coins for sale at numismatics' show at the Biltmore Hotel in Los Angeles. Police quickly arrested a couple at the show and charged them with the theft of $220,000 in coins. The couple entered pleas to receiving stolen property. Although it was not determined who stole the coins, Walch and the others were also charged with receiving stolen property.

The case dragged on for a long while and I could find no record of how it was finally resolved, but apparently it was Walch's last publicized act. Alan Walch died on January 30, 1978. He was buried in Calvary Cemetery.

Robert E. "Bobby" Walsh

Most stories of good cops turning into bad cops are tales of policemen who go bad while on the job. There was nothing in Robert Walsh's police past to indicate this was the case. Once retired, however, he did go very bad.

Robert Emmett Walsh enlisted in the Navy during World War II at the age of 15 by forging a birth certificate. He served on the USS Nashville, a light cruiser. On December 13, 1944, a kamikaze pilot, carrying two bombs, crashed into the deck of the ship killing 133 sailors and wounding 190 others. Fortunately for Walsh, he was assigned to the refurbished vessel. He returned to Cleveland after the war and on August 11, 1950, joined the Cleveland Police Department. He became a detective during his first year on the force.

His first mention in the Cleveland newspapers was on September 3, 1951, after the disappearance of 11-year-old Beverly Rose Potts. The search for the missing girl was in its second week when Walsh was mentioned. It was known that the young girl loved to visit Euclid Beach Park. On the first Sunday in September, Walsh and his partner, Arthur Bockhausen, escorted Beverly's older sister Anita and Mrs. Potts' niece Betty Marbito to the popular amusement park on the chance that she might somehow show up there. She didn't.[150] The Beverly Potts disappearance remains an open cold case to this day.

Over the next five years, Walsh was mentioned in the newspapers a number of times. On October 17, 1952, G. Albert Williams, described as a 48-year-old tax accountant for local numbers racketeers, exited his automobile to address what one newspaper called "some breach of traffic manners," at Crawford Road and Hough Avenue. When he confronted the other driver a shoving match ensued and Williams was stabbed on the inside of his left elbow. He began to bleed profusely and soon lay dying on Hough Avenue in a pool of his own blood.

Detective Walsh soon arrived at the scene and quickly stripped off his belt and used it as a tourniquet in an attempt to stop the bleeding and save Williams' life. Despite a valiant effort, Williams was dead on arrival at Mt. Sinai Hospital. Police arrested George J. Mikalaitis two days later. At trial in October 1953, Mikalaitis was found not guilty of manslaughter after two eyewitnesses testified Williams had brandished the knife and accidently stabbed himself when Mikalaitis shoved him. At trial, the defendant was represented by Edward C. Stanton and Fred W. Garmone.

In March 1954, Walsh solved one of his easier cases while investigating the armed robbery of one cab driver and the attempted robbery of another on East 89th Street. As he and his partner searched the area, a 20-year-old man came up to them at East 89th and Folsom Avenue and simply told them, "I'm the guy you're looking for."

Walsh and two other detectives had a surprise waiting for them in the late summer of 1955 when they attempted to question three young men for creating a disturbance on Euclid Avenue near East 105th Street. The young men, between the ages of 20 and 22, lived in well-to-do neighborhoods of Cleveland Heights and Shakers Heights on the East Side; one lived on Fairmount Boulevard, while another lived on wealthy South Park. When Walsh went to question one man, he pulled a blackjack and while another grabbed Walsh from behind the first man hit him over the head twice. During the beating, Walsh dropped his service revolver on the sidewalk and when he went to pick it up, a woman kicked it away. Walsh was hospitalized and was still on medical leave when he testified at the trial of the men on October 4.

After Walsh was struck, a free-for-all ensued. Soon the three young men were down on the street, beaten and bloodied, their clothes torn away. At trial their defense counsel claimed the men were arrested but did not receive their beatings until they got to the jail. Eyewitness testimony at the trial disputed that theory. Despite the vicious attack on the detectives, two of the men were convicted of resisting arrest and were given 30-days sentences in the workhouse; the third man was found guilty of assault and battery and received six months.

Later that year, Walsh worked with seasoned burglary squad detective William Lonchar in breaking up a gang of young thieves, aged 16 to 18, who were involved in the theft of nine automobiles, 11 burglaries and six safe-crackings. At a metal plant in southern Ohio, the boys had stolen $10,000 worth of copper cable and, not knowing the real value, fenced it for just $400. The detectives ended the gang's lawless spree when they arrested four of the five teenagers in a stolen car. When asked what they did with all the money they made from the thefts, which were valued at $20,000 to $30,000, one of the boys answered they spent it on "girls and gasoline."

Whether it was the beating with the blackjack, the daily hassles of being a police officer or trying to support a growing family of five on a cop's salary, "Bobby" Walsh resigned from the Cleveland Police Department on November 21, 1956. But there was another, more sinister story that floated around. Walsh's oldest son, Dennis recalls, "I was told that my father had to leave the Cleveland Police Department after he killed a guy who had knocked his father, my grandfather, Leo Eugene Walsh, to the ground and smashed his head against the curb, causing him to die from a cerebral hemorrhage, and the police department covered it up for him."

Whatever the case, the next year he was running Walsh Builders, which he operated with his brother James. From 1957 to 1959, the company was the subject of numerous complaints to the Better Business Bureau. In 1959, James Walsh and Charles L. Gamblin were indicted on two counts of grand larceny by trick for their participation in what police called a chimney repair racket, where they bilked two widows out of $5,200 and $1,100. The two men were found guilty on October 12, 1960. James Walsh was given probation. Gamblin, who was already serving a three-and-a-half year stretch in the Federal penitentiary in Milan, Michigan, would face a 1-to-7 year term in Ohio once he was released.

In December 1960, Robert Walsh was facing a more serious problem. On December 2, he was named in a secret indictment returned by a Federal Grand Jury in Cleveland. The indictment was deemed faulty because it failed to indicate the crime was committed in the Northern District of Ohio, so it was four days later that Walsh was actually arrested by Cleveland police at the request of the Secret Service, at the Coral Bar[151] located at 1988 East 105th Street, where he was employed as night manager since 1958. The indictment charged him with "aiding and abetting the manufacture of a flood of counterfeit $20 bills that swept through Ohio and other states," beginning in the spring of 1960.

By the time Walsh was indicted, six other members of the counterfeit ring were already in prison, including Charles Gamblin, who was serving his sentence in Milan. The leader of the ring, Hugh A. Lynn of Youngstown, was sentenced to ten years in Federal prison on October 20. Four others were jailed for distributing the bogus bills.[152] On December 6, before U.S. Commissioner H. A. Horn, Assistant U.S. Attorney Burt W. Griffin requested a $25,000 bail for Walsh. His lawyer, James J. Carroll, a former Assistant U.S. Attorney and future common pleas judge, protested the amount was too high. Horn set the amount at $10,000 and Walsh was released.

The trial began on April 19, 1961, in U.S. District Court in Cleveland. Federal Judge James C. Connell heard the case without a jury. In his opening statement, Burt Griffin declared the government would show that Walsh, working with Gamblin and Lynn, was part of a ring of counterfeiters who churned out $80,000 in phony $20 bills, during the spring and summer of 1960, of which Walsh received $64,000. In Carroll's opening statement, he claimed he would prove his client had no connection "in any way" to the counterfeiting gang. The defense attorney said he would show that Walsh was offered what he thought was a "legitimate printing job" at Lynn's home in Youngstown during June 1960.

On the first day of testimony, the government produced two key witnesses. Calvin D. Furlong, a salesman at Union Paper & Twine Company on East 40th Street, testified Walsh was the man he sold 5,000 sheets of bond paper to in May 1960. Marlene Schiffer, a former typist at the Addressograph-Multigraph Corporation branch in Youngstown, said Walsh had ordered repairs be made to a multilith duplicator in the spring of 1960. In both instances, Walsh used the name Marvin Hart. The government also called Hugh Lynn as a witness. He testified Walsh was the "instigator" of the printing and distributing of the fake $20 bills.

On April 25, Walsh took the stand. He denied playing any part in the counterfeiting operation at the home of Lynn. Walsh claimed instead of being the "instigator" of the ring, he "resented Lynn's proposition" that he become a member of the gang. He told the judge he met Lynn during April 1960 in the parking lot outside the Skyway Lounge in Youngstown. Lynn was accompanied by Charles Gamblin. He said the conversation was about counterfeiting racetrack mutual tickets. Walsh claimed he told both men he was not interested and left.

In early June 1960, Walsh testified, Gamblin took him and Terrence J. Hogan, a man who Walsh worked with in roofing and chimney repair in Mahoning County, to Lynn's home. Walsh said he and Hogan were shown stacks of $20 bills in the basement of the home. "I became agitated, and Gamblin attempted to explain things to me," Walsh said. The *Plain Dealer* reported the next part of his testimony:

Walsh said he became so angry he hit Gamblin. Lynn protested, Walsh said, and then he knocked Lynn out. Walsh said he tore up some phony bills and the negatives from which they were made. He said he also knocked over the press being used to make the counterfeits.

Mrs. Shirley Lynn, wife of Hugh, was in the way as he started from the basement, Walsh said, and he shoved her aside. Then he kicked a dog that was in the way and hurried out of the house.

The day after Walsh's testimony, the judge heard closing statements. At noon on April 27, Judge Connell announced a verdict of guilty. He said that Walsh "had been a good policeman who got into bad company." The judge delayed sentencing until he received a report from the court's probation office. Walsh remained free under a $10,000 bond. Attorney Carroll said an appeal would be considered.

On July 7, Judge Connell sentenced Walsh to three years in Federal prison. After Carroll told the judge the case would be taken to the U.S. Court of Appeals, he allowed Walsh to remain free on bond until the case was heard. Walsh eventually served his time at the Federal prison in Milan, Michigan. Before leaving for prison, he told his two oldest sons he was going to Germany on government business and to "help your mother out when I'm gone." The family survived on food stamps, food donations from the church on holidays and occasionally Frank "Skinny" Velotta would stop by and drop off some money. After approximately two years, Walsh returned home to Highland Heights. Walsh's friend, Alan Walch (See previous biography entry), helped him out by getting him a no-show job with Structural Iron Workers' Local 17.

From the time he returned home until mid-1966, Walsh was part of a successful burglary crew that included "Skinny" Velotta, Alfred S. "Allie" Calabrese, Pasquale "Butchie" Cisternino and Raymond Ferritto. In the book *Nobody Walks*, author Dennis M. Walsh, Robert's oldest son, recalls:

My father's criminal endeavors had steadily increased. He and his crew had been hacking through roofs in the dead of night blowtorching bank vaults for a few years. They always managed to exit in time, thanks to a police radio supplied by a friend of his still on the Cleveland PD, in exchange for a cut of the score.

Early in 1966, an FBI agent roused one of my father's confederates, Frank "Skinny" Velotta, out of bed and warned him that J. Edgar Hoover himself had sent word that if one more bank got burglarized in northeastern Ohio, Frank, my father, and Ray Ferritto would go down for it, whether they did it or not. The federal agent's threat of recrimination did not fall on deaf ears. The next we knew, we were pulling up stakes.

My siblings and I had no idea that we had been run out of town. Instead, the old man had been hyping the wonders of California for weeks.

Of this crew, Robert Walsh became closest to Ferritto. Their families became close, too. By 1966, the Walsh family had grown to seven children – five boys and two girls. Dennis Walsh remembers his father taking him and his brother, Tim, to Erie, Pennsylvania, to visit Ferritto, and to meet his family after getting out of Milan Penitentiary in the early 1960s. He also remembered an incident at their home in Highland Heights when he walked into the garage as his father, Ferritto and other members of the crew were practicing "torching a safe." After the Walsh family settled in California, Ferritto soon relocated there bringing his family with him. See Chapter Eight for Robert E. "Bobby" Walsh's involvement with Julius Petro and Ray Ferritto in California.

After the murder of Julius Petro, nearly a decade passed before Walsh was reported on again. Then it looked like the 57-year-old Walsh made up for lost time. On January 30, 1981, Walsh, his son, Tim, and Frank D'Acquisto were indicted by a Federal Grand Jury in New Orleans on 15 counts of conspiracy, embezzlement and misapplication, false statements and false entry in a bank fraud case involving Hibernia National Bank and its vice president Victor J, Lota, Jr., from which they obtained a $948,000 loan in 1980. Lota was fired from the bank in March 1980 after an FBI investigation uncovered a plot where he received "a couple of million dollars" in kickbacks from questionable loans.

An employee of the bank for 24 years, Lota was indicted in July 1980 and was facing 75 years in prison. Lota agreed to cooperate with prosecutors and in return was granted immunity from prosecution on drug charges in Florida and Louisiana. On September 11, Lota pleaded guilty to embezzling and misusing nearly $5 million in just over a year. The next month, he was sentenced to three years in prison by a Federal judge and sent to Elgin Air Force Base in Florida to serve his sentence.[153]

Victor Lota's[154] conviction resulted in a domino effect, and all of the people he had conspired with on loans soon ended up in court. D'Acquisto first received money for a real estate venture in Las Vegas after agreeing to give Lota one-third of the profits. In the loan to D'Acquisto and the Walshs, the men agreed to share the profits from distributing a plane load of marijuana and Quaaludes with Lota. Dennis Walsh explains, his father "was accused of masterminding a scheme in which a retrofitted air force transport plane that was stolen out of Burke Lakefront Airport in Cleveland would be used to smuggle four tons of marijuana and over 200,000 Quaaludes out of Columbia into Hammond, Louisiana." Prosecutors said the men used two-thirds of the $948,000 for this drug deal near Hammond.

On July 13, 1981, the Drug Enforcement Agency in Panama City, Florida issued a Federal warrant for Walsh's arrest, charging him with marijuana smuggling in Panama City and Gainesville, Florida. This was followed by the Florida Department of Law Enforcement in Tallahassee issuing a state warrant against him on the same day.

Back in Louisiana, Walsh was supposed to go on trial on July 17, 1981, in Tangipahoa Parrish, on state charges from 1979 for conspiracy to possess marijuana with intent to distribute in Hammond. Walsh was a no-show at trail and was now wanted for bail-jumping. Frank D'Acquisto pleaded guilty and received a sentence of three years. On September 8, Tim Walsh pleaded guilty to one count of making false statements to the bank. On September 23, U.S. District Judge Patrick E. Carr issued a two-year suspended sentence to Tim Walsh, telling him he would not be sent to prison, "because he apparently was pushed into the drug deal by his father."

If all this wasn't enough, that same year Bobby Walsh was charged by the Los Angeles County District Attorney with the murder of Julius Petro, which by then was eleven years old.

Over the next three years Walsh was on the lam, hiding out in California and Florida. He did not remain idle, however. In October 1983, he was indicted by a Federal Grand Jury in Cleveland for his involvement with a 2,000 pound shipment of marijuana that was seized by U.S. Customs agents from an airplane that landed in Smithville, Tennessee, in December 1980. Indicted with Walsh was Youngstown organized crime figure Orland Carabbia, who eventually pleaded guilty to one count. According to later testimony, Carabbia[155] agreed to supply the airplane and Walsh and others the marihuana.

Walsh did catch a break in July 1984 when authorities in Florida dropped the drug-smuggling charges against him. The DEA and the Florida Department of Law Enforcement explained that the charges were dropped "in light of more serious warrants elsewhere."

In *Nobody Walks*, Dennis Walsh describes a little of what was going on in the years his father was a Federal fugitive:

He always sent money home when he was gone. He paid for my law school tuition. Still, no amount of money could have atoned for the tremendous amount of grief his family had endured. He was obviously proud of me, even though he never told me directly. When notification that I had passed the California State Bar exam was mailed to my parents' house in November 1982, I received word to come by. He was on the lam but had been secretly living at home for a couple of years. He kept the car in the attached garage and would lie across the backseat while my brothers transported him to and from another car he kept across town. My mother had called and mentioned a specific code word that meant the old man wanted to see me. When I arrived, he was grinning from ear to ear. He stood up and walked over to me. "You passed the bar, Counselor," he said. He leaned over and kissed me on the cheek. I was stunned. I couldn't recall my father ever having kissed me.

During the last year Walsh was on the lam, authorities believed he spent most of his time in Florida. He would check in and out of hotels, moving constantly to avoid detection. One newspaper called him, "A fugitive disguise expert who used 25 aliases, six dates of birth, a false Japanese Airlines identification card and a toupee to evade capture."

Walsh's years on the run came to an end on the morning of Thursday, September 13, 1984, after checking into the Marriott Hotel & Marina on the 17th Street Causeway in Fort Lauderdale. Unfortunately for Walsh, his timing couldn't have been worse. He had checked into a hotel where 40 FBI agents were registered to attend an unpublicized yearly conference.

During the previous month, the FBI circulated wanted posters of Walsh to many of the hotels and motels in Florida. That morning, a hotel guest, who had seen the poster, spotted Walsh in the hotel's gift shop and told the front desk. The agents were notified by hotel personnel and three agents from the Fort Lauderdale office went to the gift shop and arrested Walsh without incident at 9:30 a.m. The agents also arrested an "unidentified companion" and escorted both people out of the hotel. They were taken to the FBI office in Fort Lauderdale, where the "companion" was questioned and released. The newspapers never indicated if the companion was a man or a woman. Walsh was then removed to the Dade Detention Center. He appeared before a U.S. Magistrate the next day. He would not be bonding out this time.

In 1984, Walsh was given a 15-year sentence for the bond jumping and three counts of embezzlement from the Hibernia National Bank in New Orleans. At one time Walsh had threatened to kill Victor Lota, the banking official who helped Walsh obtain the money, after he became a witness for the government against him. The money was used to finance a marijuana importing operation. Walsh was charged with conspiracy to smuggle marijuana into Hammond, Louisiana, but these charges were dropped in the plea agreement.

In November 1985, Walsh went on trial in U.S. District Court in Cleveland on charges of conspiracy to import and distribute marijuana. A jury deliberated over two days before returning a guilty verdict on November 19. Federal Judge John M. Manos delayed sentencing pending a pre-sentencing report. At the time, Walsh was serving the 15-year sentence for bank fraud in Louisiana.

On January 15, 1986, Judge Manos sentenced Walsh to five years in prison for conspiracy to import 2,000 pounds of marijuana; and 10 years for conspiracy to distribute it. Manos ordered the two sentences to run concurrently, but the ten year term was to run consecutively with the 15-year bank fraud sentence in Louisiana.

By the time Walsh was released from prison in 1993, the only charge still pending against him was for the murder of Julius Petro. When Ray Ferritto, with the backing of a Pennsylvania judge, refused to return to California to testify, Walsh was off the hook for the murder.

Despite all he had been through and all he had put his family through, Walsh did not retire from his life of crime. On June 12, 2000, a narcotics raid was conducted at the home of Walsh by a joint team of law enforcement officers from the Los Angeles Police Department, the Drug Enforcement Agency and the FBI. At the same time, Walsh's son, Robert "Bobby" Walsh, Jr. was arrested in Cleveland, along with 28 others around the country including Eugene "the Animal" Ciasullo, Phil Christopher and Ron Lucarelli. It was estimated that the narcotics ring had transported more than $12 million dollars in cocaine during the past two years. Their method was an ingenious one. With the help of an American Airlines employee, the cocaine was placed in passengers' luggage at Los Angeles International Airport before the bags were placed in the airplane's cargo hold. Once they arrived in Cleveland, the cocaine was removed before the luggage was placed on the conveyor belt on its way to baggage claim.

Walsh was referred to as the mastermind of the ring, despite the fact he was now 71 years-old, dealing with a bad heart and suffering from diabetes. By now, his oldest son Dennis was a defense attorney. Dennis made numerous trips to Cleveland to help negotiate the pleas of his father and younger brother. "Bobby," Jr. received a 13-year sentence, but ended up serving just three years and nine months. Robert Walsh was handed a 20-year term.

Walsh spent the last few years of his life at the Federal Medical Center in Rochester, Minnesota. Suffering from severe coronary disease, he had undergone a quadruple bypass. His condition was deemed terminal by his cardiologist. Dennis Walsh worked tirelessly to obtain a compassionate release for his father so he could die at home. Despite the effort, Robert "Bobby" Walsh died on September 29, 2003.

Thomas P. White

According to Cleveland Police Department legend, some 35 years before Clint Eastwood drove a car through the front door of a store in San Francisco, where robbers were holding hostages in the hit movie, *The Enforcer*, Detective Thomas P. White drove a detective prowl car through the front door of a Central National Bank branch at East 118th Street and Buckeye Road. Instead of gunning down all the "punks" with a .44 Magnum, "the most power handgun in the world," like Inspector "Dirty Harry" Callahan, White and his two partners arrested the stunned robbers with the use of only standard police issued .38 Special revolvers.

Thomas Patrick White was born in Cleveland on March 21, 1913. The young man, of Irish descent, grew up on Colonial Avenue on the East Side of Cleveland, which runs between East 99th and East 105th Streets. He attended Cleveland grade schools, before enrolling at Notre Dame University.

In 1937, he joined the Cleveland Police Department. During his time at the police academy, he came to the attention of legendary Safety Director Eliot Ness. After graduation, White was "handpicked" by Ness for a special six-man crime squad. Later that year, he married Rita Langdon on November 18, at St. Thomas Aquinas Church. The couple would later have a son and daughter.

White was promoted to detective in 1939. His work over the next 23 years was frequently reported in all three local newspapers. His first appearance came on January 8, 1940. A resident, who lived at the Clevelander Apartments (now torn down) at 1651 East 93rd Street, answered a payphone in the basement and was told by an anonymous caller that a basket awaited the custodian at the apartment entrance. The woman went to the Edmunds Avenue entrance where she found a grocery basket containing a two-day-old baby boy. Detective White and his partner George Reichle were sent to investigate. The child was found lightly dressed, with a thin cover over him. The first arriving officers took the baby to St. Ann's Maternity Hospital, where nurses named the child Arthur Thomas the first names of the two policemen. The child's feet nearly froze in the cold January weather, but other than that he was healthy and survived the rough arrival.

In March 1941, White and his partner, Detective James T. Reddy, were involved in the extradition of Howard Graves and Bernard Sidron, two jewel thieves from Detroit. On March 4, after "entertaining" a night club dancer from Freddie's Café, the next afternoon Graves and Sidron slugged a jewelry salesman from Chicago after he left the Cowell & Hubbard Company jewelry store. After knocking the man to the ground, they stole two cases he was carrying, which contained $15,000 worth of jewelry. The men were arrested two days later in Three Rivers, Michigan. Extradition papers were signed and Thomas White, James Reddy and Sergeant George Smythe spent St. Patrick's Day returning the duo to Cleveland. The next month both men were convicted and sentenced to 10 to 25 years in prison. The trial was heard before Cuyahoga Common Pleas Judge Frank J. Lausche, with James C. Connell representing one of the defendants. By the time the appeal was filed in November 1941, Lausche was elected mayor of Cleveland and Connell had replaced him on the Common Pleas bench. The appeal was denied in January.

In late July 1941, White and Reddy arrested Lenore McKenzie in a beer parlor on West 25th Street just hours after she was indicted by a grand jury for taking out insurance policies on two Cleveland women, without their knowledge or consent, as part of an insurance speculation scam that turned up during a state insurance investigation. In the past 12 years, McKenzie paid as much as $30 a week in premiums on at least 21 people. At present, she had collected $5,000 and had active claims for $10,000 more.

White was promoted to sergeant on March 1, 1943. After a rash of false fire alarms reported in the East 84th Street and Quincy Avenue district, during February and March 1943, Sergeant White traced footprints he found in the snow to a home on East 84th and arrested the man responsible.

In October 1944, two armed men attempted to rob a Chinese laundry at 7811 Central Avenue, only to be surprised when the owner, Yee Gin, pulled a gun from under an ironing board and started blasting. Gin told police he was sure he hit one of the men. Sergeant White, in checking with local hospitals, found out that a man received treatment at Charity Hospital for a shoulder wound. White went to the 28-year-old man's home and arrested him. He quickly ratted out his accomplice in the failed robbery.

In another celebrated story about White, in July 1945, five police cruisers and a motorcycle officer came up empty in trying to catch a speeding driver, who raced through East Side streets, reaching speeds of 70 miles-per-hour. After eluding all pursuers, the driver, 22-year-old James Mederer, decided it was safe to come to a stop at a traffic light at Crawford Road near University Circle. White pulled up next to the man in an unmarked detective car and asked Mederer, "Got a match?"

"Sure," he answered. White got out of his car, walked over to Mederer's vehicle, and calmly placed him under arrest. Mederer, a local mechanic and a repeat traffic offender, said he sped away from the pursuing police cars when he realized he was driving without a license.

In October 1945, after an armed robbery of a meat market at 1373 East 105th Street, where robbers shot at a witness who pursued them, all cars in the 4th and 5th Districts, as well as East Cleveland police, were on the lookout for the two men. A detective car with Sergeant White and Detectives Daniel McCormack and Nathan Wachs,[156] caught up with the pair on Adelbert Road, near University Hospital, just south of Euclid Avenue, and arrested them. The armed men were ex-convicts, who had served a term in the Ohio Penitentiary for robbery. One man was still holding a bag containing the $263 taken in the robbery.

On January 22, 1947, a major police department shakeup took place. New Safety Director William F. Smith, a former FBI agent, and Police Chief George J. Matowitz, made sweeping changes in the Traffic Division and moved Lieutenant Martin P. Cooney from the Homicide Squad and placed him in charge of a small unit which came to be known as the "Rackets Squad," consisting of two sergeants and eight detectives. Cooney's new assignment was to declare war on "racketeers, gangs and king-size liquor and gambling entrepreneurs." During this period in the late 1940s, as the competition in the policy rackets grew more intense, bombings and violence were occurring with more frequency. The two sergeants placed on the new squad were Thomas White and Howard Hutchings. Cooney was replaced on the Homicide Squad by Lieutenant David E. Kerr.

The new "Rackets Squad" went to work immediately harassing East Side bookies and policy game operators. In early February, Sergeant White and Detectives William Kaiser and Samuel Mears "rushed" a home on Linn Avenue on the East Side and arrested Charles Oddo, believed to be running a bookie operation. They confiscated three telephones and charged Oddo with occupying a room to record wagers, a popular charge used against bookies at that time.

An early morning stroll on Chester Avenue came to an end for White and Mears on a warm night in mid-June 1947 when the two men noticed a crowd at the entrance of the Stage Door Club. The two detectives joined the crowd after the 2:30 closing hour and watched as whiskey was served at the bar. The two arrested George Young, who described himself as part-owner of the establishment.

On June 21, Safety Director Smith issued a hoodlum pickup order to Cooney's "Rackets Squad." Before the week was out, he was frustrated because more action hadn't been taken. Smith ordered Detective Inspector Charles O. Nevel to compile a list of Cleveland "racketeers, hoodlums and known criminals." The safety director ordered copies distributed to every member of the police department so "they would have no doubt about whom to look for." In addition, Smith ordered "motion pictures" taken of racketeers so every member of the department could become familiar with their faces.

Thomas White was a true believer in what Smith was attempting to accomplish because several years later he would be championing this process and improving it. In the meantime, White, Kaiser and Mears kept up with the safety director's orders. On June 25, they arrested a man associated with the Ten-Eleven Club, and two weeks later nabbed Leroy B. Frye and charged him with keeping rooms to record bets. Ten days after this, White and Mears used a ladder to peak over a transom into a room in the Cook Building at 4614 Prospect Avenue. The two detectives arrested three men and confiscated betting slips, racing forms and six telephones. One of the arrested, Jack Green had a record of six previous arrests for keeping a room to record wagers.

When Cleveland Mayor Thomas Burke named William Smith safety director in January 1947, he left the position of assistant safety director open. Six months into the year, Burke realized the enormity of the work his new safety director was faced with. In July, Burke allowed Smith to name 27-year-old Alvin J. Sutton, Jr. to the post of Assistant Safety Director. Sutton was one of Smith's partners when he was with the FBI. Both men grew up in Cleveland Heights and worked together as agents in Cleveland and Pittsburgh. At the time Sutton was hired by Smith, he was the liaison agent between the FBI and the Cleveland police.

Sutton was a no-nonsense, dedicated, and incorruptible law enforcement officer. The first investigation he took on was the case of Lieutenant Ernest Molnar, who was believed to actually be running the policy racket in the city. Molnar went to trial in July 1948, was convicted and sent to the Ohio Penitentiary.

Sutton's new presence caused immediate friction with Lieutenant Cooney. By the middle of 1948, Sutton had mentioned on several occasions that he was not getting the co-operation he wanted from the lieutenant. At one point he accused Cooney of harassing key informants who were important to an investigation he was conducting into the policy rackets. He also believed Cooney was not pursuing one of the top policy bankers as much as he was the others.

This all came to a head on December 2, 1948, when Safety Director Smith disbanded Cooney's "Rackets Squad" before a replacement squad could even be put together. Cooney was sent packing to the First District on the far West Side, while Sergeants White and Hutchins, along with Detectives Kaiser and Mears, were all shifted to the 3rd District.

Sergeant White soon earned favor from Sutton after he and Deputy Inspector James E. McArthur helped break a case against "Shondor" Birns less than a week after a bombing attempt against his adversary Joseph Allen. Birns was charged as the mastermind of the shakedown of Allen's policy business.

In October 1950, White's memorizing of Inspector Nevel's "racketeers, hoodlums and known criminals" compilation helped him, and Detective Mears nab a "celebrated" pickpocket. The two detectives, on an unrelated assignment, spotted Louis "The Dip" Finkelstein hanging out around the corners of Chester and Vincent Avenues at East 9th Street around 11:00 one morning. Four hours later, they spotted him there again. The men watched him as he followed a young couple into a café, waited five minutes, and then walked in themselves. "The Dip" was sitting next to the lady at the bar, on which sat her purse containing $200. The detectives took Finkelstein to the station, where they found $250 in his pockets.

On June 25, 1951, Thomas P. White was promoted to lieutenant. By now he had become close with Deputy Inspector James E. McArthur, head of the Detective Bureau. There would soon be several changes in that department. The shakeup began on January 31, 1952, when 28 men in the Detective Bureau were notified they failed a recent ultimatum of "produce or else." Some were transferred to uniform duty, while others were given "beginners work" in the bureau, which resulted in several retirements. The move had the full support of Police Chief Frank W. Story, who said that in "the bureau it was common knowledge that 25% of the men carry the load while the rest drag their feet." It took a year to completely "remodel" the Detective Bureau. In announcing the changes to reporters on February 5, 1953, Inspector McArthur stated Lieutenant White, "has the assignment of coordinating the investigations and tying up loose ends."

Author's note: Thomas White is mentioned extensively in Chapter Six, which covers the arrest of Julius Petro for the Warren robbery and the ensuing trial. He is also mentioned frequently in Chapter Ten in the entries for Philip Aliberti, Anthony D'Alessio, Joseph Drago, Vincent Innocenzi and Joseph Russo.

By mid-1954, White was being hailed as the head of "special services" for Detective Chief McArthur. On June 16, McArthur and White announced to reporters they had busted a large burglary ring that specialized in jewelry stores. In arresting seven members of the gang, police said they solved the mystery of 25 burglaries throughout the state and captured Cleveland's Public Enemy #1, James M. Horay.

On September 16, 1954, *Plain Dealer* reporter Sanford Watzman revealed to Clevelanders the *Police Mug Book*. The book was borne out of the efforts of former Safety Director William Smith and Detective Inspector Nevel, but improved upon by Detective Chief McArthur and Lieutenant White. Watzman wrote:

> This society book of the underworld reads almost like the posters in your neighborhood post office. It has front and side views of each criminal and caption indicating their names, addresses, physical descriptions, the type of car they drive with its license number, their criminal specialties and gangland associates.
>
> It is a matter of pride with Detective Chief James E. McArthur that he should be able to come out with a new book so soon. He would be even happier if the 1954-55 edition were to become outdated before two more years are out.

Ten months later, Sanford Watzman was reporting on a new hot-button topic: "Loophole in Law Lets Thugs Work in Bars." The article, after an investigation by the *Plain Dealer*, revealed "a strange anomaly" in Ohio's state liquor code. While "the law makes it difficult for an ex-convict to own a tavern on paper," it doesn't prohibit them from managing or working in a tavern, bar, or café. One of the first criminals alluded to in the article was Julius Petro and referenced his "virtual take over" of Sonny's Show Bar. Lieutenant White, now being identified as "chief of the detective bureau's intelligence unit," assisted the newspaper's investigation, which compiled a list of 20 establishments that were running under this "thug" management. Criminals referred to in the article included Salvatore Poliafico, Sylvester Papalardo and "Shondor" Birns.

The latter half of the 1950s proved to be a busy time for White. The lieutenant and his squad of detectives – Sergeant Harry C. Lockwood, Walter L. Aufmuth, Joseph Kolek, James E. McHugh, Thomas E. Murphy, Harry J. Tolan, Edward J. Walsh and John Woyle – made many significant arrests. In June 1955, they helped bring down the Teller / Ritenour ring, a Bonnie & Clyde type of gang. Louis E. Teller was 27-years old, while his married partner Mrs. Lora Lee Ritenour was described as a 17-year-old "gun moll," who enjoyed drinking. Later that year the detectives brought in "lone wolf" stickup man Stephen M. Kostura after a $9,000 robbery at a Central National Bank branch on the West Side.

In April 1956, White, listed as superintendent of police communications, was involved in the filming of a staged bank robbery production at the Cleveland Trust Company branch at 4814 Euclid Avenue.[157] The film was created to give police "a complete bank robbery sequence for study and training," as well as to check the effectiveness in the new use of cameras in banks.

Lieutenant White and new Detective Chief Thomas A. Murray were part of a three-hour conference with officers of the AFL Glaziers Union on January 14, 1957. The seven union representatives and five Cleveland Police officials met in Safety Director John N. McCormick's office to discuss incidents of recent stench bombings on the West Side.

On May 5, 1957, White announced the arrests of Alfred "Allie" Calabrese and Paul Perrotti for the murder of Eldon "Pete" Shoup during a burglary in Alliance, Ohio (See Chapter Eleven).

Another piece of the Thomas White legend was added on July 8, 1957, when the *Plain Dealer* published an article titled "Criminal Hate Parade Ranks Lt. White No.1." The article, by Chief Police Reporter Robert E. Tidyman, stated McArthur created the Police Special Services Unit in 1949, and since then, "White and his men have cleaned the streets of almost every notorious crook or racketeer." Tidyman relates, "As a result of the work Lt. White and his men are doing, Cleveland 'pros' are confining their activities to suburbs and cities far from Cleveland. Many have taken up residence in California."

While commenting on the high-profile criminals White helped to remove, Tidyman provides us with this gem regarding Cleveland's "Handsomest Public Enemy":

One tale brought back by paroled prisoners returning to Cleveland from Leavenworth Federal Penitentiary is that every night before going to sleep Julius Petro, bank robber, sticks pins in a doll.

The story goes that the doll is kept under Petro's pillow. It is said to be tattered from the many pins that have been stuck in it.

The doll is said to be a white-haired, red-faced replica of Detective Lieutenant Thomas P. White, chief of Cleveland's police special services unit.

Lieutenant White and Detectives Tolan and Walsh became involved in a stolen gun case, which had its roots in Fremont, Ohio, where 175 rifles and handguns were taken during a burglary at Tex's Trading Post there. When one of the stolen weapons ended up at Sam's Loan Company at 2144 Prospect Avenue, a Cleveland pawn shop, the detectives got involved. A man from South Euclid pawned the .38 Special caliber Colt revolver there, which was found to be on the list of stolen weapons from the Fremont burglary. Police questioned the man, who said he had purchased 30 weapons from Robert S. Roskoph, and sold 19 of them to two local gun collectors.

White's detectives questioned Roskoph, a Cleveland businessman and owner of Union Towel & Supply Company, who told them he purchased the guns from William R. "Willie" Cox, described as a "Cleveland racket man and alleged muscle man for 'Shondor' Birns." When police last questioned Birns, and asked him about his occupation, he claimed he was an employee of Union Towel & Supply Company. When asked to be more specific, he said he was a salesman for them. Roskoph was arrested and charged with "gun peddling" without a city permit and was released on a $200 bail. He was later fined $100.

On April 29, 1958, the newspapers reported, "The nucleus of one of the largest safecracking operations in Greater Cleveland history was broken yesterday with the arrest of three men and the confiscation of thousands of dollars' worth of burglar tools and equipment." Arrested were Albert H. Severino, who White described as one of Cleveland's "most accomplished burglars," his brother Lawrence and Charles C. Skubovis. When the three men went to trial in January 1959, Skubovis and Albert Severino were found guilty of possessing burglary tools and sentenced to the Ohio Penitentiary; Lawrence Severino was acquitted (See Chapter Twelve: Albert Severino & Charles Skubovis).

Nine months after the conviction of Severino, *Plain Dealer* reporter Fred Mollenkopf wrote an article titled, "'Brain' Gone, Burglars Fall on Lean Days." He described how one of Cleveland's most successful burglary gangs had disintegrated due to the work of Lieutenant White and his squad. Mollenkopf stated, "White's men specialize on professional burglars and robbers. They make it their job to know the habits, quirks, comings and goings of the hoodlums and, very importantly, the cars they drive." This latter point came into use the night they were looking for a bowling alley robbery accomplice and spotted a new 1958 Lincoln that Severino had purchased only weeks earlier. Mollenkopf ended the article by stating:

The intense surveillance of White's men has had two effects: (1) The burglars can't take a chance on operating in the city. (2) They're headed for the smaller cities and towns, out of state and out of city.

To this last statement, Lieutenant White commented, "But they're making a mistake by thinking they can operate in the smaller communities. Obviously, they stick out like sore thumbs."

On Saturday, September 27, 1958, White stepped outside that morning to let his dog take a leak. The lieutenant lived in the eastern suburb of Euclid, on Kennison Avenue, which stretched from East 214th to East 222nd Street. He watched as the dog took off barking and racing toward a canvas bag sitting near a tree in his backyard. White opened the canvas bag and discovered six sticks of dynamite inside with a 50-foot fuse of which only 30 feet had burned.

Police quickly began rounding up hoods for investigation, the most prominent of whom were Severino and Skubovis. Inspector Richard R. Wagner, the new head of the Detective Bureau stated, "We don't know whether it was placed there to do damage or to intimidate." White's home was given special attention by the Euclid police. On Monday night, two telephone calls were made to the Euclid home. White's wife, Rita, answered the first one and was told, "It's not you we're after. You better get out of the house." When White answered the second call himself, he was told, "You had better get out of town."

On the day the bomb incident was made public, Anthony Buffa, a criminal with a rap sheet of 17 arrests since 1937, appeared in court. After pleading guilty to receiving stolen property he was ready to be sentenced. Following an impassioned plea from his lawyer, Adrian Fink, Common Pleas Judge Donald F. Lybarger granted Buffa probation. The police were "stunned." When informed of the decision, White threw his hands up in disgust. Inspector Wagner said he would gather the latest files on Buffa and meet with Judge Lybarger immediately. The next day, after a one-hour-and-twenty-minute hearing, featuring testimony from Lieutenant White and Sergeant John Ungvary, the judge reversed his decision and sentenced Buffa to a term of one-to-seven years in the Ohio Penitentiary. Buffa was handcuffed by a deputy sheriff and while being led out of the courtroom, he turned and spit on Lieutenant White and threatened, "I'll get you yet, you _____!"

When Vincent Innocenzi was found murdered in early August 1960, White was one of the police officers who believed the murder was a result of the continuing unrest in the gang war that was plaguing Youngstown. He may have hit the nail on the head.

Lakewood police, investigating a $10,200 home burglary, were looking to question two Cleveland men. On January 24, 1961, Lieutenant White sent Detectives Thomas E. Murphy and James P. Sweeney to pick up Angelo J. Amato, Jr. and Sam J. Vecchio – the president and secretary of Hospital Workers Local 500 – with two Lakewood detectives it tow. The detectives stopped the two men in Amato's automobile near his home on Throckley Avenue. Detectives found adding machine tapes, indicating clearinghouse numbers, in Amato's pocket, and records showing $1,070 in bets under the front seat. Lakewood detectives took the pair back to that suburb for questioning in the home burglary. Back in October 1960, White's men had arrested Amato and Vecchio in connection with two East Side home bombings during union organizing efforts at Huron Road Hospital.

August 1961 brought the baffling murder case of Louis F. Hamblin, Jr. The handsome 26-year-old lived on Eddy Road with his attractive wife and two young children. Hamblin was an ex-convict who served a term in the Moundsville Penitentiary in West Virginia for breaking and entering. Up until February 1961, Hamblin ran the Key Personnel Agency. He was last seen by his wife on Saturday night, August 12. Three nights later, his body was discovered in a ditch off a lonely country road near Remsen Corners in Medina County. He had been shot eight times. Police believed Hamblin, and two men he had served time with in Moundsville, were involved in a July 21 holdup at the Broadview Savings & Loan branch on Detroit Avenue in Rocky River, in which $39,000 was taken. When police found Hamblin's car after his murder, parked on Main Avenue in the Flats, they recovered three rubber masks. Lieutenant White discovered a check Hamblin sent to a private club at 12501 Mayfield Road in Little Italy made out for $1,000. The address was for a club known as the "Toy Shop," which was raided twice in recent weeks for selling liquor after hours, and operating gambling games. As police plowed through his sordid financial trail, Detective Chief Wagner commented, "The more you investigate this case the more you wonder not that he was killed but that he lived so long." The police theory was Hamblin was murdered by one of the two men he served time with in West Virginia. As for the motive, police believed it was over a split of the money from the Rocky River bank robbery.

In early September, the focus on the murder suspect suddenly shifted to a French-Canadian citizen using the name Edward Frank Spencer and his wife, Gina, also believed to be French-Canadian. The couple, who were living in a Bedford motel for three months, recently paid rent for six months in advance on a pink-colored bungalow on Ridge Road in North Royalton, and quickly purchased $300 worth of storm windows for the place. The two lived in the home for only a week before vacating the day after Hamblin's murder. They left behind $2,500 worth of new furniture and a sink full of empty pop bottles. Police soon discovered Hamblin was to meet Spencer when he left his Eddy Road home on August 12. Lieutenant White commented, "This looks like a good bet. If he's not [the killer], I don't know who to look for."

The Medina County prosecutor issued a warrant on September 6, charging Spencer with first-degree murder. Five days later, FBI agents, holding a fugitive warrant, arrested Spencer and Gina on a street in New Orleans. They were identified as Edward A. Smart and Marie Louise Raymond. The two were returned to the Medina County Jail, where they were questioned by White's detectives. Smart admitted to them Hamblin stopped at his house on August 12, but said he had no idea what happened to him after he left. He would not tell police what he discussed with him while he was there. Also questioning Smart were Canadian authorities, investigating a $1 million bank burglary in Montreal during the first weekend in July.

The Medina prosecutor determined he did not have enough evidence to convict Smart on murder charges, so he immediately moved to deport the two to Canada to face bank burglary charges there. Marie Raymond, just 24, was on her way back north before the end of September. Smart put up a fight, declaring he didn't know where he was born. He already entered the United States illegally once, through Brownsville, Texas, and was deported back in August 1948. His second illegal entry into the United States was also through Brownsville. On September 27, he was ordered deported, but appealed the decision. In December 1961, while his deportation order was still being appealed by the Immigration & Naturalization Service, Smart was sentenced to a 30-day jail term for entering the United States illegally.

Police were able to convict one of Hamblin's former West Virginia cell mates, Donald Ray Long, for the robbery of a Lawson's store in South Euclid. While serving that term, in June 1963, Long confessed he and Hamblin were involved in the Rocky River bank holdup. He revealed nothing about Hamblin's murder, though. Nobody was ever brought to trial for the murder of Louis F. Hamblin, Jr.

On April 8, 1963, Cleveland Police Chief Frank Story retired at the age of 72. Replaced by Richard E. Wagner, the new chief began making changes in the department immediately. A week later, on April 15, Lieutenant Thomas White was transferred to uniform duty in the 6th District. Wagner's reason for the moves was always the same, "They were for the good of the department."

Two years later, in March 1965, White left the department and joined a voter fraud squad employed by the Cuyahoga County Board of Elections. After leaving there, he headed the security department of White Motor Corporation, working there until he retired in 1976. In mid-1981, White was diagnosed with cancer. He fought bravely for four months before succumbing to it in Lakewood Hospital on November 9, 1981, at the age of 68.

END NOTES

NOTE TO READER: THE NAMES AND PLACES LISTED IN THE END NOTES DO NOT APPEAR IN THE INDEX.

Chapter One: Cleveland Birth

[1] Julius Petro's parents, Giovanni Pietroiacovo (John Petro) and Lydia Campanara, were from the province of Campobasso, in the Molise region of Italy. John and Lydia arrived in America sometime between 1907 and 1911, eventually settling in the Collinwood section of Cleveland. Their first child, a daughter, Monda Evelyn Pietroiacovo was born in Cleveland on December 15, 1920. By the time Julius was born, in June 1922, the family had shortened the name to Petro. Michael A. Petro, their last child, was born on May 17, 1926. Monda married Nicholas J. Tirabassi, in 1943. John Petro died on June 26, 1982, in Los Angeles. The death notice stated he left behind six grandchildren and seven great grand-grandchildren. Lydia Petro died on April 22, 1987, also in Los Angeles. Michael Petro died on May 17, 2002, in Las Vegas. Monda Tirabassi lived to be 95 years old, passing away on March 5, 2016.

[2] The Mansfield Reformatory, formally the Ohio State Reformatory, operated from 1896 to 1990. In 1994, the facility was used as the fictional Shawshank State Penitentiary in the hit film The Shawshank Redemption. The historic prison facility with its Romanesque architecture was the creation of Cleveland architect Levi T. Scofield, who was famous for designing the Soldiers and Sailors Monument, which adorns the southeast corner of Public Square. At Lake View Cemetery, the ornate Scofield family mausoleum, located across from Wade Chapel, is the highlight of Mausoleum Row.

[3] Michael A. Picciano graduated from Cleveland Law School in 1917. In the mid-1920s, when Ed Stanton was Cuyahoga County Prosecutor, he hired Picciano as an assistant county prosecutor. He served in that capacity from 1927 to 1929, when Stanton left office. At that time, Stanton and Picciano, along with James C. Connell, another former assistant county prosecutor, worked together in private practice for a few years. In 1933, Harry L. Davis returned to the mayor's office after leaving in 1919 for a successful run at governor of Ohio. After election to office in November 1933, Davis hired Picciano as chief police prosecutor. Picciano held that position, despite many scandals within the office, until Harold H. Burton was elected mayor in November 1935. Picciano returned to being a defense attorney and practiced law, even in semi-retirement, for the rest of his life. He died on April 13, 1977, at the age of 82.

Chapter Two: Burglary & Murder: The "Bobby" Knaus Case

[4] The Saint Francis Medal is named for Giovanni di Peitro di Bernardone (1182 to 1226), who became Saint Francis of Assisi. An Italian Catholic Friar, deacon, and preacher, he was one of the most venerated religious figures in history. Saint Francis is the Patron Saint of Animals, Merchants and Ecology, and holds many other patron saint titles.

[5] In the newspaper stories that came out after the death of Julius Petro, reporters tried to make more of the relationship between Petro and Theodore "Bobby" Knaus. One story stated that when they met at the Mansfield Reformatory, "They hit it off well together. They had the same lawless, easy-money philosophy." Their time together in the reformatory could not have been long, however, as Petro was transferred to the Ohio Penitentiary. Knaus was incarcerated until December 29, 1945, which makes the following reporting questionable: "Released, they broke into several safes and staged a number of holdups in Cleveland and out of town." Since Knaus was dead by the end of February 1946, if these events actually took place, there was a very limited window of time in which they could have occurred.

[6] When the newspapers first reported this sighting, they claimed it took place at the Green Café on Superior Avenue.

[7] The number of shell casings found would change at times between the reporting of the arrest and during the trial. The newspapers claimed that three shell casings were found inside the Petro automobile.

[8] George R. Andrews had a lengthy record in Pennsylvania. In October 1945, he claimed he was the driver of the get-away car during the hold-up attempt at the Woodhill barns of the Cleveland Transit System. He denied being involved in the actual slaying. He also confessed to murdering a girl in Cleveland and burying her body in a city dump-site. Cleveland police used a power shovel to search for the body, but could find none. While both these confessions may have been concocted, he also implicated another man, who he said broke out of a workhouse in Pennsylvania at the same time he did. The man's name was Tony Priore. Coincidentally, the name of the man Louis P. Bucci pleaded with Newport, Kentucky, police that he needed to get information to while on his deathbed was a "Tony P."

[9] Thomas Whalen, a college graduate, and former football player at Western Reserve University, had come up through the ranks of the Cleveland Police Department since joining the force in 1936. On March 2, 1946, Whalen was one of

several homicide detectives called out to the Belvoir Boulevard murder scene of Theodore "Bobby" Knaus. He accompanied the body to the Cuyahoga County Morgue.

[10] Robert L. Britton and James Griffin were two Black men from Arkansas, who relocated to Cleveland; one for a year, the other 18 months. In that time, they were responsible for five felonies including the murders of Henry Lee Webb on June 21, 1946, shot to death during a dice game holdup, and Harley Kinear, on July 12, a Nickel Plate Railroad detective, shot while preventing a box car break-in. The killing of a law enforcement officer, Kinear, and murder while perpetrating a felony were both first-degree murder offenses. The two men fled back to Arkansas where they were arrested by local authorities. A Cleveland police squad, led by Detective Lieutenant Martin P. Cooney, arrived in Arkansas on August 5. Within an hour, Cooney had a confession from Griffin. Britton held out until he arrived at Central Police Station the next day. A third man, Floyd Dace, had already confessed, but all would plead not-guilty at arraignment. On November 19, the trial for the murder of Henry Lee Webb began in the courtroom of Common Pleas Judge Julius M. Kovachy. Norman S. Minor, Cuyahoga County's first Black assistant prosecutor, handled the case for the state; Britton and Griffin were represented by Selmo Glenn and Myron W. Ulrich, respectively. Dace requested, and was granted, a separate trial. The highlight of the trial came during closing statements on November 26. While Minor was reciting the "bloody, brutal details" of the crime, Britton chose this in-opportune moment to yawn. Minor pounced on this before the defendant had a chance to close his mouth. Minor stated, "Even while we go back over these shocking facts the defendant, Britton, is yawning unconcernedly, ladies and gentlemen. Just that much concern was shown when he shot Henry Lee Webb to death and then went home to play juke box music and to shoot craps with his accomplices with the money they had got at gunpoint." The next day, the jury came back with a death-sentence verdict for Britton, 27 and Griffin, 28. Nearly a year-to-the-day later, after appeals were exhausted, both men were executed in the state penitentiary's electric chair on November 28, 1947. After a mistrial in the case of Floyd Dace, he was convicted at a second trial. Sentenced to death, the 23-year-old met the same fate as his crime associates on March 1, 1948.

[11] Frank J. Merrick was one of Cleveland's treasures when it came to law enforcement. He was born in 1894, the last of 12 siblings. He sold newspapers in Public Square at the age of nine to help his family after his father passed away. He attended St. Ignatius High School and later St. Ignatius College (now John Carroll University), but had to drop out due to finances. He went to work in the law office of prominent Cleveland attorney Francis J. Wing three days a week, while attending Cleveland Law School at night. During World War I, Merrick

worked for a branch of the U.S. Justice Department assigned to the Army on a homeland security detail. In 1918, he joined the Army and served in France as a First Sergeant. While on a detail, in August that year outside Verdun, he was wounded twice and spent the rest of the war in London, before being mustered out in May 1919.

Merrick returned to Cleveland and went into private law practice until the fall of 1920. In September, Cuyahoga County Prosecutor Roland A. Baskin appointed Merrick assistant county prosecutor. At the age of 26, he was one of the youngest men ever appointed to the county prosecutor's office. In December 1920, Merrick worked on two of the most famous cases of the time. He helped gain the convictions of members of the Mayfield Road Mob, which was involved in what the newspapers referred to as the Serra Auto Theft Ring. Among those convicted were Nicholas Angelotta, Frank "Frankie Burns" Milazzo, and Frank Motto. While Angelotta and Milazzo chose to serve their time, Motto decided to appeal his case. This decision led directly to the murders of businessmen Wilfred Sly and George Fanner on New Years' Eve day 1920. The second case was that of George "Jiggs" Losteiner, "the baddest man of Roaring-Twenties Cleveland." Losteiner was on trial for the murder of East Cleveland police officer Patrick Gaffney. Merrick worked the case with a lead prosecutor by the name of William J. Corrigan. Losteiner was convicted, but the jury voted 9 to 3 for mercy and "Jiggs" spent the rest of his life in prison. With the Republican landslide of November 1920, Republican Edward Stanton took office as Cuyahoga County prosecutor in January 1921. William Corrigan would go on the fame and fortune as a defense attorney, while Merrick became counsel for the Cleveland Automobile Club. In this capacity he helped track down the killers of Sly and Fanner, a process that would take years. In the end, however, three men would die in the electric chair for this crime including Dominic Benigno, the first leader of the Mayfield Road Mob, as well as Frank Motto.

After years as counsel for the automobile club, in January 1929, Merrick was appointed Chief Assistant Cuyahoga County Prosecutor by newly elected Democratic County Prosecutor Ray T. Miller. When Miller was elected mayor in February 1932, he named Merrick his new Director of Public Safety. In November 1933, Merrick was selected to fill a vacancy in the Municipal Court. Three years later he was elected a judge of the Common Pleas Court, remaining in that position for the next 12 years. In 1953, Merrick was appointed by Governor Frank J. Lausche to the Probate Court. Merrick remained in this position, becoming the presiding probate judge in Cuyahoga County until his retirement in 1973 at the age of 77. From 1938 to 1968, Merrick served as a member of the Cuyahoga County Democratic Executive Committee. Frank J. Merrick died on July 9, 1977, at the age of 82.

[12] Lubaloy is a wrought copper alloy composed mainly of copper and zinc. "In 1922, the Western Cartridge Company produced a copper-washed bullet-jacket-

ing called Lubaloy which stands for lubricating alloy. Lubaloy replaced standard bullet jacketing, which had been cupro-nickel coated steel or solid cupro-nickel. The original jacketing was found to be detrimental to firearm performance over time. Lumps of the hot jacketing were deposited near the end of the barrel during firing, eventually creating a hazard or destroying the barrel. The Lubaloy-Palma ammunition jacketing was a breakthrough solution to this persistent dilemma. It was composed of 90% copper, 8% zinc, and 2% tin." – *Wikipedia*

[13] Dr. Irene Levis was a professor of micro-analytical chemistry, who headed a laboratory at Frankfort University, before relocating to the United States with her husband and three children during Adolph Hitler's reign in Nazi Germany. She arrived in Cleveland in October 1938, and became the first woman faculty member at Case School of Applied Science. She was hired to teach micro-analytical chemistry at the school, using a laboratory reported to be "the only one of its kind in Cleveland and one of the few in the country." The following year, she was featured in a *Plain Dealer* article titled "Man's 'Frontier' In Science Fading." While pointing out that the school currently did not have the facilities to accommodate all the new female students, she backed away from confirming the articles premise by stating, "We don't have enough data yet." Dr. Levis made her courtroom debut in December 1940, when she testified during the trial of three safecrackers that slag found on the bottom of their shoes was consistent with slag found in the parking lot of the Carnegie Avenue fur shop they burglarized. During World War II, the new field of industrial spectroscopy opened up to woman, with much of the work requiring subtle fingers, precision, and patience, all of which were said to be "womanly qualities." In 1946, and again in 1948, she testified for the state in the murder trial of Julius Petro, amid threats to her own her life. In 1946, Dr. Levis became director of research for the National Spectrographic Laboratories, Inc. In September 1946, she introduced a course in spectroscopy at Fenn College School of Engineering. In November 1946, she testified at the trial of Thomas C. Sanfilippo, for the murder of racketeer Robert L. Firestone (see End Note 15). Using spectrograms of glass specks from an automobile window found in the trouser cuffs of Sanfilippo's pants, she tied him to the murder scene. Despite her testimony, Sanfilippo was later found not guilty. In her later years she moved to West Covina, California.

[14] "Spectroscopy pertains to the dispersion of an object's light into its component colors (i.e., energies). By performing this dissection and analysis of an object's light, astronomers can infer the physical properties of that object (such as temperature, mass, luminosity and composition)." – *University of Arizona*

[15] Dr. Clifford R. Keizer was also called as an expert witness on November 19, 1946, during the first-degree murder trial of gambler Thomas C. Sanfilippo, who

was accused of the murder of Robert L. Firestone, co-owner of the Casa Blanca night club with Cleveland racketeer Maxie Diamond. Keizer was called to testify for the defense and "presented a highly technical explanation of spectroscopic analysis and a conclusion that such a method was not infallible in the identification of glass." The prosecution claimed that glass particles found in Sanfilippo's trouser cuff matched broken glass from the death car. The jury found Sanfilippo not guilty.

Chapter Three: Green Acres Casino Robbery

[16] Emergency Clinic Hospital seems to be a mystery in itself. The hospital, which operated, from what I have been able to gather, from 1927 to 1949, doesn't seem to have a single mention in either *Cleveland: The Making of a City*, by William Ganson Rose; or *The Encyclopedia of Cleveland History*, by David D. Van Tassel and John J. Grabowski. From articles in the Cleveland *Plain Dealer*, of which it seems to be mentioned more than 500 times, the hospital stood in the Five Points section of Collinwood on the northeast corner of St. Clair and East 152nd Street. That spot is now occupied by Cleveland Fire Station No. 31. In an obituary for a Dr. John B. Hanson, from March 1, 1962, it states, "From 1918 to 1947 he was surgeon for the New York Central System here. During that period, he operated the Emergency Clinic Foundation Hospital at Five Points in the old Collinwood district."

[17] City Hospital was founded in 1837 and, after a few name changes over the years, is one of the nation's oldest medical institutions. Today, now over 180 years old, it operates as MetroHealth Medical Center. Located on Scranton Road, on the city's Near-West side, for years the hospital had a prison ward, where wounded prisoners would be taken for medical care and watched.

[18] One of Cleveland's most beloved civic, political, and legal figures, Newton Diehl Baker, Jr., following in the footsteps of his mentor Tom L. Johnson, served two terms as mayor, from 1912 to 1915. Declining to run for a third term, he retired to practice law and founded the law firm of Baker & Hostetler in January 1916. Today it remains one of the city's most prestigious law firms. Active in Democratic politics, Baker was a leading supporter of Woodrow Wilson and helped him win election in 1912. At that time, he turned down Wilson's offer to become Secretary of the Interior. Two months after his retirement as mayor, however, he accepted Wilson's appointment as Secretary of War. While in that position he had the responsibility of "drafting, organizing, outfitting, and provisioning an army of 2 million men to be sent overseas in the shortest possible time." After the war his responsibilities included demobilizing the troops and negotiating the cancellation of numerous war contracts. After five years in Washing-

ton D.C., he returned to the law firm in Cleveland in May 1921. Back home he helped found the League for Criminal Justice. He remained active in civic affairs and was a member of many charitable, educational, institutional, and corporate boards and committees throughout the remainder of his life. He died on Christmas Day 1937, at the age of 66, and was buried in Lake View Cemetery.

[19] When the Hollenden Hotel was built in Cleveland in 1885, at the corner of Superior and Bond Street (East 6th Street) it was the city's most luxurious hotel. Liberty E. Holden, owner of the *Plain Dealer* newspaper, created the corporation to build the hotel. He gave it the name Hollenden, said to be an early English form of the name Holden. The 10-story, 1,000-room hotel had a theatre, barbershop and numerous bars and clubs. It offered both temporary stay to guests and permanent housing. During the hotel's 77-year existence, it hosted overnight stays to five U.S. Presidents – William McKinley, Theodore Roosevelt, William H. Taft, Woodrow Wilson and Warren G. Harding. In addition, Albert Einstein was a guest in 1921, and in 1960 Senator John F. Kennedy gave a speech there. The hotel was also used by a number of underworld figures over the years. Just behind the hotel, on what was known as "Short Vincent" Street, were the Theatrical Bar & Grille and the Roxy Burlesque. By 1962, only 350 of the hotel's rooms were in regular use. That year the ornate hotel was demolished. A new, 14-story, 400-room Hollenden Hotel took its place. The new facility had its own parking garage. Opened on March 1, 1965, the second version of the hotel had a 24-year run before economic conditions in Cleveland hastened its demise in 1989. Three years later, the second hotel was demolished and Bank One Center, now Fifth Third Center, was constructed in its place.

[20] In 1948, twenty-eight years after the Cleveland Indians won their first World Series in 1920, they were back in it again. This time, they faced off against the Boston Braves of the National League. Going into the end of the 1948 season, the Indians were behind the Boston Red Sox by 4 and ½ games on Labor Day. During September they went on a 17 to 3 run and on October 1, Cleveland was in first place and the Red Sox were tied with the New York Yankees for second, both 1 and ½ games back. The Indians went 1 and 2 in their last three games, while the Red Sox finished the season 2 – 0. For the first time in American League history two teams finished with identical records, which led to a one-game playoff. On October 5, the two teams met in Boston for that historic playoff game. With Cleveland's Gene Bearden pitching, and shortstop / manager Lou Boudreau going 4 for 4 at the plate, the Indians beat the Red Sox 8 to 3, thus preventing an all-Boston World Series that year. In the World Series, which opened in Boston on October 6, the Indians lost the first game, but went on to win three straight and then finished it off with a win in game 6. The Boston Braves moved to Milwaukee at the end of the 1952 season and remained there through 1965 before relocating to Atlanta.

[21] Frank Budak, and his brother Joseph, would be the only people sent to jail in the aftermath of the Green Acres robbery and the murder of Sam Jerry Monachino. The brothers were arrested on October 22, 1948, for violating their Federal paroles and were brought to Cleveland from Youngstown to await their return to a Federal Penitentiary to serve out 30 more months of the sentences that they received in 1946 for income tax evasion. The brothers had been sentenced to terms of two-and-a-half years in Lewisburg Federal Prison and were released on parole on April 1, 1947. This parole period would have ended on November 21, 1948. The reports from probation officers contained information that Frank was connected with operating the Poland County Club and was reported to be the actual owner of the Green Acres. Chief Federal Probation Officer, Myron E. Patterson stated that his officer's investigation showed that the Poland Country Club was in the name of the Budak brothers' mother, "but that it is generally known that Frank operates the club." Frank was found to be connected to the Green Acres gambling den after equipment from there made its way to the Poland Country Club in the wake of the September 17, 1948, robbery. John Sanko, who operated an illegal bar at the Poland Country Club, identified himself as the owner of the Green Acres to cover for Frank Budak at that time. Joseph Budak, the older brother, was operating Club 22, located at 22 North Phelps Street in downtown Youngstown. Joseph's parole violation stemmed from an incident at the club where liquor was being served after hours. He had signed a parole agreement stating he would not "frequent places where liquor was sold, dispensed or used unlawfully." The *Vindicator* article announcing their arrests stated, "It was reported that the Youngstown underworld had made up a pool on the date the Budaks would return to prison as parole violators. The pool listed the days until Nov. 21, when the parole ended." The newspaper failed to announce who the winner was. By November 1, the brothers were back in Lewisburg to serve out their sentences. On January 6, 1950, they were released after earning six-month reprieves for being "model prisoners."

Chapter Four: Post-Bullet Hole Days

[22] Raymond Gentile had a "long record" according to police, but mostly for misdemeanors. He was an alleged associate of the notorious Alex "Shondor" Birns. In August 1958, he and two other men were in the process of trying to break into a safe at the Allen Baking Company in Warren, Ohio. Police were contacted and the men were soon trapped inside after 17 law enforcement officers surrounded the building. Sheriff's deputies discovered the men hiding under the hoods of bakery trucks.

[23] The Penn-Ohio burglary ring was the name given to a gang of professional safecrackers and robbers who operated in the Mahoning Valley and west-

ern Pennsylvania between April 1955 and June 1958. The burglaries and armed robberies were carried out by a combination of five men: Joseph Jasper "Fats" Aiello, Ronald D. Carabbia, Donald "Bull" Jones, Willie Napoli, and James Zimmerman. Assisting the gang in pulling off these burglaries was Richard Stanley, a rogue police officer from the Warren Police Department. In late 1957, Stanley was suspended and then dismissed from the police department for conduct unbecoming an officer. At this point, Stanley decided to pull off a few burglaries on his own, but was caught. He pleaded guilty to a burglary at the Warren Sanitary Milk Company in February 1959 and was sentenced to a 1-to-15-year term in the Ohio Penitentiary. Sometime between January and June 1959, Stanley gave up the members of the Penn-Ohio burglary ring. It would take the FBI to round up four of the five gang members. It would take even longer for the cases to be heard.

In May 1960, "Fats" Aiello was the first to be tried. Richard Stanley, who was serving his sentence in the Ohio Penitentiary's honor camp at Roseville, was brought back to testify. Aiello was found not guilty. James Zimmerman was tried two months later and found guilty, and received a 1-to-15-year sentence. This left Carabbia and "Bull" Jones to be tried; Napoli was still a fugitive. The case against Jones was moot, as Pennsylvania authorities were in the process of trying him for another burglary there and had a pretty airtight case against him, which also involved Joseph Drago and Phil "Fleegle" Mainer. In August 1960, Stanley was paroled from Roseville and returned home to Warren to await the next trial. In January 1961, the FBI finally caught up with Napoli, arresting him at a motel on Route 422, not far from the Ohio – Pennsylvania border.

On the night of March 23, 1961, a man crept up the outside back stair case of the duplex in which Richard Stanley, his wife, Doris, and young daughter, Darlene, were living on Charles Avenue in Warren. He tapped on the window of the backdoor. When Stanley lifted the door's window blind the man fired two .45 rounds at him. The first ripped through his face, between his nose and left eye, before exiting out the back of his head. The second bullet passed through his right shoulder. Stanley was rushed to Trumbull Memorial Hospital, a short distance away, and then taken to St. Elizabeth's Hospital in Youngstown. After two hours of surgery, he was listed as "very critical," but would survive. He was unable to identify the gunman. "Bull" Jones, Ronald Carabbia, and his cousin Dominic Senzarino were considered suspects in the shooting and were quickly picked up for questioning. The shooting of Richard Stanley would go unsolved.

In April 1961, the trial of Ronald Carabbia got underway. He was represented by Sam Petkovich and Edward L. Williams. Just 26 days after a .45 slug passed through his head, Stanley was in court to testify. When the trial was over Carabbia was found not guilty. On October 18, Willie Napoli died of a cerebral hemorrhage at the age of 43, without ever going to trial. James Zimmerman, the only Penn-Ohio burglary ring member to be convicted, finally began his sentence, after appeals were exhausted, in October 1962. – *Part of the upcoming Crimetown USA, Volume II.*

[24] Anthony Paul D'Alessio's name also appeared as Dalessio and Delessio in newspaper accounts.

[25] Today the picturesque Sovereign Hotel still exists, but is now a government-subsidized low-income housing facility for seniors known as University Towers Senior Apartments.

[26] Stan Kenton was a popular arranger, band leader, composer, and pianist whose success lasted from the 1940s into the 1970s. A New York Times article reported, "Mr. Kenton was the last major jazz-band leader to emerge from the Big Band era of 1935-45, and his was one of only a handful of bands that survived when that era came to an end." Kenton was able to survive the demise of the Big Band era artists by replacing his dance-band style with "progressive jazz." It was said that the characteristic of a Kenton band performance was the "screaming walls of brass." In 1977 Kenton fell and fractured his skull. He reportedly never fully recovered from this accident before suffering a major stroke on August 17, 1979. He died on August 25.

[27] The newspaper story about the marriage appeared in the *Cleveland Press* on December 2, 1952, at beginning of Julius Petro's robbery trial in Federal Court. The article never mentioned June Petro's maiden name, but her mother, Mrs. Lillian Guentzler testified during the trial. I was unable to locate any newspaper articles with the name June Guentzler, nor could I find any articles connecting band leader Stan Kenton with any Cleveland singers during the mid-1940s.

Chapter Five: "Very Strange!" Another Bullet Hole

[28] Sunny Acres was a long-term-care unit in the Cuyahoga County Hospital System, which opened in Warrensville Township in 1906. It was originally developed by Harris R. Cooley, Director of Charities for Cleveland, to care for patients with tuberculosis. In its first few years, it operated as a 60-bed tuberculosis hospital in a house on Richmond Road, and later became known as the Warrensville Sanatorium and expanded to 238 beds. By 1931, the facility expanded again to accommodate 430 beds. The city transferred ownership of the facility in 1942 to Cuyahoga County and the name became Sunny Acres Tuberculosis Hospital. With the development of streptomycin and other antibiotics from the mid-1940s and on, the number of tuberculosis cases declined dramatically by the late 1950s. In 1961, the Board of County Commissioners approved a program to turn the facility into an extended-care unit for the chronically ill. – *Case Western Reserve University – Encyclopedia of Cleveland History*

[29] Albert S. Wright's claim to notoriety culminated on May 3, 1950, when a Miami, Florida, judge sentenced him to five months in prison for harboring Detroit gangster Harry Fleischer in a Pompano Beach tourist camp cabin. Fleischer was a member of Detroit's infamous Purple Gang during the Prohibition Era. He was one of five men suspected of the armed robbery of the Aristocrat Club in Pontiac, Michigan, on December 2, 1944. The following month, Fleischer's participation was suspected in the brazen ambush assassination of Michigan State Senator Warren G. Hooper, on January 11, 1945, as he was driving home to Albion from a day at the state capital in Lansing. Fleischer was arrested and charged in both crimes. In July 1945, he received a five-year sentence for a murder conspiracy conviction in the Hooper case. On December 7, more than a year after the Aristocrat Club robbery, Fleischer and four others were convicted of that crime. When the men were sentenced, Fleischer received a term of 25-to-50-years in prison. The judge said he would not set bonds until a motion for a new trial was decided. Fleischer remained in prison until June 8, 1946, when a motion for a new trial was denied. Attorneys for the men immediately announced they would file an appeal, and bonds of $25,000 were set for Fleischer and two others. On October 5, 1948, the Michigan Supreme Court denied the appeal; a week later the court denied a stay of execution and the men were ordered to return to prison. On October 14, a bench warrant was issued for Fleischer and his $25,000 bond was forfeited after he failed to appear in court to turn himself in. The 46-year-old Fleischer was listed by the FBI as "one of the most badly wanted men in the country," when they began looking for him on November 1, 1948. A year later, on October 8, 1949, Fleischer was picked up in Cincinnati by two detectives investigating the theft of an automobile. He gave them a false name while being fingerprinted and police said they had no record in their files of a Harry Fleischer being wanted. He was released after police failed to connect him with the auto theft.

Cincinnati happened to be where Albert S. Wright, an Ohio parolee at the time, was living. Wright may have been followed to Florida by the FBI, or perhaps they just picked up his trail there. The bureau knew the two men had been acquainted for several years. In Florida, they kept surveillance on Wright, hoping he might lead them to the wanted man. He did. On the afternoon of January 18, 1950, agents tailed Wright after he left a Fort Lauderdale house carrying a black bag. He got into a car and drove north to Pompano Beach. Once there, Wright pulled alongside a pickup truck, stopped, and tossed the black bag into the truck before taking off. Agents followed the pickup truck to a quiet tourist camp and watched as Fleischer exited the vehicle and entered a cabin. A few minutes later, Fleischer, wearing only a pair of pants, left the cabin in the company of a woman. The couple got into the pickup truck and drove to the beach. They then got out and sprawled in the sand. Four agents, dressed like tourists, got close enough to confirm the man was Fleischer before moving in and making an arrest. The couple was placed in a car and driven to the FBI office in Miami, where they were fingered-printed and placed in a cell. Later that day, Wright, who had rented the cabin for Fleischer on January 12, was arrested and charged with harboring. Wright, sentenced to five months on May 3, was back in Cincinnati by the third week in July, where police immediately arrested him for vagrancy. Claiming he was associated with the Purple Gang, Cincinnati police said he was "so hot and high powered," they wanted to get him out of town. His arrest record showed but two arrests, neither in Detroit. As for Harry Fleischer, when he left Jackson Prison in October 1965, after serving 13 years behind bars, the prison announced that it was the first time in four decades there was no member of the Purple Gang behind bars there.

[30] John E. Dulapa first came to the attention of Michigan authorities after his arrest for the illegal trafficking of gasoline rationing coupons in December 1944. He was arrested with two other Detroit men in a Flint, Michigan, hotel room. When indicted by a Federal Grand Jury in May 1945, charged with Dulapa, who was listed as a used car salesman from Hamtramck, a suburb of Detroit, were two former Office of Price Administration (OPA) investigation agents and five others. Dulapa was found guilty and sentenced to two-and-a-half years in Federal prison and fined $15,000. By the time he was arrested with Julius Petro on May 1, 1951, the Detroit Free Press reported he had been arrested 13 times, mostly for robbery, and was questioned in the 1943 slaying of two Detroit mobsters near Mt. Clemens. Just weeks after his arrest with Petro, he was a suspect in the murder of Albert Swartz, a Detroit jeweler and fence, who was a witness against a theft ring operating out of Chicago. In December 1953, Dulapa's name came up during a corruption investigation in Hamtramck. A local police officer, Walter Bielak, was in fear for his life after revealing publicly that several high-ranking city officials were associating with known racketeers. One of those officials was Hamtramck Director of Public Safety, Martin Dulapa, the brother of John. Despite living another 43 years, that was the last time John Dulapa appeared to make the news. He died on July 8, 1996, in Garden City, Michigan.

Chapter Six: The Big Take-Down

[31] The Recreation Café at 12316 St. Clair Avenue sponsored many local sporting teams from the late 1930s into the 1960s, including baseball, basketball, and bowling. During the mid-1940s, when there was a man-power shortage due to World War II, the café posted numerous want ads for a "white" porter offering reasonable hours and a "good salary" at 65 cents an hour. On February 26, 1953, six months after Julius Petro's father's attempt to purchase the café, it was reported that a stench bomb was thrown into the place. The owners, William Bizil

and Edward Mihevic, claimed that labor trouble was not the reason. Instead, they blamed the bombing on an apparent "case of mistaken identity." On May 10, 1957, gunmen robbed the Recreation Café of more than $500 and slugged a patron, who didn't move fast enough. During the early 1960s, Mihevic kept a pickle jar next to the cash register in which he deposited half dollars he collected in change. When asked what it was for, Mihevic would say, "I'm saving them for something I've been promising myself for a long time," failing to go into any further detail. On December 26, 1961, burglars broke into the café and stole the jar, which reportedly contained $900 in half-dollar coins, along with four cases of whiskey. Today the location where the Recreation Café stood is an empty lot.

[32] It is interesting to note that when this fact first appeared in the newspapers the *Plain Dealer* wrote these bills were "not a part of the Warren loot." Since less than 25% of the bills were new and recorded, how could the newspaper know these bills were or were not a portion of the missing stolen balance?

[33] 14707 St. Clair Avenue, today is a vacant lot.

[34] 16136 St. Clair Avenue, today is a vacant lot. The Grotto Inn occupied this corner lot in 1952 when Joseph Sanzo spent some of the stolen money, he and Julius Petro obtained from their $71,000 armed robbery of a Warren banker, who was taking the money to his branch on August 14. In October 2013, the building burned to the ground after a fire which was believed to have been set on purpose.

[35] This was the reporting of the *Cleveland Press* on October 30, 1952. The *Plain Dealer* claimed Sanzo was arrested at his home by South Euclid police.

[36] John J. Kane, Jr., Frank E. Steel and Don C. Miller were all classmates at Notre Dame University and graduated from the law school there in 1925. Miller was already famous, as he was one of the vaunted Four Horsemen of Notre Dame football lore. Kane was born in Youngstown and served as assistant Mahoning County prosecutor from 1936 to 1941. He joined the U.S. Attorney's Office in 1943, working for Don Miller, who was named U.S. Attorney the year before. When Miller left the office, at the end of January 1952, Kane took over the position, serving in that capacity until March 12, 1954, some 14 months after the new Eisenhower administration took office. During that time, he oversaw the prosecution Lester E. Butzman, a wartime industrialist and obtained a tax fraud conviction against him in 1951. In late 1952, he and Steel tried Julius Petro and Joseph Sanzo for the $71,000 armed robbery of a Warren bank branch manager. After leaving the U.S. Attorney's Office, except for a few years, 1958 -1960, when he served as police prosecutor and assistant law director of Lakewood, Ohio,

Kane remained in private practice. John J. Kane, Jr. died on April 24, 1981, at the age of 81.

Born in Akron, Francis Earl Steel went home after graduation from Notre Dame law school and began his law practice. In 1928, he ran for state representative and lost. On September 11, 1933, Steel was appointed assistant county prosecutor by Summit County Prosecutor Ray B. Watters. The following November, after one year on the job, Steel ran for county prosecutor. Like the proverbial biblical verse about "no man is a prophet in his home town," Steel didn't seem to receive much respect from his fellow Akronites. Hence, this non-ringing political endorsement: "Frank E. Steel, [Herman] Werner's democratic opponent, is the most thoroughly anonymous of all the unknown attorneys constituting the present prosecutor's ineffectual staff. He has served two years without prosecuting one important case. With no record of his own, he'll have to stand on the one compiled by the whole office. And that is the worst in the recollection of living man, one so notoriously weak that the head of the office didn't even stand for re-nomination." Steel lost by more than 10,000 votes. In 1939, he was ready to try again, this time for Akron municipal judge. He lost by less than 4,000 votes to Republican candidate Thomas M. Powers.

Steel joined Kane and Miller in the Cleveland U.S. Attorney's Office in 1943. Steel excelled in narcotics and tax cases. On May 24, 1953, reporter Ted Princiotto of the *Plain Dealer* wrote an article about the assistant U.S. attorney titled: "Steel is Death to Tax Evaders." During his ten years in the office, some of his big name narcotics cases were against Angelo Amato and Sylvester "Studo" Papalardo, a former pal of Julius Petro. When Sumner Canary was appointed to replace John Kane, he announced he would not be available until mid-March. Kane and Steel were asked to stay and finish a few pending cases. The most important one was a tax evasion case against socially prominent Akron manufacturer and rubber broker, Poncet Davis, The trial would be the largest personal income tax evasion case ever tried in Cleveland history. Davis was charged with evading $738,000 in taxes from 1945 to 1949. The trial began January 19, 1954 and lasted ten days, resulting in Davis being found guilty and sentenced to five years in Federal prison by U.S. District Judge Charles J. McNamee. Before officially clearing out his desk, Steel helped prepare a number of tax evasion cases for presentation to the grand jury, among them Alex "Shondor" Birns, and Black numbers kingpin Joseph Allen. After Steel left the U.S. Attorney's Office, he joined the Cleveland law firm of Walter & Haverfield. In his new position he would be representing clients in income tax cases. Francis Earl Steel died on November 29, 1975, at the age of 74. He is buried in Holy Cross Cemetery in Akron, Ohio.

[37] "Starey," was a word used by Mrs. Abbie Alden as she described the look in Joseph Sanzo's eyes in the speeding getaway car during her testimony at the

trial of Sanzo and Julius Petro during December 1952. According to the on-line Merriam-Webster Dictionary, starey is defined as, "wild, glaring, and fixed."

[38] There were numerous discrepancies between the *Cleveland Press* and the *Plain Dealer* in the reporting. In this instance, the *Plain Dealer* identified the broker as Charles W. Schaefer, while the *Press* used the name Donald Schaefer.

[39] In this discrepancy, the *Press* referred to it as a "café-bowling alley" on St. Clair. While the Recreation Café supported several sports teams, including one for bowling, there was no indication a bowling alley was located at the St. Clair address.

[40] Another discrepancy, as the *Plain Dealer* had always maintained the money was handed to Schaefer by John Petro.

[41] The name Prijital also appeared in print as Prijitel.

[42] Euclid Beach Park was a popular Cleveland amusement park from 1894 until 1969. It started at East 156th Street and Nottingham Road and ran along the southern shore of Lake Erie. Incorporated on October 23, 1894, by a group of businessmen, it was modeled after New York City's Coney Island. In 1893, Dudley S. Humphrey II, the inventor of a popcorn maker, which seasoned the popcorn during the popping process, opened a number of popcorn stands throughout the city. From 1896 to 1899, he and his family ran a concession stand at Euclid Beach Park. During this time, the park was beginning to develop a bad reputation for its "honkytonk" type atmosphere and drunkenness. In 1901, Humphrey purchased the park and set some strict codes for behavior. Sales of beer and alcohol were abolished inside the park, and a dress code was established. In addition, new entertainment features were added, the beach and bathing facilities were expanded, and access to the park was made less expensive. The new policies drew families, and businesses were soon using the park for their company outings. In 1908, the Humphrey brothers built the Elysium, an indoor ice skating rink. The park soon hosted political gatherings, and in 1910 it was the site of "an important exhibition flight" by aviator Glen Curtis. The park remained a popular spot for nearly 60 years. By the 1960s, however, "changing lifestyles, lake pollution, rising operational costs, and racial incidents" combined to decrease attendance and receipts and eventually the demise of the park, which closed on September 28, 1969. – *The Encyclopedia of Cleveland History, second edition, compiled and edited by David D. Van Tassel and John J. Grabowski*

[43] Today this is the location of the W.O. Walker Center of the Cleveland Clinic.

[44] The Medical Record Card is the term I used for a critical defense exhibit that Dr. Spaeth used to show that Joseph Sanzo was in his office on the day of the robbery. It showed the date the patient was in the office and what was done that day. During testimony at four separate trials this piece of evidence was described in the newspapers by many names. I used the name Medical Record Card so as not to confuse the reader.

[45] In the *Plain Dealer* article reporting Grace Wilson's testimony, when it got to the part about the "third man," the newspaper added, "a man known to the FBI." This comment leads the reader to wonder if Detective Lieutenant Thomas P. White knew the name of the third participant why wasn't Wilson shown a mug shot of him; or at least question why the newspaper didn't address this.

[46] The Cleveland Crime Commission had its beginnings on January 5, 1921, when the Cleveland Foundation announced that it had hired Dr. Dean Roscoe Pound of the Harvard Law School to conduct a survey into the administration of justice in the city. The Encyclopedia of Cleveland History reports that the far-reaching survey "analyzed the work of the police, prosecutors, coroner's office, criminal courts, and correctional system; probed legal education; weighed the role of psychiatry in criminal justice; and assessed the adequacy of crime reporting in the local press." The survey was set up to review procedures within the Cleveland Police Department, investigate the judiciary system, which had developed a reputation for handing out short and suspended sentences, and investigate operating procedures in the jails.

While it produced only limited results in terms of reform, the survey did represent the first in depth study of the justice system in a major United States city. More importantly, it laid the groundwork for future studies such as the Commission on Law Observance & Enforcement, which became known as the Wickersham Committee, created in 1929 during President Herbert Hoover's first year in office. Another important result was the creation of the Cleveland Association for Criminal Justice. The association, made up of business and civic groups, served as a crime and justice watchdog in the city for the next thirty years.

Chapter Seven: The Strange Case of Dr. Spaeth

[47] Parker Kenneth Fulton was born on March 25, 1894, in Warnock, Ohio, a tiny unincorporated community located in Belmont County, on Ohio's eastern border, west of Wheeling, West Virginia. He attended public schools in Homestead, Pennsylvania, before heading to the University of Pittsburgh, graduating in 1915. Between 1915 and 1917, he attended the law schools of Ohio State University and Western Reserve University. He was admitted to the Ohio Bar in

1917. Fulton became a Cuyahoga County assistant prosecutor and in 1932 was assigned to investigate several Cleveland banking institutions and successfully prosecuted several bank officials.

In 1934, he was named a special assistant U.S. attorney and worked for U.S. District Judge Emerich B. Freed. A year later he resigned and went into private practice. As a defense attorney he represented several high profile clients, including corrupt Cleveland police lieutenant Ernest L. Molnar, and one-time Mayfield Road mob boss Alfred "Big Al" Polizzi, during his appearance before the Kefauver Committee in Cleveland during January 1951. In 1953, he represented Dr. Alexander V. Spaeth when he was indicted for perjury after his testimony at the December 1952 trial of Julius Petro and Joseph Sanzo for the robbery of a Warren bank vice president of $71,000. Before the trial began, Fulton was replaced by attorney William J. Corrigan, after he was appointed common pleas judge by Governor Frank J. Lausche to replace the late Adrian Newcomb, who passed away in April 1953.

Judge Parker K. Fulton served out Newcomb's term and ran unopposed for a new six-year term in 1954. On July 23, 1956, Fulton suffered a cerebral hemorrhage while attending a Cleveland Indians' game. He was taken to Lakewood Hospital in critical condition. Fulton remained ill over the next year. On July 28, 1957, he suffered a stroke from which he did not regain consciousness. He died on August 14 in Lakewood Hospital at the age of 63. He was buried in Holy Cross Cemetery in Brook Park.

[48] For nearly four decades, William J. Corrigan was Cleveland's most recognized defense attorney. Called an "actor" or "dramatist," the courtroom was his stage. Once when compared to Clarence Darrow, Corrigan replied, "He was a great lawyer. Why, I'm just a small-time attorney."

Corrigan was born in Cleveland on June 21, 1886. His mother was a native of Canada, her father a newspaper publisher in Manitoba. Corrigan went to school at Holy Name and later earned his bachelor's degree in 1911 from St. Ignatius College (John Carroll University). He attended law school at Baldwin-Wallace, where he helped support himself as a police reporter for the *Cleveland News*. Corrigan received his law degree in 1915 and passed the Ohio bar the same year.

In 1917, Corrigan became an assistant county prosecutor working under Samuel Doerfler. He soon found himself handling most of the major cases in the county, the "Jiggs" Losteiner trial the most prominent. In 1920, he was named chief assistant prosecutor, but resigned later that year to begin a private practice. For the next 25 years Corrigan held the title of "organized labor's attorney" as he began a long association with unions of the American Federation of Labor.

Corrigan was best known for his work in several spectacular murder trials, beginning with Sam Purpura for the murder trial of Wilfred C. Sly in May

1921. This was quickly followed by the murder trial of Eva Kaber. The evidence, testimony and witnesses left no doubt that Eva was guilty of having her husband, Dan Kaber, killed and Corrigan's sole effort was to save her from the electric chair, which he accomplished. Over the years Corrigan's cases included:

- Joseph Gogan, a wealthy industrialist accused of murdering his wife with rat poison
- Associates of notorious racketeer Alex "Shondor" Birns, who were accused of blackmail
- Labor extortionists Don Campbell and John McGee
- Police Chief George J. Matowitz during an attempt to oust him as Cleveland police chief
- Cleveland Syndicate members Morris Kleinman and Louis Rothkopf during their infamous "refusing to refuse" episode before the Kefauver Committee during hearings held in Washington D.C. in 1951

Corrigan's most famous client – bar none – was Dr. Sam Sheppard, who was accused of brutally murdering his wife Marilyn in Cleveland's most celebrated murder, surpassing the sensational case of William Potter in 1931. Sheppard was tried after a media blitz led by *Cleveland Press* editor Louis Seltzer in 1954. Convicted after a ten-week trial, Sheppard was sentenced to life in prison in the Ohio Penitentiary. Corrigan spent the remainder of his life working on appeals.

Corrigan married Marjorie Wilson on August 21, 1922. It depends on whose telling of the story you believe as to how the two met. Wilson was a reporter for the *Cleveland News* and covered several murder trials. One story has Corrigan meeting Wilson during his prosecution of "Jiggs" Losteiner. Another claims he met her while defending Eva Kaber. Whatever the case, the couple was married for nearly 40 years. In his mid-70s, Corrigan was still working. His son, William Howard Corrigan, had joined the practice, which was conducted out of the Williamson Building, located in Public Square – site of the present day Huntington Bank Building. It was here that the elder Corrigan became ill on July 27, 1961. Taken to St. Alexis Hospital by police, the 75 year-old Corrigan died the next morning. He was buried in Calvary Cemetery.

[49]James J. Carroll was born on December 6, 1916, in Sandusky, Ohio. He attended local schools and graduated from Sandusky High School. Carroll entered John Carroll University and later attended Harvard Law School. He received his law degree from Western Reserve University. After serving in the Army during World War II, Carroll began a busy career in Cleveland as a prosecutor, attorney, and judge. He first appeared the newspapers in 1953 after Sumner Canary was named U.S. Attorney here by President Dwight D. Eisenhower, replacing John J.

Kane, Jr., the Democratic U.S. Attorney. Canary named the 37-year-old Carroll as one of his assistants. In Carroll's first trial he won a conviction of counterfeiter James Epps. Over the next year he handled several more counterfeiting cases. In December 1954, he represented the government during the appeal of Dr. Alexander V. Spaeth's first of three convictions in his perjury trial (see Chapter 7). In 1955, he prosecuted members of the Teller / Ritenour ring, which was brought down by Lieutenant Thomas P. White. In 1958, Carroll stepped down as assistant U.S. attorney. While working for the law firm of Carney & Carney in the Leader Building, he ran for a four-year term as state senator in Ohio and was the top Republican vote getter. In the November election, although Carroll again was the top Republican vote earner, he received 150,000 less than the third-place Democratic candidate and only the top three vote getters achieved office.

During the late 1950s and early 1960s, Carroll was a defense attorney and represented several high-profile clients. In 1960, he handled the deportation case of Mike Giamo. During 1960-61, he defended Robert "Bobby" Walsh in his counterfeit case. In November 1961, he was defense counsel for kidnapper George E. Bentley. In June 1963, he represented Cleveland bail bondsman Dominic C. Lonardo, who was charged with impersonating an FBI agent in an attempt to track down bail-jumper Joseph J. Arrington, a former burglary partner of Vincent Innocenzi. The next month he represented attorney Vincent P. Serman and future Youngstown Mafia boss Lenine "Lenny" Strollo in another counterfeiting case. In 1965, he represented Morris R. Blane, a Cleveland lawyer with a bankruptcy practice, of fraud in the bankruptcy of Sterling Jewelry & Appliance Company, Inc. In August 1965, his clients were the three brothers of murdered Youngstown Mafia figure James Vincent "Vince" DeNiro, in a tax evasion case involving $111,000. In 1969, Carroll helped defend 19-year-old Alfred Thomas, one of four co-defendants of Fred "Ahmed" Evans, who was convicted of killing four people in the 1968 Glenville shootout.

In the spring of 1976, James Carroll ran on the Republican ticket for a common pleas court seat. Despite the many endorsements he received against incumbent opponent Judge Michael A. Sweeney, Carroll lost in another landslide. But luck was on his side as within weeks another seat became vacant. In January 1977, he was named to the seat. In December 1977, with just 11 months on the job, Carroll was assigned what would be the biggest case of his career – the Danny Greene murder trial. The trial began on February 21, 1978, and lasted until May 25, when Ronald D. Carabbia and Pasquale "Butchie" Cisternino were found guilty of the bombing murder of the flamboyant Irish hoodlum. In November 1980, Carroll was re-elected to a full six-year term. Near the end of that term, in January 1987, Carroll announced he would not seek another term. As a retired judge, he accepted cases on assignment for several years before retiring for good. James J. Carroll died on August 24, 2000, at the age of 83. He was buried in Oakland Cemetery in Sandusky, Ohio.

[50] Doctors' Hospital opened on August 6, 1946, in Cleveland Heights at the top of Cedar Hill at Euclid Heights Boulevard. To relieve the hospital-bed shortage in Cleveland in 1935, 157 physicians of the Academy of Medicine of Cleveland began a fundraising drive to build a suburban hospital. Abandoning the idea of a new structure, the Cleveland Memorial Medical Foundation purchased the Edgehill Apartment building located at 12337-49 Cedar Road., at Euclid Heights Boulevard, and converted it into a general medical and surgical hospital. By 1955, it was an accredited, modern 200-bed hospital. Doctors' Hospital was governed by a lay Board of Trustees. With a special interest in cancer research, Doctors' Hospital received research support from the Rand Corp. In 1968, the hospital was purchased by the city of Cleveland Heights for use of the land as a parking lot and fire station. In 1968 the staff and services of Doctors' Hospital moved to Mayfield Hts. (6760 Mayfield Rd.) and became known as Hillcrest Hospital (later Meridia Hillcrest Hospital). – *The Encyclopedia of Cleveland History – online – compiled and edited by David D. Van Tassel and John J. Grabowski*

Chapter Eight: The Last Years of Julius Petro

[51] Christine Koren was born in Cleveland on August 8, 1947, to Christine and Albin Koren. She grew up in the St. Clair Avenue area on the city's East Side. Around the age of 20 she moved to Los Angeles to pursue a career. While there, she met Julius Petro. About a year after his death, Koren was named Playboy Magazine's Playmate for the Month for March 1970. On February 3, 1970, a truck carrying 250,000 of Koren's centerfold photographs collided with an automobile on the Kennedy Expressway on Chicago's Northside while transporting the photos from the lithographic plant to the printing facility. The truck flipped over spilling the photographs out onto the street. Winds of 20 mph spread the photos all over the neighborhood. Nearly every newspaper in the country picked up the story. One newspaper, the Des Moines (Iowa) Register printed a portion of the centerfold showing Koren's beautiful face. In the caption they printed: "In her entirety, Miss Koren rests on a thick orange rug and hugs a pillow while wearing nothing more than a big smile." Shortly after the edition hit newsstands, Koren returned to Cleveland for what the newspapers reported was a tonsillectomy. Her picture appeared in the *Plain Dealer* as she was being "feted" at the famous Hofbrau Haus restaurant on East 55th Street. While here, the newspaper announced, she would be "guesting on Henri Bronze's polka program" via WXEN FM.

[52] Nicholas Valenti and Nicholas J. Tirabassi are characterized as "former Cleveland hoods" in this FBI report. I was unable to find any information that either man had a criminal record in Cleveland, but the reason Tirabassi may have been

hanging out with brothers Julius and Mike Petro was because he was married to their sister, Monda.

[53] Albert "Tubby" Figer was born Albert Viccara on June 15, 1927, in Rillton, Pennsylvania, an unincorporated community of less than 600 in Westmoreland County, located southeast of Pittsburgh. Three years later, at the time of the 1940 Census, the Viccara family moved to Cleveland and changed their last name to Figer. It was this name that Albert used on his World War II draft card when he registered in July 1945. As a young boy Albert, or Al, picked up the nickname "Tubby," which he would be known by his entire life.

While growing up, Figer became friends with a lot of the rising burglary stars in the Collinwood area, including Julius Petro, Frank Velotta, the Sanzo brothers – Joseph and Peter – and years later with Ray Ferritto. He was also a friend of Alan Walch, having connections with him in both Cleveland and Los Angeles. In May 1963, Figer and James "Hoola" Colavecchio were involved in the burglary of a discount store at Southland Shopping Center on Pearl Road in Middleburg Heights. The men were arrested and went to trial in March 1965. Found guilty, they were both sentenced to 4-to-47 years in prison. On October 6, 1965, the convictions were overturned, and a new trial ordered because the trial judge told the jury they could take into account the fact the two men refused to testify. The new trial began a year later on October 24, 1966, before Common Pleas Judge Hugh A. Corrigan. After a week-long trial, both men were again found guilty and sentenced to 2-to-20-years in the Ohio Penitentiary. In March 1976, Figer was linked to Peter Sanzo after he threatened attorney Harvey Rieger, who was supposed to obtain money for Sanzo from the much maligned Northern Ohio Bank. The FBI had a tape recording of Sanzo and Figer discussing what Sanzo was going to do with Rieger.

Figer was married twice and had two sons from the first marriage. In September 1974, Figer's 18-year-old son, Albert, Jr., was arrested and charged with felonious assault for the stabbing of Vincent Brookins, a Black student at Collinwood High School, following a Friday night football game. At trial, in January 1975, an all-white common pleas jury, after a four-day trial, deliberated for two days before finding Figer not guilty of the stabbing. Figer married his second wife in 1979, and shortly afterwards moved to Youngstown. He died in St. Elizabeth's Hospital after suffering a heart attack on November 12, 1983, at the age of 56. The name on his gravestone in Youngtown's Lake Park Cemetery is Albert "Tubby" Viccara.

[54] Vito Genovese was a New York City mob boss who may have met Julius Petro in one of two federal facilities, Atlanta or Springfield, Missouri. Anthony Giordano was a rising figure in the St. Louis mob when he was convicted of tax evasion in the mid-1950s. The only place Petro could have met him was in Leavenworth.

Petro had few qualities that people higher up in the Mafia would have been attracted to, unless somebody they had complete confidence in was making the introduction, which ended up being the case with Nick Licata.

[55] Alfred G. "Fred" Sica was born in New Jersey on September 11, 1915, and had his first sentence for robbery in 1934 at the age of 18. He racked up 12 arrests between 1933 and 1939, including armed robbery, assault and battery, breaking and entering, larceny, receiving stolen property, and robbery. Once he moved West, in 1942, things didn't change much. He tacked on six more arrests, including bookmaking, narcotics, and robbery. Once Mickey Cohen arrived in Los Angeles, he claimed the Sica brothers, Joe and Fred, were like lifelong partners to him. In the late 1940s, Joe and Fred Sica were suspected of "heading up a syndicate which provided the major source of heroin in California." In mid-January, sixteen people were indicted, including the Sica brothers and Abe Davidian. Back in July 1949, Davidian was being chased by state highway patrolmen during the early morning hours for a traffic violation, when he tossed a package of heroin, he had received earlier from Joe Sica, out the window. His arrest triggered the investigation leading to the indictment. By late January, it was rumored that Davidian was talking to state investigators. On February 28, a gunman put a bullet through Abe Davidian's head as he slept at his mother's home in Fresno and the state's case fell apart. Fred Sica was a suspect in the murder. On December 11, 1950, Samuel F. Rummel, attorney for Cohen, was found murdered at the door of his Hollywood hillside mansion. A gunman, hiding behind trees waiting in ambush for him to arrive home, shot him in the neck with a shotgun, killing him instantly. Fred Sica was again a suspect in this slaying. Fred became a constant figure with Cohen, traveling with him and serving as his bodyguard, dog walker and even chef. In March 1961, Fred Sica was charged in two Federal indictments with income tax evasion and making false statements about his business dealings with Cohen. In November 1961, Sica and his step-brother were arrested for gambling during a raid at a Hollywood apartment. In January 1962, Sica was indicted by another Federal Grand Jury for evading taxes on a $100,000 football betting pool. In March 1962, he went on trial on the two indictments from the previous year. He was acquitted of tax evasion, but found guilty of making a false statement about his dealings with Cohen. He was sentenced to three years in Federal prison. In April, he was acquitted of the tax evasion charges on the football betting. In February 1969, a month after the murder of Julius Petro, Sica was called before a Federal grand jury investigating the alleged doping of race horses in interstate gambling. When Mickey Cohen died on July 29, 1976, he left 15% of his estate to Fred Sica for his loyalty over the years. In 1978, the *Los Angeles Times* published a list of 92 "Reputed Mob Figures," in the state. On the list were Raymond Ferritto, Jimmy Fratianno, Fred Sica and Frank J. "Skinny" Velotta. On December 10, 1987, Fred Sica passed away at the age of 72. He was buried in Forest Lawn Memorial Park in Los Angeles.

[56] Harold "Happy" Meltzer was best known as a top lieutenant of West Coast mobster Mickey Cohen. Meltzer was born in New Jersey in 1908, and ran up a string of arrests there between 1926 and 1933, once spending two years in the Federal Penitentiary in Atlanta for a narcotics conviction in 1928. In June 1933, he was arrested on suspicion of homicide in New York City, but released. Meltzer moved West in 1945, where he connected with Cohen. Over the next four years he chalked up arrests for assault with a deadly weapon, assault with intent to kill, auto theft, bookmaking, burglary, gambling, robbery and suspicion of murder. In 1951, he had his second narcotics conviction and this time received five years in Leavenworth.

[57] State Correctional Institution – Rockview, commonly referred to as SCI Rockview is located in Benner Township, Pennsylvania, north of State College in the central part of the state. The Pennsylvania Department of Corrections prison was opened in 1915. The new facility was selected to carry out the state's executions by electrocution when the gallows were abandoned by the state. Between 1915 and 1962 the state executed 350 people in the electric chair, including the state's first woman in February 1931. In 1978, the movie *On The Yard*, starring John Heard, was filmed entirely at the prison with inmates serving as extras in the film.

[58] Again, either the author, Susan DeSantis Ferritto, or most likely, Ray Ferritto is off on the dates. Regarding Alfred "Allie" Calabrese, if she was referring to the father, he would have been serving a life sentence at this time. If she was referring to the son, he would have only been 16 or 17 years old in 1960. Robert "Bobby" Walsh was convicted of counterfeiting in July 1960 and given a sentence of three years in Federal prison. Toward the mid-1960s he would return and join a burglary crew with Frank Velotta, in which Calabrese was involved.

[59] The Ambassador Hotel, located on Wilshire Boulevard in Los Angeles, opened on January 1, 1921. For six decades the beautiful hotel "enchanted" guests with its "Mediterranean styling, tile floors, Italian stone fireplaces and semi-tropical courtyard." It was later home to the Cocoanut Grove night club, which brought many of the country's biggest names in entertainment to perform. The hotel played host to six Academy Awards ceremonies. Over the decades dozens of movies and television shows filmed scenes at the hotel including the Oscar winning film Forrest Gump. The hotel's guest list included every U.S. President from Herbert Hoover to Richard Nixon. Unfortunately, one incident at the Ambassador Hotel would provide its most notorious chapter. On June 5, 1968, presidential candidate Robert F. "Bobby" Kennedy celebrated his win in the California Democratic primary. Moments after his victory speech, he was fatally shot in the hotel's kitchen area by assassin Sirhan B. Sirhan. In the late 1980s the

hotel and the surrounding neighborhood was in decline. The hotel was closed to guests in 1989. Despite a legal struggle to preserve it, the Ambassador Hotel was demolished in 2005.

[60] Actor Steve Cochran was born Robert Alexander Cochran in 1917. He had his share of gangster roles in movies and on television. In addition to White Heat (1949), with Jimmy Cagney, he played the lead role in *I Mobster* (1959), which chronicled the rise and fall of a fictional gang boss named Joe Sante. He was also in a couple episodes of *The Untouchables* television series, as well as *Naked City* and *Burke's Law*. He appeared in nearly 40 films including *The Best Years of Our Lives* (1946), *Copacabana* (1947), *A Song is Born* (1948), *Storm Warning* (1951), *Jim Thorpe – All-American* (1951), and *The Desert Song* (1953). Known as a notorious womanizer, Cochran was said to have, "attracted tabloid attention for his tumultuous life." In 1952, Cochran threw a New Years' Eve party at his hill-top Hollywood home at 3401 Coldwater Canyon Lane. A former professional boxer, Lenwood "Buddy" Wright, an uninvited guest, showed up and was asked to leave by the actor. He refused. Cochran later testified, "I knew Buddy Wright was an ex-fighter, so I hit him with a baseball bat in self-defense." Wright sued Cochran for $400,000, but settled for $7,000. He formed his own production company in 1953, but was not very successful. In January 1965, still hoping to produce a money-making picture, Cochran left Los Angeles on his 40-foot schooner to scout locations for his latest project, *Captain O'Flynn*. The script was about "a salty old sea captain" who employed women crew members on his boat. He had taken several local girls sailing on "nautical tryouts" for roles in the picture, but found them to be too expensive. So, he decided to hire several Latino girls for the parts and try them out. On June 3, Cochran and three young women, ages 14, 19 and 25, left Acapulco, where he was living, and headed to Costa Rico on his boat, hoping to arrive there in eight days. They ran into a storm, which damaged the forward mast and slowed them down. On June 14, Cochran began complaining of severe headaches and had several fainting spells. At one point, according to the women, he became "paralyzed." The next day Cochran died. The three young women were left helpless at sea in a boat they could not sail for 12 days. On June 27, the Guatemalan Coast Guard found them and towed them to port in Champerico. Authorities there found the 48-year-old actor's body too decomposed to identify. A passport was found bearing the name Robert Alexander Cochran. An autopsy determined he died from an acute lung infection. Although rumors later arose regarding foul play in his death, no evidence was ever found to support them.

[61] "Shirt-tail relative," according to the website *World Wide Words* states, "It's usually said to refer to somebody who is a relative by marriage or is only distantly related, such as a fourth cousin, or is a family friend with honorary status

as a relative. It's fairly common in the USA and has been since the 1950s or thereabouts."

Chapter Nine: The Petro Murder Investigation

[62] On November 3, 1990, while battling cancer, Pasquale "Butchie" Cisternino died of respiratory arrest in Frazier Hospital, at the Orient Correctional Facility in Ohio. He was 56 years old. Ronald D. Carabbia, after spending 24 years in prison, was released to his wife and son on September 23, 2002, from Chillicothe Correctional Institution, in Ohio. Carabbia died on December 22, 2021, at the age of 92.

[63] Gilbert Salvador Iberri Garcetti was born on August 5, 1941, in Los Angeles. He attended local schools before enrolling in the University of Southern California. Later he received a Juris Doctorate degree from UCLA. After graduation, he joined the Los Angeles District Attorney's office where he served the next 20 years in various capacities, including trial prosecutor, deputy district attorney, and chief deputy district attorney. In 1992, Garcetti was elected Los Angeles District Attorney on the heels of the Los Angeles riots in the aftermath of the Rodney King verdict, which acquitted four police officers of the brutal beating of King. During his first term, he handled the O.J. Simpson murder trial. Garcetti won re-election in 1996, but lost overwhelmingly in 2000. That was the end of Garcetti's 32 years in the district attorney's office, and his political life. In 2013, Garcetti's son Eric was elected mayor of Los Angeles and, as of this writing, still holds the office.

[64] According to Gilbert Garcetti's 36-page investigative report, "Prior to taking their positions in the rear yard, the officers had been thoroughly briefed by their superiors concerning the danger and importance of the assignment and the probability than an attempt would be made by organized-crime figures to kill Mrs. Wolkin. The officers were told the number of guards were increased from two to three that day. The officers had been supplied with shotguns, bullet protection vests and mobile radio units for summoning help."

Chapter Ten: The Friends of Julius Petro

[65] Anthony DelGuyd was a half-brother to Joseph M. Petrangelo (See End Note #115).

[66] A frontispiece is an illustration preceding and usually facing the title page of a book or magazine.

[67] The *Police Mug Book* article appeared in the *Plain Dealer* on September 6, 1954. The book was not really a book at all, but more or less a collection of mug shot copies with additional information added, and then stapled together. The article contained some other interesting facts. The "book" was the creation of Detective Chief James E. McArthur with the help of his chief aide Detective Lieutenant Thomas P. White. It was pointed out that White was known as an "informed biographer" of the Cleveland underworld. The *Police Mug Book*, of which 1,000 copies were said to have been made of the first edition, achieved status as a police reference guide and excerpts were soon included in the civil service examination for police promotions. Despite the success and heavy reliance of the police department on the book, it should be noted that the city provided no appropriation for its publishing. It was paid for out of the pocket of McArthur. The detective chief sold copies to suburban police officials for 25 cents apiece to help offset his costs.

[68] Michael D. Roberts, a celebrated Cleveland reporter, author, and editor, began his work with the *Plain Dealer* in 1963. On November 13, his first by-line appeared covering a story about 13-year Cleveland Police veteran Patrolman Joseph Dober, who Roberts described as a veritable maestro on a crosswalk podium as he directed rush hour traffic at the corner of Euclid Avenue in Public Square. His next by-line took on a more somber tone. On November 23, the day after the assassination of President John F. Kennedy, he interviewed Clevelanders on their thoughts about the tragic events of the day before. An award-winning reporter, his work took him to Vietnam and the Middle East. He served at the newspaper's Washington D.C. bureau. In 1972, he joined Cleveland Magazine, where he wrote in depth articles about organized crime in Cleveland and served 17 years as the magazine's editor. He is the author of two books: *Thirteen Seconds: Confrontation at Kent State* (1970) with noted Cleveland-raised author and screenplay writer Joe Eszterhas; and *Hot Type, Cold Beer & Bad News: A Cleveland Reporter's Journey Through the 1960s* (2018).

[69] Today the Park Lane Lounge is the pink-colored Club Temptations, an adult entertainment lounge.

[70] 896 East 152nd Street today is a Federally owned parking lot used by the U.S. Post Office – Collinwood branch.

[71] Today this is the Fifth District Police Station.

[72] After another bombing on July 10, 1969, the *Plain Dealer* reported that it was the seventh bombing in the Collinwood neighborhood in the past 40 days. These bombings included, in addition to D'Alessio's van, June 8, a home at 276 East

171st Street; June 24, Pointview Grill, at 15242 St. Clair Avenue; June 26, Conte Bookkeeping Service, 16019 St. Clair Avenue, and Nunn-Bush Shoe Store, 15203 St. Clair Avenue; and July 10, National City Bank branch 979 East 152nd Street.

[73] The Roman Lounge at 29012 Euclid Avenue, as of 2019 is operating as a bar and restaurant named, ironically, Mugg Shotz.

[74] The name Ralph "Bull" De Biase appeared in the newspapers with many spellings. It appeared as Di Biase, DeBiase and DiBiase.

[75] In early 1953, a flurry of police graft accusations were reported in the newspapers resulting in Chief Frank W. Story requesting a grand jury investigation. The *Plain Dealer* reported on February 7, 1953, that, "It was the first time any police chief ever asked a grand jury to probe cheating charges against his own department." The initial accusation came from former vice-squad patrolman, Donald B. Catalano, who admitted he had "whitewashed" reports involving gambling operations taking place in a building at 1010 Euclid Avenue. By February 20, the probe had ballooned to include a gambling club at 9205 Kinsman Avenue (today a filling station), and an accusation of prostitution and gambling at the Goodyear Hotel at 1347 Payne Avenue (now a parking lot). After hearing testimony on February 20, it was reported that grand jury foreman, William J. Kennedy would not convene his panel again until March 9. After meeting with Assistant County Prosecutor John J. Mahon on that date, neither indicated that the inquiry into vice joints and police graft would continue. On April 25, the books were closed on the January term of the grand jury. The final report claimed that the "crooked civilian" will not usually squeal on the "crooked policeman," making it extremely difficult to root out corruption in the police department. It went on to state, "You can't have an organization as large and as old as the Cleveland police force without having a few termites in the basement and a few rats in the attic."

[76] 2408 East 25th Street today is part of the on-ramp to I-90 West across from Cleveland State University on Chester Avenue.

[77] Heinz (Henry) Bernard Ollendorff was a German Jew born in the city of Esslingen Am Neckar, located southeast of Stuttgart, in 1907. In 1929, he received a doctorate of law from the University of Heidelberg. In 1937, he was imprisoned by the Nazis and placed in solitary confinement for over a year. He and his wife were able to flee the country and get to the United States, settling in New York City. In 1940, he graduated from the New York School of Social Work at Columbia University. He moved to Cleveland and began work at the Friendly Inn Social Settlement. In 1948, he was appointed executive director of the Neighborhood

Settlement Association, which he headed until 1963. He died on February 10, 1979.

78 Benedetto "Benny" Contorno, Jr. was sent to the Ohio Penitentiary and was not heard from again until late November 1958. During a crackdown on late-night loiterers at downtown night spots, Contorno was nabbed with fellow Ohio Penitentiary parolee Philip Aliberti. Nine months later, Contorno was a member of a five-man robbery crew that hit the Glenn Fisher Jewelry store at 2380 Manchester Road in Akron on the night of August 1 (the store was still in business as of 2020). The men, four of whom were from Cleveland, entered the store, which operated out of a private home, on a Saturday night. The robbers arrived before 10:30 and went into the basement showroom, where they tied up four people and cleaned out the showcases, loading $20,000 in rings and other jewelry, along with $1,000 in cash, into three suitcases. They then went upstairs to a private residence and bound the husband and wife, who lived there.

At some point during the robbery, the men were spotted by a neighbor who summoned police. About a dozen or more of Akron's finest soon rushed to the scene and swarmed the house. One of Contorno's accomplices, George Stryanka (See End Note #120) was shot as he attempted to escape by leaping out a window with gun in hand. He was wounded in the right side and taken to Akron General Hospital, where he quickly recovered.

The men were held in the Summit County Jail on $2,500 bonds. Contorno and Stryanka, with their records, were facing serious charges. In addition to armed robbery, which carried a 10-to-25-year sentence, each was charged with breaking and entering an inhabited dwelling at night because the jewelry store was connected to a living quarters. That charge carried with it a life sentence. With the trial set for November 5, Contorno and Stryanka surprised police and Summit County Prosecutor John S. Ballard by bonding out of jail on October 20 and 24, respectively. The men used a Cleveland bail / bond firm after being unable to get an Akron bondsman to work with them. On November 4, the night before the trial was to begin, 30 county jail inmates began a hunger strike, giving no reason for their refusal to eat. Prosecutor Ballard believed it may have had something to do with the release of Contorno and Stryanka. The next day all five men pleaded guilty. The three incarcerated men were immediately sentenced by Common Pleas Judge John M. Kelly to 10-to-25-years in the Ohio Penitentiary. For some unexplained reason, the judge allowed Contorno and Stryanka to remain free until November 9, before receiving their sentences. Chief Deputy George Vaughn believed now that the hunger strike was to be a distraction and posted extra guards at the jail fearing Contorno and Stryanka might try to "spring" their robbery mates.

On the morning of November 9, Judge Kelly sentenced Contorno and Stryanka to 10-to-25-years in prison. Stryanka asked the judge for a few more days of freedom in order to complete the transfer of property to his wife. The judge denied the request. Now it was Contorno's turn to make a request. It was a novel one. He pleaded with the judge to send him to Lima State Hospital for "mental examination." Contorno told the judge he needed to find out "why I came down here from Cleveland for this thing when I had money, a good job and was about to be married." His request was also denied. Sometime after his release from prison Contorno made his way to Las Vegas. He died there on June 23, 1997, and was buried in Palm Memorial Park.

[79] Homerville is a small unincorporated community in Homer Township located in the southwest corner of Medina County.

[80] Anthony "Joe Blow" Velletto's name also appeared in newspapers as Valetto, Vellotta and Vellotto.

[81] Nathan Augustino was far from being a Cleveland "gangland figure." On August 27, 1938, Augustino was one of four hooded robbers who participated in the robbery of $1,853 from the General Motors Acceptance Corporation, located on the 11th floor of the B.F. Keith Building at 1621 Euclid Avenue. Police stopped Augustino on suspicion but let him go. Twenty minutes later they stopped him again while trying to retrieve a gun, silk hood, gloves and a sweater discarded near the scene of the robbery. In the courtroom of Common Pleas Judge Frank J. Lausche, Augustino cried on the witness stand as he accused Detectives Herbert Wachsman and Ted Carlson of threatening to "blow my brains out." After being found guilty, Augustino hurled threats at the jurors while in the corridor waiting for the elevator to the County Jail. Lausche sentenced him to 10-to-25-years in the Ohio Penitentiary. The next time Augustino was heard from was over 16 years later when a gunman slightly wounded him. Nathan Augustino passed away in June 1974.

[82] 4310 Chester Avenue today is a parking lot.

[83] White Front Provision Company was a chain of meat markets that began doing business in Cleveland in 1896. They specialized in fresh and smoked meats, poultry, and eggs. By 1931, there were 13 stores in the city. The most famous, or infamous one, stood at 3657 Central Avenue. The last time White Front Provision Company was mentioned in the newspapers was on March 4, 1973. That morning, an armed robber locked the owners, Mr. and Mrs. Ray Berg, and an employee, in a meat cooler. Mrs. Berg was able to trip a silent alarm before being locked up. As the robber was emptying the safe and a cash register, Patrolmen Harold V. Conn, Jr. and David L. Kruger were responding to the 11:45 alarm. Conn entered the store armed with a shotgun, but did not see anyone.

A moment later, the robber opened fire from behind the meat counter. Conn was wounded in the head and thigh, but managed to get off a couple of blasts as he backed out the front door. The robber raced off through backyards and got away. Conn was treated at St. Vincent Charity Hospital and released, but not before concluding, "If I had been a little taller, I'd probably be dead."

[84] Today 7107 Central Avenue is a vacant lot.

[85] Despite attempts to uncover all the criminal activities that Vincent Innocenzi was involved with during his career, at the time of his death, the *Akron Beacon Journal* reported, "Other notations on his record include burglaries in Chicago and Columbus...and suspicion and investigations charges in Cleveland Heights, Jefferson County, Shaker Heights and a host of other charges in Cleveland." No more details were provided, or uncovered by this writer.

[86] On Saturday, December 18, 1937, the Cleveland Police Department had one of its darkest nights. Patrolmen Virgil T. Bayne and Gerald N. Bode were murdered while attempting to prevent a robbery at a Buckeye Road filling station at 11:15 p.m. It was the first time in the history of the department that two officers were killed on the same day. Less than five hours after the murders, all five suspects were in custody: Carl J. Ferrito, 20; Anthony M. Gallina, 18; Anthony D. Libertore, 16; Albert A. Lippe, 25: and Neal Palatrone, 18. After an 85-mile-per-hour chase, Ferrito and Lippe were captured by Detectives Richard W. Daly and William Austin. The officers recovered four revolvers from the automobile. Libertore and Palatrone were each arrested at their homes; while Gallina was arrested at the home of his married sister.

It was decided the five young men would be tried in separate trials. On February 28, 1938, Ferrito was the first to face trial. He was found guilty of first-degree murder on March 4 and sentenced to death. He died in the electric chair, the only gang member to meet that fate, on November 3. Next came Anthony D. Libertore. He was just 16 years-old, married and the father of a 21-month-old son. He was found guilty of first-degree murder on March 11, but granted mercy by the jury due to his age. He was followed by Albert Lippe, the oldest member of the gang, on March 18. He too was found guilty of first-degree murder and sentenced to death. On January 9, 1939, Governor Martin L. Davey commuted Lippe's death sentence to life in prison. He was paroled from prison in 1965. Anthony M. Gallina's trial was next and, like the others before him, he was found guilty of first-degree murder on March 29, but received a recommendation of mercy by the jury, perhaps because of his age. On May 22, 1958, he was paroled from the Ohio Penitentiary. Neal Palatrone was the last member of the gang to be tried. His trial began on March 29. In this last trial the jury deadlocked at 8 to 4 in favor of acquittal and a mistrial was called. Palatrone testified the others were giving him a ride home from a beer parlor the night when the killings occurred and that he ran away afterwards. On May 20, he pleaded guilty to manslaughter. He was sentenced to the Ohio State Reformatory for an indeterminate sentence of 1-to-20-years. He was granted parole on October 13, 1942.

Anthony Libertore was paroled in 1958, after serving 20 years in prison. He was arrested following the murder of Vincent Innocenzi in August 1960. In May 1965, Libertore was elected business manager of Building Laborers' Local 860. He rose through the labor union ranks, becoming president of Laborers' Union 860 by the mid-1970s. He was also appointed a member of the board of trustees to the Cleveland Regional Sewer District. And then came his involvement with the effort to murder Daniel J. "Danny" Greene. Today, Anthony D. Libertore is the only cop-killer in the history of the United States to have his name on a public building.

[87] A detective working the case stated the gang would have had the whole 1962 Labor Day weekend to loot the inside of the Cleveland Trust bank branch, which contained three vaults, if not for the alertness of Patrolman John Stoyka. He claimed Stoyka may have prevented the most lucrative bank burglary in the history of the state. On September 5, bond was set at $100,000 for Arrington, due to his record of jumping bail on five separate occasions. On September 11, the grand jury issued a four-count indictment against the three men charging unlawful entry, burglary, attempting to force entry into a vault, and possession of burglary tools. Arrington was still fighting for a reduced bail and during a hearing on September 22, Assistant County Prosecutor Dennis J. McGuire argued the higher bond was necessary because of Arrington's bail jumping record. Common Pleas Judge Daniel H. Wasserman declared the higher amount was tantamount to a denial of bond, and reduced it to $50,000. Dominic C. Lonardo, owner of AAA Bail Bond Service on East 21st Street, posted the bond and Arrington immediately fled the state.

On February 8, 1963, Dominic Lonardo created his own branch of the FBI and recruited Clevelanders Richard A. Stewart and Thomas J. Myers, both with lengthy arrest records; Youngstown bondsman Mario J. Guerrier; and Youngstown crime figure Peter Manos as his "brickyard" agents. That night, posing a G-men, they stopped an automobile containing Louis Gaye and Mrs. Betty M. Flonnoy, after a high-speed chase, and removed them at gunpoint. They were taken to Gaye's home at 13013 Edmonton Avenue and held for 11 hours. Arrington had apparently escaped to Birmingham, Alabama, using an automobile Gaye had the title for. Lonardo's plan was for Gaye to contact Arrington and get the address where he was staying so the title could be sent to him. The plan worked and Arrington gave up the address. Lonardo, who was told by the court to produce Arrington for trial or forfeit the bond, gave the address to the Cleveland police, who in turn notified Birmingham authorities, who immediately arrested the fugitive. On May 9, 1963, the three men were to be tried together. Attorney John P. Butler was able to get a separate trial for his client, Charles Polizzi, since he had no prior convictions on his record. Alfred Oponowicz, like Arrington, had jumped bail, leaving Arrington to face trial alone. On May 27, a jury of two men and ten women found him guilty of malicious entry of the Cleveland Trust Bank and three other counts, and did not recommend mercy. Common Pleas Judge Hugh A. Corrigan sentenced Arrington to life in the Ohio Penitentiary. Arrington died in prison on January 24, 1970, of a heart attack at the age of 50.

On June 21, 1963, Dominic Lonardo and three of his self-appointed G-men were found guilty of posing as FBI agents and sentenced to three years in Federal prison. In September 1965, the 6th Circuit Court of Appeals reversed the conviction and granted a new trial. In January 1966, after the Appeals Court refused a rehearing, Assistant U.S. Attorney Nathaniel R. Jones filed a motion to dismiss the case after the death of one of the government's witnesses. Federal Judge Gerard E. Kalbfleisch approved the motion. Before the end of the year, Lonardo was arrested again after getting involved in another scheme. In September 1963, Charles Polizzi pleaded guilty and on December 3 was handed a sentence of 1-to-20-years in the Ohio Penitentiary.

On November 29, 1963, Alfred Oponowicz was put on the FBI's "Ten Most Wanted Fugitive's List." The next day he was suspected in the murder of Gust Georges, a wealthy vending machine business owner in Baldwin Borough, Pennsylvania; a suburb of Pittsburgh. He was captured in Painesville on December 23, 1963. On April 5, 1965, he was found guilty of the 1962 Cleveland Trust bank burglary and given two life sentences in the Ohio Penitentiary. By October 23, 1969, Oponowicz had worked his way up to trusty in the prison cafeteria before walking out that day. Doing two life sentences, not many people figured to see him back. In March 1970, on a Friday the 13th, he received his final dose of bad luck in the form of a shotgun blast from a Tallmadge patrolman after Oponowicz opened fire on him at the back of a feminine apparel store he was in the process of burglarizing. He was 43 years old.

[88] Curtis E. Chillingworth began his legal career following his return to West Palm Beach, Florida, after serving in the Navy during World War I. In 1921, at the age of 24, he served as a county judge. Two years later he was elected circuit judge, a position he held until 1955. On the night of June 14, 1955, Chillingworth and his wife, Marjorie, were having dinner in West Palm Beach, and left for their oceanfront cottage in Manalapan, around 10 p.m. The couple was reported missing the following morning when the judge failed to appear for a hearing. The ensuing investigation ruled out accidental drowning and robbery. The keys to the Chillingworth's automobile were still in the ignition. The case quickly went cold, and in 1957, they were legally declared dead. After the couple had

gone to bed that night, Floyd "Lucky" Holzapfel and Bobby Lincoln landed a small boat on the beach behind the Chillingworth's cottage. Holzapfel, armed with a handgun, knocked on the door of the cottage and when the judge answered, he forced them both at gun point down to the boat. The couple was bound and gagged, before lead weights were tied to their legs. They were then thrown overboard and drowned. During the summer of 1960, Holzapfel bragged to a friend, James Yenzer, that he knew what had happened to the judge and his wife. Yenzer then went to his friend, an ex-police officer, and told him. The two got Holzapfel drunk and got him to talk about the crime while they secretly recorded it. He was arrested on October 1, 1960. After pleading guilty to killing both the judge and his wife, on December 12, he was sentenced to death. During the investigation it came out that an ambitious municipal judge, Joseph A. Peel, Jr., who had set a path of going from state attorney, to attorney general, to governor, had hired Holzapfel to kill the judge because he saw him as someone who could interfere with his plans of advancement. Peel was brought to trial and found guilty on March 30, 1961; receiving two life sentences. In 1966, Holzapfel's death sentence was commuted to life in prison, where he died some 30 years later. Peel, dying of cancer in 1982, was paroled and before passing away gave a detailed deathbed confession. Bobby Lincoln was granted immunity, confessed, and agreed to testify. He served a 21-month Federal Prison term in Milan Michigan and was released in 1962.

[89] Carrollton, Ohio, Patrolman George Litt's name also appeared as Lilt and Litz in the newspaper reporting.

[90] Cleveland Police Lieutenant Peter M. Mihalic was assigned to the 6th District, located in Collinwood. The Cleveland *Plain Dealer*'s I-Team investigation into police misconduct in the Cleveland Police Department in March 1974 swept up Mihalic and Sergeant Dennis N. Kehn in a scheme that uncovered their participation in a burglary ring that was operating in the District. The 50-year-old Mihalic, a 25-year veteran and Kehn on the force for 12 years, were indicted on April 9, 1974, on 32 charges involving ten stores and financial institutions that were burglarized between March 28, 1971, and March 7, 1972. On July 26, both were found guilty.

[91] 5808 Whittier Avenue today is a vacant lot.

[92] 4719 Payne Avenue today is a vacant lot.

[93] The Civil Works Administration (CWA) was a creation of President Franklin D. Roosevelt's New Deal during the Great Depression of the 1930s. The short-lived program, which began in 1933, focused on creating jobs by improving or con-

structing buildings and bridges. In addition, CWA workers laid 12 million feet of sewer pipe and built or improved 259,000 miles of roads, 40,000 schools, 3,700 playgrounds, and nearly 1,000 airports. After providing employment to some four million out of work men, the program ended on March 31, 1934. It was replaced by the Works Progress Administration (WPA).

[94] 1302 Prospect Avenue today is a parking lot at the south-west corner of Prospect and East 14th Street.

[95] Peter J. Trovato, Jr. first made news on August 31, 1950, after he was arrested with eight others in what police described as a "street free-for-all" outside the Trovato home at 3824 East 149th Street (today an empty lot). The incident began when Louis Russo and his wife went to the Trovato home to try to settle a dispute with Peter. This was followed by a melee in the street with guns blazing and rocks flying. Russo and his brother Tony were wounded in the shooting and suffered head wounds from the rocks. Peter was joined by his brothers Carl and Salvatore in the fight. It was unknown which side the other four participants in the fracas were fighting on. Peter Trovato suffered a lacerated scalp wound from a flying rock. After being sentenced for the 1950 Christmas Eve burglary with Joseph Russo (no relation to the fighting Russos above), the next time Trovato was heard from was on March 2, 1962. Assistant U.S. Attorney Burt W. Griffin announced warrants were issued for Peter J. Trovato and four others who were being sought by the U.S. Secret Service for passing nearly $100,000 in counterfeit $20 bills in Cleveland and eight other cities. Two of the other warrants were for Fred Stitmon, a former muscle-man in the numbers rackets for Alex "Shondor" Birns, and Charles G. Radd. On March 14, Detective Lieutenant Thomas P. White arrested Radd and turned him over to Federal agents. On March 16, a Federal Grand Jury indicted 23 people in "what the Secret Service described as one of the best organized counterfeiting rings in history." The ring leaders were said to be Trovato, Radd and Stitmon. Trovato and Radd were sentenced to a five-year term in Federal Prison by Federal Judge James C. Connell. It was reported that Trovato was a friend of Albert H. Severino. The two of them may have met while serving time in prison. Severino was murdered in June 1967. Some 11 months later it would be Trovato who was cut down. Late on Sunday night, May 12, 1968, Trovato "fell dying" from an automobile at the corner of East 38th Street and Payne Avenue. Trovato, after received a severe beating, he was shot twice in the head, once in the chest. Since Trovato's hands and ankles were bound with tape, he was obviously not driving the car when he fell out. There was never any information released as to whether or not anyone else was seen around the automobile. A passing motorist spotted Trovato, and he was taken to St. Vincent Charity Hospital, dying just minutes after arriving. Anthony Buffa, whose car Trovato fell from, said he loaned it to Trovato on Sun-

day afternoon. Buffa identified Trovato's body at the morgue. No one was ever arrested or tried for Peter Trovato's murder. He left behind a wife and three children. He is buried in Calvary Cemetery.

[96] Edward Blythin was one of two men to serve as mayor of Cleveland without being elected to office. If the sitting mayor dies, resigns, or accepts or is elected to a higher office, the city charter calls for him to be replaced by the city law director. Such was the case in May 1920, when Mayor Harry L. Davis resigned to run for governor of Ohio. He was replaced by William S. Fitzgerald. In November 1940, Harold H. Burton was elected to the U.S. Senate. When he took office on January 3, 1941, Edward Blythin completed his unexpired term and was defeated by Common Pleas Judge Frank J. Lausche in the November 1941 mayoral election. In 1949, Blythin was elected to a seat on the Common Pleas bench. In 1954, he oversaw Cleveland's most famous murder trial, that of Dr. Samuel Sheppard for the killing of his wife Marilyn. In February 1958, Blythin was overseeing the murder trial of Cleveland Police Lieutenant Edward G. Lentz, the highest ranking officer ever murdered in the line of duty in the city. On the night of February 12, Blythin suffered a massive heart attack. Taken to Lutheran Hospital, he died on St. Valentines' Day with his son Arthur, a Cleveland police detective, at his side. He was 73 years-old. Blythin is buried in Lake View Cemetery.

[97] 10100 Woodland Avenue today an empty lot.

[98] On May 22, 1949, twelve members of a Collinwood gang attempted to enter Emergency Clinic hospital in Collinwood during off hours. It was never made clear whether they were going in to see a fellow gang member or to try to take advantage of a gang rival. The young man, who was hospitalized, was 21-year-old Albert "Tubby" Figer, the men arrested at the hospital were:

John Cirelli – charged with carrying a concealed weapon
Michael Delzoppo – charged with carrying a concealed weapon
John La Riccia – charged with carrying a concealed weapon
George Balice – charged with disorderly conduct
Eugene Constantino – charged with disorderly conduct
Anthony Contento – charged with disorderly conduct
Michael Graziano – charged with disorderly conduct
Anthony P. Lorenzo – charged with disorderly conduct
James J. Pietrantozzi – charged with disorderly conduct
Frank J. Santucci – charged with disorderly conduct
Joseph J. Sanzo – charged with disorderly conduct
Ignatius P. Tercchino – charged with disorderly conduct

[99] Today 3848 Prospect Avenue is the home of Sutton Industrial Hardware & Tool Rental.

[100] In future narcotics trials in Cleveland, where this same procedure of selling was used, the agents testified that the men pointing out where the heroin was hidden were always wearing gloves.

Chapter Eleven: Alfred Calabrese, Paul Perrotti & The "Red" Carpenter Story

[101] Today 55 South Main Street is the home of Akron-Summit County Public Library.

[102] An article in the *Plain Dealer* dated February 8, 1957, stated Eldon "Pete" Shoup was employed at the Alliance plant of Armour & Co.

[103] In the wake of the Kefauver hearings, a new Federal law was enacted by Congress which required bookies, numbers men, and sports pool operators to purchase a Federal Wagering Tax Stamp (also known as the federal gambling tax stamp). At certain intervals, the gambler had to report his earnings to the Internal Revenue Service and pay a ten percent tax on it. The tax was to be paid on the gross receipts, meaning the gambler could not deduct payouts that he made. In obtaining the stamp, the purchaser could declare himself, or herself as a "principal" or an "agent." As a principal, the purchaser indicates that they actually operate a policy business or another form of gambling activity. The gambler was instructed to purchase the $50 stamp, identify his business address, and list the names of his partners and every employee and agent. In purchasing the stamp, and providing the information, the gambler was admitting his illegal activities and where they were being carried on. Still, gamblers purchased the stamps nationwide and it's fairly certain that any declarations of income were grossly understated. Attorneys for the gamblers weren't too concerned. Most felt that if the law were ever tested in court the government would find it ruled unconstitutional because, in effect, the very purchase of the stamp was tantamount to having to testify against one's self. Hank Messick and Burt Goldblatt in *The Only Game in Town: An Illustrated History of Gambling*, state, "Government attorneys said privately that the legal eagles were probably right, and for that reason they advised the IRS and the Justice Department not to demand vigorous enforcement of the law." The new law went into effect November 1, 1951.

[104] Mount Union College, located in Alliance, Ohio, was renamed the University of Mount Union in August 2010. It was founded in 1846 as "a place where men and women could be educated with equal opportunity, science would parallel

the humanities, and there would be no distinction due to race, color or sex." Since 1993 Mount Union has become well-known for its Purple Raiders football team. The school has won a record 13 Division III National Championships, and holds the all-division record for consecutive victories – 55 from 2000 to 2003. The previous record of 54 was also held by Mount Union. The schools most famous alumnus is William McKinley, the 25th President of the United States.

[105] Early reports stated the safe contained between $6,500 and $10,000. Frank Wells claimed there was only $1,000 in it. A later newspaper story put the amount at $50,000, but this was never proven. – *Alliance Review*, November 20, 1957.

[106] The London Prison Farm, known since the mid-1960s as the London Correctional Facility, is located in Union Township in Madison County, 27 miles southwest of Columbus. Construction began on the prison in 1910, with "honor inmates" from the Ohio Penitentiary being transported to the facility to do the work. According to legend, "the original construction was with the use of human waste to make bricks." This led to the old joke about a person "shitting a brick." From 1913 to 1924, the farm served as a branch of the Ohio Penitentiary. In 1924, it became a separate facility.

[107] An article in the March 23, 1957, edition of the *Plain Dealer* stated it was a local tavern he went to.

[108] 10700 Helena Avenue today is a small parking lot one block south of St. Clair Avenue and East 107th Street.

[109] Ascot Park was a horse race track located near Cuyahoga Falls in Summit County. The track, originally operated as Northampton Park, was built along Ohio State Route 8 in 1922. It was unusual due to its length, just three-quarters of a mile long. It closed for a few years during the mid-1930s due to the Great Depression. New ownership reopened the track in 1935, and three years later changed the name to Ascot Park. In 1954, Horace S. Adams purchased the park. Adams, a Cleveland businessman, worked for seven years in the administration of Cleveland City Manager William R. Hopkins. He studied law at night and after leaving public service he founded a business management consulting firm. He became heavily involved in the motion picture industry and at one time owned ten movie theatres in Ohio and New York. He paid $1.3 million for the park and made $900,000 in improvements. Ownership of the park changed several times following Adams death in 1966. At times it was used for auctions, beauty pageants, circuses, fairs, and motorcycle races. By 1975 the facility had deteriorated to the point where it became a safety hazard. The next year, local firefighters burned down the grandstand and other buildings during training exercises.

[110] The Millersburg Military Institute, located in Millersburg, Kentucky, 3 miles northeast of Lexington, was founded in 1893 as a military boarding school. The school was active for 113 years before closing due to declining enrollment in July 2006. The United States Army Cadet Corps purchased the school in September 2008 and turned it into their national headquarters, as well as a National Cadet Training Center. It again became a military boarding school in August 2012, under the name Forest Hill Military Academy. In 2014, the U.S. Army Cadet Corps reorganized and closed the school. Efforts to keep Forest Hill Military Academy open failed and it went into bankruptcy in 2016.

[111] Today part of the Dorothy O. Jackson Terrace Apartment complex.

[112] On December 8, 1957, the Sunday after his testimony in the Eldon Shoup murder trial, Frank Stredrick was arrested by Akron police for a break-in at Weinrich's Furniture Store at 1103 South Main Street. Stredrick was free on a $2,500 bond for breaking and entering the Star Inn Café at the time. A judge set his new bond at $10,000. Stredrick was sentenced to the Ohio Penitentiary for his crimes. The next time he was heard from again was in August 1960 when his parole was announced. On December 17, 1967, Stredrick was arrested after police stopped his car and found marijuana. On May 28, he was sentenced to 2 to 15 years in the Ohio Penitentiary. By the fall of 1971, he was back on the street and involved in another crime, this time for a break-in at the Rimer's Gown Shop at 49 East Mill Street with two accomplices at 5:00 a.m. On October 2, 1975, he was one of four men arrested for a break-in at the Holland Oil Company, at 1060 South Broadway Street. Stredrick passed away in Niagara, New York, in May 1987.

[113] Joseph Pittacora and David Suarez were arrested for breaking and entering, grand larceny and possession of burglary tools for a break-in on St. Valentines' Day, 1957, at Belinski's Jewelry store at 235 2nd Street NW in Canton, Ohio. On the afternoon after the burglary, Suarez was riding a Canton city bus, when the driver noticed he was intoxicated and bleeding from a cut finger. The bus driver stopped at the Canton Police Department and dropped Suarez off. Police searched him and found 77 wedding rings identified as rings stolen from Belinski's earlier that morning. They also found a key to a cabin at the Chase Motel at 3400 Lincoln Way. When police entered, they found Pittacora and quickly obtained a search warrant for the room. In a suit case they found the burglary tools which consisted of three different size crow bars, three different size screw drivers, a hatchet, a pick and three pairs of gloves. David Suarez was found guilty of grand larceny on September 17, 1957, and sentenced to 1 to 7 year and Joseph Pittacora was found guilty of possession of burglary tools on October 7, 1957, and sentenced to 1 to 5 years. Both men were sent to the Ohio Penitentiary.

[114] In anticipation of the country's increasing effort to supply the allies before eventually entering World War II, Frederick C. Crawford, president of Thompson Products, Inc., broke ground on a government-financed factory during the spring of 1941. The $13 million facility, built on 15-acres in Euclid, opened on November 17 and began manufacturing valves and other airplane parts. This subsidiary of Thompson Products, the forerunner of TRW, Inc., operated as Thompson Aircraft Products Company, but became more commonly known as TAPCO.

[115] Joseph M. Petrangelo, on the positive side, was described as an "accomplished painter and muralist," on the negative side, police considered him a vicious and habitual armed robber and possible killer. By 1957, he had a lengthy record of arrests and convictions for armed robberies, in which death seemed to follow him. In July 1943, Petrangelo was involved in the armed robbery of the Union Tavern at 10311 Union Avenue. Soon after, police found the body of one of the robbers, David M. Hunter, Jr., in Akron with three slugs in his body. Petrangelo was a member of the Louis Teller Gang and the last of the bank robbery gang to be captured in September 1957. In June 1958, Petrangelo was a suspect in the brutal slaying of 60-year-old Rudolph Kordis, in his home at 15112 Ridpath Avenue in Collinwood. Kordis was bludgeoned about the head over 30 times with a blunt instrument after being robbed. In September 1958, Petrangelo skipped on a $10,000 bail that was posted for the armed robbery at the Play-Mor Bowling Lanes in North Collinwood. After a passerby noticed five pairs of hands in the air in the bowling alley about 1:30 a.m., he telephoned police. Petrangelo was shot in the back, while trying to escape, by Lieutenant Sidney Kershaw, and taken to the prison ward at City Hospital. Police speculated that he was afraid to go on trial because authorities in Buffalo, New York, were looking for him in a double-murder involving two brothers there. Detective Lieutenant Thomas P. White said Petrangelo lived in Buffalo at various times and was once a suspect in the murder of Dominic Mafrici in 1957 (see Chapter Ten: Dominic Mafrici & David Tiburzio biography). Meanwhile, his robbery mates in the bowling alley robbery were convicted and sentenced in October 1958. After skipping bail, Petrangelo headed south where he was arrested for armed robbery in Mississippi and sentenced to a seven-year stretch. After serving one year, he was brought back to Cleveland in leg-irons. On July 18, 1960, Petrangelo, who was convicted of the robbery at the Play-Mor Bowling Lanes, was sentenced to 10-to-20 years in the Ohio Penitentiary by Common Pleas Judge Thomas J. Parrino.

In November 1969, while still in prison, Petrangelo presented a picture he had painted of Astronaut Neil A. Armstrong to the Ohio Historical Society. The picture was then donated to the Neil A. Armstrong Aerospace Museum in Wapakoneta, Ohio. Petrangelo was paroled in August 1970. Had he finally learned his lesson? Now in his mid-50s, police said he was still "active" ...that is, until August 19, 1972, the last time he was seen alive. On Monday, August 21, residents of the Cliffview Gardens Apartments at 1925 Cliffview Road, in Collinwood, complained about a 1964 Cadillac being parked there for three or four days. At 9:00 that night, police arrived and checked the car. In the trunk they found the body of 55-year-old Joseph Petrangelo. He had been shot six times in the head. He was identified by papers in his wallet. At the time he had been living at 944 Evangeline Road with his mother, Mrs. Bessie Mariano. Despite his skill as a talented painter, the newspapers stated his "death was marked with the same violence that filled his life." The police theory for his murder was that "one of his associates might have shot him to even a debt." Petrangelo was buried in Lake View Cemetery.

[116] Roseville Prison operated as a medium security prison for 20 years – 1927 to 1933 and again from 1952 thru 1966. During its first six years, the facility housed about 300 inmates who worked at a brick factory at the prison. The town of Roseville is located in Perry County, while the prison was just across the county line in Muskingum County.

[117] Initial reports of the armed robbery at the Libbey-Owens-Ford Credit Union in Toledo stated the amount stolen was $50,000.

[118] This would be John J. Glassner's last reported court appearance as an informant. Apparently, no one gave any consideration to seeking vengeance on him for his decision to rat-out his accomplices. Of course, why go to the trouble once an informer has spilled all the beans in court. You can't un-ring the bell by killing someone. Glassner lived to be 92 years old and died at home on August 28, 2015.

[119] See End Note #95 on Peter J. Trovato for information on Charles G. Radd.

[120] George Stryanka had a lengthy criminal record. Items on his rap sheet included: auto theft, May 1940 sent to the Boys Industrial School; burglary, May 1941 sent back to the Boys Industrial School; burglary, December 1944, another arrest in Cleveland; forgery, July 1953 sentenced to 20 years at Mansfield Reformatory, paroled in May 1955; armed robbery, 1959 at the Fisher Jewelry Store (See also End Note #78) in Akron. On January 20, 1971, Stryanka and Sam Scaffidi were arrested after a woman thwarted their burglary attempt at the home of her brother in Oak Harbor, Ohio, a village located on the Portage River in Ottawa County, 11 miles west of Port Clinton. The two men were arrested and charged with breaking and entering, carrying concealed weapons and possession of burglary tools. Both pleaded not guilty and were bonded out. The preliminaries stretched out into the fall before both pleaded guilty to lesser charges and were

sentenced to prison terms. Ten years later Sam Scaffidi would be involved in organized crime activities in the Mahoning Valley working as an associate with the Joey Naples faction. As for Stryanka, things just got weirder.

In October 1989, the 66-year-old Stryanka hired two men to torch his neighbor's home in Middleburg Heights. Stryanka was upset because the neighbors had complained about his barking dogs. On October 16, a fire was set causing $40,000 in damages to the home. When police arrested Stryanka, they found loaded rifles, handguns, and thousands of rounds of ammunition in his home; one handgun was reported stolen during a Brecksville home burglary. Stryanka was facing 15 to 25 years on the arson charge alone. But there was more. Assistant Cuyahoga County Prosecutor Timothy J. McGinty said Stryanka operated a "college of crime" from his home. "We have tapes," the prosecutor related, "of Stryanka instructing younger people in the commission of crimes." McGinty went on to say the tapes were obtained from police informants who attended the classes. "We had them wired," he said. Police also discovered during their search and investigation at the house that Stryanka had found a way to bypass the water meter and was not paying for water at his residence.

On January 3, 1990, Stryanka pleaded guilty to aggravated arson and possessing weapons after being convicted of a crime. Part of the plea agreement included that Stryanka pay the Cleveland Water Department for back water bills totaling nearly $8,600. In summing up the guilty plea, McGinty declared, "This man endangered the lives of his neighbors and safety forces when he had the house set on fire. He has laughed at police long enough. He should not be eligible for parole in this century." Stryanka didn't make it to the new century; he died in Columbus, most likely while serving time in prison, on February 17, 1999. He is buried in Woodvale Cemetery in Middleburgh Heights.

Chapter Twelve: A Few Selected Biographies

[121] 12308 Mayfield Road. This property first made news in December 1928, when it was used by bondsmen Angela Taddeo Betroni and Ernest Betroni to bail out Sam Oliverio (a possible alias), who was arrested during the infamous Statler Hotel raid in which 23 Sicilian underworld figures were rounded up during what was believed to be the first Mafia meeting held in the United States. When City Manager William R. Hopkins called for an investigation into all the bond activities to release these men, it was found that this property was padlocked and subject to a liquor traffic assessment. In August 1941, while operating as the Trombetta Winery, the liquor license was revoked because it "had sold unblended foreign wines and imported wines in excess of its quota for blending purposes." By March 1947, it was known as the Midway Café and the Midway Snack Bar, which included a "back-room dice den." During the 1960s and into the 2000s, the Golden Bowl restaurant and the Mayfield theatre flanked the property. As of this writing, the space is occupied by LaCollina Little Italy apartments.

[122] S.A. Conti & Son funeral home at 2110 Murray Hill Road is now the Vitantonio-Previte funeral home.

[123] Today an open green space, part of the Thurgood Marshall Recreation Center.

[124] North Eaton is a small unincorporated community in Lorain County, just west of Columbia Station on State Route 82.

[125] Irwin "Red" Mason served his prison time, but when he got out, instead of heading west to the Golden State, he returned to Cleveland and right back to his floating poker and crap games. His last arrest came in January 1971, when he was caught with 16 others during a raid on a house at 3197 East 65th Street. Originally charged with keeping a room for gambling, Detective Sergeant Richard A. Dierker, perhaps having a soft spot for the aging gambler, allowed the charge to be reduced to visiting rooms for gambling, and he received a suspended $5 fine. Dierker claimed Mason was in the bathroom when police entered the apartment. "Because he was not at a table where others were sitting, he could not be charged with keeping rooms for gambling," Dierker reasoned. When Irwin "Red" Mason died in May 1972, after a long illness, it gave pause to several of the old-time officers and newspaper reporters to reminisce about the man they knew as the operator of the largest floating poker game in Cuyahoga County for many years. One stated, "He was not one of your hardened criminals," Lieutenant Martin P. Cooney recalled, "He just liked to gamble."

[126] William Suveges's name also appeared as Suvegas and Suvegis.

[127] The reversal of William Pollard's conviction did not mean he was free from further prosecution on the drug charges. The Appeals Court simply returned the case for retrial. I was unable to find any further updates on the matter.

[128] After a rough start in the 1950s, Michael W. Frato got his life together and by the late 1960s became the owner and president of Rubbish Systems, Inc. and AAA Rubbish Service. Beginning as a one-man operation, by 1969 the rubbish hauling firm was operating 12 trucks, and had just moved into a newly constructed heated garage to allow them a "dependable start," no matter what the weather. Located at 3017 East 83rd Street, the company had grown to where it was servicing 500 regular accounts in Cuyahoga County. Then Frato made the mistake of hooking up with Daniel J. "Danny" Greene, in his Refuse Workers Association, soon to become the Cleveland Trade Solid Waste Guild. There was soon a rift between the two men. It was never made clear what brought on the differences, but it quickly turned deadly. On Saturday night, October 30, 1971,

Frato was playing cards with friends and had parked his car at Swan's Auto Service at 2780 Mayfield Road at the corner of Coventry Road in Cleveland Heights. Frato was co-owner of the station. Just after midnight Sunday, a bomb went off in the station parking lot causing heavy damage to the station and to four cars parked there, including Frato's. The bomb also killed Arthur T. Sneperger, a 31-year-old associate of Danny Greene. Sneperger's car was parked nearby and inside was a remote to detonate a bomb. Police believed he was going to place the bomb in Frato's car when it went off in his hands. His mangled body was found nearby. While the belief was that the bomb had gone off accidentally due to a radio signal in the neighborhood, there was also a theory that Greene was waiting at Sneperger's car and set the bomb off himself because his longtime associate had recently given police a statement about Greene. What mattered to Frato was the belief that Greene was after him. He began carrying a handgun and before the month of November was over he decided the only way to come out ahead was to strike first. On November 26, Frato struck. Sitting in the passenger seat of a car believed to have been driven by August "Gus" Palladino, Jr., the two tried to ambush Greene at White City Beach, located near East 140th Street and Lake Shore Boulevard. About 10:00 that morning, Frato took three shots at Greene while he was walking his dogs, but missed. Greene pulled his .38 Special and fired twice, hitting Frato once in the right side of the head. Palladino got Frato to Mount Sinai Hospital, but it was too late to save him. Greene was soon arrested and charged with the killing, but claimed self-defense. Nearly a year went by before the case went to trial on October 5, 1972. Common Pleas Judge Herbert R. Whiting ruled the shooting was justifiable homicide.

[129] 971 East 79th Street today is a vacant lot.

[130] Albert H. Severino's name sometimes appeared in the newspapers as Albert A. Severino.

[131] 1272 Euclid Avenue is now part of the site of the Crowne Plaza Hotel in Playhouse Square. It was previously the Wyndham Hotel.

[132] The T.J. Clarke Box & Label Company is still operating at 45 Norwood Avenue in Jamestown, New York. It now operates under the name Clarke-Boxit Corporation.

[133] Adrian B. Fink was a well-respected attorney, Ohio state representative, Federal prosecutor and Common pleas judge. A U.S. Navy veteran, he served during World War II and earned two battle stars. After the war, he returned to Cleveland, where he attended Western Reserve University Law School and passed the Ohio Bar in 1948. Later that year, he married the daughter of Com-

mon Pleas Judge Daniel Wasserman. In 1950, he became a legislator for the state as member of the Ohio state house of representatives from Cuyahoga County. Two years later he joined the U.S. Department of Justice in Washington D.C. By 1955. He was back in Cleveland in a private law practice. In 1970, he was given a seat on the Common Pleas bench by Governor James Rhodes and served for seven years. He was also a member of the Cuyahoga Republican executive committee for many years. Fink passed away on June 29, 2012, at the age of 89.

[134] Lanken Avenue is located in North Collinwood. It is a short street which runs parallel to South Waterloo Road. To the east it ends at Nottingham Road; to the west it dead ends.

[135] 10011 Euclid Avenue is currently the home of United Cerebral Palsy of Cleveland.

[136] Clarence Coleman's nickname appeared at different times as both Sonny and Sunny.

[137] When most people hear the name Donald King, they immediately associate it with the wild-haired millionaire fight promoter, who made a name for himself in the 1970s and 1980s promoting such boxing stars as Muhammad Ali, Joe Frazier, George Foreman, Larry Holmes, Mike Tyson and Evander Holyfield. But most people outside of Cleveland don't realize that King first made a name for himself as a young man in the policy rackets on the East Side where he survived a bombing and shooting, while taking two lives himself in the process. In December 1954, 23-year-old "Donald the Kid," as he was known, had just returned to the rooming house where he was living at 3312 East 123rd Street, with the owner of the house. Shortly after arriving, the doorbell rang, and three men were admitted. When one pulled a gun and demanded money, King walked into another room and retrieved a revolver. King stepped back out and confronted 29-year-old Hillery Brown. Each man fired twice; Brown missed, King didn't. the three men raced out of the house. Brown's body was found 150 yards away. His companions jumped into a car bearing Michigan license plates and left their companion behind. King was held until police determined the shooting was justified. By the fall of 1955, King was considered one of the city's biggest policy operators. But it was often reported that "his customers have constantly accused him of welshing on payoffs." He was arrested numerous times for conducting a scheme of chance and participating in policy games. On May 20, 1957, a bomb exploded on the front porch of King's home at 3713 East 151st Street. When police questioned King, he told them who he believed to be responsible and why. Police immediately arrested Alex "Shondor" Birns and four other men. Trial was scheduled to begin on October 24. King would be the State's star witness. On

October 5, a man with a shotgun waited outside King's East 151st Street home. Sometime before 1:00 a.m. King walked out the backdoor to get something from his car. The gunman fired hitting King in the back of the head. Police arrived and took him to Mount Sinai Hospital, where his condition was said to be "not serious."

The trial of Birns and his co-defendants – Fred Stitmon, Elijah Abercrombie, Willie "Buckeye" Jackson and Edward Keeling – for trying to keep King's mouth shut about the bombing and the policy operation, began the last week of October. The trial was held before Common Pleas Judge Benjamin D. Nicola; with John T. Corrigan representing the state. Fred W. Garmone was counsel for Birns, while the remainder of defense counsel included Norman S. Minor, Albert Gamble, and City Councilman Charles V. Carr. Four days into the trial, a jury had yet to be seated. It was going to be a long trial. After hearing testimony for nearly four weeks, a jury of three men and nine women found one defendant not guilty, but could not come to a decision on Birns and the other three. Judge Nicola declared a mistrial. While Corrigan weighed his decision for a re-trial, King lost his home due to a tax lien, was arrested for selling whiskey illegally, and indicted for carrying a concealed weapon. Meanwhile, Fred Stitmon, the one defendant to go free, was shot and wounded in the leg. King announced that he was not interested in testifying in a second trial, and the charges against Birns and the others were dismissed. Through the early and mid-1960s, King was arrested a few more times for operating policy games. His days in the policy rackets came to an end in April 1966 after he viciously beat and stomped 32-year-old Samuel Garrett for not paying him $600 he owed. Garrett died from the beating a few days later. On February 23, 1967, King was found guilty of second-degree murder in the courtroom of Common Pleas Judge Hugh A. Corrigan, who delayed sentencing until a motion for a new trial by King's attorney, James R. Willis, could be heard. Corrigan had worked out the details of King's "revised" sentence in the privacy of his chambers. No one from the prosecutor's office, or the police department was present. There was no court reporter or stenographer to record it. The only other person was King's attorney, James Willis. The change in the sentence was not announced by Corrigan. When the media found out, it was reported to have come from a brief journal entry being filed in the clerk's office. It stated, "The verdict and judgement is modified by reducing the verdict of murder in the second degree to the lesser included offense of manslaughter." King served three years and eleven months in Marion Correctional Institution. Judge Corrigan served the rest of his life under a black cloud.

[138] Andre Alessandro's name also appeared as Allesandro, Allessandro and D'Allesandro.

[139] 3842 Scovill Avenue is now in an area occupied by the Portland-Outhwaite Recreation Center.

[140] 1800 East 17th Street, at the southwest corner of Chester Avenue, is now a parking lot surrounded by Cleveland State University.

[141] The Ohio Bureau of Criminal Identification & Investigation, also known as BCI, has been in existence since July 9, 1921. It was initially founded to maintain fingerprint files. During the early years of its existence, inmate labor was responsible for most of the work done – reviewing, indexing and the sorting and filing of fingerprint records. In 1959, a larger facility was constructed in front of the London Correctional Institute. Field agents were hired, and the name changed from the Bureau of Criminal Investigation to the Bureau of Criminal Identification & Investigation. In 1963, the operation was turned over to the Ohio State Attorney General's Office and given more responsibility. By the early 1970s, it had expanded to become the state's official crime laboratory, available on call to any police or sheriff's department in the state. There was also a BCI vehicle added, a portable investigative unit on wheels. Headquartered on the grounds of the London Correctional Institute, in addition to keeping a file of fingerprints and criminal records, the BCI personnel are experts in fingerprinting, firearms identification, lie detector tests, chemical analysis and identification, photography and other technical fields. During the 1960s and 1970s the BCI had to become experts in the growing drug culture. Over the 100 years of its existence, the BCI has added new facilities in Athens, Bowling Green, Cambridge, Richfield, and Youngstown.

[142] A veteran news journalist for 30 years, Carl Stern worked for NBC News and was public affairs director for the U.S. Department of Justice. In addition to winning the prestigious Peabody Award for radio and meritorious service to broadcasting in 1974, he also was awarded the following honors: Edmund J. Randolph Award for Public Service, U.S. Department of Justice 1996; Headliner Club Award, Network Television 1991; American Bar Association Certificate of Merit 1979, 1974; Emmy Ted Yates Award 1975; Emmy nominations, Outstanding Network TV

Broadcaster 1974, Outstanding Achievement TV News Specials 1974; American Bar Association Silver Gavel Award 1969; AFTRA George Roberts Award, Best Program 1960; and Radio-TV Mirror Best Radio Program (Midwest) 1960.

[143] The name "Day" may have been "magic" in Ohio politics, but when the second Frank S. Day got done, the name was certainly tarnished. The "magic" began with Luther Day (1813 – 1885). Perhaps Luther Day's first important move

was to marry the daughter of Rufus Paine Spalding. In 1839, Spalding was elected to the Ohio House of Representatives as a Democrat. When he was re-elected in 1841, he served as Speaker of the House. From 1849 to 1852, he served as Associate Justice of the Ohio Supreme Court. Spalding became a major contributor to the formation of the Ohio Republican Party, and in 1862 was elected to the U.S. House of Representatives (1863 to 1869).

Luther Day studied law under Rufus Spalding. In Portage County he served as Prosecuting Attorney and Common Pleas Judge. Day served in the Ohio Senate as a Republican during 1864, but stepped down that same year after he was elected to the Ohio Supreme Court, where he served until 1875.

William Rufus Day was the son of Luther. An American diplomat and jurist, he had a long record of service. A good friend and political advisor to William McKinley, Day was rewarded after McKinley became president by being named U.S. Assistant Secretary of State (1897 – 1898). In 1898, Day served as U.S. Secretary of State for five months. The next year McKinley nominated him for Judge of the U.S. Circuit Courts for the Sixth Circuit, serving in that capacity and as Judge of the U.S. Court of Appeals for the Sixth District during the same period (1899 – 1903). Day left that position when President Theodore Roosevelt nominated him for Associate Justice of the U.S. Supreme Court, which he served on from 1903 to 1922.

William Luther Day was the son of William Rufus Day and the grandson of Luther Day. He served as U.S. Attorney in Cleveland (1908 – 1911) one of the youngest men to hold that position. In 1911, President William H. Taft appointed him to U.S. District Judge, at 35, again one of the youngest men to hold that position.

Frank S. Day, while not related to the earlier Day family members who left their mark on Ohio justice and politics, was a well-known and respected jurist all the same. Frank Day was a life-long Democrat. He was elected to the Cleveland Municipal Court in 1918 and the next year was appointed to the Cuyahoga County Common Pleas Court. After a decade-long break spent in private practice, he was elected again to the Municipal Court in 1931. Three years later he ran again for a Common Pleas Court seat and was elected; holding that position until his death in 1948.

When the second Frank S. Day came along in 1938 – from where or when he didn't seem to know – he was working as a laborer on a WPA sewer project. He had an ill wife and was in desperate need of money. That's when a friend advised him, "Why don't you run for office. You've got a great political name." Who would have thought that was all it would take to propel him into a 25-year political career, and from there into prison?

[144] Mariann Colby's "long, long time" in the institution came an end on November 5, 1971. It should have ended a lot earlier according to Theodore Reshetylo,

the Lima State Hospital's director. Just 17 days after being admitted there, the doctors determined that she was not insane. She had only ended up there because of three careless judges who, while may not have wanted to send her to the electric chair, road-blocked an attempt to send her away for second-degree murder. The psychologist and psychiatrists pushed the agenda of an aggressive attorney to make the judges believe she was actually insane. Hospital records revealed that during her time there, "she had never been secluded, medicated, violent, diagnosed as psychotic, or had behavioral problems." The reason she was not released earlier, Reshetylo wrote, "was because of a fear of adverse publicity and pressure from the state attorney general's office." In the wake of the trial, Robert Colby divorced Mariann and won permanent custody of Dane. Colby remarried twice, his second wife passed away. With the third wife, he had another son, who became a doctor. Robert Colby died in Lynchburg, Virginia, at the age of 87 on May 24, 2008. Nancy Young, Cremer's mother, died on January 9, 2010, at the age of 80. In her obituary it stated she had a "lifelong dedication to serving her community, church, patriotic organizations and garden clubs," the listing of which could fill a telephone book. Her husband, John C. Young, Sr. died at the age of 85 on June 5, 2011. They are both buried near their son in Lake View Cemetery. Mariann ended up in Dublin, Ohio, located northeast of Columbus. She entered into a common law relationship with Russell Cordle, and they resided in a trailer park there. She and Dane reconnected, and he lived in Hilliard, just to the south of Dublin, until Mariann's death from a cerebral aneurism after falling and hitting her head, on March 26, 2007. She was 82. On the Find-A-Grave website, someone posted a note that the man she obsessed over before killing Cremer Young was his father John C. Young, Sr. In the book *The Insanity Defense and the Mad Murderess of Shaker Heights*, author William L. Tabac demolishes that myth, and the note should probably be removed for the sake of both families.

[145] In November 1948, Ohio voters returned Democrat Frank J. Lausche to the governor's mansion in Columbus. Lausche was born in Cleveland, where he began his legal and political career. While serving as a common pleas judge from 1936 to 1941, he was instrumental in helping to close the notorious Harvard Club and Thomas Club gambling houses. He served his first term as governor of Ohio from 1945 to 1946. He was defeated for re-election by Republican Thomas J. Herbert, before being re-elected in the fall of 1948, and would serve as governor through 1956. It would only be a matter of time before Lausche moved against the gambling clubs throughout the state.

He named the Mounds Club, in Lake County; the Pettibone Club (formerly the Arrow Club), in Geauga County; the Continental Club, in Lawrence County (the southernmost county in the state); and the Jungle Inn, in Trumbull County as the places he wanted closed; the Benore Club, in Lucas County near Toledo, was also on the governor's list. The Benore Club was the first to go in

June 1949. The following month, with State Liquor Enforcement Chief Anthony A. Rutkowski and State Liquor Director Oscar L. Fleckner leading the way, and a young agent by the name of John Kocevar in the raiding party, Thomas J. McGinty's famous Mounds Club was raided.

Next on the list was the infamous Jungle Inn in Trumbull County. The Farah brothers, John and Mike, were front men for the Cleveland Mayfield Road Mob at the Jungle Inn, which was a thorn in the side to honest law enforcement authorities since 1936. On Friday night, August 12, 1949, a squad of 19 unarmed agents entered the club and closed it. John Farah, who was managing the club that night, was furious. Someone had tipped him off to the raid and he made sure no liquor was being sold or consumed in the gambling rooms, thus making it impossible for the state liquor men to make any arrests. But the agents continued to gather the gambling equipment and waited for the county sheriff to arrive. Farah then went ballistic and ordered a guard, in a turret that overlooked the gambling tables, to shoot Rutkowski. "Kill him, kill him," he shouted. Then again, "Shoot him, shoot him." Upon hearing the shouts, the quick thinking 25-year-old agent Kocevar, who as in the cashier's cage, climbed a three-foot ladder into the turret and wrestled two shotguns away from the guard and bloodshed was averted. After that night the Jungle Inn stayed closed forever. Anthony Rutkowski, who went on to become a Municipal Judge in Cleveland, always gave credit to John Kocevar for saving his life that night.

[146] Area-Wide Paging Systems continued in business at the Lincoln Building address for a number of years. I was unable to find any articles still connecting it to John Kocevar or Joseph Linnen. The last time an article appeared about Area-Wide was in August 1976. The Lincoln Building, as of 2020, was under renovation to provide additional downtown residences.

[147] Around this time, according to Phil Christopher, he and Alan Walch became partners in the Redwood Lounge in Collinwood, with two other part-owners, whom he did not name. The lounge, located at 16137 St. Clair Avenue, was about two blocks away from where Christopher lived on Alhambra Road. Across the street, at 16136 St. Clair was the Grotto Inn, where, in September 1952, detectives recovered some of the money Julius Petro and Joseph Sanzo made off with after their Warren robbery.

[148] The Seventy-Niner's Café, named for its location on the south-east corner of East 79th Street and Hough Avenue, on Cleveland's East Side, was the flashpoint of the Hough Riots in Cleveland, which lasted from July 18 to July 23, 1966. There was unrest in the Hough neighborhood during the first half of 1966. In April, the U.S. Commission on Civil Rights conducted hearings in Cleveland. It concluded there was evidence of employment discrimination, police brutality,

poor housing, school segregation, and racism throughout the city. During the televised hearings, the belief was that Cleveland's racial powder keg was about to explode. No one could foresee that the charitable effort to help the family of a prostitute, who died of a heart attack at the age of 26, would help to ignite a deadly and costly riot. Margaret Sullivan, who had a record of a dozen prostitution arrests, plied her trade at the Seventy-Niner's Café. The café, following the murder of Benjamin Feigenbaum in February 1965, ended up in the hands of his nephews, Abe and David Feigenbaum. After Sullivan's death, her friend Louise, asked owner, Abe Feigenbaum if she could place a cigar box there to collect money for the three children Sullivan left behind. Feigenbaum, who had already banned both women from the bar for being "undesirables," denied the request. On Monday, July 18, after a heated exchange, in which "defamatory and racist language" was used, Louise was thrown out. Those were the facts of the story, what happened next had three different versions. 1) A Black man entered the café and was denied a glass of water, after which a sign stating "No Water for Niggers" was posted on the door. 2) A Black man purchased a bottle of liquor at the bar, but when he asked for a glass of ice was denied, this accounted for the posting of the "No Water for Niggers" sign. 3) A Black man entered and asked for a glass of water and after the owner denied his request, told a waitress there was "no water for niggers." At this point the co-owner posted a sign on the door simply stating, "No Ice Water." That evening, after the Feigenbaum brothers left, a robbery and some vandalism were reported at the bar and when the brothers returned, there was an angry crowd of 200-300 people outside the café. When the Feigenbaums moved inside, rocks were thrown through the windows and there was an attempt at arson that failed. Police were called on four separate occasions by the Feigenbaums, but did not come. After the Cleveland Fire Department was called, they contacted police, who finally arrived about 9:30. From that point, the crowd, growing in size, moved down Hough Avenue looting stores and setting fires as they went. The riot had begun. By the time it was over, five days later, four people had died, 50 were injured, 275 arrests were made, damage was estimated at between $1 and $2 million, and businesses between East 71st and East 93rd Street along Hough Avenue were destroyed. In a *Plain Dealer* article from July 8, 1967, a year after the riot, the newspaper wrote, "The café has since changed hands and there is a remarkable new atmosphere there along with new clientele. It has been renovated and there is political talk in the Seventy-Niner now." Today the south-east corner of East 79th Street and Hough Avenue, where the Seventy-Niner's Café once stood, is an empty lot.

[149] In this same apartment complex, 1925 Cliffview Road, police would find the body of Joseph Petrangelo on August 21, 1972. He was shot six times in the head and stuffed in the trunk of his 1964 Cadillac (See End Note #115).

[150] On the evening of August 24, 1951, ten-year-old Beverly Potts left her home at 11304 Linnet Avenue with a friend on bicycles to attend the Showagon, an annual summer event for children at nearby Halloran Park. When they arrived, the girls discovered that due to the crowd size it would be easier to maneuver around on foot, so they returned to her home, left the bicycles, and walked back to the park. This meant walking to the end of the block, where Linnet Avenue crossed West 117th Street, then turning left and walking one short block to Halloran Park. Beverly's girlfriend, Patsy Swing, had promised her parents she would be home before dark and suggested to Beverly that they leave around 8:45. Beverly told her she had permission to stay until the show was over, which ended after 9:00 p.m. Patsy went home. Beverly never did. Her disappearance and obvious abduction became a national news story, which remained fresh in the minds of Clevelanders for decades to come. The Beverly Potts disappearance remains an unsolved mystery to this day.

[151] The Coral Bar operated at 1988 East 105th Street, near the corner of Euclid Avenue, since at least the late 1940s. Outside of Robert "Bobby" Walsh's arrest there, the only activity seems to have been a citation in August 1959, while Walsh was night manager, for allowing women on the premises to solicit drinks. The only real excitement came on the night of October 18, 1967, when four or five 5th District squad cars raced to the bar following a report of a shooting. When police arrived, the shooting was still in progress, only it was professional cameramen and a lighting crew who were shooting a film outside the Coral Bar, which was written and produced by brothers Gerry and Roger Sindell, two former Clevelanders. The production manager, whose job it was to inform the proper authorities when filming was being done and where, apparently had forgotten to do so. The film, called *Double-Stop*, had a story line of: "In the suburbs of a city still reeling from race riots, a Cleveland Orchestra cellist clashes with his artist wife over whether their son should be schooled in an integrated inner-city public school." Ironically, the film debuted in May 1968, less than two months before the Glenville riots. The bar and other businesses were razed in the coming years, and today the spot is occupied by the American Cancer Society.

[152] The other four men sentenced in the counterfeiting ring were Mitchell D. Paul, three years; John R. Hennessy, two years; Lawrence Perlatti, 15 years; and Charles "Billy Fingers" Wheatley, 15 years, the last two were sentenced in U.S. District Court in Columbus.

[153] In an article from December 28, 1990, titled "Ill-gotten gains can't escape tax trap," written by reporter A.J. Cook under the column category "Tax Fables," he divulged more information regarding Victor J. Lota, Jr's. criminal activities. He

states Lota used his position as loan officer at Hibernia National Bank in New Orleans to line his pockets and help his friends. Cook reveals Lota "had become angry with the bank for reducing his authority. To get even, he circumvented its safeguard rules on large loans, which required committee approval, by making a number of smaller loans using fictitious names. During a 10-year period, Lota made unauthorized bank loans to his friends – who paid him kickbacks – and to his girlfriends." One of his girlfriends was loaned more than $1 million. With it she purchased furs, three Cadillacs, two Mercedes and $81,000 in jewelry. Some money was invested in real estate or given to her sisters to help purchase homes. When Lota was finally convicted, the IRS came looking for their share and wanted taxes on $4.7 million. Cook reports, "In the Tax Court, Lota argued the funds paid to friends were legal loans from the bank to its creditors; he was the bank's agent. The judge disagreed; Lota was not acting in the bank's interest but as a kind of Robin Hood." The court's ruling was that the unauthorized loans were taxable to Lota, while the kickbacks were not because this would tax some of the same money twice. In addition to being a syndicated columnist with his popular "Tax Fabels" piece, A.J. Cook was also an author, attorney and certified public accountant in Memphis, Tennessee, where he specialized in tax law.

[154] In the early 1980s, Victor J. Lota's scheming was found to have reached the highest levels of government. In July 1981, Francis M. "Bud" Mullen, Jr. was named Acting Administrator of the U.S. Drug Enforcement Agency (DEA). In January 1982, President Ronald Reagan announced his intention to nominate Mullen as DEA Administrator, thus initiating confirmation proceedings. Mullen had a problem, however. While he was Special Agent-in-Charge of the FBI's New Orleans office in the late 1970s, he received loans of $36,000 and $5,000 from Hibernia National Bank, which Lota had approved. The approval of the $36,000, an unsecured loan, exceeded Lota's authority.

During confirmation hearings in July 1983, by which time Mullen's confirmation had been held up more than a year, Utah Senator Orin Hatch, said the delay was due to his anger at the Justice Department's response to his inquiries into the loans to Mullen from Lota. Hatch claimed he had not received a "satisfactory answer." A Chicago Tribune front-page story on July 22 stated, "For more than a year, Hatch has been openly antagonistic to the Mullen appointment, moving frequently to shelve it." Hatch's problem with the appointee went back to 1981 when Mullen testified before the Senate Labor Committee of which Hatch was chairman. Mullen testified at a background hearing for Raymond J. Donovan, President Reagan's nominee for Secretary of Labor, that during an investigation of New Jersey organized crime figures that Donovan's name never came up on wiretaps. Mullen later admitted he lied to the committee. The Senate Judiciary Committee determined that the lie was not sufficient to reject Mullen for the position of DEA chief. In September 1983, just before the committee voted 13 – 3 to recommend him, Hatch said that Mullen had now "adequately explained" his answers. Mullen was sworn in on November 11, 1983 and served until March 1, 1985.

[155] Orland Carabbia, an older brother of Ronald D. Carabbia of Youngstown, died on April 3, 2021, in Struthers, Ohio, at the age of 93.

[156] Nathan Wachs was a fearless Cleveland police detective, who served the city for a quarter century battling bootleggers, labor racketeers, robbers, and vandals. His law enforcement style appeared to be a better fit for the Old West as there was no criminal he was afraid to face down. He was born on August 24, 1892, to Russian-born Jewish parents. According to the 1940 Census Report, Wachs attended school only through the 8th grade. When he was 19-years-old, he joined the Navy and served from 1911 to 1915. During this time, he became an excellent shot with the pistol. Years later, during World War II, he enlisted as a chief petty officer even though he was 50-years-old at the time. After his stint in the Navy, he found work as a "slab yard crane man" before joining the Cleveland Police Department in 1920.

On the night of April 21, 1921, Patrolman Elmer Sprosty, the nephew of Cleveland Safety Director Anton B. Sprosty, was six months into the job. He went on duty that night with a revolver he knew was inoperable. His beat took him to Philip Goldberg's café at 1412 Scovill Avenue, where seven men were outside engaged in drunken horseplay and one man, Robert "Bobby" Hunt, an ex-convict, was firing a gun. When Sprosty approached to break things up, several men jumped into an automobile, with two unsuspecting people, and began to drive away. Hunt, who had jumped on the running board, turned and fired three times at Sprosty fatally wounding him. Hearing the shots and racing to the scene was Patrolman Wachs, who fired five shots at the escaping car, hitting Hunt three times; one bullet ripping through his back and out his stomach. Hunt's companions drove him to the home of Jasper Polizzi, the brother of future Mayfield Road Mob leader Alfred "Big Al" Polizzi. A call was placed to Dr. Giuseppe Romano, a well-known and respected physician in the Italian community, who, ironically, would become the leader of the Mafia in Cleveland for a short time in the mid-1930s. Dr. Romano was able to save Hunt's life. Hunt later stood trial for the murder of Elmer Sprosty, and was convicted of first degree murder, but given mercy. In 1928, Hunt burned to death after setting a fire in his prison cell.

Eight months later, Wachs, while off duty, returned fire on a carload of bootleggers hitting one man in the thigh. The next month, Wachs and Patrolman George Unger fought off and then arrested six men in a café where liquor was being served. In February 1924, he was promoted from patrolman duty, in what was the 15th Precinct, to "citizen's dress" in the 2nd Precinct. Over the next 20 years he worked with men who would become some of the biggest names in the Cleveland Police Department including Charles Cavolo, John Mack, Emil Smetana and Thomas White. His partners included Henry Cowles, George Zicarelli, Phil Bova and Norman Voss. His assignments over the next two decades made for an impressive resume. In addition to involvement in armed robberies and holdups, he investigated bombings and racketeering in the dry-cleaning business; violence during the ladies garment workers strikes; bombing during the ice dealers competition; stench bombings and violence in the barber's union; tracking down a city-wide serial arsonist; violence in the Bakery Drivers Union; a shakedown in the Poultry Dealers Union; a shakedown and violence among the Kosher butcher shop owners; stench bombings in the restaurant business; violence in the milk industry; and vandalism in the painters' union. During this period, he served on units designated as the "Bomb Squad" and the "Vandal Squad."

In addition, Wachs investigated violence stirred up by Nazi sympathizers in the city during the 1930s, was involved in arrests during the occasional jail break, and helped in the investigation of the highly publicized murder of former councilman William Potter. On June 20, 1940, Wachs and partner, future police chief Richard Wagner, investigated a robbery at Boiardi's Italian Restaurant at 917 Woodland Avenue. Three gunmen entered the restaurant of the not-yet-famous Chef Boiardi (products later marketed as Chef Boyardee) and emptied cash registers and robbed patrons. In October 1942, Safety Director Frank Celebreeze had a special squad composed of Detectives Wachs, Phil Bova and Lawrence Dwyer set up to protect City Transit System operators due to a wave of assaults and robberies.

By the mid-1940s, Wachs' career was winding down. In January 1944, he and a partner were slightly injured when another driver hit their police car at Lexington Avenue and East 65th Street. In April 1945, during a boxing match at the Cleveland Arena, a "near riot and melee" broke out in the crowd and Wachs and Bova were left "bitten and bruised." In October that year, Wachs was with then Sergeant Thomas White when they captured two armed robbers on Adelbert Road. Wachs retired shortly after that. Nathan Wachs died on July 21, 1957, while living in South Euclid, he was 65-years-old. He was buried in Mayfield Cemetery in Cleveland Heights, next to historic Lake View Cemetery.

[157] 4814 Euclid Avenue is located next to the current Cleveland Agora at 5000 Euclid Avenue.

Bibliography

Books:

Demaris, Ovid – *The Last Mafioso* – 1981 – The New York Times Book Co, Inc.
DeSantis-Ferritto, Susan – *Ferritto: An Assassin Scorned* – 2012 – Ragpaper Press, Erie, PA.
DiPaolo, Dominick D. as told to Jeff Pinski – *The Unholy Murder of Ash Wednesday* – 2014 – Global Roman Publishing, Erie, PA,
May, Allan R. – *Welcome to the Jungle Inn* – 2011 – ConAllan Press, LLC, Cleveland, OH.
May, Allan R. – *CrimeTown U.S.A.* – 2013 – ConAllan Press, LLC, Cleveland, OH.
Rose, William Ganson – Cleveland: The Making of a City – 1950 – The World Publishing Company
Tabac, William L. - *The Insanity Defense and the Mad Murderess of Shaker Heights* – 2018 – The Kent State University Press
Van Tassel, David D. and John J. Grabowski – *The Encyclopedia of Cleveland History* – 1987 – Indiana University Press
Walsh, Dennis M. – *Nobody Walks* – 2013 – St. Martin's Press
Zuckerman, Michael J. – *Vengeance Is Mine* – 1987 – MacMillan Publishing Company

Newspapers:

Akron Beacon Journal
Alliance Review
Bucyrus, OH – *Telegraph Forum*
Cleveland Plain Dealer
Cleveland Press
Cleveland News
Coshocton, OH – *The Tribune*
Dayton Daily News
Detroit Free Press
Dover, OH – *Daily Reporter*
East Liverpool, OH – *Evening Review*
Freemont, OH – *News-Messenger*
Fresno Bee
Los Angeles Times
Mansfield, OH – *News-Journal*
Marysville, OH – *Journal-Tribune*
Massillon, OH – *Evening Independent*
Napa Valley Register

Newark (OH) *Advocate*
Philadelphia, OH – *Daily Times*
Pittsburgh Press
Port Clinton, OH – *New Herald*
Sacramento Bee
Salem (OH) *News*
San Bernadino County Sun
San Pedro, CA – *News-Pilot*
Sandusky Register
Tampa Bay Times
Tampa Tribune
Warren Tribune Chronicle
Wilmington News-Journal
Youngstown *Vindicator*
Zanesville, OH – *Times Recorder*

Index

Note to reader: The Index does not include names or places appearing only in "Chapter 12: A Few Selected Biographies" or "End Notes".

A-1 Martinizing, 118

Adams, Stanton, 58

Ahearn, Richard W., 244

Aiello, Joseph Jasper "Fats," 42, 298, 476(n)

Ake, Russell E., 107

Alcatraz, 93, 98, 117

Alden, Abbie, xi-xiii, 92-93, 174(p)
    biography, 357-58
    Oak Knoll encounter, 71-72, 169(p)
    Peterson testimony, 76
    trial testimony, 75-76, 87, 88, 89, 94, 98, 481(n)

Alden, H. Carter, xi-xiii, 92-93, 174(p)
    biography, 357-58
    Oak Knoll encounter, 71-72, 169(p)
    Peterson testimony, 76
    retelling of 1952 testimony, 72-73
    trial testimony, 72-75, 86, 87, 89, 94

Alpha Beta Market, 132

Aliberti, Anthony, 237

Aliberti, Lucy, 237

Aliberti, Philip W., 179(p), 249, 495(n)
    biography, 237-40
    filling station robbery, 61, 241
    Mills Jewelry Store, 240, 251
    Mug Shot Book, 207

Aliberti, Vincent, 237

Allegretti, James "Monk," 120

Allen, Joseph, 46, 227(p), 397, 461

Allen, Jr., Edward J. "Eddie," 36, 37, 38, 167(p), 412, 481(n)

Allen, Robert, 58

Alvis, Ralph, 337

Alward, Frank A., 69, 89-90, 91-92

Amato, William S. "Billy,"
    biography, 359-66
    murder of, 126-27, 365-66
    Lombardo murder, 360-62
    Lombardo murder trial, 362-64
    Los Angeles, 364-65

Ambassador Hotel, 131, 490-91(n)

Anastasia, Albert, 351

Andrews, George R., 16, 469(n)

Angelberger, Cecil, 269

Anthony's Lounge, 243

Antonelli, Michael, 239

Arrington, Joseph Jewell, 180(p), 263-65, 271, 387, 486, 498-99(n)

Artl, Joseph A., 290

Assad, Abadallah, 289, 290

Atlanta Federal Penitentiary, 117, 285, 474(n), 488(n), 490(n)

Augustino, Nathan, 221(p), 253, 496(n)
    Mug Shot Book, 207

Auker, Mrs. Harold, 70, 87

Automotive Supply & Equipment Co, 302, 303, 310, 311, 316, 327, 353

Baker, III, Newton D., 35

Baker, Jr., Newton D., 35, 473(n)

Ballard, John S., 134(p), 195(p), 309, 495(n)
    Wahoo Bar Trial I, 310-11, 313-14, 315
    Carpenter murder confession, 317, 319, 321
    Wahoo Bar Trial II, 321-22, 323, 324, 325
    Glassner sentencing, 326-27

Barbara, Joseph, 40

Baron Café, 263, 274, 275, 281

Batista, Lou, 332, 347

Battisti, Frank J., 244, 253

Batule, Casmere K., 310, 353

Beaber, John, 346, 349

Bearden, Gene, 34, 474(n)

Beavers, Diane, 293, 378

Beavers, Robert L.,293-94, 295, 296, 377, 378

Bell, Griffen B., 147

Bell, Sam, 325

Bentley, Robert F., 257

Bergen, Bus, 49, 117

Berkeley, Raymond, 248, 249, 250

Bertha's Café, 6, 156(p)

Berthlaume, Harold F., 261

Best, Howard, 333

Bevacqua, Samuel A., 35, 279-80

Bickett, William, 272

Bird, Russell M., 267, 268

Blackwell, Michael J. "Iron Mike," 48, 196(p)

Blankenship, Leslie, 339, 343

Blazy, F.W., 285

Blythin, Arthur, 290, 291, 502(n)

Blythin, Edward, 290, 291, 410, 502(n)

Bochkoros, Ann, 47

Bocci, James V., 14-15

Bombeck, Stanley, 253

Bompensiero, Frank, 119, 122, 123, 138

Bonarrigo, Anthony, 243

Bonarrigo, Joseph, 225(p), 379-80, 382, 383-84

Boys Industrial School, 5, 250, 283, 507(n)

Brancato, Frank, 242

Brenner, Michael, 144, 148, 149

Bricker, John W., 32

Brinsky, Nicholas, 311, 321, 324

Britton, Robert, 19, 470(n)

Broeckel, Charles M., 223(p), 277, 299

Brogden, Jr., Samuel, 71, 87

Brown, Earl E., 283

Brown, Harry S., 287-88

Bruce, Clifford E., 215(p), 255, 374, 375, 393

Brunswick, David, 279

Bruening, Norman L., 294, 295, 296

Bucci, Angelo, 16

Bucci, Louis P., 14, 15, 469(n)

Buckley, John J., 38

Budak, Frank, 31, 32, 37, 475(n)

Budd, Dr. John H., 106

Buddie, Robert L., 276

Buffa, Anthony, 276, 465, 501-02(n)

Buffa, James, 245-46, 247, 249

Buffa, Shirley 276

Bulkley, Estelle, 112, 113-14

Burke, James W., 64

Bush, John, 8, 22, 44

Butler, John P., 218(p), 264, 276, 369, 388, 390, 394, 440-41, 442-44, 446, 499(n)

Byrne, Matt,139

Calabrese, Alfred A. "Allie," 44, 180(p), 191(p), 193, 240, 263, 301, 356, 463
    Carpenter rats on, 316-321
    Shoup murder trial I, 327-344
    Shoup murder trial II, 345-349
    post-trial, 349-352

Calabrese, Alfred S. "Allie," 130, 143-44, 187(p), 222, 292-93, 356, 380, 381, 453, 490(n)

Calabrese, Anna, 346, 348, 356

Calabrese, Anthony, 348

Calabrese, Russell, 334

Calandra, Sr., John P., 144

Campbell, Dan, 69-70

Campbell, Ida, 62, 63, 70, 71, 87, 169(p)

Canary, Sumner, 107, 481(n), 485-86(n)

Caplea, Nicholas G., 349
Carabbia, Ronald D., 130, 186(p)
    Greene murder & conviction,
        143-44, 150, 187, 486(n),
        492 (n), 520 (n)
    Penn-Ohio burglary ring, 42,
        298, 496(n)
Cardinala, Carl, 283, 284
Cardone, Anthony "Tops," 46, 227(p),
    396-97
Carlin, Anthony C., 297
Carlin, Michael, 22, 23
Carlin, John, 297
Carmello, Angelo, 59, 251, 259
Carnegie Auto Hospital, 13, 23, 24, 26
Carpenter, Betty, 192, 302-03, 309,
    311, 312-13, 316, 320, 322,
    325, 351
Carpenter, Paul D. "Red," 180(p), 192-
    94(p), 270
    Wahoo Bar burglary, 301-04
    Shooting of Carpenter. 309-10
    Wahoo Bar Trial I, 310-14, 316
    Carpenter murder confession,
        316-21
    Wahoo Bar Trial II, 321-26
    Shoup murder trial I, 327, 329-
        34, 339-41, 343
    Shoup murder trial II, 345-47
    post-trial, 349, 351-53, 354, 356
Carr, Charles V., 280, 512(n)
Carretta, Florence, 52
Carretta, Frank, 52
Carretta, Joseph, 52, 53, 54-55, 56, 57,
245, 304, 306
Carroll, James J., 114(p), 485-86(n)
    as assistant U.S. attorney, 107,
        108-109, 112, 113, 114
    as defense counsel, 452, 453
    as common pleas judge, 141,
        143-44, 145, 187(p)
Carroll, Ronald, 136

Catavolos, Pete, 40
Celebreeze, Frank D. 214(p), 287, 288,
    393-94, 521(n)
Cernigoz, Alice, 7
Cernigoz, Bertha, 6
Cesnik, John, 42-43
Chagrin Cigarette Service Co., 242,
    243
Chapman, Abe, 125
Charney, Robert S., 145-46, 149
Chester, Bernard, 43
Chillingworth, Curtis E., 274, 499(n)
Chino, California Institute for Men,
    133, 136, 142, 184
Choma, Albert, 346
Choma, Peter, 346
Choma, Thelma, 338
Choma, William B., 336, 338, 342, 348
Christopher, Phil, 223, 277, 374, 375,
    440, 457, 516(n)
Ciarcia, Kenneth, 144
Ciasullo, Eugene "The Animal," 298,
    457
Cilenti, James V., 222(p), 277-80
    Mug Shot Book, 208
Cirelli, John, 40, 502(n)
Cisternino, Pasquale "Butchie," 130,
    187(n), 356, 453, 492(n)
    Danny Greene murder, 143, 144,
        186, 486(n)
City Hospital, 31, 32, 33, 38, 53, 54, 55,
    307, 473(n), 506(n)
Clarco, Alex, 96, 297
Clemmer Construction Co., 237, 238,
    367
Cleveland Clinic, 38, 58, 107, 279, 297,
    437, 482(n)
Clooney, George, 5
Club Verdone, 13, 26
Coats, Donald J., 255, 257
Cochran, Steve, 131, 155(p), 491(n)

Coleman, Clarence "Sonny," 227, 228(p), 399-404
Coleman, Frederick M., 294
Coleman, James C., 43
Collins, Albert, 285
Collinwood Construction Workers Social Club, 336, 339, 350
Collinwood High School, 4, 68, 170(p), 488(n)
Colucci, Olga, 26
Commorato, Anthony, 254
Connell, James C., 108, 110-11, 216(p), 452, 453, 459, 468(n), 502(n)
Contie, Jr., Leroy J., 295-96, 378-79
Contorno, Benedetto "Benny," 239, 245, 246, 247, 248-49, 495-96(n)
Contorono, Mr., 105, 106
Cooney, Martin P., 10, 14-15, 158(p), 197(p), 273, 278, 279, 287, 288, 369, 404, 460, 461, 470(n), 509(n)
Cope, Frank F., 239
Corello, Tony, 122, 123
Coreno, Thomas, 16
Corlett, Alva R., 11, 12, 13, 15, 16, 17, 18, 163(p), 222, 279, 280
Cornelius, Robert, 275
Corrigan, J.P.P., 264
Corrigan, John T., 214(p), 233, 372, 373, 390, 392, 402-03, 404, 416, 417, 418, 419, 420, 431, 432, 439, 440, 512(n)
Corrigan, William J., 102, 103-08, 178(p), 471(n), 484(n), 485(n)
Costello, Timothy J., 11
Covelli, Gerald J., 120, 121
Covelli, Louise, 120
Cowles, David L., 12, 13, 24, 27, 59, 160(p), 361, 389, 521(n)
Cox, Donald M., 306, 307, 317, 320, 333
Cragel, Michael, 283-84

Craws, Edward M., 11
Credico, Mike, 347
Creedon, Dave, 61, 237, 240
Creedon, Mary, 61
Crile Veterans Hospital, 16
Cullitan, Frank T., 12, 93, 214(p), 250
Culmer, Dave, 45
Curtis, Jr., Jesse W., 139-40
Cutright, Carroll, 194(p), 304, 310, 314, 315, 317, 319, 327, 334, 347

D'Alessio, Anthony Paul, 43, 44, 46, 61, 179(n), 239, 251, 301, 367, 477(n), 493(n)
    biography, 240-44
    deportation effort, 241-44
    Mug Shot Book, 208
D'Alessio, Geraldine, 243, 244
D'Alessio, Mary, 240, 241
Danaceau, Saul S., 249, 389, 410
Daniels, Frank, 272-73
David, Joseph, 284
Day, Frank S. (Judge), 6, 278, 287-88, 415, 514(n)
De Biase, Alfred, 248
De Biase, Ralph "Bull," 50, 55, 56, 58, 179(p), 237, 238, 249, 288, 302, 494(n)
    biography, 244-50
DelGuyd, Anthony, 237, 238, 492(n)
Delsanter, Anthony "Tony Dope," 130
DelZoppo, Michael, 40, 180(p), 381, 448, 502(n)
    Mug Shot Book, 209
DeMarco, Carla (see Shaw, Audrey)
DeMarco, Victor, 11, 17-22, 24-25, 26-27, 28, 29, 44, 162(p), 280
Demaris, Ovid, 122, 133
DeSimone, Frank, 126, 139-40
Detroit Purple Gang, 14, 478-79
DiAugustini, Frank, 273

DiCarlo, Joseph "Joe the Wolf," 31, 34, 35, 37, 164, 168(p), 266
DiGravio, John, 291
DiGravio, Pierino "Pete," 137, 138, 185(p), 291
    Mug Shot Book, 209
DiGravio, William, 138
DiMatteo, Anthony "Skully," 15-16
Diorio, Joseph, 255-57
DiPaolo, Dominick D., 142
Diplomate Apartments, 118
DiSalle, Michael V., 253
DiVito, Anthony, 61, 238
Dix, J.H., 266
Doctors' Hospital, 115, 291, 292, 487(n)
Dodge, James K., 23-24, 26, 160(p), 271-72
Doran, James M., 276
Doran, Lawrence W., 235, 273, 362, 422, 423, 424
Dougherty, Charles W., 279-80
Dovishaw, Frank "Bolo," 142,
Doyle, John, 245, 246, 247, 248
Drago, Joseph W., 6, 42, 59, 179(p)
    biography, 250-257
    Euclid car bombing, 221, 252-53
    Lorain bank robbery, 254-57
Mug Shot Book, 210
Dulapa, John, 59, 479(n)
Dunn, James, 273
Dye, Lee, 138

Eisenhower, Dwight D., 107, 480(n), 485(n)
Elser, Ralph E., 37
Emergency Clinic Hospital, 30, 38, 166, 292, 473(n), 502(n)
Emmons, Claude V.D., 310-14, 315, 321, 323, 325-27
Eschman, Martin E., 45, 261
Estrate, Marie, 8, 21-22

Euclid Beach amusement park, 82, 450, 482(n)
Ewing, Harrison W., 259

Fannin, Richard, 147
Farrior, J. Rex, 274
Fatica, Joey (aka Bob Gaylord), 45, 46, 396
Federal Medical Center at Springfield, 117, 488(n)
Federal Reserve Bank, 63, 69, 70, 88, 254
Federal Wagering Tax Stamp, 305, 330, 503(n)
Feighan, Edward F., 41, 44
Feinberg, Herbert, 260
Fernberg, Louis, 66, 175(p), 219(p), 246, 247
Ferritto, Bernadette "Bernie," 130
Ferritto, Rayme, 130
Ferritto, Raymond W., xiii, 129, 181(p), 184, 186(p), 488(n), 489(n), 490(n)
    FBI file, 121, 123, 124-25, 129
    early life, 129-30, 143
    friendship with Velotta & Walsh, 130-32, 448, 453-54
    relationship with Petro, 132
    murder of Petro, 133-36, 137, 142, 145, 148-50, 182, 186, 456
    murder of Greene, 141-44
Ferritto, Susan DeSantis, 129, 130, 142, 490(n)
Ferritto, Victor, 130
Fetzko, Father Simeon, 342, 348
Figer, Albert "Tubby," 121, 122, 292, 441, 488(n), 502(n)
    FBI files, 121, 122
Fireside Inn, 317, 330
Fisher, George, 71, 87
Five Points, 4, 13, 64, 69, 74, 82, 83, 84, 110, 116, 126, 170(p), 177, 247, 249, 473(n)

Five Torches Restaurant, 127

Florea, George, 253, 263, 265, 387

Foley, Charles J., 108, 117, 171(p), 357, 367
  robbery, 62-63, 72, 160(p), 170(p)
  trial, 69-70, 71, 87, 88

Foti, Ernest "Ernie," 195, 304, 322, 355
  Wahoo Bar burglary, 301-03
  Wahoo Bar Trial I, 308-09, 311, 313-16
  Wahoo Bar Trial II, 321, 325-26, 354

Foti, Mary M., 304, 313, 355

Frank, Aaron J., 47

Francis, Connie, 131

Fratianno, Aledena, James "Jimmy the Weasel," 122, 126, 143, 185(p), 186, 489(n)
  FBI files, 119, 122, 124, 125, 128, 129
  Petro murder, 133, 136, 137, 138, 142, 143, 148, 149
  Government informant, 141-42, 143, 186

Frederico, Salvatore A., 42

Friedman, Jerry, 44

Frindt, Jr., Edward, 22, 26

Frost, Alfred A., 290,

Fuerst, Norman A., 144

Fulton, Parker, 101, 102, 219(p), 483-84(n)

Gackowski, George, 30, 166(p), 362

Garcetti, Gilbert, 147, 492(n)

Garfield, James A., 270

Garland, Marie, 347

Garmone, Fred W., 221(p), 246-47, 370, 401-04, 450, 512(n)

Gattozzi, Gene, 81

Gattozzi, Louis, 65

Gaylord, Bob (See Fatica, Joey)

Gehringer, George H., 85

Genaro, Anthony, 285-86

Gennett, D.G., 57

Genovese, Vito, 126, 488(n)

Gentile, Raymond, 41, 475(n)

Gerber, Dr. Samuel R., 35, 159(n), 231(n), 278, 361, 409
  Knaus murder, 12, 16, 17-18, 20-21, 28
  Young murder, 422-23, 426-27

Gerding, Arthur, 289

Giordano, Anthony "Tony," 488(n)

Glassner, Ella Jean, 315

Glassner, John J., 301-02, 320, 322, 354, 507(n)
  Wahoo Bar burglary, 301, 302, 303, 326
  Wahoo Bar Trial I, 303-04, 309-11, 313-16
  Wahoo Bar Trial II, 322-23, 324, 326-27

Glassner, William, 301-02, 303, 310, 327

Gloeckner, Kurt B., 10

Gold, Gerald S., 220(p), 255, 425-27, 429-30

Gomez, David M., 149

Gordon, Neil, 32, 33

Gottfried, Albert, 325, 353-54

Gotti, John, 142

Graham, George N., 328-29, 333, 334, 338, 341-42, 344, 346, 350

Grande, Michael, 59, 180(p), 251, 259
  Mug Shot Book, 210

Gravano, Salvatore "Sammy the Bull," 142

Grdina, John, 78

Green Acres casino, 31-38, 51, 55, 126, 164, 166, 167, 475(n)

Green Café, 8-9, 10-11, 19-23, 29, 30, 33, 44, 157, 158, 469(n)

Greene, Daniel J. "Danny," xiii, 150,
     186(p), 187, 224, 356, 377-78,
     405, 435
     Murder and trial, 140-45, 486(n),
     498(n), 509-10(n)
Grieger, Edward, 40
Griesinger, John J., 276
Griffin, James, 19, 470(n)
Griffith, Jr., Lynn B., 298
Grisham Charles F. "Spider," 255-57
Grisham, Clayton L., 255-56
Grossman, Mary B., 216(p), 292
Grotto Inn, 65, 81, 170(p), 480(n),
     516(n)
Guentzler, June (see Petro, June)
Guentzler, Lillian, 83, 85, 477(n)
Gutierrez, Gabriel A., 144, 146
Guzzo, Peter, 239,

Hackley, George D. 70
Hall, John M. 266, 267
Haller, Andrew, 6
Hammerle, Norman, 249
Hankish, Paul Nathaniel, 263, 265
Hanna, Elias, 50
Hanna, Harry A., (judge) 66, 93,
     216(p); (attorney) 220(p), 296
Hargett, Edward E., 264, 298
Hargreaves, George, 310, 314
Hart, James P., 279
Helder, Robert, 2
Hess, Jr., Jacob F., 346
Hewes, George R., 112
Higgins, George V., 236
Hildebrand, Robert, 37-38
Hipple, Clarence, 64, 71
Hoffman, W.O., 27-29
Hollenden Hotel, 37, 48, 474(n)
Holt, Bill, 125
Holy Rosary Church, 314, 315, 324,
     362, 364
Horvatin, Joseph, 6

Hovancek, Joseph, 67
Huff, Harold, 298
Hughes, Alex P., 89
Hughes, Tony, 340
Hull, Peter H., 141, 145
Huron Road Hospital, 38, 100, 380, 466

Iacono, Frank, 287
Igo, Robert, 82, 84
Ilacqua, Joseph C. "Joe I," 180(p),
     224(p), 225, 238, 293-94, 295
     biography, 367-86
Innocenzi, Adolf, 270
Innocenzi, Armand, 267
Innocenzi. Edmond "Moe," 257-59,
     270
Innocenzi, Harold, 270
Innocenzi, Juanita, 266, 267, 268, 271
Innocenzi, Mario, 271
Innocenzi, Sylvio, 270, 271
Innocenzi, Vincent, 59, 179(p), 236,
     237, 272, 275, 281, 352, 387,
     486(n), 497(n), 498(n)
     Mug Shot Book, 211
     biography, 257-272
     murder of, 221, 266-72, 465

Jenkins, Richard, 144
Jeney, Emil, 23
Johnson, Olive, 316
Johnston, Robert H. 77, 408
Jones, Donald "Bull," 42, 253, 298,
     476(n)
Jones, Paul, 92, 102, 105, 285
Jungle Inn, 31, 37, 47, 168(p), 232, 430,
     515-16(n)
Jurek, Fred, 141

Kaiser, William, 206(p), 289, 460, 461
Kalbfleisch, Girard E., 255-56, 375,
     499(n)

Kane, Jr., John J., 93, 107, 175(n), 480-81(n), 486(n)
  Petro/Sanzo trial, 68, 71-72, 74-75, 76-79, 80, 82-83, 88-89
  Spaeth perjury trial, 91, 97, 100, 102, 107
Karpis, Alvin "Creepy," 63
Kaye, Ronald, 243
Kazlaukas, Dr. A.J., 21
Kefauver, Estes, 81, 484(n), 485(n), 503(n)
Kehn, Dennis N., 276, 501(n)
Keizer, Dr. Clifford R., 25, 472-73(n)
Kellner, John, 59
Kelly, John M., 353, 495
Kelly, Leroy F., 257
Keno, Stephen, 120
Kenton, Stan, 49, 154, 477(n)
Kerns, Joseph A., 23
Kerr, David E., 16, 58, 166(p), 198(p), 232(p), 362, 401, 410, 460
  Green Acres case, 33, 35-38, 51
King, John R., 48
Knaus, Dolores, 8, 22
Knaus, Theodore R. "Bobby," 30, 35, 44, 125, 138, 469-70(n)
  murder and trial, 6, 8-10, 12, 16-17, 19-24, 26, 28, 152, 156, 157, 158, 159, 160
Knecht, Harold, 11, 12
Kocevar, Daniel, 282
Kocevar, John L., 232, 430-35, 516(n)
Kocevar, Milan, 282
Kolek, Joseph, 245, 289, 463
Koren, Christine, 118-19, 133, 487(n)
Koryta, Emil, 284
Kovachy, Andrew M., 66, 216(p), 292, 398
Kovachy, Julius M., 278, 280, 470(n)
Kovacic, Victor, 295
Krause, Paul E., 60
Krause, William, 261

Krizman, Emery, 279
Krupansky, Robert B., 145, 216(p), 296, 378

LaDuca, Peter, 277-78
LaDuca, Samuel, 277
LaFatch, James, 195
Lake View Cemetery, 4, 257, 259, 270, 300, 356, 362, 364, 423, 468(n), 474(n), 502(n), 507(n), 515(n), 521(n)
LaManna, James, 14-16, 59
Lanci, Thomas P., 144
LaPolla, Dr. Anthony, 52-53, 54-55, 57
LaRiccia, Mary, 343
LaRiche, Arthur F., 345, 354, 356
  Euclid car bombing, 252
  Wahoo Bar burglary, 301-02
  Wahoo Bar Trial I, 308-11, 313, 315-16
  Shoup murder, 317-19, 321
  Wahoo Bar Trial II, 322, 324-26
  Shoup murder trial I, 329-33, 339, 340
  Shoup murder trial II, 347
  post-trials, 349, 350
LaRiche, Marilyn, 313, 324
Lauer, Laurence W., 306, 333,
Lauerhaus, Albert P. 278-79
Lausche, Frank J., 102, 459, 472, 484, 496(n), 502(n), 516(n)
Lavine, Harry C., 242, 243, 297
Laybourne, Paul C., 310-13, 322-23
Leavenworth Federal Penitentiary, xiv, 93, 96, 97, 98, 99, 117, 273, 298, 463, 488(n), 490(n)
Lehmann, John M., 241
Lemmo, Donald, 12-13, 18, 24-25, 26
Lesher, Harry, 317
Levis, Dr. Irene, 24, 25, 28, 159(p), 472(n)
Lewisburg Federal Penitentiary, 286, 475(n)

Lexune, John,
  Wahoo Bar burglary, 301-03, 309
  Wahoo Bar Trial I, 309, 310-12,
    314-16
  Wahoo Bar Trial II, 324-26
  aftermath, 326-27, 353-54
Libbey-Owens-Ford Federal Credit
Union, 310, 312, 322, 325, 327, 353-54,
    507(n)
Libertore, Anthony D., 144, 221(p),
    269, 497(n)
Licata, Nicholas, 119, 126, 127, 138-40,
    185(p), 305, 489(n)
  FBI files, 126, 129
Licavoli, James "Jack White," 130, 143,
    156, 187(p), 268, 385
Licavoli, Pete, 138, 376
Lieberman, Eleanor, 303
Lieberman, Fred, 303, 311, 322
Lima State Hospital, 16, 410, 429, 430,
    496(n), 515(n)
Litt, George, 275, 500(n)
Lockwood, Harold C., 206(p), 236, 245,
    248, 388, 463
Lonardo-Porrello Corn-Sugar War, 14
Lonardo, Angelo, 45-46
Lonardo, Angelo A. "Big Ange," 46,
    141, 142, 143, 228(p), 396,
    397, 486(n)
Lonchar, William F., 199(p), 245, 247,
    350, 401, 451
LoPresti, S.M., 279
Lorain County Savings & Trust Co.,
    254-57
Lower, Albert O., 57, 106, 319, 320,
    321, 350
Luchenberg, Joseph, 285-86
Lynch, John J., 284-85
Lynch, Patrick, 40

Macy, William H., 5
Mafrici, Dominic, 179(p), 263, 275,
    281, 302, 506(n)
  biography, 272-77
  Tampa murder, 273-74
  murder of, 275-76
Mahon, John J., 250, 362, 363, 390, 410,
    446, 494(n)
Mainer, Phillip "Fleegle," 253, 265,
    476
Malin, Betty, 341-42, 343
Mangine, Ruben, 6
Mansfield Reformatory, 6, 8, 15, 18,
    25, 156, 238, 251, 273, 370,
    390, 468(n), 469(n), 507(n)
Marcellino, Angelo, 59, 259
Marchbanks, Jr., Ray. 328, 345, 346
Marconi, Carmen S., 144
Marino, Carmen, 141, 145, 215(p)
Mashorda, Raymond S. "Legs," 37-38
Mathews, Buster H., 280
Matia, Richard F., 264
Matowitz, George J., 11, 460, 485
Mayfield Road Mob, 121, 227, 238, 258,
    271, 471(n), 484(n), 516(n),
    520(n)
McArthur, James E., 43, 45, 172(p),
    198(p), 200(p), 201(p), 408
  in pursuit of Petro and gang, 54,
    57, 58, 64, 66, 236-37, 238,
    246, 250, 289
  with Lt. Thomas White, 461, 462,
    463, 493
McCarty, William, 342
McDermott, William J., 93
McDonald, John, 58
McGonagle, Reverend John, 342
McLeod, Elizabeth, 355
McMahon, Roy F., 254, 413
McMahon, Timothy F. 102-04. 108-11,
    178(p)
McMahon, Walter, 286

McNamee, Charles J., 30, 95-97, 100-02, 176(p), 177, 297, 362-63, 481

    Petro/Sanzo trial, 67-69, 79, 81-82, 84-92, 94

McNealy, Lincoln, 259-60,

Meadows, Woodrow, 313, 315, 323, 327

Mears, Samuel, 206(p), 289, 460, 461

Meeker, Edward, 312

Meltzer, Harold "Happy," 129, 490(n)

Mernagh, John, 48

Merrell, William, 253

Merrick, Frank J., 19, 29, 246-47, 249, 250, 279, 470-71(n)

Mesnig, George F., 86, 89, 96-97, 102, 103-04, 107, 108

Messina, Joseph, 277

Mihalic, Peter M., 299, 500(n)

Milan Federal Prison, 115, 130, 451, 452, 453, 454, 500(n)

Milich, Milton V., 241, 244

Miller, Don C., 175, 480-81(n)

Miller, Roberta J. "Bobbi," 118, 135

Miller, William E. "Red," 237-38, 367

Miller's Drug Store, 82-83, 85

Millersburg Military Institute, 328, 336, 343, 505(n)

Mills Jewelry Store, 239, 240

Mines, L.A., 69, 70

Moceri, Leo, 268

Mollenkopf, Fred, 350, 464

Monachino, Margaret, 34-35, 38, 164(p)

Monachino, Sam Jerry, 164(p), 222, 277-79, 280

    murder of, 34-35, 36-37, 38, 165(p), 166, 167

Monck, Harvey R., 291, 402-03

Monica, John G. "Sparky," 129, 133-36, 143-49

    death of, 149

Monica, Lori Lynn, 145

Moore, Thomas V., 19, 30, 363

Moretti, Edward, 304, 306, 333

    Carretta robbery, 52, 55, 56, 57

Morris, Max, 86

Morrow, Vincent, 30

Mounds Club, xii, 31, 32, 34, 164, 515-16(n)

Mount Sinai Hospital, 259, 296, 438, 439, 450, 510(n), 512(n)

Mozes, Dr. E.B., 307, 333, 347

Musil, Emil, 273

Nalepa's Café, 251

Naples, Sandy, 271

Napoli, Willie, 42, 298, 476

National Industrial Laundries Co. of Newark, 44

Ness, Eliot, 196(p), 258, 270, 287, 418, 458

Nevel, Charles O., 10, 41, 158(p), 201(p), 162, 460, 461, 462

Newcomb, Adrian G., 102, 484(n)

Nichols, Mason, 287

Ninemile Creek, 9, 20, 156(p)

"Nipper," 347

Nobody Walks, 131, 133, 184, 453, 455

Ohio Penitentiary 7, 13, 19, 25, 32, 50, 185, 238, 239, 254, 259, 263, 276, 281, 286, 287, 313, 314, 326, 327, 337, 340, 349, 351, 353, 354, 355, 364, 370, 371, 390, 391, 393, 404, 412, 421, 436, 459, 461, 464, 465, 469(n), 476(n), 485(n), 488(n), 495(n), 496(n), 497(n), 499(n), 504(n), 505(n), 506(n)

Ollendorff, Henry B., 249, 494(n)

Oponowicz, Alfred, 271, 499(n)

Orban, Martin, 279

Ordovensky, Pat, 351

Orr, Stanley L., 15, 16
Osmun, John B., 285

Palumbo, Thomas L., 294, 295, 296
Paone, Albert, 310
Paone, Raymond A. 317, 320, 321
    Shoup murder trial I, 329-30,
      333, 340, 341, 345
    Shoup murder trial II, 346, 347
    post-trial, 349, 351, 352-53
Papalardo, Sam, 15
Papalardo, Sylvester "Studo," 14-15,
    53, 55, 56, 180(p), 239, 463,
    481(n)
Parrino, Thomas J., (prosecutor) 247-
    49, 250; (judge) 370, 506(n)
Park Lane Lounge, 242-43, 493(n)
Parkhill, John R., 274
Patterson, Marian, 288
Peak, James H., 14, 15, 16
Penn-Ohio Burglary Ring, 42, 296, 298,
    475-76(n)
Percoco, Liborio, 269
Perrotti, Carolyn, 335, 346
Perrotti, Margaret, 335, 337, 338, 346
Perrotti, Paul, 263, 301, 356
    Carpenter rats on, 316-321, 463
    Shoup murder trial I, 327, 329-
      331, 333-44
    Shoup murder trial II, 345-349
    post-trial, 349-352
Perrotti, Ralph, 348
Peterson, Harry K., 84, 110
Peterson, Stanley E., 72, 73, 74, 76, 88,
    173(p)
Petrangelo, Joseph M. 388, 492(n),
    506-07(n), 517(n)
Petrash, Louis, 65, 251
Petro, Darias, 49
Petro, John, 5, 28, 30, 118, 468(n),
    482(n)
    Petro/Sanzo trial, 64-66, 76-78,
      79-80, 82, 87

Petro, Juliet, 49, 82, 154(p)
Petro, Julius Anthony, xi, xiii, xiv, xv,
    2-3, 151(p), 152(p), 153(p),
    154-160, 162, 166, 169,
    171(p), 172-75, 181-82,
    184-86, 228
    early years, 5-7
    murder of Bobby Knaus, 8-9,
      10-11
    Knaus murder trials, 11-14, 16-
      20, 22, 23-27, 28-29
    murder of James Peak, 14-16
    Green Acres casino robbery, 30,
      32-34, 35-37, 38-39
    more crimes, 40-42
    stench bombs, 42-44
    car bomb, 44-45
    Sonny's Show Bar, 46-48
    June marriage, 49
    more burglaries, 50
    Carretta home invasion, 52-58
    Detroit arrest, 59-61
    filling station larceny, 61
    Warren robbery, 63-68
    Petro/Sanzo trial, 68-69
    White testimony, 79-81
    defense testimony, 81-85
    critical rebuttal, 85-87
    closing statements, delibera-
    tions & verdict, 87-93
    appeals, motions & imprison-
    ment, 93-94, 96-99
    Spaeth trials, 100, 102, 111
    Federal Prison years, 117-18
    life in Los Angeles, 118-19
    FBI files, 119-21, 122, 123-29, 138
    Ray Ferritto, 130-33
    murder of Julius Petro, 133-36
    murder investigation, 137-38,
      140-42, 143-44
    case against "Sparky Monica,
      145-150
    comparison to Eddie Coyle, 236

Petro gang members, 236-41,
    244-45, 249-51, 255, 259-60,
    280, 283, 288, 290-92, 296,
    301-03, 306, 352
Petro in Biographies:
    Aldens, 357
    William Amato, 365
    Joseph Ilacqua, 367
    Sonny's Show Bar, 396-97
    Bobby Walsh, 454-56
    Thomas White, 462, 463
Petro listed in End Notes:
    468, 469, 472, 477, 479, 480,
    481-82, 484, 487, 488-89, 516
Petro, June, 49, 82, 91, 154(p), 477(n)
Petro, Lydia, 5, 27-28, 118, 468(n)
    Petro/Sanzo trial, 65, 76, 78,
    79, 91
Petro, Michael A., 5, 48, 132, 138,
    153(p), 468(n), 488(n)
    Knaus murder trials, 19, 23, 24,
    25, 28
    Green Acres casino robbery, 30,
    31
    Carretta home invasion, 53, 54,
    55, 56, 58
    Petro/Sanzo trial, 82, 84, 89
    life in Los Angeles, 118-19
    FBI file, 119, 124-25, 126, 128-29
Petro, Monda, 5, 64, 468(n), 488(n)
Picciano, Michael A., 6, 9, 33, 161(p),
    175(p), 177, 274, 352, 468(n)
    Knaus murder & trials, 11, 17-24,
    29
    Petro/Sanzo trial, 67-69, 76, 81,
    84, 86, 88-89, 90-91, 93, 94-96,
    97, 98, 99
Pickering, Harry E., 255-56
Pilliod, Gerard, 279, 362, 363
Pinski, Jeff, 142
Pittacora, Joseph, 340, 341, 505(n)
Poland Country Club, 32, 37, 475(n)

Police Mug Book, 238, 462, 493(n)
Policy, Carmen A., 143
Polizzi, Al, 121, 484(n), 520(n)
Polizzi, Charles A. "Chuck," 271
Polizzi, Charles J., 271, 499(n)
Pollard, H.O., 252
Powers, Thomas M., 303-04, 481(n)
Presti, Charles, 251
Prijital, Henry, 81, 482(n)
Princiotto, Ted, 72, 82, 103, 481(n)
Pullen, Glenn C., 45, 228(p)
Pumphrey, Benjamin H., 336, 338, 340,
    341, 343, 348
Purvis, Joseph D., 63, 398
Putman, Norman J., 263, 351, 352
    Shoup murder trial I, 320, 328,
    329, 330, 335-43
    Shoup murder trial II, 344-46,
    347, 348
    post-trial, 349, 350, 351, 352-53

Quillin, Daniel, 356

Radd, Charles G., 354, 501(n)
Rebol, Reverend Paul, 315
Recreation Café, 64, 77, 78, 87, 479-
    80(n), 482(n)
Reed, William, 36, 37, 167(p)
Reles, Abraham "Kid Twist," 351
Ricci, Theodore, 132, 448
Roberts, Michael D., 234(p), 242, 430,
    493(n)
Robey, George W., 70
Rockefeller, John D., 270
Rockview Penitentiary, 130, 490(n)
Rockwell, Sam, 5
Roman Lounge, 244, 494(n)
Romano, Dr. Giuseppe, 142, 520(n)
Romano, Joseph, 297
Rooney, Pete, 128, 387-88
Rossetti, John, 321
Rotatori, Robert J., 215(p), 244, 375,
    385

Roth, Frederick C., 282
Rotundo, Dominic, 118
Rowdy, 136
Rudelik, Thomas "Laughing Tommy,"
    179(p), 262-63, 272, 275-76
    biography, 280-83
    Mug Shot Book, 211
Russo, Anthony, 5
Russo, Antonio, 283
Russo, Fred, 286
Russo, Joseph, 5
Russo, Joseph R., 50, 58, 59, 60, 179(p),
    245
    biography, 283-92
    death of, 291-92
Rutkowski, Anthony A., 47, 49, 316

S.A. Conti & Son, 259, 362, 364, 509(n)
Sachs, D.C., 353
Sanko, John, 31-32, 37, 475(n)
Sansavera, Joseph, 238
Sanzo, Jean, 68, 91
Sanzo, Joseph J., xii, xv, 153(p), 170,
    171(p), 172, 173, 175, 177,
    222, 239, 249, 295, 357,
    480(n), 481-82(n), 483(n),
    484(n), 488(n), 502(n), 516(n)
    biography, 292-96
    Warren robbery arrest, 64, 65,
    66, 67-68
    Petro/Sanzo trial, 68, 69, 70, 72,
    73, 74, 75, 76, 77, 81, 82, 85,
    87, 88, 89, 90, 91, 93, 94,
    95, 96, 97, 98, 99
    Spaeth testimony, 84, 86, 87, 88,
    89, 91, 92, 94. 95, 96
    Spaeth perjury trials, 100, 101,
    102, 103, 104, 105, 106, 108-
    109, 110, 111, 112, 113,
    114, 116
Savord, Edmond, 20-21, 24-25, 27
Scalish, John, 130, 187

Schaefer, Charles W., 64-65, 77-78, 79,
    82, 482(n)
Schemansee, Frank G., 60
Schmunk, Harry W., 349
Schnaufer, Doris, 287, 288,
Schultz, Allen W., 64
Schwenderman, Fred, 85
Scott, Roy W., 93
Sebek, Milo, 22-23
Sedlak, Andrew, 294
Sellars, Dr. Walter S., 33
Senate Crime Committee, 82
Senkbeil, William, 42
Sennett, Jr., James C., 112, 114-15
Serman, Vincent P., 253, 486(n)
Severino, Albert, 226(p), 251, 464-65,
    501(n), 510(n)
    biography, 387-95
    murder of, 394
Sgro, Santo, 277
Shaffer, Mary, 302, 316, 322-23
Shaw, Audrey "Audie," 265-66, 269
Sheppard, Marilyn, 108, 485(n)
Sheppard, Dr. Sam, 108, 144, 485(n),
    502(n)
Sherman, Charles, 46
Shine, Paul J., 63, 74, 93, 173(p)
Shontz & Myers, 253
Short, Joseph, 317, 320
Short, Martin, 130
Shoup, Earl, 305, 347
    murder & investigation, 306-08,
    317-19
    Shoup murder trial I, 329-35
    post-trial, 349-352
Shoup, Mrs. Earl, 333
Shoup, Eldon E. "Pete," 188(p), 190,
    304, 305, 308, 345, 349, 463,
    503(n)
    murder of, 191, 194, 222, 304,
    306, 307, 321, 324, 327, 329,
    331, 332, 335

Carpenter confesses, 316-18, 322
Shoup murder trial I, 327, 333, 339, 505(n)
Shoup murder trial II, 346, 347
aftermath, 350, 352, 353, 356
Shoup, Eldon Peter, 345
Shoup, Helen, 188, 304, 345, 349
Shoup, Regina Ann, 345
Shrull, Daniel J., 243
Sica, Fred, 127, 489
Sica, John, 266, 269
Sicafuse, Woodrow, 32
Siegel, Benjamin, 5
Silbert Joseph H., 47, 410, 411
Silver Bullet Café, 305, 332,
Simmons, Robert P., 243
Simon, Dr. S. Maurice, 53
Sinito, Thomas J., 143
Sister Pauline, 335, 336-37, 340, 343, 348
Skubovis, Charles, 180(P), 216, 464-65
Biography, 387-95
Mug Shot Book, 212
Slusser, Robert V., 42
Smith, Roger, 112
Sneiderman, Dr. Harry, 26
Somberg, Dr. Joseph S., 101
Somberg, Rose, 101
Sonny's Show Bar, 45-47, 48, 126, 227, 228, 464
biography, 396-404
Sovereign Hotel, 44, 120, 477
Spaeth, Dr. Alexander V., 100-101, 102, 177(p), 178(p)
Testimony and aftermath, 84, 86, 88, 91, 97, 99
Spaeth perjury trial I, 102-107
Spaeth perjury trial II, 107-108, 110-11
Spaeth perjury trial III, 111-16
Spaeth, Aranka, 100, 113, 114, 116
Spaeth, Helene Rita, 116

Spaulding, Genevieve, 81
St. Clair Builders Supply Co., 301, 334, 336
Stahl, Thomas D., 354
Stamphel, Edward Robert, 59, 259
Stanton, Edward C., 41, 108, 161(p), 175(p), 450, 468(n), 471(n)
Knaus murder & trials, 11, 16, 18-19, 21-22, 25-26, 29
Petro/Sanzo trial, 67, 69, 70, 74, 75-76, 80-81, 82, 84, 85, 88-91, 94, 95-97, 99
Steel, Frank E. 175(p), 241, 242, 297, 480-81(n)
Petro/Sanzo trial, 67, 69-70, 71, 76, 84, 85, 87-88
Spaeth perjury trial, 91, 97, 98, 100, 102, 104, 105, 107
Stewart, Richard A., 252-53, 271, 302, 387, 390-91, 392, 440, 442, 444, 498(n)
Stokes, Carl B. 4
Story, Frank W., 93, 166(p), 203(p), 285, 467, 494(n)
Stoyka, John, 271, 498(n)
Stredrick, Frank, 338-39, 341, 515(n)
Streepy, Jack B., 217(p), 295, 374
Strollo, Lenine "Lenny," 254, 486(n)
Struzenski, John, 238
Stuplinski, Bernard J., 255, 412
Stryanka, George, 354-55, 495(n), 507-08(n)
Suarez, David, 340, 341, 505(n)
Sullenberger, Harry, 295
Sullenberger, Ronald H., 293-96, 374, 375, 377, 378
Sweeney, Joseph M., 6, 33, 93, 96, 431
Swim, Madelyn, 113

Tablack, George D., 32
Tablack, Helen, 32
Tainow, Herbert, 44-45, 120

Tarian, Gus, 345
Tarlow, Barry, 133, 147, 148
Tartaglia, Frank, 238
    Mug Shot Book, 212
Tasker, Hal, 239
Tedrick, Delbert L., 260
Tegay, Robert "Fat Bob," 125
Terre Haute Federal Prison, 96, 97,
    108, 113
The Friends of Eddie Coyle, 236
Tholl, Joseph, xiv, 177(p), 229(p), 415
    biography, 405-437
    Petro/Sanzo trial, 86, 94-95,
        96-97
    Spaeth trials, 100, 102, 103, 104,
        108, 112
    early life, 405-06, 408
    Sprunk case, 406
    election fraud, 406-413
    murder of Gloria Ferry, 231,
        408-11
    murder of Charles Clark, 412
    Alessandro forgery, 412-13
    Frank Day corruption case, 230,
        234, 415-21
    murder of Cremer Young, 235,
        421-30
    Kocevar case, 232, 430-35
    later years and death, 435-37
Thomas, Frank, 131
Thomas, William K., 256, 257, 401,
    419-21
Thompson, Patricia Joan, 243
Tiburzio, David F., 179(p), 262, 263,
    281, 506(n)
    Mug Shot Book, 213
    biography, 272-77
    Tampa murder, 273-74
Tincher, A. Paul, 102, 104, 110, 113
Tirabassi, Nicholas J., 64, 65, 67, 77, 79,
    119, 468(n), 487(n)
Totten, Marjorie, 347

Town House night club, 42-43
Trammell III, George W., 147-49
Trafficante, Santo, 121
Trigg, Howard, 38
Trovato, Peter J., 289-90
    murder of, 501-02(n)
Trumbull Memorial Hospital, 64, 71,
    357, 476(n)
Trunk, Lloyd, 284
20th Century Cigar store, 305, 332

Uminski, Anna, 47
Union Savings & Trust Co. (Warren),
    xi, 62, 63, 69, 70, 71, 82, 169,
    171, 357

Valenti, Nicholas, 119, 487(n)
Van Vliet, W. James, 3
Vaughn, George, 267, 268, 269, 270,
    495(n)
Veale, II, Tinkham, 93
Velletto, Anthony "Joe Blow," 180(p),
    251, 252, 262, 263, 272,
    275-76, 281
    Mug Shot Book, 213
Velotta, Frank J. "Skinny," 119-20,
    121-22, 123, 124, 126, 130,
    131, 132, 133, 135-36, 137,
    181(p), 182, 185, 448, 453,
    488(n), 489(n), 490(n)
    FBI files, 119, 120-21, 122, 123,
    124-26, 127, 128-29
Vestal, Carl, 333
Viccarone, Richie, 132, 449
Vitalune, Nordi, 332
Vrabel, Steve, 350

Waddell, Gobel, 316, 317, 332
Wahoo Bar, 193-95, 301-04, 308-16,
    319, 321-24, 326-27, 331, 350,
    353-56

Walch, Alan, 122, 123, 182(p), 453, 488(n), 516(n)
   biography, 438-49
   FBI files, 122, 123, 124, 125, 129
Wallace, Frankie, 248
Walsh, Christopher, 131
Walsh, Dennis M., 131-32, 133, 136, 150, 155, 184(p), 451, 453, 454, 455, 457,
Walsh, Robert E. "Bobby," 122, 181, 182(p), 183(p), 184-86, 486(n), 490(n), 518(n)
   biography, 450-57
   FBI files, 122, 123, 124-25, 128-29
   friendship with Ferritto, 130-32
   Petro murder, 133-36, 143,145,149-50
   death of, 457
Walsh, Timothy, 136, 184, 454, 455
Warner, Ray, 192, 319
Washington, Carlos, 146-47
Waterhouse, L.G., 254
Watters, Frank, 266
Watzman, Sanford, 238, 405, 462
Weber, Paul G., 283, 345-49, 352-53
Webber, Abraham B., 47
Webber, Jean G., 47
Webber, William B., 47-48
Webber, Yetta L., 47
Weegar, Stanton N., 67, 95
Wehr, William F., 285
Weick, Paul C., 112-15
Weis, Harry, 285
Weiss, Sidney, 286
Weitzen, Joseph, 253
Wells, Frank E. "Red," 190, 191, 305-07, 308, 316, 317-19, 320, 321, 329-33, 336, 340, 346-47, 350, 352, 504(n)
Western & Southern Life Insurance Agency, 245, 246, 249
Western Penitentiary, 253

Weygandt, Carl V., 20
Whalen, Thomas, 16-18, 469(n)
Whitaker, Pat, 273-74
White Front Provision Co., 257, 258, 259, 496(n)
White, Thomas P., xiv-xv, 172(p), 205(p)
   biography, 458-67
   Warren robbery, 63, 64, 65-66, 73
   Petro/Sanzo trial, 78-81, 483(n)
   squad work, 236-37, 239, 240, 241, 251, 260, 268, 289. 291, 350, 387, 392, 486(n), 493(n), 501(n), 506(n), 521(n)
   White's legendary police stories, 458, 459, 463
   early life and career, 458-59
   promotion to sergeant, 459
   "Rackets Squad," 460-61
   promotion to lieutenant, 461
   as head of "Special Services," 462-66
   bomb, 390, 465
   murder of Louis Hamblin, 466-67
   later years and death, 467
Willard, Arthur, 36
Williams, Theodore M., 264
Wilson, Grace, 85, 87, 483(n)
Wilson, Woodrow, 35, 473(n), 474(n)
Winston, Dianne (see Miller, Roberta)
Wise, Earle E., 263
   Shoup murder trial I, 327-28, 329, 332-35, 337-43
   Shoup murder trial II, 344-46, 347-49
   post-trial, 352
Wiseman, Wilbert A., 64
Wojick, Stanley, 285-86
Wolkin, Reta M., 145-46, 148, 149, 492(n)
Woodle, Edwin F., 112, 113-15
Wright, Albert S, 59, 60-61, 478-79(n)

Made in the USA
Columbia, SC
11 March 2024

Wykoff, Harry S., 57-58

Yelsky, Leonard E., 141

Zimmerman, James "Jimmy," 96
        biography, 296-300
        Penn-Ohio burglary ring, 42,
            278, 476(n)
        murder of, 299-300
Zimmerman, June, 297
Zimmerman, May, 299
Zingale, Joseph, 34-35
Zook, Abner D., 304

*